Climate Change

International Library of Environmental Economics and Policy
General Editor: Tom Tietenberg

Titles in the Series

Climate Change

Edited by

Michael A. Toman and Brent Sohngen

Inter-American Development Bank and Ohio State University, USA

Routledge
Taylor & Francis Group

LONDON AND NEW YORK

First published 2004 by Ashgate Publishing

Reissued 2018 by Routledge
2 Park Square, Milton Park, Abingdon, Oxon OX14 4RN
711 Third Avenue, New York, NY 10017, USA

Routledge is an imprint of the Taylor & Francis Group, an informa business

First issued in paperback 2018

A Library of Congress record exists under LC control number: 2004103579

Notice:
Product or corporate names may be trademarks or registered trademarks, and are used only for identification and explanation without intent to infringe.

Publisher's Note
The publisher has gone to great lengths to ensure the quality of this reprint but points out that some imperfections in the original copies may be apparent.

Disclaimer
The publisher has made every effort to trace copyright holders and welcomes correspondence from those they have been unable to contact.

ISBN 13: 978-0-815-38808-1 (hbk)
ISBN 13: 978-1-138-61909-8 (pbk)
ISBN 13: 978-1-351-16160-2 (ebk)

Contents

PART III   POLICY DESIGN FOR GHG MITIGATION

Acknowledgements

The editors and publishers wish to thank the following for permission to use copyright material.

Ambio for the essay: P.R. Shukla (1996), 'The Modelling of Policy Options for Greenhouse Gas Mitigation in India', *Ambio*, **25**, pp. 240–48. Copyright © 1996 Royal Swedish Academy of Sciences.

American Economic Association for the essays: Brent Sohngen and Robert Mendelsohn (1998), 'Valuing the Impact of Large-Scale Ecological Change in a Market: The Effect of Climate Change on U.S. Timber', *American Economic Review*, **88**, pp. 686–710; Robert Mendelsohn, William D. Nordhaus and Daigee Shaw (1994), 'The Impact of Global Warming on Agriculture: A Ricardian Analysis', *American Economic Review*, **84**, pp. 753–71; John Quiggin and John K. Horowitz (1999), 'The Impact of Global Warming on Agriculture: A Ricardian Analysis: Comment', *American Economic Review*, **89**, pp. 1044–45; Roy Darwin (1999), 'The Impact of Global Warming on Agriculture: A Ricardian Analysis: Comment', *American Economic Review*, **89**, pp. 1049–52; Robert Mendelsohn and William Nordhaus (1999), 'The Impact of Global Warming on Agriculture: A Ricardian Analysis: Reply', *American Economic Review*, **89**, pp. 1053–55; Robert Mendelsohn and William Nordhaus (1999), 'The Impact of Global Warming on Agriculture: A Ricardian Analysis: Reply', *American Economic Review*, **89**, pp. 1046–48.

Blackwell Publishing for the essay: Andrew J. Plantinga, Thomas Mauldin and Douglas J. Miller (1999), 'An Econometric Analysis of the Costs of Sequestering Carbon in Forests', *American Journal of Agricultural Economics*', **81**, pp. 812–24. Copyright © 1999 American Agricultural Economics Association.

Allan D. Brunner (2002), 'El Niño and World Primary Commodity Prices: Warm Water or Hot Air?', *Review of Economics and Statistics*, **84**, pp. 176–83. Copyright © 2002 Allan D. Brunner.

Elsevier for the essays: William D. Nordhaus (1993), 'Rolling the "DICE": An Optimal Transition Path for Controlling Greenhouse Gases', *Resource and Energy Economics*, **15**, pp. 27–50. Copyright © 1993 Elsevier; Christian Azar and Thomas Sterner (1996), 'Discounting and Distributional Considerations in the Context of Global Warming', *Ecological Economics*, **19**, pp. 169–84. Copyright © 1996 Elsevier; Tim Roughgarden and Stephen H. Schneider (1999), 'Climate Change Policy: Quantifying Uncertainties for Damages and Optimal Carbon Taxes', *Energy Policy*, **27**, pp. 415–29. Copyright © 1999 Elsevier; Thomas C. Schelling (1995), 'Intergenerational Discounting', *Energy Policy*, **23**, pp. 395–401. Copyright © 1995 Elsevier; Zhongxiang Zhang (2000), 'Decoupling China's Carbon Emissions Increase from Economic Growth: An Economic Analysis and Policy Implications', *World Development*, **28**, pp. 739–52.

Series Preface

The *International Library of Environmental Economics and Policy* explores the influence of economics on the development of environmental and natural resource policy. In a series of twenty five volumes, the most significant journal essays in key areas of contemporary environmental and resource policy are collected. Scholars who are recognized for their expertise and contribution to the literature in the various research areas serve as volume editors and write an introductory essay that provides the context for the collection.

Volumes in the series reflect the broad strands of economic research including 1) Natural and Environmental Resources, 2) Policy Instruments and Institutions and 3) Methodology. The editors, in their introduction to each volume, provide a state-of-the-art overview of the topic and explain the influence and relevance of the collected papers on the development of policy. This reference series provides access to the economic literature that has made an enduring contribution to contemporary and natural resource policy.

TOM TIETENBERG
General Editor

Introduction

Over the years, a large and growing literature on the economics of climate change has developed, to put it mildly. There is no succinct way of summarizing this literature – different authors have focused on a wide array of issues, methods, sectors, and hypotheses. For the purposes of this book, we have categorized economic studies of climate change into three parts. Part I deals with climate change impacts on specific sectors, goods and services (including non-market values), as well as adaptation; Part II covers the costs and benefits of greenhouse gas (GHG) mitigation; and Part III discusses policy design for mitigation, including both domestic instruments and issues related to international agreements. This division is both somewhat arbitrary and involves overlaps, but seems workable.

In our selection of previously published journal essays to include in the volume, we have tried to include as wide a range of thought, and evolution of thought, as possible. This has inevitably led us to include a mix of essays ranging from 'greatest hits' in terms of citation indexes, to essays that are newer or less widely quoted but still illustrative of an important aspect of this vast topic. Inevitably as well, the requirement to include only previously published peer-reviewed journal essays, plus a constraint on volume length, have forced us to exclude many noteworthy and important pieces. With hopes of forebearance on the part of our colleagues for the consequences of Solomonic decisions on what to include and exclude, we attempt in this Introduction to provide a number of other references that complement the essays we have included here.[1]

Climate Change and its Impacts

Before turning to economic assessments of climate change impacts, we begin the volume with the short essay on the science of climate change by Houghton (Chapter 1), one of the world's leading climate scientists and a leader in the Intergovernmental Panel on Climate Change (IPCC). Houghton's essay provides a useful discussion for readers that might have a scientific background on the phenomenon. Further information can be found in the latest volume on the science of climate change published by the IPCC (Houghton *et al.*, 2001).

Several different factors distinguish various contributions to the economics of climate change and its impacts. First, it is important to characterize different types of methodologies that have been used to estimate climate change impacts. While the typical scenario for empirical economic research is to rely on a natural experiment and produce a statistical study based on a theoretical model, there are few conditions in the world that currently approximate the potential implications of climate change. It is possible, as argued by Mendelsohn *et al.* (1994), that in some sectors we can approximate the effects of climate change by exploring results across the variety of climates we currently have. Yohe and Schlesinger (Chapter 4), however, point out the difficulties that may arise if we then try to extrapolate findings from one population to another when there are substantial differences in endowments and incentives.

Furthermore, most of the physical evidence on climate change is derived from models that project changes in temperature and precipitation, changes in crop or forest yields, changes in range of pests or diseases, etc. To understand the economic implications of biophysical changes, one must carefully trace the physical or biological impacts through to economic markets. To try to capture the range of methodologies that have been suggested in the literature for estimating welfare impacts of climate change, we include studies relying on several different techniques.

The essay by Mendelsohn *et al.* reproduced as Chapter 6 of this volume, for example, uses econometrics to provide empirical evidence linking climate to economic outcomes within the agricultural sector. While the environment clearly moderates many of our activities, its influence on economic productivity had been largely unmeasured before this 1994 study. A distinctly different set of methodologies is apparent in the essay by Sohngen and Mendelsohn (Chapter 2). That research shows how physical and ecological phenomena can be integrated into economic models. In climate change research, this type of integration is perhaps more important than in other areas. Economic phenomena influence emissions; emissions influence climate change; climate influences ecosystems; and ecosystems, in turn, influence the economy.

A variety of other methods have been applied in order to estimate the implications of climate change for the economy. One of the most intriguing examples is the expert survey by Nordhaus (1994). In that study, Professor Nordhaus surveyed a set of climate experts, ranging from economists to engineers, and asked them to assess the implications of climate change for the world's gross domestic product. Although we do not include that study in this volume, it has had a substantial impact on the climate change research community. It also raises an interesting issue. Although economists have had long experience with survey techniques, the techniques have not yet been widely incorporated into the climate change impact literature. Some survey research on potential non-market impacts has appeared more recently (for example, Layton and Brown, 2000), but Nordhaus' study is one of very few.

Second, the most important contribution of economics to the climate change debate has arguably been the strong emphasis on adaptation. Economic impacts simply cannot be measured without accounting for the adaptations that people can make to climate change. Nearly all the studies included in this volume, at least to some extent, account for adaptation when estimating impacts. The recent study by Brunner (Chapter 5) clearly shows one of the most important adaptations that markets will make through price changes. That study provides empirical evidence of a link between world commodity prices and climate phenomena – namely El Niño events. Most economists agree that, if we are to adapt to climate change, it will occur because prices – either those observed on markets or shadow values on currently unpriced factors of production (such as climate) – will change.

Whilst Brunner's research shows a mechanism of adaptation within markets, significant questions about institutional adaptation to climate change loom. The difficulties of adapting services that have traditionally been provided as public goods by government institutions have not been as closely examined. An example of the difficulties that such institutions will face is provided in this volume in the essay written by Frederick and Major (Chapter 3), who explore how uncertainty is likely to influence decisions that water planners must make.

Third, economic impact estimates of climate change have occurred primarily in five sectors: agriculture, forestry, water, coastal infrastructure and energy. Although, considered alone, these sectors represent a relatively small proportion of the overall world economy, they are nevertheless arguably the most important to consider because they are all directly linked to climate, and they may be more important in specific regions of the world. Some sectors, such as agriculture and forestry, are important for other reasons entirely. Agriculture is tied to food security, which remains a critical human concern in many regions of the world today, and the world's forests hold large stores of carbon and biodiversity. This means that physical changes in the productivity of the underlying resources in these sectors can have far-reaching implications for the daily lives of people who rely on the land for income, leisure or other non-market purposes.

Within this volume, we include studies that focus on agriculture (Mendelsohn *et al.*, Chapter 6), water (Frederick and Major, Chapter 3), and forestry (Sohngen and Mendelsohn, Chapter 2) directly. The agriculture sector is definitely the most well studied, with a wide and diverse array of empirical studies exploring the implications of changes in temperature and precipitation on the productivity of specific crops. For studies in the United States, we direct readers to the seminal work of Adams *et al.* (1990, 1995) and Segerson and Dixon (1998). Studies taking a more global perspective include Rosenzweig and Parry (1994), Reilly *et al.* (1994) and Darwin *et al.* (1999).

The forestry sector has not been as widely examined, but there are a number of studies linking ecological effects to economic models. Within the United States, the study by Joyce *et al.* (1995) was the first to suggest that climate change would increase the productivity of forests and reduce prices. The study by McCarl *et al.* (2000) presents an example of a wide range of sensitivity analysis using climate models to project potential impacts, ecological models to project potential productivity changes, and an economic model to simulate the welfare implications. Globally there are two studies exploring climate change impacts – Perez-Garcia *et al.* (1997) and Sohngen *et al.* (2001).

Notably absent in this volume are studies on the impacts of climate change on energy, health and non-market sectors. Energy is partly addressed in Part II of this volume in the section on integrated assessment modelling. However, a number of good empirical studies on the potential impacts of climate change in the energy sector in the United States have appeared in the literature, including Dewees and Wilson (1990), Baxter and Calandri (1992), Rosenthal *et al.* (1995) and Morrison and Mendelsohn (1998).

Estimating welfare impacts on human health is perhaps the most complex area of climate change research because it requires measuring not only welfare effects (which is itself highly contentious – witness the continuing lively debate on the value of a human life), but also the effects of climate change on mortality and morbidity. The United Nations Intergovernmental Panel on Climate Change report presents comprehensive estimates of potential human health effects (McCarthy *et al.*, 2001), but one of the few studies to trace potential health outcomes to welfare impacts is Moore (1998), which examines mortality in the United States and uses wage rates to estimate the value of human life. Fankhauser *et al.* (1998) address the controversy of health impact valuation and other valuation controversies as they arose in the Second Assessment Report of the IPCC.

Although most of the research to date has focused on economic sectors, non-market activity may be particularly vulnerable to climate change because it does not generate income substantial enough to invest in new infrastructure. Several interesting studies have been conducted by applying different economic valuation techniques to estimate the non-market impacts of climate change. For instance, Pendleton and Mendelsohn (1999) use travel cost methods to estimate non-market impacts in angling recreation, Layton and Brown (2000) use contingent valuation to estimate non-market impacts of changes in forest structure and function, and Maddison and

Bigano (2003) use hedonics to show willingness to pay for climate in Italy. All three of these methods have been used widely to estimate impacts of other types of environmental change, but these represent the first attempts to use the methods for estimating the implications of climate change.

A fourth consideration is debate itself. Perhaps debates rise to the level of the problem, and, with climate change viewed as one of the world's most pressing environmental problems, the debate on economic impact estimation methods and results has flourished. We have chosen to highlight the debate by including several of the comments and responses to the original Mendelsohn *et al.* (1994) essay (see Chapters 7, 8, 9 and 10).

A final consideration is the issue of scale. Can estimates from individual models, developed in individual regions, be aggregated to reach a single set of estimates that represent *the* impact of climate change on the world economy? Within the literature a number of studies have considered the possibility of aggregating impacts (or have actually done it), including Nordhaus (1993), Cline (1992), Fankhauser *et al.* (1998), Mendelsohn *et al.* (2000) and Nordhaus and Boyer (2000).

However, the essay included in this volume takes a slightly different approach than the authors listed above. In Chapter 4 Yohe and Schlesinger consider the conditions under which such aggregations can occur or, as they argue, should not occur. Their thesis is that adaptive capacity differs substantively across regions, and it thus may be misleading to infer adaptive capacity from one region to another. As a result, they suggest that extrapolating welfare results from one region to another may in fact be misleading simply because the underlying economic conditions may differ widely. A different approach, taken by Tol (2001) suggests alternative methods for weighting welfare outcomes in different regions. Such an approach has strong intuitive appeal in economics.

For individuals interested in finding additional citations on climate change impacts for different market sectors, the books by Mendelsohn and Neumann (1999) and Mendelsohn (2001) provide numerous examples of different methods applied to estimating economic impacts, as well as numerous citations. Tol and Nordaus have written several excellent essays or books that review the existing literature on economic impacts (a 1999 essay by Tol is included in Part II; see also Tol *et al.*, 1998; Tol, 2002; and Nordhaus and Boyer, 2000). Finally, the latest reports from Working Groups II and III of the Intergovernmental Panel on Climate Change have extensively reviewed the impacts literature (McCarthy *et al.*, 2001; Metz *et al.*, 2001).

Evaluating the Costs and Benefits of Climate Change Mitigation

The essays collected in Part II represent examples of an extremely large and growing economics literature on the costs and benefits of climate change mitigation that has been accumulating for over a decade. The prototypical approach to this analysis is the use of integrated assessment modelling, and the opening essay paper by Nordhaus is prototypical of the approach. Integrated assessment models are constructed by linking modules that characterize:

1   how GHG emissions affect key aspects of the climate
2   how changes in climate affect a variety of ecological and economic factors of interest to human society, as illustrated by the essays in Part I

3 the economic costs of these (typically) adverse impacts over time
4 the costs of reducing GHG accumulations by altering patterns of energy use and (to some degree) other sources of GHGs in the economic system.

Each module reflects some degree of simplification of more complex processes and relationships. The models are typically global in their scale, though individual parts (in particular the representation of energy–economy relationships that give rise to costs of GHG mitigation) are usually represented at a national or regional scale.

Integrated assessment models are inherently dynamic representations of natural and economic processes over time. When applied normatively (to evaluate an 'optimal' path of GHG accumulation or mitigation), a criterion for comparing alternative paths is required. For the most part, economic applications of integrated assessment models have used a standard present value criterion – minimizing the discounted sum of climate change damage and mitigation costs over time. As discussed further below, the choice of this criterion has given rise to considerable debate amongst different groups of climate change policy analysts and advocates.

The Nordhaus (1993) model (see Chapter 11) illustrates all these key features of integrated assessment. Relatively simple equations relate global CO_2 emissions to their concentration in the atmosphere; the effect of rising GHG concentration on global average temperature; the effects of rising temperature on economic output and consumption possibilities; and the economic costs of reducing the flow of energy services to mitigate GHG emissions. To describe the effects of rising GHG concentrations on economic well-being, Nordhaus uses another relatively simple functional form and benchmarking techniques to specify the parameters. The benchmarking reflects informed judgement based on available information from more disaggregated climate change damage assessments about how warming might affect the more directly vulnerable sectors (such as agriculture) and, by extension, the less vulnerable parts.

Nordhaus himself and others have subsequently extended this 1993 model in a variety of ways, including greater geographical disaggregation, more complex specifications of damage functions and greater sophistication in the treatment of mitigation costs, including issues of technological innovation (see, for example, Nordhaus and Yang, 1996; Nordhaus and Boyer, 2000; Pizer, 1999, among others; see also Tol *et al.*, 1998).[2] Even in its relatively simple form, however, Nordhaus's 1993 model illustrates some key general insights from economic integrated assessment models. Perhaps the most striking result is the *non*-optimality of sharp curbs on GHG emissions, leading to fairly rapid stabilization and even reversal of GHG concentration, a hallmark of the debate in climate change policy venues including the Framework Convention. GHG emissions should be curbed relative to a business-as-usual baseline, but the curbing should be gradual and, according to the model, it is optimal for climate change to be allowed to continue practically indefinitely. This result is relatively robust to changes in the height or slope of the marginal damage function – a finding illustrated by studies such as Peck and Teisberg (1993) and Manne (1996).

What explains this striking finding, which would indicate that a great deal of the focus of debate in international climate policy has been misplaced? Two fundamental factors seem to be at work. One is the assumed continuity of the damage function in models such as Nordhaus's. Much of the attention given in policy debates to the need for rapid reversal of global warming trends reflects the judgement that these trends, left to run their course, will result in some kind of disaster. This disaster could be as dramatic as a sudden change in the Gulf Stream that would leave most of Europe as cold as Iceland, or it could be the unexpected collapse of global food supplies after years of more gradual stress on productivity through changes in temperature and rainfall patterns, or some other factors.

As indicated by the work of Nordhaus (1994), Gjerde *et al.* (1999) and Pizer (2003), if one inserts into an integrated assessment model the certainty or high probability of a major negative impact in the near future (something akin to the Great Depression), then optimal GHG mitigation should be correspondingly rapid and stringent. At least in the judgement of many, if not most, integrated assessment modellers, however, the scientific basis for making such an assumption in the model simply does not exist. Disasters may well occur from climate change, but both their severity and timing remain highly uncertain. More to the point, disasters in the more distant future can be assumed to be relatively much more likely than disasters in the near future (even if they remain, in an absolute sense, unlikely).

This leads to the other major factor explaining the kinds of findings for optimal GHG mitigation emerging from Nordhaus's and other similar integrated assessment models: the force of economic discounting. Controversy has surrounded not just the selection of a value for the discount rate in these models, but also the application of the present value criterion itself to judge the optimal path of GHG mitigation. We discuss this controversy more thoroughly below. For the moment, we note simply that, as illustrated by the work of Manne (1996) and Gjerde *et al.* (1999), it is difficult to get the kinds of rapid and stringent GHG mitigation emphasized in international climate policy debates out of integrated assessment models, absent a clear and immediate risk of disaster, unless the discount rate assumed in the model is extremely low (perhaps in the order of 1 per cent). Discount rates this low represent a sharp departure from what is usually assumed in economic cost–benefit analysis, even after taking into account all the fine points that normally surround the determination of time preference rates and rates of return on capital.

The essay by Tol (Chapter 12) reports results from another integrated assessment analysis, one encompassing other GHGs besides CO_2 and built up with a great deal more detail on the sources and costs of climate change damages (including agriculture, species loss, increased human mortality risks and impacts of rising sea levels. Tol's base estimates of long-term incremental damages from CO_2 emissions are roughly twice those following from Nordhaus's earlier model; damages from methane and nitrous oxide are higher since they have greater global warming potential.[3] Tol presents a careful sensitivity analysis showing how results vary for key parameters, including the discount rate. As expected, very low discount rates imply much larger damages. He also shows that aggregating damages across rich and poor regions with different weights reflecting differences in the marginal utility of income also raises aggregate damages. We return to these points below. Overall, Tol's uncertainty analysis suggests a long upper tail to the frequency density for marginal CO_2 damage costs – an important consideration if society is risk-averse to climate change.

The next three essays in Part II address specific aspects of GHG mitigation costs and benefits in more detail. The essay by Roughgarden and Schneider (Chapter 13) uses work by Nordhaus as a point of departure to argue that greater attention should be given to the possibility of severe negative outcomes in the calibration of integrated assessment outcomes. These authors argue not just that such outcomes are within the range of possibility based on expert judgement about climate change risks, but also that the consequences of such risks are important for public policy because society may be averse to bearing such risks (the standard present value criterion assumes risk neutrality), or that such risks may fall disproportionately on poorer countries.[4]

Goulder and Mathai (Chapter 14) examine how the costs of GHG mitigation can be affected by induced technical change – that is, technical change responding to increased energy prices that would follow from putting a shadow price on GHG emissions. Their analysis shows how impacts of technical change and the implications for optimal mitigation policy depend on the nature of the induced response. When the response is through learning by doing, society can benefit from more aggressive GHG mitigation that spurs cost-reducing innovation. This contrasts with the case explored in Goulder and Schneider (1999), in which redirection of innovation resources towards GHG mitigation can reduce productivity advance in other parts of the economy. Other essays, notably Fischer, Parry and Pizer (2003), address how the costs of different policy options, such as emissions permit trading or a carbon tax, are affected by accounting for induced innovation.

In Chapter 15 Kolstad discusses how the optimal GHG mitigation path in the presence of uncertainty can be affected by different kinds of option values when there is learning over time. In Kolstad's framework, while GHGs accumulate in the atmosphere, capital investment is also substantially irreversible and there is the possibility, over time, of improving estimates of climate change risks. In this case, the primary irreversibility of concern is the possibility of overinvesting in less GHG-intensive, but costlier, capital. If research does lead to upward revisions in the estimates of climate change risks, Kolstad argues, it is possible to recuperate simply by accelerating future GHG mitigation. As Fisher and Narain (2003) point out, if GHG accumulation and climate change are more irreversible, and the capital stock is more malleable than assumed by Kolstad, then the opposite conclusion follows: options are more efficiently preserved by more aggressive GHG mitigation.

The essays by Azar and Sterner (Chapter 16), Howarth (Chapter 17), and Schelling (Chapter 18) that follow each deal, in different ways, with the question raised previously about the appropriateness of the standard present value criterion for evaluating optimal GHG mitigation. Azar and Sterner argue that because of distributional considerations related to climate change within, as well as across, generations, the choice of discount rate should be lower than in a standard cost–benefit analysis. More specifically, they maintain that, because climate change is likely to disproportionately affect the poor of future generations, for whom the marginal utility of income is higher than the population average, the present value of future benefits from today's GHG mitigation should not be discounted at a rate that reflects the average rate of time preference because this understates the utility of the benefits to be realized in the future from the mitigation.

This argument is quite different than that advanced by Weitzman (1998) and Newell and Pizer (2003a), although the conclusions are similar. In those essays the focus is on discounting, reflecting the alternative rate of return on resources invested in GHG mitigation. This rate of return is uncertain, depending in particular on the effects that climate change might have on future productivity. If those effects are small, then the future rate of return will be high and investments in mitigation today will not be valuable. But if the effects of climate change on productivity are large, then the future rate of return on other investments will be smaller and highly correlated over time, and the value of mitigation today will be higher. Weitzman and Newell and Pizer show that, as a consequence, the appropriate choice of long-term discount rate for GHG mitigation analysis is lower than the certainty-equivalent rate of return on capital.

Howarth (2003) advances further along these lines by using portfolio analysis to argue that more aggressive GHG mitigation than that implied in a simple integrated assessment model is optimal, given its aggregate risk-reducing value.

Howarth (Chapter 17) moves past arguments about optimal GHG mitigation in a standard integrated assessment model by arguing, in effect, that such a specification is incomplete. Specifically, he uses an overlapping generations model of the economy benchmarked to the Nordhaus framework to highlight the intergenerational distributional implications of climate change. These implications are at best implicit in a standard growth model found in typical integrated assessment models, which basically assumes an infinitely lived representative agent. Howarth argues that these models generate a relatively moderate and slow optimal GHG mitigation path because the current generation avoids greater GHG mitigation costs and thereby pushes greater climate change impacts on to future generations. The trade-offs embodied in intergenerational distribution, he asserts, involve complex value judgements that cannot be reduced to a simple choice of discount rate. Instead, there are an infinite number of intertemporally efficient GHG mitigation paths, corresponding to different distributions of benefits and costs across generations, and society confronts the challenge of selecting a mitigation path from amongst this family.

The argument put forward by Schelling in Chapter 18 is in some ways the antithesis of Howarth's, although both would highlight the importance of intergenerational distribution and trade-offs. Schelling's analysis rests on two basic premises that challenge claims for the desirability of aggressive GHG mitigation. The first premise is that climate change is something to which society can and will largely adapt, as it already has to differences in climate across locations today and as it has to previous challenges of resource scarcity. Where adaptation is limited, Schelling argues, the problem is much more the existence of poverty that challenges adaptation of any sort than an insuperable problem deriving from climate change in and of itself. He draws from this reasoning the conclusion that a desire to mitigate climate change would be better directed at mitigating poverty in general and barriers to adaptation in particular.

Schelling's other premise is that richer and therefore relatively less vulnerable persons do not routinely signal such a high degree of altruism for poverty alleviation generally (witness, he argues, the limits on foreign aid spending in the United States and in many other wealthy countries). It therefore makes no logical sense in terms of revealed preference, he argues, to claim that large volumes of today's resources should be channelled into reducing one component of future poverty, namely climate change. Different conclusions from Schelling's would clearly follow if instead one argued (following, for example, Roughgarden and Schneider in Chapter 13) that climate change is more risky and adaptation less easy; or if one argued that there was a stronger stewardship ethic at work in the current generation, either to future generations or with respect to the ecological state of the planet itself (a global existence value of some kind).

The essay by Wigley, Richels and Edmonds (Chapter 19), dealing with the timing of GHG mitigation, is one of the most frequently quoted essays in the climate change policy literature.[5] These authors – a climate scientist and two economic policy analysts – used relatively simple models of GHG accumulation in the atmosphere and energy–economy relationships to demonstrate that different paths of GHG mitigation that achieve the same long-term target for GHG concentration can have very different economic consequences. In particular, they found that mitigation paths that start more slowly and then accelerate GHG mitigation into the future have substantially lower present value costs than alternative paths that front-load mitigation effort. The reasons advanced for the differences include: the economic advantages of temporarily deferring some GHG mitigation investments to take advantage of other investments in the economy (as reflected in the rate of discount in the model); avoiding more rapid and costly turnover of the existing GHG-producing capital stock; taking advantage of autonomous trends in energy efficiency improvement that make later investments more cost-effective for GHG mitigation than current investment; and, finally, the fact that a greater fraction of early GHG emissions to the atmosphere will be reabsorbed over time (in other words, with relatively more early emissions, nature is left to do more of the work of mitigation, and it is cost-effective to use this natural capacity).

The Wigley, Richels and Edmonds analysis has spawned an extensive follow-on literature, including a number of essays by Manne and Richels (see, for example, Manne and Richels, 1997) and other analysts (see Toman, Morgenstern and Anderson, 1999, for a review). As discussed further below, one criticism of this perspective is that it ignores sources of friction in the energy system that make a transition to a lower GHG economy more difficult than the model would suggest. A broadly similar point, underscored by the Goulder and Mathai essay (Chapter 14), is that more aggressive early GHG mitigation provides greater opportunities for endogenously bringing down the mitigation cost. This is important not just from an economic perspective, but also from a political economy perspective since, without progress in reducing the cost of GHG mitigation, the degree to which future decision-makers would sustain any initial commitments to GHG control today is open to question. Indeed, this point is often raised more directly as a criticism of analyses such as those by Wigley *et al.*, since a postponement of GHG mitigation requires faith in more aggressive action in the future, which may not be forthcoming. The difficulty with this reasoning, however, is that the cost-effectiveness of the more gradual approach implied by the Wigley *et al.* analysis is so substantial that it is difficult to see how decision-makers could avoid wanting to realize the cost savings; and, even if more aggressive action were taken today, future decision-makers could still undo the long-term impacts by doing less to mitigate in their turn.

The essay by Zhang (Chapter 20) is included in this volume not only because it is interesting in its own right, given the importance of China in the future global balance of GHG emissions, but also because it illustrates greater challenges in extending climate economic modelling and analysis to developing countries, whose economies have important structural and performance differences from those of more advanced industrial nations. The issues to be confronted in such analyses include how to address the adjustments of markets and institutions that are an inherent part of economic development, including rigidities in other factor markets and product markets as well as inefficiencies in energy markets. Zhang notes that, under business-as-usual, China is already becoming less carbon-intensive through fuel diversification and increased energy efficiency (stimulated in turn by pricing reforms). While significant cuts in total GHG emissions would be costly, China could afford to undertake target measures to further reduce the GHG intensity of economic activity.

In Chapter 21 Hyman *et al.* illustrate an important recent and still ongoing development in climate change economics – the consideration of non-CO_2 GHG abatement. Whilst CO_2 is the most important gas causing global warming, methane is also an important contributor, and several manufactured gases are extremely potent per-unit warming sources, even though the absolute emissions of these gases are quite small. From an overall cost-effectiveness perspective, therefore, inclusion of these gases, as well as CO_2, in policy targets for mitigation is important, as is storage of CO_2 in sinks such as forests. Hyman *et al.*'s essay illustrates the issues and uncertainties faced in broadening the scope of analysis beyond CO_2, and it suggests that including non-CO_2 options can greatly increase the cost-effectiveness of an overall mitigation strategy.

Since the late 1980s numerous authors have explored whether carbon sequestration in forests presents an efficient complement to energy abatement. This literature has evolved substantially over the years, as documented in Sedjo *et al.* (1995, 1997), Sohngen and Alig (2000) and Richards and Stokes (2004). Early estimates used relatively straightforward methodologies to estimate land opportunity costs and planting costs. Together with approximations of the rate of sequestration in new tree stands, the authors could estimate rates of sequestration and costs (Sedjo, 1989; Moulton and Richards, 1990). More recently, authors have evolved into using econometric and market simulation techniques.

The econometric approach is exemplified by the next two essays (Newell and Stavins, Chapter 22 and Plantinga *et al.*, Chapter 23). Both represent excellent examples that show how econometric techniques can be applied to estimate the opportunity costs of shifting land from one use (agriculture) to another (forestry). A number of authors have focused alternatively on measuring the effects of carbon sequestration policies on forestry and/or agricultural price changes. Given the dynamic nature of forest product supply, and the potential for changes in management or changes in timber rotation ages to influence carbon sequestration, these approaches involve dynamic optimization models that measure effects over time. Examples of this approach include Alig *et al.* (1997), Adams *et al.* (1999), McCarl and Schneider (2001) and Sohngen and Mendelsohn (2003).

Policy Design for GHG Mitigation

As noted in the opening paragraph of this Introduction, the line between cost–benefit analyses of GHG mitigation paths and analyses of specific mitigation instruments and strategies is somewhat artificial. That said, the essays in the first half of Part III focus more specifically on the characteristics of specific policy approaches. The essays in the second half look at some key features and challenges of international agreement to mitigate GHGs at a global level.

The essays by Parry and Williams (Chapter 24) and Pizer (Chapter 25) look in more detail at the key policy instruments usually advanced by economists for GHG mitigation – a carbon tax (in practice, a tax on the carbon content of fossil fuels) and a tradeable permits system. Parry and Williams build on a substantial prior literature in their examination of the relative cost-effectiveness of taxes, permits and other options with less flexibility, such as fixed performance standards. Their analysis considers not just conventional partial equilibrium cost-effectiveness, it also addresses the fact that different instruments generate different public revenue streams, and that these streams can be used in different ways. The authors show, in particular, that 'tax interaction effects' can make a great difference in the overall cost-effectiveness of a GHG control policy. If a policy generates revenue, such as a carbon tax or a tradeable permit system with auctioned allocation, and if the revenue is used to reduce labour and other market-distorting taxes, the result is a net cost to society of GHG mitigation that is much lower – several times lower, in some cases – than it is without the tax interaction effect.

Public finance and environmental economics are thus inextricably linked in the design of climate policy, especially when one takes into account the potential volume of revenue relative to a less ubiquitous pollutant like sulphur dioxide. (The United States, with well over 1 billion tons of carbon emitted in CO_2 every year, could raise billions of dollars of revenue each year with a \$20 per ton carbon tax, depending on how much abatement was induced.) Bovenberg and Goulder (2000) take this point one step further in their analysis of distributional impacts of GHG policy.[6] They show how, because the volume of total revenue from a carbon tax is so large, a relatively small share of this revenue could be channelled back to energy producers to reduce the adverse impacts on their profits without greatly sacrificing overall efficiency. The same outcome could be achieved by allocating a small share of total carbon permits to energy producers and then auctioning the rest. This could increase the political acceptability of GHG control, although the efficiency–distribution trade-off becomes sharper if one also attempts to compensate for adverse impacts on energy sector employment.

Chapter 25 by Pizer looks at a different facet of the design of carbon taxes or permit trading – one that goes back to Weitzman's seminal paper (1974). In the face of uncertainty about the cost of GHG control as well as the damage costs of climate change, are quantity or price instruments preferred? Extending Weitzman's logic, Pizer shows that price instruments are likely to dominate quantity instruments since the marginal damage cost of climate change attributable to a unit of current GHG emission is relatively flat. This logic is developed further by Newell and Pizer (2003b), who show that, although the long-term marginal damage of GHG accumulation may be convex, the cost per unit of current emission is essentially constant because the flow represents such a small share of the total stock in the atmosphere.

Even more interesting is Pizer's argument that a combination of price and quantity instruments may be superior to either option standing alone. A combined approach, often referred to as a 'safety valve', implies in practice a nominal ceiling on total emissions as with a tradeable permits system, but with a government commitment to supply additional permits on demand at a fixed price. If GHG mitigation cost is relatively low, the quantity standard is binding; otherwise, the limit price is the binding constraint. This approach is interesting not just because of its efficiency properties, but also because it could offer a way forward in policy debates between environmental advocates seeking hard ceilings on GHG emissions and others, such as business leaders, who are concerned about the uncertain economic consequences of such a ceiling. An interesting example of such reasoning in an international context is found in Hourcade and Ghersi (2002).

One topic not addressed in detail in any of the essays in the volume is the actual construction of carbon taxes or tradeable permit systems. As noted previously, it is generally presumed that carbon taxes would be implemented through primary energy taxes (on oil, natural gas and coal) related to the carbon content of the energy sources.[7] A similar approach could be used for a tradeable permits system – permits could be attached to the primary production or importation of fossil fuels (Fischer, Kerr and Toman, 1998). This approach is very different than the 'downstream' approach of measuring and regulating actual emissions used in the United States for SO_2 and envisaged for industrial-sector CO_2 trading within the European Union. The upstream approach, though more cost-effective and more comprehensive, also inherits any negative political baggage associated with a carbon tax, which has not exactly been widely embraced in the industrialized world. Composite approaches might then be considered which combine downstream CO_2 trading for larger sources with other measures to address the rest of GHG emissions – like fuel taxes or efficiency standards for households and transport.

Even more complicated is the development of international markets for GHG emissions. The theoretical ideal would be markets based on an agreed global allocation of allowed GHG emissions. In practice, because developing countries did not accept numerical targets for their emissions, the Kyoto Protocol envisages a mixture of emissions trading among parties in the developed world and project-based emissions reductions undertaken voluntarily to generate emissions credits in the developing world (and probably in economies in transition, such as Russia). Project-based activities, as exemplified by the Kyoto Protocol's Clean Development Mechanism (CDM), give rise to inherent difficulties in determining baseline emissions against which to calculate credits, as well as problems in safeguarding the actual generation of claimed credits over time. Against these difficulties, whilst differences in abatement cost between developed and developing countries make international emission trading a desirable possibility, expectations need to be rather modest about the realized efficiency of these transactions (see, for example, Stavins, 1997; Wiener, 1999).

In Chapter 26 Grubb takes up the issue addressed by Wigley *et al.* in Chapter 19, regarding the timing of GHG emissions, but takes as his point of departure the fact that energy systems are inherently full of inertia that, under the best of conditions, impede the selection and penetration of more efficient technologies and that the existence of more obvious distortions, like price controls and subsidies, only aggravate the problem of passing effective signals to investors to reduce GHGs. For Grubb, therefore, the case is made not only for earlier and more aggressive GHG abatement, but also for more technology-oriented interventions to avoid tying up long-lived investments in more GHG-intensive energy systems that will be regretted later. A similar argument can be found in Ha-Duong *et al.* (1997). Grubb concludes that early and more aggressive GHG mitigation is needed to avoid irreversible GHG accumulation and argues furthermore that such mitigation need not be that expensive if a proper suite of policies is used. The view that there is a lot of 'cheap lunch' available for GHG mitigation is found in Interlaboratory Working Group (1997) and Geller and Nadel (1994), as well as in a number of parts of IPCC assessments of specific sector opportunities for GHG abatement.

This view contrasts sharply with that illustrated in the essay by Jaffe and Stavins (Chapter 27). These authors draw a sharp distinction between energy efficiency and economic efficiency. Although they accept the premise that markets are by no means perfect, they also argue that much of what appears to be economically irrational investment in less energy efficient systems reflects either important attributes of the alternative systems not captured in a simple engineering–economic assessment (for example, reliability of newer versus more tested technologies) or rational responses to broader market distortions (which could include not just energy price distortions but also, in developing countries, access to reasonably functioning credit markets for initial investments).

Following on from this perspective is a more conventional economic prescription: provide good price signals to reduce GHGs, lower informational barriers to alternative technology choices and tackle broader market distortions that could impede the selection of socially more desirable energy systems. As Shukla's essay (Chapter 28) reminds us, however, these broader energy–economy relationships are likely to be considerably more complicated and difficult to make more efficient in a developing country with numerous market distortions, like India. In this setting, just deregulating energy prices, for example, could well be very costly in the absence of other measures to reduce informational and financial barriers to cost-effective technologies.

At the same time there may be many opportunities to improve energy efficiency cost-effectively, especially in small enterprises in the informal sector – although targeting policy at these sources is more difficult as well.[8]

The final four papers in the volume address different facets of climate policy at an international level. The essay by Barrett (Chapter 29) examines the difficulties of achieving substantial agreement among many countries whose joint actions are needed to significantly mitigate global GHG emissions. The 'paradox of international agreements' in this context is the high joint value of broad versus narrow participation in such agreement, but the difficulty of achieving broad participation when the benefits are spread over so many countries (in contrast, for example, to a bilateral dispute over access to a waterway). These difficulties are only made more serious when one accounts for the long-term nature of climate change, the great income disparities between rich and poor countries, and the differences in time profiles of GHG emissions – the rich countries of today are responsible for most of the emissions to date, but future emissions will come disproportionately from today's rapidly developing countries.

In Chapter 30 Rose *et al.* address the rich–poor equity issue in the context of a hypothetical international emissions trading system for GHGs and analyse a number of different equity criteria. As might be expected, while a number of rules have similar implications, a sharp distinction can be drawn between rules that essentially put a heavier weight on the well-being of poorer and less GHG-emitting developing countries (for example, through a population-based emission allocation system or an approach designed to limit net damage relative to income), and rules that put a heavier weight on the wealthier and higher-GHG developed countries (for example, grandfathering of current emissions levels). Simple equity rules do not point the way to successful international cooperation for GHG mitigation over time.

Yang (Chapter 31) explores another dimension of North–South relations with respect to climate policy – the sharing of improved technology. Such transfers are called for in both the Framework Convention and the Kyoto Protocol, although the means for effectuating them (beyond business-as-usual private transactions, including the Clean Development Mechanism) has never really been fully elucidated. Yang explores 'tied' transfers from North to South that can be used only for putting in place lower-GHG technology. While global welfare and welfare in both North and South would be better if North and South cooperatively and optimally cut GHG emissions, in the real-world situation of the Kyoto agreement and as suggested by the paradox of international agreements, it is difficult to envisage the South undertaking GHG reductions on its own in the near future. In this situation, the transfers modelled by Yang operate in a broadly similar manner to CDM projects in inducing lower-cost GHG abatement in the South than the North could achieve on its own.

Finally, Babiker *et al.* (Chapter 32) explore how the targets and mechanisms of the Kyoto Protocol might affect developing countries. Generally speaking, these effects are theoretically ambiguous – some developing countries could benefit from the increased competitiveness of certain energy-intensive sectors or capital inflows triggered by lower economic performance in the developed world, but others could be harmed by the drop in demand for their products engendered by the economic impact of GHG reductions in developing countries. Babiker *et al.* highlight how, in particular, the energy-exporting developing countries would experience losses from implementation of the Kyoto agreement and policies that might be undertaken by developed countries to reduce that and other burdens.

Conclusion

Looking at the climate change economics literature as a whole, it is easy to find examples of major uncertainties and gaps in knowledge. These gaps are not just economic, however; they are as much, or more, scientific, technological, political and philosophical. In many ways, the literature has added weight and depth to basic principles in environmental economics: the importance of considering trade-offs, of thinking comprehensively over space and time, and of harnessing incentives. At the same time, the literature has brought attention to important new insights: the challenge of international agreements, institutional barriers to good policy design, the linkages between environmental policies and public finance, and difficulties in specifying intergenerational values. One measure of the progress made by climate change economics may be the discomfort it causes across the political spectrum: liberals decry the emphasis on costs and trade-offs, while conservatives decry the insistence that long-term non-market environmental values are important. The path that the world will take over the next ten or 20 years in climate change policy remains far from clear. Our modest hope is that climate change economics plays a role in that policy evolution.

Notes

1 Available also in the literature are relatively recent surveys of the topic including Carraro (2002) and Kolstad and Toman (2004). Unfortunately, however, no survey in this field stays extremely current for very long. The most recent volumes from the Intergovernmental Panel on Climate Change (McCarthy *et al.*, 2001; Metz *et al.*, 2001) are also extremely valuable references.

2 Many of the models included in the Energy Modeling Forum's ongoing assessments of GHG mitigation costs (see Weyant and Hill, 1999 for a survey) can also operate as full integrated assessment models. The Weyant and Hill survey provides a great deal of information about why mitigation costs may differ across different model specifications, a topic to which we return below. The energy–economy models differ in both their degree of sectoral disaggregation and their representation of international trade in both goods and capital, among other factors. See, for example, McKibben *et al.* (1999) and Bernstein *et al.* (1999).

3 The conversion of other GHGs to CO_2 equivalents based on global warming potentials is in itself a complicated and controversial subject; see, for example, Reilly and Richards (1993) and Smith and Wigley (2000a, 2000b).

4 A somewhat similar line of thinking is seen in variants of what is sometimes called the 'tolerable window' or 'safe corridor' approach (see, for example, Yohe, 1997). This approach establishes certain ranges of acceptable climate change, usually reflected in the size and speed of temperature change, and then seeks within these constraints a least-cost GHG mitigation path, in contrast to the cost–benefit approach in Nordhaus-type modelling.

5 It is also, regrettably, the only one of several interesting climate policy papers from *Nature* that we were able to include in the volume, given that journal's pricing policy for republication.

6 Similar reasoning was developed in an earlier paper by Pezzey (1992).

7 This approach would have to be modified if a cost-effective technology came into existence for end-of-pipe removal and safe storage of CO_2 emissions.

8 For a more detailed illustration of these points in the context of India, see the papers in Toman *et al.* (2003).

References

Adams, D.M., Alig, R.J., McCarl, B.A., Callaway, J.M. and Winnett, S.M. (1999), 'Minimum Cost Strategies for Sequestering Carbon in Forests', *Land Economics*, **75**, pp. 360–74.

Adams, R.M., Fleming, R.A., Chang, C.C., McCarl, B.A. and Rosenzweig, C. (1995), 'A Reassessment of the Economic Effects of Global Climate-Change on U.S. Agriculture', *Climatic Change*, **30** (2), pp. 147–67.

Adams, R.M., Rosenzweig, C., Peart, R.M., Ritchie, J.T., McCarl, B.A., Glyer, J.D., Curry, R.B. Curry, Jones, J.W., Boote, K.J. and Allen, L.H. (1990), 'Global Climate Change and United-States Agriculture', *Nature*, **345** (6272), pp. 219–24.

Alig, R., Adams, D., McCarl, B., Callaway, J. and Winnett, S. (1997), 'Assessing Effects of Mitigation Strategies for Global Climate Change with an Intertemporal Model of the U.S. Forest and Agriculture Sectors', in R.A. Sedjo, R.N. Sampson and J. Wisniewski (eds), *Economics of Carbon Sequestration in Forestry*, Boca Raton: CRC Press.

Baxter, L.W. and Calandri, K. (1992), 'Global Warming and Electricity Demand – A Study of California', *Energy Policy*, **20** (3), pp. 233–44.

Bernstein, P., Montgomery, W.D. and Rutherford, T.F. (1999), 'Global Impacts of the Kyoto Agreement: Results from the MS-MRT Model', *Resource and Energy Economics*, **21** (3–4), pp. 375–414.

Bovenberg, A.L. and Goulder, L.H. (2000), 'Neutralizing the Adverse Industry Impacts of CO_2 Abatement Policies: What Does It Cost?', in C. Carraro and G. Metcalf (eds), *Behavioral and Distributional Effects of Environmental Policies: Evidence and Controversies*, Chicago, IL: University of Chicago Press.

Carraro, C. (2002), 'Climate Change Policy: Models, Controversies, and Strategies', in T. Tietenberg and H. Folmer (eds), *International Yearbook of Environmental and Resource Economics 2002/2003*, Cheltenham: Elgar.

Cline, W.R. (1992), *The Economics of Global Warming*, Washington, DC: Institute for International Economics.

Darwin, R.F., Tsigas, M., Lewandrowski, J. and Raneses, A. (1996), 'Land Use and Cover in Ecological Economics', *Ecological Economics*, **17** (3), pp. 157–81.

Dewees, D. and Wilson, T. (1990), 'Cold Houses and Warm Climates Revisited: On Keeping Warm in Chicago', *Journal of Political Economy*, **98** (3), pp. 656–63.

Fankhauser, S., Tol, R.S.J. and Pearce, D.W. (1998), 'Extensions and Alternatives to Climate Change Impact Valuation: On the Critique of IPCC Working Group III's Impact Estimates', *Environment and Development Economics*, **3** (1), pp. 59–81.

Fisher, A. and Narain, U. (2003), 'Global Warming, Endogenous Risk, and Irreversibility', *Environmental and Resource Economics*, **25** (4), pp. 395–416.

Fischer, C., Kerr, S. and Toman, M.A. (1998), 'Using Emissions Trading to Regulate U.S. Greenhouse Gas Emissions: An Overview of Policy Design and Implementation Issues', *National Tax Journal*, **51**, pp. 453–64.

Fischer, C., Parry, I.W.H. and Pizer, W.A. (2003), 'Instrument Choice for Environmental Protection When Technological Innovation is Endogenous', *Journal of Environmental Economics and Management*, **45** (3), pp. 523–45.

Geller, H. and Nadel, S. (1994), 'Market Transformation Strategies to Promote End-Use Efficiency', *Annual Review of Energy and the Environment*, **19**, pp. 301–46.

Gjerde, J., Grepperud, S. and Kverndokk, S. (1999), 'Optimal Climate Policy under the Possibility of a Catastrophe', *Resource and Energy Economics*, **21** (3–4), pp. 289–317.

Goulder, L.H. and Schneider, S.H. (1999), 'Induced Technological Change and the Attractiveness of CO_2 Abatement Policies', *Resource and Energy Economics*, **21** (3–4), pp. 211–53.

Ha-Duong, M., Grubb, M.J. and Hourcade, J.C. (1997), 'Influence of Socioeconomic Inertia and Uncertainty on Optimal CO_2 Emission Abatement', *Nature*, **390**, pp. 270–73.

Houghton, J.T., Ding, Y., Griggs, D.J., Noguer, M., van der Linden, P.J., Dai, X., Maskell, K. and Johnson, C.A. (eds) (2001), *Climate Change 2001: The Scientific Basis. Contribution of Working Group 1 to the Third Assessment Report of the Intergovernmental Panel on Climate Change*, Cambridge, UK and New York: Cambridge University Press.

Hourcade, J.C. and Ghersi, F. (2002), 'The Economics of a Lost Deal: Kyoto–The Hague–Marrakesh', *Energy Journal*, **23** (3), pp. 1–26.

Howarth, R.B. (2003), 'Discounting and Uncertainty in Climate Change Policy Analysis', *Land Economics*, **79** (3), pp. 369–81.

Interlaboratory Working Group (IWG) (1997), *Scenarios of U.S. Carbon Reductions: Potential Impacts of Energy Technologies by 2010 and Beyond*, Report LBNL-40533 and ORNL-444, Berkeley, CA and Oak Ridge, TN: Lawrence Berkeley National Laboratory and Oak Ridge National Laboratory.

Joyce, L.A., Mills, J.R., Heath, L.S., McGuire, A.D., Haynes, R.W. and Birdsey, R.A. (1995), 'Forest Sector Impacts from Changes in Forest Productivity Under Climate Change', *Journal of Biogeography*, **22**, pp. 703–13.

Kolstad, C.D. and Toman, M.A. (2004, in press), 'The Economics of Climate Policy', in J. Vincent and K.-G. Maler (eds), *Handbook of Environmental Economics*, vol. 3, Amsterdam: Elsevier.

Layton, D.F. and Brown, G. (2000), 'Heterogeneous Preferences Regarding Global Climate Change', *Review of Economics and Statistics*, **82** (4), pp. 616–24.

McCarl, B.A., Adams, D.M., Alig, R.J., Burton, D. and Chen, C. (2000), 'The Effects of Global Climate Change on the US Forest Sector: Response Functions Derived from a Dynamic Resource and Market Simulator', *Climate Research*, **15**, pp. 195–205.

McCarl, B.A. and Schneider, U. (2001), 'Greenhouse Gas Mitigation in U.S. Agriculture and Forestry', *Science*, **294**, pp. 2481–82.

McCarthy, James J., Canziani, Osvaldo F., Leary, Neil A., Dokken, David J. and White, Kasey S. *et al.* (eds) (2001), *Climate Change 2001: Impacts, Adaptation & Vulnerability. Contribution of Working Group II to the Third Assessment Report of the Intergovernmental Panel on Climate Change (IPCC)*, Cambridge: Cambridge University Press.

McKibben, R., Shackleton, R. and Wilcoxen, P.J. (1999), 'What to Expect from an International System of Tradable Permits for Carbon Emissions', *Resource and Energy Economics*, **21** (3–4), pp. 319–46.

Maddison, D.J. and Bigano, A. (1997), 'The Amenity Value of the Italian Climate', *Journal of Environmental Economics and Management*, **45** (2), pp. 319–32.

Manne, A.S. (1996), 'Hedging Strategies for Global Carbon Dioxide Abatement: A Summary of the Poll Results EMF 14 Subgroup – Analysis for Decisions under Uncertainty', in N. Nakiu'novic *et al.* (eds), *Climate Change: Integrating Science, Economics, and Policy*, Laxenburg: International Institute for Applied Systems Analysis.

Manne, A.S. and Richels, R. (1997), 'On Stabilizing CO_2 Concentrations – Cost-Effective Emission Reduction Strategies', *Environmental Modeling & Assessment*, **2** (4), pp. 251–65.

Mendelsohn, R. (2001), *Global Warming and the American Economy: A Regional Assessment of Climate Change Impacts*, Northampton, MA: Edward Elgar.

Mendelsohn, R., Morrison, W., Schlesinger, M.E. and Andronova, N.G. (2000), 'Country-Specific Market Impacts of Climate Change', *Climatic Change*, **45** (3–4), pp. 553–69.

Mendelsohn, R. and Neumann, J. (1999), *The Impact of Climate Change on the United States Economy*, Cambridge: Cambridge University Press.

Metz, B., Davidson, O., Swart, R. and Pan, J. (eds) (2001), *Climate Change 2001: Mitigation. Contribution of Working Group III to the Third Assessment Report of the Intergovernmental Panel on Climate Change (IPCC)*, Cambridge: Cambridge University Press.

Moore, T.G. (1998), 'Health and Amenity Effects of Global Warming', *Economic Inquiry*, **36**, pp. 471–88.

Morrison, W. and Mendelsohn, R. (1999), 'The Impact of Global Warming on US Energy Expenditures', in R. Mendelsohn and J.E. Neumann (eds), *The Impact of Climate Change on the United States Economy*, Cambridge: Cambridge University Press.

Moulton, R. and Richards, K. (1990), *Costs of Sequestering Carbon Through Tree Planting and Forest Management in the United States*, General Technical Report WO-58, Washington, DC: US Department of Agriculture.

Newell, R.G. and Pizer, W.A. (2003a), 'Discounting the Distant Future: How Much do Uncertain Rates Increase Valuations?', *Journal of Environmental Economics and Management*, **46** (1), pp. 52–71.

Newell, R.G. and Pizer, W.A. (2003b), 'Regulating Stock Externalities Under Uncertainty', *Journal of Environmental Economics and Management*, **45** (2S), pp. 416–32.

Nordhaus, W.D. (1994), 'Expert Opinion on Climatic-Change', *American Scientist*, **82** (1), pp. 45–51.

Nordhaus, W. and Boyer, J. (2000), *Warming the World: Economic Models of Global Warming*, Cambridge, MA: MIT Press.

Nordhaus, W.D. and Yang, Z. (1996), 'A Regional Dynamic General-Equilibrium Model of Alternative Climate-Change Strategies', *American Economic Review*, **86** (4), pp. 741–65.

Peck, S.C. and Teisberg, T.J. (1993), 'Global Warming Uncertainties and the Value of Information: An Analysis Using CETA', *Resource and Energy Economics*, **15** (1), pp. 71–97.

Pendleton, L.H. and Mendelsohn, R. (1998), 'Estimating the Economic Impact of Climate Change on the Freshwater Sportsfisheries of the Northeastern US', *Land Economics*, **74** (4), pp. 483–96.

Perez-Garcia, J., Joyce, L.A., McGuire, A.D. and Binkley, C.S. (1997), 'Economic Impact of Climatic Change on the Global Forest Sector', in R.A. Sedjo, R.N. Sampson and J. Wisniewski (eds), *Economics of Carbon Sequestration in Forestry*, Boca Raton: Lewis Publishers.

Pezzey, J. (1992), 'The Symmetry between Controlling Pollution by Price and Controlling it by Quantity', *Canadian Journal of Economics*, **25** (4), pp. 983–91.

Pizer, W.A. (1999), 'The Optimal Choice of Climate Change Policy in the Presence of Uncertainty', *Resource and Energy Economics*, **21** (3–4), pp. 255–87.

Pizer, W.A. (2003), 'Climate Change Catastrophes', Resources for the Future Discussion Paper 03-31, May, Washington, DC: Resources for the Future, available through www.rff.org.

Reilly, J.M., Hohmann, N. and Kane, S. (1994), 'Climate-Change and Agricultural Trade – Who Benefits, Who Loses', *Global Environmental Change – Human and Policy Dimensions*, **4** (1), pp. 24–36.

Reilly, J.M. and Richards, K.R. (1993), 'Climate Change Damage and the Trace Gas Index Issue', *Environmental and Resource Economics*, **3** (1), pp. 41–61.

Richards, K. and Stokes, C. (2004), 'A Review of Forest Carbon Sequestration Cost Studies: A Dozen Years of Research', *Climatic Change*, forthcoming.

Rosenthal, D.H., Gruenspecht, H.K. and Moran, E.A. (1995), 'Effects of Global Warming on Energy Use for Space Heating and Cooling in the United States', *Energy Journal*, **16** (2), pp. 77–96.

Rosenzweig, C. and Parry, M.L. (1994), 'Potential Impact of Climate-Change on World Food-Supply', *Nature*, **367** (6459), pp. 133–38.

Sedjo, R.A. (1989), 'Forests to Offset the Greenhouse Effect', *Journal of Forestry*, **87**, pp. 12–16.

Sedjo, R.A., Sampson, R.N. and Wisniewski, J. (1997), *Economics of Carbon Sequestration in Forestry*, Boca Raton: CRC Press.

Sedjo, R.A., Wisniewski, J., Sample, A.V. and Kinsman, J.D. (1995), 'The Economics of Managing Carbon via Forestry: Assessment of Existing Studies', *Environmental and Resource Economics*, **6**, pp. 139–65.

Segerson, K. and Dixon, B.L. (1999), 'Climate Change and Agriculture: The Role of Farmer Adaptation', in Robert Mendelsohn and James E. Neumann (eds), *The Impact of Climate Change on the United States Economy*, Cambridge: Cambridge University Press.

Smith, S.J. and Wigley, T.M.L. (2000a), 'Global Warming Potentials: 1. Climatic Implications of Emissions Reductions', *Climatic Change*, **44**, pp. 445–57.

Smith, S.J. and Wigley, T.M.L. (2000b), 'Global Warming Potentials: 2. Accuracy', *Climatic Change*, **44**, pp. 459–69.

Sohngen, B. and Alig, R. (2000), 'Mitigation, Adaptation, and Climate Change: Results from Recent Research on the U.S. Forest Sector', *Environmental Science and Policy*, **3**, pp. 235–48.

Sohngen, B. and Mendelsohn, R. (2003), 'An Optimal Control Model of Forest Carbon Sequestration', *American Journal of Agricultural Economics*, **85** (2), pp. 448–57.

Sohngen, B., Mendelsohn, R. and Sedjo, R. (2001), 'A Global Model of Climate Change Impacts on Timber Markets', *Journal of Agricultural and Resource Economics*, **26** (2), pp. 326–43.

Stavins, R. (1997), 'Policy Instruments for Climate Change: How Can National Governments Address a Global Problem?', *The University of Chicago Legal Forum 1997*, pp. 293–329.

Tol, R.S.J. (1999), 'The Marginal Costs of Greenhouse Gas Emissions', *Energy Journal*, **20** (1), pp. 61–81.

Tol, R.S.J. (2001), 'Equitable Cost-benefit Analysis of Climate Change Policies', *Ecological Economics*, **36** (1), pp. 71–85.

Tol, R.S.J. (2002), 'Estimates of the Damage Costs of Climate Change. Part 1: Benchmark Estimates', *Environmental and Resource Economics*, **21** (1), pp. 47–73.

Tol, R.S.J., Fankhauser, S. and Smith, J.B. (1998), 'The Scope for Adaptation to Climate Change: What Can We Learn from the Impact Literature?', *Global Environmental Change – Human and Policy Dimensions*, **8** (2), pp. 109–23.

Toman, M.A., Chakravorty, U. and Gupta, S. (eds) (2003), *India and Climate Change: Perspectives on Economics and Policy from a Developing Country*, Washington, DC: Resources for the Future.

Toman, M.A., Morgenstern, R. and Anderson, J. (1999), 'The Economics of "When" Flexibility in the Design of Greenhouse Gas Abatement Policies', *Annual Review of Energy and the Environment*, **24**, pp. 431–60.

Weitzman, M.L. (1974), 'Prices vs. Quantities', *Review of Economic Studies*, **41** (4), pp. 477–91.

Weitzman, M.L. (1998), 'Why the Far-Distant Future Should Be Discounted at Its Lowest Possible Rate', *Journal of Environmental Economics and Management*, **36** (3), pp. 201–208.

Weyant, J.P. and Hill, J. (1999), 'Introduction and Overview', *The Energy Journal*, Special Issue, pp. vii–xiiv.

Wiener, J.B. (1999), 'Global Environmental Regulation: Instrument Choice in Legal Context', *Yale Law Journal*, **108** (4), pp. 677–800.

Yohe, G.W. (1997), 'Uncertainty, Short-term Hedging, and the Tolerable Window Approach', *Global Environmental Change*, **7** (4), pp. 303–15.

Part I
Climate Change and its Impacts

[1]

The science of global warming

JOHN HOUGHTON

Hadley Centre, Meteorological Office, Berks., UK

There is strong scientific evidence that the average temperature of the earth's surface is rising as a result of the increased concentration of carbon dioxide and other greenhouse gases in the atmosphere owing to human activities, especially the burning of fossil fuels, coal, oil, and gas. This global warming will lead to substantial changes of climate, many of which will impact human communities in deleterious ways. In terms of the likely global pattern of climate change over the twenty-first century, in the absence of any mitigating action the global average temperature is likely to rise by between about 1·5 and 5·5°C and sea level by about half a metre (range 0·1–0·9 m). The hydrological cycle is likely to be more intense (leading in some places to more frequent and more intense floods and droughts) and the rate of climate change is likely to be substantially greater than the earth has experienced over at least the last ten thousand years. It is particularly to this rapid rate of change that it will be difficult for many ecosystems and for humans to adapt. Action has been taken by the world's scientists through the Intergovernmental Panel on Climate Change to assess as thoroughly as possible knowledge regarding the basic science and the impacts, including an assessment of the uncertainties. The world's governments have also taken action in setting up the Framework Convention on Climate Change (FCCC) at the Earth Summit in 1992 and at subsequent meetings of the parties to that convention, especially that at Kyoto in 1997. In order to mitigate climate change the FCCC in its article 2 has set the objective of stabilisation of the concentration of greenhouse gases in the atmosphere at a level and on a timescale consistent with the needs both of the environment and of sustainable development. Such stabilisation will eventually demand severe cuts in global emissions, for instance of carbon dioxide, to levels well below today's by the second half of the twenty-first century. To achieve the required reductions in the emissions of carbon dioxide, three possibilities are available, to sequester carbon dioxide resulting from the burning of fossil fuels rather than releasing it to the atmosphere, to become much more efficient in the generation and use of energy, and to provide for energy supply from non-fossil fuel sources. This article will summarise the science of climate change including the evidence for it and will describe the main impacts, the actions taken so far, and the further actions that are likely to be necessary to mitigate climate change.

Variations in day to day weather occur all the time; they are very much part of our lives. The climate of a region is its average weather over a period that may be a few months, a season, or a few years. Variations in climate are also very familiar to us. We describe summers as wet or dry, winters as mild, cold, or stormy, recognising that in many parts of the world the seasons vary a great deal from year to year.

Most of the variations we take for granted. Those we particularly notice are the extreme situations and the climate disasters. During recent decades, different parts of the world have experienced extreme temperatures, record floods, droughts, and windstorms. Such extremes are an important manifestation of the large natural variability of the climate; their impact has served to emphasise the vulnerability of human communities to climate variation and extremes. This is well illustrated by the unparalleled losses experienced by the insurance industry during the later years of the 1980s and the 1990s. Although there is no strong evidence that these events are outside the range of the natural variability of climate experienced in historic times, their impact has served to add more relevance to the question whether human activities (such as fossil fuel burning) are likely to lead to substantial and damaging future climate change. To obtain a perspective on climate change we shall first look at the climate of the last hundred thousand years or so, which has been dominated by the last ice age, and then look at climate trends over the last century.

The climate record over many thousands of years can be built up by analysing the composition of the ice and the air trapped in the ice obtained from different depths from cores drilled from the Antarctic or the Greenland icecaps. Figure 1 records the temperature at which the ice was laid down and the atmospheric carbon dioxide content over the last hundred and sixty thousand years from an Antarctic ice core. Currently the earth's climate is in a warm phase which began when the last ice age came to an end about twenty thousand years ago; the last warm period was about a hundred and twenty thousand years ago. The main triggers for the ice ages have been the small regular variations in the geometry of the earth's orbit about the sun which affect the distribution of solar radiation at the earth's surface. Of particular interest is the strong correlation between the atmospheric temperature and the carbon dioxide content. Part of this undoubtedly arises because the amount of carbon dioxide in the atmosphere is dependent on factors that are strongly related to the average surface temperature. But it is also true that it is not possible to understand the range of temperature variations of the past without allowing for the influ-

Climate Change

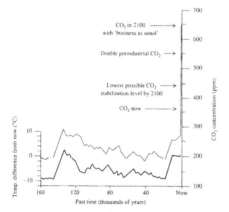

1 Observations from the Vostok ice core, showing variation of atmospheric temperature over Antarctica (it is estimated that the variation of global average temperature would be of the order of half that in the polar regions) and of atmospheric carbon dioxide concentration, for the last hundred and sixty thousand years: note the current value of carbon dioxide concentration of about 370 ppm and the likely rise during the twenty-first century under various projections of its growth

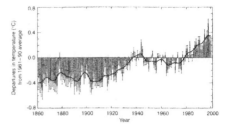

2 Changes in global annual mean surface temperature since 1860 relative to the 1961–90 average, shown by vertical bars (thin whisker bars indicate the 95% confidence range) and a smoothed curve giving the decadal average: data from thermometers

ence of carbon dioxide on atmospheric temperature through the greenhouse effect (*see* below). Note also from Fig. 1 the very rapid rise in atmospheric carbon dioxide concentration over the past two hundred years or so as a result of human activities, which has taken the concentration of this gas well outside the range of its natural variation during the last million years or more.

The changes in the average air temperature near the earth's surface over the past century or so, as established from the instrumental record, are shown in Fig. 2. Over this period this temperature has increased by somewhat more than 0·5°C, although the increase has not been uniform. There are strong indications that the increase since the 1970s is linked with the growth in the atmosphere of greenhouse gases such as carbon dioxide from anthropogenic sources. The 1990s have been particularly warm in terms of this global average temperature. Not only was 1998 the warmest year on record, but the first eight months of 1998 were the warmest of those months on record. Note also the year to year variations that are a further illustration of natural climate variability. (In Fig. 6 is shown a record constructed from proxy data for the last millennium, showing that 1998 is also likely to be the warmest year in the northern hemisphere over the last millennium.)

Greenhouse effect

That the earth's surface is kept warm by the 'greenhouse effect' has been known for nearly two centuries. But it was just one hundred years ago, in 1896, that

Svante Arrhenius, a Swedish chemist, made the first calculation of the average rise in temperature to be expected at the earth's surface if the atmospheric carbon dioxide concentration should double. His estimate of 5 or 6°C was not far out, just a little larger than current estimates that fall in the range 1·5 to 4·5°C.

The earth absorbs radiation from the sun, mainly at its surface. A balancing amount of energy is then radiated to space at longer, infrared, wavelengths. Some of the gases in the atmosphere, particularly water vapour, carbon dioxide, and methane, and clouds absorb some of the infrared radiation emitted by the surface and themselves emit radiation from higher altitudes at colder temperatures. The earth's surface is thereby kept about 30°C warmer than it would otherwise be. This is known as the greenhouse effect because the glass in a greenhouse possesses similar optical properties to the atmosphere.

Increases in the concentration of the 'greenhouse gases' will tend to lead to further warming of the surface and the lower atmosphere; this is the 'enhanced greenhouse effect'. Its approximate magnitude can be simply estimated from radiation energy balance calculations, but for detailed information, sophisticated computer models have to be used which take into account the influences of the atmospheric and oceanic circulations (*see* the section 'Has anthropogenic climate change been observed?').

It was in the late 1960s that scientists began to realise that the rate of increase of the amount of atmospheric carbon dioxide, owing to the increasing rate of burning of fossil fuels, was such that significant global warming would occur. Associated with the warming would be substantial changes in the earth's climate. By the late 1980s, wide concern was being expressed about the likely impact of climate change and it became a subject firmly on the political agenda.

Intergovernmental Panel on Climate Change

The Intergovernmental Panel on Climate Change (IPCC) was formed in 1988 jointly by two UN bodies, the World Meteorological Organization and the UN Environment Programme, to provide assessments of future climate change and its likely impact. Its first report, published in 1990, provided the scientific basis for the Framework Convention on Climate Change (FCCC) agreed at the Earth Summit held in Rio de Janeiro in June 1992 and ratified by about a hundred and sixty nations. To assist in the convention process, a comprehensive report was produced by the IPCC at the end of 1995 and a further full report published in 2001. The writing and review process of these reports has involved the leading scientists in the world in the field of climate change together with many hundreds of other scientists from many countries – in fact, a large proportion of the world's scientists who are involved in this field. The policymakers' summaries of the reports have been agreed at meetings at which delegates from up to a hundred countries have been present as well as representatives of non-governmental organisations and of the scientific community. Their findings therefore have the support both of the scientific community and of governments.

The IPCC has not only assessed the basic science of climate change but also its likely impacts on human activities and the options for adaptation to those impacts. It has also addressed how climate change can be mitigated through the reduction of emissions of greenhouse gases into the atmosphere, for instance by changes in the generation and use of energy, by the sequestration of carbon dioxide, or by reducing the emissions of methane from a variety of sources. The IPCC has also supported the work of the FCCC through its assessments of studies of the likely economic costs of the damage due to climate change and its assessments of adaptation and mitigation and of studies of the social and political implications of action and inaction. The material in this paper that summarises all aspects of the issue of anthropogenic global climate change is substantially based on the IPCC reports, in particular on the third assessment report published in 2001.

Greenhouse gases

The main greenhouse gases that are produced by human activities are carbon dioxide and methane. Their atmospheric concentrations have risen by about 30% (Fig. 3) and 150% respectively since preindustrial times, largely because of fossil fuel use, land use change (for example deforestation), and agriculture. Carbon dioxide is responsible for about two thirds of the enhanced greenhouse effect to date due to the increases in greenhouse gases. If no action is taken to mitigate emissions of carbon dioxide, the level of emissions and its atmospheric concentration will continue to rise throughout the next century (Fig. 3). Its concentration could reach 560 ppm, double its preindustrial concentration, before the year 2100.

Other greenhouse gases of importance (Fig. 4) are nitrous oxide, which has contributed about 6% to the

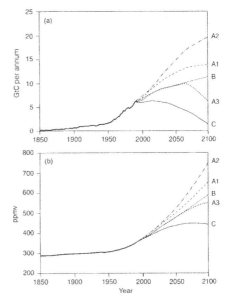

3 *a* global net carbon emissions from fossil fuel use 1850–1990 and for scenarios to 2100 (gigatonnes per annum). The scenarios make different assumptions about economic growth, fuel availability, and development of new renewable energy sources: curves A and B assume 'business as usual' (i.e. no strong pressure to reduce fossil fuel use for environmental reasons), A3 assumes rapid technical innovation to bring in non-fossil fuel sources, C is an 'ecologically driven' scenario; and *b* atmospheric carbon dioxide concentration in parts per million from 1850–1990 and for scenarios in *a* to 2100

greenhouse effect to date, the chlorofluorocarbons (CFCs), and ozone. Emissions of chlorofluorocarbons into the atmosphere have led to some destruction of the ozone layer, most dramatically illustrated by the discovery of the ozone hole over Antarctica in 1985. Because ozone is also a greenhouse gas, this ozone destruction has partially compensated for the greenhouse effect of the chlorofluorocarbons.

An important consideration is the time taken for the anthropogenic emissions of greenhouse gases to be removed from the atmosphere. For methane, the removal process is governed by chemical reactions; the lifetime of methane in the atmosphere is about ten years. On the timescales we are considering, carbon dioxide emitted into the atmosphere is not destroyed but redistributed among the carbon reservoirs, in the biosphere, and in the ocean. The carbon reservoirs exchange carbon between themselves on a wide range of timescales which vary from less than a year to decades (for exchange with the top layers of the ocean and the land biosphere) or to millennia (for the deep ocean or long lived soil pools). The

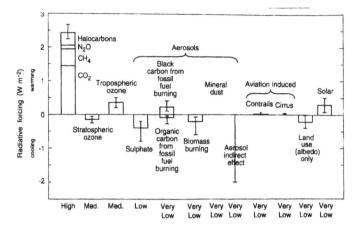

4 Estimates of globally and annually averaged anthropogenic radiative forcing resulting from changes in concentrations of greenhouse gases and aerosols from preindustrial times to 1992 and from natural changes in solar output from 1850 to the present. The indirect aerosol effect arises from the induced change in cloud properties owing to aerosols. Error bars indicate the range of uncertainty in the estimates; an indication is also provided of the degree of scientific understanding for each component. A vertical line without a rectangular bar denotes a forcing for which a best estimate cannot be given owing to the large uncertainties. Some of the radiative forcing agents are well mixed over the globe, for instance carbon dioxide, thereby perturbing the global heat balance; others represent perturbations with strong regional signatures, for instance aerosols. For this and other reasons, a simple sum of the positive and negative bars cannot be expected to yield the net effect on the climate system

large range of turnover times means that the time taken for a perturbation in the atmospheric carbon dioxide concentration to relax back to an equilibrium state cannot be described by a single time constant. Although a lifetime of about a hundred years is often quoted for atmospheric carbon dioxide so as to provide some guide, use of a single lifetime can be misleading.

Other factors influencing climate change

In recent years there has been more recognition and quantification of the role of anthropogenic aerosols (microscopic particles in the atmosphere) in climate change. Of particular importance are those which originate from the sulphur containing gases emitted from power stations – effluents which also give rise to the acid rain problem. These aerosols reflect sunlight and so tend to cool the earth's surface. However, they are very short lived (a few days) and so are concentrated near industrial regions. Locally their cooling effect can be comparable in magnitude to the warming effect of the increase of greenhouse gases. However, it is important to realise that their effect on the climate is not confined to the regions where they are concentrated, so their impact on climate change is not a simple offset to that of the greenhouse gases. Their effect in the future will be limited by the increasing recognition of the requirement to avoid the deleterious effects of acid rain.

In Fig. 4 are illustrated estimates of the globally averaged radiative forcing (a measure of influence on global climate) of aerosols from different sources compared with that due to increases in greenhouse gases, from preindustrial times to the present. Also shown is an estimate based on the best information available of the radiative forcing which may have occurred as a result of variations in the incident solar radiation during this period.

Has anthropogenic climate change been observed?

Can the observed warming in recent years be attributed to the increase in greenhouse gases? The 1990 IPCC assessment concluded that there was insufficient evidence to argue that the anthropogenic climate 'signal' had emerged from the 'noise' of climate variability. The 1995 IPCC assessment was more positive and included the sentence – agreed after a long and lively debate – 'The balance of evidence suggests a discernible human influence on climate.' Work since 1995 has provided stronger evidence that most of the warming observed over the last fifty years is attributable to human activities. Figure 5 illustrates the agreement that now exists for the global mean surface temperature for the twentieth century between observations and simulations with the best climate models that take into account both anthropogenic and natural forcings.

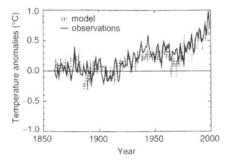

5 **Global annual mean temperature changes from 1860 to 2000 as simulated by the UK Hadley Centre climate model, compared with observations over the same period: the band of model results presented is for four runs with the same model; natural forcings included are solar variation and volcanic activity**

Modelling climate change

To ascertain the surface temperature change to be expected from an increase in radiative forcing, information about the forcing from different constituents such as those in Fig. 4 is introduced as input into a radiative transfer model of the average atmosphere. On the assumption that nothing else changes apart from the temperature of the surface and lower atmosphere, a relatively simple calculation can be made of the increase in global average surface air temperature which occurs for a radiative forcing of 4 W m^{-2}, the value appropriate to an increase of carbon dioxide concentration to 560 ppm, double its preindustrial value. It turns out to be about 1.2°C.

In reality, of course, many other factors will change, some in ways that add to the warming (positive feedbacks) others in ways that might reduce the warming (negative feedbacks). Examples of positive feedbacks which are understood reasonably well are those due to water vapour (a warmer atmosphere on average means increased water vapour content) and to changes in ice cover (decrease of ice cover means more absorption of solar radiation at the surface). The magnitude of the feedback resulting from changes in cloud cover and type, which may be positive or negative and which may vary from place to place, is still not well understood.

The situation is therefore much more complex than the simple calculation suggests. When the feedbacks are taken into account, the best estimate at the present time, should a doubling of preindustrial carbon dioxide occur, is that the rise in global average surface air temperature would be in the range 1·5 to 4·5 °C (the reason for this relatively large range is to take into account the uncertainty in the cloud feedback) with a best estimate of 2·5 °C.

When compared with the temperature changes we commonly experience, a rise of 2·5°C does not seem very large. But remember it is a rise in the *average*

temperature over the whole globe. Between the middle of an ice age and the warm periods in between ice ages, the global average temperature changes by only about 5 or 6°C (Fig. 1). So should the 2·5°C rise occur over a century or less, the change is large in the context of climate change; it would in fact represent a change of climate more rapid than has been experienced by the earth at any time during the last ten thousand years.

So far the discussion has been in terms of changes in the global average, which provides a good overall indicator of the amount and rate of climate change. However, the character of change will be far from uniform over the earth's surface; it will vary enormously with location. What concerns human communities is the detail of climate change in their particular region. To elucidate the detail of climate change, computer models of the climate system are employed. The most highly developed of these are general circulation models (GCMs) which include the basic mathematical equations describing the system physics and dynamics and which couple these for both the atmospheric and oceanic circulations. They are more complex versions of the GCMs which are employed for day to day weather forecasting. To achieve adequate resolution in space and time, they are run on the largest computers available, which can then simulate climate variations and change over model runs which cover many centuries of simulated time. In most advanced countries of the world there are laboratories where such sophisticated models are available.

The most important feature of these climate models is that they are able adequately to sum the effects arising from the wide variety of processes which occur within the atmosphere and oceans so as to give the overall response. Because all the processes are nonlinear in character they cannot be added up in any other way.

Climate models are validated by assessing how well they describe the details of current climate both in terms of its average and variability. Comparison can also be made with observations for model simulations of past climates, of major climate regimes such as those associated with the El Niño phenomena, and of climatic perturbations such as those associated with volcanic eruptions. For all these the latest models show impressive skill in simulation.

Future anthropogenic climate change

To project anthropogenic climate change into the future, estimates of future emissions of greenhouse gases are first required. These will depend on the assumptions made about such factors as the likely growth of the world economy, the availability of fossil fuels, and the degree of pressure for environmental change. For carbon dioxide, several such scenarios are illustrated in Fig. 3. The upper estimates

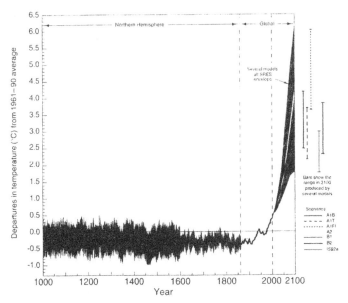

6   From 1000–1860, observations of variations in average surface temperature of the northern hemisphere
    (adequate data from the southern hemisphere not available) constructed from proxy data (tree rings,
    corals, ice cores, and historical records): the line shows the fifty year average, the grey region the 95%
    confidence limit in the annual data. Data for 1860–2000 are as in Fig. 2. From 2000 to 2100 projections
    are of globally averaged surface temperature for the six illustrative scenarios from the IPCC's 2000
    'Special report on emission scenarios' (SRES) and the earlier IPCC scenario IS92a, as estimated by a
    model with average climate sensitivity. The grey region labelled 'several models all SRES envelope'
    shows the range of results from the full range of thirty-five SRES scenarios in addition to those from a
    range of models with different climate sensitivities

assume high economic growth coupled with little
pressure for reduction in emissions for environmental
reasons. Under these scenarios emissions of carbon
dioxide into the atmosphere due to human activities,
currently about seven billion tonnes of carbon per
year, rise to up to twenty billion tonnes by the year
2100. The lowest estimate derives from a scenario
assuming strong environmental pressure, leading by
2100 to stabilisation of the carbon dioxide concentration at about 450 ppm, about 60% above its preindustrial level.

Other greenhouse gases will also increase in concentration. For instance, methane (the anthropogenic
sources of which are mainly related to cattle farming,
rice cultivation, the oil and gas industry, and landfill)
may double in concentration by 2100. Because of
other environmental problems (for example acid
rain), aerosol concentrations from anthropogenic
sources are not likely to grow substantially, and
might even on average reduce from their present level.

From the projections of the concentrations of
carbon dioxide and other greenhouse gases, estimates
may be made from climate models of the associated
increases in global mean surface air temperature.
Figure 6 shows the projections to the year 2100 for
the range of six scenarios published by the IPCC in

its special report on emission scenarios (*see* 'Further
reading'), showing increases in the range 1·4 to 5·8 °C
by 2100. Figure 6 compares these increases with the
variations in global mean surface temperature over
the past hundred and forty years as in Fig. 2 as well
as the variations for the northern hemisphere (not
enough data exist for the southern hemisphere) estimated from proxy data for the past millennium.

The greatest uncertainties in the projection of climate change in the twenty-first century arise from
our lack of knowledge of (1) the future profiles of
emissions of greenhouse gases, (2) some of the feedbacks in the climate system, especially those arising
from changes in cloudiness, (3) changes in the ocean
circulation, and (4) changes in the biosphere. Because
of these factors, projections of climate change on the
regional scale possess greater uncertainty than those
of global averages. Increased understanding of these
issues will come from combining more accurate observations possessing better coverage with careful model
simulations.

Impacts of climate change

Expressing climate change in terms of the increase in
global average temperature is not very meaningful

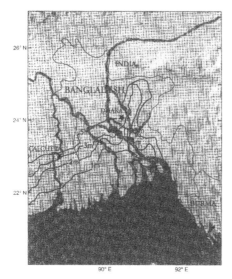

7 **Land affected in Bangladesh by various amounts of sea level rise**

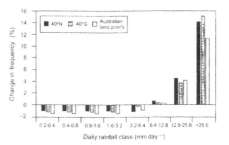

8 **Changes in frequency of occurrence of different daily rainfalls with doubled carbon dioxide concentration, as simulated by the Australian CSIRO model: note that small rates of rainfall tend to reduce, whilst large rainfall rates tend to become larger**

for most of us. What about its impacts on our lives? In some locations, the impacts may be positive. For instance, for some crops, increased carbon dioxide aids growth and at high northern latitudes the growing season will be longer. However, because humans and ecosystems have adapted closely to the current climate, most of the impacts will be deleterious. The most important impacts are likely to be on sea level, changes in rainfall, and temperature extremes. These impacts are considered in turn.

Sea level rise

The expected rise in sea level of about half a metre (range from 0·1 to 0·9 m) by the year 2100 arises mostly from the expansion of water in the oceans because of the increased temperature and the melting of glaciers; the contribution from changes in the ice sheets in the Arctic and Antarctic is expected to be small. As more of the ocean warms, sea level will continue to rise for many centuries, even if the greenhouse gas concentrations are stabilised. Adaptation, at a cost, to a rise of a metre or less will be possible in many coastal regions. However, adaptation will be extremely difficult, if not impossible, in some particularly vulnerable areas such as the delta regions of large rivers in Bangladesh (Fig. 7), Egypt, and Southern China and the many low lying islands in the Indian and Pacific oceans. The situation in many of these areas will be exacerbated because the land is sinking for other reasons, for instance tectonic movement and the extraction of groundwater, at a similar rate to the sea level rises expected from global warming. Substantial loss of land will occur in these areas and many millions of people (six million live

below the one metre contour in Bangladesh) are likely to be displaced.

Impact on water availability

Water is becoming an increasingly valuable resource. Demand for water increased by a factor of ten in the twentieth century, particularly in countries where it is extensively used for irrigation. There are already significant tensions especially in regions where the water from major river systems is shared between nations. It is not surprising that Boutros Boutros-Ghali, the former Secretary-General of the UN, has suggested that wars in the future are likely to be about water rather than oil.

A major impact of global warming is likely to be on water supplies. Warming of the earth's surface means greater evaporation and, on average, a higher water vapour content in the atmosphere that in turn leads to a more vigorous hydrological cycle. This means an increased tendency to heavy rainfall, leading to an increasing possibility of floods in some places. It also means, perhaps surprisingly, an increased tendency to less rainfall and hence periods of drought in other places, because of the interaction of the more vigorous hydrological cycle with the atmospheric circulation. Although the reliability of climate models is limited as far as regional detail is concerned, they provide some estimates of the likely effects (Fig. 8). Many parts of the world are likely to see substantial changes in rainfall patterns and the availability of soil moisture. Those likely to be most seriously affected are those with periods of particularly heavy rainfall (for example the regions covered by the Asian summer monsoon) and those with marginal rainfall.

Impacts on food and health

Studies of global food supplies in a globally warmed world tend to suggest that the global quantity of available food might not be affected by very much – some regions might be able to grow more while others grow less. However, the distribution of food pro-

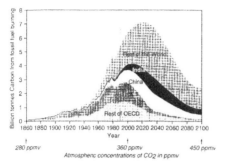

9 The 'contraction and convergence' proposal of the Global Commons Institute: global carbon emissions from fossil fuel use 1860–1990 showing share amongst groups of countries, then as projected for a scenario leading to eventual stabilisation of atmospheric carbon dioxide concentration at 450 ppm. By 2030 it is assumed that the sharing of emissions has converged to be on the basis of equal per capita emissions rights

duction will change, not least because of changed water availability. The regions likely to be adversely affected are those in developing countries in the subtropics where there are rapidly growing populations. In areas where agricultural production becomes inadequate to meet local needs there could be large numbers of environmental refugees.

Other important impacts of the likely climate change are on human health (increased heat stress and more widespread vector borne diseases such as malaria) and on the health of some ecosystems (for example forests) which will not be able to adapt rapidly enough to match the rate of climate change.

Costing the impact of climate change

It is not an easy task to estimate the likely cost to the world community of the impacts briefly listed above. For a costing to be at all realistic, especially when it is to apply to periods of decades into the future, it must account not only for direct damage but also for the possibilities of adaptation. However, even though many of the attempts at costing are relatively crude, they help to provide an idea of the size of the problem.

The most detailed cost studies of the impacts of climate change in a world with carbon dioxide concentration doubled from its preindustrial level have been carried out for the USA. For those impacts against which some value of damage can be placed (for example sea level rise, change in water supplies, increased morbidity owing to heat stress), estimates of annual cost fall in the range of about 1 to 1·5% of GDP. For other countries in the developed world, estimates of the cost of impacts are generally similar to those for the USA. For developing countries, estimates are typically larger, in the range 2 to 9% of GDP.

In considering such estimates it must be realised that there are important factors which they do not take into account. One such factor is that they apply to impacts when the carbon dioxide amount is doubled from its preindustrial value. The longer term impacts if carbon dioxide concentrations continue to rise are likely to be much greater. Another factor is that not all impacts can be quantified in terms of economic costs. This point is emphasised by concentrating on those in some developing countries who are likely to be particularly disadvantaged by anthropogenic climate change and who might become environmental refugees. One estimate is that there could be more than a hundred and fifty million such refugees by the year 2050.

Framework Convention on Climate Change

Establishment of the FCCC

The Framework Convention on Climate Change (FCCC), signed by over a hundred and sixty countries at the UN Conference on Environment and Development (the Earth Summit) held in Rio de Janeiro in June 1992, came into force on 21 March 1994. The convention sets the context in which international action regarding the issue of climate change can be pursued. It recognises the reality of global warming, recognises also the uncertainties associated with current predictions of climate change, agrees that action to mitigate the effects of climate change needs to be taken, and points out that developed countries should take the lead in this action.

In its consideration of an appropriate response to the possibility of climate change, the FCCC applies the precautionary principle. This is stated in article 3, where the parties to the convention are instructed to

take precautionary measures to anticipate, prevent or minimize the causes of climate change and mitigate its adverse effects. Where there are threats of serious or irreversible damage, lack of full scientific certainty should not be used as a reason for postponing such measures, taking into account that policies and measures to deal with climate change should be cost-effective so as to ensure global benefits at the lowest possible cost.

The FCCC mentions one particular aim and one longer term objective. The particular aim is that developed countries ('annex I countries' in FCCC parlance) should take action to return their greenhouse gas emissions, in particular those of carbon dioxide, to their 1990 levels by the year 2000. The objective stated in article 2 says:

The ultimate objective of this Convention ... is to achieve ... stabilisation of greenhouse gas concentrations in the atmosphere at a level that would prevent dangerous anthropogenic interference with the climate system. Such a level should be achieved within a time frame sufficient to allow ecosystems to adapt naturally to climate change, to ensure that food production is not threatened and to enable economic development to proceed in a sustainable manner.

In this statement of its objective, the FCCC places action concerning climate change clearly in the context of sustainable development. The balance that this implies between environmental protection on the one hand and economic development on the other must be based on the best possible scientific, economic, and technical analyses of all the factors involved. The IPCC is the international body through which the information is assessed and provided to the FCCC.

What does the requirement for the stabilisation of the atmospheric concentrations of greenhouse gases, expressed in the objective of the FCCC, imply? For methane it is easy to estimate what this would mean. For instance, to stabilise methane at today's concentration would require a reduction in anthropogenic emissions by about 8%. For carbon dioxide the situation is more complex. It is already clear from impact studies (most of which have been made for carbon dioxide concentrations of about 550 ppm) that politicians and decision makers are likely to be looking at stabilisation levels below 550 ppm. To achieve stabilisation at such levels, emissions should not rise much during the first half of the twenty-first century and should decrease substantially below today's levels during the second half of the century. An example of such a profile providing for stabilisation at about 450 ppm by the year 2100 has been given in Fig. 3 (*see* also Fig. 9).

The Framework Convention on Climate Change is rooted in the confidence that the science of climate change as expounded by the IPCC is basically sound and that adequate and appropriate technology is available to enable the necessary reductions in the emissions of greenhouse gases to occur.

Kyoto Protocol

The first conference of parties to the FCCC was held in Berlin in April 1995; it was agreed that a plan of action should be prepared for agreement in 1997. That plan was agreed by the parties in the Kyoto Protocol of December 1997. Further agreements were reached (although without the USA) in July 2001. Under the protocol, which has yet to be ratified by many countries, developed countries agreed by 2010 to reduce their emissions of greenhouse gases (all significant greenhouse gases being included in the calculation) by amounts which generally varied from 5 to 8% below their 1990 levels. The Kyoto Protocol provides for the first time for binding agreements between nations. Although the reductions provided for are modest compared with what will eventually be required, they represent an important first step in the long political process that will continue and gather momentum over the next decades. The full impact of the newly elected President Bush's announcement earlier this year that the USA would not ratify, indeed would withdraw from, the Kyoto Protocol has yet to emerge, however as the USA is responsible for almost a quarter of global emissions into the atmosphere, this change in policy represents at the very least a serious setback for the aims and objectives of the protocol.

Mitigation of climate change

Actions to mitigate climate change

To mitigate the effects of global warming, action is required to increase the sinks which remove carbon dioxide from the atmosphere (for example by reducing deforestation and increasing afforestation or by sequestration of carbon dioxide) and to reduce the emissions of both carbon dioxide and methane from anthropogenic sources.

Forestry

Over the past century the destruction of forests has contributed significantly to the increasing concentration of carbon dioxide in the atmosphere. Recent decades have seen loss of tropical forests, averaged over the globe, of about 1% per annum. Halting this deforestation (which would also be good for other reasons) and encouraging afforestation could make a significant contribution to the sequestering of carbon from the atmosphere. For instance, if an area of a hundred thousand square kilometres (approximately the area of the island of Ireland) were planted each year for forty years, by the year 2040 the area planted would be roughly equivalent to half the area of Australia. By the time the new forests matured – between forty and a hundred years after planting, depending on the type of forest – between twenty-five and fifty gigatonnes of carbon would have been sequestered, that is between 5 and 10% of the emissions of carbon into the atmosphere from fossil fuel burning over a fifty year period. Studies show that land for such a planting programme is potentially available.

Methane reduction

Methane is an important greenhouse gas: its increasing atmospheric concentration since preindustrial times has contributed about a fifth of the enhanced greenhouse effect to date. A reduction of anthropogenic emissions by around 10% would lead to stabilisation of the atmospheric methane concentration. Reductions in methane emissions can be achieved by paying attention to leaks from pipelines, by reducing the amount of waste going to landfill sites and collecting the gas it emits, by reducing deforestation, and by reducing the methane arising from agricultural sources.

Sequestration of carbon dioxide

A number of possibilities exist for sequestration of the carbon dioxide from fossil fuel emissions. The most promising is to pump it down into porous rocks, for instance into spent or partially spent gas or oil wells where it can be used to increase the gas or oil yield. Such sequestration is already occurring. For instance, a company in Norway, where there is a carbon tax, has found it economic to sequester unwanted carbon dioxide in a gas well rather than pay the tax that would be required if it were released to the atmosphere.

Energy generation and use

Two approaches are possible to reduce emissions of carbon dioxide in the energy industry: to become much more efficient in the generation and use of energy or to provide for energy supply from non-fossil fuel sources.

Substantial increases in the average efficiency of energy supply have occurred in recent years but there is plenty of room for further improvement. For instance, technologies are available for increasing the efficiencies of coal fired power stations for electricity generation (typically still no more than about 35%) and there is large potential for the growth of combined heat and power (CHP) generation (with a typical overall efficiency of around 80%).

In most energy uses, energy is employed inefficiently; only a few per cent of primary energy is turned into effective use, the rest being wasted. There is enormous potential to increase the efficiency of energy use in buildings, in industry, in domestic appliances, and in transport. Let me list some of the possibilities:

● improved design of buildings (around 35% of energy is used in buildings) through higher building standards (for example in insulation), together with the integration through changes in engineering practice of different areas of design and construction so as to minimise energy use – over half the energy used in buildings could thus be saved
● improved electrical appliances (low energy light bulbs, refrigerators with better insulation, and so on), again designed to minimise energy use
● development and marketing of more efficient vehicles, for instance hybrid vehicles (which combine small petrol or diesel engines with electric propulsion) and vehicles employing fuel cells.

The rapid development and growth of renewable energy sources (i.e. those not dependent on fossil fuels) is key to future sustainable energy provision. A number of such sources are poised for growth. In appropriate locations wind energy can be supplied at a price which is becoming competitive with fossil fuel sources. Power stations employing waste materials or renewable biomass as fuel are being developed. Solar energy, especially using photovoltaic cells as a source of electricity (with hydrogen produced electrolytically as a storage medium), is likely to become one of the major sources of world energy in due course. There are also possibilities for the development of wave and tidal energy sources.

All the developments I have mentioned require substantial research and development, a matter which is of major concern. Particularly worrying is the trend over the last ten years for reduction in R&D investment in energy supply and usage technologies. As markets have increasingly taken over energy supply, long term investment in R&D is being carried out neither by governments nor by the energy industry on the same scale as previously. For instance, since 1983 government R&D in the energy field has fallen in some developed countries by a factor of ten, and worldwide on average by a factor of three, so that it accounts now for only about 0·04% of world GNP – a very small sum compared with the capital investment in the energy industry, which runs at nearly 4% of world GNP. If the greater efficiency mentioned above and the necessary growth in renewable energy sources is to be achieved, much greater support for R&D by both industry and government must be forthcoming.

Contraction and convergence

There are three important principles that govern international action on a problem such as climate change: first is the precautionary principle, clearly embedded in the FCCC, which states that the existence of uncertainty should not preclude the taking of appropriate action; second is the principle that 'the polluter pays', which implies the imposition of measures such as carbon taxes and carbon trading arrangements; and third is the principle of equity, both international and intergenerational.

A proposal put forward by the Global Commons Institute called 'contraction and convergence' takes these three principles on board. It also illustrates well the major technical and political problems of achieving the large reductions in carbon dioxide emissions that are very likely to be necessary. Figure 9 shows the profile of global emissions that would be needed to bring stabilisation of the atmospheric carbon dioxide concentration at 450 ppm, which would in turn stabilise the climate impact, taking into account also the likely increase in other greenhouse gases, at approximately that due to doubled preindustrial carbon dioxide. That is the 'contraction' part of the proposal. The other part of the proposal addresses how the reductions are to be shared out between countries. It suggests that the simplest and fairest way to do this is to share carbon dioxide emissions equally per capita and to converge (hence 'convergence') to a situation of equal shares by, say, 2030. The diagram shows how, on this basis, emissions would be shared between countries. The further part of the proposal is that, having allocated profiles of emissions between countries, trading of these allocations would be allowed. If carried out responsibly, this trading could act to transfer economic and technical resources to developing countries, enabling their programmes of industrialisation to be carried forward in ways that have minimum impact on the environment. Although there are clearly many practical difficulties in its realisation, this 'contraction and convergence' proposal is one way in which what is necessary could be achieved.

Achievement of change and the likely cost

Figure 9 demonstrates by way of an example the enormous technical and political problems involved in any solution to the problem of achieving the necessary reduction in the use of fossil fuels. But can the world's energy industry contemplate the changes required? In a detailed study by the World Energy Council of energy generation and use next century, an 'ecologically driven' scenario is described (*see* Fig. 3) associated with which there would be a profile of carbon dioxide emissions similar to the 450 ppm stabilisation curve shown in Fig. 9. The World Energy Council show how this can be achieved – particularly by strong drives to increase energy efficiency and to develop the use of energy sources with much lower carbon dioxide emissions of the kind mentioned above. Under this scenario, by 2020, 'new' renewable energy sources make up 12% of total energy provision. Further, also by 2020, as developing countries industrialise, they are projected to roughly double their energy use and carbon dioxide emissions, while developed countries are projected to reduce their energy use by about 10% and their carbon dioxide emissions by about 30%. Estimates of the annual cost of realising such a scenario suggest figures of 1% or less of Global World Product (GWP), which is considerably less than most of the estimates which economists have made of the damage likely to result from climate change impacts.

However, with the availability of cheap energy being seen as the engine for industrial and economic growth, reductions in carbon dioxide emissions are not going to come easily. A large challenge to economists and to governments is to devise appropriate economic instruments and incentives to bring about the large increases in efficiency and the switch to non-fossil fuel energy sources which are necessary.

To achieve adequate mitigation of climate change will require commitment from all sections of the community. The challenge therefore is to scientists to improve the base of knowledge of climate change and its impacts, to governments to commit themselves to action adequately to address the problems of climate change and its mitigation, and to industry to develop and market the technologies required to reduce anthropogenic greenhouse gas emissions. The transfer of technology from developed to developing countries will also be important: the FCCC has emphasised the benefits which will accrue to industries in both the developed and developing worlds. Commitment is also required from all of us as individuals to take seriously the challenge of environmental stewardship. Furthermore, the matter is an urgent one. As the World Energy Council points out, 'the real challenge is to communicate the reality that the switch to alternative forms of supply will take many decades, and thus the realisation of the need and the commencement of the appropriate action must be *now*' [their italics].

Acknowledgements

Figures 2, 4, and 5 are reproduced from the 'Summary for policymakers' of the IPCC's 2001 report and Fig. 6 from the fourth volume of the full report ('Synthesis report'); Fig. 3 is taken from the World Energy Council's report 'Global energy perspectives' (1998, Cambridge, Cambridge University Press); and Fig. 8 comes from the IPCC's report 'Climate change 1992' (1992, Cambridge, Cambridge University Press).

Further reading

Further detailed information about global warming can be found in the IPCC reports: the most recent is 'Climate change 2001', published in four volumes ('The scientific basis', 'Impacts, adaptation and vulnerability', 'Mitigation', and 'Synthesis report') by Cambridge University Press (there is also a 'Summary for policymakers'); another important IPCC text is the 2000 'Special report on emission scenarios' (often referred to as SRES). My own book 'Global warming: the complete briefing' (2nd edn; 1997, Cambridge, Cambridge University Press) provides a comprehensive account of the science, impacts, and mitigation of climate change. A challenging assessment of the potential for increases in energy efficiency can be found in E. VON WEIZSACKER, A. B. LOVINS, and L. H. LOVINS: 'Factor four: doubling wealth, halving resource use'; 1997, London, Earthscan Publications. Detailed projections for the global energy industry are given in N. NAKICENOVIC, A. GRUBLER, and A. MACDONALD (ed.): 'Global energy perspectives'; 1998, Cambridge, Cambridge University Press.

Sir John Houghton
IPCC Working Group One
Co-Chair
Hadley Centre
Meteorological Office
London Road
Bracknell
Berks. RG12 2SY
UK

Sir John Houghton, CBE, FRS is co-chair of the Science Assessment Working Group of the Intergovernmental Panel on Climate Change. He was born at Dyserth, Clwyd and educated at Rhyl Grammar School and Jesus College, Oxford. He was Professor of Atmospheric Physics at the University of Oxford from 1976 to 1983, Chief Executive of the Meteorological Office from 1983 until his retirement in 1991, Chairman of the Royal Commission on Environmental Pollution from 1992 to 1998, and a member of the UK Government Panel on Sustainable Development from 1994 to 2000. Amongst many awards he has received gold medals from the Royal Meteorological Society and the Royal Astronomical Society, the prestigious International Meteorological Organization Prize, and honorary doctorates from a number of UK universities. He has authored several books, including 'Global warming: the complete briefing' (1997) and 'The search for God: can science help?' (1995).

[2]

Valuing the Impact of Large-Scale Ecological Change in a Market: The Effect of Climate Change on U.S. Timber

By BRENT SOHNGEN AND ROBERT MENDELSOHN *

This paper establishes a methodology for valuing the impact of large-scale ecological changes in a market. Given the large capital stocks inherent in most ecological systems, the dynamic nature of most ecological change, and the dynamic response of markets, it is critical to build dynamic models to capture the resulting effects. This paper demonstrates how to construct such a model using the impacts of climate change on U.S. timber markets as an example. Across a wide range of scenarios and models, warming is predicted to expand timber supplies and thus benefit U.S. timber markets. (JEL Q10, Q25)

Many large-scale ecosystem changes result from land management practices or pollution emissions of expanding populations and growing economies. Large-scale ecosystem changes are defined as those occurring over broad areas and potentially long time periods. They may include catastrophic forest fires, shifting from older to younger forests, soil erosion, or altered water quality and aquatic habitat. Combined, these changes are putting increased pressure on the renewable resources needed for market and nonmarket purposes. Society must weigh the costs of preventing or at least mitigating these changes against the damages these changes cause. Unfortunately, many large-scale phenomena, such as those predicted during climate change (Vegetation/Ecosystem Modeling and Analysis Project [VEMAP] Members, 1995), occur over such a large area and an extended period of time, it is difficult to value the stream of impacts.

* Sohngen: Department of Agricultural, Environmental, and Development Economics, Ohio State University, 2120 Fyffe Road, Columbus, OH 43210; Mendelsohn: School of Forestry and Environmental Studies, Yale University, 360 Prospect Street, New Haven, CT 06511. Funding for this study was provided by the Electric Power Research Institute. The authors thank Rick Freeman, Richard Haynes, Roger Sedjo, and the anonymous reviewers for comments on earlier drafts. In addition, we thank Tim Kittel and Nan Rosenbloom at the University Corporation for Atmospheric Research for help in obtaining the ecological data. The authors are solely responsible for any errors.

This paper develops methods for empirically valuing large-scale ecological change in a market for natural resource products. The approach is illustrated with a specific application to measure the impact of climate change on U.S. timber markets. Assessing the impact of climate change on timber markets is interesting for two reasons. First, it entails particularly large-scale ecosystem changes, such as a massive redistribution of the range of existing timber species and substantial changes in annual growth rates (VEMAP Members, 1995). Although these changes may differ from, or may be larger than, those expected from other ecosystem disturbances, the techniques provide important insights into valuing changes regardless of scale. Second, like the valuation of many other ecological changes, it requires dynamic, rather than steady-state, analysis.

Much of the empirical research into valuing ecological change in markets for natural resource products, however, continues to rely on steady-state analysis. Although theoretical dynamic methods are well established (Colin W. Clark, 1990), empirical fishery models, such as those by Jon M. Conrad (1989), James R. Kahn and W. Michael Kemp (1985), and Robert J. Johnston and Jon G. Sutinen (1996), all utilize static approaches. While the forestry literature has addressed dynamic stock adjustments (Kenneth S. Lyon and Roger A. Sedjo, 1983; Richard Brazee and Mendelsohn, 1990), it has not adequately considered how stocks will adjust to dynamic ecosystem changes.

In the case of climate change, for example, J. Mac Callaway et al. (1994) utilize a dynamic forest market model, but they adopt static climate and ecological models which compare the current climate to a doubled CO_2 equilibrium climate. Others, such as Linda A. Joyce et al. (1995) and John Perez-Garcia et al. (1997) all adopt static economic models that cannot capture intertemporal adaptation.

This paper distinguishes itself from this previous research by focusing specifically on the dynamic adjustment pathway. As shown, this focus turns out to have important consequences for valuing large-scale ecological change. Characterizing this dynamic adjustment pathway rests on three dynamic features. First, the stimulus of change often has an intertemporal path of its own. In our example of climate change, recent predictions suggest that temperature will increase linearly over the next century as greenhouse gases gradually accumulate in the atmosphere (see John T. Houghton et al., 1996).

Second, dynamic ecological change often entails lags and adjustments in the ecological system so that different outcomes occur over time in response to the external stimulus. In the case of climate change, forests may respond at first with widespread dieback as trees fail to adjust to new conditions, followed by a period of adaptation. To capture ecological effects, this study carefully combines climatological, biogeochemical, and biogeographical model results with an economic model to integrate findings from natural science into economic analysis.

Third, the market adjusts and adapts to the external stimulus. To adjust to large-scale change, the market can move harvests over time, plant new trees in anticipation of future needs, and salvage dying forests. The welfare outcome resulting from these complex dynamic adjustments cannot be captured accurately with static models. Given the large capital stocks involved, the dynamic nature of most ecological changes, and the dynamic response of markets, the static comparisons of Callaway et al. (1994), Joyce et al. (1995), and Perez-Garcia et al. (1997) provide poor approximations of the resulting adjustment path.

Section I constructs a dynamic economic model of U.S. timber markets, and describes how the basic model can be adapted to capture the large-scale effects of climate change. Section II then calibrates the models with market and ecological data, and simulations are developed for multiple climate, ecological, and economic scenarios. Section III presents the results, including a comparison with two static scenarios. These scenarios demonstrate that steady-state comparisons, such as those made in the earlier literature, do not capture the value of ecological impacts in timber markets accurately. In some scenarios northern forests dieback early during climate change, but market adaptation hastens forest adaptation, and it allows the positive long-run benefits of expanding southern forests to occur more quickly.

These results differ dramatically from earlier, regional studies. For example, Joel B. Smith and Dennis Tirpak (1989) predicted that climate change would damage American forests, even though they did not predict market impacts. Their prediction, however, led some economists to conclude that climate change would harm U.S. timber markets (William R. Cline, 1992; Samuel Fankhauser, 1995). More recent economic studies have been more optimistic about timber impacts (see Joyce et al., 1995; Perez-Garcia et al., 1997), but they rely on static economic models that cannot capture stock effects like dieback or shifting ecosystem boundaries.

While impact of climate change on U.S. timber markets is just one of the many sectors likely to be affected by climate change [see James Bruce et al. (1996) for a discussion of nonmarket impacts and Mendelsohn and James Neumann (1998) for a discussion of impacts on other sectors], the importance of capturing dynamic features applies to most service flows from ecosystems, including nonmarket sectors. For example, although it is unclear how public suppliers of forestland will respond to climate change, users of nonmarket services will likely make some attempt to adapt to changing circumstances. To account for the entire set of damages for the globe, one would need to aggregate estimates for different sectors and regions. While timber market damages are likely to represent only a small part of the impacts in developed economies, the dynamic methods described in this paper can be transferred to regions where timber markets are more important to national economies.

I. A Dynamic Model of Ecological Change

A. General Case

We begin by developing an ecological-economic model of a renewable resource. Because the dynamic change being measured is complex, a deterministic model is used for tractability. An interesting next step to explore would be to develop a stochastic dynamic programming model of these same decisions.

The resource we consider is composed of stocks of different organisms, $X_i(t)$. Each organism grows market products according to $V_i(a_i(t))$, where $a_i(t)$ is the age of the organism of type i in the system at time t. Following generic population and organismal biology, $V_{a_i} > 0$ and $V_{a_i a_i} < 0$ (for each organism), where the subscripts denote partial derivatives. The output at any moment of this entire system is the sum of the organisms harvested, $H_i(t)$, times the output per organism:

$$(1) \qquad Q(t) = \sum_i H_i(t) V_i(a_i(t)).$$

Demand for these products is derived from a well-behaved utility function over these and all other goods. An inverse demand function can be expressed as

$$(2) \qquad P(t) = D(Q(t), \mathbf{Z}(t)),$$

where $\mathbf{Z}(t)$ is the vector of all other goods purchased. Demand can shift over time subject to forces in the economy such as overall growth and changes in per capita income. Although there may be several different types of species or organisms, each with a distinctive yield, for simplicity of exposition, we assume that output across organisms is quality adjusted so that total quantity is simply the sum of the products of individual organisms. A more complex demand system model could be constructed to represent quality issues more carefully but would distract from the dynamic focus of this paper.

With equation (2), a Marshallian welfare measure of net consumer and producer surplus can be calculated for each time period as the area under the demand curve minus the costs of harvesting, regenerating, and holding land in each time period:

$$(3) \qquad S(Q(t), \mathbf{Z}(t), \mathbf{G}(t), \mathbf{X}(t))$$

$$= \int_0^{Q^*(t)} \{ D(Q(t), \mathbf{Z}(t)) - C(Q(t)) \} \, dQ(t)$$

$$- \sum_i \beta_i G_i(t) - \sum_i R_i(t) X_i(t),$$

where $C(Q(t))$ is the cost of harvesting, β_i is the marginal cost of regenerating an organism, $G_i(t)$ is the number of organisms regenerated, and $R_i(t)$ is a rental cost associated with holding an organism in year t. Although many ecological stocks regenerate naturally, society can enhance regeneration through investments in each period. The total size of the population at time t, $X_i(t)$, therefore will depend on the initial population size, less what is harvested, plus what is regenerated. Rent, $R_i(t)$, captures the opportunity costs associated with the use of underlying resources, such as land. In some circumstances, it may be zero because there is no opportunity cost of the resource. For example, there may be little else one can do with the oceans other than growing fish. However, for most terrestrial resources, $R_i(t)$ typically is not zero, and it plays a role in harvest and regeneration decisions. Further, total rent, $\sum_i R_i(t) X_i(t)$, varies with the size of the stock. Tracking the change in rent is particularly important during ecological change, when the size of $X_i(t)$ can shift dramatically over time. In the example used in this paper, if land shifts into forestry, society loses the returns from its previous use, which may be grazing or growing crops.

The social planner should maximize the present value of net producer and consumer surplus over time. Letting $\mathbf{G}(t) = G_i(t) \cdots G_I(t)$ and $\mathbf{X}(t) = X_i(t) \cdots X_I(t)$, this is:

$$(4) \qquad \underset{H_i(t), G_i(t)}{\text{Max}} \quad W = \int_t^\infty e^{-rt} \{ S(Q(t), \mathbf{Z}(t),$$

$$\mathbf{G}(t), \mathbf{X}(t) \} \, dt$$

subject to

$$(5) \qquad \dot{X}_i = -H_i(t) + G_i(t) \quad \forall i,$$

$$(6) \qquad X_i(0) = X_{i,0} \quad \forall i,$$

$$(7) \qquad X_i(t), H_i(t), G_i(t) \geq 0 \quad \forall i,$$

where r is the discount rate. The decision maker has two control variables, harvest amounts, $H_i(t)$, and how much to reinvest in future stock, $G_i(t)$. Equation (5) expresses the change in the size of the total population of each type of organism in each period; it is the difference between what is harvested and what is regenerated. Equation (6) is an initial condition for the stock variable, which defines not only the total stock of organisms, but also the age distribution of the initial stock. The age of the stock is distinguished by the yield function for merchantable products that accompanies each organism, $V_i(a_i(t))$. The social planner decides how much of the population to harvest, $H_i(t)$, and how much to regenerate, $G_i(t)$, at time t.

Using the maximum theorem (Lev S. Pontryagin et al., 1962), equations (4) through (7) can be solved for a set of conditions that must be satisfied in every period for a locally optimal solution of harvests (see Appendix for details):

$$(8) \qquad \dot{P}V_i(a_i(t)) + P(t)\dot{V}_i$$

$$= rP(t)V_i(a_i(t)) + R_i(t). \quad \forall i.$$

$P(t)$ is the price for a unit of organisms, and $R_i(t)$ is the rental rate of a marginal unit of resource (for example, land) required to support another unit of organisms. Organisms will be harvested along a time path where the marginal benefits of waiting an extra moment to harvest are equated with the marginal costs. The marginal benefits of waiting, the left-hand side of (8), arise from additional growth in the organism, $\dot{V}_i$, and changes in price, $\dot{P}$. Of course, if prices are declining, the marginal benefits of waiting are reduced. The marginal costs of waiting, the right-hand side of (8), include the opportunity costs of delaying har-

vests and using the resource for one more period. Note, for example, if land remains in forestry, $R_i(t)$ is the marginal opportunity cost of delaying future rotations.

Investments in future stock, $G_i(t)$, require that future marginal benefits just offset the marginal cost. The marginal benefits are simply the present value of future revenue that is expected when the new stock matures and is harvested. The marginal cost is the establishment cost, β_i, plus any resources needed to maintain the stock during its lifetime. The decision must satisfy the following first-order condition:

$$(9) \qquad \beta_i + \int_{t_0}^{t_f} [R_i(m_i)e^{-rm_i}] \, dm_i$$

$$= P(t_f)V_i(t_f - t_0)e^{-r(t_f - t_0)} \quad \forall i.$$

The impact of ecological change is calculated by comparing the present value of the stream of $S(\cdot)$ in the baseline case without the change to the same measure with the ecological change scenario. Given some forcing factor which alters species growth rates, mortality, the cost of regeneration, or the underlying opportunity cost of land (by affecting the incomes from alternative uses), the optimal dynamic path for the resource is recalculated. Comparing the present value of net welfare with and without the change provides a careful measure of large-scale ecological change.

The formulation above incorporates changes in other outputs, $\mathbf{Z}(t)$, which may accompany the resource in question. In practice, however, the vector $\mathbf{Z}(t)$ is often independent from the resource in question, so that it can be safely ignored. In cases where that is not appropriate, one needs to explore the use of a general equilibrium model to properly capture interactions across sectors (Joel D. Scheraga et al., 1993).

B. Modeling U.S. Timber Markets

In this section, we show how the general model can be applied to measure how climate change would affect U.S. timber markets. The principle of optimal forest management (Martin Faustmann, 1968; Paul A. Samuelson,

1976) is to maximize the net present value of future income over an infinite cycle of forest rotations. Faustmann analyzed a steady-state condition with constant prices and rotation lengths over time. In steady state, (8) simplifies to:

$$(10) \quad \bar{P}\dot{V}_i = r\bar{P}V_i(\bar{a}_i) + \bar{R}_i \quad \forall i.$$

Trees should be harvested when the marginal benefit of waiting, the value of annual tree growth, is equated to the marginal cost of waiting, the opportunity cost of the stock and the land. Extending this formula to dynamic prices and rotations (Brazee and Mendelsohn, 1990) leads to (8).

In timber markets, harvesting trees—one product of an ecosystem—involves completely removing individual organisms from the land. Although new trees can be grown to replace the missing individual, they must begin again at age zero. Because annual tree growth declines steadily with age (modeled by a concave yield function), given an age distribution of trees of a particular specie type, the optimal tree to harvest is the oldest member (Terry Heaps, 1984). The timber market model assumes that the oldest member is selected first.

The dynamic model of Brazee and Mendelsohn considers only a single species. In practice, however, there are many species from which the forest industry can select. The timber market model in this paper optimizes harvests across multiple species simultaneously. The model assumes that (8) is binding for all species being harvested at any moment, t.

In addition to harvesting, the model makes regeneration decisions each period. Because all species take several decades to grow to maturity and some take almost a century, this is a long-term decision. Making this decision in a dynamic model with such long foresight is clearly problematic. In the sensitivity analysis, we consequently examine an imperfect foresight scenario. With perfect foresight, the decision maker, at time t_0, follows (9) in making her regeneration decisions.

With competitive land markets, the annual land rental costs should equal the interest rate times the present value of future net income.

The present value of future net income changes as future prices and rotation ages change. If prices are rising over time, for example, the net present value of the land will increase as well, and $R_i(t)$ will increase. The stream of rental prices is consequently endogenous and cannot be treated as a constant during the period of transition.

Another problem with a long-term dynamic model is defining terminal conditions. An arbitrary future state could be imposed by fixing future demand levels and stock sizes. The system of equations described by (1), (2), (8), and (9) would eventually resolve to a steady-state Faustmann condition given this future state (Peter Berck, 1981; Heaps, 1984). The limitation of this approach is that the terminal conditions are arbitrary. In order to minimize the impact of choosing the wrong terminal conditions, we choose a terminal state that occurs very far in the future. Because current actions are not sensitive to conditions far into the future, the choice of future condition has little impact on the net present value of welfare. The terminal conditions are discussed more thoroughly at the end of Section II.

C. *Modeling Ecological Change: The Impact of Climate Change on U.S. Forests*

The impact of exogenous forces on ecosystems most often depends on the specific example considered. In this paper, we focus on the predicted impacts of climate change on U.S. forests, and consequently timber markets. This allows us to pay careful attention to the specific predictions of scientists. Forest ecologists generally predict that climate change will alter long-run growth rates and species location. However, they disagree about the dynamics of this process. Some argue that climate change will temporarily increase mortality (dieback). Trees will adjust to changing conditions by dying out prematurely and being gradually replaced. Others argue that climate change will affect only the ability of plants to regenerate in certain regions. Because the dynamic path of ecosystems is uncertain, we examine both dieback and regeneration as alternatives.

As carbon dioxide increases and climate changes, the growth rates of existing trees may gradually change. Over time, this slowly affects the size of the stock. Suppose for example that climate change affects the annual growth of a tree through the function, $\theta_i(n(t))$, which relates a climate forcing factor, $n(t)$, in time t to annual growth. The forcing factor relates CO_2 concentrations to climate in time t. Annual growth becomes:

$$(11) \quad \dot{V}_i(a_i(t), \theta_i(n(t)))$$

$$= \dot{V}_i(a_i(t))\theta_i(n(t)) \quad \forall i.$$

The size of a tree at time t is therefore:

$$(12) \quad V_i(a_i(t), \theta_i(n(t)))$$

$$= \int_0^{a_i(t)} \dot{V}_i(a_i(t))\theta_i(n(t)) \, dt \quad \forall i.$$

The size depends upon the historic influence of the forcing factor on the growth rate in each past period. The forcing factor has a unique impact on trees of different ages, and the impact is further complicated because $\theta_i(n(t))$ changes over time. A gradual forcing factor which has been in place for only a short time will tend to have only a minimal initial impact because it takes many years to alter stock size.

The change described in equation (12) will affect (8) and thus alter the harvest rate of each species. Accounting for these effects, equation (8) can be rewritten (see Appendix)

$$(13) \quad \dot{P}V_i(a_i(t), \theta_i(n(t)))$$

$$+ \theta_i(n(t))P(t)\dot{V}_i(a_i(t))$$

$$= rP(t)V_i(a_i(t), \theta_i(n(t)))$$

$$+ R_i(t, \theta_i(n(t))) \quad \forall i.$$

In (13), changing growth rates directly affect the marginal benefit of waiting and gradually alter the opportunity cost of waiting as well. Because both marginal benefits and costs of waiting adjust over long periods of time, (13) leads to a complex harvest adjustment relative to the general baseline case.

Increased mortality, dieback, is caused when climate change adjusts the boundaries

of ecosystems, leaving standing trees in the wrong climate (H. H. Shugart et al., 1986; Ronald P. Neilson et al., 1992). Under the dieback hypothesis, existing trees in the wrong climate die. The only option for the timber market is to salvage the dying trees. While ecological change could be expressed in a stochastic model, we adopt a deterministic model for tractability using a certainty equivalence approach. Given annual the mortality rate from dieback, $\delta_i(n(t))$ due to a forcing factor $n(t)$, the expected yield of an organism in year t for trees alive at the beginning of this year is

$$(14) \quad EV_i(t) = (1 - \delta_i(n(t)))V_i(t)$$

$$+ \delta_i(n(t))\gamma_i V_i(t) \quad \forall i.$$

where γ_i is the fraction of timber that dies back which can be salvaged. This change in marginal conditions affects the optimal harvest decision (see Appendix):

$$(15) \quad \dot{P}V_i(a_i(t)) + P(t)\dot{V}_i$$

$$= (r + (1 - \gamma_i)\delta_i(n_i(t)))$$

$$\times P(t)V_i(a_i(t))$$

$$+ R_i(t, \delta_i(n(t))) \quad \forall i.$$

$R_i(t, \delta_i(n(t)))$ reflects the fact that the value of land will be altered during climate change. With dieback, the cost of waiting has increased because the delay may entail loss of some stock. This causes the model to harvest stocks which are threatened by dieback earlier. This is an important adaptation because it limits the magnitude of realized dieback by harvesting trees before they die. Dieback also affects the decision to plant. Rewriting equation (9) to account for cumulative mortality (see Appendix), the decision to regenerate becomes

$$(16) \quad \beta_i + \int_{t_0}^{t_f} \left[e^{-rm_i} R(m_i, \delta(n(m_i))) \right] dm_i$$

$$= P(t_f)V_i(t_f - t_0)e^{-[r+(1-\gamma_i)\delta_i(n(t_f))](t_f - t_0)} \quad \forall i.$$

Dieback reduces the marginal benefit of re-planting species which will be subject to mortality problems today. This encourages forest owners to consider trees which are more suitable for future conditions. By replacing old species with new, more appropriate species, this market adaptation hastens the transition to a new ecosystem and mitigates some of the harmful economic impacts of dieback. However, with long-lived species, this adaptation calls for considerable foresight about the future path of climate change. It is important to consider how much foresight one can expect landowners to possess in this case. We consequently explore two alternatives: perfect foresight where landowners predict the future with accuracy, and imperfect foresight, where they make these adjustments only slowly.

The alternative dynamic pathway for ecological change has climate change affect only regeneration. Existing trees often survive well out of their natural range once they are established. Instead of relying on dieback, ecosystems may change because trees cannot regenerate in areas in which they are poorly suited. Competitive processes favor a new set of species better adjusted to the new ecological conditions. If left to natural forces alone, such an adjustment from the original stock to the new stock may take decades, if not centuries, due to the slow speed of many underlying migratory and competitive processes.

Even under the regeneration hypothesis, adaptation should still occur. Landowners considering new plantations should use (9) to determine which species will maximize present value. By selecting species which will adapt to new future conditions, the market can speed ecological adjustments. The benefits of this rational expectations planting process, however, are felt only in the distant future since it takes many decades for the trees to reach maturity.

Thus, both nature and humans will adapt to changing ecological conditions. With slowly changing growth rates, harvest decisions will be altered subtly at the margin causing harvests to shift over time. With dieback, the economic system moves away from vulnerable situations and causes a fairly rapid adjustment to more stable conditions. By influencing regeneration to favor species of higher value, the system speeds adjustment towards desirable new conditions.

This complex dynamic adjustment of ecosystems cannot be captured by simple steady-state comparisons. Figure 1 illustrates this point with four plausible cases of ecological change. All four paths have the same initial and final steady-state prices so that a comparison of the before and after steady-state conditions would imply an equal change in welfare. Prices, however, follow a very different path in each case. In case (a), massive dieback, with no salvage and slow regrowth, causes prices to jump quickly to very high levels and to decline only slowly as stocks regrow. In case (b), dieback occurs slowly so prices increase slowly. Case (c) assumes that future growth is slowly reduced. This encourages shorter rotation lengths, causing an initial increase in harvests, followed by ever smaller harvests. Case (d) involves slow dieback with high salvage harvests leading to temporary low prices and long-term high prices. Depending on the timing of high and low prices, these alternative paths would yield entirely different welfare impacts and yet the steady-state comparison would predict they all had the same value.

II. Empirical Example

Estimating the impact of climate change on timber markets requires linking information from natural science models with an empirical economic model. This set of models is listed in Table 1. We begin with two steady-state predictions of the effect of doubled CO_2 on climate in the United States, given by the models listed in Panel A. The three biogeographical models (Panel B) and three biogeochemical models (Panel C) are then used to predict nine steady-state ecological consequences for each of these climate scenarios (VEMAP Members, 1995). These steady-state results are converted to dynamic responses by first assuming a pathway for climate change, and then using the ecological literature to develop two dynamic ecosystem responses (dieback and regeneration in Panel D) to the path of climate change. This results in a set of 36 ecological responses [(two steady-state climate responses) × (nine

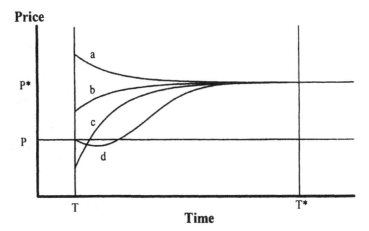

FIGURE 1. POTENTIAL DYNAMIC PATHWAYS OF THE PRICE OF A NATURAL RESOURCE ASSET DURING
A TRANSITION IN RESPONSE TO EXOGENOUSLY CHANGING FORCING FACTORS

Note: Path (a) assumes a massive dieback followed by gradual regrowth; path (b) assumes slow dieback and gradual regrowth; path (c) assumes gradual species change; and path (d) is a slow dieback with a high conversion of dead stock to markets.

steady-state ecosystem responses) × (one dynamic climate scenario) × (two dynamic ecosystem change scenarios)], which are introduced into the economic models described in Section I. The causal chain of events is from CO_2 emissions to climate change to ecological change to economic impacts on timber markets. Although there is a small feedback from the storage of carbon in forests and industrial products back to the climate model, we do not model this effect in this paper.[1]

This study focuses on measuring the impact of an effective doubling of atmospheric concentrations of carbon dioxide, allowing us to compare our results with past studies. This scenario requires us to examine a policy which stabilizes concentrations of carbon dioxide at 660 ppmv. General circulation models predict that climates across the world will change in response to such increases. We rely on

the United Kingdom Meteorological Office (UKMO) (C. A. Wilson and J. F. B. Mitchell, 1987) and Oregon State University (OSU) (Michael E. Schlesinger and Z. C. Zhao, 1989) general circulation models to predict how climates will shift in 0.5 by 0.5-degree grid cells in the United States.[2] The climate models make different predictions across the country and across seasons for multiple climatic variables (temperature, precipitation, cloud cover, etc.) for each grid cell. On average, the OSU model predicts changes of +3.0C temperature and +3.0 percent precipitation, while the UKMO model predicts changes of +6.7C temperature and +15 percent precipitation. While these averages suggest that UKMO is more severe, the two

---

[1] Sohngen et al. (1996) utilize the two sensitivity scenarios in this paper to measure forest carbon flux in the United States, rather than welfare effects. That study suggests that forests may be sources or sinks of atmospheric carbon during climate change, depending on the exact ecological changes predicted.

[2] Sohngen (1996) uses the methods of this paper to explore a wider range of climate scenarios. The qualitative results are robust, although the quantitative results generally change in proportion to the magnitude of the predicted temperature and precipitation change. Some exceptions occur, however, depending on the spatial distribution of the changes predicted by the general circulation models. Differences occur where regional changes in climate have significant impacts on the most valuable species.

TABLE 1—MODELS USED IN THE ANALYSIS

Models	Acronym
A. General circulation models	
United Kingdom Meteorological Office (Wilson and Mitchell, 1987)	UKMO
Oregon State University (Schlesinger and Zhao, 1989)	OSU
B. Biogeographical models	
Dynamic Global Phytogeography model (F. Ian Woodward et al., 1995)	DOLY
BIOME2 (I. Colin Prentice et al., 1992)	BIOME2
Mapped Atmosphere-Plant Soil System model (Neilson et al., 1992)	MAPSS
C. Biogeochemical models	
Terrestrial Ecosystem Model (Jerry M. Melillo et al., 1993)	TEM
BIOME-BioGeochemical Cycles model (Steven W. Running and Joseph C. Coughland, 1988)	BIOME-BGC
Century model (William J. Parton et al., 1988)	Century
D. Dynamic climate change scenarios	
Dieback	
Regeneration	

scenarios differ in a number of other ways, including the spatial and seasonal distribution of temperature and precipitation change. Note also that the best guess of climate scientists today is that greenhouse gases would cause a warming of only 2C by 2100 (Houghton et al., 1996).

The ecological models in this analysis rely on climate normals — long-term average weather. Although ecosystems are sensitive to changes in interannual variation or weather extremes, there is little agreement in the climate community about how greenhouse gases would change climate variation (Houghton et al., 1996). We consequently do not explore the impact of changes in variation or weather extremes in this analysis.

Following the predictions of climate scientists (Houghton et al., 1996), we assume that temperature and precipitation will change linearly from current levels in 1990 to the doubled CO_2 equilibrium levels by 2060 in each grid cell. In terms of our climate forcing factor, this entails a linear path for $n(t)$. Some grid cells will experience increases in temperature or precipitation, while others will experience

decreases. We assume that greenhouse gas policy will stabilize climates at this new equilibrium.[3] Clearly, if no control policy is undertaken, the concentration of greenhouse gases will continue to rise beyond a doubling leading to ever larger climate changes. Because expansion of concentrations well beyond 660 ppm would be the result only of policy decisions made well in the future, we do not examine these potential outcomes in this paper. In principle, however, the model could be extended to explore concentrations well beyond 660 ppm.

An international team of ecologists, known as the Vegetation/Ecosystem Modeling and Analysis Project (VEMAP Members, 1995), evaluated ecological response to the new equi-

---

[3] More recent evidence from Houghton et al. (1996) suggests that climates and ecosystems will continue to change beyond the year 2100. We explore longer-term climate changes with sensitivity analysis, but we are limited to scenarios where greenhouse gas concentrations are doubled due to the general circulation models utilized for the ecosystem analysis.

librium climates predicted by each general circulation model.[4] This project combined two types of models: biogeochemical and biogeographic (see Table 1). Biogeochemical models compute what would happen to the biological productivity of each ecosystem type. Biogeographic models predict how ecosystem types (biomes) might shift across the landscape. Because biomes have different productivity responses, these two types of models were combined to produce a single prediction of outcomes. The three biogeochemical and three biogeographic models used by VEMAP Members (1995) were used here to reflect the diversity of opinion in the quantitative ecological community. Combining a biogeochemical and a biogeographical model for each ecological prediction yields nine ecological predictions for each climate scenario.[5]

Figures 2–5 present a set of steady-state (2060) biogeographical results for the current and the UKMO climate scenarios. We have aggregated the broad regional ecosystem types of the original ecological models into four timber types: loblolly pine, Douglas fir, white pine, and ponderosa pine.[6] Figure 2 presents the distribution of ecosystems in the United States under the present climate. Figures 3–5 present the new steady-state distributions predicted by each biogeographical model for this

specific doubled CO_2 climate scenario. Although at first glance, these results suggest that loblolly pines will expand northward, the underlying climate model (UKMO) predicts higher temperatures and lower precipitation in the central–southern United States. The effect in Figures 3–5 is a large loss of existing loblolly pine stands.

The geographic changes vary by ecological model but all three biogeographical models predict a shift from northern white pines to southern loblolly pines (see Table 2). Panel A in Table 2 shows the predicted relative size of biomes after climate change compared to their current size for the three biogeographical models. Because loblolly pines are far more productive, the expansion of loblolly pines increases long-term timber supply. The biogeographical models also predict an expansion of the Douglas fir region in all cases except with the Mapped Atmosphere-Plant Soil System (MAPSS) model under the more severe UKMO climate scenario. Panel B presents predictions of the proportion of land currently in forests that shifts out of one biome and into something else during climate change, including other forest types and nonforestland.

The biogeochemistry models, in turn, are used to predict the ecosystem productivity of each biome. For each climate scenario, these models predict either increases or decreases in ecosystem productivity for each biome (Table 3). Because climate change will entail changes in both the distribution of biomes and their productivity, the changes in productivity in Table 3 are based on predicted changes in biome distribution from the three biogeographical models listed at the top of Table 3. The Terrestrial Ecosystem Model (TEM) (Panel A) predicts productivity increases in every forest type, Century (Panel B) predicts both gains and losses, but Biome-BioGeochemical Cycles (BIOME-BGC) (Panel C) under the more severe UKMO scenario predicts large productivity reductions. This range of outcomes in the ecological models is reflected in the final economic results as well.

For each long-term equilibrium scenario, we explore two dynamic ecological pathways: dieback and regeneration. In the dieback scenario, all trees which shift from one biome to

---

[4] The Vegetation/Ecosystem Modeling and Analysis Project is a multiple-party effort to assess the sensitivity of terrestrial ecosystems and vegetative processes to climatic change (VEMAP Members, 1995). This project was designed for two purposes. The first was to combine a set of different ecological models to get a sense of the range of ecosystem predictions which are possible for a given climate scenario. The second was to provide a rich source of data for economic (and other) analysis such as contained in this paper.

[5] The acronyms used to name the models in the text and tables allow us to differentiate the 36 ecological outcomes predicted by the models used. Both acronyms and references for each model used in this analysis are presented in Table 1. An overview of all six models and their climate predictions can be found in VEMAP Members (1995).

[6] Warm temperate, southern mixed forests are represented by a loblolly pine yield function; maritime temperate coniferous forests are represented by a Douglas fir yield function; cool temperate and boreal forests are represented by a white pine yield function; and continental temperate coniferous forests are represented by a ponderosa pine yield function.

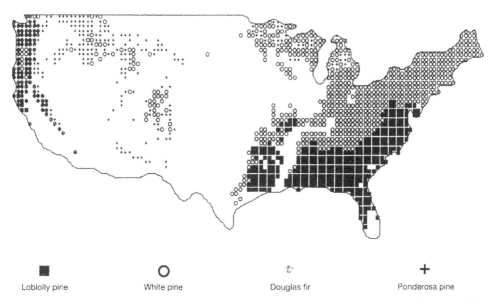

Loblolly pine   White pine   Douglas fir   Ponderosa pine

FIGURE 2. CURRENT POTENTIAL GEOGRAPHIC DISTRIBUTION OF ECOSYSTEM TYPES BASED ON AUGUST KUCHLER (1975)

another are assumed to die in the decade that the biome shifts. As can be seen in Table 2, the northern white pine and Rocky Mountain ponderosa pine regions will change a great deal under climate change. These large area changes imply high mortality rates under the dieback scenario while climate is changing.

In the regeneration scenario, biome changes do not kill trees but merely affect the speed of regeneration. Once trees are harvested, either the market will plant new species which are adapted to the new conditions or nature will slowly regenerate these lands. Acres which shift across biomes are assumed to take longer to regenerate naturally.

Each of the 36 dynamic ecosystem adjustment paths are then introduced into the economic model. Yield functions for the timber types associated with each biome type are taken from the forestry literature.[7] Species

growth rates are assumed to change proportionally with ecosystem productivity as in equation (11). The complex spatial configuration of existing stands are aggregated into an aggregate inventory by age for each species type. This inventory is grown over time using the spatial growth patterns dictated by the ecological models.

The economic model chooses harvests and replanting quantities to fit the first-order conditions (8) and (9). In addition, the model equates demand and supply each period. That is, we assume all harvested timber is consumed in the same period. Although it is technically possible to store timber once harvested, it is far more attractive to store timber in the forest where it continues to grow and is subject to a lower risk of degradation. Demand is assumed to have the following form:

$$(17) \quad Q(t) = 199 * \left(\frac{Population_t}{Population_{1990}} \right)$$
$$- 46 * \ln(P(t))$$
$$+ 28 * \ln(MGDP(t)).$$

---

[7] The loblolly pine yield function comes from Francis X. Schumacher and Theodore S. Coile (1960); Douglas fir yield is found in Richard E. McArdle et al. (1949); white pine yield is found in Suren R. Gevorkiantz and Raphael Zon (1930); and ponderosa pine is found in Walter H. Meyer (1938).

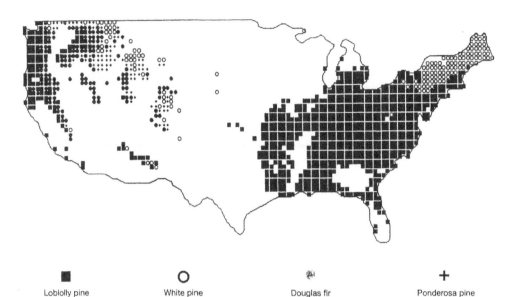

■	O	🦟	+
Loblolly pine	White pine	Douglas fir	Ponderosa pine

FIGURE 3. BIOME2 BIOGEOGRAPHICAL MODEL (PRENTICE ET AL., 1992) PREDICTION OF POTENTIAL ECOSYSTEM
DISTRIBUTION UNDER THE UKMO GENERAL CIRCULATION MODEL DOUBLED CO_2 SCENARIO

Demand shifts outward over time in response to population and manufacturing GDP (MGDP) growth. Manufacturing GDP shifts out exogenously at 1.5 percent annually. Initially population is assumed to grow 1.0 percent per year. The U.S. Bureau of the Census (1993) suggests that fertility rates will decline in the United States in the future, so we assume that population growth declines steadily to 0 percent by 2200. Price and manufacturing GDP elasticity were estimated from historical data for the period 1952 to 1988 (Darius M. Adams et al., 1988). Price elasticity of demand in (17) is −1.26, and the elasticity of manufacturing GDP per capita is 0.75. Demand is defined in terms of net domestic consumption of timber products (total demand minus net imports). We assume throughout the analysis that net imports do not change. This assumption will be relaxed in future studies which will take into account impacts around the world and trade. The ecological results upon which we rely in this study, however, are only available for the United States. The real interest rate is assumed to be 5 percent. Because the impacts of climate change are in the future, the magnitude of the present value of effects is

sensitive to the choice of interest rates. However, sensitivity analyses on the interest rate indicate that the qualitative results are robust (Sohngen, 1996).

Two management intensity levels are also included in the model. Intensively managed lands, plantations, receive high investment levels from replanting and thinning. Low-management intensity lands are more marginal timber areas which are likely to be regenerated naturally. High-intensity land classes are assumed to be managed to maximize the present value of timber net income. These landowners harvest according to the dynamic harvest and regeneration equations above. Low-intensity landholders, however, do not appear to follow Faustmann criteria, as they are observed to hold many acres of overmature timber. We assume that low-intensity landholders respond to market conditions depending upon prices by harvesting when they observe a period of high prices. The low-intensity lands are assumed to generate an upward-sloping harvest supply function for each timber type.

During climate change, high- and low-intensity lands are assumed to respond differently. After

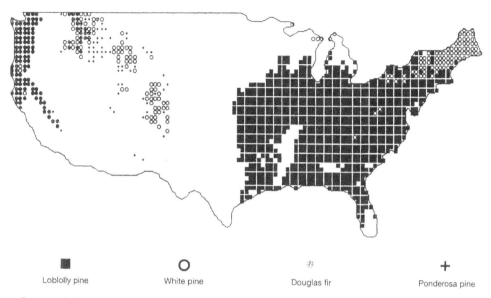

| Loblolly pine | White pine | Douglas fir | Ponderosa pine |

FIGURE 4. DOLY BIOGEOGRAPHICAL MODEL (WOODWARD ET AL., 1995) PREDICTION OF POTENTIAL ECOSYSTEM
DISTRIBUTION UNDER THE UKMO GENERAL CIRCULATION MODEL DOUBLED CO_2 SCENARIO

land dies back and converts from one biome to another, for example, high-intensity land will be regenerated quickly with the new species according to equation (9). Low-intensity land, with its reliance on natural regeneration, however, is assumed to regenerate slowly when biomes shift.[8] In addition, we assume that salvage rates, γ_i, are 75 percent on high-intensity land and 50 percent on low-intensity land.

A shooting algorithm is used to solve for equilibrium prices and harvests in each time period. Beginning with an initial stock and price, the algorithm predicts harvest age and regeneration in high-intensity land, harvest quantity from low-intensity land, and price according to the first-order conditions in (8) and (9), upward-sloping supply functions for timber from low-intensity land, and the demand equation in (17). We also allow for shifts between low-intensity and high-

intensity land in response to price. As prices increase (decrease), more (less) bare land will convert to high-intensity management. When scenarios of ecosystem change are considered, equations (13) or (15) replace (8), and equation (16) replaces (9).

These equations define a family of price paths. The optimal path out of these many possibilities is the one that leads from the initial price and harvest to the steady state. The shooting algorithm searches over a set of initial prices for one that moves the system into the new steady state in the future. If the initial price chosen is lower (higher) than the optimal initial price, the price path undershoots (overshoots) the steady state. Most paths can be dismissed quickly because prices shoot off to infinity or to 0. As we get closer to the optimal initial price, it takes more and more periods to determine if we have under- or overshot the steady state. We determine a price guess as "optimal" if the moment where under- or overshooting the steady state is so far distant that it has no impact on our measure of welfare. In general, model runs of 220 years were sufficient to estimate welfare.

[8] We use three different lags, 10 years in loblolly pines, 20 years in white pines, and 30 years in ponderosa pines and Douglas fir.

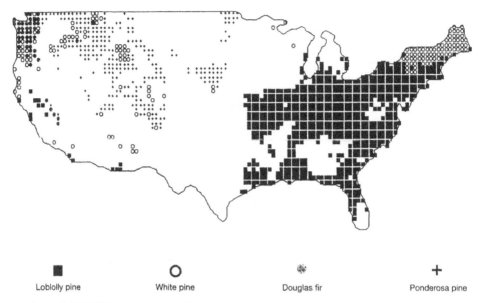

■	O	✤	+
Loblolly pine	White pine	Douglas fir	Ponderosa pine

FIGURE 5. MAPSS BIOGEOGRAPHICAL MODEL (NEILSON ET AL., 1992) PREDICTION OF POTENTIAL ECOSYSTEM DISTRIBUTION UNDER THE UKMO GENERAL CIRCULATION MODEL DOUBLED CO_2 SCENARIO

III. Results of Analysis

In order to characterize the welfare impact of the ecological changes, a baseline case without climate change is developed. The baseline case includes growth in manufacturing GDP and population as described above. Timber types are constrained to exist within the area predicted by the baseline ecological model shown in Figure 2. Prices, harvest quantities, rents, and planting are then calculated for each year. Demand grows faster than supply in the baseline scenario, so real prices climb over time even without climate change (Figure 6).

The dynamic ecological changes are then linked to the economic model using the same predictions in manufacturing GDP and population growth, so that yearly changes in timber harvest can be predicted for each of the 36 ecological scenarios. Market prices, quantities, regeneration rates, and rental rates are calculated each year. The results indicate that climate change is expected to expand aggregate timber supply in the long run under all 36 scenarios. Four of these scenarios are illustrated

in Figure 6, which shows that climate change reduces prices below the baseline in all cases. Although some of the scenarios entail productivity reductions on each acre for a given species, the geographic expansion of the highly productive loblolly pines overwhelms productivity reductions. Figure 6 illustrates this for the MAPSS & BIOME-BGC dieback and regeneration scenarios, where timber yields per acre decline (Table 3), but long-term prices are lower than in the baseline.

Comparing the net present value of the future stream of $S(\cdot)$ for each climate scenario with the baseline reveals a welfare gain under all 36 scenarios (see Table 4). Panel A in Table 4 presents the results for the dieback dynamic ecological change scenario, and Panel B presents results for the regeneration scenario. The present value of benefits range from $1 to $33 billion. The average benefits are slightly higher under the milder OSU scenario ($22 billion) than under the more severe UKMO climate scenario ($18 billion). Benefits are lower under the UKMO scenario because warmer and drier predictions for a large area of the U.S. South causes the existing

TABLE 2—STEADY-STATE ECOSYSTEM CHANGES FOR THREE BIOGEOGRAPHICAL MODELS USING
THE TWO GENERAL CIRCULATION MODEL CLIMATE RESULTS

	DOLY				BIOME2				MAPSS			
	Lob-lolly pine	Douglas fir	White pine	Pon-derosa pine	Lob-lolly pine	Douglas fir	White pine	Pon-derosa pine	Lob-lolly pine	Douglas fir	White pine	Pon-derosa pine
A. Relative size												
UKMO	1.98	1.48	0.22	0.37	1.81	2.47	0.10	0.43	1.54	0.55	0.26	1.13
OSU	1.65	1.11	0.77	0.20	1.61	1.07	0.50	0.99	1.64	0.98	0.46	1.88
B. Shifting proportion												
UKMO	0.04	0.05	0.84	0.89	0.35	0.07	0.93	0.87	0.31	0.56	0.94	0.26
OSU	0.01	0.11	0.50	0.87	0.11	0.02	0.71	0.35	0.00	0.21	0.81	0.29

Notes: "Relative size" is the ratio of the final steady-state forest area divided by the area of the initial steady state. "Shifting Proportion" is the proportion of the initial steady-state forest area that shifts out of the type and into something else, calculated as the area of forestland that converts to something else divided by the initial steady-state area. Changes for the DOLY, BIOME2, and MAPSS models with the UKMO climate scenario correspond to Figures 3–5.

range of loblolly pines to shrink. This suggests that U.S. timber markets will be slightly better off with a mild warming (average of 3C) compared to a more severe warming (average of 6C). However, one must be careful comparing the OSU and UKMO scenarios because they not only vary in severity but also in the spatial and seasonal patterns of climate change.[9]

Another interesting result in Table 4 is that the average welfare value under regeneration ($21 billion) is only slightly higher than under dieback ($18 billion). Given that over 80 percent of two regions were vulnerable to dieback, one might have expected far more severe outcomes under the dieback scenario. Three factors can explain why dieback is not more costly. First, the two most vulnerable regions to dieback, the North and the Rocky Mountains, entail low-valued species. Second, har-

vests carefully avoid the worst of dieback by removing trees prior to mortality and through salvage. Third, regeneration allows these vulnerable forests to adapt quickly to climate change by planting more productive suitable species more quickly. For example, under dieback, the low-productivity northern forests are replaced more quickly by loblolly pines than under the regeneration scenario. These factors mitigate the damages caused by the dieback dynamics.

The results from the VEMAP ecological models are noticeably more optimistic than earlier regional models. The major reason for this is that the new models are more comprehensive so that the loss of some forest types due to climate change is balanced by the gain of other forest types. Regional studies that concentrate on how local species would struggle with new climate conditions often fail to anticipate this compensating effect. For example, the U.S. Environmental Protection Agency analysis focused on the decline of northern species through dieback (Smith and Tirpak, 1989). While dying northern forests look horrendous in isolation, the gradual replacement of low-productivity hardwoods by high-productivity loblolly pines is actually beneficial. This biome shift increases overall timber supply and increases net surplus rela-

---

[9] The timber market consequences of larger CO_2 forcings for the United States is unclear for three reasons. First, the effect of larger future changes on current practices is unclear due to the role of discounting. Second, while the southern range of loblolly pine may decrease, the northern range may continue increasing. Finally, evidence from other regions suggests that subtropical regions are well suited to fast-growing plantations, and the southern United States may readily adapt to using these species during climate change.

TABLE 3—PERCENTAGE CHANGE IN STEADY-STATE ECOSYSTEM PRODUCTIVITY (TIMBER YIELD) PREDICTED BY BIOGEOCHEMICAL MODELS FOR EACH BIOME TYPE

| | Biogeographical model | | | | | | | | | | | |
| | DOLY | | | | BIOME2 | | | | MAPSS | | | |
	Loblolly pine	Douglas fir	White pine	Ponderosa pine	Loblolly pine	Douglas fir	White pine	Ponderosa pine	Loblolly pine	Douglas fir	White pine	Ponderosa pine
A. TEM												
UKMO	14	34	29	50	16	31	7	26	28	47	14	39
OSU	32	33	19	29	37	43	10	18	40	32	(2)	36
B. Century												
UKMO	(5)	(14)	7	18	(3)	(4)	(4)	14	7	(13)	(6)	19
OSU	(2)	(3)	11	21	5	9	7	6	10	0	8	0
C. BIOME-BGC												
UKMO	(29)	(19)	(18)	(11)	(19)	(29)	3	(2)	(16)	(3)	(35)	(11)
OSU	(9)	7	3	14	(2)	15	16	5	0	2	2	(19)

Notes: Changes in ecosystem productivity are conditioned on steady-state results of biogeographical models. Values in parenthesis indicate a percentage reduction in ecosystem productivity.

tive to the baseline case in the long run. Increased production in timber markets due to regrowth of this type begins to occur within 25 years of the onset of climate change. Market adaptation is also an important part of this story since investment can hasten forest adaptation and allow these positive long-run benefits to occur more quickly.

We also explore how robust the model is to alternative assumptions. We present five different scenarios in this sensitivity analysis. First, we consider a more gradual climate change scenario; allowing climates to take 150 years to reach the same equilibrium. This slower scenario is more consistent with recent findings of climate scientists (Houghton et al., 1996) who argue for milder future climate scenarios. Second, we explore what would happen if natural regeneration takes longer to shift from one biome to another. By increasing lags to 30 years in loblolly pines, 50 years in white pines, and 70 years in ponderosa pine and Douglas fir, we assume that unmanaged land remains fallow for this extensive time period once cleared. Third, we allow for higher and lower salvage rates. The high salvage scenario assumes that γ_t is 90 percent on both manage-

ment intensities, and the low salvage scenario assumes that it is 25 percent on both. Fourth, we examine imperfect forester foresight. Instead of assuming that high-intensity managed lands are replanted immediately with the best species for the future, we assume lagged regeneration rates. That is, we assume it takes foresters several years to learn how to plant for changing climatological conditions. Lags were set at 10 years in loblolly pines, 20 years in white pines, and 30 years in ponderosa pine and Douglas fir. Fifth, we consider a high demand and a low demand scenario. In the high demand scenario, demand shifts out at 2.5 percent annually, while in the low demand scenario, it is held at 1990 levels forever.

Four ecological cases are explored for the sensitivity analysis. Two ecosystem model combinations are examined which yield relatively high and low welfare values under the initial assumptions. In addition, both the dieback and the regeneration scenario are presented.[10]

---

[10] The model combinations chosen for sensitivity analysis are the Dynamic Global Phytogeography model

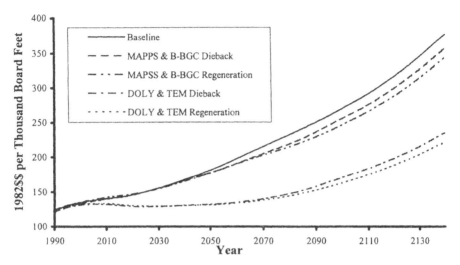

FIGURE 6. PRICE PATHS FOR THE BASELINE CASE AND FOUR ECOLOGICAL OUTCOMES FROM THE CLIMATE CHANGE PREDICTIONS OF THE UKMO GENERAL CIRCULATION MODEL

Table 5 presents the results of the sensitivity analysis. Slowing down climate change reduces the timber benefits. The delay slows the increase in loblolly pine timberland area into the distant future reducing its present value. Slowing natural regeneration on low-intensity lands that shift during climate change has only a small effect on welfare estimates because the lands which are shifting during climate change yield only small amounts of timber. Higher salvage rates substantially increase the welfare value of the dieback scenario and lower rates decrease it. The MAPSS & BIOME-BGC scenario is more sensitive to this assumption because this model predicts more dieback. Imperfect foresight by foresters reduces the expected benefits from climate change (and can even cause a small loss), but the reduction is small. Although assuming perfect foresight to anticipate climate change through planting is certainly a debatable assumption, we have chosen the two most extreme ecological scenarios for sensitivity analysis in order to bound the potential effects of imperfect foresight under alternative ecological scenarios. The welfare estimates are highly sensitive to the assumed baseline growth in the demand for timber. Rapid (slow) demand growth implies higher (lower) baseline prices, which increases (decreases) welfare effects proportionally.

In order to understand the importance of capturing the dynamics of this model, we also present the results of a steady-state comparison. We compare the steady state which would have existed in 2060 under current climate with the equilibrium which would exist in 2060 under the new climate. We use the two scenarios tested in the sensitivity analysis. The predicted change in welfare according to the steady-state comparisons is −$25.1 billion for the MAPSS & BIOME-BGC combination and +$73.6 billion in the DOLY & TEM combination. The corresponding estimates in the dynamic model are +$2.63 and +$31.2 billion, respectively. The steady-state response dramatically overstates the welfare effect.

(DOLY) (Woodward et al., 1995) and Terrestrial Eco-system Model (TEM) (Melillo et al., 1993) combination; and the Mapped Atmosphere-Plant Soil System model (MAPSS) (Neilson et al., 1992) and BIOME-BioGeochemical Cycles model (BIOME-BGC) (Running and Coughland, 1988). Results from both models were obtained under the United Kingdom Meteorological Office general circulation model (Wilson and Mitchell, 1987).

TABLE 4—CHANGE IN THE NET PRESENT VALUE OF NET MARKET SURPLUS IN TIMBER MARKETS FOR CLIMATE CHANGE CASES RELATIVE TO THE BASELINE CASE

Climate scenario	DOLY		BIOME2		MAPSS	
	Total	Percent	Total	Percent	Total	Percent
A. Dieback						
TEM						
UKMO	$30.05	10.62	$27.52	9.71	$19.10	6.74
OSU	28.94	10.21	30.16	10.64	31.77	11.21
Century						
UKMO	18.87	6.65	17.89	6.31	9.46	3.34
OSU	14.23	5.02	16.69	5.89	17.80	6.28
BIOME-BGC						
UKMO	9.35	3.30	10.31	3.64	2.63	0.93
OSU	11.86	4.19	13.72	4.84	14.52	5.12
B. Regeneration						
TEM						
UKMO	31.20	11.01	32.58	11.50	22.62	7.98
OSU	31.93	11.27	33.16	11.70	35.26	12.44
Century						
UKMO	20.47	7.22	22.99	8.11	11.03	3.89
OSU	17.11	6.04	20.34	7.18	21.92	7.74
BIOME-BGC						
UKMO	10.37	3.66	14.98	5.29	3.87	1.37
OSU	15.06	5.31	18.01	6.36	16.72	5.90

Notes: The change is measured both by the total and the percentage difference. All dollar amounts are in billions of 1982 $, U.S. currency. Net present value is measured with a discount rate of 5 percent.

Including dynamics moderates the welfare impacts for three reasons. First, the steady-state response does not capture the adjustment and adaptation of markets, especially across time. Second, the steady-state comparison does not capture the gradual changes in ecosystems over time, thereby overstating effects. Third, the steady-state response does not capture the dynamic changes in the economic baseline, so that the steady-state response assumes 2060 demand conditions immediately.[11]

[11] A similar effect would occur if 1990 economic conditions were used, except that changes would be undervalued because a lower baseline condition is used.

TABLE 5—SENSITIVITY ANALYSIS OF PRESENT VALUE CHANGES TO SEVERAL CLIMATOLOGICAL,
ECOLOGICAL, AND ECONOMIC ASSUMPTIONS

| | Ecological scenario | | | |
| | DOLY & TEM | | MAPSS & B-BGC | |
	Dieback	Regeneration	Dieback	Regeneration
Initial value of change (billions, 1982$)	$30.05	$31.20	$2.63	$3.87
1. Slow climate adjustment	16.68	16.95	3.92	(0.02)
2. Slow natural regeneration	27.79	28.99	1.73	3.00
3. Salvage				
High	35.25	31.20	8.94	3.87
Low	27.90	31.20	(2.95)	3.87
4. Imperfect foresight	25.19	27.73	(0.42)	1.66
5. Alternative baselines				
High demand	84.92	90.68	11.55	19.68
Low demand	15.17	15.88	1.26	2.67

Notes: Each of these cases are compared using the UKMO general circulation model climate change scenario.

IV. Conclusion

The dynamic ecological-economic model captures the important intertemporal features for measuring changes in market welfare arising from large-scale ecological change. The adjustment pathways for both ecosystems and economic systems are critical for measuring the welfare impacts of ecosystem change. Even when the underlying force for change is gradual and steady, the dynamics of the system play a crucial role in determining both the direction and the magnitude of the outcome. Of course, when considering ecological change, it is important to measure the nonmarket as well as the market impacts. Additional research needs to concentrate on including nonmarket services in the model and so take into account all effects.

In the specific example of the impacts of climate change on timber markets, the large-scale steady-state effects predicted by the ecological models lead to small welfare impacts over time. Although climate change can cause harmful dynamic changes in ecosystems from phenomenon like dieback, dynamic market adjustments dampen these effects. Further, the ecological models examined in this study actually predicted that the steady states would improve with greenhouse warming. All 36 combinations of ecological-climate models suggested positive results. The magnitude of the effects, however, were reasonably small with an average present value of about $20 billion. Across the different model combinations, they exhibited a wide range, from $1 billion to $33 billion of benefits. Using dynamic models, society can anticipate large-scale ecological changes, measure their consequences, and determine how best to adapt. Armed with this knowledge and a complete accounting of impacts to other market and nonmarket sectors, society can engage in an informed decision concerning whether it is best to prevent these changes or live with them.

APPENDIX

In this Appendix, we show how the first-order conditions presented for the models described in the text are derived from the maximization of market welfare, as described in equations $(1)-(7)$ in the text. The models described here are a general case with no ecological change, a case where ecological change affects timber yield, and a case where ecological change causes dieback.

General Case

The original problem was given as equations $(1)-(7)$ in the text. Net surplus is assumed to be continuous in its arguments, and $S_{H_i} \geq 0$ and $S_{H_iH_i} \leq 0$. Utilizing optimal control procedures and relying on the maximum principle (Pontryagin et al., 1962), we can characterize a solution to $(1)-(7)$ in terms of a set of necessary conditions that must hold for each stock of organisms i considered within the problem. First, let

(A1) $S(Q(t), \mathbf{Z}(t), \mathbf{G}(t), \mathbf{X}(t))$

$$= \int_0^{Q^*(t)} \{ D(Q(t), \mathbf{Z}(t)) - C(Q(t)) \} \, dQ(t)$$

$$- \sum_i \beta_i G_i(t) - \sum_i R_i(t) X_i(t)$$

and express the Hamiltonian as

(A2) $h = S(Q(t), \mathbf{Z}(t), \mathbf{G}(t), \mathbf{X}(t))$

$$- \sum_i \mu_i(t)[-H_i(t) + G_i(t)].$$

Assuming an interior solution, the following necessary conditions are derived:

(A3) $\quad S_{H_i}(\cdot) = \mu_i(t) \quad \forall i,$

(A4) $\quad S_{G_i}(\cdot) = -\mu_i(t) \quad \forall i,$

(A5) $\quad \dot{\mu}_i - r\mu_i(t) = R_i(t) \quad \forall i,$

(A6) $\quad \dot{X}_i = -H_i(t) + G_i(t) \quad \forall i.$

Equations (A3) and (A5) can be combined to obtain (note that in the following, $\forall i$ has been suppressed in most cases):

(A7) $\quad \dot{S}_{H_i} = rS_{H_i} + R_i(t).$

All organisms will be harvested at the point where the marginal gain in net surplus from waiting an additional moment to harvest just equals the marginal cost associated with holding that organism for one more period. Marginal gains in net surplus arise from organismal growth, and possibly, price growth. The sign on $\dot{S}_{H_i}$ would be uncertain, however, if prices were declining.

Assuming a linear demand function and constant marginal harvesting costs, a quadratic net surplus function can be obtained by taking the integral in (A1) to form:

(A8) $\quad S(\cdot) = k + A\left[\sum_i H_i(t)V_i(a_i(t)) \right]$

$$- \Delta\left[\sum_i H_i(t)V_i(a_i(t)) \right]^2$$

$$- \sum_i c_i H_i(t)V_i(a_i(t))$$

$$- \sum_i \beta_i G_i(t) - \sum_i R_i(t) X_i(t),$$

where k is a constant of integration. Differentiating (A8) with respect to $H_i(t)$ results in

(A9) $\quad S_{H_i(t)}$

$$= \left[A - 2\Delta\left(\sum_i H_i(t)V_i(a_i(t)) \right) \right]$$

$$\times V_i(a_i(t)) - c_i V_i(a_i(t)).$$

The term $A - 2\Delta(\sum_i H_i(t)V_i(a_i(t)))$ on the right-hand side of (A9) is the marginal benefit of harvesting one additional unit of organisms. In a competitive market, this is equal to the price, so that:

(A10) $\quad S_{H_i(t)} = (P^L(t) - c_i)V_i(a_i(t)).$

In timber markets, $P^L(t)$ is the price of a log of harvested timber. The value $P^L - c_i$ is therefore the value of uncut timber logs that are still standing in a forest. Letting

(A11) $\quad P(t) = P^L(t) - c_i,$

(A9) can be redefined by finding dS_{H_i}/dt and substituting. The result is

$$(A12) \quad \dot{P}V_i(a_i(t)) + P(t)\dot{V}_i$$
$$= rP(t)V_i(a_i(t)) + R_i(t),$$

which is equation (8) in the text.

Differentiating (A8) with respect to $G_i(t)$ yields

$$(A13) \qquad S_{G_i} = -\beta_i.$$

Recognizing that $\mu_i(t)$ is the marginal net surplus of holding one additional acre of land until the next regeneration decision,

$$(A14) \quad \mu_i(t_0) = P(t_f)V_i(t_f - t_0)e^{-r(t_f-t_0)}$$
$$- \int_{t_0}^{t_f} \{ R_i(m_i)e^{-rm_i} \} dm_i,$$

then equation (9) in the text can be derived from (A4), (A13), and (A14) as

$$(A15) \quad \beta_i + \int_{t_0}^{t_f} \{ R_i(m_i)e^{-rm_i} \} dm$$
$$= P(t_f)V_i(t_f - t_0)e^{-r(t_f-t_0)}.$$

Ecological Change: Productivity

Here, we consider the derivation of equation (13) in the text, where the yield of merchantable products from the ecosystem changes over time. Different species are likely to experience different changes in growth. Recalling that $\theta_i(n(t))$ relates climate forcing to a change in annual growth, the new yield function is redefined as:

$$(A16) \quad V_i(a_i(t), \theta_i(n(t)))$$
$$= \int_0^{a_i(t)} \dot{V}_i(a_i(t))\theta_i(n(t)) dt.$$

(A16) can be introduced into the net surplus function, so that (A8) becomes

$$(A17) \quad S(\cdot) = k + A\left[\sum_i H_i(t) \right.$$
$$\times \left(\int_0^{a_i(t)} \{ \dot{V}_i(a_i(t)) \, \theta_i(n(t)) \} dt \right) \right]$$
$$- \Delta\left[\sum_i H_i(t) \right.$$
$$\times \left(\int_0^{a_i(t)} \{ \dot{V}_i(a_i(t))\theta_i(n(t)) \} dt \right) \right]^2$$
$$- \sum_i c_i H_i(t)$$
$$\times \left(\int_0^{a_i(t)} \{ \dot{V}_i(a_i(t))\theta_i(n(t)) \} dt \right)$$
$$- \sum_i \beta_i G_i(t) - \sum_i R_i(t)X_i(t).$$

Differentiating net surplus with respect to $H_i(t)$, and noting the relationship in (A11), an equation similar to (A10) can be derived:

$$(A18) \quad S_{H_i(t)} = P(t)\left(\int_0^{a_i(t)} \{ \dot{V}_i(a_i(t)) \right.$$
$$\times \theta_i(n(t)) \} dt \right)$$
$$= P(t)V_i(a_i(t), \theta_i(n(t))).$$

Finding dS_{H_i}/dt and substituting that result into (A7), produces equation (13) in the text:

$$(A19) \quad \dot{P}V_i(a_i(t), \theta_i(n(t)))$$
$$+ \theta_i(n(t))P(t)\dot{V}_i(a_i(t))$$
$$= rP(t)V_i(a_i(t), \theta_i(n(t)))$$
$$+ R_i(t, \theta_i(n(t))).$$

Note that $dV_i(a_i(t), \theta_i(n(t)))/dt = \dot{V}_i(a_i(t))\theta_i(n(t))$.

Regeneration will also be altered to account for changes in growth rates. Equation (A4) above can be solved to account for the altered yield function. This leads to the following condition:

(A20)

$$\beta_i + \int_{t_0}^{t_f} \left\{ R_i(m_i, \theta_i(n(m_i))) e^{-rm_i} \right\} dm_i$$

$$= \left(P(t_f) \int_{t_0}^{t_f} \left\{ \dot{V}_i(m_i) \theta_i(n(m_i)) \right\} dm_i \right)$$

$$\times e^{-r(t_f - t_0)}.$$

Ecological Change: Dieback

This section shows how dieback will affect marginal harvest and regeneration decisions. Although it is possible to model dieback as a stochastic problem, we instead analyze a deterministic analogue to the stochastic problem. This allows a direct comparison to the baseline model, and it provides for a more tractable numerical solution. We begin by describing how an expression for expected yield is obtained.

Letting $\delta_i(n(t))$ be mortality from exogenous dieback due to forcing factor $n(t)$ and γ_i be the proportion of timber that can be salvaged if it dies back, the expected yield for a tree alive at the beginning of a year is given by

(A21) $E[V_i(a_i(t))]$

$$= (1 - \delta_i(n(t))) V_i(a_i(t))$$

$$+ \delta_i(n(t)) \gamma_i V_i(a_i(t)).$$

Over all the time that a tree is subjected to the possibility of dieback, this is

(A22) $E[V_i(a_i(t))] = V_i(a_i(t))$

$$\times \prod_{a_i(0)}^{a_i(t)} (1 - (1 - \gamma_i) \delta_i(n(t))).$$

In continuous time, this can be expressed as

(A23) $E[V_i(a_i(t))]$

$$= V_i(a_i(t)) e^{-(1 - \gamma_i)\delta_i(n(t))a_i(t)}.$$

Equation (A23) can be incorporated into (A8) to obtain

$$(A24) \quad S(\cdot) = k + A\left[\sum_i H_i(t)(V_i(a_i(t))\right.$$

$$\left. \times e^{-(1 - \gamma_i)\delta_i(n(t))a_i(t)} \right)\right]$$

$$- A\left[\sum_i H_i(t)(V_i(a_i(t))\right.$$

$$\left. \times e^{-(1 - \gamma_i)\delta_i(n(t))a_i(t)} \right)\right]^2$$

$$- \sum_i c_i H_i(t)(V_i(a_i(t))$$

$$\times e^{-(1 - \gamma_i)\delta_i(n(t))a_i(t)}$$

$$- \sum_i \beta_i G_i(t) - \sum_i R_i(t) X_i(t).$$

Differentiating net surplus with respect to $H_i(t)$ and t allows us to obtain the following result:

$$(A25) \quad \dot{S}_{H_i} = \frac{d}{dt}[PV_i(a_i(t))$$

$$\times e^{-(1 - \gamma_i)\delta_i(n(t))a_i(t)}]$$

$$= \{ \dot{P}V_i(a_i(t)) + P\dot{V}_i$$

$$- (1 - \gamma_i)\delta_i(n(t)) PV_i(a_i(t)) \}$$

$$\times e^{-(1 - \gamma_i)\delta_i(n(t))a_i(t)}.$$

Combining (A25) with (A3) and (A5) produces equation (15) in the text:

$$(A26) \quad \dot{P}V_i(a_i(t)) + P(t)\dot{V}_i$$

$$= (r + (1 - \gamma_i)\delta_i(n(t)))$$

$$\times P(t)V_i(a_i(t))$$

$$+ R_i((t), \delta_i(n(t))),$$

Equation (16) in the text is found by noting that (A14) becomes

$$(A27) \quad \mu_i(t_0) = P(t_f)V(t_f - t_0)$$

$$\times e^{-[r+(1-\gamma_i)\delta_i(n(t_f))](t_f - t_0)}$$

$$- \int_{t_0}^{t_f} \{ R_i(m_i, \delta_i(n(m_i)))$$

$$\times e^{-[r+(1-\gamma_i)\delta_i(n(m_i))]m_i} \} dm_i$$

and combining (A27) with (A13) and (A4).

REFERENCES

Adams, Darius M.; Jackson, K. C. and Haynes, Richard W. "Production, Consumption and Prices of Softwood Products in North America: Regional Time Series Data, 1950–1985." *Resource Bulletin PNW-RB-151*, U.S. Department of Agriculture, Forest Service, Portland, OR, 1988.

Berck, Peter. "Optimal Management of Renewable Resources with Growing Demand and Stock Externalities." *Journal of Environmental Economics and Management*, June 1981, 8(2), pp. 105–17.

Brazee, Richard and Mendelsohn, Robert. "A Dynamic Model of Timber Markets." *Forest Science*, June 1990, 36(2), pp. 255–64.

Bruce, James; Lee, Hoesung and Haites, Eric, eds. *Climate change 1995: The economic and social dimensions of climate change.* Cambridge: Cambridge University Press, 1996.

Callaway, J. Mac; Smith, Joel and Keefe, Sally. "The Economic Effects of Climate Change for U.S. Forests." U.S. Environmental Protection Agency, Adaptation Branch, Climate Change Division, Office of Policy, Planning, and Evaluation, Washington, DC, 1994.

Clark, Colin W. *Mathematical bioeconomics: The optimal management of renewable resources*, 2nd Ed. New York: Wiley, 1990.

Cline, William R. *The economics of global warming.* Washington, DC: Institute for International Economics, 1992.

Conrad, Jon M. "Bioeconomics and the Bowhead Whale." *Journal of Political Economy*, August 1989, 97(4), pp. 974–87.

Fankhauser, Samuel. *Valuing climate change: The economics of the greenhouse.* London: Earthscan, 1995.

Faustmann, Martin. "On the Determination of the Value which Forest Land and Immature Stands Pose for Forestry," in Michael Gane, ed., *Martin Faustmann and the evolution of discounted cash flow.* Oxford: Commonwealth Forestry Institute, Oxford University, 1968, pp. 27–55.

Gevorkiantz, Suren R. and Zon, Raphael. "Second-Growth White Pine in Wisconsin: Its Growth, Yield, and Commercial Possibilities." *Research Bulletin 98*, University of Wisconsin, Agricultural Experiment Station, 1930.

Heaps, Terry. "The Forestry Maximum Principle." *Journal of Economic Dynamics and Control*, May 1984, 7(2), pp. 686–99.

Houghton, John T.; Filho, L. G. Meira; Callander, Bruce A.; Harris, Neil; Kattenberg, Arie and Maskell, Kathy, eds. *Climate change 1995: The science of climate change.* Cambridge: Cambridge University Press, 1996.

Johnston, Robert J. and Sutinen, Jon G. "Uncertain Biomass Shift and Collapse: Implications for Harvest Policy in the Fishery." *Land Economics*, November 1996, 72(4), pp. 500–18.

Joyce, Linda A.; Mills, John R.; Heath, Linda S., McGuire, A. David; Haynes, Richard W. and Birdsey, Richard A. "Forest Sector Impacts from Changes in Forest Productivity Under Climate Change." *Journal of Biogeography*, July/September 1995, 22(4/5), pp. 703–13.

Kahn, James R. and Kemp, W. Michael. "Economic Losses Associated with the Degradation of an Ecosystem: The Case of Submerged Aquatic Vegetation in Chesapeake Bay." *Journal of Environmental Economics and Management*, September 1985, 12(3), pp. 246–63.

Kuchler, August W. *Potential natural vegetation of the United States*, 2nd Ed. New York: American Geographical Society, 1975.

Lyon, Kenneth S. and Sedjo, Roger A. "An Optimal Control Theory Model to Estimate the Regional Long Term Supply of Timber." *Forest Science*, December 1983, 29(4), pp. 798–812.

McArdle, Richard E.; Meyer, Walter H. and Bruce, Donald. "The Yield of Douglas Fir in the Pacific Northwest." *Revised Technical Bulletin Number 201*, U.S. Department of Agriculture, Washington, DC, 1949.

Melillo, Jerry M.; McGuire, A. David; Kicklighter, David W.; Moore, Berrien III; Vorosmarty, Charles J and Schloss, Annette L. "Global Climate Change and Terrestrial Net Primary Production." *Nature*, May 20, 1993, *363*(6426), pp. 234–40.

Mendelsohn, Robert and Neumann, James. *The market impact of climate change on the U.S. economy*. Cambridge: Cambridge University Press, 1998.

Meyer, Walter H. "Yield of Even-Aged Stands of Ponderosa Pine." *Technical Bulletin Number 630*, U.S. Department of Agriculture, Washington, DC, 1938.

Neilson, Ronald P.; King, George A. and Koerper, Greg. "Toward a Rule-Based Biome Model." *Landscape Ecology*, April 1992, *7*(1), pp. 27–43.

Parton, William J.; Stewart, J. W. B. and Cole, C. Vernon. "Dynamics of C, N, P and S in Grassland Soils: A Model." *Biogeochemistry*, 1988, *5*(1), pp. 109–31.

Perez-Garcia, John; Joyce, Linda A.; Binkley, Clark S. and McGuire, Andrew D. "Economic Impacts of Climatic Change on the Global Forest Sector: An Integrated Ecological Economic Assessment," in R. Neil Sampson, Roger A. Sedjo, and Joseph Wisniewski, eds., *Reviews in environmental science and technology*. Boca Raton, FL: CRC Press, 1997, pp. 5123–38.

Pontryagin, Lev S.; Boltyanskii, V. S.; Gamkrelidze, R. V. and Mischenko, E. F. *The mathematical theory of optimal processes*. New York: Wiley, 1962.

Prentice, I. Colin; Cramer, Wolfgang; Harrison, Sandy P.; Leemans, Rik; Monserud, Robert A. and Solomon, Allen M. "A Global Biome Model Based on Plant Physiology and Dominance, Soil Properties and Climate." *Journal of Biogeography*, March 1992, *19*(2), pp. 117–34.

Running, Steven W. and Coughland, Joseph C. "A General Model of Forest Ecosystem Processes for Regional Applications. I. Hydrologic Balance, Canopy Gas Exchange and Primary Productivity Processes." *Ecological Modeling*, August 1988, *42*(2), pp. 125–54.

Samuelson, Paul A. "Economics of Forestry in an Evolving Society." *Economic Inquiry*, December 1976, *14*(4), pp. 466–92.

Scheraga, Joel D.; Leary, Neal A.; Goettle, R. J.; Jorgenson, Dale W. and Wilcoxen, Peter J. "Macroeconomic Modeling and the Assessment of Climate Change Impacts," in Yoichi Kaya, N. Nalicenovic, and William D. Nordhaus, eds., *Costs, impacts, and benefits of CO$_2$ mitigation*. Laxenburg, Austria: International Institute for Applied Systems Analysis (IIASA) Collaborative Paper Series, CP93-2, 1993, pp. 107–32.

Schlesinger, Michael E. and Zhao, Z. C. "Seasonal Climate Changes Induced by Doubled CO$_2$ as Simulated by the OSU Atmospheric GCM-Mixed Layer Ocean Model." *Journal of Climate*, February 1989, *2*(2), pp. 459–95.

Schumacher, Francis X. and Coile, Theodore S. "Growth and Yield of Natural Stands of Southern Pines." School of Forestry and Environmental Studies, Duke University, Durham, NC, 1960.

Shugart, H. H.; Antonovsky, M. Ya.; Jarvis, P. G. and Sandford, A. P. "CO$_2$, Climatic Change, and Forest Ecosystems," in Bert Bolin, Bo R. Doos, Jill Jager, and Richard A. Warrick, eds., *The greenhouse effect, climatic change and ecosystems*. Chichester, U.K.: Wiley, 1986, pp. 475–521.

Smith, Joel B. and Tirpak, Dennis. "The Potential Effects of Global Climate Change on the United States." EPA-230-05-89-050, U.S. Environmental Protection Agency, Washington, DC, 1989.

Sohngen, Brent L. "Integrating Ecology and Economics: The Economic Impact of Climate Change on Timber Markets in the United States." Ph.D. dissertation, Yale University, 1996.

Sohngen, Brent; Mendelsohn, Robert and Neilson, Ronald. "CO$_2$ Emissions from Forests During Climate Change: Including the Role of Markets." Mimeo, Yale University, 1996.

U.S. Bureau of the Census, Department of Commerce. *Population projections of the United States, by age, sex, race and hispanic origin: 1993 to 2050*. Washington,

DC: U.S. Government Printing Office, 1993.

Vegetation/Ecosystem Modeling and Analysis Project (VEMAP) Members. "Vegetation/ Ecosystem Modeling and Analysis Project (VEMAP): Comparing Biogeography and Biogeochemistry Models in a Continental-Scale Study of Terrestrial Ecosystem Responses to Climate Change and CO_2 Doubling." *Global Biogeochemical Cycles*, December 1995, *9*(4), pp. 407–37.

Wilson, C. A. and Mitchell, J. F. B. "A Doubled CO_2 Climate Sensitivity Experiment with a Global Climate Model Including a Simple Ocean." *Journal of Geophysical Research*, November 20, 1987, *92*(D11), pp. 13,315–343.

Woodward, F. Ian; Smith, Thomas M. and Emanuel, William R. "A Global Land Primary Productivity and Phytobiogeography Model." *Global Biogeochemical Cycles*, December 1995, *9*(4), pp. 471–90.

[3]

CLIMATE CHANGE AND WATER RESOURCES

KENNETH D. FREDERICK
Resources for the Future, 1616 P Street, NW, Washington, DC 20036

DAVID C. MAJOR
Sarah Lawrence College, 1 Mead Way, Bronxville, NY 10708-5999

Abstract. Current perspectives on global climate change based on recent reports of the Intergovernmental Panel on Climate Change (IPCC) are presented. Impacts of a greenhouse warming that are likely to affect water planning and evaluation include changes in precipitation and runoff patterns, sea level rise, land use and population shifts following from these effects, and changes in water demands. Irrigation water demands are particularly sensitive to changes in precipitation, temperature, and carbon dioxide levels. Despite recent advances in climate change science, great uncertainty remains as to how and when climate will change and how these changes will affect the supply and demand for water at the river basin and watershed levels, which are of most interest to planners. To place the climate-induced uncertainties in perspective, the influence on the supply and demand for water of non-climate factors such as population, technology, economic conditions, social and political factors, and the values society places on alternative water uses are considered.

1. Introduction

This paper provides an introduction to global climate change and its implications for water resources. This and the following paper on planning methods serve as background for the rest of the volume. Recent conclusions of the Intergovernmental Panel on Climate Change (IPCC) about greenhouse gas emissions and their likely climate impacts are summarized. The impacts on water supplies of changes in temperature, precipitation, carbon dioxide, and sea levels are examined along with the impacts of these climate variables on water for irrigation and for domestic, industrial, and thermoelectric power uses. Non-climate factors influencing the availability and use of water are also considered, to provide some perspective as to the relative magnitude of and the uncertainties surrounding the climate impacts.

2. Global Climate Change

Considerable progress has been made in recent years in understanding climate change science. Some of the conclusions from the Intergovernmental Panel on Climate Change (1996a) are presented below.

8   KENNETH D. FREDERICK AND DAVID C. MAJOR

- Atmospheric concentrations of long-lived greenhouse gases have increased significantly since pre-industrial times, tending to warm the surface and produce other climate changes.
- The most important of these gases are carbon dioxide (CO_2), methane (CH_4), and nitrous oxide (N_2O) which have increased about 30%, 145%, and 15% respectively over the last 250 years. Human activities such as fossil fuel use, land-use change, and agriculture are largely responsible for these trends.
- Tropospheric aerosols from fossil fuel combustion, biomass burning, and other sources tend to have a cooling effect that is focused in particular regions. However, in contrast to the long-lived greenhouse gases that remain in the atmosphere for decades to centuries, these aerosols are very short-lived in the atmosphere.
- Although year-to-year variations in weather at any one location are large, important systematic changes for large areas over periods of decades and longer are evident. Global mean surface temperature has increased by about 0.3 to 0.6°C over the past century. The ability to quantify the human influence on global climate remains limited in part because of the problems of separating it from the noise of natural climate variability. "Nevertheless, the balance of evidence suggests that there is a discernible human influence on global climate" (Intergovernmental Panel on Climate Change, 1996a, p. 5).
- Based on the IPCC's mid-range emission scenario and best estimate as to climate sensitivity, models project an increase in global mean surface temperature of about 2°C relative to 1990 by the year 2100. Combining the lowest IPCC emission scenario with a low value of climate sensitivity reduces the projected increase in temperature to about 1°C by 2100. On the other hand, combining the highest IPCC emission scenario with a high climate sensitivity results in a projected warming of about 3.5°C.
- Warmer temperatures will accelerate the hydrological cycle, altering in uncertain ways the prospects for more extreme droughts and/or floods. An increase in precipitation intensity resulting in more extreme rainfall events is a possibility. But the hydrological changes are more speculative than the temperature projections.
- Average sea level under the mid-range IPCC emission scenario is expected to rise about 50 cm by 2100. The high and low IPCC scenarios give a range of 15 to 95 cm rise in sea level.

3. Impacts of Climate Change on Water Supplies

There is broad agreement that a greenhouse warming will have major impacts on water resources. Possible impacts that may especially affect water planning and project evaluation include changes in precipitation and runoff patterns, sea level rise, and land use and population shifts that may follow from these effects. Warmer

CLIMATE CHANGE AND WATER RESOURCES 9

temperatures will accelerate the hydrologic cycle, altering precipitation, the magnitude and timing of runoff, and the intensity and frequency of floods and droughts. Higher temperatures will also increase evapotranspiration rates and alter soil moisture and infiltration rates. Uncertainties abound, however, especially at geographic scales of particular relevance for water resource planning. While the timing and magnitude of the global temperature changes are uncertain, even less is known about climate changes and their impacts at the basin and watershed levels. General circulation models (GCMs), the principal tools relating changes in atmospheric chemistry to changes in climate variables such as temperature and precipitation, do not provide the requisite degree of region-specific information.

3.1. IPCC RESULTS

The IPCC Working Group II (Intergovernmental Panel on Climate Change, 1996b) review of evidence regarding the impacts of a greenhouse warming on water suggests the following:

- The timing and regional patterns of precipitation events will change, and more intense precipitation events are likely.
- GCMs project that a 1.5 to 4.5°C rise in global mean temperature would increase global mean precipitation about 3 to 15 percent.
- Although the regional distribution is uncertain, precipitation is expected to increase in higher latitudes, particularly in winter. This conclusion extends to the mid-latitudes in most cases.
- Even in areas with increased precipitation, higher evaporation rates may lead to reduced runoff.
- More annual runoff due to increased precipitation is likely in the high latitudes. Some lower latitude basins, however, may experience reductions in runoff due to a combination of increased evaporation and decreased precipitation.
- Although potential evapotranspiration (ET) rises with air temperature, actual ET may increase or decrease according to the availability of moisture.
- GCMs and hydrologic impact studies provide evidence of an increase in flood frequencies with global warming. The amount of increase for any given climate scenario is uncertain, and impacts will vary among basins. Floods may become less frequent in some areas.
- The frequency and severity of droughts could increase in some areas as a result of a decrease in total rainfall, more frequent dry spells, and higher evapotranspiration.
- The hydrology of arid and semiarid areas is particularly sensitive to climate variations.
- Seasonal disruptions in water supplies of mountainous areas, where snowmelt is an important source of spring and summer runoff, might result if more precipitation falls as rain rather than snow and the length of the snow storage season is reduced.

10   KENNETH D. FREDERICK AND DAVID C. MAJOR

- Water quality problems are likely to increase where streamflow declines.

One clear message from the IPCC assessment of the effects of climate change on hydrologic regimes is that the prospect of a greenhouse warming adds to the considerable uncertainty already confronting water planners. Uncertainties as to the impacts of climate change on water availability are evident in Table I depicting water availability per capita in 21 countries as of 1990 and forecasts for 2050 under four climate scenarios: the present climate and three GCM transient climate results. The ratio of the highest and lowest GCM-derived water availability forecasts is 1.3 or higher in 13 of the 21 countries and 2.7 or higher in 6 countries.

Hydrological uncertainties attributable to changing atmospheric chemistry are likely to persist for the foreseeable future, pending major improvements in our understanding of the impacts of atmospheric greenhouse gases on climate and hydrology at the river basin and watershed levels. In the meantime, analysis of various climate change scenarios can provide planners with some idea of the range of hydrological changes that may occur. The results of several such studies are summarized below.

3.2. HYDROLOGIC SENSITIVITY TO THE CLIMATE

The American Association for the Advancement of Science (AAAS) panel on Climate Variability, Climate Change and the Planning and Management of U.S. Water Resources undertook several studies to evaluate the effects of global climate change on water supplies. The panel's final report (Waggoner, 1990) examines the effects of climate change and CO_2 enrichment on evapotranspiration, the effects of the climate on flow, and the impacts of flow on available supplies. This report also evaluates the impacts of climate change on floods and drought, irrigation, water quality, recreation, wildlife, urban water, and electricity generation.

In this work, Schneider, Gleick, and Mearns (1990) conclude that the range of likely changes in average annual precipitation associated with an equivalent doubling of atmospheric CO_2 for any given region might be on the order of plus or minus 20 percent. The range of likely changes in regional runoff and soil moisture are on the order of plus or minus 50 percent. Advances in global climate modeling made since that assessment have done little to reduce the uncertainty regarding the impacts of increasing atmospheric greenhouse gases on regional water supplies.

Changes in runoff are the direct result of changes in precipitation and evaporation (which is strongly influenced by temperature). Schaake (1990) used water balance models of hydrologic processes to investigate the influence of climate on streamflows in the United States. Flow sensitivity to climate variables differs widely for different locations and climates. Schaake's estimates of the elasticities of runoff with respect to precipitation and temperature (i.e., the percentage change in runoff resulting from a 1 percent change in precipitation and temperature) range from less than 1 to as high as 10. The runoff elasticities are higher for drier climates, and the elasticity with respect to precipitation is greater than that for

CLIMATE CHANGE AND WATER RESOURCES 11

evapotranspiration. Thus, a warming alone will decrease runoff much less than a warming accompanied by a decrease in precipitation. Schaake's study of the Animas River Basin in southwestern Colorado suggests that the elasticity of annual runoff to a change in precipitation is 1.9 while the elasticity of runoff with respect to evapotranspiration is -0.7.

Table I
Water availability (m^3/yr/per capita) in 2050 for the present climatic conditions and for three transient climate scenarios[1]

Country	Present Climate (1990)	Present Climate (2050)	Scenario Range (2050)
China	2,500	1,630	1,550-1,780
Cyprus	1,280	820	620-850
France	4,110	3,620	2,510-2,970
Haiti	1,700	650	280-840
India	1,930	1,050	1,060-1,420
Japan	3,210	3,060	2,940-3,470
Kenya	640	170	210-250
Madagascar	3,330	710	480-730
Mexico	4,270	2,100	1,740-2,010
Peru	1,860	880	690-1,020
Poland	1,470	1,250	980-1,860
Saudi Arabia	310	80	30-140
South Africa	1,320	540	150-500
Spain	3,310	3,090	1,820-2,200
Sri Lanka	2,500	1,520	1,440-4,900
Thailand	3,380	2,220	590-3070
Togo	3,400	900	550-880
Turkey	3,070	1,240	700-1,910
Ukraine	4,050	3,480	2,830-3,990
United Kingdom	2,650	2,430	2,190-2,520
Vietnam	6,880	2,970	2,680-3,140

[1]The transient climate scenarios are based on general circulation models of the Geophysical Fluid Dynamics Laboratory (GFDL) in Princeton, N.J., USA; the United Kingdom Meteorological Office (UKMO) in Bracknell, UK; and the Max Planck Institute for Meteorology (MPI) in Hamburg, Germany.

Source: IPCC, 1966b, p. 478.

12   KENNETH D. FREDERICK AND DAVID C. MAJOR

Other simulation studies of the effects of changes in climate variables on hydrologic processes have been performed for a number of river basins and subbasins. Hypothetical climate scenarios commonly include increases in average temperatures of 1° to 4° C and increases and decreases in precipitation of 10 and 20 percent. Other studies use GCM results to generate climate scenarios. These simulation studies estimate the impacts of the underlying climate-change assumptions on water resources; they offer no guidance as to the likelihood that the climate-change assumptions will be realized. While they are not intended to be predictions or forecasts of future events, these studies are instructive as to the possible magnitude of, and the uncertainty surrounding, the implications of a greenhouse warming.

As an example, estimated impacts of alternative temperature and precipitation changes on annual runoff in several semiarid rivers are summarized in Table II, adapted from Nash and Gleick (1993). These studies suggest that relatively small changes in temperature and precipitation can have large effects on runoff. With no change in precipitation, estimated runoff declines by 3 to 12 percent with a 2° C increase in temperature and by 7 to 21 percent with a 4° C increase in temperature. These results are consistent with Schaake's (1990) and Karl and Riebsame's (1989) conclusion that runoff is more sensitive to changes in precipitation than to temperature. Nevertheless, a 10 percent increase in precipitation does not fully offset the negative impacts on runoff attributable to a 4° C increase in temperature in three of the five rivers for which this climate scenario was studied. The Pease River runoff estimates are the most extreme example of the sensitivity of runoff to precipitation. With a 1° C rise in temperature, runoff declines by 50 percent given a 10 percent decline in precipitation and increases by 50 percent given a 10 percent increase in precipitation.

Many of the climate impact studies reviewed by the IPCC (1996b) highlight the vulnerability of water resource systems to climate variables and suggest that small changes in these variables could lead to large changes in system performance. Most notably, isolated single-reservoir systems in arid and semiarid regions are extremely sensitive and less able to adapt to climate impacts that could vary from decreases in reservoir yields in excess of 50 percent to seasonal flooding.

In contrast, another set of studies undertaken largely in the United States and based on the most recent transient GCM simulations suggests "that even with the large variability in future climate represented by the three transient GCM experiments, most of the systems investigated possess the robustness and resilience to withstand those changes, and adequate institutional capacity exists to adapt to changes in growth, demands, and climate" (IPCC, 1996b, 475). The differences between the two sets of studies are attributable primarily to two factors. First, the climate scenarios produced by the transient GCMs tended to produce smaller changes than those based on earlier GCM results. Second, highly integrated systems are inherently more robust than isolated single-reservoir systems. However, much of the world's water is managed through single-source, single-purpose systems.

CLIMATE CHANGE AND WATER RESOURCES 13

Table II
Impacts of climatic changes on mean annual runoff in semiarid river basins

Change in Precipitation		Change in Temperature			
		T+1°	T+2°	T+3°	T+4°
		Percent Change in Mean Annual Runoff			
	Pease River [1]	-50		-50	
	Great Basin Rivers [2]		-17 to -28		
	Sacramento River [3]		-18		-21
-10%	Inflow to Lake Powell [4]		-24		-32
	White River		-13		-17
	East River		-19		-25
	Animas River		-17		
	Sacramento River		-3		-7
	Inflow to Lake Powell		-12		-21
0	White River		-4		-8
	East River		-9		-16
	Animas River		-7		-14
	Pease River	+50		+35	
	Sacramento River		+12		+7
+10%	Inflow to Lake Powell		+1		-10
	White River		+7		+1
	East River		+1		-3
	Animas River		+3		-5

Notes: [1] All Pease River results from Nemec and Schaake, 1982.
[2] All Great Basin Rivers results from Flaschka, et al., 1987.
[3] All Sacramento River results from Gleick, 1986, 1987b.
[4] All Lake Powell, White, East, and Animas River results from Nash and Gleick, 1993.

Source: Adapted from Nash and Gleick, 1993.

Uncertainties as to how the climate will change and how societies will adapt to these changes are challenges that all climate impact studies confront. Estimates of climate impacts several decades in the future are highly uncertain. However, one of the more likely impacts of a greenhouse warming on regional hydrology involves areas where winter snowfall is the primary source of precipitation and spring and summer snowmelt are the primary sources of streamflow. Such regions are likely to see a distinct shift in the relative amounts of snow and rain and in the timing of

14   KENNETH D. FREDERICK AND DAVID C. MAJOR

snowmelt due to higher temperatures. The resulting changes in runoff patterns could greatly alter the likelihood of flooding and the availability of water during peak-demand periods such as the irrigation season. This type of seasonal effect was identified by Gleick (1988) for basins in the western United States.

3.3. SEA LEVEL RISE

Impacts on water resources will also come from rising sea levels due to thermal expansion of the oceans and increased melting of glaciers and land ice. The global sea level increased some 10 to 20 centimeters (cm) during the past century, largely due to the melting of land-based ice sheets and glaciers (U.S. Congress, Office of Technology Assessment, 1993). The most recent IPCC results suggest average sea level might rise another 15 to 95 cm by the year 2100, with a best guess of about 50 cm (Intergovernmental Panel on Climate Change, 1996a).

Higher sea levels and increased storm surges could adversely impact freshwater supplies in some coastal areas. Saline water profiles in river mouths and deltas would be pushed farther inland, and coastal aquifers would face an increased threat of saltwater intrusion. The intrusion of saltwater into current freshwater supplies could jeopardize the quality of water for some domestic, industrial, and agricultural users. For example, sea level rise would aggravate water-supply problems in several coastal areas in the United States, including Long Island, Cape Cod, New Jersey shore communities, and the Florida cities of Miami, Tampa, and Jacksonville.

Rising sea levels pose a threat to critical freshwater supplies in California. The Sacramento-San Joaquin Delta, which is already under stress, is a major source of water for the farms and cities of southern California and the San Joaquin Valley. It is also the habitat for scores of fish species, several of which have been so weakened that they have either been granted protection or are being considered for listing under the federal Endangered Species Act. Saltwater intrusion from San Francisco Bay threatens the Delta's ecology as well as its use as a freshwater source. Over the last century, an "apparent" sea level rise of 17 cm in San Francisco Bay (the result of an actual sea-level rise of approximately 12 cm and ground subsidence of about 5 cm) has exacerbated these water supply and environmental problems.

Two critical factors for limiting the intrusion of saltwater are sufficient freshwater flows from the Delta to the Bay and the levees protecting the more than 500,000 acres of islands within the Delta. These islands are now rich farmlands that were created around the turn of the century out of the marshland that originally characterized much of the Delta. The gradual compaction of the Delta's peat soils has caused many of the islands to fall well below sea level. Maintaining the levees is important both to protect lives and property on these islands and to prevent saltwater from intruding into the Delta. When a levee breaks, as happens on average about twice a year, freshwater that would otherwise help prevent saltwater from entering into the Delta floods onto the land. Any widescale failure of these levees would increase salinity levels in the Delta, threatening the ecosystem and water for the farms and cities to the south. Sea level rise would aggravate already serious problems; additional scarce freshwater supplies would be required to prevent saltwater intrusion into the Delta, and it would become increasingly difficult and expensive to maintain the more than 1,100 miles of levees protecting the islands located in the Delta (U.S. Congress, Office of Technology Assessment, 1993).

3.4. CARBON DIOXIDE EFFECTS

A growing body of research suggests that atmospheric carbon dioxide (CO_2) levels may affect water availability through its influence on vegetation. Controlled experiments indicate that elevated CO_2 concentrations increase the resistance of plant stomata to water vapor transport, resulting in decreased transpiration per unit of leaf area. Some experiments suggest that a doubling of CO_2 will increase stomatal resistance and reduce transpiration by about 50 percent on average (Rosenberg et al., 1990). On the other hand, CO_2 also has been demonstrated to increase plant growth, leading to a larger area of transpiring tissue and a corresponding increase in transpiration. Other factors that might offset any potential increases in plant water-use efficiency are a potential increase in leaf temperatures due to reduced transpiration rates and species changes in vegetation communities (Ayers et al., 1993; Rosenberg et al., 1990). The net effect of opposing influences on water supplies would depend on the type of vegetation and other interacting factors, such as soil type and climate.

The Erosion Productivity Impact Calculator (EPIC) model has been used to examine the likely impacts of CO_2 enrichment on runoff in the Missouri River Basin (Frederick et al., 1993). EPIC (a generic crop simulator originally developed to model runoff, soil erosion, crop productivity, and the interactions among them) includes detailed treatment of hydrologic processes. The model was adapted to allow for the impacts of alternative CO_2 levels on transpiration and plant growth and used to estimate runoff from various land covers and soil types within the Missouri Basin under three alternative climate scenarios. The results suggest that the increased stomatal resistance associated with CO_2 enrichment would increase runoff, especially from land in perennial crops such as alfalfa and wheatgrass. This positive CO_2 effect, however, would offset only a small fraction of the decrease in streamflows resulting from the higher temperature and lower precipitation rates that characterized the climate change scenario used in the study.

4. Impacts of Global Climate Change on Water Demand

Precipitation, temperature, and carbon dioxide levels can affect the demand for as well as the supply of water. This section considers how changes in these climate variables might impact the demand for various uses of water.

16   KENNETH D. FREDERICK AND DAVID C. MAJOR

4.1. IRRIGATION WATER USE

Irrigation is the largest use of water in the United States, accounting for 41 percent of all withdrawals and 81 percent of consumptive use. In the water-scarce 17 western states irrigation accounts for 77 percent of withdrawals and 85 percent of consumptive use (Solley, Pierce, and Perlman, 1993). Irrigation is also the most climate-sensitive water use. The profitability of irrigated relative to dryland farming tends to increase as conditions become hotter and drier and crop yields produced under dryland conditions decline. In areas with available and affordable water supplies, hotter and drier conditions would likely lead both to an increase in the land under irrigation and to an increase in the amount of water applied per irrigated acre. As noted above, CO_2 enrichment would tend to increase both the water-use efficiency of the plants and the growth of the plant, with less certain impacts on water use per unit of land.

Simulation results using the EPIC model for growing grains in Nebraska and Kansas under the different climate conditions existing in the 1931-40 and 1951-80 periods suggest the potential advantages of applying more water under hotter and drier conditions. Estimated irrigation water use averaged 39 percent higher on corn in Nebraska and 14 percent higher on corn, wheat, and sorghum in Kansas under the hotter and drier 1931-40 climate than under the 1951-80 climate. Temperatures averaged about 1 degree C higher and precipitation averaged about 4 inches less during the 1931-40 period (Frederick, 1991a).

When allowance is made for the impacts of higher levels of atmospheric CO_2 on transpiration rates, these increases in irrigation water use are dampened somewhat. Adapting the EPIC model to allow for an increase in CO_2 from 350 to 450 parts per million reduces estimated water use for irrigation in Kansas and Nebraska by an average of 7 percent under the 1931-40 climate (Frederick, 1991a).

McCabe and Wolock (1992) used an irrigation model (based on a modified Thornthwaite water balance model) to simulate the effects of hypothetical changes in temperature, precipitation, and stomatal resistance on annual plant water use in a humid-temperate climate. Hypothetical climate scenarios included combinations of temperature changes of 0, +2, +4, and +6° C; precipitation changes of 0, +/-10, and +/-20 percent; and a stomatal resistance factor of 0, 20 and 40 percent. Their results suggest that increases in mean annual water use are strongly associated with increases in temperature and less strongly associated with decreases in precipitation. When temperature and precipitation are the only changes, water use increased, even with 20 percent more precipitation and a 2° C warming. Their results also suggest that plant water use is even more sensitive to changes in stomatal resistance than to temperature. Decreases in water use resulting from greater stomatal resistance resulted in less water use for all scenarios except those with the smaller (20 percent) increase in stomatal resistance and temperature increases of at least 4° C.

Herrington's (1996) analysis of the impacts of climate change on the demand for water in England and Wales concluded that a 1.1° C rise in temperature would increase water demand by 12 percent for agriculture and 4 percent for both golf courses and other parks.

4.2. DOMESTIC WATER USE

Domestic water use accounts for 8 percent of withdrawals and 6 percent of consumptive use in the United States (Solley, Pierce, and Perlman, 1993). Domestic use, especially outdoor use for watering lawns and gardens, is somewhat sensitive to changes in temperature and precipitation. A survey of the water demand literature identified 13 studies that examine the effects of climate variables on residential/municipal water use (Schefter, undated). The estimated temperature and precipitation elasticities of the demand for water varied widely depending on the region, season, and whether the estimates differentiated between indoor and outdoor or urban and suburban uses. The elasticity estimates suggest that a 1 percent rise in temperature would increase residential water use from 0.02 to 3.8 percent and a 1 percent decrease in precipitation would increase residential water use from 0.02 to 0.31 percent.

A study of urban water use in four Wasatch Front counties of Utah found that potential evapotranspiration and rainfall best explain changes in residential water use attributable to the climate. Higher evapotranspiration attributable to a temperature rise of about 2.2 ° C (4° F) increased residential water demand by an estimated 2.8 percent during the summer season and by as much as 8 percent during the month of June. A temperature increase of 4.4 ° C (8 ° F) increased demand by 5 percent in the summer and as much as 16 percent in June (Hughes, Wang, and Hansen, 1994).

Herrington's (1996) analysis of the impacts of climate change on the demand for water in England and Wales concluded that global warming would have significant impacts on only three domestic water uses -- showering, lawn sprinkling, and other garden use. His forecasts for the year 2021 indicated that a 1.1°C increase in temperature would increase water demand by 12 percent for showers, 35 percent for lawn sprinkling, and 19 percent for other garden use. These changes produce a 4 percent increase in total domestic water use.

Boland (this volume) examined the impacts on urban water use in the Washington, DC metropolitan area in the year 2030 of five climate scenarios derived from GCM results and a stationary climate scenario. The forecasts of annual water use under the five climate change scenarios ranged from -8 to +11 percent of the stationary climate forecast. The moisture deficit for the June to August period under the various climate scenarios is a critical factor in the water use forecasts. The forecast of an 8 percent reduction in water use from the stationary climate case was from the only GCM scenario with a lower average summer moisture deficit.

4.3. INDUSTRIAL AND THERMOELECTRIC POWER WATER USES

Industrial use - which includes water for purposes such as processing, washing, and cooling in facilities that manufacture products - accounts for 7 percent of withdrawals and 4 percent of consumptive use in the United States. Thermoelectric power use - which includes water used for cooling to condense the steam that drives the turbines in the generation of electric power with fossil fuel, nuclear, or geothermal energy - accounts for 39 percent of all water withdrawals but only 4 percent of consumptive use in the United States (Solley, Pierce, and Perlman, 1993).

Global warming could have important implications for these water uses. A rise in water temperature would reduce the efficiency of cooling systems and, therefore, might result in an increased demand for cooling water. If aquatic ecosystems were threatened by higher water temperatures resulting from either a global warming or returnflows of cooling water, these uses might be subjected to more stringent environmental regulations. More than 95 percent of the freshwater withdrawn for industrial and thermoelectric power use is returned to ground and surface water sources.

A possible response to the imposition of stricter regulations on returnflows would be to switch from once-through cooling systems to cooling towers and cooling ponds that return little or no water to the source. While the water withdrawals would drop sharply as a result of such a switch, there is little difference in the consumptive use of water for these cooling technologies. The evaporative losses occur on site with cooling towers and ponds. In a once-through system more of the evaporation occurs off-site and is attributable to the increased temperature of the receiving water body (Miller, 1990).

A global warming would also have indirect effects on industrial and thermoelectric power uses. Summer energy use for air conditioning would rise, and winter demand for space heating would decline. Changes in the temporal and perhaps the spatial demand for energy would alter the demand for cooling water.

4.4. INSTREAM USES

The impacts of a greenhouse warming on the quantity, quality, and timing of runoff would affect instream water uses such as aquatic ecosystem maintenance, instream water quality, hydroelectric power generation, navigation, and recreation. They might also affect, either directly or indirectly, water demands. For example, changes in streamflows would affect actual and potential hydroelectric power generation, which in turn would affect the demand for substitute sources of electricity. Since thermoelectric cooling is one of the largest withdrawal uses of water, shifts in hydroelectric power production could have a significant impact on the demand for water within a watershed.

A warming would increase the potential length of the navigation season on some northern lakes and rivers, especially the Great Lakes. To the extent that lake depth and river flow are constraints on navigation, there may be an increased demand for water to facilitate navigation during the extended ice-free period. Similarly, the changed climate might alter seasonal water demands associated with recreational uses such as swimming, boating, and fishing.

5. Non-Climate Factors Influencing Future Water Supply and Demand

Climate is only one of many factors that will affect the future supply and demand for water. Population, technology, economic conditions, social and political factors, and the values society places on alternative water uses are important determinants of supply and demand conditions, and, indeed, may be more important determinants than those attributable to climate change (Intergovernmental Panel on Climate Change, 1996b; Goklany, 1995; Stakhiv, 1996).

A wide range of non-climate factors affects the quantity and quality of freshwater supplies. Groundwater stocks are depleted when pumping exceeds recharge rates, and both surface and groundwater supplies are degraded when the capacity of an aquatic system to assimilate pollutants is exceeded. On the other hand, the effective supply of water can be augmented by investments to develop, protect, and restore supplies. Investments in infrastructure such as dams and canals can capture water that otherwise would be unavailable for use. The United States is currently spending billions of dollars annually to protect and restore the quality of water supplies. And upgrading water through recycling and desalting to a quality suitable for human use is becoming increasingly common.

Population growth will be a major, if not the most important, determinant of future water availability in the developing world. Countries with high population growth rates will experience sharp declines in per capita water availability regardless of the assumed climate scenario. For example, per capita water availability in the year 2050 in Kenya and Madagascar would decline to 27 and 21 percent respectively of their 1990 levels under stationary climate conditions, anticipated population growth, and no allowance for possible development of water resource systems (see Table I).

For the first three-quarters of this century, population and economic growth were the primary factors underlying changes in water use in the United States. Estimated total offstream water use rose from 40 to 420 billion gallons per day (bgd) from 1900 to 1975 (Frederick, 1991b). Although population and the economy have continued to grow, other factors have emerged to dampen and even reverse the growth of water withdrawals. By 1990, total offstream use of 408 bgd was estimated to be 3 percent below the level fifteen years earlier (Solley, Pierce, and Perlman, 1993). This decline in offstream water use in the United States, which was largely unforeseen by water planners, is attributed to a number of forces that have altered water use in recent decades. These include the growing scarcity and rising costs of the resource, higher values being placed by society on protecting and restoring

20   KENNETH D. FREDERICK AND DAVID C. MAJOR

instream flows and uses, environmental regulations inhibiting new water infrastructure developments, and development and adoption of water-conserving technologies.

Our ability to foresee how non-climate factors will influence the future supply and demand for freshwater is probably not any better than our current ability to foresee how a greenhouse-induced climate change will affect regional water supplies. Indeed, if the past record of forecasting water use is any guide, great uncertainties are likely to stem from the non-climate variables, and these uncertainties may be greater than those associated with climate variables. As illustrated in Figure 1, few people anticipated that U.S. water withdrawals would start to level off in the mid-1970s, and then decline. This comparison between actual freshwater withdrawals in the United States and the range of forecasts that influenced water programming and budgeting several decades ago indicates how uncertain and, in many cases, inaccurate such forecasts can be. Yet, these forecasts, by prestigious institutions, established a baseline against which national, regional, and watershed level impact analyses were conducted (Stakhiv, 1996). Projections made in 1960 by the Senate Select Committee on National Water Resources overestimated 1980 water use (as estimated by the U.S. Geological Survey) by 137 percent for industrial and 22 percent for thermoelectric uses and underestimated irrigation use by 20 percent and municipal use by 15 percent. In 1968, the U.S. Water Resources Council's projections of water withdrawals for 1980 were 68 percent too high for industrial, 6 percent too high for irrigation, and 11 percent too low for thermoelectric uses. The Council's projections in the Second National Water Assessment (U.S. Water Resources Council, 1978) for 1985 water use were 23 percent too high for industrial, 20 percent too high for irrigation, 27 percent too low for thermoelectric, and 18 percent too low for municipal use (Waggoner and Schefter, 1990). The prediction errors for individual basins were, in general, greater than the errors for the United States as a whole.

The difficulties of projecting changes in water use a decade or two in the future offer little confidence as to our ability to project over periods that might be used in climate impact studies. The populations, incomes, and life styles that create demands for water are likely to change substantially over the time horizon within which global climate change will have significant impacts. The additional changes that will result from global climate change must be added to these largely unknowable changes. What, for example, will be the demand 40 years from now for water-based recreation in the Northeastern United States? What will be the demand for energy in the Southwest? These questions suggest the importance of sensitivity analysis, the evaluation of uncertainty, and the concept of robustness in project evaluation, with or without climate change.

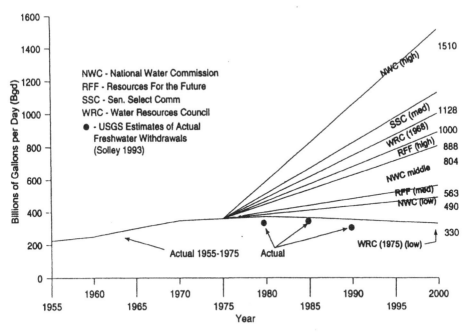

Figure 1. Historic and projected fresh water withdrawals 1955-2000.
Source: Stakhiv, 1996.

6. Summary

The IPCC's mid-range emission scenario and best estimate as to climate sensitivity suggest that global mean surface temperature will increase by about 2°C by the year 2100 relative to 1990. Warmer temperatures will accelerate the hydrologic cycle, with uncertain implications for precipitation, runoff, and the intensity and frequency of floods and droughts, especially at the basin and watershed levels of most interest to planners. Simulation studies suggest that relatively small changes in temperature and precipitation can have large effects on runoff, especially in semiarid areas. Sea level rise and increased storm surges could adversely impact water supplies in some coastal areas. Increased stomatal resistance associated with elevated levels of atmospheric CO_2 could increase runoff. However, this positive CO_2 effect would likely offset only a small fraction of the decrease in streamflows that would result from higher temperatures and lower precipitation rates. Precipitation, temperature, and carbon dioxide levels have important but uncertain effects on the demand for as well as the supply of water. While the prospect of climate change adds uncertainty to water planning, climate is only one of many factors influencing the future supply and demand for water. Population, technology, economic conditions, social and political factors, and the values society places on alternative water uses may be more important for the future availability and use of water.

Acknowledgments

Eugene Stakhiv provided insightful comments as well as source materials that were helpful in the preparation of this paper. Two anonymous reviewers also provided useful comments.

References

Ayers, M.A., Wolock, D.M., McCabe, G.J., Hay, L.E., and Tasker, G.D.: 1993, 'Sensitivity of Water Resources in the Delaware Basin to Climate Variability and Change', Open File Report 92-52, U.S. Geological Survey, West Trenton, NJ.

Boland, J.J.: 'Assessing Urban Water Use and the Role of Water Conservation Measures Under Climate Uncertainty', *Climatic Change* **37** (this volume).

Flaschka, I.M., Stockton, C.W., and Boggess, W.R.: 1987, 'Climatic Variation and Surface Water Resources in the Great Basin Region', *Water Resources Bulletin* **23**, 47-57.

Frederick, K.D.: 1991a, 'Processes for Identifying Regional Influences of and Responses to Increasing Atmospheric CO2 and Climate Change - The MINK Project', Report IV - Water Resources, DOE/RL/01830T-H10, Office of Energy Research, U.S. Department of Energy, Washington, D.C.

Frederick, K.D.: 1991b, 'Water Resources: Increasing Demand and Scarce Supplies', in Frederick, K.D. and Sedjo, R.A., eds., *America's Renewable Resources: Historical Trends and Current Challenges*, Resources for the Future, Washington, D.C.

Frederick, K.D., McKenney, M.S., Rosenberg, N.J., and Balzer, D.K.: 1993, 'Estimating the Effects of Climate Change and Carbon Dioxide on Water Supplies in the Missouri River Basin', Discussion Paper, ENR 93-18, Resources for the Future, Washington, D.C.

Gleick, P.H.: 1986, 'Methods for Evaluating the Regional Hydrologic Impacts of Global Climatic Changes', *J. of Hydrology* **88**, 99-116.

Gleick, P.H.: 1987, 'Regional Hydrologic Consequences of Increases in Atmospheric CO_2 and Other Trace Gases', *Climatic Change* **10**, 137-161.

Gleick, P.H.: 1988, 'Regional Hydrologic Impacts of Global Climatic Changes', in Whitehead, E.E., Hutchinson, C.F., Timmermann, B.N., and Varady, R.G. eds., *Arid Lands: Today and Tomorrow*, Proceedings of an International Research and Development Conference, Tucson, Arizona, October 20-25, 1985, Westview/Bellhaven Press, Boulder, Colo.

Goklany, I.M.: 1995, 'Strategies to Enhance Adaptability: Technological Change, Sustainable Growth and Free Trade', *Climatic Change* **30**: 427-449.

Herrington, P.: 1996, *Climate Change and the Demand for Water*, Department of the Environment, HMSO. London.

Hughes, T., Wang, Y.M., and Hansen, R.: 1994, *Impacts of Projected Climate Change on Urban Water Use: An Application Using the Wasatch Front Water Demand and Supply Model*, U.S. Bureau of Reclamation, Provo, Utah.

Intergovernmental Panel on Climate Change: 1996a, *Climate Change 1995: The Science of Climate Change: Contribution of Working Group I to the Second Assessment Report of the Intergovernmental Panel on Climate Change*, Cambridge University Press.

Intergovernmental Panel on Climate Change: 1996b, *Climate Change 1995: Impacts, Adaptations and Mitigation of Climate Change: Scientific-Technical Analyses: Contribution of Working Group II to the Second Assessment Report of the Intergovernmental Panel on Climate Change*, Cambridge University Press.

Karl, T.R. and Riebsame, W.E.: 1989, 'The impact of decadal fluctuations in mean precipitation and temperature on runoff: a sensitivity study over the United States', *Climatic Change*, **15**, 423-447.

McCabe, G.J. Jr. and Wolock, D.M.: 1992, 'Sensitivity of Irrigation Demand in a Humid-Temperate Region to Hypothetical Climatic Change', *Water Resources Bulletin* **28**, 3, May/June, 535-543.

Miller, K.A.: 1990, 'Water, Electricity, and Institutional Change', in Waggoner, P.E., ed., *Climate Change and U.S. Water Resources*, 367-393, John Wiley and Sons, New York.

Nash, L.L. and Gleick, P.H.: 1993, 'The Colorado River Basin and Climatic Change: The Sensitivity of Streamflow and Water Supply to Variations in Temperature and Precipitation', EPA 230-R-93-009, U.S. Environmental Protection Agency, Washington, D.C.

Nemec, J., and Schaake, J.C. jr.: 1982, 'Sensitivity of Water Resource Systems to Climatic Variation', *Hydrological Sciences* **17**, 327-343.

Rosenberg, N.J., Kimball, B.A., Martin, P., and Cooper, C.F.: 1990, 'From Climate and CO_2 Enrichment to Evapotranspiration', in Waggoner, P.E., ed., *Climate Change and U.S. Water Resources*, 151-175, John Wiley and Sons, New York.

Schaake, J.: 1990, 'From Climate to Flow', in Waggoner, P.E., ed., *Climate Change and U.S. Water Resources*, 177-206, John Wiley and Sons, New York.

Schefter, J.: n.d., 'Selected Estimates of Effect of Climate Variables on Residential/Municipal Water Demand', Unpublished table provided by the author, U.S. Geological Survey, Reston, VA.

Schneider, S.H., Gleick, P.H., and Mearns, L.O.: 1990, 'Prospects for Climate Change', in Waggoner, P.E., ed., *Climate Change and U.S. Water Resources*, 41-73, John Wiley and Sons, New York.

Solley, W.B., Pierce, R.R., and Perlman, H.A.: 1993, *Estimated Use of Water in the United States*, U.S. Geological Survey Circular 1081, U.S. Government Printing Office, Washington, D.C.

Stakhiv, E.Z.: 1996, 'Managing Water Resources for Climate Change Adaptation', in Smith, J.B., Bhatti, N., Menzhulin, G.V., Benioff, R., Campos, M., Jallow, B., Rijsberman, F., Budyko, M.I., Dixon, R.K., eds. *Adapting to Climate Change: Assessment and Issues*, 243-264, Springer, New York.

U.S. Congress, Office of Technology Assessment: 1993, *Preparing for an Uncertain Climate*, Vol. I, OTA-O-567,. U.S. Government Printing Office, Washington, D.C.

U.S. Water Resources Council: 1978, *The Nation's Water Resources 1975-2000*, U.S. Government Printing Office, Washington, D.C.

Waggoner, P.E., ed.: 1990, *Climate Change and U.S. Water Resources*,: John Wiley and Sons, New York.

Waggoner, P.E. and Schefter, J.: 1990, 'Future Water Use in the Present Climate', in Waggoner, P.E., ed., *Climate Change and U.S. Water Resources*, 19-39, John Wiley & Sons, New York.

[4]

The economic geography of the impacts of climate change

Gary Yohe* and Michael Schlesinger**

Abstract

Our ability to understand the geographical dispersion of the impacts of climate change has not yet progressed to the point of being able to quantify costs and benefits distributed across globe along one or more climate scenarios in any meaningful way. We respond to this chaotic state of affairs by offering a brief introduction to the potential impacts of a changing climate along five geographically dispersed portraits of how the future climate might evolve and by presenting a modern approach to contemplating vulnerability to climate impacts that has been designed explicitly to reflect geographic diversity and uncertainty. Three case studies are offered to provide direct evidence of the potential value of adaptation in reducing the cost of climate impacts, the versatility of thinking about the determinants of adaptive capacity for specific regions or sectors, and the feasibility of exploring both across a wide range of 'not-implausible' climate and socio-economic scenarios. Three overarching themes emerge: adaptation matters, geographic diversity is critical, and enormous uncertainty must be recognized and accommodated.

Keywords: climate change, adaptive capacity, scenarios, value of information
JEL classifications: I3, O2, Q2, R1.
Date accepted: 27 December 2001

1. Introduction

The contribution of Working Group II to Third Assessment Report of the Intergovernmental Panel on Climate Change (IPCC, 2001b) devoted nearly 1000 pages of text to a thorough assessment of the current literature on the potential impacts of climate change and climate variability.[1] Organized across seven different sectors and eight different regions, their work provides immediate access to the 'state of the art' in evaluating the vulnerabilities of communities, nations, and regions to possible climate futures—at least as of the year 2000. The present paper will not try to duplicate the

---

*John E. Andrus Professor of Economics, Wesleyan University, 238 Church Street, Middletown, CT 06459; USA. *email* < gyohe@wesleyan.edu >
**Department of Atmospheric Sciences, MC 223, University of Illinois at Urbana-Champaign, 105 S. Gregory Street, Urbana, IL 61801 USA.
email < schlesin@atmos.uiuc.edu >

1   The first IPCC assessment (IPCC, 1990) began the process of reviewing the scientific literature in support of what became the United Nations Framework Convention on Climate Change. It was augmented by a supplementary report (IPCC, 1992) and subsequently followed in three parts by the Second Assessment Report, the SAR, in the middle of the decade (IPCC (1996a), (1996b), and (1996c)). The Third Assessment Report also appeared in three parts. Working Group I focused on the natural science of climate change (IPCC, 2001a). Working Group II concentrated on impacts and adaptation (IPCC, 2001b); and Working Group III reported on the state of our understanding about mitigation (IPCC, 2001c).

IPCC coverage. It will, instead, focus attention on a few of the strengths and weaknesses in our current understanding that are most germane to the economic paradigm in an effort to highlight how economists might be able to exploit those strengths and overcome those weaknesses.

Few impact analyses have, for example, looked at transient change, so few have accounted for how different rates of change might influence costs and damages. Few impact studies have recognized fully the wide range of uncertainty that colors our vision of future climate, so few have investigated robust responses that might accommodate wide ranges of possible change. Few studies have provided insight into the implications of location-specific and path dependent social, political, and economic environments in determining the capacity of these systems to adapt to change, so few have accommodated the implications of global diversity. These and other topics surely lie within the purview and interest of the economic community.

This list of shortcomings, drawn from an economist's perspective, could easily be extended, but we must recognize from the start that researchers from other disciplines would construct different lists. It follows that all contributing disciplines must recognize the limitations imposed on their approaches to the problem by deficiencies in understanding or methodological coverage that are beyond their control. An economist might think that it would be productive at this point to express the Third Assessment Report in terms of costs and benefits distributed across globe along one or two specific climate change scenarios. To do so, however, would be both imprudent and impossible. It would be impossible to pick one climate scenario and still reflect the enormous uncertainties that cloud our understanding of how future climate might unfold even if we knew how the pattern of world development and associated changes in land-use over the next 50 years or so. It would also be impossible to translate any global climate change scenario into regional portraits that span the globe with sufficient resolution to inform impacts research at local levels. Finally, our ability to predict how communities and/or nations might adapt to those impacts over time is still in an embryonic stage, so translating exposure into vulnerability across the globe is currently beyond our reach, as well.

We respond to this chaotic state of affairs by offering a brief introduction to the potential impacts of a changing climate in the first section before turning to five geographically dispersed portraits of how the future climate might evolve in Section 2. Section 3 then presents a modern approach to contemplating vulnerability to climate impacts that has been designed explicitly to reflect geographic diversity and uncertainty. Three case studies are then offered in Section 4. They have been chosen to provide direct evidence of the potential value of adaptation in reducing the cost of climate impacts, the versatility of thinking about the determinants of adaptive capacity for specific regions or sectors, and the feasibility of exploring both across a wide range of 'not-implausible' climate and socio-economic scenarios. Concluding remarks simply reiterate three overarching themes: adaptation matters, geographic diversity is critical, and enormous uncertainty must and can be recognized and accommodated.

2. Introduction to the potential impacts of climate change

Schneider (1989) contains perhaps the most concise explanation of how the Earth's atmosphere works to maintain an inhabitable temperature and how it might be altered by human activity. Clouds and particles in the atmosphere, together with the Earth's surface, reflect roughly 30% of the incoming solar energy, but the remaining 70% of the energy is absorbed. This heats the surface of the Earth and the atmosphere, and it is then re-emitted in the infrared spectrum. An energy balance for the planet is achieved by this radiation, but only after energy trapped by clouds and greenhouse gases (GHGs) warms its surface. In fact, pre-industrial concentrations of GHGs made the Earth about 33 °C warmer than it would have been otherwise, and increased concentrations can further warm the planet. Since it is now understood that concentrations are increasing from human activity, the fundamental questions are clear. How much higher will temperatures climb, and how fast? How will this warming be distributed across the globe? Will some regions warm more quickly than others? Will other regions actually grow colder? How will higher temperatures affect sea levels? How might precipitation patterns change? Could warming change the frequencies and geographical distributions of extreme (weather) events? Might there be abrupt changes in climate?

Figure 1 displays a stylized overview of the most recent thinking on the impacts of climate change. It shows that the risks of adverse impacts from climate change measured along five dimensions increase with the magnitude of climate change indexed by increases in global-mean temperature. In all cases, white regions indicate no or neutral impacts and no risk, while increasingly shaded regions reflect increasingly negative impacts and significant risk. Two of the critical dimensions identified in Fig. 1 involve estimates of economic damage: 'Aggregate Impacts' and the 'Distribution of Impacts'. They are loose reflections of a literature that has, over the past decade or so, recorded estimates of the economic consequences of climate change with increasing geographical resolution but not necessarily with increasing accuracy. Published estimates show modest and, in some instances, positive impacts on market-based sectors with small temperature increases, but they also show that the impacts of even small climate change will not be evenly distributed across the globe. Developing countries will, in particular, be more vulnerable to the negative potential of climate change, and this raises the possibility that impacts could exacerbate income inequality between and even within countries. With larger increases in temperature, moreover, negative impacts would be exaggerated while net positive impacts in even developed countries would begin to decline and eventually turn negative (IPCC, 2001b, ch.19).

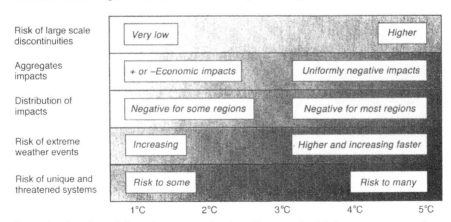

Figure 1. Overview of climate impacts as a function of increases in global mean temperature. Areas with darker shading indicate larger and more dangerous impacts and associated risks. *Source*: early versions of what became Fig. 19-7 in IPCC (2001b).

Table 1 records some of the estimates that support these conclusions; positive numbers denote benefits while negative numbers reflect costs. As a point of reference, notice that the estimates reported in 1995 by the IPCC in its Second Assessment Report (IPCC, 1996b) were dominated by declines in agricultural production for high and low climate sensitivities. Agriculture is, of course, a sector whose current practices would likely be threatened by higher temperatures and less precipitation. Most of the early estimates for agriculture (as well as for other sectors) were, however, drawn from vulnerability studies that paid little attention to the ability of humans and their institutions to reduce economic damage and expand economic opportunity by adapting. Moreover, most of the early studies relied on relatively primitive methods of tracking the different regional consequences of a 2.5 °C increase in global-mean temperature. It is well known that some regions would see temperatures increase by more than 2.5 degrees while others might actually get cooler, but there is no consensus about exactly how these differences will be distributed. It is also well understood that some areas would get wetter while others got drier. It is equally well understood that sea

Table 1. Indicative world impacts by region (in percent of current GDP)

	IPCC SAR (2.5 °C)	Mendelsohn et al. (1.5 °C)	Mendelsohn et al. (2.5 °C)	Nordhaus & Boyer (2.5 °C)	Tol (1.0 °C)
North America					3.4 (1.2)
United States			0.3	−0.5	
OECD Europe					3.7 (2.2)
EU				−2.8	
OECD Pacific					1.0 (1.1)
Japan			−0.1	−0.5	
Eastern Europe/FSU					2.0 (3.8)
Eastern Europe				−0.7	
Russia			11.1	0.7	
Middle East				−2.0	1.1 (2.2)
Latin America					−0.1 (0.6)
Brazil		−1.4			
South/Southest Asia					−1.7 (1.1)
India			−2.0	−4.9	
China			1.8	−0.2	2.1 (5.0)
Africa				−3.9	−4.1 (2.2)
Developed countries	{−1.0, −1.5}	0.12	0.30		
Developing countries	{−2.0, −9.0}	0.05	−0.17		
World	{−1.5, −2.0}	0.09	0.10	−1.5	2.3 (1.0)

Source: Table 19-4, IPCC(2001b).

level would rise in some places and fall elsewhere (where the coastline is actually rising at present). Finally, few of the early studies were able to consider the effects of changes in humidity, frequency of extreme temperature events, or any of the other more subtle physical ramifications of global warming.

More recent cost estimates have begun to take a few small steps designed to overcome these shortcomings. The second column of Table 1 presents regional cost estimates of market impacts published recently by Mendelsohn et al. (2000) for a 2.5 °C global-mean warming and a 50 cm increase in sea level. Notice that the overall annual effect on world economic activity, a 0.1% increase, is opposite in sign to the decreases reported in the Second Assessment. Effects on agriculture still dominate the Mendelsohn regional estimates, but their regional distribution has made the largest impression on the research community. Table 1 shows, for example, that North America, Russia, and China could benefit from warming while India, Brazil, and Japan would suffer harm. It is important to understand, however, that Mendelsohn and his coauthors extrapolated statistical summaries of how various regions in developed countries have coped with their current climates to describe how other regions might respond if their climates changed and if they adapted perfectly and if relative prices were unchanged.

The third column of Table 1 reports comparable results from Nordhaus and Boyer (2000) for the same 2.5 °C global-mean warming and 50 cm increase in sea level. They reported losses almost everywhere, but not because they were less sanguine about the ability of adaptive behavior to ameliorate damage and exploit benefits. Estimated damages are, instead, higher because Nordhaus and Boyer included rough representations of losses driven by extreme events (whose frequencies and distributions might change with the climate) as well as the reflections of the risk of sudden and severe change in the climate, itself.

The last column of Table 1 records cost estimates from Tol (1999) for a 1 degree warming in even greater geographical detail. Notice that Tol also reports standard deviations in parentheses; these values are best interpreted as the lower bounds of model-based uncertainty. Only Latin America, southern and Southeast Asia, and Africa suffer losses in his work, and many regions (including China again) benefit substantially. Modest warming might, it would seem, be a good thing; but we cannot leap to that conclusion too quickly. The reported standard deviations indicate a 66% likelihood based on model uncertainty that the true impact of a 1 degree warming would lie within a range that frequently includes zero.

The Nordhaus and Boyer (2000) estimates reveal the potential economic power of two other lines of evidence identified in Fig. 1. We know very little about one—the possibility that climate change might be sudden rather than smooth as the global mean temperature climbs. This possibility will be the focus of intensive research over the next few years.[2] We know a little more about the second—the likelihood that even smooth change might increase the frequencies and/or intensity of extreme (weather) events. We will see in a later section that the changes in those frequencies may be important triggers

---

2 Several possible events that could be related to warming and could also produce sudden changes in climate have been identified in the recent literature. They include a shutdown of the thermohaline circulation in the Atlantic Ocean, a disintegration of the West Antarctic Ice Sheet, a runaway carbon cycle, some transformation of the distribution of continental monsoons, qualitative modifications in cyclical weather patterns like ENSO, a destabilization of the international political order, an so on. See Chapter 19 of IPCC (2001b) for brief descriptions of each.

for economically motivated adaptation. For now, Table 2 summarizes a literature that is full of conjectures that many sectors could be highly sensitivity to a wide range of climate extremes. Few of the studies in that literature have made those claims with much confidence, though, particularly when it comes to attributing changes in the distribution of extreme events to anthropogenic climate change.

The fifth line of evidence highlighted in Fig. 1 reflects the expert judgement that 'we have high confidence that the overall patterns and processes of observations reveal a widespread and coherent impact of 20th century climate changes on many physical and biological systems' (IPCC, 2001b, pp. 914–915). The Third Assessment Report selected 56 of the 200 studies that related trends in impacts to trends in regional climate at various locations around the globe to support this claim on the basis of specific criteria related to time frame and natural variability.[3] These 56 studies investigated approximately 660 distinct natural processes and/or species. Many dealt with decadal to century-long trends in sea ice and glaciers. Others looked at change in terrestrial or marine ecosystems over at least 20 years. More than 59% reported changes in response to climate that were consistent with well-established expectations of a climate-driven impact. Roughly 5% showed responses in unexpected directions, and 36% showed no statistically significant correlation with a climate variable.

The general conclusion to be drawn from Fig. 1 is simple: climate will continue to change as the globe warms and it will produce demonstrable effects. The analyses that support this conclusion were, however, generally constructed from static snapshots of impacts for specific changes in global mean temperature. They therefore missed the time dependence of associated costs, and they subsumed enormous uncertainty about the geographical distributions of changes in critical climate variables other than mean temperature. As a result, these studies are particularly difficult to interpret from a global perspective because different regions of the world will warm, and sometime cool, at different rates. Researchers have, of course, honestly acknowledged that they have been looking through a lens clouded by uncertainty, geographical diversity, and site-specific path dependence. Theirs is not, therefore, the last word on future impacts. Indeed, we have just begun to confront the problem of exploring the full suite of geographically distributed economic implications.

3. Looking at future climate

The first step in this process continues to focus attention on future climate. Climate change over the long-term will be driven by complex dynamic systems about which our understanding is, at best, limited. Demographic patterns, socio-economic development, future land-use and forestry practices, political evolution, and technological change will all drive emissions of greenhouse gases and sulfur dioxide over the requisite century-long time horizon; each driver is a source of enormous uncertainty. The climate implications of these emissions will, in turn, be determined by the sensitivity of the climate system to corresponding changes in the associated atmospheric concentrations of greenhouse gases and by the radiative forcing associated with sulfate aerosols—two more sources of uncertainty. As the research community approaches the climate issue, therefore, it must work with scenarios that reflect these and other underlying uncertainties.

---

3 See Fig. SPM-1 in IPCC (2001b) and the text of Chapter 19 for details.

Table 2. Extreme climate-related phenomena—observed and projected[a]

Climate phenomena	Observed changes	Projected changes	Type of event	Time scale	Sensitive sectors
Higher maximum temperatures	likely	very likely	heat waves droughts	daily/weekly monthly/seasonal	electric/settlements forests/agriculture/water/electricity/tourism/health
Higher minimum temperatures	very likely	very likely	frost/frozen land	daily/monthly	agriculture/energy/health/transport
More intense precipitation events	likely in mid/high latitudes medium likelihood	very likely very likely uncertain uncertain	flash floods floods and mudslides snow/ice hailstorms	hourly/daily weekly/monthly hourly/weekly hourly	settlements agriculture/forests/transport/water/settlements/tourism same agriculture/property
Increased summer drying	likely in a few areas	likely in mid-latitude interiors	drought subsidence wildfires	monthly/seasonal	forests/agriculture/water hydro/settlements
El Nino events	inconclusive	likely	droughts or floods	various	forests/agriculture/water hydro/settlements
Asian summer monsoons	not treated in IPCC (2001a)	likely	droughts or floods	seasonal	forests/agriculture/water hydro/settlements

[a]Likelihood refers to confidence judgments used in IPCC (2001a): very likely (> 90% chance); likely (66%–90% chance) and medium (33%–66% chance).
Source: Table TS-4; IPCC (2001b).

3.1. Future emissions of GHGs and the SRES scenarios

The *Special Report on Emissions Scenarios* (IPCC, 2000) describes forty 'SRES scenarios' that were developed to replace the earlier IS92 scenarios in a way that more accurately represents our understanding of these uncertainties. The SRES scenarios exclude 'surprise' or 'disaster' scenarios, but each is firmly rooted in one of four different 'narrative storylines' that cover a wide range of demographic, economic, and technological futures. The A1 'Rich World' storyline describes a future with very rapid economic growth supporting a global population that peaks mid-century. New and more efficient technologies are produced and introduced easily while significant capacity building across the globe results in significant reductions in regional differences in per capita income. The A2 'Divided World' storyline meanwhile describes a world that continues to be extremely self-reliant and heterogeneous. Economic development is regionally oriented so that economic growth and technological change are more fragmented and slower. The B1 'Sustainable Development' storyline mirrors A1 somewhat, but adds rapid changes in economic structure toward information and service economies. Material intensity declines with the introduction of clean and efficient technology driven in part by global solutions to economic, social and environmental sustainability, and equity. Finally, the B2 'Dynamics as Usual' storyline brings the same orientation toward sustainability and social equity to a world that focuses its attention regionally much in the same way envisioned in A2. Each individual scenario reflects its parent storyline and describes consistently a particular variant in the relationship between socio-economic drivers and the emission of GHGs and sulfur dioxide. Moreover, the entire collection of scenarios spans much of the range of carbon emissions through 2100 reported in the published literature through 1999. It must be noted, however, that none of the SRES scenarios include mitigation initiatives like those that would be required if the United Nations Framework on Climate Change (UNFCCC) or the Kyoto Protocol were implemented.

Figure 2 presents portraits of representatives of the four SRES storylines reported by Schlesinger et al. (2000) in terms of population, per capita annual gross world product, primary energy intensity, carbon intensity, and carbon emissions.[4] Panel (a) also includes a trajectory for the noninterventionist 'Business As Usual' IS92a scenario from IPCC (1992). Population and per capita annual income are larger in 2100 than 1990 for each scenario, but energy intensity and carbon intensity always decline over this time frame. Carbon emissions display paths that grow monotonically for three scenarios (A1, A2, and IS92a). Emissions peak mid-century for the B1 and B2 scenarios, though, and actually fall below 1990 levels by 2100 for the B1 variant. Figure 3 displays associated concentration trajectories for critical GHGs in panels (a) through (c).[5] Carbon dioxide

---

4   The A1 representative was produced by the Asian-Pacific Integrated Model (AIM) (see Morita et al., 1998); the A2 scenario by the Atmospheric Stabilization Framework (ASF) (see Pepper et al., 1998); the B1 scenario by the IMAGE2 model (see Alcamo et al., 1998) and the B2 scenario by the MESSAGE model (see Gritsevskii and Gruebler, 1998).

5   The carbon dioxide concentrations trajectories depicted in Panel A were produced from the carbon-cycle model of the Center for International Climate and Environment Research—Oslo (CICERO) (see Alfsen and Berntsen, 1999); the model, based on the work by Joos et al. (1996) was provided by T. K. Berntsen and J. S. Fuglestvedt. M. J. Prather calculated the methane and nitrous oxide concentrations depicted in Panels B and C. The equivalent carbon dioxide (ECD) values were computed from the equations in Table 1 of Myhre et al. (1998).

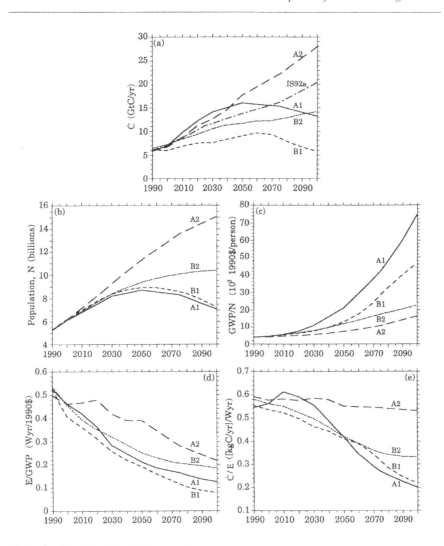

Figure 2. Portraits of the SRES scenarios.
Panels (a) through (e) display global carbon emissions (gigatons of carbon per year), world population (in billions of people), per capita gross world product (in thousands of 1990 $ per person), global energy consumption (in Watts per year) per dollar of gross world product, and global carbon emissions per unit of energy consumption (in kilograms of carbon per Watt per year) along representatives of the four SRES storylines, respectively. The A1 'Rich World' storyline describes a globally integrated future with very rapid economic growth supporting a global population that peaks mid-century. The A2 'Divided World' storyline describes a world with the same economic growth inhibited by extremely self-reliant and heterogeneous regions. The B1 'Sustainable Development' storyline incorporates rapid changes in economic structure toward information and service economies to an integrated future. The B2 'Dynamics as Usual' storyline brings the same orientation toward sustainability and social equity to a world that focuses its attention regionally much in the same way envisioned in A2. The original 'Business as Usual' IS92a is also depicted in panel (a) for reference. *Source*: Fig. 1 in Schlesinger et al. (2000).

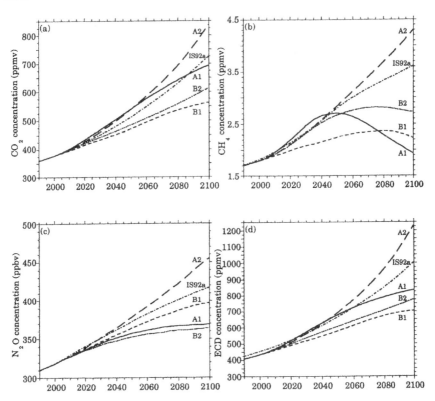

Figure 3. Greenhouse gas emissions and equivalent carbon dioxide equivalents for the SRES and IS92a scenarios.
Concentrations of critical GHGs are portrayed in panels (a) through (c). They are denominated in parts per million in volume (ppmv) or parts per billion for nitrous oxide (ppmb) along the SRES and IS92a scenarios that were depicted in Fig. 2. Panel (d) shows corresponding concentrations in terms of equivalent carbon dioxide units—concentrations of carbon dioxide that would be required to produce the same radiative forcing as the actual combinations of CO_2, methane, and nitrous oxide. *Source*: Fig. 9 in Schlesinger et al. (2000).

concentrations range from 552 ppmv for the B1 scenario to 836 ppmv for the A2 scenario—a range that misses about 30% of the trajectories published prior to the SRES initiative. Panel (d) shows the combined radiative forcing of these compounds along each scenario denominated in equivalent carbon dioxide units (ECD)—the amount of carbon dioxide required to give the same radiative forcing as the three compounds are taken together.

Figure 4 relates the ECD trajectories of Fig. 3 to changes in the global mean surface-air temperature for three different climate sensitivities. These sensitivities, defined in terms of warming associated with doubling pre-industrial atmospheric concentrations of carbon dioxide, are a fundamental source of uncertainty. Our understanding can do little more than bound its value between 1.4 °C on the low side and 5.2 °C on the high side (IPCC, 2001a). Notice that the temperature trajectories for any climate sensitivity are not really distinguishable through the middle of the 21st century. There are,

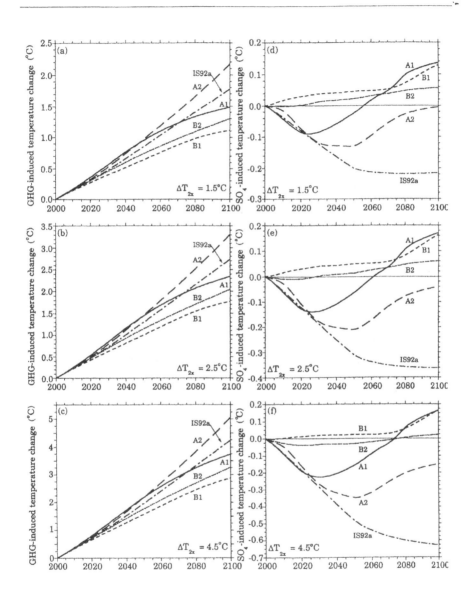

Figure 4. Changes in global mean temperature driven by GHG emissions with alternative climate sensitivities for the SRES and IS92a scenarios.

Transient temperature change scenarios are portrayed for the SRES and IS92a scenarios that were depicted in Fig. 2. Climate sensitivity is reflected in terms of change in global mean temperature that would be associated with a doubling of effective carbon dioxide concentrations. This parameter, denoted ΔT_{2x}, assumes values of 1.5 °C, 2.5 °C, and 4.5 °C, respectively, in panels (a) through (c). Panels (d) through (f) show the corresponding influence of sulfate aerosols along the same scenarios. *Source:* Fig. 10 in Schlesinger et al. (2000).

322 · *Yohe and Schlesinger*

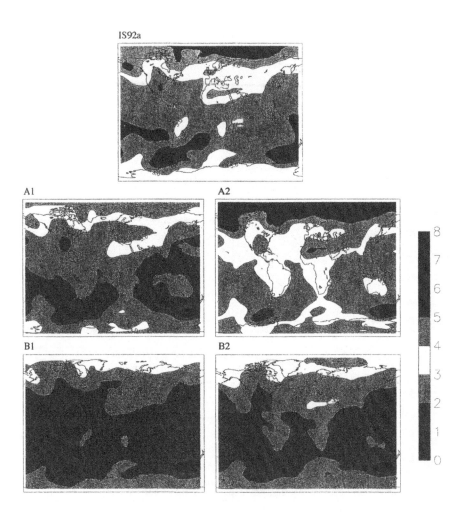

Figure 5. Geographical distribution of annual surface-air temperature change in 2100 relative to 2000 driven by GHG emissions with a climate sensitivity of 2.5 °C for the SRES and IS92a scenarios. Regional temperature changes through 2100 are depicted according to the scale on the right for the SRES and IS92a scenarios that were depicted in Fig. 2. The scale indicates temperature increase from a low of 0 °C to a high of 8 °C in colors that run from green through yellow, red, and dark purple. *Source*: Fig. 12 in Schlesinger et al. (2000).

however, differences across scenarios over the longer term. Estimates of total warming through 2100 range from 1.1 °C along the B1 scenario with climate sensitivity set equal to 1.5 °C to 5.0 °C along the A2 scenario with climate sensitivity set equal to 4.5 °C. Schlesinger et al. (2000) shows that about 41% of this 3.9 °C temperature range for 2100 can be attributed to scenario uncertainty derived from alternative views of social-political-economic development; but the source of the remaining 59% lies squarely in our fundamental uncertainty about climate sensitivity.

Figure 5 finally presents geographical distributions of surface temperature change in 2100 relative to 2000 for the four SRES representative scenarios and the IS92a scenario due to GHGs alone with a climate sensitivity of 2.5 °C.[6] GHG-induced warming is smallest in the tropical latitudes and increases toward both poles. Warming also increases across the scenarios from B1 through B2, A1, IS92a and finally A2. Scenario uncertainty clearly translates into larger geographical uncertainty, particularly in the Arctic, even after ignoring uncertainty about climate sensitivity.

3.2. The future role of sulfate aerosols

The recent literature has emphasized a growing recognition that emissions of sulfur dioxide could play a large role in determining future climate change (IPCC, 2001a). The same set of representative SRES scenarios can be employed to explore this possibility and to demonstrate how quickly our perceptions of future climate can change. Figure 6 displays the corresponding trajectories for SO_2 emissions; notice that the four SRES paths differ significantly from the one associated with IS92a. Panels (d) through (f) in Fig. 4 show their effect on global mean temperature. Figure 7 combines the effects of GHGs and sulfates to display net changes in global-mean surface-air temperature and sea level, respectively, for three climate sensitivities. Combined estimates of total warming and sea level rise range from 1.2 °C and 27 cm along the B1 scenario with a climate sensitivity equal to 1.5 °C to 4.9 °C and 72 cm along the A2 scenario with a climate sensitivity equal to 4.5 °C. About 38% of the temperature range and 31% of the sea level range can be attributed to scenario uncertainty derived from alternative views of social-political-economic development; but the source of the remaining variation continues to lie squarely in our fundamental uncertainty about climate sensitivity.

Figure 8 brings the combined trajectories to bear on the issue of geographical distribution. The patterns are similar to the ones portrayed in Fig. 5 for GHGs, but it is important to note that the higher sulfate emissions of IS92a serve to reduce warming in the Arctic. If the new SRES scenarios are more representative of how the future might evolve, then lower sulfate trajectories can be expected to have a significant effect on climate projections, particularly when geographic dispersion is included in the analysis. Figure 8 also shows that all regions warm along all scenarios, but by differing amounts even for specific climate sensitivities. The increases for a 2.5 °C sensitivity, for example, range from 1.6 °C to 2.7 °C across scenarios B1 to A2 in the Southern Hemisphere and

---

6 These scenarios are the products of simulations performed separately for doubled CO_2 concentration and independent SO_2 emissions by the University of Illinois at Urbana-Champaign (UIUC) general circulation/mixed-layer-ocean model. Each case was normalized by its corresponding global-mean surface temperature change and time trajectories of global-mean surface temperature simulated by an energy-balance-climate/upwelling-diffusion-ocean (EBC/UDO) model. See Schlesinger et al. (2000) for descriptions of the content of these models.

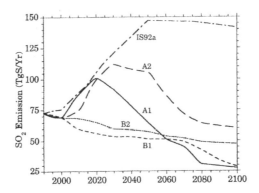

Figure 6. Sulfur dioxide emissions for the SRES and IS92a scenarios.
Emissions of sulfur dioxide denominated in terragrams of sulfur (TgS) per year for the SRES and IS92a scenarios that were depicted in Fig. 2. *Source*: Fig. 1 in Schlesinger et al. (2000).

from 3.1 °C to 5.3 °C in Siberia. These large differences for specific regions appear in spite of little differentiation in global mean temperature.

3.3. Summarizing future climate for impacts analysis

IPCC (2001b) recorded ranges of exposure in terms of possible rates of change in precipitation and temperature, respectively, for 32 major geographical regions across the SRES storylines with climate sensitivities ranging from 1.5 °C to 4.5 °C.[7] Wide ranges of uncertainty in both of these critical indicators of climate change were obvious for all regions. It is still not obvious, however, if these uncertainties matter in terms of socio-economic impacts. Large reductions in precipitation, measured in percentage terms, would have little effect in the Sahara, for example, but reductions in precipitation across eastern Africa could have significant implications for flow in the Nile and, as a result, for political stability and economic sustainability in the Nile Basin. Indeed, Strzepek et al. (2001) produced the range of 'not-implausible' scenarios for flow in the Nile depicted in Fig. 9. Drawn from climate scenarios that span the range of output from the SRES storylines, they include one trajectory with a 20% increase in the flow of the Nile into Lake Nasser by 2100; but they also include other trajectories with reductions as large as 80%. Could Egypt and the other countries of the Nile Basin adapt to these futures? That remains to be seen.

4. Adaptive capacity and improved geographical resolution

Many existing studies have been criticized for overstating the power of adaptation to reduce climate-related costs because their authors have applied statistical models drawn from the developed world to the economic environments of the developing world. These studies have assumed, at least implicitly, that the adaptive strategies that are available and practicable in the market sectors of the world's developed economies would

---

7   See Fig. TS-3 in IPCC (2001b) and associated text for a summary discussion.

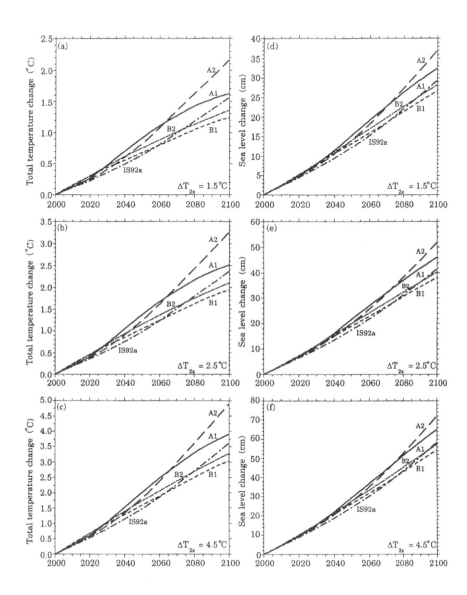

Figure 7. Changes in global mean temperature and sea level rise driven by GHG emissions and sulfate aerosol emissions with alternative climate sensitivities for the SRES and IS92a scenarios. Panels (a) through (c) portray changes in global mean temperature along the SRES and IS92a scenarios that were depicted in Fig. 2 for climate sensitivities (ΔT_{2x}) equal to 1.5 °C, 2.5 °C, and 4.5 °C, respectively. Panels (d) through (f) display the corresponding trajectories for sea level rise in centimeters. *Source:* Fig. 11 in Schlesinger et al. (2000).

IS92a

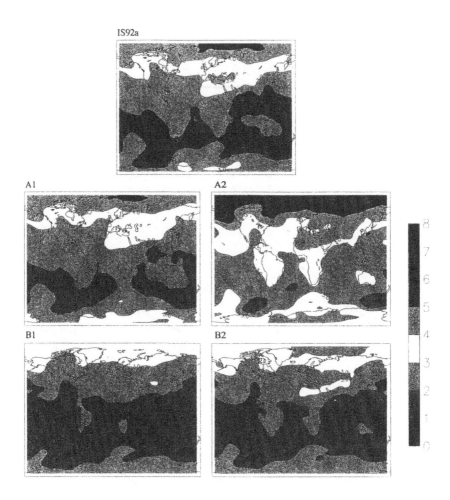

Figure 8. Geographical distribution of annual surface-air temperature change in 2100 relative to 2000 driven by GHG emissions and sulfate aerosols with a climate sensitivity of 2.5 °C for the SRES and IS92a scenarios. Regional temperature changes through 2100 are depicted according to the scale on the right for the SRES and IS92a scenarios that were depicted in Fig. 2. The scale indicates temperature increase from a low of 0 °C to a high of 8 °C in colors that run from green through yellow, red, and dark purple. *Source*: Fig. 18 in Schlesinger et al. (2000).

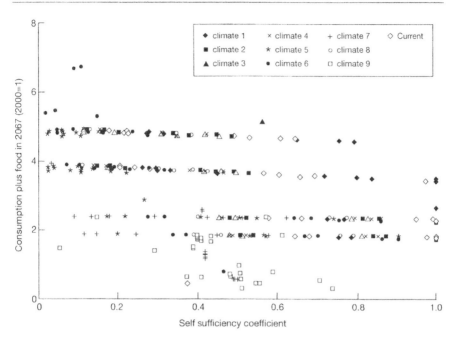

Figure 9. Annual flow into Lake Nasser along 'not implausible' climate futures (2000 flow=1). Projections of annual flow from the upper Nile into Lake Nasser along nine climate scenarios that were chosen to span a range of 'not implausible' futures. The futures were drawn to represent the variability displayed in a collection of over 600 runs of a hydrologic model calibrated by Yates and Strzepek (1998) to accept precipitation and temperature output from 14 regional global circulation models along five different emissions scenarios with three alternative climate sensitivities and sulfate forcing coefficients. *Source*: Fig. 4 in Strzepek et al. (2001).

routinely be available to people who inhabit the world's developing countries. These are people who may face similar climate related stresses in the future, but they will face them in the context of extraordinarily dissimilar socio-economic circumstances.

In addition to the obvious diversity in economic context, any system's environment varies from day to day, month to month, year to year, decade to decade, and so on (see Mearns, et al., 1997; or Karl and Knight, 1998). It follows that changes in the mean conditions that define those environments can actually be experienced most noticeably through changes in the nature and/or frequency of variable conditions that materialize across short time scales and that adaptation necessarily involves reaction to this sort of variability. This is the fundamental point in Hewitt and Burton (1971), Kane et al. (1992), Yohe et al. (1996), Downing (1996), and Yohe and Schlesinger (1998). Some researchers, like Smithers and Smit (1997), Downing et al. (1997), and Smit et al. (1999), use the concept of 'hazard' to capture these sorts of stimuli, and claim that adaptation is warranted whenever either changes in mean conditions or changes in variability have significant consequences. For most systems, though, changes in mean conditions over short periods of time fall within a 'coping range'—a range of circumstances within which, by virtue of the underlying resilience of the system, significant consequences are not observed (see Downing et al. (1997) or Pittock and Jones (2000)). There are limits to

328 • *Yohe and Schlesinger*

resilience for even the most robust of systems, of course. It is therefore critically important to understand the boundaries of systems' resilience; how, exactly, are the thresholds beyond which the consequences of experienced conditions become significant actually determined?

A unifying vulnerability model with which to explore this question across a wide range of contexts has begun to emerge.[8] Any system's vulnerability to climate change and climate variability will be determined by *its exposure to the impacts of climate, its baseline sensitivity to those impacts, and its adaptive capacity.* All three of these factors are clearly dependent on specific circumstances that can be path dependent and geographically idiosyncratic, and therein lies the rub. The determinants of adaptive capacity, for example, include:

1. The range of available technological options for adaptation.
2. The availability of resources and their distribution across the population.
3. The structure of critical institutions, the derivative allocation of decision-making authority, and the decision criteria that would be employed.
4. The stock of human capital including education and personal security.
5. The stock of social capital including the definition of property rights.
6. The system's access to risk spreading processes.
7. The ability of decision-makers to manage information, the processes by which these decision-makers determine which information is credible, and the credibility of the decision-makers, themselves, and
8. The public's perceived attribution of the source of stress and the significance of exposure to its local manifestations.

Table 3 summarizes the state of our knowledge about the distribution of adaptive capacity across many of the major regions of the globe. The numbers recorded in each box are designed to refer the reader back to the relevant determinant listed above, but those links hardly convey the major insight to be drawn from the table. The paucity of entries in the adaptive capacity column accomplishes this task. The open space there is visual evidence that the research community has a long way to go before it can claim to understand how each region might be able to cope with exposure to uncertain climate change as well as current and uncertain future climate variability.

5. Estimating of the economic cost of climate change with adaptation

Three themes have emerged from careful consideration of the content of Table 3 in the context of the vulnerability model just described; and each can be viewed as a challenge for the research community. First of all, adaptation can reduce the economic cost of exposure to climate change and climate variability, but adaptation cannot be expected to eliminate all of those costs. Secondly, the potential role of adaptation in reducing costs depends on the adaptive capacity of the exposed community, region, or sector and the certainty with which that community, region or sector can predict future climate and separate its signal from the noise of climate variability. Finally, a third theme follows from the second. The uncertainty that confounds climate researchers confounds

---

8   See Chapter 18 in IPCC (2001b) for a thorough discussion of these points.

Table 3. TAR (WGII-IPCC, 2001) Summary of adaptation and adaptive capacity*

Sector/region	Adaptation	Adaptive capacity
Africa (Ch. 10)	Regional assessments of vulnerability, impacts and adaptation are required to fill gaps in information. 7&8 Adaptation options include: increase irrigation efficiency through canal linings and better management, more reuse of drainage water, better use of the Nile valley aquifer, changes in crop types, development of western desert groundwater resources, and desalination. 1 Specific measures in water resources, coastal resources, forests, ecosystems, and agriculture would enhance the flexibility of resources to adapt and have net benefits greater than costs. 3 The use of improved technologies in agriculture, e.g. irrigation and crop husbandry, would result in better adaptation. 4, 6 & 7 The most promising adaptation strategies to declining tree resources include: natural regeneration of local species, energy-efficient cook-stoves, sustainable forest management, and community based natural resource management. 1, 3, 4, & 7 A risk sharing approach between countries will strengthen adaptation strategies. 4, 6, & 7	Adaptive capacity was largely influenced by the ability to communicate potential risks to vulnerable communities and the ability to react as a result of perceived risks. 5 & 8 A critical factor is the ability to mobilize emergency evacuation. 2 & 3
Asia (Ch. 11)	Priority issues, that could lead to catastrophic impacts for temperate and tropical Asian counties include: sea level rise, potentially more intense cyclones, and threats to ecosystems and biodiversity. A macro strategy involves rapid development to increase income levels, education, and technical skills, and improve public food distribution, disaster preparedness, and management and health care systems. 4 & 6 A micro strategy involves modifying the management of sensitive sectors by developing new institutions or modifying existing institutions that promote adaptation and modifying climate sensitive infrastructures. 3 & 7 Crucial for countries with large populations are food security, disaster preparedness and management, soil conservation, and human health sectors. 2, 3, 4, 6, & 7	Poor resource and infrastructure bases (disparities in income level, weak financial mechanism, technological gaps, cultural diversity) exist in most developing countries in Asia and hinder adaptive capacity. 2 & 6 Adaptive approaches include: strengthening legal and institutional frameworks, removing pre-existing market distortions, correcting market failures (such as inadequate economic valuation of biodiversity), and promoting public participation and education. 3 & 8 Adaptive capacity varies between countries depending upon social structure, culture and economic capacity, and level of environmental disruptions. 3 Limiting factors include: institutional inertia, a scarcity of technological adaptation options and additional economic burden. 1, 2, & 3

Continued

Table 3. TAR (WGII-IPCC, 2001) Summary of adaptation and adaptive capacity* (continued)

Sector/region	Adaptation	Adaptive capacity
	Adaptations proposed for human health, which involves improving the health care system, are already required to address the current human health situation in several Asian countries. 3	
	Implementation of adaptation measures is hindered by the economic policies and conditions, e.g. taxes, subsidies, and regulations, that shape decision making, development strategies, and resource-use patterns. 4	
	Adaptation depends upon the affordability of adaptive measures, the existence of appropriate institutions, access to technology, and biophysical constraints, such as land and water resource availability, soil characteristics, genetic diversity for crop breeding (e.g. development of heat-resistant cultivars) and topography.	
	Adaptation measures for present day variability include: sea defences, institutional adaptations, plant breeding and the adoption of new technologies in agriculture. 1	
	Adaptation will require increased access to appropriate technologies, information, and adequate financing. 7	
	Anticipation and planning is required to prevent capital-intensive development of infrastructures or technologies that are ill-suited to future conditions, and missed opportunities to lower the cost of adaptation. 3 & 6	
Latin America (Ch. 14)	Several strategies for adaptation are shared between countries. 1	
	Adaptation measures in the fishery sector include: changing the species capture (e.g. switching from anchovy to tuna fish to reduce losses due to sea water warming), and price increases (to reduce losses to 40%). 1	
	Adaptation to flooding in water shortage areas includes the creation of artificial lakes through the damming of excess water. 2 & 3	

| Small island states (Ch. 17) | Coastal assets will be further stressed with the projected increase in sea level. The three categories of strategies for adaptation to sea level rise are: retreat, accommodate, and protect.
Progress will require the integration of appropriate risk reduction strategies with other sectoral policy initiatives in areas such as sustainable development planning, disaster prevention and management, integral coastal management, and health care planning. 7
Adaptation measures such as retreat to higher ground, raising of the land, and the use of building set backs appear to have little practical utility, especially when hindered by limited physical size. 1
Measures for reducing the severity of health threats include: the implementation of effective health education programs, preventative maintenance and improvement of health care facilities, cost-effective sewerage and solid waste management practices, and disaster preparedness plans. 3 & 6
Support from policy-makers and the general public is essential for implementing adaptive measures. 7
Raising public awareness and understanding about climate change and sea level rise, and the need for appropriate adaptation is necessary. 8 | Given their size and limited individual capacities, external technical, financial, and other assistance is necessary. 2, 5, & 7
Regional cooperation has been proposed as an effective means of designing and implementing adaptation measures and building adaptive capacities (e.g. Caribbean Planning for Adaptation to Global Climate Change). 3
Legitimate concerns have been raised due to the limited resources and low adaptive capacity in SIS. 2
The main concern about capacity is the challenge of meeting the social and economic needs of their populations in a manner that is sustainable. 4, 5, & 6
Low adaptive capacity is the result of a combination of physical size, limited access to capital and technology, and a shortage of human resource skills. 1, 2, & 5
Other factors affecting capacity include: lack of tenure security, limited access to traditional resources for construction, overcrowding, preparedness, and level of traditional knowledge. 4 & 5 |

*The numbers recorded with each entry in the table identify the most relevant determinants of adaptive capacity. The determinants are described in the text; in short, though, the associations are as follows: (1) technological options; (2) resource availability and distribution; (3) institutional structure; (4) human capital; (5) social capital; (6) access to risk spreading mechanisms; (7) ability to manage information; (8) public perception.
Source: drawn from Table 18-7, IPCC (2001b).

policy makers, as well. Methods must be devised that accommodate a wide range of uncertainty and ambiguity even as researchers struggle to understand the relative efficacy of adaptation across the globe from the perspective of those policy makers. This section will review three case studies chosen from the authors' experience to illustrate these themes and to offer at least one method with which their inherent challenges might be overcome.

5.1. The economic cost of sea level rise along the developed coastline of the United States

A series of studies that estimated the economic cost of sea level rise on developed property in the United States can provide evidence of the importance of adaptation and the implications of recognizing extreme events in that context. The series began when Yohe (1989) produced estimates of the cost for the United States under the assumption that none of its coastline would be protected. This earliest work reported only the current value of all of the property that would, without any intervention, be inundated by rising seas through the year 2100. Yohe et al. (1996) subsequently reported estimates for the same representative sample of coastal locations that were derived from a model that allowed property values to appreciate over time and included decisions to protect or to abandon property at a very micro-level. Even with no foresight and therefore no autonomous adaptation, planned adaptation based on cost-benefit analyses of protection options reduced economic costs by 90% along sea level rise scenarios that spanned the IPCC-SAR range of possibilities through the year 2100 (10 cm to 90 cm).[9] Adding perfect foresight allowed market-based autonomous adaptation to reduce estimated costs by another seven percentage points across the same wide range of sea level futures.[10] In both cases, though, some residual damage remained because not all property was protected and because protection was not free. The difference between the first two estimates reflects the significant role that planned adaptation can play in affecting the costs associated with climate change. The difference between the second two estimates reflects the significant role that autonomous adaptation can play in augmenting those plans.

Subsequent work by West and Dowlatabadi (1999) inserted a stochastic time series of coastal storms into the same methodology and applied the resulting model to a representative community; their results offer preliminary insight into how climate variability and extreme events might influence estimates of the economic cost of climate change. In their model, storms could destroy or damage property directly by rain and wind or indirectly from erosion; but damaged structures could be rebuilt if the expected value of reconstruction exceeded the cost. This decision rule allowed the same structure to exist multiple times in multiple storms (and it could be a structure that would ultimately be abandoned in the face of rising seas). It also allowed a property destroyed by a storm not to be rebuilt so that damage could be correctly attributed to storms and

---

9   Planned adaptation worked to protect property when the cost of that protection was less than the cost of abandonment, but residual losses in property that was nonetheless abandoned (between 10% and 33% of the developed coastline depending upon the sea level trajectory) were observed.

10 Autonomous adaptation worked to depreciate the value of threatened structures to zero if they were to be abandoned. These structures may or may not have been protected without this depreciation and with property value appreciation and so autonomous adaptation produced a measurable efficiency gain.

not to rising seas. Running multiple manifestations of the same stochastic storm profile over 50 years with and without sea level rise showed that the cost that could be attributed to rising seas could increase costs by as much as 50% (relative to the perfect foresight base). But the cost could also fall by as much as 10% if large storms claimed significant property before the rising seas took their toll.

5.2. Applying the concept of adaptive capacity

Informed by a Workshop on Adaptation in Coastal Zones held in Charleston, South Carolina in Februrary of 1999, Dowlatabadi and Yohe (2000) argue that adaptation to sea level rise and coastal storms along the North American coastline can be expected to be so effective in reducing the economic cost of sea level rise because adaptive capacity is so high. Indeed, a coastal community located on the Atlantic shore would score high marks for each determinant. Protection options are plentiful. Resources are available. Local planning and emergency management agencies are well supported by a federal infrastructure and can process information well. Property rights are well defined. Property owners have direct access to private and public insurance; and the public at large recognizes the risk of living near the ocean. The relative efficacy of protective measures may be questionable, particularly along the open coastline, but long-term retreat from the sea is also a viable option in most states. It remains to be seen, however, if organizing research around the determinants of adaptive capacity would be an effective diagnostic tool in cases where the evidence is not as clear as it is in the United States.

Tol et al. (2001) report on an extensive assessment of adaptation against the increased risk of climate-induced flooding in the Rhine Delta; and their work can support an instructive application of the vulnerability model to examine this issue. Six feasible options for the Netherlands were identified by major consultancies: (1) store excess water in Germany; (2) accept more frequent floods; (3) build higher dikes; (4) deepen and widen the river bed; (5) dig a fourth river mouth; and (6) dig a bypass and create a northerly diversion.

Just as in the United States, macro-scale forces tend to dominate in this Dutch setting. Resources would be available for any option. The Netherlands is the eleventh largest economy in the world (by PPP), and the distribution of resources across the population is irrelevant because flood protection is administered by the national government. The structure of critical institutions, the derivative allocation of decision-making authority, and the decision criteria could be more problematic, however. Water management and land use planning are administered by separate agencies; as a result, pressure to expand into the flood plain can limit the options for water management because of conflicts among many stakeholders. Indeed, public works are increasingly decided through direct participation of the population; long postponements result, and radical solutions are disadvantaged. The stock of human capital, including education and personal security, is very high in the Netherlands, though; and Dutch water engineers are among the best in the world. The stock of social capital is also high. The Netherlands is a consensus-oriented society in which the collective need is an effective counterweight to individual interests. Property rights are clearly defined, and the judiciary is independent. The system's access to formal risk spreading processes is limited because flood insurance cannot be purchased. Decision-makers are quite capable of managing information and determining which is credible; as a result, their decisions are generally taken to be credible. Dutch bureaucrats are typically well educated and supported by able consultancies; but an 'old-boy' network of professors, civil servants, and consultants controls water management practices. The public, as well as the water managers, are well aware of climate change and its implications for flood risk.

Table 4 offers expert judgment into how these macro-scale observations might be translated into the micro-scale determinants of each of the options. The strength of each determinant was scored on a subjective scale from 0 on the low side to 5 on the high side. The low score for storing water is a reflection of the international cooperation that would be required to implement and to manage such a scheme. Accepting floods, creating a fourth mouth for the river, and constructing a bypass also scored low marks, but their deficiencies were far less ubiquitous; instead, specific determinants like distributional ramifications and/or risk spreading were sources of weakness. Higher dikes and manipulating the river bed were awarded higher scores, but neither is perfect. Indeed, manipulating the river bed would appear to be most feasible, but it is hampered by a relatively low efficacy factor; i.e., such a plan could not eliminate the risk of flooding. On the other hand, higher dikes face participation difficulties on the feasibility side, but could offer extremely effective flood protection. The results of organizing an examination of adaptive capacity around its underlying determinants are thus surprisingly pessimistic. Each alternative, for one reason or another, has a weakness that can be discovered by a process that looks at each determinant in turn.

5.3. Coping with enormous uncertainty

The third and final application looks at adaptation under enormous uncertainty in a different context—a less well developed economy contemplating macro-scale adaptations to climate change. Strzepek et al. (2001) described a process by which 'not implausible' climate scenarios were selected for Egypt as the first step of a project designed ultimately to conduct detailed integrated assessments of their impacts across a range of similarly 'not implausible' socio-economic scenarios.[11] Recall that Fig. 10 displays nine representative climate scenarios in terms of flow into Lake Nasser. Each was driven by specific assumptions about GHG and sulfate emissions, climate and sulfate aerosol sensitivities, and the results of some specific global circulation model; but each was selected for its value in representing a wide range of futures that cannot, as yet, be discarded as completely impossible. Taken together, they span a range of outputs produced by running COSMIC for rainfall and temperature for nine upstream countries through a hydrological model authored by David Yates and Kenneth Strzepek; and they provide an arena in which the robustness of alternative adaptations and the value of climate information can be evaluated.[12]

A careful review of Fig. 9 sets the stage for thinking about the ramifications of alternative socioeconomic scenarios, especially with a view towards framing experiments designed to investigate the role of three possible macro-scale adaptations: municipal recycling, drip irrigation, and groundwater pumping. Scenario 1 could produce favorable outcomes from climate change as long as potential floodwaters could

---

11 The method employed to select the representative scenarios is fully developed in Yohe et al. (1999).
12 See Yates and Strzepek (1998) for a description of the hydrologic model and Strzepek et al. (2001) for its accommodation of COSMIC inputs; see Schlesinger and Williams (1998) for a description of COSMIC.

Table 4. Evaluating the determinants of adaptive capacity for flood control options along lower Rhine delta[a]

Determinant	Store water	Accept floods	Higher dikes	River bed	4th Mouth	Bypass
2. Resources	1	3	4	4	1	1
3. Institutions	1	1	3	4	1	2
4. Human capital	1	2	5	4	4	3
5. Social capital	1	3	4	5	2	2
6. Risk spreading	2	1	5	4	4	3
7. Information	1	2	4	4	2	2
8 Awareness	3	3	5	5	3	3
Feasibility factor[b]	1	1	3	4	1	1
Efficacy factor[c]	0.8	1.0	1.0	0.6	0.8	0.6

Notes:
[a]The numbers recorded in the table indicate subjective ratings of the strength of each determinant of adaptive capacity for each adaptation option on a scale from 1 (very weak) to 5 (very strong). The numbers preceding each determinant refer back to the list in the text.
[b]The feasibility factor is an overall ranking index; it is the minimum of the subjective ratings across all determinants.
[c]The efficacy factor is a subjective judgment of likelihood that the indicated option will effectively eliminate the threat of flooding.
Source: Yohe and Tol (2002).

be diverted into vacant and domestic regions of the Sahara Desert. Flow into Lake Nasser would be stable along this scenario through 2030 and then climb over the next 70 years. Scenarios 2 and 3 would be relatively benign. Flow would fall by roughly 8% by 2030, but that level would be maintained across the rest of the 22nd century. Scenarios 4 and 8 would also portend modest climate change with a gradual decline by 2100 of approximately 12%. Scenario 6 offers the first portrait of serious shortfall in Nile flow. Flow would fall by 25% by 2025, thereby tracking even the worst climate outcomes over the near-term; but it would decline only gradually thereafter for a total reduction of 40% by 2100. Scenario 5 tracks scenario 6 through 2025, but subsequent reductions would be more severe. Indeed, flow into Lake Nasser would be 55% and 65% lower then the present value by 2067 and 2100, respectively. Finally, scenarios 7 and 9 would produce the worst outcomes in terms of climate change. Near-term reductions of 30% by 2025 are not much worse than 5 and 6; but flow falls by 75% by 2067 and by 80% around the turn of the next century.

Motivated by an understanding of the critical role played by the determinants of adaptive capacity, Strzepek et al. (2001) highlighted the potential significance of high-capital and low-capital futures in evaluating the potential for effective adaptation. Variation across socio-economic futures captured this distinction in a Ramsey-style growth model with three different population trajectories and high or low settings for three critical parameters: nonagricultural productivity growth, growth in agricultural yields, and investment efficiency. Since domestic food security is a critical policy objective of the Egyptian government, favorable and unfavorable terms of trade were also considered. Fig. 10 displays the results of running the growth model without

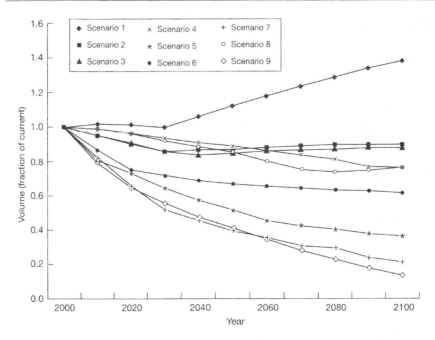

Figure 10. Economic output for Egypt along 'Not Implausible' Climate and Socio-Economic Futures.
The vertical axis reflects an index of the sum of consumption goods and food available to the Egyptian population in the year 2067 as a fraction of 2000 totals for over 900 climate/socio-economic scenarios. The horizontal axis indicates the proportion of total food consumption actually grown domestically. *Source*: Fig. 3 in Yohe et al. (2002).

adaptation for 600 combinations of climate and socio-economic futures in terms of an index of Egyptian food self-sufficiency and total food plus consumable good consumption in the year 2067.[13]

Allowing adaptation to climate along 36 of the 600+ scenarios, themselves selected to represent of the diversity displayed in Fig. 10, showed that adaptation could make a significant difference in Egypt, especially for pessimistic climate scenarios. Panel A of Fig. 11, for example, links outcomes in 2067 with and without adaptation for four socio-economic scenarios for the middle population trajectory along climate scenario 3. Notice that the value of adaptation is seen most clearly in terms of increased food self-sufficiency, sometimes at the expense of some economic activity. Panel B meanwhile links outcomes for the same scenarios for the same population trajectory along the most pessimistic climate future—scenario 9. Here, adaptation was devoted to increasing economic activity. Moreover, food security suffers in three cases, and quite substantially

---

13 The year 2067 was chosen for display because it reflects a point in the relatively distant future by which time the nine climate scenarios had, for the most part, diverged. The implications of climate and socioeconomic circumstances were therefore fully represented. The self sufficiency coefficient reflects the proportion of total food consumption supported by domestic food production.

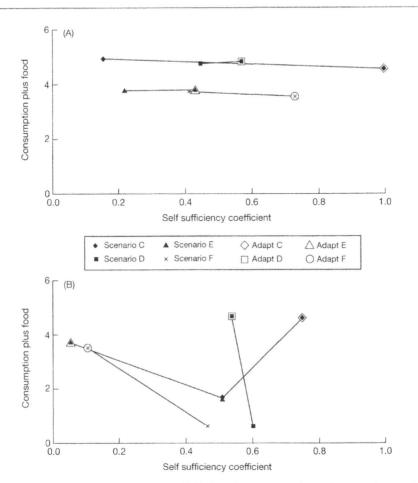

Figure 11. Panel A displays outcomes in 2067 along four representative socio-economic scenarios and climate scenario 3 depicted in Fig. 9 with median expected population growth. Smaller points indicate outcomes without adaptation; larger points connected by dotted lines indicate outcomes with efficient adaptation (drip irrigation and municipal recycling). Panel B displays comparable results along climate scenario 9; adaptation now includes groundwater pumping beginning around 2025 and significant reallocation of domestic investment in anticipation of the enormous investment required to deliver this water to major population centers.

in two where economic robustness is hampered by inefficient investment (scenarios E and F). In fact, only along scenario C, marked by high efficiency in investment and the agricultural sector, could both policy objectives improve with adaptation. The results therefore show that socio-economic context of the sort suggested by the determinants of adaptive capacity mattered. Indeed, scenarios hampered by inefficient investment displayed diminished capacities to adapt along either the food security or the economic activity scale, or both. It is, finally, significant that food security was the major beneficiary of adaptation to all climates but the most severe.

How much would it be worth to the Egyptian economy to know that it should expect climate scenario 3 rather than 9, or the other way around? The value information like that is critically dependent upon the specific properties of the adaptative response under consideration. Improved ex ante information can hold negligible value for adaptations that are tied directly to direct observations of current circumstances as the future unfolds *as long as the appropriate signal of change can be effectively distinguished from the surrounding noise.* Improved information can, by way of contrast, be enormously valuable for adaptations that involve significant investment in infrastructure and/or significant reallocations of resources in anticipation of that investment. Drip irrigation and municipal recycling fell relatively well into the first category; either would involve modest investment in small projects that could efficiently come on line as climate change produced incremental need. Drilling for groundwater below the Sahara and pumping it to where it would be needed would, however, lie squarely in the second.

Reflecting current expectations of the Egyptian Ministry of Water and Irrigation, the growth model undertook direct investment in pumping groundwater only when five-year average flows into Lake Nasser fell 25% below current levels, but that turned out to be only half of the story. The perfect foresight assumed in its Ramsey formulation allowed the economy to reallocate capital between the agricultural and non-agricultural sectors well in advance of that date. As a result, information that could support early differentiation between two strikingly different climate futures could be expressed as measurable fractions of current GDP—roughly 0.5% of current GDP in present value. In addition, planning for bad news and adapting to good was shown to be a better choice than the other way around. Indeed, increased climate variability made it even better to 'plan for the worst' because it made the climate signal more difficult to detect and therefore delayed possible 'midcourse' corrections in adaptation and investment plans.

6. Concluding remarks

We began with a warning that it would be imprudent to reflect the content of the Third Assessment Report in terms of costs and benefits distributed across globe along one or two specific climate change scenarios. It is a warning that is entirely consistent with one of the fundamental conclusions of that report:

> Current knowledge of adaptation and adaptive capacity is insufficient for reliable prediction of adaptations; it also is insufficient for rigorous evaluation of planned adaptation options, measures and policies of governments . . . Given the scope and variety of specific adaptation options across sectors, individuals, communities and locations, as well as the variety of participants—public and private—involved in most adaptation initiatives, it is probably infeasible to systematically evaluate lists of adaptation measures; improving and applying knowledge on the constraints and opportunities for enhancing adaptive capacity is necessary to reduce vulnerabilities associated with climate change. (p. 880)

This is not to say that all is lost. The take-home message is simply that future research has a long way to go if it is to come to grips with the diversity of the socio-political-economic environments that produce wide ranges of sensitivities and imply enormous variances in adaptive capacity. Geographic diversity and enormous uncertainty are the sources of challenge for building and exercising methods so that the next assessment of the state of knowledge will not be so pessimistic. It goes without saying that geographically centered economic research has a significant role to play here.

Acknowledgements

The US National Science Foundation supported this work through its funding of the Center for Integrated Study of the Human Dimensions of Global Change at Carnegie Mellon University under Cooperative Agreement SBR 95–21914. Much of Sections 2 and 3 were drawn from extensive collaboration with the Lead Authors of Chapters 18 and 19 of the IPCC (2001b) and Chapter 1 of IPCC (2001c). Contributions in this regard by Ian Burton, Saleemul Huq, Richard Klein, Olga Pilifosova, Barry Smit, Joel Smith, John Weyant, and Richard Tol are gratefully acknowledged. Thanks are offered, as well, to Tammy Pau and Courtney Yohe for their help in preparing the manuscript and working to make it intelligible. Two referees and Richard Arnott also contributed to the content of the paper and to its presentation. Notwithstanding the influence of all of these, errors in this presentation reside at the authors' doorsteps. The authors also gratefully acknowledge that Figures 2 through 8 were reprinted from *Technological Forecasting and Social Change*, Volume 65, Schlesinger, M.E., Malyshev, S., Rozanov, E., Yang, F., Andronova, N.G., deVries, B., Grubler, A., Jiang, K., Masui, T., Morita, T., Penner, J., Pepper, W., Sankovski, A., Shang, Y., 'Geographical Distributions of Temperature Change for Scenarios of Greenhouse Gas and Sulfur Dioxide Emissions'. 167–193, 2000, with permission of Elsevier Science.

References

Alcamo, J., Leemans, R., Kreileman, E. (eds.) (1998) *Global Change Scenarios of the 21st Century: Results from the IMAGE 2.1 Model.* London: Elsevier Science.

Alfsen, K. H., Berntsen, T. K. (1999) Modeling atmospheric carbon concentrations, Working Paper No. 1, CICERO, Oslo, Norway.

Dowlatabadi, H., Yohe, G. (2000) The who-how of adaptation: towards more realistic impact assessments. *Global Environmental Change* 10: 214–227.

Downing, T. E. (ed.) (1996) *Climate Change and World Food Security.* Berlin: Springer.

Downing, T. E., Ringius, L, Hulme, M., Waughray, D. (1997) Adapting to climate change in Africa. *Mitigation and Adaptation Strategies for Global Change* 2: 19–44.

Gritsevskii, A., Gruebler, A. (1998) *The Scenario Generator: A Tool for Scenario Formulation and Model Linkages.* Laxenburg. Austria: International Institute for Applied Systems Analysis.

Hewitt, J., Burton, I. (1971) *The Hazardousness of a Place: A Regional Ecology of Damaging Events.* Toronto: University of Toronto.

Intergovernmental Panel on Climate Change (IPCC) (1990) *1990: Climate Change: The IPCC Scientific Assessment.* Cambridge: Cambridge University Press.

IPCC (1992) *1992: Climate Change: The Supplementary Report to the IPCC Scientific Assessment.* Cambridge: Cambridge University Press.

IPCC (1996a) *1995—The Science of Climate Change, Contribution of Working Group I to the Second Scientific Assessment of the Intergovernmental Panel on Climate Change.* Cambridge: Cambridge University Press.

IPCC (1996b) *1995—Impacts, Adaptation and Mitigation of Climate Change: Scientific-Technical Analyses, Contribution of Working Group II to the Second Scientific Assessment of the Intergovernmental Panel on Climate Change.* Cambridge: Cambridge University Press.

IPCC (1996c) *Climate Change 1995—Economic and Social Dimensions of Climate Change, Contribution of Working Group III to the Second Scientific Assessment of the Intergovernmental Panel on Climate Change.* Cambridge: Cambridge University Press.

IPCC (2000) *2000: Special Report on Emissions Scenarios.* Cambridge: Cambridge University Press.

340 • *Yohe and Schlesinger*

IPCC (2001a) *2000—The Science of Climate Change—The Contribution of Working Group I to the Third Scientific Assessment of the Intergovernmental Panel on Climate Change.* Cambridge: Cambridge University Press.

IPCC (2001b) *2000—Impacts, Adaptation, and Vulnerability—The Contribution of Working Group II to the Third Scientific Assessment of the Intergovernmental Panel on Climate Change.* Cambridge: Cambridge University Press.

IPCC (2001c) *2000—Mitigation—The Contribution of Working Group III to the Third Scientific Assessment of the Intergovernmental Panel on Climate Change.* Cambridge: Cambridge University Press.

Joos, F., Bruno, M., Fink, R., Siegenthaler, U., Stocker, T. F., Quere, C. L., Sarmiento, J. L. (1996) An efficient and accurate representation of complex oceanic and biospheric models of anthropogenic carbon uptake. *Tellus* 48: 397–417.

Kane, S. J., Reilly, J., Tobey, J. (1992) An empirical study of the economic effects of climate change on world agriculture. *Climatic Change* 21: 17–35.

Karl, T. R., Knight, R. W. (1998) Secular trends of precipitation amount, frequency and intensity in the United States. *Bulletin of the American Meteorological Society* 79: 231–241.

Mearns, L. O., Rosenzweig, C., Goldberg, R. (1997) Mean and variance change in climate scenarios: methods, agricultural applications and measures of uncertainty. *Climatic Change* 34: 367–396.

Mendelsohn, R., Morrison, W., Schlesinger, M. E., Andronova, N. G. (2000) Country-specific market impacts of climate change. *Climatic Change* 45: 553–569.

Morita, T., Matsuoka, Y., Jiang, K., Masui, T., Takahashi, K., Kainuma, M., Pandey, R. (1998) *Quantification of IPCC-SRES Storylines Using the AIM/Emission-Linkage Model.* Japan: National Institute for Environmental Studies.

Myhre, G., Highwood, E. J., Shine, K. P., Stordal, F. (1998) New estimates of radiative forcing due to well mixed greenhouse gases. *Geophysics Research Letter* 25: 2715–2718.

Nordhaus, W. D., Boyer, J. (2000) *Warming the World: Economics Models of Climate Change.* Cambridge MA: MIT Press.

Pepper, W., Barbour, W., Sankovski, A., Graatz, B. (1998) No-policy greenhouse gas scenarios: revisiting IPCC 1992. *Environmental Science and Policy* 1: 289–312.

Pittock, B., Jones, R. N. (2000) Adaptation to what and why? *Environmental Monitoring and Assessment* 61: 9–35.

Schlesinger, M. E., Williams, L. (1998) COSMIC—country specific model for intertemporal climate. Palo Alto, CA: Computer Software, Electric Power Research Institute.

Schlesinger, M. E., Malyshev, S., Rozanov, E., Yang, F., Andronova, N. G., deVries, B., Grubler, A., Jiang, K., Masui, T., Morita, T., Penner, J., Pepper, W., Sankovski, A., Shang, Y. (2000) Geographical distributions of temperature change for scenarios of greenhouse gas and sulfur dioxide emissions. *Technological Forecasting and Social Change* 65: 167–193.

Schneider, S. (1989) The changing climate. In *Managing the Planet—Readings from Scientific American.* New York: W.H. Freeman and Company, 25–39.

Smit, B., Burton, I., Klein, R., Street, R. (1999) The science of adaptation: a framework for assessment. *Mitigation and Adaptation Strategies for Global Change* 4: 119–213.

Smithers, J., Smit, B. (1997) Human adaptation to climatic variability and change. *Global Environmental Change* 7: 129–146.

Strzepek, K., Yates, D., Yohe, G., Tol, R. S. J., Mader, N. (2001) Constructing 'not implausible' climate and economic scenarios for Egypt. *Integrated Assessment* forthcoming.

Tol, R. S. J. (1999) New estimates of the damage costs of climate change, parts I and II. Working Papers D99-01 and D99-02, Institute for Environmental Studies, Vrije Universiteit, Amsterdam.

Tol, R. S. J., van der Grijp, N. M., Olsthoorn, A. A., van der Werff, P. E. (2001) Adapting to climate change: a case study on riverine flood risks in the Netherlands. In R. S. J. Tol and A. A. Olsthoorn (eds) *Floods, Flood Management and Climate Change in the Netherlands.* Amsterdam: Institute for Environmental Studies, Vrije Universiteit.

West, J., Dowlatabadi, H. (1999) On assessing the economic impacts of sea-level rise on developed coasts. In T. Downing, A. Osthoorn, and R. S. J. Tol (eds) *Climate Change and Risk.* London: Routledge, 205–220.

Yates, D., Strzepek, K. (1998) Modeling the Nile basin under climate change. *Journal of Hydrologic Engineering* 3: 98–108.

Yohe, G. (1989) The cost of not holding back the sea—economic vulnerability. *Ocean and Shoreline Management* 15: 233–255.

Yohe, G., Schlesinger, M. (1998) Sea level change: the expected economic cost of protection or abandonment in the Unites States. *Climatic Change* 38: 447–472.

Yohe, G., Tol, R. (2002) Indicators for social and economic coping capacity—moving toward a working definition of adaptive capacity. *Global Environmental Change* forthcoming.

Yohe, G., Neumann, J. E., Marshall, P., Amaden, H. (1996) The economic cost of greenhouse induced sea level rise for developed property in the United States. *Climatic Change* 32: 387–410.

Yohe, G., Jacobsen, M., Gapotchenko, T. (1999) Spanning 'not-implausible' futures to assess relative vulnerability to climate change and climate variability. *Global Environmental Change* 9: 233–249.

Yohe, G., Strzepek, K, Pau, T., Yohe, C. (2002) Bringing economic analysis to bear on adaptation: the Egyptian case study. In *Proceedings of the PIK Workshop on Enhancing the Capacity of Developing Countries to Adapt to Climate Change.* Potsdam: Potsdam Institute for Climate Impact Research.

[5]

El Niño and World Primary Commodity Prices: Warm Water or Hot Air?

Allan D. Brunner*

Abstract——This paper examines the historical effects of the El Niño–Southern Oscillation (ENSO) cycle on world prices and economic activity. The primary focus is on world real non-oil primary commodity prices, although the effects on G-7 consumer price inflation and GDP growth are also considered. This paper has several distinct advantages over previous studies. First, several econometric models are estimated using fairly broad measures of prices and economic activity. Second, the models include continuous measures of ENSO intensity (sea surface temperature and sea-level air pressure anomalies in the Pacific Ocean) rather than dummy variable measures. Finally, confidence intervals are constructed for all estimated effects of ENSO on world prices and economic activity. The analysis indicates that ENSO has economically important and statistically significant effects on world real commodity prices. A one-standard-deviation positive surprise in ENSO, for example, raises real commodity price inflation about 3.5 to 4 percentage points. Moreover, ENSO appears to account for almost 20% of commodity price inflation movements over the past several years. ENSO also has some explanatory power for world consumer price inflation and world economic activity, accounting for approximately 10% to 20% of movements in those variables.

I. Introduction

This paper examines the historical effects of the El Niño–Southern Oscillation (ENSO) cycle on world primary commodity prices, as well as other measures of world economic activity. There is, of course, an extensive literature devoted to estimating the effects of weather on economic activity. The bulk of this work concerns the effects of relatively high-frequency changes in weather on economic activity. Although the importance of weather varies by geographic region and by industrial sector,[1] a plethora of studies have documented the effects of precipitation and temperature on agricultural production,[2] energy demand,[3] and construction activity.[4] In addition, Saunders (1993) found that Wall Street weather has significant psychological effects on daily stock market returns.

There is also a great deal of interest in the effects of low-frequency weather developments on economic activity. Following Jevons (1884), a number of studies examined the relationship between sunspot cycles (11-year to 100-year cycles) and atmospheric changes, crop production, and broader measures of economic activity. More recently, economists have turned their attention to the possible economic consequences of global warming; see Mendelsohn,

Nordhaus, and Shaw (1994), Cline (1996), and their cited references.

Surprisingly, little attention has been directed toward understanding the significance of medium-frequency weather fluctuations, such as ENSO events. Some of the notable exceptions are Handler (1983), Adams et al. (1995), Debelle and Stevens (1995), and Solow et al. (1997). These studies are of only limited use, however, in understanding the importance of ENSO to the world economy. First, they focused on a small number of commodities and certain geographical areas thought to be significantly affected by ENSO. Consequently, one cannot conclude whether ENSO has any implications for broader measures of prices and economic activity. Second, none of these studies put confidence bounds on their calculated effects. As a result, it is difficult to draw any firm conclusions about the statistical importance of these phenomena for prices and economic activity. Finally, these studies used dummy variables to designate years in which there was unusual climactic activity.[5] Thus, relatively weak ENSO events were averaged with more-severe episodes, and La Niña events were either ignored or were treated as symmetric to El Niño events. In any case, this likely biased the estimated effects toward zero and toward insignificance.

This paper makes several important contributions to this literature. First, several simple econometric models are constructed to study the global economic consequences of the ENSO cycle. The primary focus of these models is on the effects on world real non-oil primary commodity prices (as measured by IMF commodity price indices), although the effects on G-7 consumer price inflation and GDP growth are also considered. Second, the models include continuous measures of ENSO intensity (sea surface temperature and sea-level air pressure anomalies in the Pacific Ocean) rather than dummy variable measures. Finally, confidence intervals are constructed for all estimated effects of ENSO on world prices and economic activity.

The analysis indicates that ENSO has economically important and statistically significant effects on world commodity prices. A one-standard-deviation positive surprise in ENSO, for example, raises real commodity price inflation about 3.5 to 4 percentage points. Moreover, ENSO appears to account for almost 20% of commodity price inflation movements over the past several years. ENSO also has some explanatory power for world consumer price inflation and world economic activity, accounting for about 10% to 20% of movements in those variables.

Received for publication May 12, 1999. Revision accepted for publication October 23, 2000.

* International Monetary Fund.

I would like to thank Neil Ericsson, Caroline Freund, Bill Helkie, Dave Howard, Karen Johnson, Eric Leeper, Andy Levin, John Rosine, Ted Truman, and three anonymous referees for extensive comments on earlier versions of this paper. This paper was written while I was a staff economist at the Board of Governors of the Federal Reserve System. The views expressed in this paper are mine and do not necessarily reflect those held by any member of either institution. I am responsible for any errors.

[1] See Norrbin and Schlagenhauf (1988).

[2] This literature dates back to at least Day (1965).

[3] See Lawrence and Aigner (1979), EPRI (1981, 1983), Engle et al. (1986), and Maddala et al. (1997).

[4] See, for example, Solomou and Wu (1997).

[5] Debelle and Stevens—using a continuous measure to model Australian output—is one exception.

The remainder of this paper is organized as follows. Section II briefly reviews the general characteristics of ENSO events and describes the ENSO measures used in the econometric analysis. Section III describes the econometric approach, and section IV discusses the estimated effects of ENSO on commodity prices, world consumer price inflation, and world economic activity. Concluding remarks are provided in section V.

II. ENSO and World Commodity Prices

During "normal" seasons in the tropical Pacific, a persistent high-pressure system is located off the west coast of South America and a persistent low-pressure system off the east coast of Australia. As a result, the prevailing surface winds in the tropical Pacific are "easterlies," blowing from east to west. These winds tend to push warm surface water from the eastern and central regions of the equatorial Pacific toward Asia and Australia, providing these regions with precipitation that is useful for both agricultural and industrial uses. In the eastern regions of the Pacific, cold, nutrient-rich water comes up from below to replace the displaced warmer water, leading to ideal living conditions for many cold-water tropical fish and providing an economic livelihood for the South American fishing industry.

Periodically, these patterns are disrupted by anomalous shifts in atmospheric pressures and sea surface temperatures in the Pacific. Occasionally, during La Niñas, the high- and low-pressure systems intensify, the prevailing easterlies become stronger, and ocean temperatures plummet. At other times, during El Niños, the low- and high-pressure systems actually switch positions, causing the easterlies to weaken and often become westerlies. In that case, warm surface water accumulates and often gets pushed toward the Pacific coasts of the Americas. This complex, cyclical interaction between the atmosphere and the ocean in the Pacific is called the El Niño–Southern Oscillation (ENSO).

The intensity of an ENSO event can be measured in several ways. Two widely cited measures of an ENSO's severity are sea surface temperature (SST) anomalies— deviations between sea surface temperatures in a given region and the region's historical average—and Southern Oscillation Index (SOI) anomalies, which are deviations between air-pressure differentials in the South Pacific and their historical averages.[6] SOI anomalies for the Pacific and SST anomalies for the so-called "Niño3.4" region (a central region of the Pacific) are illustrated in figure 1.[7] As the chart shows, the two measures are highly but not perfectly correlated. Indeed, the measures offer a somewhat different view of the 1997–1998 El Niño event. The SST anomaly

FIGURE 1.—TWO MEASURES OF ENSO INTENSITY

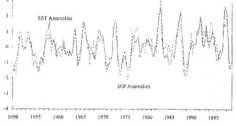

measure reached an all-time high in late 1997, whereas the SOI anomaly measure is in line with previous El Niño episodes.

The chart also indicates that the time series properties of ENSO events are similar to those for business cycles. Most importantly, the ENSO cycle is characterized by two alternating but persistent phases: the El Niño and the La Niña phases. El Niños, for example, typically occur at intervals of three to seven years and last about two years. They also vary greatly in their intensity. The 1982–83 and 1997–98 El Niños were quite severe and had devastating effects in many regions of the world, whereas the 1994–95 El Niño was relatively mild.

Although ENSO events arise in the Pacific Ocean, they have far-reaching effects on the world's weather. The experience of the 1982–83 El Niño highlights the possible consequences of a severe ENSO event.[8] That episode began in May 1982, when easterly winds weakened and shifted to westerlies. As warm surface water accumulated off the Pacific coasts of the Americas, many tropical fish were killed and others were sent to colder regions, thus harming fishing industries (especially anchovy and sardine industries) from Chile to British Columbia.

In addition, the 1982–83 El Niño created important global atmospheric disturbances, as high-altitude jet stream winds were altered, affecting weather patterns in Asia, in North and South America, and as far away as Africa. Ecuador and Peru, for example, received about seven years worth of rain in four months, causing extensive flooding and the destruction of several cities. In contrast, India, Indonesia, Malaysia, and Australia suffered droughts and disastrous forest fires. Abnormal wind patterns steered typhoons toward Hawaii and Tahiti rather than toward the Asian continent. In the United States, winter storms battered southern California and caused widespread flooding across many of the southern states, while more northern states experienced unseasonably mild weather.

---

[6] Other measures of ENSO's severity include sea-level air temperature and windspeed anomalies.

[7] This paper uses SST and SOI data from 1950 to the present. Although these measures are available intermittently back to the late 1800s, data prior to WWII are not directly comparable to more recent data, and they are often deemed unreliable.

[8] The most recent El Niño paralleled the 1982–83 episode in most respects. La Niñas generally produce climate anomalies that are opposite to those of El Niños.

FIGURE 2.—IMF COMMODITY PRICE INFLATION AND SST ANOMALIES

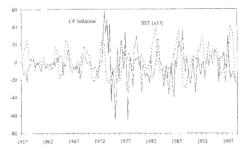

A substantial amount of anecdotal evidence suggests that ENSO events have an important influence on the world's production of primary commodities. Some of ENSO's effects on commodity production are direct. For example, during the most recent El Niño, extensive rainfall washed away rice crops in Ecuador and flooded copper mines in Chile and Peru. Drought conditions parched Australian wheat crops and resulted in forest fires in Indonesia. The El Niño had important indirect influences, as well. For example, excess moisture led to pestilential attacks on California vegetables. Drought shut down some mining firms in Indonesia that relied on hydroelectric power and waterway transportation, and drought prevented heavy ships from passing through the Panama Canal, which relies on water from nearby lakes to raise and lower ships. Analogously, La Niñas also have both direct and indirect influences.

Despite the ample anecdotal evidence, however, only a few economic studies have focused on the possible consequences of ENSO for world economic activity—for world production, prices, and international trade. This paper provides an important step in that direction by focusing on the link between ENSO and world commodity prices and, to a lesser extent, world inflation and economic activity.

Figure 2 charts the recent historical relationship between a measure of **real** commodity price inflation (the solid line) and the SST measure of ENSO intensity (the dashed line).[9] The commodity price measure is derived using the IMF's index of non-oil primary commodity prices and the average CPI inflation rate for the G-7 countries.[10] There is a surprisingly close association between SST anomalies and commodity price changes, given the large array of other factors that are likely to affect commodity prices (for example, world economic activity). As figure 2 indicates, El Niños are generally associated with subsequent real commodity price increases, whereas La Niñas are associated with price de-

clines. The 1982–83 El Niño had a very dramatic effect on commodity prices, although the 1972–73 and 1986–87 El Niño events were also important contributors to commodity price inflation in those years. For La Niñas, the 1973–74 and 1987–88 events were particularly influential on commodity price deflation in those years.

Much of the correlation between ENSO and commodity prices is accounted for by the food component of the overall index (not graphed), although there is a weaker correlation between the ENSO indexes and agricultural raw material prices and metals prices. These results are roughly consistent with the anecdotal evidence just discussed. During the 1982–83 El Niño event, for example, grain and oilseed prices rose sharply in late 1982 and early 1983, both because of droughts in Asia and Australia and because of the displaced fish population. (Soybean meal is a close substitute for fishmeal.) Supply disruptions in Southeast Asia (droughts) and South America (floods) also put some upward pressures on copper prices. Finally, cocoa and (to a lesser extent) coffee prices were pushed up due to dry conditions in Malaysia and Indonesia and due to excessive rainfall in South America.

Figure 3 charts the historical relationship between SST anomalies and G-7 inflation and GDP growth rates. These relationships are not as tight as the relationship between measures of ENSO and world commodity prices. Nevertheless, there is a small positive relationship between the

FIGURE 3.—G-7 INFLATION AND GDP AND SST ANOMALIES

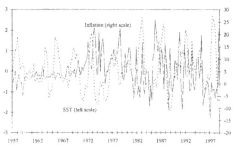

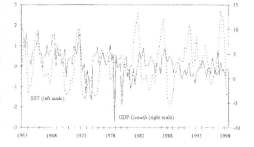

[9] Because most measures of ENSO are highly correlated, most of the following analysis focuses on just the SST measure. Results using the SOI measure are available in Brunner (2000).

[10] With the exception of the ENSO measures, all variables were constructed using the IMF's *International Financial Statistics*. See the appendix for a description of the data.

ENSO and both inflation and economic growth, especially during the particularly strong phases of the cycle that were discussed earlier.

III. The Econometric Approach

To better gauge the effects of ENSO events on world prices and growth, several vector autoregressive (VAR) models were estimated. Each four-variable VAR model contained $ENSO_t$, a measure of ENSO intensity. $ENSO_t$ was either the SST anomaly or the SOI anomaly measure. Each model also included the average CPI inflation rate (π_t^g) and the average GDP growth rate (Δy_t) for the G-7 countries. Finally, each VAR contained a measure of real commodity price inflation ($\pi_t^{cp} - \pi_t^g$). The real commodity price inflation measures were based either on the IMF's five index measures of non-oil primary commodity prices (foods, beverages, agricultural raw materials, metals, and all non-oil commodities) or on one of the 33 individual commodity prices that compose the overall index.

The models were of the following form:

$$ENSO_t = \mu_s + A_{11}(L)\,ENSO_{t-1} + \epsilon_t \qquad (1)$$

$$X_t = \phi_s + A_{21}(L)\,ENSO_t + A_{22}(L)\,X_{t-1} + \eta_t$$

where

$$\begin{bmatrix} \epsilon_t \\ \eta_t \end{bmatrix} \sim N\left(\begin{bmatrix} 0 \\ 0 \end{bmatrix}, \begin{bmatrix} \sigma_\epsilon^2 & 0 \\ 0 & \Sigma_\eta \end{bmatrix} \right) \qquad (2)$$

and where $ENSO_t$ represents a measure of $ENSO$ intensity; $X_t = [\pi_t^{cp} - \pi_t^g \ \pi_t^g \ \Delta y_t]$; μ_s and ϕ_s are seasonally varying constants; $A_{11}(L)$, $A_{21}(L)$, and $A_{22}(L)$ are polynomials in L, the lag operator; ϵ_t is a exogenous shock to $ENSO_t$; and η_t is a 3×1 vector of innovations to X_t.

Several aspects of the specification in equation (1) and (2) deserve discussion. First, it seems reasonable that ENSO events are not influenced contemporaneously by economic events. Thus, $ENSO_t$ is assumed to be weakly exogenous, affecting X_t contemporaneously but not vice versa. This assumption also identifies the ENSO shocks (ϵ_t) as being orthogonal shocks; that is, ϵ_t and η_t are assumed to be uncorrelated. Second, the idea that ENSO events are strictly exogenous—as shown in equation (1)—is a testable hypothesis given the assumption of weak exogeneity. Indeed, Wald tests revealed $ENSO_t$ is uncorrelated with lags of X_t at conventional significance levels. Third, Σ_η is expected to be nondiagonal; that is, the individual innovations within η_t are correlated. However, because the focus of this analysis is entirely on the role of ϵ_t (which is uncorrelated with η_t), it is not necessary to make any orthogonalizing assumptions about η_t. Finally, it should be noted that the economic variables in equation (1) are expressed as first differences. Augmented Dickey-Fuller tests indicated that the ENSO measures are I(0), whereas the economic variables are I(1) in log levels and I(0) in first differences. Because there was

TABLE 1.—GRANGER CASUALITY TESTS FOR IMPORTANCE OF ENSO TO WORLD ECONOMIC ACTIVITY

$$X_t = \Phi_s + A_{21}(L)\,ENSO_t + A_{22}(L)\,X_{t-1} + \text{H}_t$$

IMF Commodity Price Index	Significance Level of $\chi^2(18)$ Test for $A_{21}(L) = 0$ where:	
	$ENSO_t = SST_t$	$ENSO_t = SOI_t$
All primary commodities	0.07	<0.01
Food	<0.01	<0.01
Beverages	0.03	<0.01
Average raw materials	0.20	0.01
Metals	<0.01	<0.01

no evidence of cointegration among the variables in log levels, the economic variables were expressed in first-difference form.

The VAR models were estimated using quarterly data from 1963 through 1998. Based on a sequence of general-to-specific likelihood ratio tests, it was determined that an appropriate lag length for all of the VARs is six quarterly lags.[11] The estimated model coefficients showed some evidence of instability, mostly associated with the equations describing the evolution of consumer price inflation. This is not too surprising given the high and volatile inflation rates seen in the 1970s relative to the lower and fairly stable rates seen in the rest of the sample period. (See figure 3.)

IV. The Estimation Results

Does ENSO have any explanatory power for the economic variables in the models? Table 1 presents the results of Granger causality tests for the importance of ENSO for each of the ten VAR models. The first column of the table denotes the commodity price measure (π_t^{cp}) used in the VAR model, and the second and third columns represent the two different measures of ENSO intensity ($ENSO_t$). Each of the ten entries in the table denotes the respective significance level of a χ^2 test for whether $A_{21}(L)$ in equation (1) is statistically different from zero.

A couple of aspects of the results in table 1 are worth noting. The SOI anomaly measure of ENSO intensity appears to have a much stronger statistical relationship with the economic variables than the SST anomaly measure does. This is true regardless of which commodity price measure is being used. On the other hand, the statistical significance of the SST measure is somewhat sensitive to the commodity price measure that is being included in the VAR model. In particular, the SST measure is not statistically significant at the 5% level when all primary commodity prices or when agricultural raw material prices are included in the model. The statistical importance of the SST measure is somewhat stronger, however, when prices of food, beverages, and metals are included.

---

[11] The Schwarz and Akaike information criteria yielded the same choice of lag lengths.

180 THE REVIEW OF ECONOMICS AND STATISTICS

FIGURE 4.—THE EFFECTS OF A SURPRISE IN SST

Effects on SST

Effects on Real Commodity Price Inflation

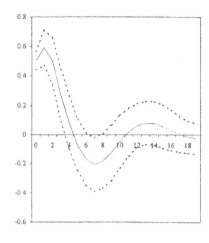
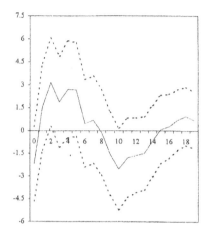

Effects on CPI Inflation

Effects on GDP Growth

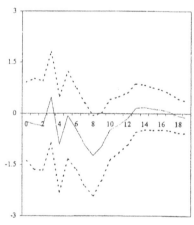
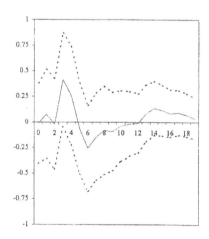

Dashed lines denote 2-standard deviation confidence bounds.

Figure 4 report the impulse response functions associated with surprises in ENSO for one of the ten estimated models. The model illustrated by figure 4 included SST anomalies and the real commodity price inflation rate for all primary commodities, as well as the average CPI inflation rate and GDP growth rate for the G-7 countries. The solid lines in the figure indicate the impulse responses for a one-standard-deviation surprise in the SST measure, and the dashed lines denote two-standard-deviation confidence intervals for each impulse response function.

As shown in the upper left panel, a positive ENSO surprise has very persistent effects, leading to raised sea

EL NIÑO AND WORLD PRIMARY COMMODITY PRICES: WARM WATER OR HOT AIR?   181

TABLE 2.—CONTRIBUTION OF SST TO THE VARIANCES
OF THE ECONOMIC VARIABLES

Economic Variable	Percentage of k-step-ahead Forecast Error Variance Attributable to SST	
	$k = 4$	$k = 16$
Commodity price inflation		
All primary commodities	**9.3** (4.7)	**18.1** (7.3)
Food	**12.3** (5.0)	**21.3** (6.9)
Beverages	4.2 (3.0)	**10.9** (4.8)
Average raw materials	6.3 (3.7)	**13.8** (6.2)
Metals	**9.3** (4.2)	**17.6** (6.6)
CPI inflation (G-7 countries)	3.7 (2.6)	**13.0** (6.0)
GDP growth (G-7 countries)	5.3 (3.4)	**10.0** (4.7)

Standard errors are in parentheses. Boldface indicates significance at 5% level.

surface temperatures (above their historical averages) for four subsequent quarters after the initial surprise. The upper right panel shows that a one-standard-deviation positive ENSO surprise raises commodity price inflation (in real terms) an estimated 3.5 to 4 percentage points two quarters after the initial surprise. Commodity prices fall by a similar amount in the second and third years after the initial surprise.[12] A similar pattern is evident for other measures of commodity prices (not shown). Not surprisingly, prices for food commodities are affected the most by ENSO, although prices of beverages, agricultural raw materials, and metals are also pushed up and then down.

The lower left panel of figure 4 indicates that ENSO has a similar "up-then-down" effect on overall prices among the G-7 countries, although the effect is much weaker and only marginally significant from zero for SOI measure. This relatively subdued influence on overall consumer prices is not unexpected because primary commodities account for only a fraction of overall finished good costs. Finally, as shown in the lower right panel, economic activity in the G-7 countries appears to be stimulated by a positive ENSO shock—raising GDP growth as much as one-half of a percentage point—although these effects are significant at only the 10% level. The stimulatory effects of an El Niño event on G-7 economic activity are somewhat surprising. One possible explanation for this result is that there is a measurable increase in investment spending (especially residential construction). The United States, for example, experiences wind storms and flooding during El Niños, which generally increase residential investment afterwards. On the other hand, this result could be capturing increased aggregate demand from other countries (for food, housing materials, machinery, equipment, and so on) that are devastated by El Niño events. In any case, this possible relationship deserves further investigation.

Although the Granger causality tests and the impulse response functions point to a strong statistical relationship between ENSO and world commodity prices and, to a lesser extent, to a statistically significant relationship between

[12] The hypothesis of no long-run effect on commodity price levels cannot be rejected.

ENSO and world inflation and economic activity, they provide no indication of economic significance. Table 2 and figure 5 provide evidence that ENSO has substantial economic importance. Each of the ten estimated VARs was used to calculate k-step-ahead dynamic forecasts for real commodity price inflation, world CPI inflation, and world economic activity for each time period in the data sample. The resulting forecast errors were then decomposed into the portion attributable to ENSO (ϵ_t) and the portion attributable to all other factors (η_t). The variances of these forecast errors were also decomposed in a similar manner.[13]

The results of the variance decomposition exercise for four- and sixteen-quarter-ahead forecasts are presented in table 2 for the case of SST anomalies.[14] The results can be summarized as follows. First, ENSO appears to account for a substantial amount of variation in the economic variables, regardless of which measure of ENSO is used, although the SOI anomalies generally have a stronger and more statistically significant influence. Second, in the short run, ENSO's

[13] The only assumption required to calculate these decompositions is that ENSO is weakly (contemporaneously) exogenous with respect to the other three variables in the VAR. As discussed previously, however, this paper models ENSO as strictly exogenous.

[14] SOI anomalies produced very similar results. An appendix with those results and impulse response functions for all commodities is available on request.

FIGURE 5.—THE HISTORICAL CONTRIBUTIONS OF SST ANOMALIES

a) Contributions to Real Commodity Price Inflation

b) Contributions to G7 CPI Inflation

c) Contributions to G7 GDP Growth

Solid line represents four-quarter-ahead forecast error; dashed line represents contribution of SST.

TABLE 3.—PRIMARY COMMODITIES MOST AFFECTED BY SST

Commodity	Percentage of k-step-ahead Forecast Error Variance Attributable to SST	
	$k = 4$	$k = 16$
Coconut oil	9.8 (4.8)	33.7 (9.4)
Tobacco	13.8 (6.4)	27.3 (9.4)
Fish meal	8.7 (5.0)	26.1 (9.9)
Palm oil	8.4 (4.2)	23.1 (7.5)
Rice	16.3 (6.4)	20.8 (6.8)
Soybean oil	11.3 (4.8)	19.7 (7.1)
Iron ore	16.7 (5.6)	19.1 (5.9)
Rubber	3.9 (2.5)	18.8 (7.9)
Wheat	6.6 (3.6)	18.8 (6.4)
Soybeans	13.7 (5.4)	17.4 (5.5)
Maize	8.5 (4.5)	17.3 (6.4)
Zinc	4.6 (3.0)	16.0 (6.8)
Wool (fine)	10.9 (6.0)	15.6 (7.2)
Groundnut oil	5.8 (3.5)	15.1 (6.4)
Copper	8.3 (3.9)	15.0 (5.5)

Standard errors are in parentheses. Boldface indicates significance at 5% level.

influence is mostly on food prices, accounting for between 12% and 14% of the four-quarter-ahead forecast error variance in these prices. ENSO appears to have little effect on G-7 economic activity, and the two ENSO measures provide conflicting information about the short-run effects on G-7 inflation.

Third, ENSO's influence is much stronger over the longer horizon, accounting for almost 20% of the variation in real primary commodity prices, which is quite consistent with the anecdotal evidence discussed previously. Most of the effects on commodity prices are attributable to ENSO's effects on food prices, and more than 20% of the variation in these prices are accounted for by ENSO shocks. Beverage, metal, and agricultural raw material prices are also moved around a bit by both ENSO measures, although the confidence bounds for these estimates are somewhat wider and the two ENSO measures do not agree as closely. Similarly, the ENSO measures also provide a wide range of estimates for the effects on CPI inflation (13% to 18%) and economic activity (10% to 13%).

Table 3 shows the contribution of SST anomalies to those commodities most affected by ENSO events. The table conforms well with the anecdotal evidence discussed in section II. Coconut oil is the most affected commodity, with ENSO accounting for about one-third of its variance. Other oils (palm, soybean, and groundnut) are also highly affected, as are several other food items (rice, wheat, soybeans, and maize). Other tropical commodity prices (fish meal and rubber prices) and some metals (iron ore and copper) also appear to be influenced by ENSO events.

Finally, figure 5 presents the historical decomposition of the forecast errors for the three economic variables with respect to SST anomalies. The solid line in each panel represents the four-quarter-ahead forecast error for each variable at each point in time, and the dashed line denotes the portion of that error than can be attributed to SST shocks. The results are consistent with the previous ones.

The upper panel shows that most of the estimated effects of ENSO on commodity prices are associated with the 1982–83 and 1986–87 El Niño events. Although ENSO likely had important effects on commodity prices during the 1970s, these effects were overwhelmed by other factors, such as the oil price shocks and subsequent goods price inflation. The lower panels indicate that, although ENSO has had some influence on overall price inflation and economic activity in the past couple of decades, that influence is not as economically and statistically important as its influence on commodity prices.

V. Conclusion

This paper examined the historical effects of ENSO on world prices and world economic activity. The primary focus was on world real primary commodity prices, although the effects on G-7 consumer price inflation and GNP growth were also considered. This paper has several distinct advantages over previous studies. First, econometric models were estimated using fairly broad measures of economic activity. Second, the models included continuous measures of ENSO intensity (sea surface temperature and sea-level air-pressure anomalies in the Pacific Ocean) rather than dummy variable measures. Finally, confidence intervals were constructed for all estimated effects of ENSO on world prices and economic activity.

The analysis indicates that ENSO has a economically important and statistically significant effect on world real commodity prices. A one-standard-deviation positive surprise in ENSO, for example, raises commodity price inflation about 3.5 to 4 percentage points. Moreover, ENSO appears to account for almost 20% of real commodity price inflation movements over the past several years. ENSO also has some explanatory power for world consumer price inflation and world economic activity, accounting for about 10% to 20% of movements in those variables.

REFERENCES

Adams, Richard M., Kelly J. Bryant, Bruce A. McCarl, David Legler, James O'Brien, Andrew Solow, and Rodney Weiher, "Value of Improved Long-Range Weather Information," *Contemporary Economic Policy* 13 (1995), 10–19.

Brunner, Allan D., "El Niño and World Primary Commodity Prices: Warm Water or Hot Air?" International Monetary Fund working paper (2000).

Cline, William R., "The Impact of Global Warming on Agriculture: Comment," *The American Economic Review* 86:5 (1996), 1309–1311.

Day, R. H., "Probability Distributions of Field Crops," *Journal of Farm Economics* 47:3 (1965), 713–743.

Debelle, Guy, and Glenn Stevens, "Monetary Policy Goals for Inflation in Australia," Reserve Bank of Australia Research discussion paper no. 9503 (1995).

Engle, Robert F., C. W. J. Granger, John Rice, and Andrew Weiss, "Semiparametric Estimates of the Relation between Weather and Electricity Sales," *Journal of the American Statistical Association* 81 (1986), 310–320.

Electric Power Research Institute, "Regional Load-Curve Models: QUERI's Model Specification, Estimation and Validation," EA-1672, Palo Alto, CA (1981).

———, "Weather Normalization of Electricity Sales," EA-3142, Palo Alto, CA (1983).

Handler, Paul, "Climatic Anomalies in the Tropical Pacific Ocean and Corn Yields in the United States," *Science* 20 (1983), 1155–1156.

Jevons, W. Stanely, "Commercial Crises and Sunspots" (pp. *Investigations in Currencies and Finance,* edited by H. S. Foxwell, London: McMillan and Company, Ltd.

Lawrence, Anthony, and Dennis Aigner (Eds.), "Modelling and Forecasting Time-of-Day and Seasonal Electricity Demands," *Journal of Econometrics* 9:1–2 (1979),

Maddala, G. S., Robert P. Trost, Hongyi Li, and Frederick Joutz, "Estimation of Short-run and Long-run Elasticitities of Energy Demand from Panel Data Using Shrinkage Estimators," *Journal of Business and Economic Statistics,* 15 (January 1997), 90–100.

Mendelsohn, Robert, William Nordhaus, and Daigee Shaw, "The Impact of Global Warming on Agriculture: A Ricardian Analysis," *The American Economic Review* 84 (1994), 753–771.

Norrbin, Stefan C., and Don E. Schlagenhauf, "An Inquiry Into the Sources of Macroeconomic Fluctuations," *Journal of Monetary Economics* 22 (1988), 43–70.

Saunders, Edward M, "Stock Prices and Wall Street Weather," *The American Economic Review* 83:5 (1993), 1337–1345.

Solomou, Solomos, and Weike Wu, "The Impact of Weather on the Construction Sector Output Variations, 1955–1989," DAE working papers no. 9722, University of Cambridge, Cambridge, UK (1997).

Solow, Andrew, Richard F. Adams, Kelly J. Bryant, David Legler, James O'Brien, Bruce A. McCarl, William Nayda, and Rodney Weiher, "The Value of Improved ENSO Prediction to U.S. Agriculture," *Climatic Change* 39 (1998), 47–60.

DATA APPENDIX

This appendix describes the data that were used in this paper.

ENSO Measures

Sea surface temperatures (SST) and Southern Oscillation index (SOI) measures were obtained from NOAA's Climate Prediction Center database. The data were standardized by subtracting seasonal means and dividing by seasonal standard deviations.

Commodity Prices

The commodity price indexes were obtained from the IMF's *International Financial Statistics* database. The overall index, for example, is a weighted average of over 30 non-oil primary commodity prices, including foods (33 percent), beverages (7 percent), agricultural raw materials (32 percent), metals (27 percent), and fertilizers (1 percent). The weights are based on world export earnings for each commodity.

Consumer Prices and GDP

Consumer price and GDP indexes for the G-7 countries (Canada, France, Germany, Italy, Japan, the United Kingdom, and the United States) were also obtained from the IMF's *International Financial Statistics* database. Weighted indexes for the G-7 as a whole were constructed using weights based on PPP-adjusted income for each country.

[6]

The Impact of Global Warming on Agriculture:
A Ricardian Analysis

By Robert Mendelsohn, William D. Nordhaus, and Daigee Shaw*

We measure the economic impact of climate on land prices. Using cross-sectional data on climate, farmland prices, and other economic and geophysical data for almost 3,000 counties in the United States, we find that higher temperatures in all seasons except autumn reduce average farm values, while more precipitation outside of autumn increases farm values. Applying the model to a global-warming scenario shows a significantly lower estimated impact of global warming on U.S. agriculture than the traditional production-function approach and, in one case, suggests that, even without CO_2 fertilization, global warming may have economic benefits for agriculture. (JEL Q10, Q25)

Over the last decade, scientists have extensively studied the greenhouse effect, which holds that the accumulation of carbon dioxide (CO_2) and other greenhouse gases (GHG's) is expected to produce global warming and other significant climatic changes over the next century. Numerous studies indicate major impacts on agriculture, especially if there is significant midcontinental drying and warming in the U.S. heartland.[1] Virtually every estimate of economic impacts relies on a technique we denote the production-function approach.

This study compares the traditional production-function approach to estimating the impacts of climate change with a new "Ricardian" approach that examines the impact of climate and other variables on land values and farm revenues. The traditional approach to estimating the impact of climate change relies upon empirical or experimental production functions to predict environmental damage (hence its label in this study as the production-function approach).[2] This approach takes an underlying production function and estimates impacts by varying one or a few input variables, such as temperature, precipitation, and carbon dioxide levels. The estimates might rely on extremely carefully calibrated crop-yield models (such as CERES or SOYGRO) to determine the impact upon yields; the results often predict severe yield reductions as a result of global warming.

While providing a useful baseline for estimating the impact of climate change on farming, these studies have an inherent bias and will tend to overestimate the damage. This bias is sometimes called the "dumb-farmer scenario" to suggest that it omits a

*Mendelsohn: School of Forestry and Environmental Studies and the Department of Economics, Yale University, 360 Prospect Street, New Haven, CT 06511; Nordhaus: Department of Economics and Cowles Foundation, Yale University, P.O. Box 1972, Yale Station, New Haven, CT 06511; Shaw: Institute of Economics, Academia Sinica, Taipei, Republic of China. We thank the National Science Foundation and Economic Research Service, USDA, for funding this project, although all views are the authors' alone. We also thank John Miranowski, Daniel Hellerstein, John Reilly, Katherine Segerson, Paul Waggoner, and referees for their assistance and advice, and we thank Susan Helms for producing the color maps in this paper. Correspondence regarding the paper should be addressed to Mendelsohn at the above address.

[1] See particularly the reports of the Intergovernmental Panel on Climate Change (1990) and the National Academy of Sciences Panel on Greenhouse Warming (1992).

[2] Important studies include John Callaway et al. (1982), W. Decker et al. 1986, Richard Adams et al. (1988, 1990), Adams (1989), D. Rind et al. (1990), and Cynthia Rosenzweig and Martin L. Parry (1994). For useful surveys, see National Research Council (1983), Joel Smith and Dennis Tirpak (1989), National Academy of Sciences (1992), and William Cline (1992).

754   THE AMERICAN ECONOMIC REVIEW   SEPTEMBER 1994

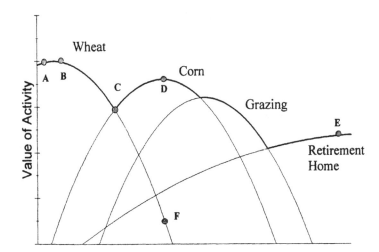

Temperature or Environmental Variable

FIGURE 1. BIAS IN PRODUCTION-FUNCTION STUDIES

variety of the adaptations that farmers customarily make in response to changing economic and environmental conditions. Most studies assume little adaptation and simply calculate the impact of changing temperature on farm yields. Others allow limited changes in fertilizer application, irrigation, or cultivars (see William Easterling et al., 1991). None permits a full adjustment to changing environmental conditions by the farmer. For example, the literature does not consider the introduction of completely new crops (such as tropical crops in the south); technological change; changes in land use from farming to livestock, grassland, or forestry; or conversion to cities, retirement homes, campsites, or the 1,001 other productive uses of land in a modern postindustrial society.

By not permitting a complete range of adjustments, previous studies have overestimated damages from environmental changes. Figure 1 shows the hypothetical values of output in four different sectors as a function of a single environmental variable, temperature, in order to illustrate the general nature of the bias. In each case, we

assume that the production-function approach yields an accurate assessment of the economic value of the activity as a function of temperature. The four functions provide a simplified example of how the value of wheat, corn, grazing, and retirement homes might look as a function of the temperature. For example, the curve to the far left is a hypothetical "wheat production function," showing how the value of wheat varies with temperature, rising from cold temperatures such as point A, then peaking at point B, finally falling as temperatures rise too high. A production-function approach would estimate the value of wheat production at different temperatures along this curve.

The bias in the production-function approach arises because it fails to allow for economic substitution as conditions change. For example, when the temperature rises above point C, adaptive and profit-maximizing farmers will switch from wheat to corn. As temperature rises, the production-function approach might calculate that the yield has fallen to F in wheat, but wheat is in reality no longer produced; the realized value is actually much higher, at point D

VOL. 84 NO. 4   *MENDELSOHN ET AL.: IMPACT OF GLOBAL WARMING*   755

where corn is now produced. At a slightly higher temperature, the land is no longer optimally used for corn but switches to grazing, and production-function estimates that do not allow for this conversion will again overestimate the losses from climate change. Finally, at point E, even the best agricultural model will predict that the land is unsuitable for farming or grazing and that the damage is severe. A more complete approach might find that the land has been converted to retirement villages, to which old folks flock so they can putter around in the warm winters and dry climates.

All this is of course illustrative. However, it makes the crucial point that the production-function approach will overestimate the damages from climate change because it does not, and indeed cannot, take into account the infinite variety of substitutions, adaptations, and old and new activities that may displace no-longer-advantageous activities as climate changes.

In this study, we develop a new technique that in principle can correct for the bias in the production-function technique by using economic data on the value of land. We call this the *Ricardian approach*, in which, instead of studying yields of specific crops, we examine how climate in different places affects the net rent or value of farmland. By directly measuring farm prices or revenues, we account for the direct impacts of climate on yields of different crops as well as the indirect substitution of different inputs, introduction of different activities, and other potential adaptations to different climates. If markets are functioning properly, the Ricardian approach will allow us to measure the economic value of different activities and therefore to verify whether the economic impacts implied by the production-function approach are reproduced in the field.

The results of the Ricardian approach can be seen in Figure 1. We assume that the "value" measured along the vertical axis is the net yield per acre of land; more precisely, it is the value of output less the value of all inputs (excluding land rents). Under competitive markets, the land rent will be equal to the net yield of the highest and

best use of the land. This rent will in fact be equal to the heavy solid line in Figure 1. We label the solid line in Figure 1 the "best-use value function."

In general, we do not observe market land rents because land rent is generally a small component of the total profits. However, with farms, land rents tend to be a large fraction of total costs and can be estimated with reasonable precision. Farm value is the present value of future rents, so if the interest rate, rate of capital gains, and capital per acre are equal for all parcels, then farm value will be proportional to the land rent. Therefore, by observing the relationship of farm values to climatic and other variables, we can infer the shape of the solid, best-use value function in Figure 1.[3]

This study measures the effect of climatic variables on agriculture. We examine both climatic data and a variety of fundamental geographical, geophysical, agricultural, economic, and demographic factors to determine the intrinsic value of climate on farmland. The units of observation are U.S. counties in the lower 48 states. We examine the effect of climatic variables as well as nonclimatic variables on both land values and farm revenue, and the analysis includes a number of urban variables in order to measure the potential effect of development upon agricultural land values. The analysis suggests that climate has a systematic impact on agricultural rents through temperature and precipitation. These effects tend to be highly nonlinear and vary dramatically by season. The paper concludes with a discussion of the impacts of global warming on American farms.

I. Measuring the Effect of Climate on Agriculture

Using the Ricardian technique, we estimate the value of climate in U.S. agriculture. Agriculture is the most appealing application of the Ricardian technique both because of the significant impact of climate

---

[3] The analytical basis for the present empirical study is presented in Mendelsohn et al. (1993).

on agricultural productivity and because of the extensive county-level data on farm inputs and outputs.

Sources and Methods

The basic hypothesis is that climate shifts the production function for crops. Farmers at particular sites take environmental variables like climate as given and adjust their inputs and outputs accordingly. Moreover, we assume perfect competition in both product and input markets. Most important, we assume that the economy has completely adapted to the given climate so that land prices have attained the long-run equilibrium that is associated with each county's climate.

For the most part, the data are actual county averages, from the *1982 U.S. Census of Agriculture*, so that there are no major issues involved in obtaining information on these variables.[4] The *County and City Data Book* (U.S. Bureau of the Census, 1988) and the computer tapes of those data are the sources for much of the agricultural data used here, including values of farm products sold per acre, farm land and building values,[5] and information on market inputs for farms in every county in the United States. In addition, in many specifications, we include social, demographic, and economic data on each of the counties; these as well are drawn from the *County and City Data Book*.

Data about soils were extracted from the National Resource Inventory (NRI) with the kind assistance of Daniel Hellerstein and Noel Gollehon of the U.S. Department of Agriculture. The NRI is an extensive survey of land characteristics in the United States. For almost 800,000 sites, NRI has collected soil samples, or land characteristics, each providing a measure of salinity, permeability, moisture capacity, clay content, sand content, flood probability, soil erosion

(K-factor), rain erosion (R-factor), slope length, wind erosion, whether or not the land is a wetland, and numerous other variables that are not used in this analysis. Each sample also contains an expansion factor, which is an estimate of the amount of land the sample represents in that county. Using these expansion factors, we aggregate these data to yield an overall county estimate for each soil variable.

Climatic data pose more difficult issues. They are available by meteorological station rather than by county, so it was necessary to estimate county-average climates. To begin with, climate data were obtained from the National Climatic Data Center, which gathers data from 5,511 meteorological stations throughout the United States. These stations form a dense set of observations for most regions of the United States, with the exception of some of the desert Southwest. The data include information on precipitation and temperature for each month from 1951 through 1980. Since the purpose of this study is to predict the impacts of climate changes on agriculture, we focus on the long-run impacts of precipitation and temperature on agriculture, not year-to-year variations in weather. We consequently examine the "normal" climatological variables —the 30-year average of each climatic variable for every station. In this analysis, we collect data on normal daily mean temperature and normal monthly precipitation for January, April, July, and October. We focus on these four months in order to capture seasonal effects of each variable. For example, cold January temperatures may be important as a control on insect pests, warm-but-not-hot summers may be good for crop growth, and warm October temperatures may assist in crop harvesting.

In order to link the agricultural data which are organized by county and the climate data which are organized by station, we conduct a spatial statistical analysis that examines the determinants of the climate of each county. Although the specific climatic variables we analyze in this study have been measured frequently, there are some counties with no weather stations and others with several. Some of the weather stations

---

[4]Appendix A contains complete descriptions and definitions of the variables used in this study.

[5]The definition and source of the farm value variable is critical to this study, and its derivation is described in Appendix B.

TABLE 1—INTERPOLATION FOR COUNTY CLIMATE MEASURES (FRESNO, CA)

| | Temperature | | | Precipitation | | |
Independent variable	April	July	October	April	July	October
Constant	131,535	231,764	124,970	−58,846	−184,063*	16,551
Longitude	−32.8*	−59.6*	−29.2	26.7	45.2*	1.96
Latitude	−13.2	−18.2	−16.8	−19.6	21.7*	−16.33
Latitude squared	1.9×10^{-4}	2.8×10^{-4}	4.1×10^{-4}	1.6×10^{-3}	-3.1×10^{-4}	$1.6 \times 10^{-3*}$
Longitude squared	$2.0 \times 10^{-3*}$	$3.8 \times 10^{-3*}$	1.7×10^{-3}	-2.3×10^{-3}	$-2.7 \times 10^{-3*}$	-3.9×10^{-4}
Longitude × latitude	1.8×10^{-3}	$2.8 \times 10^{-3*}$	2.1×10^{-3}	1.5×10^{-3}	$-2.9 \times 10^{-3*}$	1.1×10^{-3}
Altitude	−0.56*	−1.44*	−1.00*	0.525	1.28*	1.48*
Altitude squared	$-1.6 \times 10^{-6*}$	$-3.0 \times 10^{-6*}$	$-2.3 \times 10^{-6*}$	$-3.7 \times 10^{-6*}$	$-6.5 \times 10^{-7*}$	$-2.4 \times 10^{-6*}$
Latitude × altitude	4.3×10^{-5}	8.8×10^{-5}	$7.7 \times 10^{-5*}$	-4.8×10^{-5}	$-1.1 \times 10^{-4*}$	$-1.1 \times 10^{-4*}$
Longitude × altitude	6.2×10^{-5}	$1.8 \times 10^{-4*}$	$1.1 \times 10^{-4*}$	-4.6×10^{-5}	$-1.5 \times 10^{-4*}$	$-1.7 \times 10^{-4*}$
Distance	−40.4*	−74.5*	−35.2	−5.47	59.4*	−26.6
Distance squared	2.6×10^{-3}	4.2×10^{-3}	2.2×10^{-3}	2.9×10^{-3}	$-4.9 \times 10^{-3*}$	$4.8 \times 10^{-3*}$
Distance × longitude	$5.2 \times 10^{-3*}$	$9.6 \times 10^{-3*}$	4.2×10^{-3}	-1.3×10^{-3}	$-6.7 \times 10^{-3*}$	2.6×10^{-3}
Distance × latitude	2.0×10^{-3}	3.7×10^{-3}	2.3×10^{-3}	4.3×10^{-3}	$-4.9 \times 10^{-3*}$	2.7×10^{-3}
Distance × altitude	6.7×10^{-5}	1.3×10^{-4}	$9.7 \times 10^{-5*}$	-1.9×10^{-4}	$-7.0 \times 10^{-5*}$	$-2.3 \times 10^{-4*}$
Adjusted R^2:	0.999	0.998	0.999	0.796	0.777	0.706
Standard error:	0.13	0.24	0.13	0.54	0.13	0.30
Number of observations:	331	331	331	525	525	525

Notes: Temperature is measured in Fahrenheit, and precipitation is in inches per month.
*Statistically significant at the 5-percent level.

are not in representative locations, such as the station on the top of Mt. Washington. Furthermore, some counties are large enough or contain sufficient topographical complexity that there is variation of climate within the county. We therefore proceeded by constructing an average climate for each county.

First, we assume that all the weather stations within 500 miles of the geographic center of the county provide some useful climate information. The 500-mile circle invariably draws in many stations, so that our measure does not depend too heavily on any one station.

Second, we estimate a climate surface in the vicinity of the county by running a weighted regression across all weather stations within 500 miles. The weight is the inverse of the square root of a station's distance from the county center because we recognize that closer stations contain more information about the climate of the center. We estimate a separate regression for each county since the set of stations within 500 miles and the weights (distances) are unique for each county. The dependent variables

are the monthly normal temperatures and precipitation amounts for January, April, July, and October for the 30-year period. The independent variables include latitude, longitude, altitude, and distance from closest shoreline. The regression fits a second-order polynomial over these four basic variables, including interactive terms, so that there are 14 final variables in the regression, plus a constant term. Eight regressions (4 seasons × 2 measures) for each of 3,000 counties leads to over 24,000 estimated regressions.

Third, we calculate the predicted value of each climatic variable for the geographic center of the county. The predicted values of normal precipitation and temperature from the climate regressions are the independent variables for climate in the property-value regressions. This complicated interpolation procedure is intended to provide geographically accurate estimates of the climatic variables for each county.

The estimates of the climate parameters for individual counties are too numerous to present, but we show two selected counties in Tables 1 and 2. These show the indepen-

TABLE 2—INTERPOLATION FOR COUNTY CLIMATE MEASURES (DES MOINES, IOWA)

Independent variable	Temperature			Precipitation		
	April	July	October	April	July	October
Constant	6,425	5,006	8,967	−32,243	77,324*	41,650
Longitude	−0.919	−1.12	−2.55	7.72	−15.8*	−9.61
Latitude	−2.48	−0.829	−1.55	10.0	−32.9*	−16.32
Latitude squared	2.5×10^{-4}	2.0×10^{-5}	3.2×10^{-5}	-9.7×10^{-4}	$3.2 \times 10^{-3*}$	1.6×10^{-3}
Longitude squared	3.7×10^{-5}	8.1×10^{-5}	2.0×10^{-4}	-4.9×10^{-4}	6.8×10^{-4}	5.9×10^{-4}
Longitude × latitude	2.0×10^{-4}	1.0×10^{-4}	2.4×10^{-4}	-9.9×10^{-4}	$3.8 \times 10^{-3*}$	1.8×10^{-3}
Altitude	−0.13	0.046	0.34*	0.353	3.02*	2.09*
Altitude squared	-1.2×10^{-6}	$-1.3 \times 10^{-6*}$	$1.6 \times 10^{-6*}$	$1.1 \times 10^{-5*}$	-1.5×10^{-6}	$2.1 \times 10^{-5*}$
Latitude × altitude	2.1×10^{-5}	-1.6×10^{-5}	$-6.9 \times 10^{-5*}$	-1.2×10^{-4}	$-5.7 \times 10^{-4*}$	$-2.8 \times 10^{-4*}$
Longitude × altitude	1.1×10^{-5}	-9.7×10^{-6}	$-4.9 \times 10^{-5*}$	-3.1×10^{-5}	$-3.6 \times 10^{-4*}$	$-3.2 \times 10^{-4*}$
Distance	1.14	−1.17	−0.564	−0.150	26.8	18.6
Distance squared	1.8×10^{-4}	-3.1×10^{-4}	-1.9×10^{-4}	5.8×10^{-4}	-1.2×10^{-3}	1.4×10^{-3}
Distance × longitude	-4.4×10^{-5}	1.9×10^{-4}	-1.2×10^{-4}	-4.1×10^{-4}	-2.7×10^{-3}	-1.9×10^{-3}
Distance × latitude	-3.6×10^{-4}	2.2×10^{-4}	9.0×10^{-5}	4.2×10^{-4}	$-5.4 \times 10^{-3*}$	-3.8×10^{-3}
Distance × altitude	-2.2×10^{-5}	3.2×10^{-5}	$9.9 \times 10^{-5*}$	-1.7×10^{-4}	$6.9 \times 10^{-4*}$	$3.6 \times 10^{-4*}$
Adjusted R^2:	0.999	0.999	0.999	0.989	0.987	0.976
Standard error:	0.04	0.04	0.04	0.14	0.17	0.15
Number of observations:	928	928	928	1,477	1,477	1,477

Notes: Temperature is measured in Fahrenheit, and precipitation is in inches per month.
  *Statistically significant at the 5-percent level.

dent variables as well as the coefficients and summary regression statistics for Fresno, California, and Des Moines, Iowa. Note that more coefficients are significant in the Fresno regressions than in the Des Moines regressions. There is more variation across the sample in Fresno because of the effects of the coast and nearby mountain ranges. Although there are more significant coefficients in the California regression, the Iowa regression has a better overall fit and smaller standard errors. In general, the fit east of 100 degrees longitude (the east slope of the Rocky Mountains) was tighter than in the West.

In order to gain some sense of the reliability of this geographic approximation method, we predicted the climate for each of the weather stations. Dropping the weather station itself, we predicted the climatic variables for the station from all stations within 500 miles in the manner explained above. Comparing these results with the actual measurements from each station reveals that the approximation method predicts between 87 percent and 97 percent of the variation in precipitation in the

continental United States and between 97 percent and 99 percent of the variation in temperature. It should be noted that, even in a statistically stationary environment, the observations of "climate" themselves contain error because they contain only 30 observations. Depending upon the relative importance of idiosyncratic error in climate versus misspecification error in our equation, the predictions might actually be superior to the recorded observations themselves. In any case, the predictions serve as sophisticated interpolations of the climate between stations.

II. Empirical Analysis

The Ricardian approach estimates the importance of climate and other variables on farmland values. As noted above, land values are the expected present value of future rents. There is little reason for the riskless interest rate to vary across counties in the United States, but the risk and capital-gains components of land value might vary considerably. For example, California agricultural land near growing cities might well have a larger capital-gains component than would rural land in an economically stagnant coal-mining region of Appalachia. Moreover, there are major potential errors in measurement of land values since values are estimated by farmers, and such estimates are often unreliable. However, there is no reason to believe that the errors of measurement are correlated with independent data such as temperature or precipitation. The major effect of measurement errors will be imprecision of the econometric estimates rather than bias in the estimation of the coefficients or in the estimate of the economic value of climate on agriculture.

We regress land values on climate, soil, and socioeconomic variables to estimate the best-value function across different counties. There are 2,933 cross-sectional observations. The means have been removed from the independent variables in this regression. The quadratic climate variables are consequently easier to interpret. The linear term reflects the marginal value of climate evaluated at the U.S. mean, while the quadratic term shows how that marginal effect will change as one moves away from the mean.

We present several regressions in Table 3. In order to give a sense of the importance of the nonfarm variables in the model, we begin with a model that contains only climate variables. The first set of regressions in Table 3 is a quadratic model that includes the eight measures of climate (four months of precipitation and temperature). For each variable, linear and quadratic terms are included to reflect the nonlinearities that are apparent from field studies.

In the remainder of regressions, we include urban, soil, and other environmental variables to control for extraneous factors influencing land values and farm revenues. This raises the question of how the counties should be weighted. A first set of regressions uses the *cropland weights*, in which observations are weighted by the percentage of each county in cropland. Counties with a large fraction of cropland should provide a better reading on price determination because other influences, such as cities or forests, are minimized; these results are particularly useful for the grain belt. A second set of regressions uses *crop-revenue weights*; that is, observations are weighted by the aggregate value of crop revenue in each county. This second weighting scheme emphasizes those counties that are most important to total agricultural production, even though some of the counties might have their land values affected by large neighboring cities; it also places greater weight on counties where more valuable crops are grown. On the whole, the cropland measure tends to emphasize the corn, wheat, and soybean belt and therefore reflects the influence of climate on the grains. The crop-revenue weights, by contrast, give more influence to the truck farms and citrus belt of the coast lands, and the crop-revenue regressions thus reflect a broader definition of agriculture.

The results of this analysis are shown in columns (ii)–(v) of Table 3. The squared terms for most of the climate variables are significant, implying that the observed relationships are nonlinear. However, some of the squared terms are positive, especially for precipitation, implying that there is a minimally productive level of precipitation and that either more or less precipitation will increase land values. The negative quadratic coefficient implies that there is an optimal level of a climatic variable from which the value function decreases in both directions.

The overall impact of climate as measured by the marginal impacts is largely the same across the different models, although the quantitative estimates vary. All models suggest that higher winter and summer temperatures are harmful for crops; that higher fall temperatures and higher winter and spring rainfall are beneficial for crops; but that higher summer or fall rainfall is harmful. The two weighting schemes differ, however, in terms of their assessment of the relative importance of winter versus summer temperature. The cropland model finds higher winter temperatures less harmful, valuing a 1°F increase by between $89 and $103 per acre, whereas the crop-revenue model finds this effect more harmful, with estimated impacts between $138 and $160

TABLE 3—REGRESSION MODELS EXPLAINING FARM VALUES

	Cropland weights			Crop-revenue weights	
Independent variables	1982 (i)	1982 (ii)	1978 (iii)	1982 (iv)	1978 (v)
Constant	1,490 (71.20)	1,329 (60.18)	1,173 (57.95)	1,451 (46.36)	1,307 (52.82)
January temperature	−57.0 (6.22)	−88.6 (9.94)	−103 (12.55)	−160 (12.97)	−138 (13.83)
January temperature squared	−0.33 (1.43)	−1.34 (6.39)	−2.11 (11.03)	−2.68 (9.86)	−3.00 (14.11)
April temperature	−137 (10.81)	−18.0 (1.56)	23.6 (2.23)	13.6 (1.00)	31.8 (2.92)
April temperature squared	−7.32 (9.42)	−4.90 (7.43)	−4.31 (7.11)	−6.69 (9.44)	−6.63 (11.59)
July temperature	−167 (13.10)	−155 (14.50)	−177 (18.07)	−87.7 (6.80)	−132 (12.55)
July temperature squared	−3.81 (5.08)	−2.95 (4.68)	−3.87 (6.69)	−0.30 (0.53)	−1.27 (2.82)
October temperature	351.9 (19.37)	192 (11.08)	175 (11.01)	217 (8.89)	198 (9.94)
October temperature squared	6.91 (6.38)	6.62 (7.09)	7.65 (8.93)	12.4 (12.50)	12.4 (15.92)
January rain	75.1 (3.28)	85.0 (3.88)	56.5 (2.81)	280 (9.59)	172 (7.31)
January rain squared	−5.66 (1.86)	2.73 (0.95)	2.20 (0.82)	−10.8 (3.64)	−4.09 (1.72)
April rain	110 (4.03)	104 (4.44)	128 (5.91)	82.8 (2.34)	113 (4.05)
April rain squared	−10.8 (1.17)	−16.5 (1.96)	−10.8 (1.41)	−62.1 (5.52)	−30.6 (3.35)
July rain	−25.6 (1.87)	−34.5 (2.63)	−11.3 (0.94)	−116 (6.06)	−5.28 (0.34)
July rain squared	19.5 (3.42)	52.0 (9.43)	37.8 (7.54)	57.0 (8.20)	34.8 (6.08)
October rain	−2.30 (0.09)	−50.3 (2.25)	−91.6 (4.45)	−124 (3.80)	−135 (5.15)
October rain squared	−39.9 (2.65)	2.28 (0.17)	0.25 (0.02)	171 (14.17)	106 (11.25)
Income per capita		71.0 (15.25)	65.3 (15.30)	48.5 (6.36)	47.1 (7.39)
Density		1.30 (18.51)	1.05 (16.03)	1.53 (18.14)	1.17 (17.66)
Density squared		-1.72×10^{-4} (5.31)	-9.33×10^{-5} (3.22)	-2.04×10^{-4} (7.47)	-9.38×10^{-5} (4.57)
Latitude		−90.5 (6.12)	−94.4 (6.95)	−105 (5.43)	−85.8 (5.33)
Altitude		−0.167 (6.09)	−0.161 (6.41)	−0.163 (4.72)	−0.149 (5.20)
Salinity		−684 (3.34)	−416 (2.20)	−582 (2.59)	−153 (0.81)
Flood-prone		−163 (3.34)	−309 (6.98)	−663 (8.59)	−740 (11.99)
Wetland		−58.2 (0.47)	−57.5 (0.51)	762 (4.41)	230 (1.72)
Soil erosion		−1,258 (6.20)	−1,513 (8.14)	−2,690 (8.21)	−2,944 (11.23)
Slope length		17.3 (2.91)	13.7 (2.49)	54.0 (6.24)	30.9 (4.54)
Sand		−139 (2.72)	−35.9 (0.77)	−288 (4.16)	−213 (3.95)
Clay		86.2 (4.08)	67.3 (3.47)	−7.90 (0.22)	−18.0 (0.63)
Moisture capacity		0.377 (9.69)	0.510 (14.21)	0.206 (3.82)	0.450 (10.07)
Permeability		−0.002 (1.06)	−0.005 (2.53)	−0.013 (5.58)	−0.017 (8.61)
Adjusted R^2:	0.671	0.782	0.784	0.836	0.835
Number of observations:	2,938	2,938	2,941	2,941	2,941

Notes: The dependent variable is the value of land and buildings per acre. All regressions are weighted. Values in parenthesis are t statistics.

per acre. However, a 1°F increase in summer temperature decreases farm values by only $88–$132 according to the crop-revenue model but by between $155 and $177 in the cropland model. Except for spring rains, the crop-revenue model suggests that rain has a much larger effect on land value than the cropland model. For example, the crop-revenue model suggests that winter rain increases farm values between $172 and $280 per monthly inch, whereas the cropland model suggests an effect between $57 and $85 per monthly inch.

The predicted overall effects from the existing climate across the United States are shown in Figures 2 and 3. These maps show the *Ricardian values of climate* by county in 1982, that is, the partial effect of climate on property values. To construct each map, we begin with the difference between the estimated climate for each county and the national average climate. We then multiply these differences by the estimated coefficients in Table 3 and sum them across the climate variables. Figures 2 and 3 show the estimated contribution of climate to the farmland value in each county. The results match folk wisdom about farm values (for example, the infamous 100th meridian of American history can be seen sharply in Figure 2). The most valuable climates are along the west coast, the corn belt near Chicago, and the northeast. The least valuable areas are the southwest and southeast regions. Both figures show almost identical geographic patterns, indicating that the results are stable; similar results were also found using 1978 data.

The control variables in Table 3 provide a rich set of results in and of themselves. Economic and soil variables play a role in determining the value of farms. Farm values are higher in denser, growing, and wealthier counties because of higher local demand for food and the potential for conversion of land to nonfarm uses. Farm values respond as expected to other environmental factors such as solar flux (latitude) and altitude. Salinity, likelihood of flooding, presence of wetlands, and soil erosion all act negatively as expected. Slope length was slightly bene-

ficial to land values. Irrigation is left out of the regressions shown in Table 3 because irrigation is clearly an endogenous reaction to climate. However, when included, irrigation is a strongly positive variable, increasing land values substantially; which is not surprising, given the crucial importance of irrigation in many areas of the arid West.[6]

One hypothesis suggested in the theory section is that the impacts of environmental effects would be exaggerated by a gross-revenue model. We explore this hypothesis in Table 4 by regressing the same climate and contol variables on the gross revenue earned from crops. The marginal effects in Table 4 for the farm-revenue model suggest similar seasonal patterns as the farm-value equation with the exception of spring. Warmer Aprils reduce farm revenues, whereas they increase farm values. Wetter springs, good for farm values, reduce farm revenues according to the cropland model but increase farm revenues according to the crop-revenue model.

The magnitude of damages predicted by the gross-revenue model, however, are generally larger than the effects predicted by the Ricardian model. To compare the two approaches, we need to translate the annual rents into land value using the discount rate defined in Section II. Based on asset returns and farm earnings, a real discount rate of 5 percent per annum appears most suitable.[7] At this discount rate, the marginal coefficients in Table 4 should be multiplied

---

[6] Including irrigation does not significantly change the results of the paper.

[7] According to Roger Ibbotson and Gary Brinson (1987), farmland prices over the period 1947–1984 had a compound annual return (income and capital gains) of 9.6 percent while the GNP deflator rose at an average of 4.4 percent annually. This produces an average real yield of 4.99 percent per annum. By comparison, all real-estate investments had an average real yield of 4.4 percent per annum over this period. Another comparison is the rate of profit on farms, defined as the net income of farms divided by total value of farms and farmland. For the three census years of 1974, 1978, and 1982, the average rate of profit on farms was 5.02 percent per annum.

TABLE 4—REGRESSION MODELS EXPLAINING FARM REVENUES

Independent variables	Cropland weights		Crop-revenue weights	
	1982 (i)	1978 (ii)	1982 (iii)	1978 (iv)
Constant	180	143	213	186
	(31.37)	(28.09)	(16.61)	(16.27)
January temperature	−11.6	−6.65	16.1	16.4
	(5.00)	(3.21)	(3.19)	(3.55)
January temperature squared	−0.048	0.006	0.867	0.659
	(0.88)	(0.13)	(7.80)	(6.71)
April temperature	−23.5	−20.3	−47.7	−39.3
	(7.89)	(7.63)	(8.62)	(7.83)
April temperature squared	−1.31	−1.12	−2.74	−2.26
	(7.67)	(7.43)	(9.43)	(8.55)
July temperature	−27.2	−21.5	−10.0	−7.20
	(9.85)	(8.66)	(1.90)	(1.49)
July temperature squared	0.053	−0.166	1.27	0.341
	(0.32)	(1.14)	(5.52)	(1.65)
October temperature	51.3	41.4	−2.12	2.92
	(11.43)	(10.43)	(0.21)	(0.32)
October temperature squared	0.637	0.598	−0.025	0.569
	(2.62)	(2.85)	(0.06)	(1.58)
January rain	30.1	21.4	−28.9	−11.5
	(5.29)	(4.26)	(2.42)	(1.06)
January rain squared	−4.10	−2.93	−4.08	−3.33
	(5.49)	(4.49)	(3.36)	(3.04)
April rain	−22.5	−23.2	47.5	16.0
	(3.67)	(4.29)	(3.28)	(1.24)
April rain squared	−2.46	4.65	−5.73	2.65
	(1.12)	(2.39)	(1.24)	(0.63)
July rain	−3.29	2.12	−64.5	−33.3
	(0.97)	(0.70)	(8.25)	(4.61)
July rain squared	10.8	6.74	22.8	13.2
	(6.93)	(5.23)	(8.03)	(5.02)
October rain	−40.2	−16.1	−44.4	−16.3
	(6.93)	(3.17)	(3.32)	(1.35)
October rain squared	27.2	17.4	33.8	9.32
	(7.73)	(5.62)	(6.84)	(2.15)
Income per capita	0.568	0.803	3.37	8.24
	(0.47)	(0.73)	(1.08)	(2.81)
Density	0.172	0.133	0.457	0.280
	(9.46)	(8.47)	(13.28)	(9.14)
Density squared	2.86×10^{-6}	2.92×10^{-6}	-4.47×10^{-5}	-1.92×10^{-5}
	(0.34)	(0.43)	(3.99)	(2.03)
Latitude	−24.3	−15.4	−72.6	−41.6
	(6.28)	(4.44)	(9.15)	(5.59)
Altitude	−0.049	−0.033	−0.096	−0.059
	(6.91)	(5.03)	(6.78)	(4.47)
Salinity	−156	−149	−502	−427
	(2.97)	(3.23)	(5.44)	(4.90)
Flood-prone	29.8	25.4	−40.7	−1.45
	(2.36)	(2.27)	(1.29)	(0.05)
Wetland	70.9	64.8	234	115
	(2.21)	(2.32)	(3.31)	(1.86)
Soil erosion	−169	−74.5	−413	−360
	(3.18)	(1.60)	(3.08)	(2.98)
Slope length	−1.18	−1.21	−15.3	−13.5
	(0.73)	(0.85)	(4.33)	(4.31)
Sand	28.7	32.3	70.3	46.7
	(2.18)	(2.84)	(2.49)	(1.88)
Clay	11.1	12.3	−48.1	−31.8
	(1.99)	(2.49)	(3.32)	(2.43)
Moisture capacity	0.062	0.050	0.101	0.058
	(6.10)	(5.49)	(4.57)	(2.79)
Permeability	0.001	0.001	−0.001	−0.005
	(2.22)	(2.15)	(6.94)	(5.30)
Adjusted R^2:	0.525	0.509	0.800	0.762
Number of observations:	2,834	2,443	2,834	2,443

Notes: The dependent variable is the gross value of crop revenue per acre per year. All regressions are weighted. Values in parenthesis are t statistics.

TABLE 5—PREDICTED IMPACT OF GLOBAL WARMING ON FARMLAND VALUES AND FARM RENTS

Year	Weight	Change in farmland values (billions of dollars, 1982 prices)		Change in farmland rents (percentage of 1982 farm marketings)	
		Impact	Truncated impact	Impact	Truncated impact
1982	Cropland	− $125.2	− $118.8	− 4.4	− 4.2
1978	Cropland	− $162.8	− $141.4	− 5.7	− 4.9
1982	Crop revenue	$34.5	$34.8	1.2	1.2
1978	Crop revenue	− $14.0	$21.0	− 0.5	0.7

Notes: The global-warming scenario is a uniform 5°F increase with a uniform 8-percent precipitation increase. The "impact" column shows the estimated loss; the "truncated impact" columns show the impact when the loss in farmland value in each county is limited to the original value of the land. The last two columns are annualized impacts, as explained in the text, as a percentage of 1982 farm marketings.

by 20 to make them comparable with the present-value estimates in Table 3. Making this adjustment, a 1°F increase in summer temperature decreases the present value of farms by between $140 and $540 according to the gross-revenue model but only between $88 and $177 according to the Ricardian models.

One concern with the Ricardian approach to climate effects is that the results may not be robust over time and that the weather and economic factors in a given year may have distorted the results. We consequently estimated the model again using data from 1978. These values have been converted to 1982 dollars using the GNP deflator obtained from the *1991 Economic Report of the President*. The 1978 results are surprisingly similar to the findings using the 1982 data. The control variables have similar impacts in both years. Evaluating the marginal effects of climate in 1978 at the national mean and comparing the results with 1982 shows that the climatic variables are also similar in 1978 and 1982 with few exceptions. The pattern of climate effects on agriculture is stable over time, but apparently some factors can alter the magnitude of the effects from year to year.

III. Implications for Greenhouse Warming

The Ricardian analysis in the previous section shows that climate has complicated effects on agriculture, highly nonlinear and varying by season. An important application of this analysis is to project the impact of global warming on American agriculture. For this projection, we take a conventional CO_2 doubling scenario, which is associated with a 5°F increase in global mean surface temperature (see Intergovernmental Panel on Climate Change, 1990; National Academy of Sciences Panel on Greenhouse Warming, 1992). According to most projections, such an increase will occur sometime in the second half of the next century if current trends continue. According to the survey by the Intergovernmental Panel on Climate Change, a 5°F temperature increase will be accompanied by an 8-percent average increase in precipitation. These changes are applied uniformly by season and region to the United States in the calculations that follow. In principle, they show the impact of climate change including all adaptations, although they omit the impact of CO_2 fertilization and price effects.

Table 5 shows the results of this experiment for the two years and sets of weights. The "impact" columns show the estimated impact of global warming on farmland values; the "truncated impact" columns truncate these losses if they drive land values below zero. This truncated impact is the preferred economic measure. The estimates diverge dramatically depending upon whether cropland or crop revenues are used for weighting. Under the cropland weights, the loss in land value from warming ranges from $119 billion to $141 billion; assuming that the annual crop loss is 5 percent of this value,[8] the annual loss ranges from $6 billion to $8 billion (in 1982 prices at 1978 or 1982 levels of output). Relating this value to gross farm income in 1982 of $164 billion, the annual damage is in the neighborhood of 4–5 percent. The cropland model emphasizes the unattractiveness of a warmer climate for an agriculture that emphasizes grains, which have relatively low value per acre and thrive in the relatively cool climate of the northern United States.

Strikingly different results emerge if we use the crop-revenue approach. For these, the net impact of warming (again without CO_2 fertilization) is slightly positive, suggesting an increase of $20–$35 billion in farmland values. Annualizing these capital values, this suggests a gain of between $1 billion and $2 billion per year. As a fraction of 1982 revenue, this amounts to about a 1-percent gain. The differing results arise because the crop-revenue approach weights relatively more heavily the irrigated lands of the West and South that thrive in a Mediterranean and subtropical climate, a climate that will become relatively more abundant with a warming. Including this broader set of crops and adaptations paints a more optimistic picture because the gains from the sunbelt crops tend to offset the losses in the marginal grain regions.

The striking difference between the crop-revenue and cropland approaches is a useful reminder of how we can be misled by our mental images. The specter of global warming calls up the vista of corn blistering on the stalk or desiccated wheat fields. Yet the major grains so vulnerable to drought—wheat and corn—represented only $22.5 billion of the $143 billion of farm marketings in 1982. Our results suggest that the vulnerability of American agriculture to climate change may be exaggerated if the analysis is limited to the major grains. A broader vision should also include the warm-weather crops such as cotton, fruits, vegetables, rice, hay, and grapes in addition to other sectors such as livestock and poultry. Whereas past production-function studies focus ominously on the vulnerable cool-weather grains, the comprehensive crop-revenue Ricardian model reminds us that the irrigated warm-weather crops may be a silver lining behind the climate-change cloud.

Figures 4 and 5 provide geographic detail for these global-warming scenarios. According to the cropland model shown in Figure 4, warming will be particularly harmful for the entire southern part of the United States and will only be beneficial to the northern fringe of the country. The crop-revenue model of Figure 5 suggests, by contrast, that global warming will be beneficial to California and the citrus belt of the Southeast as well as the corn and wheat belts of the Midwest. Global warming will be harmful, in this model, only to the relatively unimportant mountainous regions of Appalachia and the Rocky Mountains.

It will be useful to compare these estimates with results from other studies. In its analysis, Smith and Tirpak (1989) surveyed a number of different climate and agriculture models to estimate the impact of CO_2 doubling. Omitting CO_2 fertilization, the EPA concluded that the impact would lie in the range of $6 billion to $34 billion per year (in 1982 prices). Cline (1992) used two different approaches, the EPA estimate and a modification of Rind et al. (1990), both of which project losses of $20 billion per year without CO_2 fertilization. It is instructive to note that these studies all rely on the production-function approach and apply it to grains; these estimates therefore are closest to our cropland model, and as was predicted in the theoretical section above, they show a higher estimate of damage for that universe than the Ricardian approach—approximately triple the estimates in Table 5. By excluding the nongrain, warm-weather crops, these studies further bias upward the estimates of damage, as is shown by the

---

[8]See the discussion of this issue in the last section and in footnote 6.

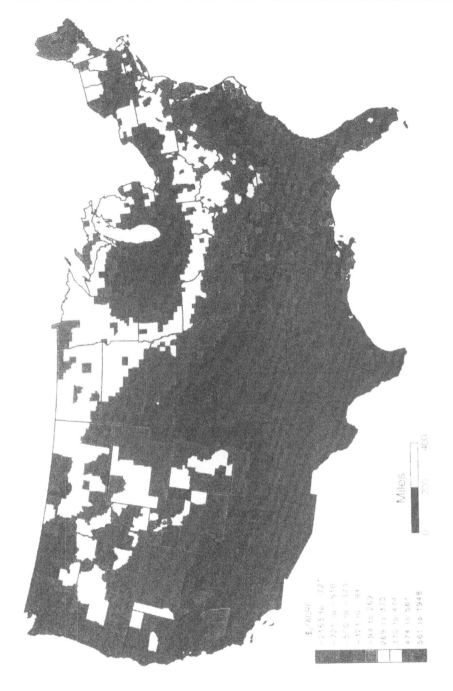

FIGURE 2. INFLUENCE OF CURRENT CLIMATE ON FARM VALUES: CROPLAND WEIGHTS

Note: Farm value is measured as the difference in dollars per acre from the sample average, 1982 prices.

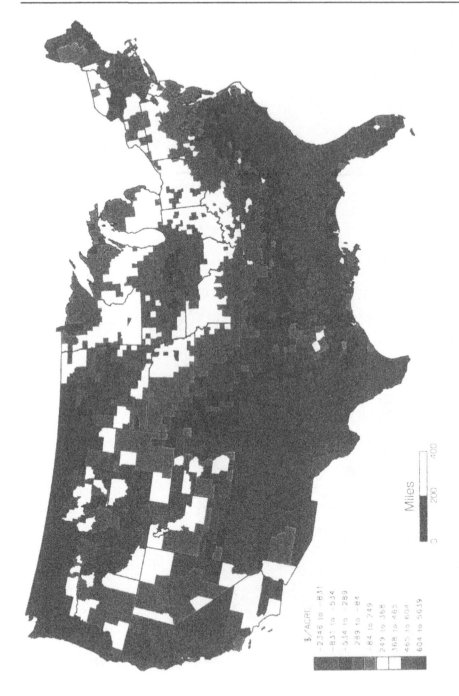

FIGURE 3. INFLUENCE OF CURRENT CLIMATE ON FARM VALUES: CROP-REVENUE WEIGHTS

Note: Farm value is measured as the difference in dollars per acre from the sample average, 1982 prices.

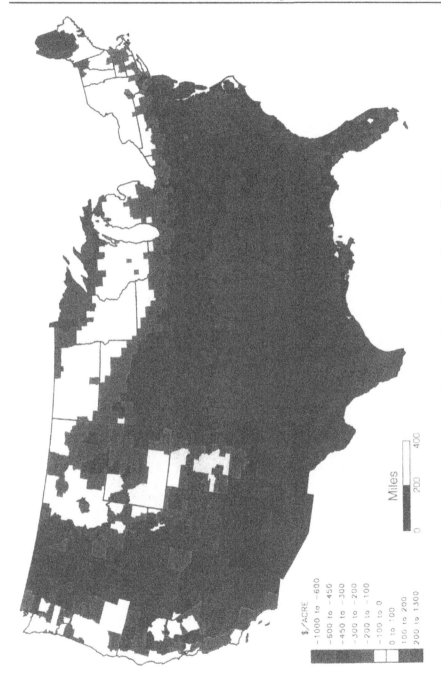

FIGURE 4. CHANGE IN FARM VALUE FROM GLOBAL WARMING: CROPLAND WEIGHTS

Note: The map shows the change in terms of dollars per acre for a 5° F uniform warming and an 8-percent increase in precipitation, 1982 prices.

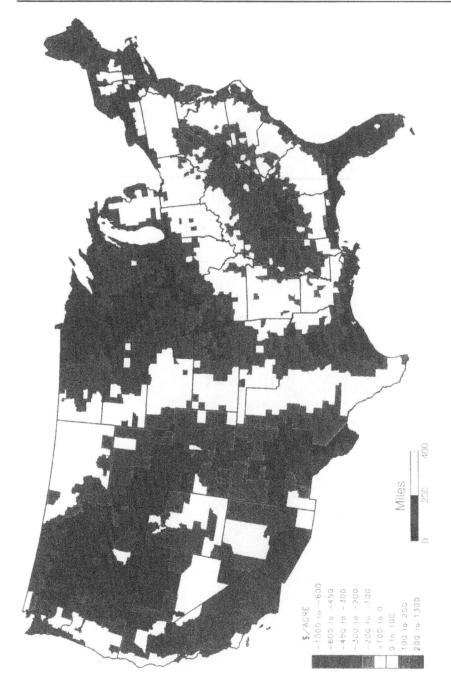

FIGURE 5. CHANGE IN FARM VALUE FROM GLOBAL WARMING: CROP-REVENUE WEIGHTS

Notes: The map shows the change in terms of dollars per acre for a 5°F uniform warming and an 8-percent increase in precipitation, 1982 prices.

comparison between the cropland and the crop-revenue models.

The results in Table 5 are based on a highly stylized global-warming scenario and are therefore quite tentative. In research underway, we are drawing estimated global-warming results from large-scale general circulation models; these should allow differentiation among broad regions of the United States. In addition, the effects of CO_2 fertilization should be included, for some studies indicate that this may produce a significant increase in yields. Other omitted variables are the effect of extremes and ranges in climatic variables as well as the effect of changes in irrigation. Notwithstanding these omissions, the present paper does provide a benchmark for projecting the impact of global warming on American agriculture. Using the narrow definition of crops, the negative impact is estimated to lie between 4 percent and 6 percent of the value of farm ouput. Using a more inclusive definition that weights warm-weather crops and irrigated agriculture more heavily, our projections suggest that global warming may be slightly beneficial to American agriculture.

APPENDIX A: DEFINITIONS OF MAJOR
VARIABLES USED IN THIS STUDY

Constant: a term equal to 1

January temperature: normal daily mean temperature (°F) from 1951 to 1980 in the month of January

January temperature squared: value of January temperature squared

April temperature: normal daily mean temperature (°F) from 1951 to 1980 in the month of April

April temperature squared: value of April temperature squared

July temperature: normal daily mean temperature (°F) from 1951 to 1980 in the month of July

July temperature squared: value of July temperature squared

October temperature: normal daily mean temperature (°F) from 1951 to 1980 in the month of October

October temperature squared: value of October temperature squared

January rain: normal precipitation (inches) from 1951 to 1980 in the month of January

January rain squared: value of January rain squared

April rain: normal precipitation (inches) from 1951 to 1980 in the month of April

April rain squared: value of April rain squared

July rain: normal precipitation (inches) from 1951 to 1980 in the month of July

July rain squared: value of July rain squared

October rain: normal precipitation (inches) from 1951 to 1980 in the month of October

October rain squared: value of October rain squared

Income per capita: annual personal income per person in the county, 1984

Density: resident population per square mile, 1980

Density squared: value of density squared

Latitude: latitude measured in degrees from southernmost point in United States

Altitude: height from sea level (feet)

Migration: net of incoming people minus outgoing people from 1980 to 1986 for the county

Salinity: percentage of land that needs special treatment because of salt/alkaline minerals in the soils

Flood prone: percentage of land that is prone to flooding

Irrigated: percentage of land where irrigation provides at least 50% of water needs

Wetland: percentage of land considered wetland

Soil erosion: K-factor soil (erodibility factor) in hundredths of inches

Slope length: length of slope (feet) (not steepness)

Wind erosion: measure of wind erosion (hundredths of inches)

Farm value: estimate of the current market value of farmland including buildings expressed in dollars per acre, 1982

Farm revenue: gross revenue from crops sold in 1982 in dollars per acre

Sdist: linear distance from the nearest shoreline

Long: longitude measured in degrees from the easternmost point of the United States

Permeability: soil permeability (inches per hour)

Moisture capacity: available water capacity (inches/pound)

APPENDIX B: DATA ON FARMS AND VALUE OF LAND AND BUILDINGS[9]

The data on farms and on farmland values are central to this study. This appendix describes the definition and sources of the data. The current definition of a farm, first used for the *1974 Census of Agriculture* final reports, is any place from which $1,000 or more of agricultural products were sold or normally would have been sold during the census year. Land in farms is an operating-unit concept and includes land owned and operated as well as land rented from others. The acreage designated as "land in farms" consists primarily of agricultural land used for crops, pasture, or grazing. It also includes woodland and wasteland not actually under cultivation or used for pasture or grazing, provided it was part of the farm operator's total operation.

The land is defined to lie in the operator's principal county, that is, the county where the largest value of agricultural products was raised or produced. Irrigated land includes land watered by any artificial or controlled means, such as sprinklers, furrows or ditches, and spreader dikes. Cropland includes land from which crops were harvested or hay was cut, land in orchards, citrus groves, vineyards, nurseries, and greenhouses, land used only for pasture or grazing that could have been used for crops without additional improvement, and all land planted in crops that were grazed before the crops reached maturity. Also included were all cropland used for rotation pasture and lands in government diversion programs that were pastured.

Respondents were asked to report their estimate of the current market value of land and buildings owned, rented, or leased from others, and of land rented or leased to others. Market value refers to the respondent's estimate of what the land and buildings would sell for under current market conditions. If the value of land and buildings was not reported, it was estimated during processing by using the average value of land and buildings from a similar farm in the same geographic area.

The value of products sold by farms represents the gross market value before taxes and production expenses of all agricultural products sold or removed from the place regardless of who received the payment. In addition, it includes the loan value received in 1982 for placing commodities in the Commodity Credit Corporation loan program.

REFERENCES

Adams, Richard. "Global Climate Change and Agriculture: An Economic Perspective." *American Journal of Agricultural Economics,* December 1989, *71*(5), pp. 1272–79.

Adams, Richard; McCarl, Bruce; Dudek, Daniel and Glyer, David. "Implications of Global Climate Change for Western Agriculture." *Western Journal of Agricultural Economics,* December 1988, *13*(2), pp. 348–56.

Adams, Richard; Rosenzweig, Cynthia; Pearl, Robert; Ritchie, Joe; McCarl, Bruce; Glyer, David; Curry, Bruce; Jones, James; Boote, Kenneth and Allen, Hartwell. "Global Climate Change and U.S. Agriculture." *Nature,* 17 May 1990, *345*(6272), pp. 219–24.

Callaway, John; Cronin, F.; Currie, J. and Tawil, J. "An Analysis of Methods and Models for Assessing the Direct and Indirect Economic Impacts of CO_2-Induced Environmental Changes in the Agricultural Sector of the U.S. Economy." Pacific Northwest Laboratory (Richland, WA) Working Paper No. PNL-4384, 1982.

Cline, William. *The economics of global warming.* Washington, DC: Institute of Inter-

---

[9]This description is drawn from the *City and County Data Book,* and the underlying data are from *1982 Census of Agriculture* (U.S. Bureau of the Census, 1984).

national Economics, 1992.

Decker, W.; Jones, V. and Achutuni, R. *The impact of climate change from increased atmospheric carbon dioxide on American agriculture*, DOE/NBB-0077. Washington, DC: U.S. Department of Energy, 1986.

Easterling, William, III; McKenney, Mary; Rosenberg, Norman and Lemon, Kathleen. *Processes for identifying regional influences of and responses to increasing atmospheric CO$_2$ and climate change — The MINK project — Report IIB*, DOE/RL/01830T-H8. Washington, DC: U.S. Department of Energy, 1991.

Ibbotson, Roger and Brinson, Gary. *Investment markets*. New York: McGraw-Hill, 1987.

Intergovernmental Panel on Climate Change. *Climate change: The IPCC scientific assessment* (J. T. Houghton, G. J. Jenkins, and J. J. Ephraums, eds.). New York: Cambridge University Press, 1990.

Mendelsohn, Robert; Nordhaus, William and Shaw, Dai Gee. "The Impact of Climate on Agriculture: A Ricardian Approach," in Yoichi Kaya, Nebojsa Nakicenovic, William Nordhaus, and Ferenc Toth, eds., *Costs, impacts, and benefits of CO$_2$ mitigation*. Laxemburg, Austria: International Institute of Applied Systems Analysis, 1993, pp. 173–208.

National Academy of Sciences Panel on Greenhouse Warming. *Policy implications of greenhouse warming: Mitigation, adaptation, and the science base*. Washington, DC: National Academy Press, 1992.

National Research Council. *Changing climate*. Washington, DC: National Academy Press, 1983.

Rind, D.; Goldberg, R.; Hansen, J.; Rosenzweig, Cynthia and Ruedy, R. "Potential Evapotranspiration and the Likelihood of Future Drought." *Journal of Geophysical Research*, June 1990, *95*(D7), pp. 9983–10004.

Rozenzweig, Cynthia and Parry, Martin L. "Potential Impact of Climate Change on World Food Supply." *Nature*, 13 January 1994, *367*(6459), pp. 133–38.

Smith, Joel and Tirpak, Dennis, eds. *The potential effects of global climate change on the United States: Report to Congress*, EPA-230-05-89-050. Washington, DC: Environmental Protection Agency, 1989.

U.S. Bureau of the Census. *1982 Census of Agriculture*. Washington, DC: U.S. Government Printing Office, 1984.

_____. *County and city data book*. Washington, DC: U.S. Government Printing Office, 1988.

[7]

The Impact of Global Warming on Agriculture: A Ricardian Analysis: Comment

By John Quiggin and John K. Horowitz*

To assess the desirability of policies to reduce greenhouse gas emissions, it is necessary to estimate the costs that climate change is likely to impose. A number of studies have estimated the costs of climate change to agriculture by modeling changes in yield on the assumption that the existing pattern of land use will remain unchanged. Robert Mendelsohn et al. (1994), hereafter MNS, call this the "dumb-farmer scenario" and observe that costs derived in this way represent an upper-bound estimate for the costs of climate change. As an alternative, MNS propose a "Ricardian" approach, based on comparative static estimates of the change in equilibrium rents to land associated with a one-time change in climatic conditions. MNS estimate that a 5°F increase in mean temperatures will yield changes in farmland rents ranging from a 4.9-percent loss to a 1.2-percent gain.

The main purpose of this note is to observe that, just as the "dumb-farmer scenario" implicitly assumes infinite adjustment costs and therefore yields an upper-bound estimate, the "Ricardian" approach implicitly assumes zero adjustment costs and therefore yields a lower-bound estimate of the costs of climate change. Before developing this point, it is necessary to observe that the model estimated by MNS is not well-behaved. This leads to some difficulties in explaining the logic of the distinction between the MNS comparative static and a more appropriate dynamic model.

The comparative static approach allows us, in principle, to calculate the optimal temperature for U.S. agriculture, when there are zero adjustment costs. For this calculation to be made, however, it is necessary that the implied tech-

nology have the concavity properties required for the existence of a global optimum. For the model estimated by MNS, where land values are a quadratic function of temperatures, the relevant condition is that the quadratic term should be negative. In the equations estimated by MNS, this condition is not satisfied, since the quadratic term for October is typically positive.

Using equation (iv) of MNS Table 3, we can calculate that the deviations from the means of January, April, and July temperatures that maximize farm values are −30°, 1°, and −146°F. Mean January, April, and July temperatures in the United States are roughly 37°, 56°, and 78°. Therefore, the optimal temperatures for January, April, and July are in the neighborhood of 7°, 57°, and −68°, while no finite optimum exists for October temperatures. These unusual results presumably reflect estimation problems, probably arising from multicollinearity. Whatever the cause, it is evident that, although the MNS equations fit the data reasonably well, they will not, in general, be well-behaved for data points lying outside the range of the data set used in estimation. This casts doubt on the accuracy of comparative static estimates of costs of global warming derived from the MNS model.

Even if the MNS model produced accurate comparative static estimates, however, these estimates would not provide an appropriate basis for estimating the costs of global warming or for assessing policies designed to mitigate warming. The question addressed by MNS may be stated as, "If temperatures were and always had been 5°F higher, what difference would it make to the net social surplus arising from US agriculture?" But the effect of a 5°F change would be very different if the climate were 5°F warmer *next year*, than if mean temperatures rose by 0.01°F per year over 500 years. The difference between these cases is in the costs that would be incurred in adjusting to the new climate, not in the overall temperature increase. The MNS

* Quiggin: Department of Economics, James Cook University, Townsville, Queensland 4811, Australia; Horowitz: Department of Agricultural and Resource Economics, University of Maryland, College Park, MD 20742. We thank the National Science Foundation and the Australian Research Council for support.

analysis cannot distinguish between these two cases.

There are strong reasons to expect that a comparative static approach will yield small estimates of global warming's impact on agriculture. Agriculture is possible under a wide range of climate conditions, and the United States contains both regions where low temperatures are the main limiting factor and regions where high temperatures are the main limiting factor. In a well-behaved version of the MNS model, this fact would be reflected by an observation that actual climatic conditions in the United States are above the estimated temperature optimum in some counties and below it in others. Temperature change would be expected to be disadvantageous in the former areas but beneficial in the latter, and if land area is approximately uniformly distributed across regions then global warming will have a small effect on aggregate output, when adjustment costs are ignored.

Therefore, economists should focus attention on the costs of adjustment, which are necessarily positive. If, in the example of MNS, land currently used for wheat and corn is to be turned over, first to grazing and then to retirement homes, it will be necessary for farmers with crop-specific skills to move (presumably northward) or acquire new skills, and for items of capital stock such as grain elevators and flour mills to be relocated or scrapped. How large these adjustment costs will be is as yet unanswered, but the comparative static analysis can give no indication of their magnitude.

There are also practical difficulties with the comparative static approach. The MNS approach is based on differences between the current climate and that predicted to prevail with higher greenhouse gas concentrations. By contrast, a fully dynamic assessment will focus attention on the rate of change of temperature and other climate variables rather than their level. Users of the static approach must not only select an (implicit) estimate of the rate of change of temperature but also a cutoff date at which to make the calculation. This will produce either noncomparable estimates across different studies, if different stopping dates are chosen, or an unjustified focus on a particular date.

Adjustment costs might be estimated in two ways. First, a micro-level examination of capital stocks and depreciation rates could be used to estimate the rate at which climate-specific capital would need to be scrapped in order to achieve the necessary rate of adjustment. For agriculture, it seems likely that the largest costs would arise with respect to irrigation. As MNS note, irrigation is an endogenous response to climate, but it is a response characterized by large stocks of long-lived capital. A significant change in temperature or rainfall patterns could render many existing investments useless.

An alternative approach to the estimation of adjustment costs could focus on observed responses to changes in relative prices. Changes in relative yields arising from climate change are, from the point of view of profit-maximizing farmers, similar to changes in relative prices. However, estimation difficulties would arise from the fact that changes in climate are more persistent than changes in prices.

In summary, the main costs of global warming are almost sure to be adjustment costs. Economic analysis of global warming should focus on the rate of temperature change, not temperature level. Such an analysis is more difficult than the comparative static analysis offered by MNS. However, it is likely to give us a very different, and more accurate, picture of the impact of global warming.

REFERENCES

Mendelsohn, Robert; Nordhaus, William D. and Shaw, Daigee. "The Impact of Global Warming on Agriculture: A Ricardian Analysis." *American Economic Review*, September 1994, *84* (4), pp. 753–71.

[8]

The Impact of Global Warming on Agriculture: A Ricardian Analysis: Reply

By ROBERT MENDELSOHN AND WILLIAM NORDHAUS*

In Mendelsohn et al. (1994), hereafter MNS, we suggested a "Ricardian" approach to measuring the impact of global warming on agriculture. Under this approach, we first estimated the impact of climate on agricultural land values and then predicted the impacts of climate change on agriculture using these estimated relationships.

John Quiggin and John K. Horowitz (1999), hereafter Q&H, raise three concerns about the Ricardian method. First, they note that it is important to measure damages across time and not rely strictly on comparative statics since the warming is predicted to move gradually over a very long time period. Second, they note that one of the costs of adapting to climate change is adjustment costs; these are not included in our estimates and could be important. Third, they argue that some of the second-order seasonal terms in the estimates are positive, not negative as expected, which in their view raises questions about interpolation of the results outside the range of the data.

1. The fact that damages from a stock externality such as those due to greenhouse gases should be modeled using a dynamic analysis is surely valid; we have emphasized that point repeatedly in our research over the last two decades (see Nordhaus, 1979, 1991, 1994). Indeed, we prefer to analyze climate-change policy as an optimal control problem which requires careful attention to the dynamics of the underlying processes.

Empirical understanding of the dynamics, alas, is not that easy. One of the most elusive aspects of global warming is estimation of the impact of climate change on relevant economic outcomes, where deriving meaningful measures

has proven extremely difficult. Virtually every study of impacts takes the comparative statics or "snapshot" approach, where a modified climate is imposed upon a given (usually today's) economic structure. The static comparative structure is, in our view, a useful first step and is the approach we took in our Ricardian model in MNS. More recent work (Mendelsohn and Michael Schlesinger, 1999) presents climate-response functions that can serve as building blocks for future dynamic analyses of impacts. It must be emphasized, however, that reliable estimates of the transition cost of climate change are extremely fragile because we have but the most rudimentary understanding of both climate dynamics and farmer dynamics.

2. Q&H are also correct in emphasizing the importance of adjustment costs in estimating impacts. Climate-change impacts in sectors with large and long-lived capital stocks may involve significant adjustment costs. The studies by Brent Sohngen and Mendelsohn (1998) of timber stocks and Gary Yohe et al. (1996) of coastal structures both indicate that dynamic models of adjustment are important in these two sectors. However, both coastal structures and timber resources involve huge capital stocks which are difficult to adjust. The same dominance of capital structures is not as apparent in the agricultural sector more generally. We are consequently skeptical whether adjustment costs will ultimately prove to be an important issue in assessing the effects of climate change on agriculture. One way of addressing adjustment costs alluded to by Q&H is to determine the impact of interannual fluctuations in temperature and precipitation. This has been quantified in another Ricardian study (Mendelsohn et al., 1996), which indicated climate (especially temperature) variance caused large agricultural damages. However, interannual temperature variation is a poor proxy for climate change. According to current projections, greenhouse warming is expected to increase

* Mendelsohn: School of Forestry and Environmental Studies, Marsh Hall, Yale University, 360 Prospect Street, New Haven, CT 06511; Nordhaus: Department of Economics, Yale University, P.O. Box 208268, New Haven, CT 06511.

U.S. temperature between 1°C and 3.5°C over the next century. The issue is whether a projected change which is this slow is likely to cause large adjustment costs to an industry as adaptable as agriculture appears to be.

Adjustment is costly primarily because of farm-specific capital. Farmers do have substantial capital investments, but in equipment like tractors and harvesters that have relatively short economic lifetimes. Over a century, farmers can roll over most of their capital stock several times as they adapt to the changing climate, and adjustment costs for this capital are likely to be trivially small. Some agricultural capital, particularly structures and soils, may have longer lifetimes, and some local climate changes may not be smooth and gradual. However, there is no evidence that adjustment costs associated with a change of 0.01 to 0.035°C per year would entail significant adjustment costs. To put this in perspective, the U.S. Department of Commerce estimates that the current-dollar value of farm structures in 1982, the year of our central estimate, was $150 billion.[1] Assuming that the effective lifetime of this capital is reduced from 50 years to 40 years (a desperately pessimistic assumption), the annualized economic cost of this life-shortening would be $0.45 billion. This number is more than an order of magnitude smaller than the uncertainty among the different impact estimates using the Ricardian model. Short-term weather fluctuations, such as those seen in the 1930's, are likely to be much more important for adjustment costs than those associated with global warming over the next half century.

3. Q&H also note that the MNS coefficients for the quadratic terms on temperature have positive values, implying that farm values are convex with respect to temperature. Common sense would suggest a concave temperature response function. In further work, we have explored why the climate-response function in MNS does not have the expected concavity. The original MNS study estimated the response of land values to climate given the existing land in crops. Subsequent research (Mendelsohn et al., 1996) has shown that climate also affects the

fraction of land which is devoted to crops. In extremely cold, hot, or dry climates, less land is used for farming. Taking this into account, the agricultural response function to temperature has the expected hill shape. That is, the second-order terms with respect to temperature are negative as expected (Mendelsohn et al., 1996). Projecting both to polar regions and tropical regions, the expanded model predicts that the temperate zone has the most valuable agricultural climate.

Q&H are concerned that MNS might have understated the damages from climate change and may mislead analysts concerning the seriousness of the economic consequences of global warming. However, subsequent research suggests that MNS may actually have presented too pessimistic an outlook for U.S. agriculture. Perhaps the most important factor excluded from the MNS model is CO_2 fertilization. Current research indicates that the buildup of atmospheric CO_2 is likely to have major beneficial impacts on crop growth. Recent agronomic studies which include adaptation and carbon fertilization confirm these results (Richard Adams et al., 1998). The original MNS study was controversial because it was one of the first impact studies to predict warming would be beneficial. However, subsequent studies that include full adaptation (such as Adams et al., 1999) find agricultural results that are consistent with MNS.

Our view is that the major open questions about the impacts of global warming lie largely outside the U.S. agricultural sector. Indeed, many studies have concluded that the impact of climate change on the market sectors in the United States are likely to be modest over the next century (Mendelsohn and James Neumann, 1998). The major uncertainties about impacts are nonmarket impacts (health, aesthetics, ecosystem changes, and the potential for catastrophic changes) and the impacts on poor and tropical countries. Research on these areas will be a fruitful area for economic research for many years to come.

REFERENCES

Adams, Richard; McCarl, Bruce; Segerson, Kathleen; Rosenzweig, Cynthia; Bryant, K.; Dixon, Bruce; Conner, R.; Evenson, Robert

[1] These data are available at the BEA web site at http://www.bea.doc.gov/bea/dn2.htm.

1048 THE AMERICAN ECONOMIC REVIEW SEPTEMBER 1999

and Ojima, Dennis. "The Economic Effect of Climate Change on U.S. Agriculture," in Robert Mendelsohn and James Neumann, eds., *The impact of climate change on the United States economy.* Cambridge: Cambridge University Press, 1998, pp. 18–54.

Mendelsohn, Robert and Neumann, James, eds. *The impact of climate change on the United States economy.* Cambridge: Cambridge University Press, 1998.

Mendelsohn, Robert; Nordhaus, William D. and Shaw, Daigee. "The Impact of Global Warming on Agriculture: A Ricardian Analysis." *American Economic Review*, September 1994, *84* (4), pp. 753–71.

_____. "Climate Impacts on Aggregate Farm Values: Accounting for Adaptation." *Journal of Agricultural and Forest Meteorology*, June 1996, *80*(1), pp. 55–66.

Mendelsohn, Robert and Schlesinger, Michael. "Climate-Response Functions." *Ambio*, June 1999, 27(4), pp. 362–66.

Nordhaus, William. *The efficient use of energy resources.* New Haven, CT: Yale University Press, 1979.

_____. "To Slow or Not to Slow: The Economics of the Greenhouse Effect." *Economic Journal*, July 1991, *101* (407), pp. 920–37.

_____. *Managing the global commons: The economics of climate change.* Cambridge, MA: MIT Press, 1994.

Quiggin, John and Horowitz, John K. "The Impact of Global Warming on Agriculture: A Ricardian Analysis: Comment." *American Economic Review*, September 1999, *89* (4), pp. 1044–45.

Sohngen, Brent and Mendelsohn, Robert. "Valuing the Impact of Large-Scale Ecological Change: The Effect of Climate Change on U.S. Timber." *American Economic Review*, September 1998, *88* (4), pp. 686–710.

Yohe, Gary; Neumann, James; Marshall, Paul and Ameden, Holly. "The Economic Cost of Sea Level Rise on U.S. Coastal Properties from Climatic Change." *Climatic Change*, April 1996, *32*(4), pp. 387–410.

[9]

The Impact of Global Warming on Agriculture: A Ricardian Analysis: Comment

By Roy Darwin*

In 1994, Robert Mendelsohn et al., hereafter MNS, presented what they term the "Ricardian" approach for estimating the impact of global climate change on land values. With appropriate caveats, this approach can provide useful information about the economic effects of climate-induced agricultural changes when traditional welfare measures are not available (Darwin, 1999). I am concerned, however, that MNS's 1994 models produce estimates that violate basic agricultural and/or economic principles. This is especially true of their preferred model, which greatly overestimates the value of warm-weather agriculture in the United States.

The two most-cited models in MNS (1994) use 1982 values of farm real estate per acre at the county level as their dependent variable. Climatic influences are captured by linear and quadratic terms for temperature and precipitation in January, April, July, and October. Control variables account for differences in soils, altitude, and proximity to markets. One MNS model uses cropland and the other uses crop revenues to weight observations during estimation.[1] Cropland weights, i.e., the percentage of each county in cropland, tend to emphasize grain production, which thrives in the Midwest and the relatively cool climate of the northern United States. Crop-revenue weights, i.e., the value of crop products sold by farms each county, tend to emphasize the irrigated lands of the coastal West and South where Mediterranean and subtropical climates are found. I refer to these models as the cropland model and crop-revenue model, respectively. MNS claim that the crop-revenue model is more inclusive and reflects a broader definition of agriculture than the cropland model.

The basic agricultural principle implicit in the Ricardian approach is that the underlying functional form of the relationship between temperature and agricultural productivity is hill-shaped (MNS, 1996). Where temperatures are generally low, say around 0°C, land is not very suitable for agricultural production and the value of such land approaches zero. As temperatures increase above 0°C, agricultural possibilities and farmland value increase assuming that soil moisture conditions are suitable. Above some optimal temperature, however, agricultural productivity and farmland value begin to decline. At relatively high temperatures, land again becomes unsuitable for agricultural production (even with sufficient water) and farmland value is low. However, the models presented in MNS (1994) are not fully consistent with this basic Ricardian principle (see MNS, 1996). While MNS's cropland model is consistent with the principle, their crop-revenue model is not (see Darwin, 1999). The omission of an important variable—irrigation—is a likely reason.

Although the value of irrigation capital, legal rights to, and the availability of, irrigation water determines farmland value, MNS's 1994 models omit irrigation variables. As a result, the effect of irrigation on farmland value is inappropriately captured by the coefficients on their climate and geography variables. This approach results in biased parameters on climate variables within the counties and fails to account for other relevant climate variables. To illustrate these problems, let farmland value, V, be:

$$(1) \qquad V = a_0 + b_1 T_{gs} + b_2 P_{gs}$$
$$+ b_3 P_{ngs} + b_4 I$$

* U.S. Department of Agriculture, Economic Research Service, 1800 M Street, NW, Room 4180, Washington, DC 20036. The views expressed herein do not necessarily reflect those of the U.S. Department of Agriculture.

[1] Crop revenue is the value of crop products sold by farms and consists of the gross market value of all crops sold or removed from the place regardless of who received payment.

1050   THE AMERICAN ECONOMIC REVIEW   SEPTEMBER 1999

where T_{gs} is temperature during the growing season, P_{gs} is precipitation during the growing season, P_{ngs} is precipitation during the nongrowing season (part of which may replenish soil moisture), and I is irrigation. Assuming b_1, b_2, and $b_3 >$ or ≤ 0, and $b_4 > 0$ provides the greatest generality for an individual county.

Also let the availability of irrigation, I, be:

$$(2) \quad I = a_1 + b_5 T_{gs} + b_6 P_{gs} + b_7 P_{ngs}$$
$$+ b_8 P_{othr} + b_9 T_{othr}$$

where P_{othr} is precipitation that serves as a source of irrigation water from outside the county and T_{othr} is the temperature of areas where P_{othr} falls or its runoff passes through. Irrigation systems are more likely to exist in counties where temperature and precipitation during the growing season are, respectively, relatively high and low, so $b_5 > 0$ and $b_6 < 0$. Irrigation water is more likely to be available in counties where precipitation occurs during the nongrowing season or outside the county so $b_7 > 0$ and $b_8 > 0$. Higher temperatures in other areas are likely to reduce the availability of irrigation water on average because they reduce runoff by increasing evapotranspiration so $b_9 < 0$. This negative relationship is strengthened if snowpack, which naturally helps to store water precipitated during nongrowing seasons until it is needed during growing seasons, is a major component of a county's agricultural system.

Substituting equation (2) into equation (1) and rearranging yields:

$$(3) \quad V = (a_0 + b_4 a_1 + b_4 b_8 P_{othr}$$
$$+ b_4 b_9 T_{othr}) + (b_1 + b_4 b_5) T_{gs}$$
$$+ (b_2 + b_4 b_6) P_{gs}$$
$$+ (b_3 + b_4 b_7) P_{ngs}$$

where $(b_1 + b_4 b_5) > b_1$, $(b_2 + b_4 b_6) < b_2$, and $(b_3 + b_4 b_7) > b_3$. The intercept term in equation (3) shows that MNS's models do not estimate the effects on farmland values that global climate change might have when irrigation water originates outside the county in

which it is used. Snowpack in the Sierra Nevada Mountains, for example, is an important source of California's irrigation water. Increased precipitation in these mountains would mean greater supplies of irrigation water. Rising temperatures in these mountains on the other hand could reduce overall snowpack or release meltwater from snowpack sooner than needed. Rising temperatures in lowland areas through which this water passes would also reduce the amount of water available for irrigation. The net effect could easily be a net loss in farmland values which neither the cropland nor crop-revenue model could distinguish.

Equation (3) also shows that reduced-form parameters on climate variables in counties that rely heavily on irrigation differ from parameters on climate variables in counties where irrigation is not necessary. Combining irrigated and nonirrigated counties while ignoring these differences results in biased estimates of b_1, b_2, and b_3. Although likely to occur in both models, parameters will be biased more in the crop-revenue model because of its greater emphasis on irrigated areas. Temperature increases in July and October (which is part of the growing season for some vegetables and fruits in the truck farm and citrus-fruit belt), for example, are less harmful or more beneficial, respectively, in the crop-revenue than in the cropland model. Also, precipitation increases in January are more beneficial in the crop-revenue than in the cropland model, while an additional inch of July rain is beneficial in the cropland model, but harmful in the crop-revenue model. This bias reenforces the crop-revenue model's intended emphasis on warm-weather agriculture.

The bias toward warm-weather agriculture in the crop-revenue model is reenforced in other ways as well. Both models, for example, neglect U.S. livestock and poultry production. Cropland weights ignore permanent pasture, while crop-revenue weights disregard livestock sales. The latter generated 53 percent of farm revenues in 1982. Thirty-nine percent of livestock and poultry sales, however, occurred in eight grain-belt states—Illinois, Indiana, Iowa, Kansas, Minnesota, Missouri, Nebraska, and Wisconsin, while only 10 per-

VOL. 89 NO. 4   DARWIN: IMPACT OF GLOBAL WARMING, COMMENT   1051

cent of livestock-related sales occurred in the coastal states of California, Florida, Oregon, and Washington (U.S. Bureau of the Census [USBC], 1984). In addition, crop-revenue weights exclude the value of crops harvested and fed directly to livestock on the same farm. These crops include grass consumed by livestock on cropland pasture (i.e., pasture that could have been used for crops without additional improvement) as well as most hay and corn silage. Finally, it is important to note that temperate-weather crops were twice as important as warm-weather crops to U.S. agriculture in 1982. Grain-belt crops like maize, soybeans, and wheat made up 51 percent of crop sales, while fruits and vegetables made up only 16 percent and cotton and tobacco made up only 10 percent of crop sales in 1982 (USBC, 1984). These facts contradict MNS's claim that the crop-revenue model is more inclusive and reflects a broader definition of agriculture than the cropland model. Instead they indicate that the crop-revenue model greatly overemphasizes warm-weather agriculture.

Last but not least, estimates from MNS's models violate a basic economic principle, e.g., farmland values must be positive (or equal to zero). Estimated changes in farmland values based on results from 16 general circulation climate models range from $-\$1,522$ billion to $\$413$ billion and from $-\$969$ billion to $\$1,209$ billion, respectively, for the cropland and crop-revenue models (Mendelsohn and Nordhaus, 1996). The total nominal value of farm real estate in 1982, however, was only $\$763.2$ billion (USBC, 1984). This implies that MNS's models predict negative farmland values in some counties under global climate change. MNS recognized this problem in their 1994 article, where they provided "truncated" impacts, in which losses in farmland value at the county level were limited to the original value of the land, as preferred economic measures. Truncation, however, focuses on only half the problem. The mechanisms that generate invalid damages almost certainly generate invalid benefits as well. This would be especially true for the crop-revenue model with its overemphasis on warm-weather agriculture.

Mendelsohn and Nordhaus (1996) pointed

out that getting the size of the economic shock right with the Ricardian approach is important. The issues raised in this paper indicate that both MNS's cropland and crop-revenue models have difficulty in getting the size of the shock right. Fortunately the problems discussed here are correctable. The first step is to include a term that eliminates the bias caused by ignoring irrigation.[2] One way is to recognize that $V = s_1 V_1 + s_2 V_2$, where s_i is the share of land type i, and $i = (1, 2)$ represents nonirrigated and irrigated land, respectively. Calculate s_2 using irrigated farmland per county (USBC, 1984). Then substitute an equation like equation (1), but without the irrigation term, for nonirrigated land values, V_1, and multiply by s_1. The second step (to be taken in addition to step one) is to use more neutral weights on the observations. Farmland weights, i.e., the total amount of farmland in each county, for example, would reduce the influence of the relatively small counties located in the Midwest grain belt that an unweighted estimation would generate without discriminating against livestock production.[3] The third step is to implement estimation procedures that explicitly recognize that farmland values are positive. One approach would be to collect climate, soil, and other data for U.S. counties with no farmland, e.g., where the value of farmland equals zero, and estimate a Tobit model; another would be to specify the dependent variable as the natural logarithm of farmland values (G. S. Maddala, 1983). In any event, because the standard error of a prediction based on linear regression models increases the further away the values of the independent variables are from their means (Maddala, 1977), practitioners of the Ricardian approach should report standard errors of their models and confidence limits for projections to facilitate more meaningful

---

[2] In their 1994 paper, MNS said that they included irrigation in some of their models, but they did not describe how or present results.

[3] MNS (1996) presented some farmland-weighted models of farmland values that included variation terms in addition to deviations (and squared deviations) from means of climate variables as independent variables. The models did not include irrigation.

assessments of the agricultural effects of global climate change.

REFERENCES

Darwin, Roy F. "A FARMer's View of the Ricardian Approach to Measuring Agricultural Effects of Climatic Change." *Climatic Change*, April 1999, *41*(3–4), pp. 371–411.

Maddala, G. S. *Econometrics.* New York: McGraw-Hill, 1977.

_____. *Limited-dependent and qualitative variables in econometrics.* Cambridge: Cambridge University Press, 1983.

Mendelsohn, Robert and Nordhaus, William. "The Impact of Global Warming on Agriculture: Reply." *American Economic Review,* December 1996, *86* (5), pp. 1312–15.

Mendelsohn, Robert; Nordhaus, William D. and Shaw, Daigee. "The Impact of Global Warming on Agriculture: A Ricardian Analysis." *American Economic Review,* September 1994, *84* (4), pp. 753–71.

_____. "Climate Impacts on Aggregate Farm Value: Accounting for Adaptation." *Journal of Agricultural and Forest Meteorology,* June 1996, *80*(1), pp. 55–66.

U.S. Bureau of the Census, Department of Commerce. *1982 census of agriculture.* Washington, DC: U.S. Government Printing Office, 1984.

[10]

The Impact of Global Warming on Agriculture: A Ricardian Analysis: Reply

By ROBERT MENDELSOHN AND WILLIAM NORDHAUS*

The original Ricardian study (Mendelsohn et al., 1994) (MNS) was significant because it was one of the first studies to demonstrate that cross-sectional evidence could provide quantitative estimates of the economic effects of climate. The study was also significant because it was one of the first empirical studies to demonstrate that warming could be beneficial. Although other climate studies of agriculture and forestry now obtain similar results (Mendelsohn and James Neumann, 1998), these findings were more controversial five years ago. The MNS study also revealed, however, that cross-sectional analyses are demanding and can profit from constructive criticism.

Roy Darwin (1999) raises several points in his note on the Ricardian model. First, he notes that the estimated crop-revenue model in MNS is not hill-shaped with respect to temperature as expected. The sum of the second-order coefficients on temperature in MNS is positive (see Table 1). He speculates that the omission of irrigation from the analysis is the likely cause of this problem. He further speculates that the omission of irrigation has biased the climate coefficients especially in the crop-revenue weighted regression. Finally, he recommends including livestock in the Ricardian regression.

In this note, we follow Darwin's suggestion and include irrigation in the Ricardian model. As a point of comparison, two columns in Table 1 present the original MNS model with cropland weighting and crop-revenue weighting. Two additional columns regress the percent of irrigated farmland on the independent variables of the model. The predicted frequency of irrigation from these regressions is

then entered as a new independent variable into the Ricardian model.

The irrigation regressions provide some interesting insights. In both irrigation equations, warmer winter, spring, and summer temperatures reduce the probability of irrigation. Irrigation increases only with warmer falls. Irrigation is used to take advantage of warm falls, not to grow crops in warmer climates. Irrigation increases with winter precipitation but falls with precipitation in all other seasons. This result confirms Darwin's hypothesis that irrigation is a substitute for low rainfall during the growing season and is more likely in places with non-growing season rains. The positive coefficients on flood prone and wetland areas further confirm that irrigation is more likely in places with access to outside water supplies.

The key regressions, however, are the Ricardian models with the second-stage irrigation variable included. The new cropland model is hardly distinguishable from the original model. The irrigation variable is insignificant and the climate variables have barely changed. Including irrigation has no effect on the cropland model. This is not that surprising given that only 3 percent of U.S. farmland is irrigated. Irrigation does not explain the variation in land value across the U.S. landscape.

Irrigation is important in the crop-revenue model. The irrigation coefficient is highly significant and large, suggesting an irrigated acre is worth $910 more than a dryland acre. Irrigation is more important in the crop-revenue model because irrigated acres are highly productive and so they are relatively more important. Including irrigation has also changed the climate coefficients. The marginal effect of an increase in annual temperature has risen from $-$17 to $+$4, an insignificant increase. The marginal effect of an increase in annual precipitation has risen from $123 to $218, a significant increase. Including irrigation in the Ricardian model increases the beneficial

* Mendelsohn: School of Forestry and Environmental Studies, Marsh Hall, Yale University, 360 Prospect Street, New Haven, CT 06511; Nordhaus: Department of Economics, Yale University, P.O. Box 208268, New Haven, CT 06511.

TABLE 1——RICARDIAN MODELS WITH AND WITHOUT IRRIGATION[a]

Independent variables	Cropland weights			Crop-revenue weights		
	Farm value	Percent irrigation	Farm value	Farm value	Percent irrigation	Farm value
January temperature	−88.7	−6.41	−89.6	−160	−9.74	−133
	(9.95)	(3.64)	(9.86)	(13.21)	(5.02)	(11.45)
January temperature squared	−1.34	−0.14	−1.37	−2.68	−0.22	−1.88
	(6.41)	(3.33)	(6.31)	(10.04)	(5.10)	(7.28)
April temperature	−17.8	−14.6	−20.5	13.6	−6.81	91.1
	(1.55)	(6.42)	(1.62)	(1.02)	(3.19)	(6.79)
April temperature squared	−4.90	−0.47	−4.98	−6.69	−0.56	−4.66
	(7.43)	(3.60)	(7.34)	(9.61)	(4.97)	(6.93)
July temperature	−155	−2.46	−155	−87.7	−0.28	−128
	(14.51)	(1.16)	(14.52)	(6.92)	(0.14)	(10.42)
July temperature squared	−2.96	−0.77	−3.14	−0.30	−0.64	0.17
	(4.69)	(6.16)	(4.31)	(0.54)	(7.17)	(0.32)
October temperature	192	21.9	195	217	23.7	174
	(11.09)	(6.40)	(10.47)	(9.06)	(6.16)	(7.58)
October temperature squared	6.63	0.91	6.81	12.4	1.59	7.89
	(7.10)	(4.91)	(6.81)	(12.73)	(10.22)	(8.24)
January rain	85.1	15.7	87.7	280	26.4	199
	(3.88)	(3.63)	(3.90)	(9.77)	(5.73)	(7.21)
January rain squared	2.74	0.90	2.99	−10.8	−0.18	−8.91
	(0.95)	(1.58)	(1.02)	(3.71)	(0.37)	(3.21)
April rain	104	−8.27	101	82.8	−12.9	126
	(4.40)	(1.77)	(4.21)	(2.38)	(2.31)	(3.81)
April rain squared	−16.2	−8.84	−14.2	−62.1	8.69	−63.3
	(1.92)	(5.30)	(1.52)	(5.63)	(4.89)	(6.02)
July rain	−34.6	−21.5	−38.7	−116	−20.8	−39.7
	(2.63)	(8.27)	(2.51)	(6.17)	(6.91)	(2.16)
July rain squared	51.9	3.56	51.9	57.0	1.01	29.2
	(9.41)	(3.26)	(9.40)	(8.35)	(0.92)	(4.36)
October rain	−50.0	−14.4	−53.2	−124	0.41	−67.5
	(2.23)	(3.24)	(2.29)	(3.87)	(0.08)	(2.20)
October rain squared	2.13	6.38	3.06	171	10.5	119
	(0.16)	(2.36)	(0.22)	(14.43)	(5.51)	(10.22)
Control variables						
Constant	1,330	45.7	1,340	1,450	56.4	1,480
	(60.18)	(10.47)	(44.61)	(47.22)	(11.42)	(50.52)
Income per capita	71.1	−2.42	70.5	48.5	−2.23	686
	(15.24)	(2.63)	(14.83)	(6.48)	(1.85)	(9.50)
Density	1,300	0.02	1,310	1,530	0.01	1,470
	(18.51)	(1.56)	(18.48)	(18.48)	(0.57)	(18.71)
Density squared	−172	−0.01	−172	−204	−0.01	−181
	(5.31)	(0.91)	(5.33)	(7.61)	(1.96)	(7.07)
Solar radiation	−90.6	−14.1	−93.2	−105	−3.53	−15.0
	(6.12)	(4.81)	(5.94)	(5.53)	(1.15)	(0.79)
Altitude	−167	7.78	−167	−163	17.5	15.3
	(6.10)	(1.43)	(6.10)	(4.80)	(3.21)	(0.45)
Salinity	−683	−192	−733	−582	−122	−1,230
	(3.33)	(4.72)	(3.21)	(2.63)	(3.43)	(5.77)
Flood prone	−164	36.7	−157	−663	9.07	−618
	(3.41)	(3.86)	(3.07)	(8.75)	(0.74)	(8.57)
Wetland	−58.4	132	−30.3	762	150	669
	(0.48)	(5.45)	(0.22)	(4.49)	(5.50)	(4.13)
Soil erosion	−1,260	58.2	−1,240	−2,690	112	−3,350
	(6.21)	(1.45)	(6.05)	(8.37)	(2.17)	(10.85)
Slope length	17.3	18.4	23.1	54.0	31.0	−21.5
	(2.90)	(15.54)	(1.79)	(6.35)	(22.68)	(2.33)
Sand	−138	31.6	−132	−288	−13.3	−255
	(2.72)	(3.13)	(2.54)	(4.24)	(1.22)	(3.94)
Clay	86.4	0.36	87.0	−7.90	9.59	−30.2
	(4.09)	(0.08)	(4.11)	(0.23)	(1.71)	(0.91)
Water capacity	378	−0.86	380	206	−60.6	222
	(9.69)	(0.11)	(9.67)	(3.89)	(7.14)	(4.41)
Permeability	−2.50	2.64	−1.76	−12.7	3.00	−39.1
	(1.07)	(5.74)	(0.64)	(5.68)	(8.32)	(14.93)
Irrigation	—	—	−193	—	—	911
			(0.51)			(17.42)
Adjusted R^2	0.779	0.436	0.779	0.837	0.764	0.852
Observations	2,938	2,938	2,938	2,938	2,938	2,938

[a] Values in parentheses are t-statistics.

effect of higher temperatures and especially precipitation. Because irrigation is a substitute for precipitation, it may seem odd that precipitation is more valuable with irrigation in the model. Irrigation, however, involves substantial capital investments that increase the purchase price or observed land value of farms. By introducing irrigation explicitly in the model, one controls for these additional investments. The value of low precipitation farms (with more irrigation) falls, taking into account irrigation capital, making precipitation more valuable.

Darwin's concern that irrigation should be included in the Ricardian crop-revenue model is confirmed. However, contrary to his expectation, the original model was not too optimistic about temperature and precipitation. It was slightly too pessimistic. Predictions of the effects of warming increase slightly with irrigation in the Ricardian model. For example, a 2°C, 8-percent precipitation warming, according to the crop-revenue model in MNS, increases crop net revenues by 3.3 percent while the new model predicts an increase in crop net revenues of 10.4 percent.

Interestingly, the second-order terms on temperature in the crop-revenue equation continue to be positive in Table 1 even with irrigation. The problem with the shape of this function is not due to irrigation. What is missing in Table 1 is a function describing the effect of climate on the probability that land is being farmed. When aggregate farm value per acre of land is used as the dependent variable in a Ricardian analysis, the second-order temperature coefficients have the correct sign (Mendelsohn et al., 1996).

Despite Darwin's concern with the crop-revenue model, we continue to favor this model over the cropland model. We feel it is more representative of the agricultural sector, even though it may be less representative of

the landscape. Crop-revenue weights distribute the influence of all crops according to their contribution to GNP. There is no evidence that crop-revenue weights give warm-weather crops too much influence. As Darwin himself notes, over half of crop revenues belong to the grain-growing states and only one-fourth of crop revenues come from warm-weather crops.

It is important to remember that the Ricardian model was designed to measure the influence of climate on crops. Darwin's suggestions to include livestock in the crop model would probably only muddy the waters since there is no reason to expect that livestock would have the same relationship with climate as crops. The crop model already accounts for the influence that crop production may have on livestock production. In order to measure the effect of climate on livestock; it would be best to estimate an independent regression of livestock net income on climate.

REFERENCES

Darwin, Roy. "The Impact of Global Warming on Agriculture: A Ricardian Analysis: Comment." *American Economic Review*, September 1999, *89*(4), 1049–52.

Mendelsohn, Robert; Nordhaus, William D. and Shaw, Daigee. "The Impact of Global Warming on Agriculture: A Ricardian Analysis." *American Economic Review*, September 1994, *84*(4), pp. 753–71.

_____. "Climate Impacts on Aggregate Farm Values: Accounting for Adaptation." *Journal of Agricultural and Forest Meteorology*, June 1996, *80*(1), pp. 55–66.

Mendelsohn, Robert and Neumann, James, eds. *The impact of climate change on the United States economy.* Cambridge: Cambridge University Press, 1998.

Part II
Evaluating the Costs and Benefits of Climate Change Mitigation

[11]

Rolling the 'DICE': An optimal transition path for controlling greenhouse gases*

William D. Nordhaus

Yale University, New Haven, CT 06520, USA

Final version received November 1992

Economic analyses of efficient policies to slow climate change require combining economic and scientific approaches. The present study presents a dynamic integrated climate-economy ('DICE') model. This model can be used to investigate alternative approaches to slowing climate change. Evaluation of five policies suggest that a modest carbon tax would be an efficient approach to slow global warming, while rigid emissions-stabilization approaches would impose significant net economic costs.

1. Introduction

The threat of climate change has become a major economic and political issue, symbolic of growing concerns that humans are making irreversible and potentially calamitous interventions in life-support systems. Climatologists and other scientists have warned that the accumulation of carbon dioxide (CO_2) and other greenhouse gases (GHGs) is likely to lead to global warming and other significant climatic changes over the next century. Many scientific bodies, along with a growing chorus of environmentalists and governments, are calling for severe curbs on the emissions of greenhouse gases, as for example the reports of the Intergovernmental Panel on Climate Change [IPPC (1990)] and the Second World Climate Conference (October 1990). Governments have recently approved a 'framework treaty' on climate change to monitor trends and national efforts, and this treaty formed the centerpiece of the 'Earth Summit' held in Rio in June 1992.

To date, the calls to arms and treaty negotiations have progressed more or

Correspondence to: Professor William D. Nordhaus, Cowles Foundation, Yale University, Box 1972, Yale Station, New Haven, CT 06520, USA.

*This research was supported by the National Science Foundation. The author is grateful for helpful suggestions from Jesse Ausubel, Richard Cooper, William Hogan, Allan Manne, Thomas Schelling, Stephen Schneider, Paul Waggoner, and John Weyant, and for patient research assistance from Zili Yang.

less independently of economic studies of the costs and benefits of measures to slow greenhouse warming. Over the last few years, however, a growing (but not unanimous) body of evidence has pointed to the likelihood that greenhouse warming will have only modest economic impacts in industrial countries, while programs to cut GHG emissions will impose substantial costs. Like two ships passing in the night, the economic studies and the treaty negotiations seems to be proceeding independently under their own steam.

Notwithstanding the difficulties of marrying the economic analysis with the policy process, the need to address the potential issues raised by future climate change is daunting for those who take policy analysis seriously. It raises formidable issues of data, modeling, uncertainty, international coordination, and institutional design. In addition, the economic stakes are enormous, involving investments on the order of hundreds of billions of dollars a year to slow or prevent climate change.

In earlier studies, I developed a simple cost–benefit framework for determining the optimal 'steady-state' control of CO_2 and other greenhouse gases.[1] This earlier study came to a middle-of-the-road conclusion that the threat of greenhouse warming was sufficient to justify modest steps to slow the pace of climate change, but I found that the calls for draconian cuts in GHG emissions by 50% or more were not warranted by the current scientific and economic evidence on costs and impacts.

The earlier studies had a number of shortcomings, but one of the most significant from an analytical point of view was the inadequate treatment of the dynamics of the economy and the climate. The steady-state approach is unsatisfactory primarily because of the extraordinarily long time lags involved in the reaction of the climate and economy to greenhouse gas emissions. Current scientific estimates indicate that the major GHGs have an atmospheric residence time over 100 years; moreover, because of the great thermal inertia of the oceans, the climate appears to have a lag of several decades behind the changes in GHG concentrations; and there are long lags in introduction of new technologies in human economies to changing economic conditions. It would appear, therefore, that the dynamics are of the essence and that an examination of the steady state may provide misleading conclusions for the steps that we should take at the dawn of the age of greenhouse warming.

The plan of the present study is to develop a dynamic, global model of both the impacts of and policies to slow global warming. It is an integrated model that incorporates both the dynamics of emissions and impacts and the economic costs of policies to curb emissions. We call it the *DICE model* as

---

[1]The latest version appears in abbreviated form in Nordhaus (1991a) and in greater detail in Nordhaus (1991b).

an acronym for a 'Dynamic Integrated Climate-Economy model'.[2] This new model is an advance over earlier studies in that it allows for different policies in the transition path from those in the ultimate steady state. It does this through the extension of the standard tools of modern optimal economic growth theory and adding to this analysis both a climate sector and a closed-loop interaction between the climate and the economy. The model is sufficiently small as to be transparent (or at least translucent), to allow a range of sensitivity analyses, and to be available for a number of further extensions.

The purpose of this paper is to lay out in details the structure of the model and the nature of the assumptions. The first section lays out the algebra of the model in simplified form. The following sections derive the parameters of the model in detail. The final sections then show some empirical runs of the model and provide estimates of the optimal policy along with some alternative approaches.

2. Methodology

Existing empirical studies of the interaction between climate change and economic growth have generally been of a partial-equilibrium or static nature. Much economic work has to date analyzed the costs of different GHG restrictions. Estimating the economic and other impacts of greenhouse warming has proved extremely difficult. I have attempted to summarize the results of studies for the United States [see Nordhaus (1991c)], but these remain incomplete in a number of respects.

The present study constructs a dynamic optimization model for estimating the optimal path of reductions of GHG gases. The basic approach is to use a Ramsey model of optimal economic growth with certain adjustments and to estimate the optimal path for both capital accumulation and GHG-emission reductions. The resulting trajectory can be interpreted as either (i) the most efficient path for slowing climate change given initial endowments or (ii) as the competitive equilibrium among market economies where the externalities are internalized using the appropriate social shadow prices for GHGs. We first describe the approach verbally and then present the model in equation form.

In intuitive language, the approach is the following. Begin with the market sector of the economy. The global economy is assumed to produce a composite commodity. This means that countries can differ in their quantita-

---

[2]The complete model is presented in a forthcoming book [Nordhaus (1993a)]. In addition, the theoretical underpinnings of the model are developed in a companion paper, Nordhaus (1993b), which developed an optimal growth model in which to analyze the issue of the optimal response to the threat of climate change under conditions of certainty.

tive attributes, but there cannot be large differences in the composition or relative proportions of different commodities. While this is a restrictive assumption, preliminary work with a more complete multi-country model suggests that aggregation does not affect the major conclusions.

Our composite economy is endowed with an initial stock of capital, labor, and technology, and all industries behave competitively. Each country maximizes an intertemporal objective function, identical in each region, which is the sum of discounted utilities of per capita consumption times population. Output is produced by a Cobb–Douglas production function in capital, labor, and technology. Population growth and technological change are exogenous, while capital accumulation is determined by optimizing the flow of consumption over time.

The next part of the model introduces a number of relationships that attempt to capture the major forces affecting climate change. This part includes an emissions equation, a concentrations equation, a climate equation, a damage relationship, and a cost function for reducing emissions. Emissions represent all GHG emissions, although they are most easily interpreted as CO_2. Uncontrolled emissions are a slowly declining fraction of gross output; this assumption is consistent with a complex set of assumptions about the underlying production functions. GHG emissions can be controlled by increasing the prices of factors or outputs that are GHG-intensive.[3]

Atmospheric concentrations are increased with emissions, with concentrations reduced with an atmospheric residence time of 120 years. Climate change is represented by realized global mean surface temperature, which uses an equilibrium relationship drawn from the consensus of climate modelers and a lag given by a recent coupled ocean-atmospheric models. The economic impacts of climate change are assumed to be increasing in the realized temperature increase.

We note that this model has one major shortcoming as a representation of economic and political reality. It assumes that the public goods nature of climate change is somehow overcome. That is, it assumes that, through some mechanism, countries internalize in their *national* decision making the *global* costs of their emissions decisions. This seems unlikely, but the current solution has the virtue of calculating the equilibrium that would emerge were each country to behave in such a farsighted and altruistic fashion.

---

[3]One concern that has arisen about this set of assumptions is whether it is consistent with fundamental laws of physics. Is it possible, in other words, to have an indefinite decline in emissions-output ratios? In principle, the answer is clearly yes because output is measured in 'utils' (or, more precisely, in ratios of marginal utilities), not in physical terms. Reductions arise if the composition of output moves toward goods and services that have lower intensities of constrained physical units (away from copper wire and toward moving a few electrons in fibers). Moreover, the waste of energy in current economic activity is prodigious.

3. Model

3.1. Basic outline[4]

In estimating the efficient path of capital accumulation and emissions reduction, we use the following model and assumptions. The different regions of the world are aggregated together and we analyze the optimal policy for the average individual. Clearly, this assumption misses much of the current dilemma and debate between developed and poor countries, and it also averages out the losers and the winners from climate change. The defense of this assumption is that this study is concerned with the efficient *intertemporal* policies, not with the issues concerning the distribution of income across countries or people.

The model operates in steps of 10 years centered on 1965, 1975, 1985, ..., 2095, ... The model is calibrated by fitting the solution for the first three decades to the actual data for 1965, 1975 and 1985 and is then optimizing for capital accumulation and GHG emissions in the future. This approach assumes that it is desirable to maximize a social welfare function that is the discounted sum of the utilities of per capita consumption. The major decision is about the level of consumption today, where abstaining from consumption today increases consumption for future generations. In technical language, we desire to maximize the objective function:

$$\max_{\{c(t)\}} \sum_t U[c(t), P(t)](1 + \rho)^{-t}, \tag{1}$$

which is the discounted sum of the utilities of consumption, $U[c(t), P(t)]$, summed over the relevant time horizon. Here U is the flow of utility or social well-being, $c(t)$ is the flow of consumption per capita at time t, $P(t)$ is the level of population at time t, and ρ is the pure rate of social time preference.[5]

The maximization is subject to a number of constraints. The first set

---

[4]This section presents the bare bones of a longer study which documents the data, assumptions, and literature more fully. The longer study is currently available in Nordhaus (1992) and will be forthcoming as a monograph from MIT Press in Nordhaus (1993a).

[5]No issue is more controversial than the role of discounting in long-term environmental problems. Much confusion arises because of the failure to distinguish between time discounting and goods discounting, a distinction that is well handled in the Ramsey model. Time discounting refers to the trade-off between the utility or well-being of different generations and is represented by the pure rate of time preference, ρ, in the objective function. However, most social decisions involve goods and services rather than well-being. Society must decide whether to make an investment aimed at reducing today's consumption in order to increase consumption in the future; this approach is one of goods discounting, and the intertemporal price is reflected in the real interest rate, r. In the framework used here, with no population growth, with a growth rate of real income at rate g, and in steady state, goods discounting is related to time discounting by the equilibrium formula $r = \rho + \alpha g$.

represents economic constraints, while the second is the novel set of climate-emissions constraints.

3.2. Economic constraints[6]

The first set of constraints is those relating to the growth of output. Economists will recognize these as a standard model of optimal economic growth known as the 'Ramsey model' [Ramsey (1928); Solow (1988)]. The first equation is the definition of utility, which is equal to the size of population [$P(t)$] times the utility of per capita consumption $u[c(t)]$. We take a power function to represent the form of the utility function:

$$U[c(t), P(t)] = P(t)\{[c(t)]^{1-\alpha} - 1\}/(1-\alpha). \tag{2}$$

In this equation, the parameter α is a measure of the social valuation of different levels of consumption, which we call the 'rate of inequality aversion'. When $\alpha = 0$, the utility function is linear and there is no social aversion to inequality; as α gets large, the social attitude becomes increasingly egalitarian. In the experiments reported here, we take $\alpha = 1$, which is the logarithmic or Bernoullian utility function.

Output [$Q(t)$] is given by a standard Cobb–Douglas production function in capital in technology [$A(t)$], capital [$K(t)$], and labor, which is proportional to population. The term $\Omega(t)$ relates to climatic impacts and will be described in eq. (12):

$$Q(t) = \Omega(t)A(t)K(t)^{\gamma}P(t)^{1-\gamma}, \tag{3}$$

where γ is the elasticity of output with respect to capital. We assume constant returns to scale in capital and labor.

The next equation shows the disposition of output between consumption [$C(t)$] and gross investment [$I(t)$]:

$$C(t) = Q(t) - I(t). \tag{4}$$

This simply notes that output can be devoted either to investment or to consumption.

The next equation is the definition of per capita consumption:

$$c(t) = C(t)/P(t). \tag{5}$$

Finally, we have the capital balance equation for the capital stock:

---

[6]This section presents a summary of a more extensive analysis of the DICE model. The full documentation is given in Nordhaus (1993a).

$$K(t) = (1 - \delta_K)K(t-1) + I(t), \tag{6}$$

where δ_K is the rate of depreciation of the capital stock.

3.3. Climate-emissions-damage equations

The next set of constraints will be unfamiliar to most economists and consists of a simple representation of the relationship between economic activity, emissions, concentrations, and climate change. As with the economic relationships, these equations are highly aggregated.

3.3.1. Emissions

The first equation links greenhouse-gas emissions to economic activity. In the analysis that follows, we translate each of the GHGs into its CO_2 equivalent. To aggregate the different GHGs, we use a measure of the total warming potential, which is the contribution of a GHG to global warming summed over the indefinite future. Approximately 80% of the total warming potential is due to CO_2, and we therefore put most of our effort into analyzing that gas.

In modeling GHG emissions, I assume that the ratio of uncontrolled GHG emissions to gross output is a slowly moving parameter represented by $\sigma(t)$. In what follows, we assume that the exogenous decline in σ is 1.25% per annum. GHG emissions can be reduced through a wide range of policies. We represent the rate of emissions reduction by an 'emissions control factor', $\mu(t)$. This is the fractional reduction of emissions relative to the uncontrolled level. One of the key questions investigated here is the optimal trajectory of emissions control. The emissions equation is given as:

$$E(t) = [1 - \mu(t)]\sigma(t)Q(t). \tag{7}$$

In this equation, $E(t)$ is GHG emissions, $\sigma(t)$ is determined from historical data, and it is assumed that GHG emissions were uncontrolled through 1990. The variable $\mu(t)$ is determined by the optimization.

3.3.2. Concentrations

The next relationship in the economy–climate nexus represents the accumulation of GHGs in the atmosphere. For the non-CO_2 GHGs, the issues are relatively straightforward issues of estimating the atmospheric lifetimes or chemical transformations. We concentrate here on CO_2 because that is likely to be the most important gas for greenhouse warming. I assume that CO_2 accumulation and transportation can be represented as a system of boxes in which each of the boxes is well mixed. The background study [Nordhaus (1992a, 1993)] shows that this can be represented by the following equation:

$$M(t) = \beta E(t) + (1 - \delta_M) M(t - 1),\tag{8}$$

where $M(t)$ is the change in concentrations from pre-industrial times, β is the marginal atmospheric retention ratio, and δ_M is the rate of transfer from the quickly mixing reservoirs to the deep ocean. This equation is the GHG analog of the capital accumulation equation. Atmospheric concentrations in a period are determined by last period's concentrations $[M(t-1)]$ times $(1 - \delta_M)$, where δ_M is the rate of removal of GHGs. We have estimated this relationship on historical data (1860–1985) and derived the following equation:

$$M(t) - 0.9917 M(t - 1) = 0.64 E(t) \qquad R^2 = 0.803, \text{SEE} = 0.519$$
$$(0.015)\tag{8'}$$

This is the equation we use in the model.

3.3.3. Climate change

The next step concerns the relationship between the accumulation of greenhouse gases and climate change. Climate modelers have developed a wide variety of approaches for estimating the impact of rising GHGs on climatic variables. On the whole, existing models are, unfortunately, much too complex to be included in economic models. Another difficulty with current general circulation models (GCMs) is that they have generally been used to estimate the equilibrium impact of a change in CO_2 concentrations upon the level of temperature and other variables. For economic analyses, it is essential to understand the dynamics or transient properties of the response of climate to GHG concentrations.

The basic approach is to develop a small model that captures the summary relationship between GHG concentrations and the dynamics of climate change. In what follows, we represent the climate system by a multi-layer system; more precisely, there are three layers – the atmosphere, the mixed layer of the oceans, and the deep oceans – each of which is assumed to be well mixed. The accumulation of GHGs warms the atmospheric layer, which then warms the mixed ocean, which in turn diffuses into the deep oceans. The lags in the system are primarily due to the thermal inertia of the three layers. We can write the model as follows:

$$T_1(t) = T_1(t-1) + (1/R_1)\{F(t) - \lambda T_1(t-1) -$$

$$(R_2/\tau_2)[T_1(t-1) - T_2(t-1)]\},$$

$$\text{(9)}$$

$$T_2(t) = T_2(t-1) + (1/R_2)\{(R_2/\tau_2)[T_1(t-1) - T_2(t-1)]\},$$

where $T_i(t)$ = temperature of layer i in period t (relative to the pre-industrial period); $i = 1$ for the atmosphere and upper oceans (rapidly mixed layer) and $i = 2$ for the deep oceans; $F(t)$ = radiative forcing in the atmosphere (relative to the pre-industrial period); R_i = the thermal capacity of the different layers; τ_2 = the transfer rate from the upper layer to the lower layer; and λ = feedback parameter.

The next step is to find the appropriate numerical representation of the simplified climate model in (9). We estimate the parameters in (9) by calibrating the smaller model to transient runs from larger GCMs and by comparing the predictions with historical data. Unfortunately, the models disagee by a wide margin, and the historical data are even further at variance from the climate models. In the study here, we use the results from a study by Schlesinger and Jiang (1990) for calibration purposes. This study has a temperature–CO_2 sensitivity of 3°C for CO_2 doubling, which is close to that of the scientific consensus [see National Academy of Sciences (1992)].

3.3.4. Impacts

The next link in the chain is the impact of climate change on human and natural systems. Estimating the damages from greenhouse warming has proven extremely difficult. An early discussion is contained in Schelling (1983), EPA summarized a number of studies (1989), and I put those studies into the context of the national-income accounts in Nordhaus (1991b). The overall assessment of the cost of greenhouse warming in the U.S. was that the net economic damage from a 3°C warming is likely to be around 0.25% of national income for the United States in terms of those variables could be quantified. This figure is clearly incomplete, for it neglects a number of areas that are either inadequately studied or inherently unquantifiable. As a rough adjustment, I increased this number to around 1% of total U.S. output to allow for these unmeasured and unquantifiable factors. Making adjustments for output composition in different countries, I further raised the estimated impact to 1.33% of global output for all countries. In addition, there is evidence that the impact increases nonlinearly as the temperature increases, and we assume that the relationship is quadratic. Therefore, the final relationship between global temperature increase and income loss is:

$$d(t) = 0.0133[T(t)/3]^2 Q(t), \qquad \text{(10)}$$

where $d(t)$ is the loss of global output from greenhouse warming. Although there is much controversy about the parameters of (10), using alternative estimates of impacts does not change the basic results markedly.[7]

3.3.5. Cost of emissions reduction

The last major link in the chain is the costs of reduction of greenhouse gases. This is the one area that has been extensively studied and, while not without controversy, the general shape of the cost function has been sketched on a number of occasions. There are numerous estimates, particularly for CO_2, of the cost of reducing GHGs; see the extensive surveys in EPA (1990), Nordhaus (1991c), Dean and Hoeller (1992), Amano (1992), EC (1992a, b) and the results of EMF-12.[8] Using current annual emissions of 8 billion tons of CO_2 equivalent, my survey suggested that a modest reduction of GHG emissions can be obtained at low cost. After 10% reduction, however, the curve rises as more costly measures are required. A 50% reduction in GHG emissions is estimated to cost almost $200 billion per year in today's global economy, or around 1% of world output. This estimate is understated to the extent that policies are inefficient or are implemented in a crash program. The final form of the equation used in the model is:

$$TC(t)/GNP(t) = b_1 \mu(t)^{b2} = 0.0686 \mu(t)^{2.887} \tag{11}$$

where μ is the fractional reduction in GHG emissions and TC/GNP is the total cost of the reduction as a fraction of world output.[9]

Combining the cost and damage relationships, we have the Ω relationship in the production function as follows:

$$\Omega(t) = [1 - b_1 \mu(t)^{b2}]/[1 + d(t)]$$

[7]A thorough review of impacts by Cline (1992) finds an estimated impacts of 1.1% of GNP for a 2.5°C warming as opposed to the estimate of 1% for 3°C warming by the present author. A more recent unpublished study by Fankhauser (1992) estimates total impacts of a doubling of CO_2 would lead to a 1.3% cost to the US, a 1.4% cost to the OECD, and a 1.5% cost to the world. Because estimating the impacts of climate change has proven extremely difficult, the present author is in the process of undertaking a survey of experts on the economic impacts of climate change on human and non-human systems. At the mid-point of the survey, the 'trimmed mean' of the experts' estimate of the impact of a 3°C warming is approximately 20% higher than the estimate used in the DICE model while the experts' estimate of the impact of a 6°C warming is about 30% lower than that in the DICE model. One major concern of most respondents is that the impact is thought to be considerably higher for low-income countries than in high-income countries.

[8]The most systematic study is the model comparison study of the Stanford Energy Modelling Forum 12 under the general direction of John Weyant. The results of this study have been presented informally and conform for the most part to the survey in Nordhaus (1991c).

[9]Alternative views of the costs of mitigation are contained in National Academy of Sciences (1992) and Cline (1992). The major difference among studies concerns the possibility of zero-cost or low-cost mitigation in areas where informational deficiencies or market failures hinder reaping all cost-beneficial investments in energy conservation. National Academy of Sciences (1992) estimates these to range between 10 and 40% of U.S. GHG emissions, whereas this study is at the lower end of that range.

$$= [1 - 0.0686\mu(t)^{2.887}]/[1 + 0.00144T(t)^2]. \tag{12}$$

4. Data, calibration, and sensitivity analysis[10]

4.1. Fitting the model

This section describes briefly the sources of the data used for the model and the calibration of the model to the data. Data on the major variables were collected for three years, 1965, 1975 and 1985, while future periods are estimated by the calculations described above. Data on population, GNP, consumption, and investment are obtained from existing data sources of the World Bank, UNESCO, the OECD and the U.S. and other national governments.

The parameters of the Cobb–Douglas production function are obtained by assuming that the output-elasticity of capital is 0.25 and then by estimating the level and rate of Hicks-neutral technological change directly as a residual. The utility function is assumed to be logarithmic, and the rate of social time preference is taken to be three percent per year. This preference function leads to predictions of the rate of return on capital and the gross savings rate that are close to observed levels.

Assumptions about future growth trends are as follows: the rate of growth of population is assumed to decrease slowly, stabilizing at 10.5 billion people in the 22nd century. The rate of growth of total factor productivity is calculated to be 1.3% per annum in the 1960–1989 period. This rate is assumed to decline slowly over the coming decades.

The model has been run using the 486 version of the GAMS algorithm on various 386 compatible machines. The canonical runs presented below use a 40-period calculation with terminal valuations (or transversality conditions) on carbon, capital, and atmospheric temperature; these terminal valuations were obtained from a 60-period run and are sufficient to stabilize the solution for the first 20 periods. The canonical 40-period run can be solved in about two minutes on an Intel 486/33 processor.

Optimization models of the kind analyzed here have proven extremely resistant to conventional econometric estimation. In the place of a formal statistical procedure, we have simply chosen parameters so that the values taken by the model in the first three periods are tolerably close to actual data. The current solution matches global GNP, emissions, GHG concentrations, and even estimates of global temperature change reasonably well for the historical periods.

---

[10]The details of the data are described in Nordhaus (1993a).

4.2. Sensitivity analyses

The DICE model contains many parameters and assumptions that will affect the projections and policy conclusions. The present study presents the central or 'best-guess' case and does not at this stage include sensitivity analyses. In work underway, however, an extensive and systematic attempt to evaluate the major uncertainties has been undertaken, and that analysis will be presented in Nordhaus (1993a). A brief description of the approach and tentative results of the sensitivity analysis will be provided here.

The sensitivity analysis first screens each of the parameters and major model components in the DICE model to determine which are important for economic, environmental, and policy variables. Among the two dozen parameters, nine which have the most impact upon key outcomes are then selected for detailed analysis – these nine including parameters such as population and productivity growth, the parameters of the climate, emissions, and concentrations modules, and the rate of time preference. A Monte Carlo run then provides estimates of the uncertainty due to each parameter as well as the underlying uncertainty about the major variables (such as temperature, GHG concentrations, and GHG control rates). The major results of this stage to data are that the results are modestly sensitive to alternative values of major variables. Among the important variables that produce large uncertainties are population and productivity growth, the trend in the GHG emissions–output ratio, and the pure rate of time preference.[11]

The final stage of the analysis is to determine the impact upon the optimal policy of uncertainty. Should we pay an 'insurance premium' to reflect the impact of uncertainty, non-linearity, and risk aversion upon our optimal policy? While the research on the issue is still underway, it appears that the uncertainty about the size and impacts of future climate change would add a significant risk premium to, perhaps even doubling, the 'best guess' policies analyzed here.

5. Policy experiments

We now describe the different scenarios or policy experiments to which the model is applied.

---

[11]Many readers of this and associated studies have expressed concern that the results are inherent in assuming too high a 'discount rate'. While there is some merit in this point, the whole story is more complicated. In the first point, the distinction between time discounting and goods discounting is often obscured. While people may raise ethical objections to time preference in the form of a high pure rate of time preference, there is no analogous objection to a high rate of goods discounting in the form of a high real interest rate where that reflects rapid growth of living standards. Second, when the pure rate of time preference is lowered to 0.1% per year while adjusting the rate of inequality aversion to maintain the same real rate of interest, there is only a modest change in the optimal policy (either the carbon tax or the GHG control rate). The change in the optimal policy occurs because an increase in the net savings rate drives down the real interest rate.

5.1. No controls ('baseline')

The first run is one in which there are no policies taken to slow or reverse greenhouse warming. Individuals would adapt to the changing climate, but governments would take no steps to curb greenhouse-gas emissions or to internalize the greenhouse externality. This policy is one which has been followed for the most part by nations through 1989.

5.2. Optimal policy

The second case undertakes to construct economically efficient or 'optimal' policies to slow climate change. This run maximizes the present value of economic welfare; more precisely, this case maximizes the discounted value of utility in (1) subject to the constraints and relationships in (2) to (12). This policy can be thought of as one in which the nations of the world gather to set the efficient policy for internalizing the greenhouse externality. It is assumed that the policy is efficiently implemented, say through uniform carbon taxation, in the decade beginning 1990.

5.3. Ten-year delay of optimal policy

This policy is one which delays implementing the optimal policy for ten years. This policy examines the issue of the costs and benefits of delaying implementing policies until our knowledge about the greenhouse effect, along with its costs and benefits, is more secure. This approach has been advocated by the U.S. government during the Bush administration. In this scenario, we assume that sufficient information is in hand so that the optimal policy is implemented beginning in the decade starting in 2000.

5.4. Twenty percent emissions reductions from 1990 levels

Many environmentalists and some governments are proposing a substantial cut in CO_2 or GHG emissions. One target that has been prominently mentioned is a 20% cut in emissions. This is interpreted here as a 20% cut of the combination of CFC and CO_2 emissions from 1990 levels, where these are converted to a CO_2-equivalent basis. In quantitative terms, this represents an emissions limitation of 6.8 billion tons per year of CO_2 equivalent. This policy has no particular analytical, scientific, or economic merit, but it has the virtue of simplicity; it implies a growing percentage reduction in the future given a growing uncontrolled emissions path.

Table 1

Impact of alternative policies on discounted consumption.

Run no.	Description	Discounted value of consumption, 1990 [trillions of 1989 US $]	Difference from no controls [billions of $]	Percent difference
1	No controls	731.694	0	0.000
2	Optimal policy	731.965	271	0.037
3	Ten-year delay	731.937	243	0.033
4	Stabilize emission	720.786	(10.908)	−1.491
5	Geoengineering	737.296	5.602	0.766

5.5. Geoengineering

A final policy would be to determine the benefit of a technology which would provide costless mitigation of climate change. This could occur, for example, if some of the geoengineering options proved technically feasible and environmentally benign. Two interesting proposals include shooting smart mirrors into space with 16-inch naval rifles or seeding the oceans with iron to accelerate carbon sequestration.[12] An alternative interpretation would be that the greenhouse effect has no harmful economic effects. This scenario is useful as a baseline to determine the overall economic impact of greenhouse warming and of policies to combat warming.

6. Results and conclusions

We now summarize the overall results for the five scenarios described above. A longer description of the model and a presentation of the numerical results is contained in Nordhaus (1993a).

6.1. Overall results

Table 1 shows the overall evaluation of the different policies. The first column shows the discounted value of consumption for the five paths. This is calculated as the present value of consumption after 1990 discounted at the market rate of return on capital (discounted back to 1990 in 1989 prices).

The optimal policy in row 2 has greater value than the three other policies in rows 1, 3 and 4.[13] The optimal policy has a net benefit of $271 billion relative to a policy in which no controls are undertaken. This number is

---

[12]The issues of geoengineering are discussed in National Academy of Sciences (1992).

[13]The values in column 3 for run *i* are equal to the present value of consumption for run 1 plus the algebraic difference in the attained value of the objective function from run *i* to run 1.

absolutely large, although it is only 0.037% of the discounted value of the consumption. The cost of delaying the optimal policy by ten years is estimated to be $28 billion.

The environmentalists policy of reducing emissions 20% below 1990 levels is extremely costly. We estimate that this policy will cost $10.9 trillion in present value terms. This constitutes 1.5% of the total discounted value of consumption.

The last row shows the overall economic impact of climate change. The net damage from global warming is estimated to be $5.9 trillion relative to the optimal policy and $5.6 trillion relative to a policy of no controls. These represent 0.81 and 0.77% of the discounted value of consumption.

In general, these numbers are mind-numbing in absolute size – largely because we are considering global output over the indefinite future. On the other hand, with the exception of the policy of stabilizing emissions, the numbers are modest relative to the total size of the global economy.

6.2 Emissions and concentrations

We next show some of the details of the model runs. Figs. 1 and 2 show the emissions control rates in different scenarios. These show the extent to which GHG emissions are reduced below their uncontrolled levels. In the optimal path, the rate of emissions reduction is approximately 10% of GHG emissions in the near future, rising to 15% late in the next century. (Recall that this is primarily CO_2 emissions.) The environmental path of a 20% cut in emissions from the 1990 level shows steeply rising control rates, with the rate of control reaching 70% by the end of the next century.

Fig. 3 shows projected CO_2-equivalent atmospheric concentrations in billions of tons CO_2 equivalent (again, this includes both CO_2 and CFCs). The impact of the optimal control strategy is noticeable, reducing concentrations by a little more than 100 billion tons at the end of the next century. Note that even with emissions stabilized at 80% of 1990 levels, the atmospheric concentrations of CO_2-equivalent concentrations continue to rise. The ten-year delay in implementing greenhouse gas restraints show virtually no difference from the optimal path and is not included in the graph.

6.3. Global temperature

Fig. 4 shows the resulting projected increase in realized mean global surface temperatures (relative to temperatures in the 19th century). The uncontrolled path shows an initial increase of around 0.6°C today, rising to 3.1°C by 2100.

The optimal path shows a modest decline in the growth rate of global

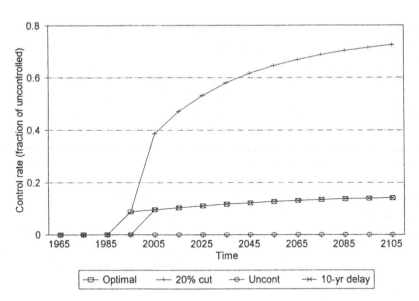

Fig. 1. Greenhouse-gas control rate (reduction in GHG emissions).

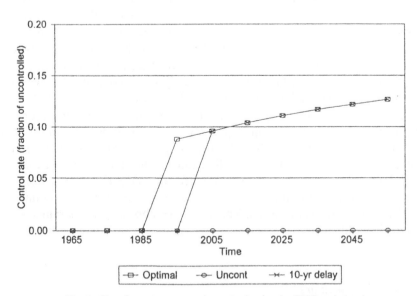

Fig. 2. Greenhouse-gas control rate (reduction in GHG emissions).

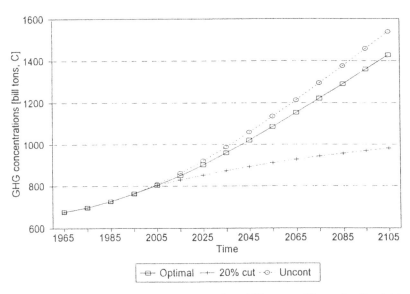

Fig. 3. Atmospheric greenhouse gas concentrations (billion tons CO_2 equiv., C weight).

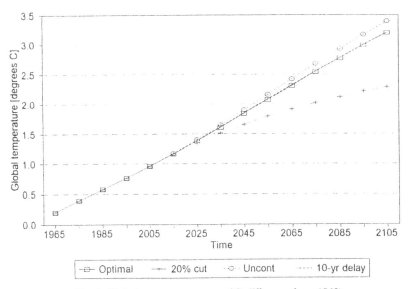

Fig. 4. Global mean temperature ($^\circ$C, difference from 1860).

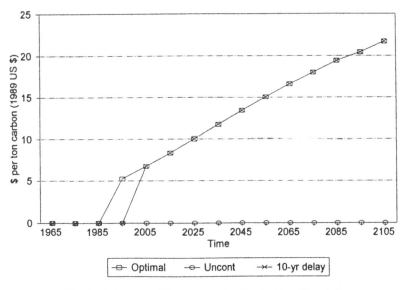

Fig. 5. Carbon tax, different scenarios (tax in $ ton C equiv.).

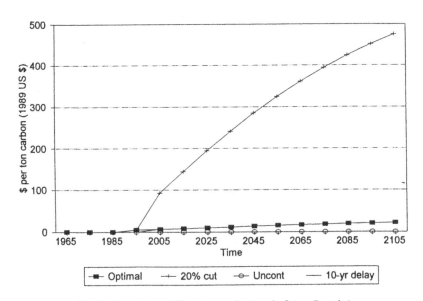

Fig. 6. Carbon tax, different scenarios (tax in $ ton C equiv.)

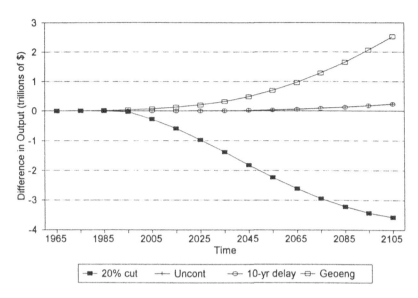

Fig. 7. Differences in global output (from baseline, trillions 1989 US $).

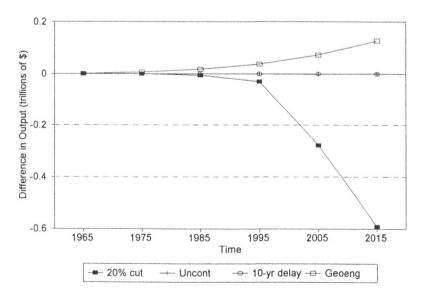

Fig. 8. Differences in global output (from baseline, trillions 1989 US $).

temperatures, with a rise of about 0.2°C less than the uncontrolled path by the end of the next century. The policy that cuts emissions to 80% of the 1990 level shows continued growth in temperatures, rising to 2.25°C by the end of the next century. This surprising result shows that even draconian policies will slow climate change only modestly. The reason is primarily because of the momentum in the system from existing concentrations of GHGs.

6.4. Carbon taxes

Figs. 5 and 6 show the carbon tax that would be necessary to implement each of the policies. The carbon tax should be thought of as the tax (or its regulatory equivalent) that would be necessary to raise fossil fuel and other prices sufficiently to induce economic agents to substitute other goods and services for carbon-intensive ones.

The optimal path shows a carbon tax of around $5 per ton carbon (or the equivalent in other GHGs) for the first control period, 1990–1999. For reference, a $10 per ton carbon tax will raise coal prices by $7 per ton, about 25% at current U.S. coal prices. The carbon tax increases gradually over time to around $20 per ton carbon by the end of the next century. The rising tax primarily reflects the rising level of global output rather than increasingly stringent control efforts.

The ten-year delay has a zero tax in the fourth period, but then is virtually indistinguishable from the optimal policy. The policy of no mitigation obviously has a zero carbon tax. Fig. 6 shows the trajectory of the policy that cut emissions 20% from 1990 levels. This tax reaches about $100 per ton early in the 21st century and climbs to almost $500 per ton by the end of the next century. Clearly, very substantial fiscal or regulatory steps are necessary to bring about a trajectory with constant CO_2 emissions.

6.5. Output

Figs. 7 and 8 show the impact of different policies on output. The first shows the estimates for the entire period while the second zooms in on the first few periods. For these calculations, the value of output is 'green' gross world output (GGWP). Conceptually, GGWP equals output less the flow of damages from climate change less the costs of mitigation. The surprising result of these figures is that the difference between a policy of no controls and the optimal policy is relatively small through the next century. The flow impact, relative to the optimum, is somewhat less than one percent of real output at the maximum. Of course, the actual damage (equal to the

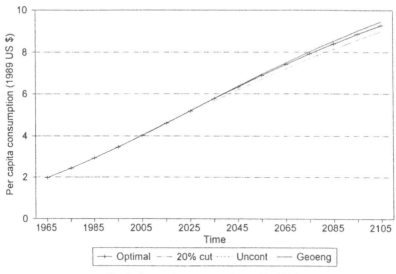

Fig. 9. Per capita consumption (1989 US $).

difference between the 'no controls' and the 'geoengineering') is much larger than the cost of no controls relative to the optimum. But the latter appears small because a fair amount of economic cost would occur even in the optimal trajectory.

While the difference between the no-controls and the optimal policies is small, there are big stakes in both the geoengineering option and in the environmental option. The impact of a geoengineering solution would be quite substantial – because it would cut the costs of both climate damage and of mitigation.

There is also potential for a major waste of resources if the greenhouse policies go too far. Fig. 7 shows the impact on green world output of going too far in the control of greenhouse gases – leading to *net* losses in output of over $3 trillion annually by the end of the next century.

Finally, fig. 9 shows the trajectory of real consumption per capita in the four cases. The striking feature of this figure is that, even though there are differences among the cases studied here, the overall economic growth projected over the coming years swamps the projected impacts of climate change or of the policies to offset climate change. In these scenarios, future generations may be worse off as a result of climate change, but they are still likely to be much better off than current generations. In looking at this graph, I was reminded of Tom Schelling's remark a few years ago that the difference between a climate-change an a no-climate-change scenario would be thinner than the line drawn by a number 2 pencil used to draw the curves. Thanks to the improved resolution of computerized graphics, we can now barely spot the difference!

7. Summary and conclusion

The present study has investigated the implications of economic growth on the environment as well as the economic impact of different environmental control strategies upon the global economy. This study takes the approach that an efficient strategy for coping with greenhouse warming must weigh the costs and benefits of different policies in an intertemporal framework. Using this approach, the major results and reservations are the following.

This study has examined five different approaches to GHG control: no control, an economic optimization, geoengineering, stabilization of emissions, and a ten-year delay in undertaking climate-change policies. Among these five, the rank order from a pure economic point of view at the present time is geoengineering, economic optimum, ten-year delay, no controls, and stabilizing emissions. The advantage of geoengineering over other policies is enormous, although this result assumes the existence of an environmentally benign geoengineering option. The policies of no controls, the economic optimum, ten-year delay, and emissions stabilization have differential impacts that are less than one percent of discounted consumption.

It is instructive to compare these results with those from other economic studies. The studies of Manne and Richels (1990, 1992), Peck and Teisberg (1991), and Kolstad (1992) find conclusions that are roughly similar to those reported here. All these studies contain explicit or implicit relationships between emissions control rates and carbon taxes; the relationships are broadly similar to those found in figs. 1, 2 and 5 of this paper, although papers with more detailed energy sectors have more complex dynamics than those seen here. The studies by Jorgenson and Wilcoxen (1991 expecially) show a lower set of carbon taxes needed to reduce GHG emissions than those shown here in part because of the induced innovation in the Jorgenson–Wilcoxen model.

Three other studies – those of Cline (1992), Peck and Teisberg (1991), Kolstad (1992) as well as earlier studies by the present author (1979, 1991a, b) – also determine the optimal emissions control rates and carbon taxes. With the exception of Cline (1992), all the earlier studies show optimal policies in the general range of those determined here. A study by Hammitt et al. (1992) traces out alternative control strategies to attain certain temperature constraints; while not determining an optimal path, this study concludes that a 'moderate reduction strategy' is less costly than an 'aggressive' approach if either the temperature–concentrations sensitivity $(1/\lambda)$ is low or if the allowable temperature change is above 3°C. The study of Cline (1992), by contrast, has much higher control rates. The more stringent controls in the Cline study are due to a number of features – primarily, however, because the Cline result is not grounded in explicit intertemporal optimization and assumes a rate of time preference that is lower than would be consistent with observed real interest rates.[14]

It must be emphasized that the present analysis has a number of important qualifications. The most important shortcoming is that the damage function, particularly the response of developing countries and natural ecosystems to climate change, is poorly understood at present; moreover, the potential for catastrophic climatic change, for which precise mechanisms and probabilities have not been determined, cannot currently be ruled out. Furthermore, the calculations omit other potential market failures, such as ozone depletion, air pollution, and R&D, which might reinforce the logic behind greenhouse gas reduction or carbon taxes. Issues of sensitivity analysis with respect to either parameters or components of the model have not been addressed in this study, although an examination of these issues is underway, as discussed above. And finally, this study abstracts from issues of uncertainty, in which risk aversion and the possibility of learning may modify the stringency and timing of control strategies. Notwithstanding these qualifications, the optimal-growth approach may help clarify the questions and help identify the scientific, economic and policy issues that must underpin any rational decision.

[14]See the discussion in footnote 5 above.

References

Amano, A., 1992, Economic costs of reducing CO_2 emissions: A study of modeling experience in Japan, Paper presented to the International Workshop on Costs, Impacts, and Possible Benefits of CO_2 Mitigation, IIASA, Laxenburg, Austria, September.

Cline, W., 1992, The economics of global warming (Institute of International Economics, Washington, DC).

Dean, A. and P. Hoeller, 1992, Costs of reducing CO_2 emissions: Evidence from six global models, OECD/GD (92) 140 (Organisation for Economic Co-operation and Development, Paris) processed.

EPA, 1989, U.S. Environmental Protection Agency, The potential effects of global climate change on the United States: Report to Congress, EPA-230-05-89-050, Dec.

EPA, 1990, D.A. Lashof and D.A. Tirpak, eds., Policy options for stabilizing global climate (Hemisphere, New York).

EC, 1992a, The economics of limiting CO_2 emissions, Commission of the European Communities, Special Edition no. 1 (ECSC-EEC-EAEC, Brussels).

EC, 1992b, The climate challenge: Economic aspects of the community's strategy for limiting CO_2 emissions, Commission of the European Communities, no. 51 (ECSC-EEC-EAEC, Brussels) May.

Fankhauser, S., 1992, The economic costs of global warming: Some monetary estimates, Paper presented to the International Workshop on Costs Impacts, and Possible Benefits of CO_2 Mitigation, IIASA, Laxenburg, Austria, Sept.

Hammitt, J.K., R.J. Lempert and M.E. Schlesinger, 1992, A sequential-decision strategy for abating climate change, Nature 357, 28 May, 315–318.

IPCC, 1990, Intergovernmental panel on climate change, climate change: The IPCC scientific assessment, J.T. Houghton, G.J. Jenkins and J.J. Ephraums, eds. (Cambridge University Press, New York).

Jorgenson, D.W. and P.J. Wilcoxen, 1991, Reducing U.S. carbon dioxide emissions: The cost of different goals, in: J.R. Moroney, ed., Energy, growth and the environment (JAI Press, Greenwich, CT) 125–128.

Kolstad, C.D., 1992, Looking vs. leaping: The timing of CO_2 control in the face of uncertainty and learning, Paper presented to the International Workshop on Costs, Impacts, and Possible Benefits of CO_2 Mitigation, IIASA, Laxenburg, Austria, Sept.

Manne, A.S. and R.G. Richels, 1990, CO_2 emission limits: An economic cost analysis for the U.S.A., The Energy Journal 11, no. 2, 51–74.

Manne, A.S. and R.G. Richels, 1992, Buying greenhouse insurance: The economic costs of CO_2 emission limits (MIT Press, Cambridge, MA).

National Academy of Sciences, 1992, Committee on Science, Engineering and Public Policy, policy implications of greenhouse warming: Mititagion, adaptation, and the science base (National Academy Press, Washington, DC).

National Research Council, 1983, Changing climate (National Academy Press, Washington, DC).

Nordhaus, W.D., 1979, The efficient use of energy resources (Yale University Press, New Haven, CT).

Nordhaus, W.D., 1991a, A sketch of the economics of the greenhouse effect, The American Economic Review 81, no. 2, 146–150.

Nordhaus, W.D., 1991b, To slow or not to slow: The economics of the greenhouse effect, The Economic Journal 101, July, 920–937.

Nordhaus, W.D., 1991c, A survey of the costs of reduction of greenhouse gases, The Energy Journal 12, no. 1, 37–65.

Nordhaus, W.D., 1992, Explaining the 'DICE': Background paper on dynamic integrated model of climate change and the economy, Mimeo. (Yale University, New Haven, CT).

Nordhaus, W.D., 1993a, Managing the global commons: The economics of global warming (MIT Press, Cambridge, MA) forthcoming.

Nordhaus, W.D., 1993b, How much should we invest to slow climate change?, in: H. Giersch, ed., Policies on economic growth (Springer-Verlag, Berlin) forthcoming.

Ramsey, F.P., 1928, A mathematical theory of saving, The Economic Journal, Dec., 543–559.

Peck, S.C. and T.J. Teisberg, 1991, CETA: A model for carbon emissions trajectory assessment, The Energy Journal 13, no. 1, 55–77.

Schelling, T.C., 1983, Climatic change: Implications for welfare and policy, in: National Research Council, 1983, 449–482.

Schlesinger, M.E. and X. Jiang, 1990, Simple model representation of atmosphere–ocean GCMs and estimation of the time scale of CO_2-induced climate change, Journal of Climate 3, Dec., 12.

Solow, R.M., 1988, Growth theory: An exposition (Oxford University Press, New York).

[12]

The Marginal Costs
of Greenhouse Gas Emissions

Richard S. J. Tol*

Estimates of the marginal costs of greenhouse gas emissions are an important input to the decision how much society would want to spend on greenhouse gas emission reduction. Marginal cost estimates in the literature range between $5 and $25 per tonne of carbon. Using similar assumptions, the FUND model finds marginal costs of $9-23/tC, depending on the discount rate. If the aggregation of impacts over countries accounts for inequalities in income distribution or for risk aversion, marginal costs would rise by about a factor of 3. Marginal costs per region are an order of magnitude smaller than global marginal costs. The ratios between the marginal costs of CO_2 and those of CH_4 and N_2O are roughly equal to the global warming potentials of these gases. The uncertainty about the marginal costs is large and right-skewed. The expected value of the marginal costs lies about 35% above the best guess, the 95-percentile about 250%.

1. INTRODUCTION

The impacts of climatic change are usually presented as a total, annual effect of some assumed change in temperature, precipitation etc., often associated with a doubling of the atmospheric concentration of carbon dioxide (Pearce et al., 1996; Watson et al., 1996). This is insightful, but for many applications one would rather be interested in the impact caused by a small perturbation in greenhouse gas emissions, for instance to set a Pigouvian tax on such emissions. This paper presents new estimates of the marginal costs of emissions of carbon dioxide, methane and nitrous oxide, and discusses their sensitivities and uncertainties, based on version 1.6 of the *Climate Framework for Uncertainty, Negotiation and Distribution (FUND)*.

The Energy Journal, Vol. 20, No. 1. Copyright © 1999 by the IAEE. All rights reserved.

Comments by Tom Downing, Nick Eyre, Vlaus Pennings and two anonymous referees, and financial support by EC-DGXII under contract no. J0S3-CT95-0002 are gratefully acknowledged.

*   Institute for Environmental Studies, Vrije Universiteit, De Boelelaan 1115, 1081 HV Amsterdam, The Netherlands. E-mail: richard.tol@ivm.vu.nl

An overview and discussion of earlier estimates of the marginal costs of greenhouse gas emissions, particularly carbon dioxide, can be found in Pearce et al. (1996) and, much shorter, in Section 3. The estimates of this paper are based on largely the same climate change impact literature as those reviewed by Pearce et al. (1996). However, the model used here (Tol, 1996) is considerably more dynamic and complicated than the models used by earlier studies. Also, a sensitivity analysis is added, and due care is given to the aggregation of impact estimates over regions with disparate per capita income levels.

The paper is organized as follows. Section 2 briefly discusses the model. See Tol (1997) for a further discussion. Section 3 presents the results and compares them to the literature. Section 4 performs a sensitivity analysis. Section 5 does an uncertainty analysis. Section 6 concludes.

2. THE MODEL

Essentially, *FUND* consists of a set of exogenous scenarios and endogenous perturbations, specified for nine major world-regions, namely OECD-America, OECD-Europe, OECD-Pacific, Central and Eastern Europe and the former Soviet Union, Middle East, Latin America, South and South-East Asia, Centrally Planned Asia, and Africa.

The model runs from 1950 to 2200, in time steps of a year. The prime reason for extending the simulation period into the past is the necessity to initialize the climate change impact module. In *FUND*, some climate change impacts are assumed to depend on the impact of the year before, so as to reflect the process of adaptation to climate change. Without a proper initialization, climate change impacts are thus misrepresented in the first decades. Scenarios for the period 1950-1990 are based on historical observation, namely the *IMAGE* 100-year database (Batjes and Goldewijk, 1994). The period 1990-2100 is based on the IS92a scenario, with IS92d and IS92f as alternatives (Leggett et al., 1992). Note that the original IPCC scenarios had to be adjusted to fit *FUND*'s nine regions and yearly time-step. The period 2100-2200 is based on extrapolation of the population, economic and technological trends in 2050-2100, that is, a gradual shift to a steady state of population, economy and technology. The model and scenarios are so far extrapolated that the results for the period 2100-2200 are not to be relied upon. This period is used here only for purposes of sensitivity analysis.

The scenarios concern economic growth, population growth, urban population, autonomous energy efficiency improvements, decarbonization of energy use, and methane and nitrous oxide emissions.

The scenarios of economic and population growth are perturbed by the impact of climate change. Population falls with climate change deaths, resulting from changes in heat stress, cold stress, malaria, and tropical cyclones. Heat and cold stress are assumed to affect only the elderly, non-reproductive population; heat stress only affects urban population. Population also changes with climate-induced migration between the regions. Economic impacts of climate change are modelled as deadweight losses to disposable income. Scenarios are only slightly perturbed by climate change impacts, however, so that income and population are largely endogenous. Such feedbacks are, in this paper, only included as a sensitivity analysis.

The endogenous parts of *FUND* consist of the atmospheric concentrations of carbon dioxide, methane and nitrous oxide, the global mean temperature, and the impact of climate change on coastal zones, agriculture, extreme weather, natural ecosystems and malaria.

Methane and nitrous oxide are taken up in the atmosphere, and then geometrically depleted:

$$C_t = C_{t-1} + \alpha E_t - \beta(C_{t-1} - C_{pre}) \tag{1}$$

where C denotes concentration, E emissions, t year, and *pre* pre-industrial. Table 1 displays the parameters for both gases.

Table 1. Parameters of Equation (1)

gas	α^a	β^b	pre-industrial concentration
methane (CH_4)	0.3597	1/8.6	790 ppb
nitrous oxide (N_2O)	0.2079	1/120	285 ppb

[a] The parameter α translates emissions (in million metric tonnes of CH_4 or N_2O) into concentrations (in parts per billion by volume).
[b] The parameter β determines how fast concentrations return to their pre-industrial (and assumedly equilibrium) concentrations; $1/\beta$ is the atmospheric life-time (in years) of the gases.

The carbon cycle is a five-box model:

$$Box_{i,t} = \rho_i Box_{i,t-1} + 0.000471\alpha_i E_t \tag{2a}$$

with

$$C_t = \sum_{i=1}^{5} \alpha_i Box_{i,t} \tag{2b}$$

where α_i denotes the fraction of emissions E (in million metric tonnes of carbon) that is allocated to box i (0.13, 0.20, 0.32, 0.25 and 0.10, respectively) and ρ

the decay-rate of the boxes (ρ = exp(-1/lifetime), with average life-times infinity, 363, 74, 17 and 2 years, respectively). Thus, 13% of total emissions remains forever in the atmospheric, while 10% has an average life-time of two years. The parameters are after Hammitt et al. (1992). The model is due to Maier-Reimer and Hasselmann (1987). Carbon dioxide concentrations are measured in parts per million by volume.

Radiative forcing for carbon dioxide, methane and nitrous oxide are based on Shine et al. (1990). The global mean temperature T is governed by a geometric build-up to its equilibrium (determined by radiative forcing RF), with a life-time of 50 years. In the base case, global mean temperature rises in equilibrium by 2.5°C for a doubling of carbon dioxide equivalents, so:

$$ T_t = \left[1 - \frac{1}{50} \right] T_{t-1} + \frac{1}{50} \frac{2.5}{6.3 \cdot \ln(2)} RF_t \qquad (3) $$

Global mean sea level is also geometric, with its equilibrium determined by the temperature and a life-time of 50 years. These life-times result from a calibration to the central estimates of temperature and sea level for the IS92a scenario of Kattenberg et al. (1996). *FUND* also calculates hurricane activity, winter precipitation, and winter storm activity because these feed into the damage module. These factors depend linearly on the global mean temperature. The central estimates are that hurricane activity remains unchanged (cf. Kattenberg et al., 1996), winter precipitation increases 10% for a global warming of 2.5°C (cf. Penning-Rowsell et al., 1998), and winter storm activity increases by 6% (cf. Dorland et al., 1998).

The climate impact module is fully described in Tol (1996). Impacts include sea level rise (dryland loss, wetland loss, coastal protection, migration), agriculture, heat stress, cold stress, malaria, tropical cyclones, extratropical storms, river floods, and unmanaged ecosystems (cf. Tol, 1995; Pearce et al., 1996). Each of these impacts is modelled separately. The damage module has two units of measurement: people and money. Mortality changes (heat stress, malaria, tropical cyclones, cold stress), and people migrate. These effects, like all impacts, are monetized. Impacts can be due to either the rate of change (benchmarked at 0.04°C/yr) or the level of change (benchmarked at 2.5°C). Impacts in the rate of change can be interpreted as the costs of adaptation. Impacts in the level of change can be interpreted as the (dis)advantages of the new climate relative to the current one. Benchmark estimates can be found in Table 2. Note that—in contrast to the economic impact literature (Pearce et al., 1996)—*FUND*'s benchmark estimates do not have an intuitive interpretation: trying to capture the essence of a complicated, dynamic model in one single figure is bound to fail.

Table 2.
Monetized Estimates of the Impact of Global Warming (in 10^9 US$)

region	species	life	agriculture	sea	extreme	total
level	(global mean temperature: +2.5°C; sea level: +50 cm; hurricane activity: +25%; winter precipitation: +10%; extratropical storm intensity: +10%)					
OECD-A	0.0	-1.0	-5.3	0.9	2.5	-2.9
OECD-E	0.0	-1.1	-6.0	0.3	0.3	-6.5
OECD-P	0.0	-0.5	-6.1	1.5	5.5	0.3
CEE&fSU	0.0	3.7	-23.2	0.1	0.2	-19.1
ME	0.0	3.5	3.1	0.1	0.0	6.6
LA	0.0	67.0	7.3	0.2	0.0	74.5
S&SEA	0.0	81.4	15.8	0.2	0.6	98.8
CPA	0.0	58.4	-22.2	0.0	0.1	36.3
AFR	0.0	22.5	5.4	0.1	0.0	28.0
rate	(global mean temperature: 0.04°C/year; other variables follow)					
OECD-A	0.3	0.2	0.3	0.2	0.2	1.2
OECD-E	0.3	0.2	0.0	0.2	0.0	0.7
OECD-P	0.2	0.1	0.0	0.3	0.4	1.0
CEE&fSU	0.1	0.1	0.0	0.0	0.0	0.2
ME	0.0	0.0	0.1	0.0	0.0	0.2
LA	0.0	0.4	0.1	0.1	0.0	0.6
S&SEA	0.0	0.3	0.1	0.1	0.0	0.6
CPA	0.0	0.2	0.3	0.0	0.0	0.5
AFR	0.0	0.0	0.1	0.0	0.0	0.2

Source: After Tol (1995, 1996).

Damage in the rate of temperature change fades at speeds indicated in Table 3. Damage is calculated through a second-order polynomial in climatic change. So, damage D_t (of a certain impact category) in year t equals

$$D_t = \alpha_t \frac{T_t - T_{base-year}}{T_{benchmark}} + \beta_t \left[\frac{T_t - T_{base-year}}{T_{benchmark}} \right]^2 \tag{4a}$$

or

$$D_t = \gamma_t \frac{\Delta T_t}{\Delta T_{benchmark}} + \delta_t \left[\frac{\Delta T_t}{\Delta T_{benchmark}} \right]^2 + \rho D_{t-1} \tag{4b}$$

where T denotes temperature (or another climate parameter); α, β, γ and δ are parameters (which may change over time); and ρ is another parameter which controls the rate of adaptation. Note that *total damage* per region per year is the sum over a number of equations like (5) and (6). Total impacts thus depend on both level and rate of change.

Table 3. Duration of Damage per Category[a]

category	years	category	years
species loss	100	immigration	5
agriculture	10	emigration	5
coastal protection	50	wetland (tangible)	10
life loss	15	wetland (intangible)	50
tropical cyclones	5	dryland	50

[a] Damage is assumed to decline geometrically at a rate of 1-1/life-time.
Source: After Tol (1996).

Damage is distinguished between tangible (market) and intangible (non-market) effects. Tangible damages affect investment and consumption; through investment, economic growth is affected; through consumption, welfare is affected. Intangible damages affect welfare. Relative vulnerability to climate change changes with economic development in many ways. The importance of agriculture falls with per capita income growth, and so do malaria incidence and the inclination to migrate. Heat stress increases with urbanization. The valuation of impacts on non-marketed goods and services increases with per capita income. Impacts vary across regions, and values vary as well. Impacts in one region are not valued in other regions. The one exception is the impact of climate change on ecosystems: Regional monetary impacts are a function of global rather than regional changes in ecosystems.

The reader should keep in mind the relative strengths of the many assumptions to go into any estimate of the marginal costs of climate change. The atmospheric chemistry and climate change parts are relatively undisputed. The economic and population scenarios are very uncertain. The dynamics of the climate change impact module are speculative. The quality of the impact estimates also vary between impact categories and regions. The impacts of climate change on agriculture and sea level rise are relatively well-established, whereas impacts on health and unmanaged ecosystems are hardly understood. Monetisation of non-market impacts introduces great uncertainties. Lacking local studies, impact estimates on less-developed countries are largely based on extrapolation from results for OECD countries.

3. THE MARGINAL COSTS OF GREENHOUSE GAS EMISSIONS

A limited number of estimates of the marginal costs of CO_2 emissions can be found in the literature. They have been assembled in the Second Assessment Report of Working Group III of the Intergovernmental Panel on Climate Change (Pearce et al., 1996). This assessment is reproduced in Table 4. For comparison, results from this study are added. Two types of marginal cost estimation methods are distinguished. One is based on the average additional cost of a small perturbation of an exogenous "business-as-usual" scenario (commonly IPCC's IS92a or something very similar). The other is based on the shadow value of carbon dioxide emissions along an optimal emission path. Since optimal and no-control trajectories lie very close to one another (e.g., Manne et al., 1995; Nordhaus and Yang, 1996; Peck and Teisberg, 1994; Tol, 1997), the difference is small in practice.

The estimates of Table 4 show a wide range. The upper bound of Cline can be explained by (*i*) high benchmark estimates of climate change; (*ii*) a long time horizon combined with a low discount rate; and (*iii*) constant vulnerability to climate change. Ayres and Walter's estimate is on the high side because they use a low discount rate and OECD values for the whole world, e.g., to value health risks. Nordhaus shows that the expected value of marginal costs is higher than the best guess[1] value, because uncertainties are asymmetric and relationships non-linear (cf. Tol, 1995, and Section 5). Fankhauser's estimates are expected values, centred around a discount rate of 3%.

---

1. A best guess estimate of climate change impact is the value that is obtained when all underlying parameters (e.g., temperature rise, change in crop yield, value of a statistical life) assume their central estimate. Because these central estimates may be means, modi, medians, or best guesses, and because processes are non-linear, the term best guess has no probabilistic interpretation, nor an unambiguous relation to modus, mean or median.

Table 4. The Marginal Costs of CO_2 Emissions[a]

Study	Type[b]	1991-2000	2001-2010	2011-2020	2021-2030
Nordhaus 91[c]	MC		7.3 (0.3-65.9)		
Ayres and Walter[c]	MC		30-35		
Nordhaus 94	CBA				
- best guess		5.3	6.8	8.6	10.0
- expected value		12.0	18.0	26.5	n.a.
Cline	CBA	5.8-124	7.6-154	9.8-186	11.8-221
Peck and Teisberg	CBA	10-12	12-14	14-18	18-22
Fankhauser	MC	20.3 (6.2-45.2)	22.8 (7.4-52.9)	25.3 (8.3-58.4)	27.8 (9.2-64.2)
Maddison	CBA	5.9	8.1	11.1	14.7
	MC	6.1	8.4	11.5	15.2
This study[d]	MC	11	13	15	18

[a] current (1990) value $\$^{1990}$/tC; figures in brackets denote 90% confidence intervals; net present values are discounted to the period of emission.

[b] MC = marginal cost study, i.e., estimate is based on a slight perturbation of a baseline; CBA = cost-benefit study, i.e., estimate is based on a shadow value.

[c] Time of emission not explicitly considered.

[d] Time horizon 2100; discounted to start of decade; discount rate: 5%; scenario: IS92a; simple sum; no higher order effects.

Sources: Pearce et al. (1996); see also Ayres and Walter (1991), Nordhaus (1991, 1994), Cline (1992, 1993), Peck and Teisberg (1991), Fankhauser (1995) and Maddison (1995).

Table 5 presents the marginal costs of climate change according to *FUND*, using a simple summation of the impact across its nine regions. For a discount rate of 3-5%, the marginal costs of carbon dioxide emissions are comparable to those that can be found in Table 4. The figures for *FUND* displayed in Table 4 assume a discount rate of 5% per year. Table 5 also presents marginal damage estimates for methane and nitrous oxide. Usually, greenhouse gases are converted from one to another using their global warming potentials (GWP). The GWP of a gas is defined as the time integral of radiative forcing per unit emission divided by the same integral for carbon dioxide. Schmalensee (1993) and Richards and Reilly (1993) criticized the concept of GWP because the relationship between radiative forcing and impact may well be highly non-linear and because time discounting is ignored. The global damage potential is defined similar to the GWP, with radiative forcing replaced by impact and discounting introduced. In fact, the global damage potential is the ratio of the marginal damages. Table 6 displays global damage potentials as estimated with *FUND* and as reported in the literature. Results are very similar, despite the fact that *FUND*'s impact module depends also on the rate of climate change and vulnerability is a function of socio-economic development.

Table 5. Marginal Damages for CO_2, CH_4 and N_2O Emissions[a]

Discount rate	0%	1%	3%	5%	10%
Carbon dioxide ($/tC)					
1995-2004	142	73	23	9	2
2005-2014	149	72	20	7	1
Methane ($/t$CH_4$)					
1995-2004	147	141	89	52	16
2005-2014	264	186	87	41	8
Nitrous oxide ($/t$N_2O$)					
1995-2004	15,468	7,559	2,201	817	140
2005-2014	16,313	7,632	1,975	631	71

[a] Damages discounted to 1990; time horizon: 2100; model *FUND*1.6; scenario: IS92a; simple sum; no higher order effects.
Source: Own calculations.

Table 6. Global Damage Potential, Impact per Tonne of CH_4 and N_2O Relative to Impact per Tonne of CO_2

	FUND[a]	Kandlikar[b]	Fankhauser[c]	Hammitt[d]	GWP[e]
CH_4	14	12	20	11	25
N_2O	348	282	333	355	320

[a] Emissions between 1995 and 2004; time horizon: 2100; discount rate: 3%; model: *FUND*1.6; scenario: IS92a; simple sum; no higher order effects.
[b] Time horizon: 100 years; discount rate: 2%; scenario: IS92a; quadratic damages.
[c] Emissions between 1991 and 2000; time horizon: 2100; GDP is calculated as ratio of mean marginal damages.
[d] Emissions in 1995; time horizon: 2100; discount rate: 3%; scenario: IS92a; middle case.
[e] Time horizon: 100 years.
Sources: Own calculations, Kandlikar (1995, 1996), Fankhauser (1995), Hammitt et al. (1996), Schimel et al. (1996).

The estimates of Table 5 are based on different values for different regions (e.g., for human mortality risks). This may be considered inequitable (e.g., Masood, 1995), and may be inconsistent with the view of a global decision-maker (who would treat all equal, like regional decision-makers are assumed to do within their regions, and as national decision-makers commonly do within their countries). It is also inconsistent with basic welfare theory, since simply adding monetary values across disparate income levels assumes that utility is a linear function of monetary income. Following Fankhauser et al. (1997), equity-weights are used in aggregating regional impact. Equity-weights express the relative importance of small changes in regional impacts in an hypothesized global welfare function. In this analysis, regional welfare is the natural logarithm of per capita income—a mild form of risk aversion—and global welfare is the sum of regional welfare. Alternatively, global welfare may be interpreted as the product of regional welfare, a mild form of adversity to income inequality. The equity-weights are then the inverse of per-capita income (relative to its global average), so:

$$D_{world} = \sum_{regions} D_{region} \frac{Y_{world}}{Y_{region}} \qquad (5)$$

where D denotes damage and Y per-capita income. Since per-unit values are generally assumed to be approximately linear in per-capita income, equity-weighted per-unit values are approximately the same for all regions, and equal to their global average. Table 7 shows the result of this for marginal damage of greenhouse gas emissions. Marginal impacts increase by a factor of slightly less than 3. This increase is solely due to the fact that, above, a "dollar to a rich man" is assumed equal to a "dollar to a poor man." With equity-weights, the welfare equivalents are compared, so that the "dollar to a poor man" counts more. In Fankhauser et al. (1997), it is shown that if the income distribution itself also counts, damage estimates increase even further. However, it is hard to find empirical support for a preference for international income redistribution.

Table 7.
Equity-weighted Marginal Damages for CO_2, CH_4 and N_2O Emissions[a]

Discount rate	0%	1%	3%	5%	10%
Carbon dioxide ($/tC)					
1995-2004	317	171	60	26	6
2005-2014	311	157	48	18	3
Methane ($/tCH$_4$)					
1995-2004	660	517	295	170	52
2005-2014	831	556	252	120	24
Nitrous oxide ($/tN$_2$O)					
1995-2004	32,735	16,862	5,459	2,217	434
2005-2014	32,785	15,994	4,510	1,556	197

[a] Damages discounted to 1990; time horizon: 2100; model: *FUND*1.6; scenario: IS92a; equity-weighted; no higher order effects. *Source:* Own calculations.

4. SENSITIVITY ANALYSIS

Figure 1 presents the results of a sensitivity analysis around the equity-weighted marginal costs of emissions in the decade 1995-2004 discount at 3% per annum (cf. also Table A1 in the appendix). The discount rate is clearly the most important parameter.

Figure 1. Sensitivity of the Marginal Costs of Carbon Dioxide The base case uses a discount rate of 3% and a time horizon of 2100, for equity-weighted, first-order damages of emissions in the period 1995-2004, according to *FUND* 1.6 evolving around IS92a with a climate sensitivity of 2.5°C. See Table A1

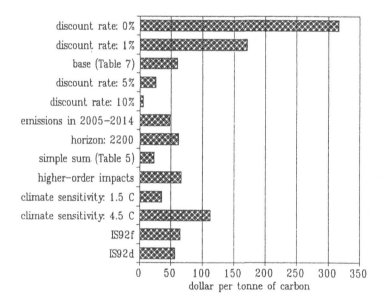

Postponing emissions by 10 years slightly reduces the marginal costs, primarily because they are discounted for 10 more years. However, the estimate for the zero per cent discount rate reveals that undiscounted marginal costs are also somewhat lower, because of a slower rate of climate change in the future and reduced vulnerability.

Extending the horizon to 2200 makes little difference, except for the zero discount rate. Yearly marginal damages become negative in the second half of the 22nd century. The reason is as follows. Marginal costs are estimated by slightly increasing emissions in the period 1995-2004. Higher emissions in the early years lead to higher concentrations for all later years. Because of the saturation of the spectral window of carbon dioxide (i.e., temperatures depend on the natural logarithm of atmospheric concentrations), the rate at which temperature rises, falls at the long term because of higher initial emissions. This reduces damages in the rate of change. Damages in the level of change remain largely the same.

Equity weights matter a great deal as damage in poorer countries counts much more in the global total. Including the effect of climate change on economic growth adds a little to the marginal estimates, but not sufficiently so to justify an in-depth analysis; lacking much insight, higher-order effects have been included in a very *ad hoc* way (cf. Section 2). Perturbing the climate sensitivity has an obvious and substantive influence on the marginal damages. If *FUND* runs with a higher (IS92f) or lower (IS92d) emission scenario, marginal costs are higher or lower. The effect is not large, partly because the difference in climate change only becomes substantial in the long run, and partly because IS92d leads to a more equitable income distribution than IS92a (so impact in developing countries is less–because of overall lower vulnerability–and counts less–because of lower equity weights) while IS92f has overall higher economic growth rates.

Figure 2 presents the marginal damages over the period 1990-2100, and their breakdown over the regions, for a discount rate of 3% (cf. also Table A2). South and Southeast Asia contributes most to world damage, followed by Latin America and Africa. The OECD is relatively less vulnerable to climate change, particularly if the difference in income levels are taken into account. Central and Eastern Europe and the former Soviet Union are net beneficiaries of climate change.

Figure 3 presents the marginal damages, and their breakdown over the impact categories (cf. also Table A3). Sea level rise is the most important category. Extreme weather, particularly the balance of heat and cold stress, comes second, and increases in importance over time. Agriculture is a net beneficiary of climate change. Figure 4 repeats Figure 3, this time equity-weighted (cf. also Table A4). The importance of species loss falls, as this is mostly valued in the richer regions. Agriculture switches sign, indicating that poorer regions are losers here, and rich regions winners.

Figure 2. Share of FUND's Nine Regions in the Global Marginal Costs of Carbon Emissions, Discounted at 3%. See Table A2

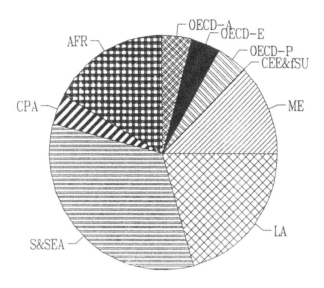

Figure 3. Sectorial Disaggregation of Global Marginal Costs (Simple Sum), for Different Discount Rates. See Table A3 and Figure 4

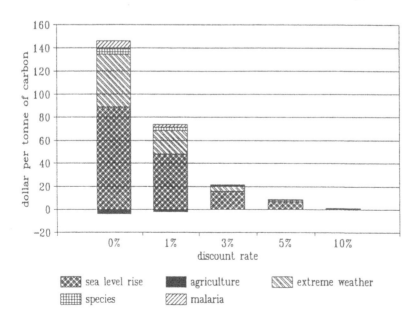

Figure 4. Sectorial Disaggregation of Global Marginal Costs (Equity Weighted) for Different Discount Rates. See Table A3 & Figure 4

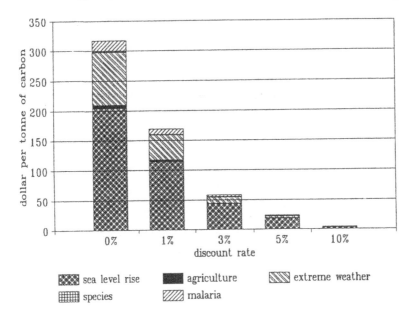

5. UNCERTAINTY ANALYSIS

The quantification of the uncertainties about the parameters of *FUND* is largely based on expert knowledge, that is, my qualitative interpretation of an informal selection of the literature and informal talks with topical experts. Table 8 provides an overview of the assumptions made for the analysis of parameter uncertainty. The modal values equal the best guesses. Distribution and spread are based on the knowledge of the present author, which is informally based on the literature. Parameters are assumed to be independent, across both regions and sectors. In some cases, it is hard to think of correlations (e.g., between heat stress and sea level rise). In other cases, the sign of the correlation is unclear (e.g., worse than expected impacts of US agriculture may be a boon for European agriculture, but may also be due to a pest overlooked both in the US and Europe). In any case, estimating correlations between unknown parameters is a daunting task.

Table 8.
Description of Parameter Uncertainty; Units are Given in Brackets

parameter	distribution	characteristics		parameters	
climate sensitivity	gamma	mode	2.50	α	8.1270
(°C/doubling CO_2)		mean	2.85	β	0.3508
		std.dev.	1.00		
sea level sensitivity	gamma	mode	0.31	α	5.9957
(m/°C)		mean	0.36	β	0.0613
		std.dev.	0.15		
hurricane sensitivity	normal	mean	0.00	μ	0.00
(index, °C)		std.dev.	0.10	σ	0.10
flood sensitivity	normal	mean	0.04	μ	0.04
(index, per °C)		std.dev.	0.04	σ	0.04
storm sensitivity	normal	mean	0.02	μ	0.02
(index, per °C)		std.dev.	0.02	σ	0.02
atm. life-time CH_4	triangular	mode	8.6	a	8.0
(year)		mean	10.2	b	16.0
		std.dev.	1.3	c	8.6
atm. life-time N_2O	triangular	mode	120	a	100
(year)		mean	130	b	170
		std.dev.	15	c	120
life-time temperature	triangular	mode	50	a	25
life-time sea level		mean	58	b	100
(year)		std.dev.	16	c	50
atm. life-times CO_2	normal[a]	mean	363; 74; 17; 2	μ	mean
(year)		std.dev.	half mean	σ	std.dev.
driving scenarios[b]	normal	mean	1.0	μ	1.0
(growth rate)		std.dev.	0.1	σ	0.1
impacts[c]	normal	mean	1.0	μ	1.0
(dollar, people)		std.dev.	0.5	σ	0.5
VOSL[d]	gamma	mean	1.0	α	2.6180
(dollar)		std.dev.	1.0	β	0.6180
life-time impacts	normal[a]	mean	Table 4	μ	mean
(year)		std.dev.	quarter mean	σ	std.dev.

[a] Knotted (truncated) at zero.

[b] Multiplier of economic growth, population growth, AEEI, ACEI and exogenous emissions land-use change.

[c] Multiplier of impact due to/on species, heat, cold, malaria, agriculture, hurricane (life and property), floods, winter storms, migration, coastal protection, dry land, wet land.

[d] Value of a statistical life; multiplier of VOSL, which is time and region-dependent, equalling 240 times the per capita income.

Table 9 presents the results of a Monte Carlo analysis applying the uncertainty assumptions described in Table 8 to marginal impact estimates of *FUND*. The Monte Carlo analysis is done with 2500 replications, the largest number that can be conveniently handled given the author's resources—there is no sign of instability of the estimates. For comparison, Table 9 also displays the best guess (i.e., the marginal costs with all parameters set at their central estimate). The best guess is a conservative estimate of the marginal costs of CO_2. The mean estimate is higher than the best guess by some 35%, because uncertainties are asymmetric and relationships non-linear (cf. Tol, 1996). The uncertainty about the marginal costs is also asymmetric (right-skewed) so that median and modal marginal costs are smaller that the mean. For small discount rates, the mode also lies above the best guess. Mode (the most likely value of the marginal costs) and best guess (the marginal costs if all parameters are set to their most likely value) deviate in a non-linear system. The uncertainty is large, as is revealed by the standard deviation and the confidence intervals. The coefficient of variation varies around 2/3. The upper bound of the 95% interval lies at more than 2.5 times the best guess, and more than 2 times the mean. The uncertainty is so large mainly because of the non-linearities in the system and the convolution of uncertainties. The many impact categories and regions, varied independently of one another, dampen the overall uncertainty. Interestingly, even the one-percentile marginal costs is positive, although the distributions of Table 8 do allow for the enhanced greenhouse effect to have a positive effect. Figure 5 display the frequency distribution of the marginal costs for a 3% discount rate, along with a fitted Lognormal distribution.

Table 9. Characteristics of the Uncertainty about the Marginal Costs of Carbon Dioxide Emissions (in $/tC)

discount rate	0%	1%	3%	5%	10%
Best guess	317	171	60	26	6
Mean	465	244	82	35	7
Median	405	210	70	29	6
Mode	340	190	54	22	5
Std.Deviation	267	143	51	22	5
1-percentile	106	54	17	7	1
5-percentile	158	81	26	11	2
95-percentile	962	512	178	77	17
99-percentile	1390	744	259	114	26
Geometric mean	6.0	5.3	4.2	3.4	1.8
Geometric std.dev.	1.7	1.8	1.8	1.8	1.9

[a] Damages discounted to 1990; emissions in 1995-2004; model: *FUND*1.6; scenario: IS92a; time horizon: 2100; equity-weighted; no higher order effects.
Source: Own calculations.

Figure 5. Uncertainty About the Marginal Costs of Carbon Dioxide Emissions (in \$/tC). Damages discounted to 1990 at 3%; emissions in 1995-2004; model: *FUND* 1.6; scenario IS92a; time horizon: 2100; equity-weighted; no higher order effects

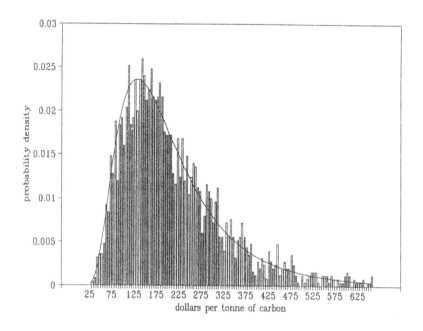

6. CONCLUSIONS

The marginal costs of emissions of carbon dioxide, methane, and nitrous oxide, as estimated by *FUND*, are highly sensitive to variations in the underlying assumptions. The literature review of the IPCC (Pearce et al., 1996) found that estimates of the marginal costs of CO_2 emissions lie between \$5 and \$125 per tonne of carbon, with the majority of the estimates in the lower end of this range, i.e., below \$25/tC. For discount rates of 3% to 5%, *FUND*'s estimates fall well in this lower range, with values of \$23/tC and \$9/tC, respectively. On the one hand, this reconfirms the IPCC review: *FUND* has a different structure than the models on which earlier estimates were based. On the other hand, one should keep in mind that the studies underlying *FUND* are largely the same as the studies underlying earlier marginal cost estimates.

Regional differentiation of values may be unacceptable from a global decision maker's point of view. Assuming that people are not risk averse is inconsistent with empirical studies. Correcting for this in aggregating monetised impacts, marginal costs rise to \$60/tC and \$26/tC for discount rates of 3% and 5%, respectively.

Alternatively, global values may be little relevant for regional decision makers. The marginal costs to the OECD, the supposed main actor in near-term climate policies, are an order of magnitude lower than the global marginal costs.

The marginal costs of methane and nitrous oxide emissions are considerably higher than those of carbon dioxide. The ratios of the marginal costs of CH_4 and N_2O to CO_2 roughly equal the global warming potentials of these gases.

The uncertainty about the marginal costs is high. The mean cost is some 35% higher than the best guess cost, the 95% confidence bound some 250%. This, and the sensitivity of the results to 'ethical' choices about discount rates and aggregation, indicates that it is hard to base firm emission reduction policy advice on current knowledge of the impact of climate change. Nevertheless, the central estimates suggest a policy that is less ambitious than is currently on the political table.

APPENDIX

Table A1.
Sensitivity Analysis Marginal Damage of CO_2 Emissions (\$/tC)[a]

case discount rate	0%	1%	3%	5%	10%
base (Table 7)	317	171	60	26	6
emissions in 2005-2014	311	157	48	18	3
horizon: 2200	243	172	62	26	6
simple sum (Table 5)	142	·73	23	9	2
higher order impacts	360	192	66	28	6
climate sensitivity: 1.5°C	186	101	35	15	3
climate sensitivity: 4.5°C	590	318	112	49	11
IS92f	348	187	65	28	6
IS92d	288	156	56	25	6

[a] Damage discounted to 1990; emissions in 1995-2004; model: *FUND*1.6; scenario: IS92a; time horizon: 2100; equity weighted; no higher order effects.
Source: Own calculations.

Table A2. Regional Marginal Damages over the Period 1990-2100[a]

Region	0%	1%	3%	5%	10%
OECD-A	5	3	1	1	0
OECD-E	7	4	1	1	0
OECD-P	4	2	1	0	0
CEE&fSU	-2	-1	0	0	0
ME	15	8	3	1	0
LA	28	15	5	2	0
S&SEA	54	26	8	3	1
CPA	8	3	1	0	0
AFR	23	12	4	1	0
World	142	73	23	9	2

[a] Damages discounted to 1990; emissions in 1995-2004; model: *FUND*1.6; scenario: IS92a; time horizon: 2100; simple sum; no higher order effects.
Source: Own calculations.

Table A3. Sectoral Marginal Damages Using Simple Summation[a]

Sector	0%	1%	3%	5%	10%
Sea level rise[b]	89	48	16	7	1
Agriculture	-4	-2	0	0	0
Extreme weather[c]	46	21	5	2	0
Species	5	3	1	1	0
Malaria	7	3	1	0	0
Total	142	73	23	9	2

[a] Damages discounted to 1990; emissions in 1995-2004; model: *FUND*1.6; scenario: IS92a; time horizon: 2100; simple sum; no higher order effects.
[b] Coastal protection, dryland loss, wetland loss and migration.
[c] Hurricanes, extratropical wind storms, river floods, hot spells, cold spells.
Source: Own calculations.

Table A4.
Sectoral Marginal Damages Using Equity-weighted Summation[a]

Sector	0%	1%	3%	5%	10%
Sea level rise[b]	204	115	43	19	4
Agriculture	6	3	1	0	0
Extreme weather[c]	88	42	12	5	1
Species	1	1	0	0	0
Malaria	19	10	4	2	0
Total	316	171	60	26	6

[a] Damages discounted to 1990; emissions in 1995-2004; model: *FUND*1.6; scenario: IS92a; time horizon: 2100; equity-weighted; no higher order effects.
[b] Coastal protection, dryland loss, wetland loss and migration.
[c] Hurricanes, extratropical wind storms, river floods, hot spells, cold spells.
Source: Own calculations.

REFERENCES

Ayres, R.U. and J. Walter (1991). "The Greenhouse Effect: Damages, Costs and Abatement." *Environmental and Resource Economics* 1: 237-270.

Batjes, J.J. and C.G.M. Goldewijk (1994). *The IMAGE 2 Hundred Year (1890-1990) Database of the Global Environment (HYDE)*, 410100082, RIVM, Bilthoven.

Cline, W.R. (1992). *Optimal Carbon Emissions over Time: Experiments with the Nordhaus DICE Model* (draft).

Cline, W.R. (1993). *Modeling Economically Efficient Abatement of Greenhouse Gases* (draft).

Dorland, C., R.S.J. Tol, A.A. Olsthoorn, and J.P. Palutikof (1998). "An Analysis of Storm Impacts in The Netherlands," in T.E. Downing, A.A. Olsthoorn, and R.S.J. Tol, (eds.) *Climate, Change and Risk*. London: Routledge.

Fankhauser, S. (1995). *Valuing Climate Change - The Economics of the Greenhouse*, London: EarthScan.

Fankhauser, S., R.S.J. Tol, and D.W. Pearce (1997). "The Aggregation of Climate Change Damages: A Welfare Theoretic Approach." *Environmental and Resource Economics* 10: 249-266.

Hammitt, J.K., R.J. Lempert and M.E. Schlesinger (1992). "A Sequential-Decision Strategy for Abating Climate Change." *Nature* 357: 315-318.

Hammitt, J.K., A.K. Jain, J.L. Adams, and D.J. Wuebbles (1996). "A Welfare-Based Index for Assessing Environmental Effects of Greenhouse-Gas Emissions." *Nature* 381: 301-303.

Kandlikar, M. (1995). "The Relative Role of Trace Gas Emissions in Greenhouse Abatement Policies." *Energy Policy* 23(10): 879-883.

Kandlikar, M. (1996). "Indices for Comparing Greenhouse Gas Emissions: Integrating Science and Economics." *Energy Economics* 18: 265-281.

Kattenberg, A., F. Giorgi, H. Grassl, G.A. Meehl, J.F.B. Mitchell, R.J. Stouffer, T. Tokioka, A.J. Weaver, and T.M.L. Wigley (1996). "Climate Models - Projections of Future Climate," in J.T. Houghton, L.G. Meiro Filho, B.A. Callander, N. Harris, A. Kattenberg, and K. Maskell, (eds.) *Climate Change 1995: The Science of Climate Change -- Contribution of Working Group I to the Second Assessment Report of the Intergovernmental Panel on Climate Change*. Cambridge: Cambridge University Press.

Leggett, J., W.J. Pepper, and R.J. Swart (1992). "Emissions Scenarios for the IPCC: An Update," in J.T. Houghton, B.A. Callander and S.K. Varney, (eds.) *Climate Change 1992 - The Supplementary Report to the IPCC Scientific Assessment.* Cambridge: Cambridge University Press.

Maddison, D.J. (1995). "A Cost-Benefit Analysis of Slowing Climate Change." *Energy Policy* 23 (4/5): 337-346.

Maier-Reimer, E. and K. Hasselmann (1987). "Transport and Storage of Carbon in the Ocean: An Inorganic Ocean Circulation Carbon Cycle Model." *Climate Dynamics* 2: 63-90.

Manne, A.S., R. Mendelsohn, and R.G. Richels (1995). "MERGE - A Model for Evaluating Regional and Global Effects of GHG Reduction Policies." *Energy Policy* 23(1): 17-34.

Masood, E. (1995). "Developing Countries Dispute Use of Figures of Climate Change Impact." *Nature* 376: 374.

Nordhaus, W.D. (1994). *Managing the Global Commons: The Economics of Climate Change.* Cambridge, MA: The MIT Press.

Nordhaus, W.D. and Z. Yang (1996). "RICE: A Regional Dynamic General Equilibrium Model of Optimal Climate-Change Policy." *American Economic Review* 86(4): 741-765.

Pearce, D.W., W.R. Cline, A.N. Achanta, S. Fankhauser, R.K. Pachauri, R.S.J. Tol, and P. Vellinga (1996). "The Social Costs of Climate Change: Greenhouse Damage and the Benefits of Control," in J.P. Bruce, H. Lee, and E.F. Haites, (eds.) *Climate Change 1995: Economic and Social Dimensions -- Contribution of Working Group III to the Second Assessment Report of the Intergovernmental Panel on Climate Change.* Cambridge: Cambridge University Press.

Peck, S.C. and T.J. Teisberg (1991). "CETA: A Model for Carbon Emissions Trajectory Assessment." *The Energy Journal* 13(1): 55-77.

Peck, S.C. and T.J. Teisberg (1994). "Optimal Carbon Emissions Trajectories When Damages Depend on the Rate or Level of Global Warming." *Climatic Change* 28: 289-314.

Penning-Rowsell, E., J.W. Handmer, and S. Tapsell (1998). "Extreme Events and Climate Change: Floods," in T.E. Downing, A.A. Olsthoorn, and R.S.J. Tol (eds.) *Climate, Change and Risk.* London: Routledge.

Reilly, J.M. and K.R. Richards (1993). "Climate Change Damage and the Trace Gas Index Issue." *Environmental and Resource Economics* 3: 41-61.

Schimel, D., D. Alves, I. Enting, M. Heimann, F. Joos, M. Raynaud, R. Derwent, D. Ehhalt, P. Fraser, E. Sanhueza, X. Zhou, P. Jonas, R. Charlson, H. Rodhe, S. Sadasivan, K.P. Shine, Y. Fouquart, V. Ramaswamy, S. Solomon, J. Srinivasan, D. Albritton, I. Isaksen, M. Lal, and D. Wuebbles (1996). "Radiative Forcing of Climate Change," in J.T. Houghton, L.G. Meiro Filho, B.A. Callander, N. Harris, A. Kattenberg, and K. Maskell (eds.) *Climate Change 1995: The Science of Climate Change -- Contribution of Working Group I to the Second Assessment Report of the Intergovernmental Panel on Climate Change.* Cambridge: Cambridge University Press.

Schmalensee, R. (1993). "Symposium on Global Climate Change." *Journal of Economic Perspectives* 7(4): 3-10.

Shine, K.P., R.G. Derwent, D.J. Wuebbles, and J.-J. Morcrette (1990). "Radiative Forcing of Climate," in J.T. Houghton, G.J. Jenkins, and J.J. Ephraums, (eds.) *Climate Change - The IPCC Scientific Assessment.* Cambridge: Cambridge University Press.

Tol, R.S.J. (1995). "The Damage Costs of Climate Change Toward More Comprehensive Calculations." *Environmental and Resource Economics* 5: 353-374.

Tol, R.S.J. (1996). "The Damage Costs of Climate Change Towards a Dynamic Representation." *Ecological Economics* 19: 67-90.

Tol, R.S.J. (1997). "On the Optimal Control of Carbon Dioxide Emissions -- An Application of FUND." *Environmental Modelling and Assessment* 2: 151-163.

Watson, R.T., M.C. Zinyowera, and R.H. Moss (1996). *Climate Change 1995: Impacts, Adaptation, and Mitigation of Climate Change--Scientific-Technical Analysis--Contribution of Working Group II to the Second Assessment Report of the Intergovernmental Panel on Climate Change.* Cambridge: Cambridge University Press.

[13]

Climate change policy: quantifying uncertainties for damages and optimal carbon taxes

Tim Roughgarden[a,1], Stephen H. Schneider[b,*]

[a]*Department of Computer Science, Cornell University, Ithaca, NY 14853 USA*
[b]*Department of Biological Sciences, Institute for International Studies, Stanford University, Stanford, CA 94305 USA*

Received 10 March 1998

Abstract

Controversy surrounds climate change policy analyses because of uncertainties in climatic effects, impacts, mitigation costs and their distributions. Here we address uncertainties in impacts, and provide a method for quantitative estimation of the policy implications of such uncertainties. To calculate an "optimal" control rate or carbon tax a climate-economy model can be used on estimates of climate damages resulting from warming scenarios and several other key assumptions. The dynamic integrated climate-economy (DICE) model, in its original specification, suggested that an efficient policy for slowing global warming would incorporate only a relatively modest amount of abatement of greenhouse gas emissions, via the mechanism of a small (about $5 per ton initially) carbon tax. Here, the DICE model is reformulated to reflect several alternate published estimates and opinions of the possible damages from climatic change. Our analyses show that incorporating most of these alternate damage estimates into DICE results in a significantly more aggressive optimal policy than that suggested by the original model using a single damage function. In addition, statistical distributions of these damage estimates are constructed and used in a probabilistic analysis of optimal carbon tax rates, resulting in mostly much larger (but occasionally smaller) carbon taxes than those of DICE using point values of damage estimates. In view of the large uncertainties in estimates of climate damages, a probabilistic formulation that links many of the structural and data uncertainties and thus acknowledges the wide range of "optimal" policies is essential to policy analysis, since point values or "best guesses" deny policy makers the opportunity to consider low probability, but policy-relevant, outliers. Our presentation is offered as a prototypical example of a method to represent such uncertainties explicitly in an integrated assessment. © 1999 Published by Elsevier Science Ltd. All rights reserved.

Keywords: Optimal carbon tax; Climate policy; Greenhouse gas abatement; Integrated assessment of climate change

1. Introduction

With increasing evidence that anthropogenic emissions of greenhouse gases will lead to an increase in surface temperature, increased hydrologic extremes, and possibly several other climatic effects (Houghton *et al.*, 1996), research has been increasingly focused on the potential impacts of climatic change.

Some express deep concern over the possibility of catastrophic damage from changes in ocean circulation, a melting of the West Antarctic Ice Sheet, and other improbable but plausible changes in climate-related systems (Broecker, 1997; Schneider *et al.*, 1998). Concerns for significant climate damage motivates advocacy for reducing the amount of global greenhouse gas emissions (especially carbon dioxide, CO_2, the most important greenhouse gas), to below so-called "business as usual" (BAU) baseline projections (Azar and Rodhe, 1997). The primary proposed mechanism is by economic incentives — typically a carbon tax — to promote less carbon-intensive fuels and to develop alternatives (e.g., Schneider and Goulder (1997)) discuss costs of a carbon tax versus direct research and development subsidies). Others seem confident that humans will be largely capable of adapting to most projected changes and argue that short-term growth should not be restricted much to reduce climatic change (Schelling, 1983).

---
* Corresponding author. Tel: + 650-725-9978; fax: + 650-725-4387.
E-mail address: shs@leland.stanford.edu (S.H. Schneider)
[1] This research was conducted while the author was at the Institute for International Studies, Stanford University.

416   T. Roughgarden, S.H. Schneider / Energy Policy 27 (1999) 415–429

There are many uncertainties in estimated climatic change effects, impacts, and costs of carbon abatement. Moreover, there is little agreement on how to place a dollar value on the non-market impacts of climatic change, such as the loss of human life, biodiversity, or ecosystem services. There is also debate regarding what kinds and what values of discount rates should be applied in cost–benefit studies (Chapman et al., 1995; Hasselmann et al., 1997; Nordhaus, 1997). Nevertheless, several studies suggest that climatic change will have only minor economic impacts, and that an optimal policy would therefore incorporate only modest controls on greenhouse gas emissions (Kolstad, 1993; Nordhaus, 1991; Peck and Teisberg, 1992). However, many of these "modest controls" conclusions are based on point estimate values — that is, results which are derived from a series of "best guesses". This point estimate method fails to account for the wide range of plausible values for many parameters. Since policy making in the business, health and security sectors often is based on hedging against low probability but high consequence outcomes, any climate policy analytic tools that represent best guess point values or limited (i.e., "truncated") ranges of outcomes restrict the ability of policy makers to make strategic hedges against such risky outlier events. In this paper, we demonstrate a method to include the wide range of outcomes and show their implications for climate policy.

Clearly, given the many uncertainties and unexplored assumptions in conventional economic analysis (Azar, 1996; Brown, 1997; Grubb, 1997; Jenkins, 1996; Repetto and Austin, 1997; Schneider, 1997), it is necessary to formally develop and apply a variety of methods to explore a range of possible conclusions. Thus, we will demonstrate in explicit detail here quantitative methods that can be used to explicitly incorporate a wide range of uncertainty estimates (including outliers) of the impacts of climatic change. In addition, little attention has been given to the non-market impacts of climatic change, and the implications of modeling market and non-market impacts separately (Daily, 1997; Tol, 1995). However, some studies have tried to incorporate aspects of such uncertainties (Manne and Richels, 1994; Morgan and Dowlatabadi, 1996; Nordhaus, 1994b; Peck and Teisberg, 1995), finding that their inclusion typically increases the magnitude of "optimal" abatement efforts. This study goes beyond these previous attempts by including the full range of climate damage estimates (i.e., not truncating the distribution to exclude outlier estimates) and/or by performing a Monte Carlo simulation based on published climate damage distributions, which yields a statistical distribution of optimal policy responses.

We focus on key assumptions made in earlier analyses — specifically, in the pioneering model of Nordhaus (DICE) — and determine the sensitivity of the model's conclusions to plausible alternative assumptions. In par-

ticular, we consider the climatic change impact estimates published by several researchers and experts, and construct several reformulated DICE models to reflect a variety of these estimates and opinions. We then compare the results and policy implications of the reformulated models to those of the previous studies. We conclude that the policy community must be sure that a wide range of estimated outcomes are explicitly represented in any policy analysis so that strategic hedging may be one of the policy options considered.

2. Integrated assessment

There are several Integrated Assessment models (IAMs) that have been used for the analysis of emission control policies. These models vary in complexity, structure, and the numerical values of key parameters. Indeed, no IAM can credibly deal with all important factors nor cover the wide range of value-laden alternatives that need to be considered in real-world policy-making (for example, see the review by Schneider (1997) or the special issue edited by Filar et al. (1998)). Nevertheless, IAMs can provide insights via sensitivity analyses of key uncertain parameters, structural elements, and value choices. The DICE model is a well known, well documented and relatively simple IAM. The transparency of the model allows for several reformulations and extensions, which will be important for our purposes of displaying quantitative methods of presenting uncertainties and demonstrating that policy makers need to be aware of the full range of potential outcomes. Although the simplicity of this approach precludes taking the quantitative results literally, the qualitative insights from our presentation will hopefully prove useful to the climate policy-making community.

3. The DICE model

All of the quantitative analyses here use the Dynamic Integrated model of Climate and the Economy (the DICE model), as described by Nordhaus (1992). A short overview of the model is given in Appendix A. Put briefly, DICE optimizes the trade-off between the costs of climatic change and the costs of restricting greenhouse gas emissions. Here we only reconsider the former cost, and examine DICE's sensitivity to the formulation of the damage term (Eq. (A.8) in Appendix A) with several alternate damage functions. One attempt to quantify the importance of the damages of climatic change appears in Nordhaus and Popp (1997). That study demonstrates that improved estimates of climate damages are more valuable than improved estimates of any other parameter in the DICE model. This paper extends their conclusion by adding a sensitivity analysis of DICE policy

T. Roughgarden, S.H. Schneider / Energy Policy 27 (1999) 415–429   417

conclusions to alternate published damage estimates (including outliers which might imply strategic hedging policies), thereby providing a wide range of plausible optimal policies in the presence of uncertainty in the magnitude of climatic damage.

The DICE model was originally designed to compare the economic effects of several different policies regarding the control of anthropogenic carbon dioxide emissions. One such policy is a "Business-As-Usual" (BAU) or baseline scenario, where no efforts are made to control greenhouse gas emissions. In terms of Eq. (A.5) in Appendix A, this scenario fixes the endogenous control rate $\mu(t) = 0$ for all t. We will sometimes refer to this as the "no-controls" constraint. In this scenario, there is no emissions abatement (and thus no abatement costs), but we anticipate the temperature increase, and hence the damage from climatic change, to be higher.

In the "optimal" policy scenario, the "no-controls" constraint is relaxed, and $\mu(t)$ is determined endogenously. In this scenario, DICE is free to trade off the costs of climatic change with those of emissions abatement. If the costs of global warming are relatively small, the incentive to mitigate carbon emissions will also be small, so we would expect $\mu(t)$ to be close to zero (i.e., the BAU scenario would be close to the optimal one). If the impacts of climatic change are great, however, we would expect $\mu(t)$ to be much closer to 1, implying that "Business-As-Usual" would be a relatively poor policy, from the point of view of optimizing economic efficiency.

Discounted consumption is used by Nordhaus as the primary criterion for comparing different model results. "Discounted consumption" here refers to all consumption occurring after 1989, discounted to 1990 by the rate of interest on goods and services calculated in the standard optimal DICE run. Since utility is an increasing function of consumption, in this formulation larger quantities of discounted consumption are taken as more desirable — a premise challenged by some (e.g., Brown, 1997; Jenkins, 1996) but accepted here for the purposes of our analysis and to demonstrate policy implications from including a wide range of outcomes.

Discounted consumption can also serve as an indicator of the severity of climatic change (since unmitigated warming will decrease production, and hence consumption). Because of the large scale (hundreds of trillions of dollars) for discounted consumption from 1990 to 2100, sometimes different formulations of climatic damage will have little impact (percentagewise) on total discounted consumption, even though the absolute evolving differences over time can be quite large and thus have important short- and long-term policy ramifications.

Optimal emission control rates, the values of $\mu(t)$ for the optimizing run of a model, are a second important

indicator of the consequences of climatic damage. An "optimal policy" is one which uses these values of $\mu(t)$. This optimal policy can be achieved via an "optimal carbon tax" value. In other words, we are interested in the level of carbon tax that would induce the optimal values of $\mu(t)$.

The optimal carbon tax can be calculated as a ratio of "shadow prices" (or "dual variables") of the model's nonlinear program. The shadow price of consumption (C_m) is equivalent to the increase in the model's objective function (Eq. (A.1) in Appendix A) from one additional unit of consumption (relative to the optimal level), and the shadow price of carbon emissions (E_m) represents the increase in utility from one additional unit of carbon emissions. Thus, by taking the ratio of these shadow prices (E_m/C_m), we derive the implicit price of carbon per unit of consumption, which provides a calculation of the carbon tax.

4. Nordhaus's damage function

There are currently many different estimates and countless opinions regarding the economic impacts of global warming. The DICE model includes a climate damage function based on Nordhaus's personal estimate. We first compare this function with those of several other damage estimation studies, and later add in the opinions of eighteen experts surveyed by Nordhaus in a subsequent study (Nordhaus, 1994a).

In deriving a damage function for his DICE model, Nordhaus first estimated the effect of a 3°C warming on US income. Based on the results in Nordhaus (1991), Nordhaus used a 0.25% loss of GDP as the starting estimate for this value. Due to the difficulty in quantifying all of the probable damage from climatic change, especially non-market damage, this may be an overly conservative guess. To account for this, Nordhaus raised the estimate to 1% of US income. This value may still be too conservative for a global model (such as DICE), since damage estimates for the United States are likely to be considerably less than those for countries which have a greater dependence on agriculture and a more limited ability to adapt to climatic change (as is the case with many less developed countries (Bruce et al., 1996)). A second adjustment was then made to extrapolate a global estimate from the domestic estimate, and a total (negative) impact of 1.33% to global output was used by Nordhaus for a 3°C warming in the DICE model.

We are also interested in the relationship between damage and warming as warming increases beyond the 3°C value. Recognizing that disproportionally larger damages have been hypothesized for larger climate changes than for smaller ones, Nordhaus assumed

418 T. Roughgarden, S.H. Schneider · Energy Policy 27 (1999) 415–429

Table 1
A comparison of IPCC damage estimates for a CO_2-doubling scenario (damage is for US only)

Researcher	Warming (°C)	Damage (% of GDP)
Cline	2.5	1.1
Fankhauser	2.5	1.3
Nordhaus	3.0	1.0
Titus	4.0	2.5
Tol	2.5	1.5

Both temperature increase and the corresponding amount of damage are estimated.
Source: Bruce et al., (1996).

a quadratic function. This yields the following damage function for the original DICE model:

$$d_N(t) = 0.0133[\Delta T(t)/3]^2 \qquad (1)$$

where $d_N(t)$ is the fractional loss of global output, and $\Delta T(t)$ is the rise in average global temperature.

5. Alternate damage functions

Other experts have made independent estimates of the damage of global warming. This section uses the results of several of these studies to derive alternative damage functions for use in the DICE model.

Table 1 presents an overview of recent damage estimates for a doubling of CO_2 levels by Cline (1992); Fankhauser (1995); Titus (1992) and Tol (1995). Detailed breakdowns of these estimates have been published by the IPCC (Bruce et al., 1996). However, these values only consider damage to the United States, and only describe a damage function for a single temperature increase value. To derive continuous functions consistent with DICE, we borrow the assumptions from Nordhaus's approach — that total damage to the global output will be a factor of one-third greater than the damage to United States output, and that damage is a quadratic function of global warming, with zero damage for an unchanging climate. Under these assumptions, the damage functions for these four estimates are as follows:

$$d_C(t) = 0.0146[\Delta T(t)/2.5]^2, \qquad (2)$$

$$d_F(t) = 0.0173[\Delta T(t)/2.5]^2, \qquad (3)$$

$$d_{Ti}(t) = 0.03325[\Delta T(t)/4.0]^2, \qquad (4)$$

$$d_{To}(t) = 0.0200[\Delta T(t)/2.5]^2. \qquad (5)$$

The relative character of all five damage functions is shown in Fig. 1a. The functions spread out considerably with more than 3°C of warming. The function used in the original DICE model is the most conservative of the five.

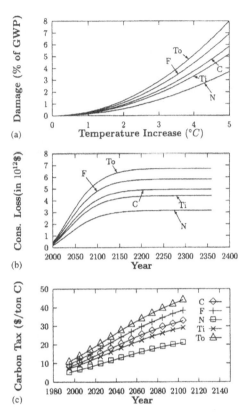

(a)

(b)

(c)

Fig. 1. The DICE model reformulated with damage functions derived from damage estimates by Cline (C), Fankhauser (F), Nordhaus (N), Titus (Ti), and Tol (To). The original model used the damage function derived from Nordhaus's personal damage estimates (N). Figure 1a displays the damage functions derived from published IPCC damage estimates (Bruce et al., 1996). Fig. 1b shows the loss of discounted consumption in the BAU scenario for each of the damage functions in Fig. 1a (where discounted consumption is all consumption occurring after 1989, discounted to 1990 by the rate of interest on goods and services calculated in the standard optimal DICE run). In essence, these curves represent the damage of unmitigated climate change. Of course, the curves shown here represent only a small fraction of overall consumption (the largest difference between the highest and lowest curves is less than 1% of total discounted consumption). Fig. 1c gives optimal carbon tax levels corresponding to each of the damage functions in Fig. 1a.

6. IPCC damage functions in DICE

Fig. 1b presents the loss of discounted consumption due to climate damage in the "Business As Usual" (BAU) policy scenario, where no action is taken to mitigate the buildup of atmospheric greenhouse gases. These curves

T. Roughgarden, S.H. Schneider / Energy Policy 27 (1999) 415–429 419

also represent the gross benefit of complete climatic change abatement associated with each damage function in the DICE model (since complete abatement would reduce the damage from climatic change to zero). Since a relatively large amount of climate-induced damage results in less income, and hence less consumption, the more severe damage functions result in a greater losses of discounted consumption, and hence a larger economic incentive for climatic change abatement.

We next consider the "optimal" policy scenario (i.e., we remove the "no-controls" constraint), in order to compare the levels of optimal emission control rates (the level of mitigation) and optimal carbon taxes (the mechanism used to induce the mitigation) for each of the damage estimates. Fig. 1c shows the values of the optimal carbon taxes associated with each damage function (Eqs. (1)–(5)).

With the original damage function (Eq. (1)), the DICE model calculates modest carbon taxes — less than 10 1990 US dollars per ton of carbon over the next two decades, with a tax of just over 20 dollars by the end of the 21st century. By contrast, these numbers double when the DICE model is run with the damage estimates of Fankhauser or Tol (Eqs. (3) and (5)). Similarly, the optimal emission control rates for model runs with Fankhauser or Tol damage estimates are over 50% higher than those in the canonical DICE run.

7. Damage functions from an expert survey

A second source for estimates of damage from climatic change is an expert survey conducted by Nordhaus (1994a). Nineteen experts from the natural sciences, the social sciences, technology, and economics were questioned about the economic impacts, distributional effects, and non-market effects of global warming. For all questions, three scenarios were considered: a 3°C warming by 2090 (scenario A); a 6°C warming by 2175 (scenario B); and a 6°C warming by 2090 (scenario C). Here we concentrate on the experts' opinions regarding economic impacts in scenarios A and C. (This data is shown in Table 2 (Nordhaus, 1993). Respondent 19 is not included because he did not complete this portion of the survey.)

8. Disciplinary background affects damage functions

The survey respondents were categorized by Nordhaus as natural scientists, environmental economists, and "other social scientists" (a group composed primarily of "mainstream" economists). As the final rows of Table 2 show, there is considerable variation in opinion between researchers of these different fields. The natural scientists' average damage estimate is far more pessimistic for the world economy than that of the social scientists, and the

Table 2
Expert opinion on climate change (in %GWP loss)

Respondent number	Scenario A			Scenario C		
	10%ile	50%ile	90%ile	10%ile	50%ile	90%ile
1	0.7	1.3	8.8	1.4	2.6	14.1
2	− 0.3	1.3	6.0	2.0	3.8	15.0
3	0.1	0.3	0.6	0.2	0.8	3.0
4	− 0.5	1.5	5.0	− 0.5	4.0	9.0
5	3.3	16.3	31.3	6.5	30.0	62.5
6	1.2	1.9	3.6	3.0	6.0	18.0
7	0.0	2.5	6.0	2.0	5.0	15.0
8	10.0	21.0	30.0	20.0	62.0	100.0
9	− 1.0	1.5	8.0	0.0	4.0	15.0
10	1.0	5.0	14.0	4.0	15.0	30.0
11	0.8	1.8	5.0	2.8	6.4	17.0
12	1.0	2.0	5.0	3.0	6.0	15.0
13	− 1.0	3.0	8.0	1.0	6.0	15.0
14	0.0	0.0	0.8	0.0	2.0	5.0
15	− 2.0	2.0	6.0	3.0	10.0	17.0
16	− 0.5	0.5	1.0	2.0	3.5	5.0
17	− 0.5	0.3	0.5	− 1.0	1.0	5.0
18	0.0	2.0	4.0	10.0	20.0	30.0
Mean	0.7	3.6	8.0	3.3	10.4	21.7
Nat. Sci.	5.5	13.0	22.0	12.0	38.5	65.0
Env. Econ.	1.2	6.6	14.3	3.2	13.3	31.8
Other	− 0.1	1.5	4.4	2.0	3.9	12.7

Source: Nordhaus, 1993.

420   *T. Roughgarden, S.H. Schneider / Energy Policy 27 (1999) 415–429*

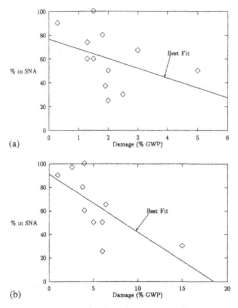

(a)

(b)

Fig. 2. Best estimates of survey respondents for total climate damage plotted against respondents' predictions for the percentage of damage occurring in the standard national accounts. Fig. 2a presents results for Scenario A (a 3°C warming by 2090), and Fig. 2b shows estimates for Scenario C (a 6°C warming by 2090). Several respondents did not complete this portion of the survey. Note that there is a strong suggestion that respondents estimating large climate damages are more likely to assign a large proportion of such damages to non-market categories.

environmental economists average an estimate between the other two. Additionally, Fig. 2 plots climate damage estimates versus market damage estimates for all respondents except the "outliers" (i.e., excluding two respondents who estimated less than a 0.3% loss of GWP from 3°C of warming, and two respondents who estimated more than a 15% loss of GWP from 3°C of warming). Fig. 2 shows that respondents who estimated a large amount of climate damage were more likely to place a larger proportion of those damages outside of the standard national accounts (i.e., large damage estimates implied large non-market damages).

The differences across disciplines in the survey results have been previously noted (Nordhaus, 1994a; Peck and Teisberg, 1995). Indeed, Peck and Teisberg have used the survey respondents' estimates of a "high-consequence outcome" (one defined as a sustained loss of global output of 25% or more) to incorporate risk into the CETA model (Peck and Teisberg, 1995).

Some researches have argued that any decision analytic survey in which groups of respondents appear to

hold to different paradigms should avoid aggregating experts; the estimates of each paradigmatically different group should be presented separately (Keith, 1996; Morgan and Henrion, 1990; Paté-Cornell, 1996). Unfortunately, when the survey participants are grouped together by discipline, the smaller pools (e.g., natural scientists) consist of only a few individuals. Because of the small sample size, much of our analysis aggregates the estimates of all of the experts, despite the strong caveat (but in Fig. 3 we do show a "traceable account" of the subgroups that we subsequently aggregate into one summary distribution in Fig. 4). On the other hand, drawbacks of considering each paradigmatically distinct group separately are pointed out in Titus (1997).

The data from Nordhaus's survey can be used to derive several new damage functions. In particular, we can use the estimates from scenarios A and C as two data points (for $\Delta T(t) = 3$ and $\Delta T(t) = 6$, respectively). With our previous assumption of zero damage for a zero-warming scenario, we have a third data point at $\Delta T(t) = 0$. We can then derive a unique continuous damage function for each set of three data points. One should note that the assumption of a quadratic relationship between damage and warming that we borrowed from Nordhaus and used above is now relaxed. That is, unlike our previous "assumed quadratic" functions, the exponents of these "curve fit" damage functions follow directly from the data. However, this analysis still only considers functions of a single term of the form ax^b. A dual-term approach to quantifying damage has been discussed in Roughgarden (1997). There, the DICE model was reformulated to include one market damage term and one non-market damage term. Non-market damage affected global utility directly, rather than indirectly through income (as is the case in the original specification of DICE). Preliminary analyses suggest that the DICE model is much more sensitive to the magnitude of the damage function than to a partitioning of the damage function into market and non-market components. A similar, less extensive analysis appears in Tol (1994).

We begin by deriving damage functions for each of the disciplines represented in the survey. The 50th percentile estimates from Table 2 yield the following damage functions for the natural scientists, the environmental economists, the other social scientists, and the entire group of respondents:

$$d_{NS}(t) = 0.0231\Delta T(t)^{1.57}, \tag{6}$$

$$d_{EE}(t) = 0.0218\Delta T(t)^{1.01}, \tag{7}$$

$$d_{SS}(t) = 0.0022\Delta T(t)^{1.87}, \tag{8}$$

$$d_{All}(t) = 0.0067\Delta T(t)^{1.53}. \tag{9}$$

These functions are shown graphically in Fig. 3a, together with the original DICE damage function for comparison. The DICE damage function is similar to that of

T. Roughgarden, S.H. Schneider / Energy Policy 27 (1999) 415–429   421

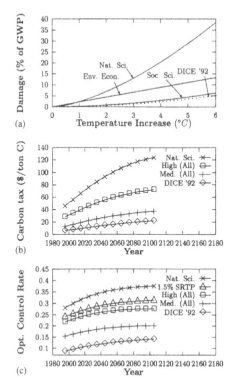

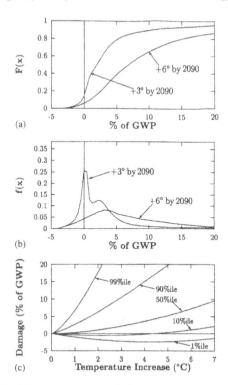

Fig. 3. The DICE model reformulated with damage functions derived from damage estimates given by experts. Fig. 3a shows the "disciplinary damage functions" derived from an expert survey (Nordhaus, 1994a), for natural scientists ("Nat. Sci."), environmental economists ("Env. Econ."), and other social scientists ("Soc. Sci."), primarily conventional economists. The original DICE damage function ("DICE '92") is also shown for comparison. In Figs. 3b and c, optimal policy given the median damage estimates of natural scientists ($\times$) is compared with optimal policies with the high (90th percentile) damage estimates of all of the experts ($\square$), the median damage estimates of all of the experts ($+$), and with the damage estimates used in the original DICE model ($\diamond$). Fig. 3b gives optimal carbon tax levels for each group of damage estimates, and Fig. 3c displays the corresponding optimal emission control rates. The increases in global average temperature by 2105 associated with these policies are 2.77°C, 2.94°C, 3.10°C, and 3.20°C, respectively, suggesting that even the largest control rate abates only a modest fraction of the projected climate changes. In addition, Fig. 3c shows optimal control rates with the median damage estimates of all experts and a 1.5% social rate of time preference ($\triangle$)—half the value used for (+).

Fig. 4. "Aggregate expert damage distributions" for warming scenarios A (3° by 2090) and C (6° by 2090). These distributions are used to derive "randomly sampled" damage functions for use in a probabilistic analysis of the DICE model under uncertainty. Figs. 4a and b show the cumulative distribution functions and probability density functions, respectively, of the damage distributions. Fig. 4c displays several example damage functions used in the Monte Carlo simulation. The "50%ile" damage function (for example) is the function through all of the following: the origin (since we assume zero damage with no temperature increase), the median of the damage distribution for scenario A at $\Delta T(t) = 3°C$, and the median of the damage distribution for scenario C at $\Delta T(t) = 6°C$.

the social scientists, and is substantially more optimistic than the other three functions.

It is interesting to note that differences of opinion show up primarily in the coefficients of these functions, rather than in the exponents. For example, Eq. (7) (for the

environmental economists) is nearly linear and Eq. (8) (for other social scientists) is nearly quadratic. However, this fact is overshadowed by the order of magnitude difference between the two equations' coefficients — in the warming range that we are interested in, the former equation has a much greater value than the latter. Overall, the experts seem to largely agree that there is a non-linear relationship between damage and warming, but that there is less than quadratic dependence on $\Delta T(t)$. This contrasts to the less than linear damage functions in a survey of non-expert home owners in California (Berk and Schulman, 1991).

422 *T. Roughgarden, S.H. Schneider / Energy Policy 27 (1999) 415–429*

The second group of functions compares the low, middle, and high estimates of the respondents. Here, we disregard the backgrounds of the participants and concentrate solely on the spread of all respondents' aggregated estimates. The following equations are derived from the aggregated averages for the 10th, 50th, and 90th percentile damage estimates:

$$d_{10}(t) = 0.0006\Delta T(t)^{2.24}, \tag{10}$$

$$d_{50}(t) = 0.0067\Delta T(t)^{1.53}, \tag{11}$$

$$d_{90}(t) = 0.0164\Delta T(t)^{1.44}. \tag{12}$$

Note that, by definition, Eqs. (9) and (11) are identical.

9. Survey damage functions in DICE

Next, we discuss the effects of replacing the original DICE damage function (Eq. (1)) with Eq. (6), the natural scientists' 50th percentile response, and with Eq. (12), the entire survey group's 90th percentile estimate of damages. This "optimistic versus pessimistic" contrast (see Fig. 3b) is useful for examining the importance of the large differences in opinion regarding the potential impacts of climatic change on policy (i.e., optimal carbon taxes).

The first analysis of DICE with each of the above three damage functions compares the net present value of consumption after 1990 in the BAU policy scenario, where no efforts are made to slow climatic change. In this case, we would expect the model runs with pessimistic damage functions to exhibit decreased consumption, due to increased damage from unmitigated global warming. Reformulating DICE with the damage function given by Eq. (12) results in a 2.8% loss in discounted consumption, and using the damage function given by Eq. (6) causes a 4.4% loss in discounted consumption (relative to a world without climate-induced damage). Thus, the benefit of emissions control in the reformulated DICE models is several times higher than that in the original DICE model (where a BAU policy resulted in a less than 0.5% loss in discounted consumption). We examine the effects of these incentives to abate carbon by rerunning the DICE model and including the possibility of policies that restrict carbon emissions (i.e., we consider the "optimal" policy scenario).

Using the damage function from the 90th percentile estimates of all of the experts, DICE calculates about three times as much carbon taxes as in the more optimistic scenario. With the damage function based on natural scientists' 50th percentile estimates, optimal carbon taxes (Fig. 3b) are about six times as large as those in the optimistic scenario. The values of optimal control rates for these two models (Fig. 3c) range from two to three times higher than those in the original model. The average of the median estimates (i.e., Eq. (11)) yields results

closer to those of the DICE model, but still gives higher values for optimal control rates and carbon taxes.

Finally, several researchers argue that a low (or even zero) rate of social time preference is appropriate for the DICE model, on the basis that it is philosophically indefensible to value the welfare of future generations less than the welfare of the present generation (even if this yields a discount rate inconsistent with observed economic behavior, such as the global savings rate) (Azar and Sterner, 1996; Cline, 1992). Thus, as a pure sensitivity analysis comparison, in Fig. 3c we include a curve in which the 3% social rate of time preference of DICE (ρ in Eq. (A.1) of Appendix A) is replaced by a smaller rate (1.5%). We also use Eq. (11) (i.e., the aggregate median) as a damage function. The resulting increase in optimal emission control rates is larger than that caused by using the experts' 90th percentile damage estimates (as reflected in Eq. (12)) in place of the experts' median estimates (Eq. (11)), showing a high sensitivity to a small change in ρ.

A more thorough sensitivity analysis of the DICE model to the social rate of time preference was performed in Chapman et al. (1995). This study found that a zero rate of social time preference leads to an optimal control rate almost three times that of the original DICE model. Additionally, it shows that replacing the decreasing function $\sigma(t)$ in Eq. (A.5) of Appendix A (the CO_2-equivalent emissions per unit of output without controls) with a constant function causes a similar increase in optimal control rates. Finally, the study by Kaufmann (1997) demonstrates that alternate assumptions about the transfer of carbon from the atmosphere to the ocean yield increased climate damages, and hence a more stringent optimal policy. However, our purpose here is not to address the structural assumptions or parameters in DICE that are both debatable and have large impacts on policy options, but to concentrate on damage function sensitivity and the implications of ignoring outliers.

10. Subjective probability distributions of survey respondents

To this point we have derived damage functions for particular estimates of the respondents to Nordhaus's survey. However, this approach does not capture all of the information in the results of the survey. Each respondent gives a subjective probability distribution for damage in each warming scenario, rather than simply point estimates. Thus, we can combine these distributions and construct an aggregated "expert probability distribution" for damage from climatic change. We do not suggest that the resulting functions should be viewed as particularly "credible", as expert opinion on climate damage will likely change markedly as new research reshapes subjective opinions (Schneider, 1997). Further, this "aggregate expert opinion" should not be considered a "consensus"

T. Roughgarden, S.H. Schneider / Energy Policy 27 (1999) 415-429   423

among experts, since several survey respondents would undoubtedly strongly disagree with the properties of the aggregate damage distributions. We do, however, believe that this analysis technique in which uncertainties are explicitly displayed provides much better insights to policy-makers viewing integrated assessments than simple point values. Moreover, it is useful to look at the implications of the spread of opinions in considering decision-making under uncertainty of the severity of climatic damage, in particular the opportunity to consider strategic hedging policies to deal with extreme event possibilities.

In Nordhaus's survey, each respondent gives low (10th percentile), median or "best guess" (50th percentile), and high (90th percentile) estimates for damage in each scenario. As before, we restrict our attention to scenario A (a 3°C warming by 2090) and scenario C (a 6°C warming by 2090). One obvious distribution to consider is the symmetric normal distribution. However, the skewness of the estimates must be considered. An easy way to check for skewness is to compare each best guess estimate to the average of the respective low and high estimates. If a respondent's estimates are symmetric, these two values should be equal — that is, the chance of overestimating climatic damage by a given amount should be the same as that of underestimating damage by the same amount.

Referring back to Table 2, we see that, of the 36 sets of 10th, 50th, and 90th percentile estimates, only 5 sets of estimates suggest a symmetric distribution (respondent 16 in scenario C, and respondents 15 and 18 in both scenarios). Four sets of estimates exhibit left-skewness (a best guess estimate which is greater than the average of the low and high estimates), and the remaining 27 sets of estimates exhibit right-skewness (a best guess estimate which is smaller than the average of the other two). Thus, the bulk of the (both optimistic and pessimistic) experts thought that their best guess for climatic damage had a greater chance of being a large underestimate than a large overestimate; in other terms, a higher probability of a "nasty surprise" than a "pleasant surprise" (Schneider *et al.*, 1998).

Given the skewness of the data, we fit a Weibull distribution to the damage estimates of each survey respondent.

11. Aggregate damage distributions for 3°C and 6°C warming scenarios

To construct an aggregate damage distribution, a range of relevant damage levels is first identified. "Relevant" is defined here as within 1.5 standard deviations of *some* expert's best estimate. Using this definition, we consider damage estimates from -2.7% to 33.9% of GWP in scenario A, and from -1.4% to 100% of GWP in scenario C. It should be noted that distributions for

both warming scenarios will consider the possibility of a net benefit from climatic change (from increased agricultural yields, new discoveries of or access to minerals in the polar regions, reduced cold season health impacts, etc.).

To finish the construction of an aggregate distribution, we must simply "add up" the subjective probability distributions and normalize their sum. This requires a "discretization" of the probability distributions, as they are not easily summed in closed form. This is done by partitioning the range of relevant damage levels into 100 subranges, and splitting up each probability distribution across the subranges. Then, we simply normalize by the number of respondents (18) to ensure that the total value of the range will be equal to 1. The result can then be considered a discrete approximation to the aggregate damage distribution, with each subrange approximating the value of the probability density function (PDF) of the aggregate distribution at a single point.

More formally, we can describe this approximate aggregate distribution as follows. Denote the cumulative distribution function (CDF) of the ith subjective probability distribution as F_i, and the subrange with left endpoint x_1 and right endpoint x_2 as $S_{1,2}$. Then the value of $S_{1,2}$ is given by

$$S_{1,2} = \frac{\sum_{i=1}^{18} (F_i(x_2) - F_i(x_1))}{18} \tag{13}$$

$S_{1,2}$ can be considered an approximation of $\tilde{f}((x_1 + x_2)/2)$, where $\tilde{f}$ denotes the actual (continuous) probability density function of the aggregate damage distribution.

The CDFs for damage in scenarios A and C are given in Fig. 4a (labelled $F(x)$) and the PDFs are given in Fig. 4b (labelled $f(x)$).

A striking feature of both distributions is their right skewness (i.e., "surprise potential"). For the 3°C warming scenario, the mode of the distribution (the peak of the PDF) is very close to zero, indicating that for this statistic aggregated expert opinion suggests that the benefits of climatic change are likely to offset most of the costs. Looking at the CDF, however, we see that there is a significant ($> 10\%$) chance of a loss of more than 10% of the gross world product in this scenario. For scenario C, the shape of the distribution is similar. According to the aggregated expert opinion, there is a 50% chance of experiencing less than 6% GWP loss from 6°C of warming, but a 4% chance that the climatic change in this scenario will cut global output in half — an unfathomable economic catastrophe!

Nordhaus also used right-skewed damage distributions in his formal sensitivity analysis of the DICE model (Nordhaus, 1994b) based on the expert opinion expressed in his survey (Nordhaus, 1994a). Our analysis differs from Nordhaus's in that we use an input distribution based

424 *T. Roughgarden, S.H. Schneider / Energy Policy 27 (1999) 415–429*

solely on expert opinion, rather than one centered around Nordhaus's personal damage estimate. In addition, we consider the damage estimates of all 18 survey respondents, whereas Nordhaus ignored the "outliers", considering only the "trimmed mean" of the survey results (a statistic that ignored the three highest and three lowest estimates, markedly changing the output distribution). Moreover, since all of the participating natural scientists were among the pessimistic outliers, our distributions reflect the beliefs of a group not represented by the damage distributions of Nordhaus (1994b). Including the opinions of natural scientists in the construction of the damage distributions yields an increased asymmetry in the probability density functions and higher expected damages given a particular temperature increase. This in turn increases the expected value of both optimal control rates and optimal carbon taxes. Whose opinions will turn out to be more credible is empirically testable, of course, by "performing the experiment" of substantial climate change over the next century. Whether or not to take that risk is a value judgement we will not confront in this article, but one that policy makers contemplating ratification of the Kyoto protocol will have to confront (for the personal views on this subject by one of the authors, see Schneider (1998)).

12. Damage functions from distributions

The general approach for deriving a damage function from random damage estimates is similar to the one outlined earlier: given damage estimates for $\Delta T(t) = 3$ and $\Delta T(t) = 6$, assume no damage for $\Delta T(t) = 0$, and derive a function through the three data points of the form ax^b. In most cases, the procedure is identical to the one used above to derive damage functions from the point estimates of the survey respondents; the details are deferred to Appendix B.

Five damage functions derived from random samples of the damage distributions are presented in Fig. 4c. For contrast, damage functions from the 1st, 10th, 50th, 90th, and 99th percentile damage estimates are shown. The 1st and 10th percentile damage functions were derived from Eqs. (B.4)–(B.7) in Appendix B (since they must pass through negative damage estimates), while the other three functions are derived from Eqs. (B.1)–(B.3) in Appendix B.

13. Results from a Monte Carlo simulation

Using the methods of the previous section, we can now perform a probabilistic analysis with the expert opinions from Nordhaus's survey. This section discusses the results of a Monte Carlo simulation, a simulation which generates data from a series of "runs". In this analysis, each of one thousand runs selects random input parameters, drawn from the previously derived damage distributions, reformulates the DICE model with a damage function derived by the method outlined in Appendix B, and runs the new model to generate data for the optimal and BAU scenarios. This exercise is useful for evaluating the effects of the uncertainty of the economic costs (market and non-market, as both were implicit in Nordhaus's survey) of climatic change on the output of the DICE model. In particular, the data from the simulation runs yield an output distribution, which will allow a comparison between the standard DICE model and the opinions expressed in Nordhaus's survey. This comparison is more comprehensive than that for Fig. 3, where the analyses relied solely on specific point estimates of expert opinion, rather than on entire subjective probability distributions.

14. Optimal carbon taxes

We have already seen that the damage distributions derived from the aforementioned expert survey have large variances in the magnitude of damage from unmitigated climatic change. We now consider the distribution of optimal policy, in the form of carbon taxes, associated with these damage distributions.

Using the results of the Monte Carlo simulation, distributions for optimal carbon taxes in the years 1995, 2055, and 2105 were derived. The CDFs for these distributions are shown in Figs. 5a, c and e, and the PDFs are given in Figs. 5b, d, and f. Points showing the optimal carbon taxes calculated by the original DICE model are shown for comparison.

All three distributions show a heavy concentration of results near 0. For the year 1995, nearly a quarter of the simulation runs give an optimal tax level less than that of the original DICE run (5.24 1990 US dollars per ton of carbon). For 2055 and 2105, this fraction of relatively optimistic runs is slightly higher (where the original DICE model gave optimal carbon taxes of 15.04 and 21.73 1990 US dollars, respectively).

However, all three optimal carbon tax distributions suggest a non-negligible probability that a large carbon tax is needed for optimal response to potential climatic change. One quarter of the simulation runs "recommend" a 1995 carbon tax of at least $50 per ton of carbon, which is a tenfold increase from the optimal tax in the canonical run. About 15% of the runs give similarly enhanced tax levels for 2055 and 2105. In the most pessimistic damage runs, optimal carbon taxes start at nearly $200 per ton in 1995, and climb to nearly $500 per ton by the end of the 21st century. We reiterate that all of these carbon tax rates are "optimal", and differ only by the damage function assumed.

T. Roughgarden, S.H. Schneider / Energy Policy 27 (1999) 415–429   425

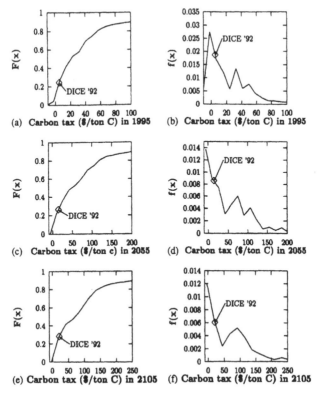

Fig. 5. Results of the Monte Carlo simulation based on surveyed experts (Nordhaus, 1994a), presented as distributions of optimal carbon tax levels. Figs. 5a and b give the cumulative distribution function, $F(x)$, and probability density function, $f(x)$, respectively, for optimal taxes in 1995. Figs. 5c and d show similar functions for optimal taxes in 2055; Figs. 5e and f display the corresponding functions for 2105.

15. Comparison of results with DICE

Several comparisons between our optimal carbon tax distributions and the output of the original DICE model can be made, using the data summarized in Table 3 and Fig. 5.

Comparing the mode (the most frequent value) of the output distribution with the results of the original DICE model, it seems that DICE is a good representative of the expert opinion expressed in Nordhaus's survey. The modes of the optimal carbon tax distributions are near zero, close to DICE's recommendation for a relatively light carbon tax. However, the other properties of the output distributions justify very different policies. The median and mean of the optimal carbon tax distributions range from three to eight times as high as those featured in the original DICE run.

The differences between the modes of the output distributions and their medians and means can be attributed to their lack of symmetry. As a result of the preponder-

Table 3
Comparison of Monte Carlo simulation results with the standard DICE model

Source of data	Optimal Carbon Tax ($/ton C)		
	1995	2055	2105
DICE	5.24	15.04	21.73
Median	22.85	51.72	66.98
Mean	40.42	84.10	109.73
"Surprise"	193.29	383.39	517.09

Note: "Surprise" values are 95th percentile results. Explicitly including low probability, high consequence outcomes alerts policy makers to consider strategic hedging options to reduce the risk of experiencing catastrophic outlier events.

ance of right-skewness of the opinions given in Nordhaus's survey, discussed earlier (e.g., Fig. 4), the output distributions include a non-negligible probability of extremely severe damage from climatic change. These long, heavy tails (which we label "Surprise" in Table 3) pull the medians and means of the distributions away from the modes.

The differences between the output distribution and the results of the original DICE model are particularly obvious when we consider the tails of the output distributions. We take the 95th percentile results from the output distributions as representatives of these tails. Referring back to Table 3, we see that the "surprise" estimates for optimal carbon taxes are over twenty times the level of those in the canonical run.

These differences are caused by two different effects. First, the means of these distributions (4.04% and 11.22% of GWP damage for scenarios A and C, respectively) are much higher than the damage estimates used in DICE (1.33% and 5.32%). Thus, most of our Monte Carlo runs will use more pessimistic damage functions than that of the original DICE model. Second, the non-linearities of the model will, on average, push optimal carbon taxes even higher. Intuitively, damage functions derived from these damage distributions will never cause far more optimistic results than those with the original DICE damage function, but they will occasionally result in far more pessimistic outcomes. These occasional "catastrophic" damage functions will lead to a relatively pessimistic expected value of output. In other words, the significant chance of a "surprise" (Schneider *et al.*, 1998) causes a much higher level of "optimal" abatement, relative to the original DICE formulation.

In addition, we analyzed the effects of the relative severity of the average survey damage estimate versus those of the non-linearities of the DICE model in a probabilistic analysis. Approximately one third of the difference between the optimal carbon taxes of DICE and the means of our optimal carbon tax distributions are accounted for by the relatively high survey damage estimates, and the remaining two-thirds of the difference can be attributed to the non-linearities in the model.

16. Conclusions

By including a wide range of published climate damage estimates and applying them to a simple, but well-known, climate-economy integrated assessment model, we make explicit to policy makers the wide range of "optimal" climate abatement policy options that this analytic approach provides. Our analysis shows that the original DICE model is a fairly good representative of the most frequent estimates from the Monte Carlo analysis based on Nordhaus's survey of experts, but DICE with Nordhaus's original damage function is far more optimistic (i.e., suggests a lower carbon rate) than the bulk of the distribution of expert opinion. In a sense, the original

DICE carbon tax may be regarded as a point estimate between the mode and median of the distribution of expert opinion. However, this point estimate ignores the chance that, as estimated by 18 experts, climatic change could cause a disastrous amount of damage, a chance that most of the survey respondents clearly consider non-negligible. In other words, output from a single model run does not display all the information available nor does it offer sufficient information to provide the insights needed for well-informed policy decisions. One cannot simply look at a recommendation for a "five dollars per ton carbon tax" and claim that higher carbon taxes are "necessarily less economically efficient". As we have shown, such a relatively low carbon tax results from using a relatively optimistic damage estimate, and from ignoring the uncertainty of the magnitude of impacts from climatic change. Instead, a wide range of possible scenarios, including low-probability, beneficial and high-risk scenarios, must be explicitly considered. In particular, strategic hedging policies to deal with the 95th percentile, high damage outcome may well be chosen by policy makers, just as individuals or firms purchase insurance against low probability catastrophic outcomes. Regardless of the risk proneness or risk averseness of the individual decision maker, the characterization and range of uncertainties of the information provided by decision analysis tools must be made explicit and transparent to policy-makers (Moss and Schneider, 1997). This range of uncertainty should also include estimates for the subjective probability of varying climatic effects (e.g., Morgan and Keith, 1995), damage estimates (e.g., this article), discount rates (e.g., Cline, 1992; Chapman *et al.*, 1995), carbon cycle effects on CO_2 uptake (e.g., Kaufmann, 1997), and the sensitivity of the economy to structural changes such as induced technological change (e.g., Grubb, 1997; Repetto and Austin, 1997; Goulder and Schneider, 1999). The end result of any set of integrated assessment modeling exercises will be, as always, the subjective choice of a decision-maker (Schneider, 1997), but a more comprehensive analysis with uncertainties in all major components explicitly categorized and displayed will hopefully lead to a better-informed choice, including the options for strategic hedging against low probability, high consequence events.

Acknowledgements

We appreciate the many useful discussions with Larry Goulder. We thank Christian Azar, Michael Dalton, Robert Kaufmann, and Billy Pizer for numerous helpful comments on an earlier draft of this paper. We also thank Bill Nordhaus for permission to use his survey data and Steve Fetter for suggesting the use of the Weibull distribution. This work was partially supported by Winslow Foundation Award, SPO number 18744.

T. Roughgarden, S.H. Schneider / Energy Policy 27 (1999) 415–429   427

Appendix A. The DICE model

The DICE model is an intertemporal, optimal-growth model of the global economy, first published in Nordhaus (1992). More specifically, the model maximizes utility by choosing values for three decision variables (consumption, investment, and emissions control) subject to several economic and geophysical constraints. The exact form of the objective functions is given by:

$$\max U = \sum_t \frac{P(t) \ln(C(t)/P(t))}{(1 + \rho)^t} \qquad (A.1)$$

where U is discounted utility, $P(t)$ is the population size at time t, $C(t)$ is global consumption at time t, and ρ is the social rate of time preference. In words, utility is a function of per capita consumption, discounted at rate ρ. The values of $P(t)$ are taken as exogenous, with population levels stabilizing around 10.6 billion people in the 24th century. ρ is also taken exogenously as 3%.

Global output, $Y(t)$, is given by a Cobb–Douglas production function:

$$Y(t) = \Omega(t)A(t)L(t)^{1-\gamma}K(t)^\gamma \qquad (A.2)$$

where $A(t)$ represents technology, $L(t)$ is labor, $K(t)$ is capital, and γ is capital elasticity. $\Omega(t)$ relates production to the costs of emission control and the costs of climatic change, and will be discussed below. γ is assumed to be 0.25. $L(t)$ is assumed to be equal to $P(t)$, the population size. $A(t)$ is taken to be an exogenously increasing function, but with decreasing growth. In other words, as with population size, productivity is taken to be increasing but leveling off.

Global output is then endogenously divided among consumption and investment:

$$Y(t) = C(t) + I(t) \qquad (A.3)$$

and the level of investment affects the future capital stock:

$$K(t) = (1 - \delta_K)K(t-1) + I(t-1) \qquad (A.4)$$

where δ_K is the rate of depreciation of the capital stock, taken exogenously to be 0.10. Since the model uses time increments of 10 yr, time t is 10 years after time $t - 1$.

The economic side of DICE interacts with the climatic side through greenhouse gas emissions. Specifically, emissions are taken to be a function of output:

$$E(t) = [1 - \mu(t)]\sigma(t)Y(t) \qquad (A.5)$$

where $\mu(t)$ is the endogenous control rate and $\sigma(t)$ is the CO_2-equivalent emissions per unit of output without controls. $\sigma(t)$ is taken exogenously as a decreasing function, due to historical trends of increasing energy efficiency and substitution for carbon-intensive fuels.

The magnitude of climatic change depends on the stock of greenhouse gases in the atmosphere ($M(t)$), not the flow of gases to the atmosphere (i.e., $E(t)$):

$$M(t) - M_{pre} = \eta E(t-1) + (1 - \delta_M)[M(t) - M_{pre}] \qquad (A.6)$$

where M_{pre} is the preindustrial level of the stock, η is the marginal atmospheric retention ratio, and δ_M is the rate of transfer of carbon to the deep oceans. M_{pre}, η, and δ_M are given as 590 billion tons of carbon equivalent, 0.64, and 0.0833 per decade, respectively.

As greenhouse gases accumulate, the amount of radiation near the Earth's surface increases. This relationship is

$$F(t) = 4.1\{\log[M(t)/590]/\log(2)\} + O(t) \qquad (A.7)$$

where $F(t)$ is radiative forcing in watts per square meter and $O(t)$ is exogenous forcings from other greenhouse gases (primarily CH_4 and N_2O). $F(t)$ is then related to a global average surface temperature increase $\Delta T(t)$ via equations which describe the heat transfer between the atmosphere, upper oceans, and deep oceans. One assumption of these equations is that a doubling of CO_2 levels will lead to a 3°C warming — a quantity known as the "climate sensitivity"; variations in this important parameter are easy to incorporate into DICE. Further details regarding the relationship between $F(t)$ and $\Delta T(t)$ can be found in Schneider and Thompson (1981).

It is through $\Delta T(t)$ that the climate side of the DICE model provides feedback to the economic side. Specifically, using temperature as an indicator for climatic change, damage from climatic change is given by

$$d(t) = \alpha_1 \, \Delta T(t)^{\alpha_2} \qquad (A.8)$$

where $d(t)$ is in fractional loss of global output, and α_1 and α_2 are estimated as 0.00148 and 2, respectively.

The amount of temperature increase, and hence the amount of damage from climatic change, can be influenced by choosing $\mu(t)$. However, controlling emissions also carries a cost:

$$TC(t) = \beta_1 \mu(t)^{\beta_2} \qquad (A.9)$$

where $TC(t)$ is in fractional loss of global output, and β_1 and β_2 given by Nordhaus as 0.0686 and 2.887, respectively. This implies that a small (< 10%) reduction in emissions can be achieved with relatively low cost, but drastic cuts are fairly expensive (e.g., a 50% cut in emissions would cost about 1% of global output). Although these values are debatable (e.g., Repetto and Austin, 1997), we use the original DICE formulation in order to focus on the sensitivity of policy options to alternative damage functions.

These two costs are combined in the $\Omega(t)$ term

$$\Omega(t) = \frac{1 - TC(t)}{1 + d(t)}. \qquad (A.10)$$

428 *T. Roughgarden, S.H. Schneider / Energy Policy 27 (1999) 415–429*

It is worth noting that $\Omega(t)$ does not fully capture the damages of the $d(t)$ term, since $1/(1 + d(t))$ is a reasonable approximation of $1 - d(t)$ only for small values of $d(t)$. In the extreme case, with $d(t) = 1$, the world "only" experiences a 50% reduction in output due to damage from climatic change, rather than a complete loss of global output. However, since the original model is being used here to analyze the consequences of uncertainties in damage functions and to display methods to present uncertainties quantitatively, we do not reformulate $\Omega(t)$ in this study.

This completes the linking of the economic and climatic sides of the DICE model.

Appendix B. Deriving damage functions from damage distributions

In this appendix, we describe the derivation of the damage functions used in our probabilistic analysis of the DICE model.

Given positive damage estimates from the scenario A and scenario C damage distributions (call the estimates y_3 and y_6, respectively), the corresponding damage function is given by

$$d(t) = a\Delta T(t)^b \tag{B.1}$$

where

$$a = y_6/6^b \tag{B.2}$$

$$b = \frac{\log(y_6/y_3)}{\log 2}. \tag{B.3}$$

About 10% of the time, however, at least one of the damage estimates is negative — that is, a net benefit from climatic change is predicted. In this case, there is no longer a function of the form ax^b which contains the three damage estimates $(0, y_3, \text{ and } y_6)$. However, the three estimates can be described by a function with the form $a(x + c)^b + d$ (roughly, a translated parabola). We cannot, however, solve for all four variables (a, b, c, d) with only three data points. As a result, we reassert the assumption that damage is a quadratic function of temperature increase (i.e., we fix $b = 2$). Now we can derive a damage function from y_3 and y_6 as follows:

$$d(t) = a(\Delta T(t) + c)^2 + d \tag{B.4}$$

where

$$a = \frac{y_6 - 2y_3}{18}, \tag{B.5}$$

$$c = \frac{y_3 - 9a}{6a}, \tag{B.6}$$

$$d = -ac^2. \tag{B.7}$$

References

Azar, C., 1996. Technological change and the long-run cost of reducing CO_2 emissions, INSEAD Working paper, France.

Azar, C., Rodhe, H., 1997. Targets for stabilization of atmospheric CO_2. Science 276, 1818–1819.

Azar, C., Sterner, T., 1996. Discounting and distributional considerations in the context of global warming. Ecological Economics 19, 169–184.

Berk, R.A., Schulman, D., 1991. Public perceptions of global warming. Climatic Change 29, 1–33.

Broecker, W.S., 1997. Thermohaline circulation, the achilles heel of our climate system: will man-made CO_2 upset the current balance?. Science 278, 1582–1588.

Brown, P.G., 1997. Stewardship of climate. Climatic Change 37, 329–334.

Bruce, J.P., Lee, H., Haites, E.F. (Eds.), 1996. Climate Change 1995: Economic and Social Dimensions of Climate Change. Intergovernmental Panel on Climate Change, Cambridge University Press, Cambridge.

Chapman, D., Suri, V., Hall, S.G., 1995. Rolling dice for the future of the planet. Contemporary Economic Policy 13, 1–9.

Cline, W.R., 1992. The Economics of Global Warming. Institute for International Economics, Washington D.C.

Daily, G.C., 1997. Nature's Services: Societal Dependence on Natural Ecosystems. Island Press, Washington D.C.

Fankhauser, S., 1995. Valuing Climate Change: The Economics of the Greenhouse. Earthscan, London.

Filar, J.A., Rotmans, J., Vrieze, K. (Eds.), 1998. Environmental Modeling and Assessment 3, 135–207 (special issue on integrated assessment).

Goulder, L.H., Schneider, S.H., 1999. Induced Technological Change and the attractiveness of CO_2 abatement policies, Resource and Energy Economics 21, 211–253.

Grubb, M., 1997. Technologies, energy systems and the timing of CO_2 emissions abatement: an overview of the economic issues. Energy Policy 25, 159–172.

Hasselmann, K., Hasselmann, S., Giering, R., Ocana, V., von Storch, H., 1997. Sensitivity study of optimal CO_2 emission paths using a simplified Structural Integrated Assessment Model (SIAM). Climatic Change 37, 345–386.

Houghton, J.T., Meira Filho, L.G., Callander, B.A., Harris, N., Kattenberg, A., Maskell, K. (Eds.), 1996. Climate Change 1995: The Science of Climate Change. Intergovernmental Panel on Climate Change. Cambridge University Press, Cambridge.

Jenkins, T.N., 1996. Democratising the global economy by ecologicalising economics: the example of global warming. Ecological Economics 16, 227–238.

Kaufmann, R.K., 1997. Assessing the DICE model: uncertainty associated with the emission and retention of greenhouse gases. Climatic Change 35, 435–448.

Keith, D., 1996. When is it appropriate to combine expert judgements?. (an editorial essay) Climatic Change 33, 139–143.

Kolstad, C.D., 1993. Looking vs. leaping: the timing of CO_2 control in the face of uncertainty and learning. In: Kaya, Y., Nakicenovic, N., Nordhaus, W.D., Toth, F.L. (Eds.), Costs, Impacts, and Benefits of CO_2 Mitigation. International Institute for Systems Analysis, Laxenburg, Austria.

Manne, A.S., Richels, R., 1994. The costs of stabilizing global CO_2 emissions: a probabilistic analysis based on expert judgements. The Energy Journal 15, 31–56.

Morgan, D., Keith, D., 1995. Subjective judgments by climate experts. Environmental Science and Technology 29, 468–476.

Morgan, M.G., Dowlatabadi, H., 1996. Learning from integrated assessment of climate change. Climatic Change 34, 337–368.

T. Roughgarden, S.H. Schneider / Energy Policy 27 (1999) 415–429   429

Morgan, M.G., Henrion, M., 1990. Uncertainty: A Guide to Dealing with Uncertainty in Quantitative Risk and Policy Analysis. Cambridge University Press, New York.

Moss, R.H., Schneider, S.H., 1997. Characterizing and communicating scientific uncertainty: Building on the IPCC second assessment. In: Hassol, S.J., Katzenberger, J. (Eds.), Elements of Change 1996. Aspen Global Change Institute, Aspen, CO, pp. 90–135. http://www.gcrio.org/agci-home.html.

Nordhaus, W.D., 1991. To slow or not to slow: the economics of the greenhouse effect. The Economics Journal 101, 920–937.

Nordhaus, W.D., 1992. An optimal transition path for controlling greenhouse gases. Science 258, 1315–1319.

Nordhaus, W.D., 1993. Survey on uncertainties associated with potential climate change, Final draft.

Nordhaus, W.D., 1994a. Expert opinion on climatic change. American Scientist 82, 45–51.

Nordhaus, W.D., 1994b. Managing the Global Commons: The Economics of Climate Change, MIT Press, Cambridge, MA.

Nordhaus, W.D., 1997. Discounting in economics and climate change (an editorial comment). Climatic Change 37, 315–328.

Nordhaus, W.D., Popp, D., 1997. What is the value of scientific knowledge?: an application to global warming using the PRICE Model. The Energy Journal 18, 1–45.

Paté-Cornell, M.E., 1996. Uncertainties in global climate change estimates (an editorial essay). Climatic Change 33, 145–149.

Peck, S.C., Teisberg, T.J., 1992. CETA: a model for carbon emissions trajectory assessment. The Energy Journal 13, 55–77.

Peck, S.C., Teisberg, T.J., 1995. Optimal CO_2 control policy with stochastic losses from temperature rise. Climatic Change 31, 19–34.

Repetto, T., Austin, D., 1997. The Costs of Climate Protection: A Guide for the Perplexed, World Resources Institute, Washington D.C.

Roughgarden, T., 1997. Quantifying the damage of climatic change: implications for the DICE model. Honors Thesis, Stanford University. Available at http://www.cs.cornell.edu/timr.

Schelling, T.C., 1983. Climatic change: implications for welfare and policy. In: Climate Change. National Academy Press, Washington D.C., pp. 449–482.

Schneider, S.H., 1997. Integrated assessment modeling of global climate change: transparent rational tool for policy making or opaque screen hiding value-laden assumptions? Environmental Modeling and Assessment 2, 229–248.

Schneider, S.H., 1998. Kyoto protocol: the unfinished agenda (an editorial essay). Climatic Change 39, 1–21.

Schneider, S.H., Goulder, L.H., 1997. Achieving low-cost emissions targets. Nature 389, 13–14.

Schneider, S.H., Thompson, S.L., 1981. Atmospheric CO_2 and climate: importance of the transient response. Journal of Geophysical Research 86, 3135–3147.

Schneider, S.H., Turner II, B.L., Morehouse Garriga, H., 1998. Imaginable surprise in global change science, Journal of Risk Research, 1(2), 165–185.

Titus, J.G., 1992. The cost of climate change to the United States. In: Majumdar, S.K., Kalkstein, L.S., Yarnal, B., Miller, E.W., Rosenfeld, L.M. (Eds.), Global Climate Change: Implications, Challenges, and Mitigation Measures. Pennsylvania Academy of Science, Easton, PA.

Titus, J.G., 1997. Probabilities in sea level rise projections. In: Hassol, S.J., Katzenberger, J. (Eds.), Elements of Change 1996. Aspen Global Change Institute, Aspen, CO.

Tol, R.S.J., 1994. The damage costs of climate change: a note on tangibles and intangibles, applied to DICE. Energy Policy 22, 436–438.

Tol, R.S.J., 1995. The damage costs of climate change: towards more comprehensive calculations. Environmental and Resource Economics 5, 353–374.

[14]

Optimal CO_2 Abatement in the Presence of Induced Technological Change

Lawrence H. Goulder[1] and Koshy Mathai

Department of Economics, Stanford University, Stanford, California 94305

Received August 4, 1998; revised June 18, 1999

This paper explores the significance of policy-induced technological change for the design of carbon-abatement policies. We derive analytical expressions characterizing optimal CO_2 abatement and carbon tax profiles under different specifications for the channels through which technological progress occurs. We consider both R & D-based and learning-by-doing-based knowledge accumulation, and we examine each specification under both a cost-effectiveness and a benefit–cost policy criterion.

We show analytically in a cost-effectiveness setting that the presence of induced technological change (ITC) always implies a lower time profile of optimal carbon taxes. The same is true in a benefit–cost setting as long as damages are convex in the atmospheric CO_2 concentration. The impact of ITC on the optimal abatement path varies. When knowledge is gained through R & D investments, the presence of ITC justifies shifting some abatement from the present to the future. However, when knowledge is accumulated via learning-by-doing the impact on the timing of abatement is analytically ambiguous.

Illustrative numerical simulations indicate that the impact of ITC upon overall costs and optimal carbon taxes can be quite large in a cost-effectiveness setting but typically is much smaller under a benefit–cost policy criterion. The impact of ITC on the timing of abatement is very slight, but the effect (applicable in the benefit–cost case) on cumulative abatement over time can be large, especially when knowledge is generated through learning-by doing.
© 2000 Academic Press

Key Words: climate policy; carbon tax; technological change.

1. INTRODUCTION

Over the past decade considerable efforts have been directed toward evaluating alternative policies to reduce the atmospheric accumulation of greenhouse gases, particularly carbon dioxide (CO_2). Initial assessments tended to disregard interconnections between technological change and CO_2-abatement policies, treating the rate of technological progress as autonomous—that is, unrelated to policy changes or associated changes in relative prices. Recently, however, several researchers have emphasized that CO_2 policies and the rate of technological change are connected: to the extent that public policies affect the prices of carbon-based fuels, they affect incentives to invest in research and development (R & D) aimed at

[1] Address correspondence to: Lawrence H. Goulder, Department of Economics, Stanford University, Stanford, CA 94305. E-mail: goulder@leland.stanford.edu. We have benefitted from very helpful comments from Michael Dalton, Michael Grubb, Chad Jones, Alan Manne, Robert Mendelsohn, William Nordhaus, Richard Richels, Stephen Schneider, Sjak Smulders, David Wheeler, and an anonymous referee. Financial support from Department of Energy Grant DE-FG03-95ER62104 and National Science Foundation Grant SBR9310362 is gratefully acknowledged.

bringing alternative fuels on line earlier or at lower cost. Such policies may also prompt R & D oriented toward the discovery of new production methods that require less of *any* kind of fuel. Moreover, climate policies can affect the growth of knowledge through impacts on learning by doing (LBD): to the extent that these policies affect producers' experience with alternative energy fuels or energy-conserving processes, they can influence the rate of advancement of knowledge.

Thus, through impacts on patterns of both R & D spending and learning by doing, climate policy can alter the path of knowledge acquisition. What does this connection imply for the design of CO_2-abatement policy? In particular, how do the optimal timing and extent of carbon emissions abatement, as well as the optimal time path of carbon taxes, change when we recognize the possibility of induced technological change (ITC)?

Policymakers and researchers are divided on these questions. Wigley *et al.* [31] have argued that the prospect of technological change justifies relatively little current abatement of CO_2 emissions: better to wait until scientific advances make such abatement less costly. In contrast, Ha-Duong *et al.* [8] have maintained that the potential for ITC justifies relatively more abatement in the near term, in light of the ability of current abatement activities to contribute to learning by doing. Yet another possibility is that ITC makes it optimal to increase abatement in all periods and thus achieve more ambitious overall targets for atmospheric CO_2 concentrations.

In addition to these disagreements on the optimal profile for abatement, there are differing viewpoints concerning the optimal carbon tax profile. One frequently heard claim is that induced technological change justifies a higher carbon tax trajectory than would be optimal in the absence of ITC. The argument is that in the presence of ITC, carbon taxes not only confer the usual environmental benefit by forcing agents to internalize the previously external costs from CO_2 emissions, but also yield the benefit of faster innovation, particularly in the supply of alternative energy technologies.[2] Another possibility, however, is that with technological progress, a lower carbon tax profile is all that is needed to achieve desired levels of abatement.

This paper aims to clarify the issues underlying these controversies. We derive analytical expressions characterizing the optimal paths of emissions abatement and carbon taxes under different specifications for the channels through which knowledge is accumulated, considering both *R & D-based* and *learning-by-doing-based* knowledge accumulation. We examine each of these specifications under two different optimization criteria: the *cost-effectiveness* criterion of obtaining by a specified date and thereafter maintaining, at minimum cost, a given target for the atmospheric CO_2 concentration; and the *benefit–cost* criterion under which we also choose the optimal concentration target, thus obtaining the path of carbon abatement that maximizes the benefits from avoided climate damages net of abatement

---

[2] Some have suggested that the innovation-related benefits from a carbon tax might be as large as the direct abatement costs associated with such a tax. If this were the case, then the overall cost (ignoring environmental benefits) of a carbon tax would be zero. Porter and van der Linde [25] advance a general argument consistent with this view, maintaining that environmental regulation often stimulates substantial technological progress and leads to significant long-run cost savings that make the overall costs of regulation trivial or even negative.

costs.[3] To gain a sense of plausible magnitudes, we also perform illustrative numerical simulations.

Our analysis is in the spirit of two studies by Nordhaus [16, 17]—the first to obtain analytical expressions for the optimal carbon tax trajectory—as well as more recent work by Farzin and Tahvonnen [4], Farzin [3], Peck and Wan [23], Sinclair [28], and Ulph and Ulph [29]. Our paper also complements work by Nordhaus [18], Nordhaus and Yang [20], and Peck and Teisberg [21, 22], in which numerical methods are used to obtain the optimal carbon abatement and carbon tax profiles under different exogenous technological specifications.[4] Another related paper is by Kolstad [12], who solves numerically for optimal emissions trajectories in the presence of endogenous learning. Kolstad's paper differs from ours, however, in that it focuses on learning that reduces uncertainty about CO$_2$-related damages, rather than on learning that improves abatement technologies and thus reduces abatement costs. Finally, our paper is closely related to the previously mentioned studies by Wigley *et al.* [31] and Ha-Duong *et al.* [8], as well as to working papers by Grubb [7], Goulder and Schneider [6], and Nordhaus [19] that analyze the implications of induced technological change for optimal climate policy.

The present investigation differs from each of these other studies in three ways. First, it derives *analytical* results revealing the impact of ITC on optimal time profiles for carbon taxes and carbon abatement. Second, it considers, in a unified framework, two channels for knowledge accumulation (R & D and learning by doing) and two policy criteria (cost-effectiveness and benefit–cost). In the model, policymakers (or the social planner) choose optimal paths of carbon abatement and carbon taxes, taking into account the impact of these taxes on technological progress and future abatement costs. Finally, it employs both analytical and numerical methods in an integrated, complementary way.

The analytical model reveals (contrary to what some analysts have suggested) that the presence of ITC generally implies a lower time profile of optimal carbon taxes.[5] The impact of ITC on the optimal abatement path varies. When knowledge is gained through R & D investments, the presence of ITC justifies shifting some abatement from the present to the future. However, when knowledge reflects learning by doing, the impact on the timing of abatement is analytically ambiguous.

When the government employs the benefit–cost policy criterion, the presence of ITC justifies greater overall (cumulative) abatement than would be warranted in its absence. This does not imply, however, that abatement rises in every period: when knowledge accumulation results from R & D expenditure, the presence of ITC implies a reduction of near-term abatement efforts, despite the overall increase in the scale of abatement over time.

Our numerical simulations reinforce the qualitative predictions of the analytical model. The quantitative impact on overall costs and optimal carbon taxes can be quite large in a cost-effectiveness setting but typically is much smaller under a benefit–cost policy criterion. The weak effect on the tax rate in the benefit–cost case reflects the relatively trivial impact of ITC on optimal CO$_2$ concentrations,

---

[3]This is equivalent to minimizing the sum of abatement costs and CO$_2$-related damages to the environment.

[4]The present paper also complements that of Manne and Richels [14], who employ a multiregion computable general equilibrium model to solve for Pareto-efficient paths of carbon abatement and taxes.

[5]However, in a benefit–cost setting, the opposite could be true if damages were concave in the atmospheric CO$_2$ concentration.

4   GOULDER AND MATHAI

associated marginal damages, and (hence) the optimal tax rate. As for the optimal abatement path, the impact of ITC on the timing of abatement is very weak, but the effect on overall abatement (which applies in the benefit–cost case) can be large, especially when knowledge is accumulated via learning-by-doing.

The rest of the paper is organized as follows. Section 2 lays out the analytical model and applies it to the case in which the policy criterion is cost-effectiveness. Section 3 applies the model to the situation in which policymakers employ the broader benefit–cost criterion. Section 4 presents and interprets results from numerical simulations and includes a sensitivity analysis. The final section offers conclusions and indicates directions for future research.

2. OPTIMAL POLICY UNDER THE COST-EFFECTIVENESS CRITERION

In this section we consider optimal abatement when the policy criterion is cost-effectiveness (CE). We assume that producers are competitive and minimize costs. Let $C(A_t, H_t)$ be the economy's (aggregate) abatement-cost function, where A_t is abatement at time t and H_t is the stock of knowledge—or alternatively, the level of technology—at time t. We assume $C_A(\cdot) > 0$, $C_{AA}(\cdot) > 0$, $C_H(\cdot) < 0$, and $C_{AH}(\cdot) < 0$. The last two properties imply that increased knowledge reduces, respectively, total and marginal costs of abatement. Later on, we consider the implications of alternative assumptions. We also allow for the possibility that costs may depend on the relative amount of abatement (A_t/E_t^0) rather than the absolute level (A_t). In this case baseline emissions become an argument of the cost function. For expositional simplicity, however, we usually suppress E_t^0 from the cost function in the main text.

2.1. *Technological Change via R & D*

2.1.1. *The Problem and Basic Characteristics of the Solution*

Within our cost-effectiveness analysis, we consider two modes of knowledge accumulation. The first specification assumes that to accumulate knowledge, the economy must devote resources to research and development. We refer to this as the CE_R specification (where "R" indicates that the channel for knowledge accumulation is R & D). The planner's problem is to choose the time-paths of abatement and R & D investment that minimize the costs of achieving the concentration target.[6] Formally, the optimization problem is

$$\min_{A_t, I_t} \int_0^\infty \left(C(A_t, H_t) + p(I_t)I_t \right) e^{-rt} \, dt \qquad (1)$$

$$\text{s.t.} \qquad \dot{S}_t = -\delta S_t + E_t^0 - A_t \qquad (2)$$

[6]Our analysis focuses on the social planner's problem. We disregard the market failure associated with knowledge spillovers, that is, with the inability of firms to appropriate the full social returns on their investments in knowledge. Our model implicitly assumes that any market failures associated with this appropriability problem have already been addressed through public policies.

OPTIMAL CO$_2$ ABATEMENT 5

$$\dot{H}_t = \alpha_t H_t + k\Psi(I_t, H_t) \qquad (3)$$

$$S_0, H_0 \text{ given}$$

$$\text{and} \quad S_t \leq \bar{S} \quad \forall t \geq T \qquad (4)$$

where A_t is abatement, I_t is investment in knowledge (i.e., R & D expenditure), S_t is the CO$_2$ concentration, H_t is the knowledge stock, $p(\cdot)$ is the real price of investment resources, r is the interest rate, δ is the natural rate of "removal" of atmospheric CO$_2$, E_t^0 is baseline emissions, α_t is the rate of *autonomous* technological progress, and k is a parameter that, as discussed below, indicates whether *induced* technological progress is present as well.

Expression (1) indicates that the objective is to minimize the discounted sum of abatement costs and expenditure on R & D into the infinite future. Expression (2) states that the change in the CO$_2$ concentration is equal to the contribution from current emissions ($E_t^0 - A_t$) net of natural removal (δS_t).[7]

Expression (3) describes the evolution of the knowledge stock (H_t), that is, the process of technological change. In the case where $k > 0$, the planner will choose an optimal profile for investments in R & D consistent with meeting the concentration target at minimum cost. These R & D investments (I_t) serve to increase the stock of knowledge (H_t) through the knowledge-accumulation function ($\Psi(\cdot)$). This profile of investment can be interpreted as the *additional* R & D investment that the optimal carbon tax would induce on the part of competitive firms. Thus, the $k > 0$ case is the induced technological change, or "ITC" case. We also consider the situation where $k = 0$ and there is no possibility of induced technological change because the connection between additional R & D investments and the stock of knowledge is severed. We call this the no-ITC or "NITC" case. In much of this paper, we will compare optimal abatement and carbon tax paths between the ITC and NITC cases. In addition to induced technological change, we also allow for *autonomous* technological change at the rate α_t: even if there were no climate policies in place, it seems reasonable to assume that some technological progress would still occur. There may be nonclimate reasons for such progress, such as a desire on the part of firms to economize on costly fuel inputs.

Expression (4) shows that the target CO$_2$ concentration, $\bar{S}$, must be met by time T and maintained after that point in time. We assume $p(\cdot)$ is nondecreasing in I_t; that is, the average cost of R & D investment increases with the level of R & D. This captures in reduced form the idea that there is an increasing opportunity cost (to other sectors of the economy) of employing scientists and engineers to devise new abatement technologies.[8] We also assume that the knowledge-accumulation function $\Psi(\cdot)$ has the following properties: $\Psi(\cdot) > 0$, $\Psi_I(\cdot) > 0$, and $\Psi_{II}(\cdot) < 0$.

The current-value Hamiltonian associated with the optimization problem for $t < T$ is[9]

$$\mathcal{H}_t = -(C(A_t, H_t) + p(I_t)I_t) - \tau_t(-\delta S_t + E_t^0 - A_t) + \mu_t(\alpha_t + k\Psi(I, H_t))$$

[7]For analytical convenience, we postulate a simple stock-flow relationship here. A more complicated equation of motion, such as the one introduced in the numerical simulations, would not alter the qualitative analytical results obtained here.

[8]This issue is discussed in greater detail by Goulder and Schneider [6].

[9]This Hamiltonian actually corresponds to the problem of maximizing the negative of costs.

6   GOULDER AND MATHAI

where $-r_t$ and μ_t are the shadow values of S_t and H_t, respectively. For $t \geq T$, however, we must form the following Lagrangian:

$$\mathcal{L}_t = \mathcal{H}_t + \eta_t(\bar{S} - S_t).$$

From the maximum principle, we obtain a set of first-order conditions, assuming an interior solution, as well as costate equations, state equations, and transversality conditions. Two key equations are

$$C_A(\cdot) = \tau_t \tag{5}$$

and

$$\dot{\tau}_t = \begin{cases} (r + \delta)\tau_t & \text{for } t < T \\ (r + \delta)\tau_t - \eta_t & \text{for } t \geq T. \end{cases} \tag{6}$$

In this problem, $-\tau_t$ is the shadow value of a small additional amount of CO_2 at time t. This shadow value is negative, since CO_2 is a "bad" from the policymaker's perspective. Thus τ_t represents the (positive) shadow *cost* of CO_2 or, equivalently, the benefit from an incremental amount of abatement (a small reduction in the CO_2 concentration). In a decentralized competitive economy in which all other market failures have been corrected, the optimal carbon tax is τ_t, the shadow cost of CO_2. By Eq. (5), this is equal to the marginal abatement cost at the optimal level of abatement. Equation (5) states that abatement should be pursued to the point at which marginal cost equals marginal benefit, while Eq. (6) states that the optimal carbon tax grows at the rate $(r + \delta)$ (at least for points in time up until T).[10] The two equations together imply that in an optimal program, the discounted marginal costs of abatement must be equal at all points in time (up to T), where the appropriate discount rate is $(r + \delta)$.[11] In the Appendix we demonstrate that this corresponds to an optimal abatement profile that slopes upward over time (whether or not there is induced technological change) so long as baseline emissions are not declining "too rapidly."

2.1.2. *Implications of ITC*

We now examine the effect of ITC on abatement costs and on the optimal carbon tax and abatement profiles. We do this by considering the significance of a change in the parameter k. As mentioned above, the case of $k = 0$ corresponds to a scenario with no induced technological change (the NITC scenario), while positive values of k imply the presence of induced technological change (the ITC

[10] After T, matters are complicated by the η_t term in Eq. (6).

[11] The appropriate discount rate is not simply r. Consider an arbitrary path of emissions leading to a given concentration S_T at the time T. Since CO_2 is removed naturally, altering this path by increasing emissions slightly at time t and reducing emissions slightly at a later time t' leads to greater overall removal and thus leads to a CO_2 concentration at time T that is less than S_T. Equivalently (as seen in the sensitivity analysis in Section 3), S_T can be achieved with less cumulative emissions abatement if the path of abatement is oriented more toward the future. Hence there is a value to postponing abatement beyond that implied by interest rate, r; this additional value is captured in the appearance of δ in the discount rate.

scenario). Our analysis will focus on incremental increases in k from the point $k = 0$.[12]

If (as is assumed) $C_H(\cdot) < 0$, then additional knowledge is clearly valuable (i.e., the multiplier μ is positive). When $k = 0$, all of the growth in knowledge is due to the autonomous term, and knowledge grows at the rate α_t. In contrast, for strictly positive values of k, the planner will find it optimal for society to accumulate at least some additional knowledge, assuming an interior solution.[13] This additional knowledge causes a decrease[14] in optimized costs to a degree dictated by μ_t. Thus, as would be expected, the introduction of the ITC option lowers the costs of achieving the given concentration target.

Next we examine the impact of introducing ITC on the optimal time profiles of abatement and carbon taxes. Differentiating Eq. (5) with respect to k and rearranging, we obtain

$$\frac{dA_t}{dk} = \frac{d\tau_t/dk - C_{AH}(\cdot)\, dH_t/dk}{C_{AA}(\cdot)}. \tag{7}$$

For the moment, assume that the first term in the numerator is zero, i.e., that ITC has no impact on the shadow cost of CO_2. Under this assumption, we are left only with what we shall refer to as the *knowledge-growth effect*: to the extent that knowledge has increased as a result of ITC ($dH_t/dk > 0$) and has thus reduced marginal abatement costs ($-C_{AH}(\cdot) > 0$), abatement tends to rise.[15]

The knowledge-growth effect is represented in Fig. 1 by the upward pivot of the abatement profile from the initial path 1 to path 2. At time 0 path 2 coincides with the initial path because knowledge is initially fixed at H_0: there can be no knowledge-growth effect at time 0.[16] The distance between paths 1 and 2 grows over time, representing the fact that the knowledge-growth effect becomes larger over time. This follows from the fact that there is no depreciation of knowledge in our model: whatever additional knowledge was induced by ITC at time t remains at time $t' > t$, and there might have been a further increment to knowledge at this later time.

Note that path 2 involves more abatement in every period than does the first path. Given that the same $\bar{S}$ constraint holds and that the initial path satisfied this constraint, path 2 clearly cannot be optimal. Path 2 was obtained under the assumption that the introduction of ITC had no impact on the shadow cost of CO_2. In fact, however (as shown in the Appendix), under the maintained assumption that

---

[12] The focus here on differential changes does not limit the generality of the analysis. Our analytical results are independent of the initial value of k. Given the smooth nature of our problem, results that hold for small changes in k around any initial value will carry over qualitatively for large changes around the point 0. This is confirmed in the numerical simulations.

[13] A corner solution arises if even the first increment of knowledge has marginal returns smaller than marginal costs. In this case, the social planner does not invest in additional knowledge; even here, though, we know that knowledge at least will not decrease from the baseline path.

[14] Throughout, when we use the words "increase" and "decrease" we will mean nonstrict increases and decreases, thus including the possibility that the variable stays constant.

[15] Note that the denominator of Eq. (7) is positive by assumption.

[16] We are stating that $dH_0/dk = 0$. This simply expresses the notion that the initial value for H_t (i.e., H_0) is not affected by different values for k. It remains true, however, that dH_t/dt is positive at all points in time. Even at time 0, the time-derivative of H_t is positive as a result of autonomous knowledge growth and induced investment in knowledge.

8   GOULDER AND MATHAI

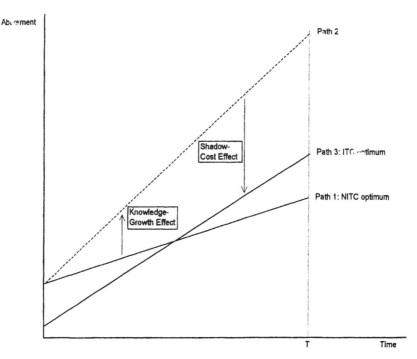

FIG. 1.   Knowledge-growth and shadow-cost effects (drawn for CE_R model).

$C_{AH}(\cdot) < 0$, the shadow cost of CO_2 at all points in time decreases in magnitude in the presence of ITC: $d\tau_t/dk \leq 0 \ \forall t$. The basic explanation for this *shadow-cost effect* is as follows. If we are armed with the potential to develop new technologies rapidly through ITC, the prospect of being given an additional amount of CO_2 at time t and still being expected to meet the $\bar{S}$ constraint by time T is less worrisome than it would be if we had only autonomously advancing abatement technologies at our disposal.[17] Note that since the optimal carbon tax is the shadow cost of CO_2, it follows that the presence of ITC lowers carbon taxes.

This result contradicts the notion that the induced-innovation benefit from carbon taxes justifies a higher carbon tax rate. Figure 2 demonstrates our result heuristically by offering a static representation of this dynamic problem.[18] Cost-effective abatement (depicted in the upper panel) is achieved by a carbon tax set equal to the marginal abatement cost (MC) at the desired level of abatement. Technological progress causes the MC curve to pivot down, thus implying a lower optimal tax: it now takes a lower tax to yield the same amount of abatement. Note that this result depends on the assumption that *marginal* abatement costs are lowered by technological progress; i.e., $C_{AH} < 0$. It is possible to conceive of new

---

[17] The decline in the shadow cost reflects the maximum potential of the ITC option over the entire time horizon; i.e., the fall in the shadow cost corresponds to optimal R & D, as is sensible in this model of an optimizing planner.

[18] The figure is not meant to represent a single year in the program, but rather an independent one-period analogue to our abatement problem.

OPTIMAL CO$_2$ ABATEMENT   9

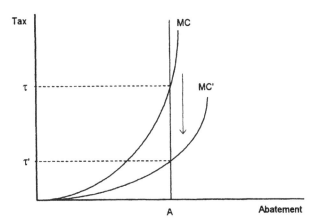

Cost-Effectiveness Case

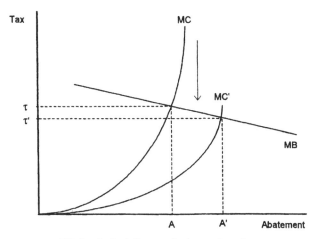

Benefit-Cost Case

FIG. 2. Optimal climate policy in a static setting.

technologies that involve higher marginal abatement costs but that are nonetheless attractive because of lower fixed (and overall) abatement costs; however, this seems to be an unusual case.

Now we return to our analysis of the impact of ITC on abatement. The shadow-cost effect, reflected in the first term of the numerator in Eq. (7), shows up in Fig. 1 as the downward shift from path 2 to path 3. The shift is not parallel: as shown in the Appendix, tax rates at later points in time fall by greater absolute amounts than do early taxes, in such a way as to preserve the carbon tax growth rate at $(r + \delta)$. The downward shift is of a magnitude such that path 3 lies neither completely above nor completely below path 1: if it did, it would imply either overshooting or undershooting the constraint $\bar{S}$, which is likely to be suboptimal.[19] Together, the knowledge-growth and shadow-cost effects imply a new optimal abatement path that is steeper than the initial one: abatement is postponed from the present into the future.[20] Intuitively, ITC reduces the cost of future abatement relative to current abatement and thus makes postponing (some) current abatement more attractive. Thus, in a cost-effectiveness setting with R & D-based technological change, our analysis supports the claim of Wigley *et al.* [31] that future technological developments justify a more gradual approach to abatement.

At any given time t, we cannot be sure whether abatement rises or falls—this depends on whether the knowledge-growth effect or the shadow-cost effect dominates at that particular moment. But we can say something definite about abatement at time 0. Because knowledge is initially fixed at H_0, only the shadow-cost effect comes into play at time 0:

$$\frac{dA_0}{dk} = \frac{d\tau_0/dk}{C_{AA}(\cdot)} \leq 0. \tag{8}$$

Thus, *initial* abatement weakly declines as a result of ITC.

These results depend on our assumption that $C_{AH}(\cdot) < 0$—that knowledge lowers marginal abatement costs. However, the possibility that $C_{AH}(\cdot) > 0$ cannot be ruled out. In this case (which we find somewhat implausible), ITC raises marginal costs, but presumably lowers total costs through greatly reduced sunk costs. Under these circumstances, the shadow-cost effect is positive and the presence of ITC raises the optimal carbon tax. The net effect of an increase in k on abatement at any arbitrary time t is (again) ambiguous, but initial abatement unambiguously rises.

2.1.3. Summary

Our results to this point are as follows. First, the solution to the cost-minimization problem (for any value of k) involves carbon taxes that rise over time at the rate $(r + \delta)$ for $t < T$, and that grow more slowly, and perhaps even decline, afterward. Second, the optimal abatement profile is upward sloping for $t < T$, as long as baseline emissions are not too steeply declining. Finally, assuming that ITC reduces marginal (and total) abatement costs, opening the ITC option causes optimized costs to fall, makes the entire carbon tax path fall (and by an equal proportion at all t), and causes initial abatement to fall and later abatement to rise. Table I summarizes the results regarding the implications of ITC.

---

[19] If baseline emissions were to rise sharply after T, then given the convexity of the abatement cost function, it might be optimal to more than meet the $\bar{S}$ requirement at time T to reduce the amount of abatement required afterward. However, it is the case nevertheless that one curve cannot lie above or below another over the entire infinite horizon: perpetual over- or undershooting of the constraint cannot be optimal.

[20] In characterizing the path as "steeper" we do not mean that the slope of the new path is everywhere greater than that of the old path. In fact, in the numerical simulations we will see that this is often not the case. We simply mean that, loosely speaking, less abatement is undertaken early on, and more later on.

TABLE I

Summary of Analytical Results

Policy criterion	Channel for technological change	Impacts of induced technological change on optimal solution	
		Tax path[a]	Abatement path
Cost-effectiveness	R & D	Falls by an equal proportion at all t	A_0 falls and later A rises; "steepening" of path
	LBD	Falls by an equal proportion at all t	Ambiguous effect on A_0 and on slope of path
Benefit–cost	R & D	Falls	A_0 falls; cumulative abatement rises; "steepening" of path
	LBD	Falls	Ambiguous effect on A_0; cumulative abatement increases

[a]Assuming damages are a convex function of the CO_2 concentration.

2.2. *Technological Change via Learning by Doing*

2.2.1. *The Problem and Basic Characteristics of the Solution*

Here we analyze a variant of the model presented above; now abatement itself yields improvements in technology. This is the "CE_L" model, where the "L" refers to learning by doing. The optimization problem is now

$$\min_{A_t} \int_0^\infty C(A_t, H_t) e^{-rt}\, dt$$

$$\text{s.t.} \quad \dot{S}_t = -\delta S_t + E_t^0 - A_t$$

$$\dot{H}_t = \alpha_t H_t + k\Psi(A_t, H_t)$$

$$S_0, H_0 \text{ given}$$

$$\text{and} \quad S_t \leq \bar{S} \quad \forall t \geq T.$$

This problem is virtually the same as the CE_R model of the previous section, except for a change in the $\Psi(\cdot)$ function: now induced knowledge growth is a function of the current level of abatement rather than R & D investment. Equivalently, current knowledge depends on cumulative abatement, which is regarded as a measure of experience. The first-order condition for abatement is now given by

$$C_A(\cdot) - \mu_t k\Psi_A(\cdot) = \tau_t. \tag{9}$$

Equation (9) states that the marginal benefit of abatement (τ_t, the value of the implied reduction in the CO_2 concentration) should equal the gross marginal cost of abatement ($C_A(\cdot)$) adjusted for the cost-reduction associated with the learning by doing stemming from that abatement ($\mu_t k\Psi_A(\cdot)$).

12   GOULDER AND MATHAI

As in the CE_R model, the optimal carbon tax here is equal to τ_t.[21] Since the costate equation for τ_t is unchanged from before, we can refer to earlier results and conclude that the carbon tax grows at the rate $(r + \delta)$ for $t < T$, and that it grows more slowly, and perhaps declines, thereafter.

Although the CE_R and CE_L models are similar as regards the carbon tax path, they differ with respect to the characteristics of the optimal abatement path. In particular, it is no longer unambiguously true that the abatement path is positively sloped for $t < T$, even in the case in which baseline emissions are growing over time. This is demonstrated in the Appendix; the basic reason is that the cost-reduction due to learning by doing does not necessarily grow with time.[22]

2.2.2. *Implications of ITC*

Now consider what happens to the optimal tax and abatement paths when we introduce ITC, i.e., increase k from the point $k = 0$. As before, our assumption that $C_H(\cdot) < 0$ directly implies that the presence of ITC causes optimized costs to fall. Perhaps more substantively, under the assumption that $C_{AH}(\cdot) < 0$, we again find that the presence of ITC causes the shadow cost of the CO_2 concentration, and thus the optimal carbon tax, to decline (and increasingly so for higher t).

To analyze the impact of ITC on the abatement path, we differentiate Eq. (9) with respect to k. Evaluating this at $k = 0$ yields

$$\frac{dA_t}{dk} = \frac{d\tau_t/dk + \mu_t \Psi_A(\cdot) - C_{AH}(\cdot)\, dH_t/dk}{C_{AA}(\cdot)}. \tag{10}$$

As in the CE_R model, we observe the negative shadow-cost effect $(d\tau_t/dk)$ and the positive knowledge-growth effect $(-C_{AH}(\cdot)\, dH_t/dk)$. In our LBD specification, however, the presence of ITC has an additional, positive effect on abatement which we term the *learning-by-doing effect* ($\mu_t \Psi_A(\cdot)$). This effect reflects the fact that in the learning-by-doing specification, there is an additional marginal benefit (the learning) from abatement. Other things being equal, this further marginal benefit justifies additional abatement. Thus, under this specification the presence of ITC has three effects on abatement, one negative (the shadow-cost effect), and two positive (the knowledge-growth and learning-by-doing effects).[23] The net effect is ambiguous. Even at time 0, when the knowledge-growth effect does not come into play, we are still left with the opposing shadow-cost and learning-by-doing effects:

$$\frac{dA_o}{dk} = \frac{d\tau_o/dk + \mu_0 \Psi_A(\cdot)}{C_{AA}(\cdot)}.$$

---

[21] We have assumed no spillovers in the model (or at least none that have not been fully addressed by other government policies); the cost-reduction from learning by doing is fully appropriated by agents.

[22] In an NITC scenario, the abatement path will unambiguously slope upward for $t < T$, given that baseline emissions do not decline too rapidly. See the Appendix for details.

[23] Evaluating at an arbitrary nonzero initial value of k adds extra terms which are difficult to sign. Unlike in the R & D-specification, here we cannot be fully confident that our differential analysis around the point $k = 0$ carries over to the case of large increases in k from 0. However, the numerical simulations below indicate that the qualitative results obtained here carry through even for large changes in k.

Thus, in contract to the CE–R model, the presence of ITC no longer implies unambiguously that initial abatement will fall. If the learning-by-doing effect is strong enough, initial abatement rises. (This in fact happens in most of the numerical simulations presented in Section 4.)[24] These results offer partial support for Ha-Duong *et al.*'s [8] claim that because of learning by doing, ITC justifies higher initial abatement. Higher initial abatement may be justified, but this is not always the case.

2.2.3. *Summary*

We can summarize our results for the CE–L case as follows. The optimal carbon tax grows at the rate $(r + \delta)$ for $t < T$, but will grow more slowly, and perhaps even decline, after that. The slope of the optimal abatement path is of ambiguous sign throughout (unless we are in an NITC scenario, in which case abatement unambiguously rises over time, at least for $t < T$, if baseline emissions do not decline too rapidly). The presence of ITC lowers optimized costs and makes the entire carbon tax path fall by an equal proportion at all $t < T$. The impact on initial abatement is analytically ambiguous. These effects of ITC are noted in Table I.

3. OPTIMAL POLICY UNDER THE BENEFIT – COST CRITERION

We now analyze optimal tax and abatement profiles in a benefit–cost (BC) framework. No longer is there an exogenously given concentration target; rather the object is to minimize the sum of abatement costs, investment costs (in the R & D model), *and damages from CO$_2$* over an infinite horizon.

3.1. *Technological Change via R & D*

3.1.1. *The Problem and Basic Characteristics of the Solution*

In the R & D-based specification (hereafter referred to as the BC–R model), the problem is

$$\min_{A_t, I_t} \int_0^\infty (C(A_t, H_t) + p(I_t)I_t + D(S_t))e^{-rt}\, dt$$

$$\text{s.t.} \quad \dot{S}_t = -\delta S_t + E_t^0 - A_t$$

$$\dot{H}_t = \alpha_t H_t + k\Psi(I_t, H_t)$$

$$\text{and} \quad S_0, H_0 \text{ given,}$$

where $D(S_t)$ is the damage function, assumed to have the following properties: $D'(\cdot) > 0$ and $D''(\cdot) > 0$. This is not completely uncontroversial. Although most would accept that damages are a convex function of climate change, it is also widely felt—see, e.g., Dickinson and Cicerone [1]—that climate change forcing is a

---

[24] The learning-by-doing effect can be quite large, as abatement, by increasing the stock of knowledge, lowers the cost of future abatement over the entire remaining time horizon.

14   GOULDER AND MATHAI

concave function of changes in the atmospheric CO_2 concentration. Thus our $D(\cdot)$ function—relating damages to concentrations—could be concave. The shape of the damage function is critical in predicting the impacts of ITC.

The current-value Hamiltonian associated with the optimization problem is

$$\mathcal{H}_t = -\left(C(A_t, H_t) + p(I_t)I_t + D(S_t)\right) - \tau_t\left(-\delta \dot{S}_t + E_t^0 - A_t\right)$$
$$+ \mu_t\left(\alpha_t + k\Psi(I_t, H_t)\right).$$

From the maximum principle, assuming an interior solution, we obtain a set of necessary conditions, of which the most important to us are

$$C_A(\cdot) = \tau_t \tag{11}$$

and

$$\dot{\tau}_t = (r + \delta)\tau_t - D'(\cdot). \tag{12}$$

As before, $-\tau_t$ is the negative shadow value of a small additional amount of CO_2. Hence τ_t again represents the marginal benefit of abatement. Equation (11) thus states that abatement should be pursued up to the point at which marginal cost equals marginal benefit. Equation (12) can be integrated, using the relevant transversality condition as a boundary condition, to obtain

$$\tau_t = \int_t^\infty D'(S_s) e^{-(r+\delta)(s-t)} \, ds. \tag{13}$$

Equation (13) states that the shadow cost of an increment to the CO_2 concentration equals the discounted sum of marginal damages that this increment would inflict over all future time. Alternatively, the marginal benefit from incremental CO_2 abatement equals the discounted sum of the avoided damages attributable to such abatement.

As in the CE_R model, the optimal carbon tax is equal to τ_t, and thus, by Eq. (11), to the marginal abatement cost at the optimum. Using Eq. (13), we demonstrate in the Appendix that in the BC_R model, the optimal carbon tax may either rise or fall over time. This contrasts with the results from the cost-effectiveness models, in which the optimal carbon tax rose at the rate $(r + \delta)$ (at least for $t < T$). The reason for the ambiguity is that although there is a tendency for the BC_R shadow cost to grow at the rate $(r + \delta)$, there is also a tendency for it to decline over time because an extra amount of CO_2 later on would inflict marginal damages over a shorter time horizon. The Appendix shows that given the convex damage function which we think reasonable, a sufficient condition ensuring that the tax path slopes upward is that the optimized path of CO_2 also slopes upward.

Given rising taxes and a baseline emissions path that rises (or at least does not fall too rapidly), we can also demonstrate that optimal abatement rises; otherwise, the slope of the abatement path is ambiguous. (See the Appendix for details.)

3.1.2. *Implications of ITC*

As before, the presence of ITC leads to lower optimized total costs (where these now include CO_2-related damages as well as abatement and investment costs). Just as before (and as proven in the Appendix), if we assume that knowledge reduces the marginal costs of abatement, the shadow-cost of CO_2 declines in the presence of ITC: $d\tau_t/dk \leq 0$. The intuition is similar to what it was in both the CE_R and CE_L models. Technological progress makes marginal abatement cheaper. Thus, when R & D investments are capable of yielding advanced technologies ($k > 0$), the prospect of being given an additional amount of CO_2 is less worrisome than it would be if we knew only more primitive abatement technologies would be available ($k = 0$). Since the optimal carbon tax is the shadow cost of CO_2, the presence of ITC lowers carbon taxes (the shadow-cost effect).[25] In this benefit–cost setting, we can also appeal to another piece of intuition. When ITC gives us the prospect of having more advanced technologies at our disposal, it makes sense that we would aim for more ambitious CO_2 concentration targets. Given a convex damage function, this would imply that marginal damages would be lower in the ITC world, and thus, by Eq. (13), optimal carbon taxes would be lower as well.

The result that ITC lowers optimal carbon taxes is perhaps surprising. Earlier, in a cost-effectiveness setting, we dismissed the claim that the presence of ITC should increase optimal taxes by appealing to a simple static graph; this graph showed that with ITC, it took a lower tax to achieve the same required level of abatement. But one might still have expected that in the broader, benefit–cost setting, if technology progressed sufficiently, it would make sense to *increase* the amount of abatement, and thus the optimal tax would increase.

The lower panel of Fig. 2 heuristically indicates that this notion is incorrect, at least under the assumption that the damage function is convex in the CO_2 concentration. The optimal amount of abatement and the optimal carbon tax are given by the intersection of the upward sloping MC curve and the downward sloping marginal abatement benefit (MB) curve.[26] If the MC curve were to pivot downward as a result of technological progress, the optimal amount of abatement would increase, but the optimal carbon tax would fall because we move to a lower point on the marginal benefit (marginal damage) curve.

If the damage function were linear, implying a flat marginal damage schedule, then the MC pivot would increase the optimal amount of abatement while leaving the optimal carbon tax unchanged. On the other hand, if damages were concave in the CO_2 concentration, then the MB curve would be upward sloping, and it is possible to envision a scenario in which a technology-driven fall in the MC schedule could actually increase the optimal carbon tax.[27]

Next we examine the implications of increasing k. Using the same approach as in the CE_R model, we obtain

$$\frac{dA_t}{dk} = \frac{d\tau_t/dk - C_{AH}(\cdot)\,dH_t/dk}{C_{AA}(\cdot)}. \tag{14}$$

---

[25] Unlike in the cost-effectiveness models, however, it is not necessarily true that taxes later on fall by greater amounts than do early taxes. See the Appendix.

[26] This MB curve conveys the same information as the schedule of marginal damages from additions to the stock of CO_2.

[27] See Repetto [26] for a discussion of nonconvex damages. Also note that, as before, if technological progress were to raise the MC schedule, then even with convex damages, the optimal carbon tax would rise (and the optimal scale of abatement would fall). This is confirmed in the Appendix.

16   GOULDER AND MATHAI

Once again, the impact of ITC on abatement at time t is ambiguous because the shadow-cost effect and the knowledge-growth effect oppose one another. At time 0, however, the stock of knowledge is fixed at H_0, and thus only the shadow-cost effect comes into play:

$$\frac{dA_0}{dk} = \frac{d\tau_0/dk}{C_{AA}(\cdot)} \leq 0. \tag{15}$$

Thus initial abatement declines as a result of ITC (although this result is reversed if $C_{AH}(\cdot) < 0$).

In the cost-effectiveness analyses, where we had a fixed terminal constraint, $\bar{S}$, we knew that over the entire time horizon, cumulative abatement would be approximately the same under both ITC and NITC scenarios.[28] This implied that the shadow-cost and knowledge-growth effects would approximately balance one another out over the entire horizon; in terms of Fig. 1, the area under path 1 would roughly approximate the area under path 3.

In the benefit–cost framework, however, this is not the case. As demonstrated in the Appendix, the overall scale of abatement over the entire infinite horizon increases; that is to say, the knowledge-growth effect dominates the shadow-cost effect on average. Since CO_2 inflicts environmental damages, it seems reasonable that in the presence of ITC, which makes emissions abatement cheaper, the optimal balance of benefits and costs of emissions abatement would be struck at a higher level of abatement (on average) than would be optimal in the NITC scenario. This result is perhaps not very surprising.[29] Perhaps a more unexpected result is that *initial* abatement still falls, no matter how "large" or powerful the ITC option. Equation (14) indicates that this occurs because there is no separate analytical term representing an upward shift of abatement at all points in time. Rather, the increased scale of abatement is reflected completely in the steepening of the abatement path resulting from the interaction between the knowledge-growth and shadow-cost effects.

3.1.3. *Summary*

We have obtained the following main results for the BC_R case. First, the optimal carbon tax may either rise or fall over time, but if concentrations of CO_2 are increasing through time, then (given a convex damage function) the optimal carbon tax rises as well. Optimal abatement may either rise or fall over time, but, as long as baseline emissions are not falling too rapidly over time, it will rise if the carbon tax is rising. Second, as summarized in Table I, introducing the ITC option lowers optimized net costs and causes the entire carbon tax path to fall. Initial

---

[28] We say "approximately" because natural removal implies that two abatement paths leading to $\bar{S}$ need not involve exactly the same cumulative abatement. In fact, as will be seen in the sensitivity analysis in Section 4, paths which concentrate relatively more abatement in the future need less cumulative abatement to reach the same $\bar{S}$ constraint because they take better advantage of natural removal than do more heavily "front-loaded" abatement paths.

[29] What may be surprising, however, is that the result depends on the convexity of the damage function. With concave damages and a marginal damage schedule steeper than marginal cost (unlikely, given that we have a stock pollutant), a downward pivot in the marginal cost schedule could lead to less abatement.

abatement also falls, but cumulative abatement over the entire horizon rises; hence ITC implies a "steeper" abatement path.

3.2. *Technological Change via Learning by Doing*

Finally, we examine an LBD specification in a benefit–cost framework (the BC_L model).

3.2.1. *The Problem and Basic Characteristics of the Solution*

The optimization problem is now

$$\min_{A_t} \int_0^\infty (C(A_t, H_t) + D(S_t))e^{-rt}\, dt$$

$$\text{s.t.} \quad \dot{S}_t = -\delta S_t + E_t^0 - A_t$$

$$\dot{H}_t = \alpha_t H_t + k\Psi(A_t, H_t)$$

$$\text{and} \quad S_0, H_0 \text{ given.}$$

Thus, CO$_2$-related damages are part of the minimand, and abatement effort contributes to the change in the knowledge stock. The optimality conditions are the same as in the BC_R model, with one major change: the first-order condition for abatement is now

$$C_A(\cdot) - \mu_t k\Psi_A(\cdot) = \tau_t, \tag{16}$$

which is just as it was in the CE_L model (Eq. (9)).

As in the BC_R model, the slope of the carbon tax path is ambiguous (though it will be positive if the optimized CO$_2$ concentration rises over time, given convex damages). Thus the slope of the abatement path is ambiguous as well.

3.2.2. *Implications of ITC*

As always, the presence of ITC lowers overall optimized costs as well as the profile of optimal carbon taxes (assuming $C_H(\cdot) < 0$ and $C_{AH}(\cdot) < 0$). The impact of ITC on abatement is given by[30]

$$\frac{dA_t}{dk} = \frac{d\tau_t/dk + \mu_t \Psi_A(\cdot) - C_{AH}(\cdot)\, dH_t/dk}{C_{AA}(\cdot)}.$$

As in the CE_L model, ITC has three effects on abatement: the negative shadow-cost effect ($d\tau_t/dk$), the positive learning-by-doing effect ($\mu_t\Psi_A(\cdot)$), and the positive knowledge-growth effect ($-C_{AH}(\cdot)\, dH_t/dk$). The net effect on abatement at an arbitrary point in time t (including $t = 0$) is clearly ambiguous. At

---

[30]As in the CE_L analysis, we restrict our attention to the neighborhood around $k = 0$.

18   GOULDER AND MATHAI

$t = 0$, in particular, the knowledge-growth effect drops out, leaving the negative shadow-cost and positive learning-by-doing effects

$$\frac{dA_0}{dk} = \frac{d\tau_0/dk + \mu_0 \Psi_A(\cdot)}{C_{AA}(\cdot)}$$

and we cannot even claim that *initial* abatement declines unambiguously.

Although the components of the analysis here are the same as in the corresponding cost-effectiveness case, their overall impact is different. In the CE_L model, since the overall scale of abatement was approximately the same in both ITC and NITC scenarios, all three effects roughly balanced out over the entire horizon. In contrast, in this benefit–cost case, cumulative abatement increases.[31] Thus, on average the learning-by-doing and knowledge-growth effects dominate the shadow-cost effect.

3.2.3. *Summary*

The key results are as follows. The slope of the optimal carbon tax path is ambiguous. However, if the optimized CO_2 concentration rises (given a convex damage function), the tax rises as well. These results are similar to those in the CE_L model. Moreover, the slope of the optimal abatement path is of ambiguous sign throughout (unless we are in an NITC world with rising taxes and baseline emissions that are not declining too rapidly). As noted in Table I, although introducing the ITC option makes overall costs and the entire carbon tax path fall, it could lead to an increase in initial abatement. Furthermore, cumulative abatement over the entire time horizon increases.

4. NUMERICAL SIMULATIONS

Here we perform numerical simulations to gauge the quantitative significance of our results. We postulate functional forms and parameter values and solve for optimal paths. We then conduct sensitivity analysis to assess the robustness of our results. The numerical simulations reinforce our analytical findings and also point up several striking empirical regularities, as discussed below. We begin this section by describing the choice of functional forms and the methods used to calibrate the various parameters of the model. We then present and discuss the numerical results.

4.1. *Functional Forms and Parameter Values*

The numerical model is solved at 10-year intervals, with the year 2000 as the initial year. Although the planner's time horizon is infinite, we actually simulate over 41 periods (400 years) and impose steady-state conditions in the last simulated

---

[31] See the Appendix for details.

period. This enables us to project forward the values of this last period and thereby determine benefits and costs into the infinite future.[32]

The CO$_2$ concentration in 2000 is taken to be 360 parts per million by volume (ppmv), following the projections of the Intergovernmental Panel on Climate Change (IPCC) [9]. Baseline emissions for the period 2000 to 2100 roughly follow the IPCC's IS92(a) central scenario. After that time, we adopt a hump-shaped profile that peaks at 26 gigatons of carbon (GtC) in 2125 and flattens out to 18 GtC by 2200.[33]

In the analytical section, we assumed for expositional clarity that CO$_2$ in the atmosphere is naturally "removed" at a constant exponential rate. In the numerical simulations, we adopt Nordhaus' [18] slightly more complex and realistic model, which applies short-term and long-term removal rates to the flow and "stock" of emissions, respectively.[34]

$$\dot{S}_t = \beta\left(E_t^0 - A_t\right) - \delta\left(S_t - PIL\right)$$

$$\text{where} \quad \beta = 0.64$$

$$\text{and} \quad \delta = 0.008.$$

Thus, only 64% of current emissions actually contribute to the augmentation of atmospheric CO$_2$, and the portion of the current CO$_2$ concentration in excess of the preindustrial level ($PIL = 278$ ppmv) is removed naturally at a rate of 0.8% per annum.

For our benefit–cost simulations, we need to specify a CO$_2$ damage function. We assume this function to be quadratic and, following Nordhaus [18], who reviewed damage estimates from a number of studies, calibrate the remaining scale parameter so that a doubling of the atmospheric CO$_2$ concentration implies a loss of 1.33% of world output each year. Thus we have

$$D(S_t) = M_D S_t^{\alpha_D}$$

$$\text{where} \quad M_D = 0.0012$$

$$\text{and} \quad \alpha_D = 2.$$

---

[32] Specifically, we impose the requirement that the CO$_2$ concentration remain constant after the last period. For this to occur, abatement must also remain constant (given that baseline emissions are constant at that point in time). In the R & D simulations, we also impose the steady-state constraint that investment go to zero. Even when these constraints are imposed, our model does not yield a steady state with constant abatement costs because the stock of knowledge continues to grow; this continued growth is due both to autonomous technological change and (in the LBD simulations) to the increments to knowledge stemming from continued experience with abatement. In solving the numerical model, we assume that abatement costs beyond the last simulation period are constant, even though the analytical structure of the model implies that abatement costs would fall as knowledge continued to accumulate. Thus our approach overestimates the true future costs. We have verified that this inconsistency has no numerical significance by comparing numerical results under this approach with those from simulations that assume costs after year 2400 are zero and thus underestimate future costs. These two alternative specifications bound the truth about future costs. The numerical results under these two very different approaches are indistinguishable: discounting over a 400-year horizon makes the terminal conditions unimportant in practice.

[33] This profile is patterned after a scenario used by Manne and Richels [15].

[34] Some scholars endorse more complex formulations, such as the five-box model of Maier-Reimer and Hasselmann [13].

The functional form assumed for the abatement-cost function is

$$C(A_t, H_t) = M_C \frac{A_t^{\alpha_{C1}}}{\left(E_t^0 - A_t\right)^{\alpha_{C2}}} \frac{1}{H_t}.$$

This form has the properties assumed in the analytical model, including the feature that knowledge lowers marginal abatement costs ($C_{AH}(\cdot) < 0$). It also has the property that marginal costs tend to infinity as abatement approaches 100% of baseline emissions.[35] We choose the parameters M_C, α_{C1}, and α_{C2} to meet the requirements that (1) a 25% emissions reduction in 2020 should cost between 0.5 and 4% of global GDP[36] and (2) the present value (at a 5% discount rate) of global abatement costs for reaching $S_t = 550$ ppmv by 2200 (in an NITC world) should be roughly \$600 billion (Manne and Richels [15]). The parameter values that best meet these requirements are $M_C = 83$, $\alpha_{C1} = 3$, and $\alpha_{C2} = 2$, but calibration of the cost function remains an area of considerable uncertainty, and sensitivity analyses in this respect are particularly important.

Following estimates common in the literature,[37] we take the rate of autonomous technological progress to be 0.5% per annum: $\alpha_t = 0.005$. The knowledge accumulation function exhibits the properties discussed in the analytical section and is given, in the R & D simulations, by

$$\Psi(I_t, H_t) = M_\Psi I_t^\gamma H_t^\phi$$

$$\text{where} \qquad M_\Psi = 0.0022$$

$$\gamma = 0.5$$

$$\text{and} \qquad \phi = 0.5.$$

H_0, the initial knowledge stock, is normalized to unity. In the learning-by-doing simulations, the knowledge accumulation function is the same, with A_t replacing I_t. The function we use is fairly standard in the endogenous growth literature.[38] γ is chosen to be 0.5 to indicate diminishing returns to R & D investment,[39] while ϕ, which dictates the intertemporal knowledge spillover, is set to 0.5, a central value of the range typically seen in the literature. As ϕ is positive, it indicates that knowledge accumulation today makes future accumulation easier. This is the "standing on shoulders" case which has been used, for example, by Nordhaus [19]. It contrasts with the case where $\phi < 0$, which implies a limited pool of ideas which are slowly "fished out"—current knowledge accumulation makes future accumulation more difficult. M_Ψ is calibrated so that the cost-savings from ITC are approximately 30% in the CE_R model. This is consistent with Manne and Richels

---

[35] There is no backstop technology in the model.

[36] These calculations are based on results of a literature review in EPRI [2] and are extrapolated to the global economy.

[37] See Manne and Richels [14, 15].

[38] See, for example, Romer [27], Jones [10], or Jones and Williams [11]. We are grateful to William Nordhaus and Chad Jones for recommending this function and alerting us to its usefulness.

[39] Jones and Williams [11] dub this the "stepping on toes effect," for "an increase in R & D effort induces duplication that reduces the average productivity of R & D."

[14], who compare the costs of carbon abatement under different assumptions about technological progress.[40]

We assume that the price of investment funds is

$$p(I_t) = I_t.$$

Thus the average cost of R & D investment increases with scale; as mentioned earlier, this captures the idea that drawing scientists away from R & D in other sectors involves increasing costs. Following Manne and Richels [15], we take the discount rate to be 5%.[41] Finally, we model the NITC cases by setting $k = 0$ and the ITC cases by setting $k = 1$.

4.2. Central Cases

4.2.1. CE_R Simulation

In the cost-effectiveness cases (CE_R and CE_L), the concentration target $(\bar{S})$ is 550 ppmv, which must be reached by 2200. This scenario has received considerable attention in policy discussions. We first consider results for the CE_R case, both with and without ITC. The upper-left panels of Figs. 3 and 4 depict, respectively, the optimal abatement and carbon tax paths in this case.

Abatement. As predicted by the analytical model, the optimal abatement paths slope upwards for most of the horizon until 2200, the year in which the constraint is first imposed.[42] Figure 3 shows that the presence of ITC leads to a slightly "steeper" abatement profile, with less abatement during the first 125 years and more abatement after that. However, the effect of ITC on abatement is almost imperceptible. The minuteness of this "abatement-timing effect" is noteworthy, particularly in light of the fact that ITC lowers the discounted average costs of abatement by 30%. The sensitivity analysis below will show that the weakness of ITC's abatement-timing effect is robust to different parameter specifications.

Carbon Tax. The upper-left panel of Fig. 4 shows that the optimal carbon tax starts at a few dollars per ton and grows exponentially. Although not evident from the figure alone, the tax grows at the rate $(r + \delta)$, just as predicted by the analytical model. While ITC's impact on abatement was extremely small, its effect

---

[40] In the work by Manne and Richels [14, p. 64], GDP costs of abatement policy are approximately 90% lower in an optimistic technology scenario than in the central-case technology scenario. This difference in GDP costs does not account for the costs of developing the improved technologies that distinguish the optimistic scenario from the central-case scenario. We assume that R & D investments have a social rate of return of 50% (as in Nordhaus [19]) and then calculate the net cost savings from technological progress to be roughly 30%. (The R & D costs that generate 0.90 of abatement-cost savings amount to (1/1.5)0.90. Thus, the net cost savings from technological progress is given by $0.90 - (1/1.5)0.90 = 0.30$. We assume that this figure is relevant to the induced technological change which we study in our paper, and we then choose M_Ψ to generate this level of savings.

[41] The discount rate represents, in this context, the marginal product of capital, rather than the pure rate of time preference.

[42] A slight decline begins around 2170, as baseline emissions are declining rapidly at this point; this is fully consonant with the analytical model. In both the ITC and NITC cases, the level of abatement drops discontinuously in the year 2200 and stays constant thereafter, maintaining the CO₂ concentration at the level $\bar{S}$. The constraint on the year-2200 concentration forces this discontinuity.

22   GOULDER AND MATHAI

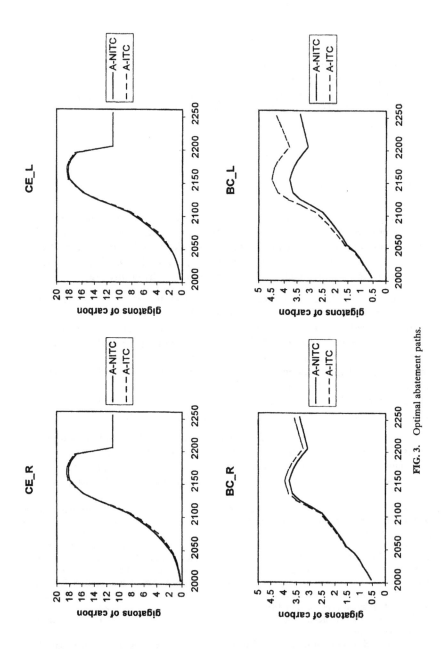

FIG. 3.   Optimal abatement paths.

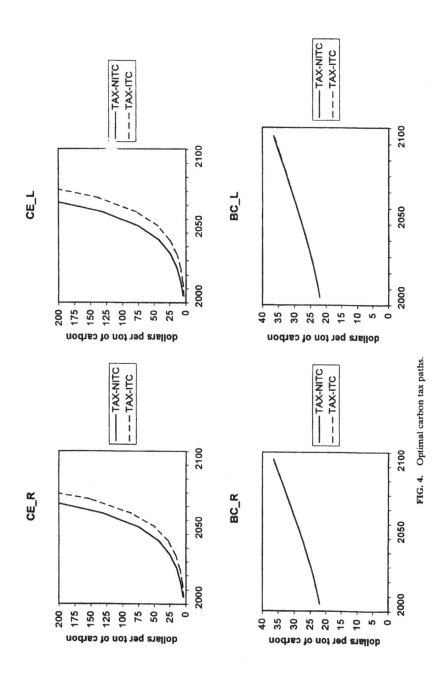

FIG. 4. Optimal carbon tax paths.

24   GOULDER AND MATHAI

on the optimal tax is pronounced. The presence of ITC lowers the optimal carbon tax path at all points in time up to 2200 by about 35%, roughly in line with the 30% cost savings mentioned earlier.

4.2.2. *CE_L Simulation*

The upper-right panels of Figs. 3 and 4 depict the abatement and tax paths for the CE_L case. The results here are broadly similar to those in the CE_R case just discussed. Again the optimal abatement paths slope upward,[43] the optimal carbon tax rises at the rate $(r + \delta)$, and the presence of ITC causes a slight steepening of the abatement path and a sizable downward shift in the tax path. Here ITC implies a reduction in total costs of about 39% and a comparable (41%) lowering of the optimal carbon tax path.

Some differences between the CE_R and CE_L cases deserve mention. First, under learning by doing, the presence of ITC has an even smaller effect on optimal abatement timing than it does under R & D. This makes sense because the basic tendency toward postponing some abatement from the present to the future is offset in the CE_L case by the learning-by-doing effect, which prompts more abatement now in order to accumulate experience-based knowledge. (In fact, this learning-by-doing effect is large enough to cause initial abatement to rise in the CE_L simulation). A second difference is that ITC has a larger impact on taxes and costs in the CE_L case than it does in the CE_R case. This reflects the fact that under LBD-based ITC, technological progress comes about as a "free" by-product of abatement, rather than as a result of costly expenditures on R & D.

4.2.3. *BC_R Simulation*

We now turn to the benefit–cost cases. The lower-left panels of Figs. 3 and 4 depict the optimal abatement and tax paths in the BC_R model.

Abatement. The analytical model indicated that as long as taxes were rising and baseline emissions not declining "too rapidly," the abatement path would rise. In our simulations, abatement rises over the interval 2000–2150 and falls after that, largely matching the pattern of baseline emissions. As shown in Fig. 3, in the presence or absence of ITC, there is much less abatement here than in the CE cases (note the different scales used on the vertical axes). Correspondingly, the CO_2 concentration in 2200 that results from the optimal abatement path is above 800 ppmv, considerably higher than the 550 ppmv imposed in the CE simulations. These differences imply that the 550 ppmv target in the cost-effective analysis—a target given much attention in policy discussion—is too stringent from an efficiency point of view (given the parameters used here for the cost and damage functions). The presence of ITC implies a slight increase in the overall scale of abatement and steepening of the abatement path. Nonetheless, initial abatement falls (though only slightly). These outcomes all square with the predictions of the analytical model.

Carbon Tax. The lower left-panel of Fig. 4 shows that the optimal carbon tax profile is roughly linear in this simulation. This contrasts with the exponential shape in the CE simulations and conforms to the analysis of Section 3. Recall that

---

[43] Recall that the analytical model was unable to guarantee this result for the ITC scenario.

the shadow cost of the CO$_2$ concentration (i.e., the carbon tax) is given by the sum of marginal damages that a small additional amount of CO$_2$ would cause into the infinite future, discounted at the rate $(r + \delta)$. Although the shadow cost tends to rise at the rate $(r + \delta)$, this is offset by the fact that as time goes on, less time remains over which the incremental amount of CO$_2$ can inflict marginal damages. The combination of these two effects produces a linear carbon tax profile.

Again in striking contrast to the CE simulations, the impact of ITC on the optimal carbon tax path is virtually imperceptible in the BC_R central case. There are two reasons for the difference. First, as suggested by Fig. 2, the adjustment due to ITC is in both the quantity (that is, abatement) and price (tax) dimensions; in the CE cases, in contrast, adjustment can only occur in the price dimension because of the constraint on the terminal CO$_2$ concentration. In our central case, the marginal damage curve is very flat over the relevant range. As a result, nearly all of the adjustment to ITC in the BC cases comes via changes in the level of abatement.[44]

The second reason is more subtle and relates to the fact that the $\bar{S}$ constraint imposed in the cost-effectiveness scenarios is too stringent, as indicated by the fact that $\bar{S}$ is significantly lower than the optimal concentration for the year 2200 that emerges from the benefit–cost simulation. Consequently, levels of abatement are generally much higher in the cost-effectiveness cases, which implies that the potential gains from improved technology are also higher. Thus in the cost-effectiveness cases, it pays to accumulate more knowledge than it does in the benefit–cost settings. This implies that the downward pivot of the MC curve and associated impact on the carbon tax are larger in these cases.

Finally, the presence of ITC has an extremely small (2%) impact on average costs of abatement in the benefit–cost cases; as before, this contrasts with the result in the cost-effectiveness cases. Given that ITC in the benefit–cost cases has a small impact on the carbon tax, and in fact on the entire marginal abatement cost schedule, it should not be surprising that it has a correspondingly small impact on average costs. Similarly, the ITC-induced percentage increase in the net benefits of climate policy is very small.[45]

In a working paper circulated contemporaneously with early drafts of this paper, Nordhaus [19] independently obtained the result that, in a benefit–cost context, the presence of ITC has an imperceptible impact on the optimal carbon tax and on the net benefits from carbon abatement policy. Our BC results conform to Nordhaus', although, as discussed below, we obtain different results under alternative parameterizations.[46]

---

[44] In the central case, when the MC curve is relatively steep, the effect on abatement is not very large either.

[45] In other words, the net benefits of optimal abatement relative to a baseline of no abatement whatsoever, are scarcely bigger in an ITC scenario than they are in an NITC scenario.

[46] Nordhaus obtains his result in a dynamic optimization model in which technological change is driven by R & D expenditure. Some differences between the Nordhaus study and the present study are worth noting. His analysis explicitly models a production function, while ours represents production (or ease of substitution) in reduced form through the abatement-cost function. This enables us to obtain analytical results where Nordhaus relies solely on numerical simulations. Another difference is that the Nordhaus study considers only the BC_R case. In contrast, the present study considers both the benefit–cost and cost-effectiveness cases, and considers learning-by-doing- as well as R & D-based technological change. The present paper's attention to alternative policy specifications and knowledge-generation channels, along with the broad sensitivity analysis below, enable it to map out more broadly the conditions under which ITC has (or does not have) a significant impact on economic outcomes.

4.2.4. BC_L Simulation

Finally, we consider the BC_L case. The results for this case are displayed in the lower-right panels of Figs. 3 and 4. The effect of ITC on abatement (Fig. 3) is similar to the effect in the BC_R case, although the impact is somewhat more pronounced.[47] Initial abatement rises, indicating that the learning-by-doing effect outweighs the shadow-cost effect. Once again, the presence of ITC has a virtually imperceptible impact on the optimal carbon tax path, average costs per unit of abatement, and net benefits. The explanation is the same as that given in the BC_R case.

4.3. Sensitivity Analysis

Here we examine the sensitivity of the numerical results to changes in key parameters. For each of the four models, we examine six sets of variants of the central case. Table II presents summary statistics describing, in each variant, the percentage impact that ITC has on the abatement profile, the cumulative amount of abatement over the period 2000–2200, the terminal CO_2 concentration, the tax profile, and overall costs per unit of abatement. We report the impacts on abatement and taxes in the years 2000, 2050, and 2200 (or 2190).[48] For the benefit–cost cases, we also report the percentage impact of ITC on the net benefits of optimal climate policy relative to a zero-abatement baseline.

A higher discount rate (case 2a) reduces the importance of future benefits or costs relative to current ones. Since the costs of ITC are borne today, whereas the benefits are spread more uniformly through time, a higher discount rate tends to reduce the net benefits from ITC. This means that there will be less knowledge accumulation, which implies that the abatement-timing effect (the pivoting of the abatement path) is smaller. The reduced attractiveness of ITC implies, in the benefit–cost cases, that there will be a smaller impact on the overall scale of abatement as well. The opposite results hold under a lower discount rate (case 2b).

The next variant involves changes either in the constraint on year-2000 concentrations (in the cost-effectiveness cases) or in the parameters of the damage function (in the benefit–cost cases). In a cost-effectiveness setting, a tighter concentration constraint (case 3a) enforces greater overall abatement and therefore entails higher marginal costs of abatement. This confers higher value to ITC in terms of greater cost savings. The reverse applies when the constraint is more lax (case 3b).[49] In the benefit–cost simulations, case 3a imposes higher curvature on the damage function.[50] Thus the marginal damage function is steeper in the relevant range. As a result, ITC has a larger impact on the optimal carbon tax and there is less impact on quantity (abatement). Case 3b imposes a linear damage

---

[47] As when we compared the CE_R and CE_L models, this difference is due to the fact that ITC is "free" under an LBD specification but costly under R & D.

[48] In the cost-effectiveness simulations, we report these results for the year 2190; the year-2200 statistic is uninformative as both abatement and taxes in this first year of the constraint are identical across ITC and NITC runs.

[49] In Case 3b, the value 836.39 is chosen to match the optimized value of the year-2200 CO_2 concentration in the NITC scenario of the BC_R simulation.

[50] The multiplicative parameter in the damage function is recalibrated so that the cumulative amount of abatement in the NITC run remains constant.

TABLE II

Sensitivity Analysis (Percentage Changes, ITC Case Relative to NITC Case)

Policy Criterion: Cost-Effectiveness

CE_R Model

	Abatement in year			Cumulative abatement	CO_2 concn. in 2200	Tax in year			Cost per unit of abatement
	2000	2050	2190			2000	2050	2190	
1. Central Case	−18.47	−12.39	1.46	−0.89	0.00	−34.83	−34.83	−34.83	−29.83
2a. $r = 0.075$	−14.92	−12.02	1.04	−0.60	0.00	−27.88	−27.88	−27.88	−24.14
2b. $r = 0.025$	−21.63	−11.18	2.09	−1.32	0.00	−44.49	−44.49	−44.49	−37.87
3a. $\bar{S} = 350$	−19.69	−4.16	0.52	−0.78	0.00	−57.14	−57.14	−57.14	−52.85
3b. $\bar{S} = 836.39$	−4.63	−3.98	0.97	−0.26	0.00	−9.06	−9.06	−9.06	−6.76
4a. $C = 12.14 * A^4/((E − A)^2 * H)$	−12.04	−8.35	1.52	−0.90	0.00	−34.74	−34.74	−34.74	−29.39
4b. $C = 105.7 * A^2 \zeta/H$	−39.30	−31.89	0.00	−0.28	0.00	−39.30	−39.30	−39.30	−36.05
4c. $C = 438.4 * A^{1.5}/H$	0.00	−51.21		−0.06	0.00	−37.75	−37.75	−37.75	−36.19
5a. $M_\Psi = 0.0058$	−31.35	−21.16	2.31	−1.48	0.00	−54.43	−54.43	−54.43	−48.83
5b. $M_\Psi = 0.0015$	−9.74	−6.51	0.81	−0.47	0.00	−19.37	−19.37	−19.37	−15.97
6a. $\phi = 0.75$	−21.72	−15.27	2.00	−1.14	0.00	−40.14	−40.14	−40.14	−34.53
6b. $\phi = -0.5$	−10.96	−6.08	0.53	−0.39	0.00	−21.64	−21.64	−21.64	−18.20
7a. $\alpha_t = 0.01$	−12.71	−8.15	0.76	−0.50	0.00	−24.56	−24.56	−24.56	−20.43
7b. $\alpha_t = 0.00$	−25.60	−17.86	2.59	−1.47	0.00	−46.68	−46.68	−46.68	−41.28

CE_L Model

	Abatement in year			Cumulative abatement	CO_2 concn. in 2200	Tax in year			Cost per unit of abatement
	2000	2050	2190			2000	2050	2190	
1. Central Case	19.63	−6.01	1.32	−0.53	0.00	−41.15	−41.15	−41.15	−39.06
2a. $r = 0.075$	47.40	−2.00	0.86	−0.35	0.00	−36.36	−36.36	−36.36	−34.70
2b. $r = 0.025$	1.37	−7.25	2.06	−0.84	0.00	−46.25	−46.25	−46.25	−43.65
3a. $\bar{S} = 350$	−8.88	−2.48	0.31	−0.42	0.00	−42.44	−42.44	−42.44	−42.57
3b. $\bar{S} = 836.39$	79.70	15.92	1.77	−0.05	0.00	−24.88	−24.88	−24.88	−22.08
4a. $C = 12.14 * A^4/((E − A)^2 * H)$	0.34	−6.02	1.37	−0.65	0.00	−44.21	−44.21	−44.21	−42.40
4b. $C = 105.7 * A^2 \zeta/H$	613.85	122.37	0.00	0.29	0.00	−27.10	−27.10	−27.10	−25.74
4c. $C = 438.4 * A^{1.5}/H$	15109.73	3003.29		0.18	0.00	−20.12	−20.12	−20.12	−18.73
5a. $M_\Psi = 0.0058$	18.04	−11.05	2.08	−0.95	0.00	−60.02	−60.02	−60.02	−57.79
5b. $M_\Psi = 0.0015$	16.30	−3.18	0.79	−0.29	0.00	−25.85	−25.85	−25.85	−24.26
6a. $\phi = 0.75$	18.24	−7.66	1.77	−0.71	0.00	−46.17	−46.17	−46.17	−43.95
6b. $\phi = -0.5$	24.25	−2.10	0.50	−0.16	0.00	−27.81	−27.81	−27.81	−26.05
7a. $\alpha_t = 0.01$	29.68	−3.07	0.83	−0.30	0.00	−33.94	−33.94	−33.94	−31.88
7b. $\alpha_t = 0.00$	9.11	−9.56	2.03	−0.88	0.00	−49.00	−49.00	−49.00	−46.96

TABLE II—(Continued)

Policy Criterion: Benefit–Cost

BC_R Model

	Abatement in year			Cumulative abatement	CO_2 concn. in 2200	Tax in year			Cost per unit of abatement	Net benefits
	2000	2050	2200			2000	2050	2200		
1. Central case	-0.00	1.59	5.77	3.73	-0.45	-0.01	-0.06	-0.52	-2.29	0.74
2a. $r = 0.075$	-0.00	1.04	4.08	2.57	-0.25	-0.00	-0.03	-0.27	-2.04	0.25
2b. $r = 0.025$	-0.03	3.01	9.63	6.41	-1.04	-0.07	-0.25	-1.24	-1.06	3.16
3a. $D = 1.14E^{-6} * S^3$	-0.01	1.42	5.43	3.56	-0.44	-0.02	-0.11	-1.02	-2.01	0.84
3b. $D = 1.64 * S$	0.00	1.80	6.14	3.92	-0.46	0.00	0.00	0.00	-2.55	0.67
3c. $D = 85.3 * S^{0.5}$	0.00	1.93	6.35	4.03	-0.47	0.00	0.04	0.26	-2.67	0.65
4a. $C = 47.62 * A^4/((E - A)^2 * H)$	-0.00	1.06	3.90	2.39	-0.28	-0.01	-0.05	-0.33	-1.43	0.41
4b. $C = 2.441 * A^2/H$	-0.02	4.29	17.58	11.00	-1.39	-0.02	-0.16	-1.89	-7.59	1.62
4c. $C = 5.608 * A^{1.5}/H$	-0.04	7.90	34.46	25.71	-3.52	-0.02	-0.17	-5.15	-15.35	4.59
5a. $M_\psi = 0.0058$	-0.01	3.97	13.97	9.15	-1.10	-0.02	-0.15	-1.26	-5.32	1.83
5b. $M_\psi = 0.0015$	-0.00	0.66	2.43	1.57	-0.19	-0.00	-0.03	-0.22	-0.99	0.31
6a. $\phi = 0.75$	-0.00	1.66	6.94	4.26	-0.52	-0.01	-0.07	-0.61	-2.71	0.78
6a. $\phi = -0.5$	-0.00	1.37	3.15	2.41	-0.28	-0.01	-0.05	-0.31	-1.25	0.61
7a. $\alpha_t = 0.01$	-0.00	1.42	3.75	2.83	-0.44	-0.01	-0.06	-0.51	-1.56	0.68
7b. $\alpha_t = 0.00$	-0.00	1.79	8.74	4.82	-0.45	-0.01	-0.06	-0.51	-3.19	0.79

BC_L Model

	Abatement in year			Cumulative abatement	CO_2 concn. in 2200	Tax in year			Cost per unit of abatement	Net benefits
	2000	2050	2200			2000	2050	2200		
1. Central case	0.47	5.61	23.64	14.45	-1.76	-0.03	-0.22	-2.06	-8.98	3.23
2a. $r = 0.075$	0.22	5.00	22.54	13.64	-1.34	-0.01	-0.13	-1.53	-10.21	1.50
2b. $r = 0.025$	1.69	6.91	24.67	15.57	-2.54	-0.19	-0.61	-3.12	-5.03	8.95
3a. $D = 1.114E^{-6} * S^3$	0.57	5.22	21.80	13.73	-1.69	-0.06	-0.41	-3.95	-7.95	3.78
3b. $D = 1.64 * S$	0.41	6.03	25.65	15.14	-1.81	0.00	0.00	-0.00	-9.91	2.80
3c. $D = 85.3 * S^{0.5}$	0.38	6.26	26.74	15.48	-1.84	0.02	0.13	1.07	-10.32	2.63
4a. $C = 47.62 * A^4/((E - A)^2 * H)$	0.23	4.38	17.41	10.35	-1.23	-0.03	-0.20	-1.44	-6.78	2.15
4b. $C = 2.441 * A^2/H$	1.55	15.47	74.51	43.18	-5.53	-0.10	-0.59	-7.75	-23.15	15.02
4c. $C = 5.608 * A^{1.5}/H$	3.86	23.16	141.78	93.45	-13.03	-0.07	-0.52	-18.99	-37.16	15.02
5a. $M_\psi = 0.0058$	0.93	11.17	45.82	28.43	-3.45	-0.06	-0.45	-4.02	-15.74	6.43
5b. $M_\psi = 0.0015$	0.25	2.91	12.39	7.52	-0.92	-0.02	-0.12	-1.07	-4.98	1.67
6a. $\phi = 0.75$	0.48	5.87	29.17	16.74	-2.06	-0.03	-0.24	-2.46	-10.55	3.42
6a. $\phi = -0.5$	0.45	4.76	12.63	9.16	-1.08	-0.03	-0.18	-1.21	-5.24	2.67
7a. $\alpha_t = 0.01$	0.48	5.08	16.66	11.66	-1.85	-0.03	-0.23	-2.16	-6.99	3.07
7b. $\alpha_t = 0.00$	0.46	6.18	32.65	17.44	-1.62	-0.03	-0.22	-1.88	-11.05	3.37

function, so that the marginal damage schedule is perfectly flat. In this case, there is no impact on the optimal carbon tax profile. All of the adjustment occurs in quantity (abatement). Even in this case, however, the effect on the abatement levels is quite small because the marginal cost curve is quite steep. Finally, in case 3c (applicable only in the BC simulations), we introduce a concave damage function, so that the marginal damage curve is upward sloping in abatement (but still flatter than the MC curve). As expected, taxes *rise* in this case.

In cases 4a, 4b, and 4c we alter the curvature of the cost function such that the *marginal* cost curve is, respectively, more convex than in the central case, strictly linear (less convex), and concave (much less convex). For the CE models, M_C in cases 4a, 4b, and 4c is calibrated such that the optimal tax path in the NITC world coincides with what it was in the central case.[51] For the BC models, M_C is calibrated such that the total amount of NITC abatement over the period 2000–2200 stays constant. Changes in the curvature of the cost function are most important to the results of the BC simulations. In case 4a, the marginal cost function is convex and steep in the relevant range. As a result, the downward-pivot of this function caused by ITC does not greatly alter the optimal levels of abatement. In contrast, when the marginal cost function is linear or concave (cases 4b and 4c) and much flatter in the relevant range, ITC has pronounced effects on optimal abatement. Indeed, in the concave case, ITC implies a 26% increase in cumulative abatement in the BC_R model and a 93% increase in the BC_L model! These larger impacts on abatement are associated with significant effects on average costs (costs per unit of abatement) and on the net benefits from optimal abatement. Thus, even if ITC's impact on the tax profile is small (a result attributable to the flatness of the marginal damage schedule), it may have a significant impact on abatement levels, abatement costs, and net benefits if the marginal cost function is concave and flat in the relevant range. Further research regarding the shape of the abatement cost schedule would seem necessary before one could confidently accept the Nordhaus [19] conclusion that ITC has only negligible effects.

In variants 5a and 5b we change the ease of accumulating knowledge when ITC is present by altering the multiplicative parameter M_Ψ in the $\Psi(\cdot)$ function. As expected, when the ITC option is made more powerful (case 5a), the effects of ITC are magnified. The reverse occurs when the ITC option is made weaker (case 5b).

Next, in variants 6a and 6b we consider alternative values for ϕ, which governs the intertemporal knowledge spillover. The central value is 0.5, indicating some degree of "standing on shoulders." Case 6a involves a value of 0.75 (a stronger positive intertemporal spillover); as expected, the effects of ITC are magnified, though only by a small amount. In case 6b, we set ϕ to -0.5 (which represents "fishing out"); here, the opposite holds, and the effects of ITC are (slightly) diminished.

Finally, in variants 7a and 7b we consider alternative rates of autonomous technological progress. The effects of ITC are muted, the higher the rate of autonomous technological change. This is highly sensible, given the idea of diminishing returns to R & D investments or LBD efforts.

---

[51] Thus we are assuring, for comparability across the cases, that the MC curve always intersects the vertical constraint (in the upper panel of Fig. 2) at the same point.

5. CONCLUSIONS

This paper has employed analytical and numerical models to examine the implications of induced technological change for the optimal design of CO_2-abatement policy. We obtain optimal time profiles for carbon taxes and CO_2 abatement under two channels for knowledge accumulation—R & D-based and LBD-based technological progress—and under both a cost-effectiveness and a benefit–cost policy criterion.

The analytical model reveals, in contrast with some recent claims, that the presence of ITC generally lowers the time profile of optimal carbon taxes. The impact of ITC on the optimal abatement path varies: when knowledge is gained through R & D investments, some abatement is shifted from the present to the future, but if the channel for knowledge-growth is learning by doing, the impact on the timing of abatement is analytically ambiguous.

When the government employs the benefit–cost policy criterion, the presence of ITC justifies greater overall (cumulative) abatement than would be warranted in its absence. However, ITC does not always promote greater abatement in all periods. When knowledge accumulation results from R & D expenditure, the presence of ITC implies a reduction in near-term abatement, despite the increase in overall abatement.

The numerical simulations reinforce the qualitative predictions of the analytical model. The quantitative impacts depend critically on whether the government is adopting the cost-effectiveness criterion or the benefit–cost criterion. ITC's effect on overall costs and optimal carbon taxes can be quite large in a cost-effectiveness setting: thus, policy-evaluation models that neglect ITC can seriously overstate both the costs of reaching stipulated concentration targets and the carbon taxes needed to elicit the desired abatement. On the other hand, the impact on costs and taxes is typically much smaller under a benefit–cost policy criterion. The weak effect on the tax rate in the benefit–cost case reflects the relatively trivial impact of ITC on CO_2 concentrations, associated marginal damages, and (hence) the optimal tax rate. As for the optimal abatement path, the impact of ITC on the timing of abatement is very weak, but the effect (present in the benefit–cost case) on total abatement over time can be large, especially when knowledge is accumulated via learning by doing.

Our work abstracts from some important issues. One is uncertainty. We have assumed both that knowledge accumulation is a deterministic process and that the cost of damage functions are perfectly known. In doing so, we have avoided difficult issues of abatement timing relating to irreversibilities and the associated need to trade off the "sunk costs and sunk benefits" of abatement policy.[52]

In addition, in this model the sole policy instrument available to the decision maker (social planner) is a tax on CO_2 emissions. It would be useful to extend the model to include two instruments: viz., a carbon tax and a subsidy to R & D. This would allow explorations of public policies that simultaneously consider two market failures—one attributable to the external costs from emissions of CO_2, and one attributable to knowledge spillovers, which force a wedge between the social and private returns to R & D. In this broader model, one could investigate optimal

---

[52] See Pindyck [24] and Ulph and Ulph [30].

combinations of carbon taxes and subsidies to R & D. It would also permit investigations of second-best policies: for example, optimal R & D subsidies in a situation in which the government is not able to levy a carbon tax. This approximates the situation implied by recent policy proposals of the Clinton administration.

APPENDIX A

A.1. *The Cost-Effectiveness Criterion*

A.1.1. *Technological Change via R & D*

We first demonstrate the basic characteristics of the slope of the optimal abatement path. We then go on to establish the implications of ITC. To determine how abatement changes over time, we differentiate the first-order condition governing abatement with respect to t. Note that the abatement-cost function is not necessarily time-stationary because costs may depend on baseline emissions, which usually vary through time. Differentiating Eq. (5) with respect to t yields

$$C_{AA}(\cdot)\dot{A}_t + C_{AH}(\cdot)\dot{H}_t + \frac{\delta C_A(\cdot)}{\delta t} = \dot{\tau}_t$$

$$\Leftrightarrow \quad \dot{A}_t = \frac{\dot{\tau}_t - C_{AH}(\cdot)\dot{H}_t - C_{AE}(\cdot)\dot{E}_t^0}{C_{AA}(\cdot)}.$$

We have established that for $t < T$, $\dot{\tau}_t > 0$ (see Eq. (6)), and we know that $\dot{H}_t \geq 0$. Previously we had assumed that $C_{AH}(\cdot) < 0$ and $C_{AA}(\cdot) > 0$. If costs do not depend on the level of emissions, then $C_{AE}(\cdot) = 0$ and Eq. (17) implies that abatement increases over time ($\dot{A}_t \geq 0$).

It is plausible that $C_{AE}(\cdot) < 0$, namely that the marginal cost of a fixed amount of abatement is greater, the lower the level of baseline emissions. This is consistent with the idea that abatement costs depend on relative, rather than absolute, levels of abatement. In this circumstance, $\dot{A}_t \geq 0$ so long as baseline emissions are not declining "too rapidly."

Next we move to the ITC/NITC comparison. Under the assumption that $C_{AH}(\cdot) < 0$, we prove the claim that $d\tau_0/dk \leq 0$. Suppose the opposite, i.e., suppose that

$$\frac{d\tau_0}{dk} > 0. \tag{17}$$

Equation (6) in the main text can be integrated, using the relevant transversality condition as a boundary condition, to obtain the following expression:

$$\tau_t = \int_{\max[t,\,T]}^{\infty} \eta_s e^{-(r+\delta)(s-t)} \, ds. \tag{18}$$

η_t, the multiplier on the $\bar{S}$ constraint, is zero if the constraint does not bind, and is typically positive, representing the shadow value of relaxing the constraint, if the constraint does bind. Thus, Eq. (18) states that the shadow cost of having a small additional amount of CO_2 at time t is dictated by how binding the $\bar{S}$ constraints are into the infinite future.[53] Combining Eq. (18) with our supposition (17) yields (assuming the proper regularity conditions hold)

$$\int_T^\infty \frac{d\eta_s}{dk} e^{-(r+\delta)s}\, ds > 0, \tag{19}$$

which states that overall, the $\bar{S}$ constraints from T onward become more binding, or costly. The supposition that τ_0 rises implies, from Eq. (8), that A_0 also rises. Noting from Eq. (6) that $\tau_t = \tau_0 e^{(r+\delta)t}$ for $t < T$, we see that our supposition implies that τ_t rises for all $t < T$. This in turn implies, from Eq. (7) (since $-C_{AH}(\cdot)dH_t/dk$ is clearly nonnegative), that A_t strictly rises for all $t < T$. In fact, as we shall now show, A_t strictly rises for all t, even beyond T. If abatement has strictly risen at every point in time up until T, then we know that S_T is now strictly less than it used to be in the NITC scenario, and thus certainly strictly less than $\bar{S}$. This itself is acceptable: it is easy to imagine situations in which, given a convex abatement-cost function and an emissions baseline that rises sharply after time T, an optimal program involves undershooting the constraint at the first point in time when it is imposed. However, the fact that S_T is now strictly less than $\bar{S}$ implies, by complementary slackness, that $\eta_T = 0$, and thus, since η_T is always nonnegative, that η_T is less than or equal to its value before the increase in k. In other words, $d\eta_T/dk \leq 0$. But we know from Eq. (19) that the constraints from T onward are, on the whole, more binding, and thus we can now conclude, for sufficiently small ϵ' and all $\epsilon \in (0, \epsilon')$ as well, that

$$\int_{T+\epsilon}^\infty \frac{d\eta_s}{dk} e^{-(r+\delta)s}\, ds > 0 \quad \Leftrightarrow \quad \frac{d\tau_{T+\epsilon}}{dk} > 0 \quad \Leftrightarrow \quad \frac{dA_{T+\epsilon}}{dk} > 0.$$

Now we know that abatement has strictly risen for all $t < T + \epsilon$. The above argument can be repeated, in the style of a proof by induction, to show that $dS_{T+\epsilon}/dk < 0$, implying that $d\eta_{T+\epsilon}/dk \leq 0$, and that, in turn, $dA_t/dk > 0\ \forall t$. Our supposition that $d\tau_0/dk > 0$ has led us to the conclusion that abatement rises at all points in time. Given that the initial program satisfied the constraints, a new program in which abatement is higher at every point clearly cannot be optimal. Thus we have a contradiction. We may conclude that $d\tau_0/dk \leq 0$, and thus that $dA_0/dk \leq 0$. Since the multiplier simply grows at the constant rate $(r + \delta)$ until time T, we have also shown that $d\tau_t/dk \leq 0\ \forall t < T$, and in fact, that the absolute fall in the multiplier increases with t over this time range, but in such a way as to preserve the growth rate as $(r + \delta)$.

Note that if we had assumed $C_{AH}(\cdot) > 0$, then the above proof could be reversed to show that initial abatement and the entire tax path weakly rise. We would find that, in contrast to the normal case, ITC would cause a "flattening" rather than a "steepening" of the optimal abatement profile.

---

[53]As noted in the main text, this is in contrast to the benefit–cost cases, in which the shadow cost is given by the discounted sum of the marginal damages that a small additional amount of CO_2 would cause into the infinite future.

A.1.2. *Technological Change via Learning by Doing*

We start by establishing the slope of the optimal abatement path. It is necessary, however, first to examine the profile of μ_t, the shadow value of knowledge. The costate equation for μ_t, which is the same in both the CE_R and CE_L models, states that

$$\dot{\mu}_t = \mu_t(r - \alpha_t - k\Psi_H(\cdot)) + C_H(\cdot).$$

The shadow value grows at r because it is a *current-value* multiplier. The value of knowledge falls at α_t because new knowledge is being generated autonomously at that rate. Next, depending on the sign of $\Psi_H(\cdot)$—that is, depending on whether knowledge accumulation is characterized by "standing on shoulders" or "fishing out"—there is a third tendency for the shadow value either to fall or to rise over time. For example, when $\Psi_H(\cdot) < 0$, the "fishing out" case where further knowledge accumulation becomes more difficult the larger the current stock of knowledge, it is preferable to suffer this disadvantage over as short a time interval as possible. Thus in this case, the shadow value tends to rise over time. The opposite holds in the "standing on shoulders" case where $\Psi_H(\cdot) > 0$. Finally, since $C_H(\cdot) < 0$, there is a tendency for the shadow value of knowledge to fall over time because we have a shorter time range over which the knowledge will serve to reduce abatement costs. These four effects combine to make the slope of the μ_t path ambiguous in sign.

We now focus on the slope of the optimal abatement path in the CE_L model. Differentiating Eq. (9) and rearranging, we obtain

$$\dot{A}_t = \frac{\dot{\tau}_t + \dot{\mu}_t k\Psi_A(\cdot) + (\Psi_{AH}(\cdot)\mu_t k - C_{AH}(\cdot))\dot{H}_t - C_{AE}(\cdot)\dot{E}_t^0}{C_{AA}(\cdot) - \mu_t k\Psi_{AA}(\cdot)}.$$

The denominator is positive, but the numerator is of ambiguous sign because of the second and third terms. If we consider an NITC scenario in which $k = 0$, then we obtain

$$\dot{A}_t = \frac{\dot{\tau}_t - C_{AH}(\cdot)\dot{H}_t}{C_{AA}(\cdot)} - C_{AE}(\cdot)\dot{E}_t^0,$$

which, at least for $t < T$, is clearly positive, as discussed above, as long as $\dot{E}_t^0$ is not too negative. In the general LBD case with ITC, however, the optimal abatement path may very well slope downward (even if the emissions baseline is growing over time), in contrast to the R & D case.[54]

Now we examine the implications of ITC. The proof that $d\tau_0/dk \leq 0$ proceeds along the same lines as in the CE_R appendix. We suppose that τ_0 strictly rises, and this implies that abatement rises for all t, which cannot be optimal. (The extra learning-by-doing effect in Eq. (10) is positive and thus only strengthens the link

---

[54]Our numerical solutions confirm, however, that the abatement path typically does slope upward, even in the ITC learning-by-doing case.

between τ_t's rising and A_t's rising.[55] We conclude, as in the CE$-$R model, that the entire path of carbon taxes falls, and increasingly so for higher t (up to T). As noted in the text, however, this finding is not enough to assure us that initial abatement also falls.

A.2. The Benefit–Cost Criterion

A.2.1. Technological Change via R & D

First let us analyze the slope of the carbon tax path. We rearrange Eq. (12) to see that

$$\dot{\tau}_t = (r + \delta)\tau_t - D'(\cdot). \tag{20}$$

The first term on the right-hand side contributes to growth in τ_t, while the second contributes to its decline over time (an additional amount of CO_2 later on inflicts marginal damages over a shorter horizon). It is thus possible for the optimal carbon tax to decline over time.

Let us now consider the conditions under which the carbon tax will necessarily rise. Substituting Eq. (13) into Eq. (20) yields

$$\dot{\tau}_t = (r + \delta)e^{(r+\delta)t}\int_t^\infty D'(S_s)e^{-(r+\delta)s}\,ds - D'(S_t). \tag{21}$$

If we had a linear damage function, such that $D'(S_s)$ were constant and equal to $D'(S_t)$ for all $s > t$, then the first term in Eq. (21) would reduce to $D'(S_t)$, and we would conclude that $\dot{\tau}_t = 0$; i.e., the optimal tax path would be flat. If, however, $D'(S_s) > D'(S_t)\ \forall s > t$, the first term in Eq. (21) would be larger than $D'(S_t)$, and the tax path would be upward sloping. Given the convex damage function which we (and others, typically) assume, having an optimized S_t path that slopes upward ensures $D'(S_s) > D'(S_t)\ \forall S > t$, and is thus a sufficient condition for having an upward sloping tax path. Given that many other authors' simulations involve a steadily increasing optimized CO_2 concentration, it is easy to see why the literature frequently obtains optimal carbon taxes that forever rise.

What can we say about the slope of the abatement path in the BC$-$R model? Differentiating equation (11) with respect to t and rearranging, we obtain, as in the CE$-$R model,

$$\dot{A}_t = \frac{\dot{\tau}_t - C_{AH}(\cdot)\dot{H}_t - C_{AE}(\cdot)\dot{E}_t^0}{C_{AA}(\cdot)}.$$

The denominator and the second term in the numerator[56] are clearly positive, but the ambiguous slope of the optimal carbon tax path prevents us from concluding that optimized abatement must always rise over time. Once again, if the optimized S_t path is rising and the damage function is convex, then taxes rise, and thus so

---

[55] The learning-by-doing effect, however, prevents us from reversing the proof for the $C_{AH} > 0$ case. In that case, under a learning-by-doing specification, we cannot conclude anything about the impact of ITC on taxes or abatement.

[56] Assuming $C_{AH}(\cdot) < 0$.

does abatement, as long as the emission baseline is not declining too rapidly. As we see in our numerical simulations of the BC-R model, even though taxes are always rising, the optimal abatement profile actually slopes down during the time when baseline emissions are steeply decreasing.

Now we turn to the analysis of the implications of ITC; i.e., the effects of increasing k. We shall prove that $d\tau_0/dk \leq 0$, that $dA_0/dk \leq 0$, that the overall scale of abatement increases when we raise k, that the abatement path thus becomes steeper, and that $d\tau_t/dk \leq 0 \; \forall t$. If we were to assume that knowledge *raises* marginal abatement costs ($C_{AH}(\cdot) \geq 0$), then the entire proof could be reversed to demonstrate that taxes rise, initial abatement rises, the overall scale of abatement falls, and the abatement path thus becomes flatter.

Suppose that τ_0 rises, and that thus, by Eq. (15), A_0 rises as well. We have, using Eq. (13) and (11),

$$\frac{d\tau_0}{dk} > 0 \quad \Leftrightarrow \quad \int_0^\infty \frac{dD'(S_s)}{dk} e^{-(r+\delta)s}\, ds > 0 \tag{22}$$

$$\Leftrightarrow \quad \int_0^\infty D''(S_s) \frac{dS_s}{dk} e^{-(r+\delta)s}\, ds > 0$$

$$\Leftrightarrow \quad \int_0^\infty D''(S_s) e^{-(r+\delta)s} \int_0^s \frac{dA_m}{dk} e^{-\delta(s-m)}\, dm\, ds < 0. \tag{23}$$

Given our convex damage function, this last equation (23) means that the overall scale of abatement becomes less ambitious when k rises.

For $t > 0$, we can use similar steps to obtain

$$\frac{d\tau_t}{dk} = -\int_t^\infty D''(S_s) e^{-(r+\delta)(s-t)} \int_0^s \frac{dA_m}{dk} e^{-\delta(s-m)}\, dm\, ds$$

$$\Leftrightarrow \quad \frac{d}{dt}\left(\frac{d\tau_t}{dk}\right) = -(r+\delta)\int_t^\infty D''(S_s) e^{-(r+\delta)(s-t)} \int_0^s \frac{dA_m}{dk} e^{-\delta(s-m)}\, dm\, ds$$

$$+ D''(S_t)\int_0^t \frac{dA_m}{dk} e^{-\delta(t-m)}\, dm. \tag{24}$$

Note that $d(d\tau_t/dk)/dt$ is clearly positive if each of the two terms on the right hand side of Eq. (24) is positive. Given Eq. (23), the first term is definitely nonnegative if

$$\int_0^t D''(S_s) e^{-(r+\delta)s} \int_0^s \frac{dA_m}{dk} e^{-\delta(s-m)}\, dm\, ds \geq 0.$$

The second term is clearly positive, assuming a convex damage function, if

$$\int_0^t \frac{dA_m}{dk} e^{-\delta(t-m)}\, dm \geq 0.$$

We thus are led to the following lemma. Given our assumption that the initial tax rises (Eq. (22)), and assuming a convex damage function, then

$$\int_0^t D''(S_s) e^{-(r+\delta)s} \int_0^s \frac{dA_m}{dk} e^{-\delta(s-m)} \, dm \, ds \geq 0 \tag{25}$$

and

$$\int_0^t \frac{dA_m}{dk} e^{-\delta(t-m)} \, dm \geq 0. \tag{26}$$

These together imply

$$\frac{d}{dt}\left(\frac{d\tau_t}{dk}\right) \geq 0.$$

Equations (22) and (15) together tell us that $dA_0/dk > 0$. This means (using inductive reasoning much like that used in the CE–R appendix),[57] that sufficiency conditions (25) and (26) hold for $t = \epsilon$ sufficiently close to 0, and also for $t = \epsilon'$ $\forall \epsilon' \in (0, \epsilon)$. Thus we conclude that

$$\frac{d}{dt}\left(\frac{d\tau_\epsilon}{dk}\right) \geq 0 \quad \Leftrightarrow \quad \frac{d\tau_\epsilon}{dk} \geq \frac{d\tau_0}{dk} > 0 \quad \Leftrightarrow \quad \frac{dA_\epsilon}{dk} > 0,$$

where this last implication is only strengthened by the $-C_{AH}(\cdot) \, dH_\epsilon/dk$ effect in Eq. (15). The whole chain of reasoning can be repeated inductively to imply that abatement strictly rises at every point in time. This, however, contradicts Eq. (23), which says that the overall scale of abatement is less ambitious. Thus, our supposition must be wrong. Thus, we conclude that τ_0 (weakly) falls, A_0 falls, a more ambitious overall scale of abatement is adopted, and the abatement path becomes "steeper," all as a result of the increase in k. That is to say,

$$\frac{d\tau_0}{dk} \leq 0$$

$$\frac{dA_0}{dk} \leq 0$$

and

$$\int_0^\infty D''(S_s) e^{-(r+\delta)s} \int_0^s \frac{dA_m}{dk} e^{-\delta(s-m)} \, dm \, ds \geq 0. \tag{27}$$

Using arguments similar to those used above, it is also possible to demonstrate that the entire path of carbon taxes must weakly fall: $d\tau_t/dk \leq 0$ $\forall t$. This does not mean, however, that *abatement* always weakly falls; the growth in H_t as a result of k counters the effect of the weakly falling carbon taxes, and we know, in fact, that overall we end up with a weakly more ambitious abatement path.

---

[57] Where we used a small ϵ and appealed to continuity to justify an inductive proof in a continuous-time problem.

OPTIMAL CO_2 ABATEMENT 37

A.2.2. *Technological Change via Learning by Doing*

Using methods virtually identical to those in the previous sections, we prove that (1) the carbon tax falls at all points in time, including time 0, (2) the impact on A_0 is ambiguous, and (3) the overall scale of abatement increases. Please refer to earlier sections of the Appendix corresponding to the CE_L and BC_R models; the proofs here are not substantively different.

REFERENCES

1. R. E. Dickinson and R. J. Cicerone, Future global warming from atmospheric trace gases, *Nature* January, 109–115 (1986).
2. Electric Power Research Institute (EPRI), "Economic Impacts of Carbon Taxes: Detailed Results," EPRI TR-104430-V2, November (1994).
3. Y. H. Farzin, Optimal pricing of environmental and natural resource use with stock externalities, *J. Public Econom.* **62**, 31–57 (1996).
4. Y. H. Farzin, and O. Tahvonnen, Global carbon cycle and the optimal time path of a carbon tax, *Oxford Econom. Papers* **48**, 515–536 (1996).
5. L. H. Goulder and K. Mathai, "Optimal CO_2 Abatement in the Presence of Induced Technological Change," NBER Working Paper 6494, Cambridge, MA, April (1998).
6. L. H. Goulder and S. Schneider, Induced technological change, crowding out, and the attractiveness of CO_2 emissions abatement, *Resour. Energy Econom.* **21**, 211–253 (1999).
7. M. Grubb, Technologies, energy systems, and the timing of CO_2 abatement: An overview of economic issues, submitted for publication (1996).
8. M. Ha-Duong, M. Grubb, and J.-C Hourcade, "Optimal Emmision Paths Towards CO_2 Stabilization and the Cost of Deferring Abatement: The influence of Inertia and Uncertaintly," working paper, CIRED, Montrouge, France (1996).
9. Intergovernmental Panel on Climate Change, "Climate Change 1994: Radiative Forcing of Climate Change, and An Evaluation of the IPCC 1S92 Emission Scenarios," (J. T. Houghton, L. G. Meira Filho, J. Bruce, H. Lee, B. A Callander, E. Haites, N. Harris, and K. Maskell, Eds.) Cambridge University Press, Cambridge UK (1995).
10. C. I. Jones, "Human Capital, Ideas, and Economic Growth," working paper, VIII Villa Mondragone International Economic Seminar, Rome, June 25–27 (1996).
11. C. I. Jones and J. Williams, "Too Much of a Good Thing?," working paper, Stanford University (1996).
12. C. D. Kolstad, Learning and stock effects in environmental regulation: The case of greenhouse gas emissions, J. Environ. Econom. Management **31**, 1–18 (1996).
13. E. Maier-Reimer and K. Hasselmann, Transport and Storage in the Ocean: An Inorganic Ocean-Circulation Carbon Cycle Model, *Climate Dynam.* **2**, 63–90 (1987).
14. A. Manne and R. Richels, "Buying Greenhouse Insurance: The Economic Costs of CO_2 Emission Limits," MIT Press, Cambridge, MA (1992).
15. A. Manne and R. Richels, "Toward the Stabilization of CO_2 Concentrations: Cost-Effective Emission Reduction Strategies," working paper, Electric Power Research Institute, Palo Alto, CA (1997).
16. W. D. Nordhaus, "Thinking about Carbon Dioxide: Theoretical and Empirical Aspects of Optimal Growth Strategies," Cowles Foundation Discussion Paper No. 565, Yale University, October (1980).
17. W. D. Nordhaus, How fast should we graze the global commons?, *Amer. Econom. Rev.* **172**, 242–246 (1980).
18. W. D. Nordhaus, "Managing the Global Commons: The Economics of Climate Change," MIT Press, Cambridge, MA (1994).
19. W. D. Nordhaus, "Modeling Induced Innovation in Climate-Change Policy," working paper, NBER Summer Institute, PEG Workshop (1997).
20. W. D. Nordhaus and Z. Yang, A Regional dynamic general-equilibrium model of alternative climate change strategies, *Amer. Econom. Rev.* **86**, 741–765 (1996).

38   GOULDER AND MATHAI

21. S. C. Peck and T. J. Teisberg, CETA: A model for carbon emissions trajectory assessment, *Energy J.* **13**, 71–91 (1992).
22. S. C. Peck and T. J. Teisberg, Optimal carbon emissions trajectories when damages depend on the rate or level of global warning, *Climatic Change* **28**, 289–314 (1994).
23. S. C. Peck and Y. S. Wan, "Analytical Solutions of Simple Optimal Greenhouse Gas Emission Models," working paper, Electric Power Research Institute, Palo Alto, CA (1996).
24. R. S. Pindyck,"Sunk Costs and Sunk Benefits in Environmental Policy," working paper, MIT (1993).
25. M. E. Porter and C. van der Linde, Toward a new conception of the environment–competitiveness relationship, *J. Econom. Perspectives* **9**, 97–118 (1995).
26. R. Repetto, The policy implications of non-convex environmental damages: A smog control case study, *J. Environ. Management* **14**, 13–29 (1987).
27. P. M. Romer, Endogenous technological change, *J. Polit. Economy* **98**, S71–102 (1990).
28. P. J. N. Sinclair, On the optimum trend of fossil fuel taxation, *Oxford Econom. Papers* **46**, 869–877 (1994).
29. A. Ulph and D. Ulph, The optimal time path of a carbon tax, *Oxford Econom. Papers* **46**, 857–868 (1994).
30. A. Ulph and D. Ulph, Global warming, irreversibility and learning, *Econom. J.* **107**, 636–650 (1997).
31. T. M. L. Wigley, R. Richels, and J. Edmonds, Economic and environmental choices in the stabilization of atmospheric CO_2 concentrations, *Nature* **18**, January (1996).

[15]

Learning and Stock Effects in Environmental Regulation: The Case of Greenhouse Gas Emissions

CHARLES D. KOLSTAD*

Department of Economics, University of California, Santa Barbara, California 93106-9210

Received March 24, 1994; revised April 14, 1995

This paper concerns the optimal regulation of greenhouse gases that lead to global climate change. In particular, we focus on uncertainty and learning (which, over time, resolves uncertainty). We present an empirical stochastic model of climate–economy interactions and present results on the tension between postponing control until more is known vs acting now before irreversible climate change takes place. Uncertainty in our model is in the damage caused by global warming. The results suggest that a temporary carbon tax may dominate a permanent one because a temporary tax may induce increased flexibility. © 1996 Academic Press, Inc.

I. INTRODUCTION

Uncertainty is a dominant characteristic of environmental externalities, including the accumulation of greenhouse gases leading to climate change. We understand well neither the effects of climate change nor the costs of controlling greenhouse gases. This is one reason considerable sums are expended in trying to better understand this problem. An additional factor frequently comes into play having to do with the cumulative or stock effects of greenhouse gases. It is not the *emissions* of greenhouse gases that *directly* cause adverse effects; rather it is the stock of these gases that may lead to climate change and these stocks change slowly with a great deal of inertia. The process of emitting is not readily reversible. These two aspects of the problem—stock effects and uncertainty—lead to a tension between instituting control and delaying control.[1] Some in society will desire control of greenhouse gases before climate change is well understood, citing the irreversible nature of additions to the global stock of greenhouse gases. Others in society may urge delaying control until the problem is clearly delineated. If, *ex post*, the problem turns out to be less severe than expected then those urging delay will have been proved correct (*ex post*). If on the other hand, the problem turns out to be more severe than expected, then delay can be very costly indeed.

Irreversibilities in climate change have many facets; stock effects are one type of irreversibility. At the simplest level, some investments in controls on greenhouse

* Research supported in part by a grant from the Research Board of the University of Illinois, by NSF Grant SBR-94-96303, by USAID cooperative agreement DHR-5555-A-00-1086, and by DOE Grant DE-FG03-94ER61944. Comments and suggestions by John Braden, Lars Mathiesen, Michael Schlesinger, two anonymous referees and an associate editor have been appreciated. I am grateful to Prof. William Nordhaus for providing an early version of the 'DICE' model.

[1] There are other examples with these basic characteristics: hazardous wastes and groundwater, acid rain, species extinction, pesticide accumulation, and the list could go on.

gas emissions are irreversible—one cannot uninvest in a CO_2 scrubber. Environmental irreversibilities are more multidimensional. On the one hand, the fact that CO_2 emissions contribute to the long-lived CO_2 stock and cannot be "unemitted" is an irreversibility analogous to the capital irreversibility. However, there may be environmental effects triggered by a buildup of CO_2 that are irreversible: an ice age, a shift in the Gulf Stream, or the extinction of a species. The focus of this paper is on stock-type irreversibilities.

Uncertainty gives rise to two quite different issues, often confused. One relates to risk aversion. It would appear that the disutility from low-probability severe climate damage may not be equivalent to the disutility from the certain wasting of a corresponding amount of control capital; thus a risk averse decision maker might find it optimal to "bias" control decisions toward over-control, relative to the deterministic case. In this case, the fact that one cannot uninvest control capital or actively remove carbon from the atmosphere is irrelevant to the optimal regulatory strategy.

A second and quite distinct issue relates to uncertainty where that uncertainty is being resolved over time; i.e., information is being acquired over time. Since control decisions are not made at one time for all future times, but rather sequentially over time, today's decision may well be influenced by learning. In this case, stock effects, either environmental or in control capital investment, may significantly affect the optimal level of control today. The literature on irreversibilities tells us that with learning, we should avoid decisions that restrict future options.

This paper concerns the latter issue, one of the most fundamental questions in the climate change/greenhouse gas control policy arena: what delay or acceleration of the generation of greenhouse gases should be pursued when uncertainty exists and learning is taking place? Thus this paper seeks to determine how the *fact* that we are learning about climate change influences our actions *today* to control greenhouse gases. In our application, there is uncertainty on the damage from climate change. While there has been some work related to this question [29, 34, 35, 37, 38, 41, 42], explicit treatment of the learning process has yet to appear in the empirical literature on climate change.[2] Our approach to the problem is to adapt a simple optimal growth economy-climate model [35, 37] to include uncertainty and learning.

There are two major results of this paper. One is that we are unable to find any significant stock effect associated with greenhouse gas accumulation, where by stock effect we mean an effect associated with an inability to reduce the stock of greenhouse gas. The rate of change of the climate is just too slow. In retrospect, should we turn out to be emitting slightly too much today, then that can be corrected in the future by emitting slightly too little. Thus if greenhouse gas emission control decisions are perfectly reversible, then there should be no bias in greenhouse gas control, upward or downward, relative to the deterministic case. In other words, uncertainty and learning are second order effects.

A second result is that there is a modest stock effect associated with sunk control capital. In other words, when control capital investment is not reversible, then the capital stock effect appears to be stronger than the environmental stock effect.

---

[2] Hammitt *et al.* [16] and Manne and Richels [28, 29] have examined the costs of delaying action until more is known.

Thus we should bias emission control downward, relative to the deterministic case. This might suggest that we should do little to control greenhouse gases. While this is one interpretation, another interpretation is that greenhouse policies that result in *reversible* actions are to be preferred (all other things being equal) to those involving capital investments that are long-lived and not easily reversed. For example, a permanent carbon tax may be dominated by a temporary carbon tax.

The next section of the paper reviews some important contributions to the theoretical literature on learning, as well as existing empirical analyses of climate change and learning. The subsequent section presents our model of optimal regulation. We then examine the case of uncertainty in the disutility of pollution and, finally, the results.

II. BACKGROUND

The basic issues here are (a) how stock effects determine current period emissions, (b) how optimal emission policies for greenhouse gas can be computed, and (c) how learning can be represented in a model of pollution accumulation in an economy. The first two of these issues are considered in this section. We defer learning to the subsequent section.

A. Irreversibilities and Stock Externalities

A major literature has developed in the area of investment under uncertainty in the presence of externalities. Arrow and Fisher [1] initiated much of the work in this area by focusing on a two period model with uncertainty about the benefits of an environmental asset that is to be exploited (e.g., a canyon flooded to make electricity). With some uncertainty resolved between the two periods and the impossibility of undoing development of the environmental asset, it turns out to be optimal to bias development in favor of preservation of the environmental asset. Henry [17] published similar results. In essence, taking an irreversible action has a cost in terms of reducing the value of information. Arrow and Fisher [1] introduced the notion of quasi-option value, the value of the information gained by waiting before exploiting the environmental asset. Since then, there has been considerable literature on irreversibilities and on quasi-option value (e.g., see [3, 10, 11, 13, 31]). Of course there is also a large literature in finance on option value. In particular, a number of recent papers concern the optimal timing of capital investments (e.g., oil field development) when learning is taking place (e.g., oil field exploration); see Paddock *et al.* [40].

Another related literature, primarily from the early 1970s, concerns optimal growth in the presence of environmental externalities, particularly stock externalities. This was a natural extension of the optimal growth models that were popular in the 1960s and early 1970s (and earlier—see [46]). An important and characteristic paper in this genre is that of Keeler *et al.* [19]. In that paper a simple optimal growth model is posited where utility is a function of consumption and a stock of pollution. Optimal paths for accumulation of capital and pollution are developed for several different types of pollution control. Other papers of this type include [6, 12, 44, 45, 48]. Cropper [4] also considers such a model of optimal growth but focuses on catastrophic environmental effects—the ultimate in irreversibilities. See also Viscusi and Zeckhauser [51].

4   CHARLES D. KOLSTAD

The general problem we are examining is one where a regulator must make a
sequence of decisions, acquiring information between each decision. This is not a
new problem. In fact, one of the first papers illuminating this question is Simon
[47], who showed that if the objective is quadratic, uncertainty is Gaussian and the
problem is unconstrained, then uncertainty and/or learning are irrelevant to
today's decision. Malinvaud [25] generalized this somewhat, showing that if one
allows any well-behaved objective but requires uncertainty to be small, then the
same result emerges. In both of these cases, irreversibilities in terms of today's
actions constraining tomorrow's opportunities are not allowed. Freixas and Laffont
[14] showed that under very special conditions, if today's actions constrain tomorrow's opportunities, then there should be a bias in today's decisions when learning
is occurring, relative to the no-learning case. The most general theory was developed by Epstein [9]. His result was that curvature of benefits and costs determine
the sign of the bias and that learning can induce a bias in the absence of an
irreversibility. His result has been applied in the climate change context by Ulph
and Ulph [50] and Kolstad [21].

B. Climate–Economy Models and Learning

Economic models have played a critical role in the formulation of environmental
policy in the United States over the past three decades. The main function of these
models has been to simulate the economy's response to particular environmental
regulations. In the arena of climate change policy, a number of economic models
have been developed, particularly over the last 5 years.

We should acknowledge that one of the first economics papers on the subject of
global warming was Nordhaus [32] and the first models were developed by Nordhaus and Yohe [33] and Edmonds and Reilly [8]. We refer the reader to the survey
by Weyant [52] for a comprehensive discussion of the applied economic models for
examining climate policy.[3] We focus here on several papers that have addressed
the specific question of the effect of uncertainty and learning on climate change
policy.

Peck *et al.* [42] was one of the first papers to explicitly examine learning in the
context of climate change. However, analysis of this issue within the context of an
empirical model had to wait for the development of the Peck and Teisberg [41, 43]
model of climate and the economy. In [42], the model is used to compute the value
of information on climate uncertainty. They find particularly valuable information
about the warming rate and damages, although that value is not much diminished
if the information is acquired as late as 50 years from the present. In other words,
there is no rush to resolve uncertainty.

Hammitt *et al.* [16, 24] have conducted analyses of the optimal sequential
decision strategy when there is uncertainty about climate sensitivity and the target
for an equilibrium temperature rise, uncertainty which is assumed to be resolved in
the next decade. Their model is not an optimal growth model but rather a simple

---

[3] Because the field is changing so rapidly, even the Weyant [52] survey misses some work in this area.
In particular, Nordhaus [34, 37, 38] has produced several models of the climate and economy, evolving
into the DICE model—Dynamic Integrated Climate–Economy Model. Furthermore, the Global 2100
model of Manne and Richels [29] has recently metamorphosed into a model ("MERGE") with more
explicit accounting of damages [27].

THE OPTIMAL REGULATION OF GREENHOUSE GASES 5

decision analytic framework. In [16], the authors conclude that moderate emission controls should be pursued unless climate sensitivity is high while the target for emission increases is low. In [24], the model is modified to include abrupt climate changes; the conclusions remain qualitatively valid.

Manne and Richels [29] explicitly examine how an optimal decision (within an optimal growth framework) will be changed by the acquisition of information. They focus on the resolution of uncertainty about climate damage. Although the primary contribution of their work is to establish a framework for analyzing this issue, in that their results are highly dependent on specific assumptions, they do demonstrate that there can be a large payoff from improved information. Furthermore, their results suggest that information acquisition is preferred to precautionary emissions reductions.

III. A STOCHASTIC MODEL WITH LEARNING

In this section we will introduce a stochastic, discrete time optimal growth model in the spirit of Ramsey [46]. What makes the problem more complex is that learning is a stochastic process whereby as every decade passes, more is learned, although we do not know *ex ante* what that will be. Thus the state of knowledge evolves as a stochastic process. We first introduce the optimal growth model and then incorporate a specific type of learning into the model.

A. A Stochastic Growth Model

In this section we present a general model of the dynamic evolution of an economy, incorporating emission control, pollution accumulation, and pollution damage. To a large extent it is a standard optimal growth model, although some aspects having to do with the climate are nonstandard. It is based and draws heavily on the climate–economy model of Professor William Nordhaus [35–38]. His model is deterministic however, and our model is stochastic.

The model is not regionally differentiated and involves the maximization of the worldwide net present value of expected per capita utility (for a representative consumer), summed over the population. Utility is enhanced by consumption and depressed by pollution damage. Output can be channeled to consumption, emission control, or investment. Knowledge is represented by the probability vector on states of the world and that knowledge follows a random walk through time, associated with learning. In other words, the probability vector evolves over time depending on the uncertain outcome of learning.

There are two ways to represent a problem such as this. One is to use dynamic programming, solving the Bellman equation [49]. The other is to formulate a stochastic programming problem, which is our approach. Essentially, one must look at all possible trajectories learning might take in the future and condition all variables on the learning that has taken place up to the point in time where the variable's value is determined. It is standard [7] to write the variables as functions of *histories* of the stochastic process; i.e., the realization of the random variable up to a point in time.

Thus assume that there are several states of the world (s) with knowledge represented by a probability vector on those states. The variable h_t is the history of

6   CHARLES D. KOLSTAD

learning and we will define precisely how knowledge evolves with learning. The
model follows with the variables and parameters defined in Table I.
    Maximize the expected net present value of utility:

$$\max_{I,E} \sum_{t} (1+\rho)^{-t} \sum_{h_t} \mu(h_t, t) \sum_{s} \pi_s(h_t, t) u[c(h_t, t), d(h_t, t), s] L(t) \quad (1)$$

$$\text{s.t.} \quad I(t, h_t), E(t, h_t) \geq 0, \quad (2a)$$

given the consumption identity

$$c(t, h_t) = [Y(t, h_t) - I(t, h_t)]/L(t); \quad (2b)$$

the production function

$$Y(t, h_t) = f[K(t, h_t), L(t), E(t, h_t), t]; \quad (2c)$$

damage from climate change

$$d(t, h_t) = g[T(t, h_t), Y(t, h_t)]/L(t); \quad (2d)$$

sunk nature of abatement

$$(1 - \delta_E)[\sigma(t)Y(h_t, t) - E(h_t, t)]$$
$$\leq [\sigma(t+1)Y(h_{t+1}, t+1) - E(h_{t+1}, t+1)]; \quad (2e)$$

TABLE I

Model Variables and Parameters

I	Investment (trillion $ per decade)	(control)
E	Emissions of greenhouse gases (gigatons per decade)	(control)
K	Capital stock (trillion $)	(state)
M	Stock of greenhouse gases (gigatons)	(state)
T	Mean atmosphere temperature (°C relative to base)	(state)
O	Mean deep ocean temperature (°C relative to base)	(state)
c	Per capita consumption (thousands of $)	
d	Per capita climate damage (thousands of $)	
Y	Gross output of goods and services (trillion $ per decade)	
ρ	Pure social rate of time preference (0.01 or 0.03 per annum)	
h	History of learning	
δ_K	Capital depreciation rate (0.35 per decade)	
δ_M	Greenhouse gas stock decay rate (0.0833 per decade)	
δ_E	Emission control depreciation rate (parameter)	
L	population/labor supply (billions, $L > 0$)	
σ	Greenhouse gas emissions–output ratio, uncontrolled ($\dot{\sigma} < 0$)	
t	Time/technology (decades)	
s	State of the world	
β	Greenhouse gas emission factor (0.64)	
π_s	Probability of state s given learning history h_t: $\sum \pi_s = 1$	
μ	Probability of learning history h_t	
λ	Rate of learning (0 = no learning; 1 = complete learning in one period).	

THE OPTIMAL REGULATION OF GREENHOUSE GASES 7

capital accumulation

$$K(t + 1, h_{t+1}) = (1 - \delta_K)K(t, h_t) + I(t, h_t);\tag{2f}$$

greenhouse gas accumulation

$$M(t + 1, h_{t+1}) = (1 - \delta_M)M(t, h_t) + \beta E(t, h_t);\tag{3a}$$

atmospheric temperature evolution

$$T(t + 1, h_{t+1}) = s[T(t, h_t), M(t, h_t), O(t, h_t)];\tag{3b}$$

ocean temperature evolution

$$O(t + 1, h_{t+1}) = r[T(t, h_t), O(t, h_t)].\tag{3c}$$

Equations (1)–(2) constitute the basic economic model and Eqs. (3) describe the evolution of the climate. Equation (2e) captures the extent to which emission control decisions are irreversible. Uncontrolled emissions are σY. We assume investment in emission control capital is proportional to controlled emissions, $\sigma Y - E$. Control capital in period $t + 1$ is bounded from below by the previous period's control capital (represented by controlled emissions), depreciated by $1 - \delta_E$. Note that if δ_E is zero, Eq. (2e) requires that next period's controlled emissions must be at least as great as this period's controlled emissions; in other words, you cannot reverse a decision to control emissions. If δ_E is equal to 1, Eq. (2e) simply states that controlled emissions cannot be negative, a rather innocuous assumption. The intermediate territory with δ_E between zero and one corresponds to partial reversibility of emission control decisions.

Analogous to δ_E is δ_M, found in Eq. (3a). This variable controls the persistence of the stock of CO_2: a small value of δ_M corresponds to a very pronounced stock effect. A value of δ_M close to 1 implies that the pollutant is not a stock pollutant but rather a flow that does not accumulate.

The links between the economic model and the climate are E and T. Emissions in Eq. (2c) are good in that they allow increased output. However, emissions (E) increase CO_2 levels (M) which increase temperature (T) which causes damage (d) which yields disutility (Eq. (2d)). The goal is to choose the investment path and emission path that maximize expected utility. The specific functional forms of the functions f, g, s, and r in Eqs. (2c), (2d), (3b), and (3c) are described in the Appendix. We note here that environment damage is quadratic in the temperature change. Damage is of course reversible in the stock of pollution but much less so with respect to the flow of pollution because of the difficulty in quickly changing the stock.

B. Learning

There are three basic types of learning which are potentially applicable to global warming. One is active learning whereby observations on the state of the economy/climate convey information about uncertainty. Thus by perturbing emissions, one can obtain information about uncertain parameters (e.g., see [2] or, for an application to climate change, [5]). A second type of learning is purchased learning whereby knowledge is purchased and the amount of knowledge purchased (R & D

8   CHARLES D. KOLSTAD

expenditures) depends on its cost and benefits (see [15]). A third type of learning can be called autonomous learning where the mere passage of time reduces uncertainty. It is this third type of learning that we examine in this paper.

1. *Information structures.* The typical approach to including autonomous learning in models of irreversibility is to posit a two or three period model where uncertainty changes from one period to the next. Miller and Lad [31] use a two period model with an *ex ante* probability distribution on period i benefits (b_i) of $f(b_1, b_2)$. After observing period one benefits, the *ex post* marginal distribution is obtained: $f(b_1, b_2 \mid b_1)$. While this is clearly learning, we need a way to parameterize the rate of learning so that the effects of the *rate* of learning can be deduced.

Jones and Ostroy [18], Olson [39], and Marshak and Miyasawa [30] provide such a framework through the concept of an ordering on information structures. Start with a set of possible states of nature and a probability vector associated with those states of nature being realized. Add to this the receipt of an informative message, and a vector of probabilities of receiving specific messages. The information in the message is a conditional probability on states of nature. An information structure consists of a prior on states of nature, a vector of probabilities of receiving specific messages, and, for each message, and *ex post* probability of states of nature. Of two information structures with the same prior on states of nature, the one that has the greater variability in terms of possible posteriors is viewed as being "more informative." This is equivalent to the more informative structure yielding a higher attainable expected utility when the consumption bundle depends on the state of nature (more flexibility can only be advantageous [18]). Thus if two learning processes are associated with two comparable information structures, then the structure that is more informative corresponds to greater learning.

To quantify this concept of learning further, suppose there is a set of possible states of nature, indexed by $s = 1, \ldots, S$. Furthermore, suppose there is a finite set, Y, of possible "messages" containing information on the state of nature. Suppose the prior on receiving particular messages is q (dimension equal to the size of Y) and the conditional probability on states of nature (after the message $y \epsilon Y$ has been received) is $\pi(y)$. We use the term "prior" to refer to a probability distribution on states, before the message is received and "posterior" to refer to distributions on states of nature after a message has been received. Let Π be a matrix with columns consisting of $\pi(y)$ with a different column for each y. Thus Π has S rows and the same number of columns as members of Y. (Π, q) is an information structure. A first goal is to develop an economically relevant ordering on information structures. A standard definition of the comparative value of information is provided by [18] (see also [23]).

2. *A special parameterization of learning.* We consider a special restriction on the set of comparable information structures. In particular, if there are S possible states of nature, we assume a message consists of a noisy signal as to the true state of nature and thus there are S possible noisy signals. Let $\lambda \epsilon [0, 1]$ reflect the level of information in the signal with 0 being no information and 1 being perfect information. Thus given a prior $\bar{\pi}$ we define the *star-shaped* information structure

THE OPTIMAL REGULATION OF GREENHOUSE GASES 9

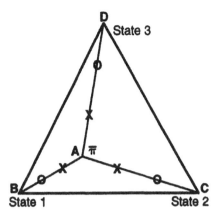

FIG. 1. Star-shaped spreading of beliefs from $\bar{\pi}$.

(Π, q) where $q \equiv \bar{\pi}$ and the sth column of Π is

$$\pi^S = (1 - \lambda)\bar{\pi} + \lambda e_s, \tag{4}$$

where e_s consists of all 0's except for a 1 in the sth position. Clearly $E_y[\pi(y)] = \Pi q = \bar{\pi}$. Furthermore if $\lambda = 0$, each column of Π is $\bar{\pi}$ and if $\lambda = 1$, $\Pi = I$.

As an example, suppose you can receive one of three messages indicating whether the state of nature is 1, 2, or 3. We are now assuming that the number of possible messages equals the number of possible states of nature. A message that conveys the maximum amount of information would resolve all uncertainty on the state of nature. If the message is too noisy to contain any information, then the posterior on states of nature is the same as the prior. This is illustrated in Fig. 1 where the simplex of probabilities on states of nature is shown. The prior is $\bar{\pi}$. The set of posteriors associated with a star-shaped spreading of beliefs, spread all the way out to the vertices, is shown by the three lines radiating out from $\bar{\pi}$. Perfect learning would move you to one of the three vertices following receipt of the message. Less learning would move you to one of the three points marked with circles. Even less learning would move you to one of the three points marked with x's after receiving the message.

The advantage of representing learning by this star-shaped spreading of beliefs is that the process can be parameterized by the λ in Eq. (4). The disadvantage is that we have eliminated perfectly legitimate and orderable learning processes (emanating from $\bar{\pi}$ in Fig. 1).

C. Learning in the Optimal Growth Model

Introducing learning into our stochastic growth model involves introducing a second set of states corresponding to different paths that learning might take; i.e., sequences of messages that might be received. Each message yields a different outcome of the learning process where an outcome is a new probability vector on states of nature, $\pi(t)$. As before, let Y_t be the set of possible single period outcomes (messages) of the learning process at time t. At any point in time, to know the current state of knowledge it is essential to know the learning that has preceded t.[4] We call this the history of learning, $H_t = \{(y_0, \ldots, y_t) \mid y_i \varepsilon Y_i \ \forall 0 \le i \le t\}$. Notationally, H_t contains the learning that has occurred by time period t (before decisions are taken in time period t). An element of H_t is a particular history, h_t. For instance, consider a 10 period world in which learning can proceed in three directions $\{-1, 0, 1\}$ at any point in time. One possible history would be $(0, 1, -1, -1, -1, 1, 0, 1, 1, 0)$.

If we partition any h_t as (h_{t-1}, y_t), then we define the "predecessor" and "most recent" functions, $\varphi: H_t \to H_{t-1}$ and $\psi: H_t \to T_t$ as $\varphi(h_t) = h_{t-1}$, $\psi(h_t) = y_t$. The function ψ indicates the most recent learning whereas φ indicates learning that occurred earlier. This allows one to functionally represent the learning path and to compute the probability vector on states of the world, $\pi(h_t, t)$. Define the transition matrix $\Pi_t(h_t)$ such that each column is a posterior probability vector corresponding to a different element of the message space, Y_{t+1}. Thus $\pi(h_t, t)$ is the column of $\Pi_{t-1}(\varphi(h_t))$ corresponding to $\psi(h_t)$. Furthermore if $q_t(h_t)$ is the probability vector associated with different elements of Y_{t+1}, then

$$\pi(h_t, t) = \Pi_t(h_t) q_t(h_t). \tag{5}$$

$[\Pi_t(h_t), q_t(h_t)]$ is an information structure as described earlier. In our model, we define $q_t(h_t) \equiv \pi(h_t, t)$. Thus the probability of receiving a message that reinforces state i is the same as the prior on state i.

It is "easy" to modify the stochastic growth model (1)–(3) to incorporate this learning. Two things remain to be specified: how the probability vector (π) evolves and the probability (μ) of a specific history (learning path) occurring. Following Eq. (4),

$$\pi(h_{t+1}, t+1) = \begin{cases} (1 - \lambda)\pi(h_t, t) + \lambda e_s, & \text{if } s = \hat{s} \\ (1 - \lambda)\pi(h_t, t) & \text{otherwise} \end{cases} \tag{6a}$$

$$\mu(h_{t+1}, t+1) = \mu(h_t, t)\pi_{\hat{s}}(h_t, t), \tag{6b}$$

where

$$\hat{s} = \psi(h_{t+1}), \tag{7a}$$

$$h_t = \varphi(h_{t+1}), \tag{7b}$$

where e_s is a vector of 0's and 1's with a 1 in the sth position and 0 in the rest of the positions, and λ is the rate of learning. As indicated above, we assume the message space is the same as the space of possible states of the world. Thus messages are noisy indications of the true state of the world. Thus for each possible learning path, we know the probability vector on states of nature *and* the probability of that learning path actually occurring. Since Eqs. (6) are defined recursively, initial values need to be defined for π and μ. π is of course the prior

---

[4] Of course the current state of knowledge can be characterized by the probability on states of nature. However, this is an infinite set whereas the possible learning histories are finite. Finiteness is more amenable to stochastic programming which is the solution approach used here.

THE OPTIMAL REGULATION OF GREENHOUSE GASES 11

on states of nature and the initial μ corresponds to q in the previous discussion, which is also equal to the prior on states of nature.

There are many ways uncertainty can enter a model such as this. As indicated above, we assume uncertainty in the damage from global warming.[5] Specifically, we write utility as

$$u[c(t), d(t), s] = \log[c(t) - \Delta_s d(t)]. \tag{8}$$

We further assume there are two states of the world, B and L, corresponding to global warming being a big problem (B) vs global warming being a little problem (L). Learning can proceed to reinforce B or reinforce L. We arbitrarily assume $\pi_B(t = 0) = 0.2$ and $\pi_L(t = 0) = 0.8$ with $\Delta_b = 5$ and $\Delta_L = 0$. Although arbitrary, this yields an expected value of Δ of 1 and reflects the fact that damage could be serious. The variance of Δ is 4. The expected variance declines with time, at faster rates for larger λ (see [22]).[6]

IV. RESULTS

The model described above has been implemented using time points at 10-year intervals beginning in 1965.[7] The first three points (1965–1985) are used as calibration and control of emissions is fixed at zero. Optimal emission control levels are computed beginning in 1995. Learning occurs in 1995–2005 and 2005–2015. No learning occurs thereafter (but uncertainty persists).

The model described in the previous section is an infinite horizon model. Only finite horizon models can be solved as stochastic programs so we have chosen to approximate the infinite horizon model with a 20 period/200 year finite horizon model. As has been shown elsewhere [22], the control level in 1995 is essentially independent of horizon length, when the length is in excess of 20 periods. Model (1)–(8) was solved as a function of δ_E and λ.

Focusing on the year 1995, with reversible emission control rates (i.e., $\delta_E = 1$), we find that optimal control levels for greenhouse gases are virtually unaffected by the rate of learning. If one over-controls today, then that error can be corrected in the future. Thus the fact that learning is taking place does not impact current decisions to control emission.

Figure 2 shows the optimal 1995 control rate as a function of the learning rate (0 = no learning; 1 = complete resolution of uncertainty in one period). The control rate is the fraction emissions have been reduced, relative to the uncontrolled level of emissions.[8] Three curves are shown in the figure, corresponding to

[5] Uncertainty in damage is commonly examined (see [16, 29]) although many other types of uncertainty are possible and are important. Clearly there is uncertainty in control costs. There is uncertainty in how the climate evolves. There is uncertainty in how the economy evolves. Peck and Teisberg [43] discuss some of the different types of uncertainty.

[6] For instance, for $\lambda = 0.5$, the expected variance declines from 4 to 2.3 in two periods.

[7] The model is a stochastic programming model, solved using GAMS/MINOS. I am grateful to Lars Mathiesen for suggesting this approach.

[8] The control rate is defined more precisely in the Appendix (Eq. A-2).

12   CHARLES D. KOLSTAD

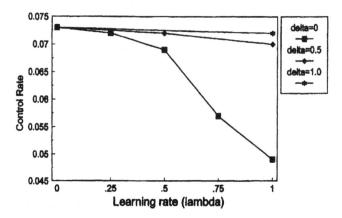

FIG. 2.   1995 greenhouse gas control levels (rate of time preference = 3%).

different values of δ_E, the abatement capital depreciation rate.[9] The first thing to note is that the capital stock effect is real and has an effect on current control decisions. With no learning, there is no difference in the optimal decisions for the three δ_E values. In fact the control level is the same as it would be in the deterministic case. However, with more rapid learning, it makes sense to reduce control levels when abatement capital investment is irreversible. When abatement capital is perfectly reversible ($\delta_E = 1$), then learning has virtually no effect on the optimal control level. In other words, the environmental stock effect, associated with greenhouse gas accumulation, does not appear.

It could be that this failure to find an environmental stock effect is due to discounting the future at 3% per annum—a small rate but one which adds up over 100 years. When the rate of time preference is decreased to 1% per annum, the desirable level of control increases—from 7 to 15% for the case of no learning. However, the same pattern as found in Fig. 2 persists. Irreversible control capital has a significant influence on optimal levels of control in 1995 but the environmental stock effect just does not materialize.

Why doesn't the accumulation of greenhouse gas emissions lead to an environmental stock effect? To answer this question, we perturbed the optimal trajectory of control levels. In particular, we considered two cases with suboptimal control levels in 1995 and 2005 with a return to an optimal path after that. One is an approximate doubling of control to 15% for the 1995–2005 period and the other is no control for that period. Remarkably, this substantial deviation from optimality in 1995–2005 has little effect on subsequent emission control levels (see [20]).

Why is this? One reason is that costs and damages in the stochastic model are such that the optimal level of greenhouse gas abatement is very insensitive to the total stock of greenhouse gases. The simple reason is that while damage from greenhouse gases increases with the stock, and in fact is quadratic in temperature change, the present value of damage is quite linear over a fairly broad range in

---

[9] To provide intuition on δ_E, abatement capital with a lifetime of 10, 20, 30, 40 or 50 years, depreciating at the same percentage per decade, leaving 10% residual value at the end of its life, would correspond to a δ_E of 0.90, 0.68, 0.54, 0.44 and 0.37 respectively.

current stocks of greenhouse gases. This is illustrated in Fig. 3 where the loss in the present value of utility (in monetary units) is shown from an exogenous addition of 50 to 100 megatons of greenhouse gas in 1995. Keep in mind that greenhouse gas emissions are less than 10 megatons per year and that we allow future emissions subsequently to adjust optimally to a larger stock of gases. As is also illustrated in the figure, marginal damage is almost constant over a wide range of stocks of greenhouse gases. Figure 4 reproduces the marginal damage curve from Fig. 3 (although writing it as a function of the emission control rate) and superimposes the marginal cost of control. Note from Figs. 3 and 4 that suboptimal emissions in one period will have virtually no effect on optimal emissions in the next period because of the insensitivity of marginal damage to the stock size and the fairly large slope of the marginal control cost function.

This suggests that if damages were more nonlinear, the results might be different. To investigate this, we executed the model using damages proportional to the third, fourth, and fifth power of the temperature change, rather than just the square. We found negligible effect.[10] We conclude that even if damages are nonlinear in the stock, and there are long time delays in stocks being translated into effects, then damages will still be roughly linear in current period emissions. This means that something like Fig. 4 applies.

Getting back to the stock effect, recall that it has to do with the stock nature of greenhouse gases, and the fact that one cannot negatively emit; i.e., one cannot reverse emissions by negatively emitting in the future. Consequently, the effect can occur only if one might wish to negatively emit in the future. But because future emissions are so slightly influenced by today's actions, there is no scenario under

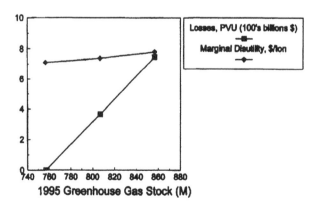

FIG. 3. Marginal and total disutility as a function of stock of greenhouse gases.

[10] We considered the extreme cases of complete learning in one period and no learning. More nonlinear damages resulted in increased current period emissions. For the 3% rate of time preference case, current period emission control increased from 7 to 18%. We also found that learning had an effect in the high curvature case when there was no stock effect, consistent with the results of Ulph and Ulph [50]. To eliminate this effect, we modified the no-learning case to be exactly the same as the learning case except that control levels at any point in time were constrained to be the same over all learning histories.

14   CHARLES D. KOLSTAD

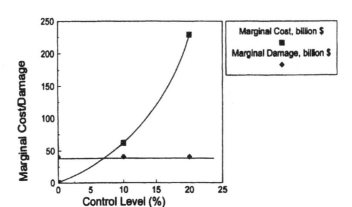

FIG. 4.   Marginal cost, marginal damage vs 1995 control rate.

which it would be optimal to negatively emit in the future to correct over-emissions today. This is the crux of why there is no such effect with regard to emissions.[11] This point is also made in [50].

Finally, we can fall back on Malinvaud's [25] result that when uncertainty is small, it makes no difference in optimal decisions. This seems to apply here since learning and uncertainty have very modest effects on outcomes.

It is interesting to compare this result to that of Manne and Richels [29]. While their model is substantially different from ours, they show that immediate resolution of uncertainty (very rapid learning) results in lower emission control rates (higher emissions) than when uncertainty is not resolved. This is qualitatively the same as our result.

V. POLICY IMPLICATIONS AND CONCLUSIONS

In this paper we have addressed the question of whether the stock nature of greenhouse gas emissions or the sunk nature of control costs lead to a bias in today's decisions regarding the control of greenhouse gases. Certainly the political debate has emphasized irreversibilities, either in control capital or climate change, and has suggested these irreversibilities have profound effect on control decisions made today. To answer the question, we have developed a stochastic model of greenhouse gas control and parameterized the rate of learning.

We find only qualified support for such positions. In particular, we find no evidence of a stock effect from greenhouse gases affecting today's control decisions. Of course the stock effect is only one type of environmental irreversibility. We have not examined irreversible changes in the climate or irreversibilities in damage. Such irreversibilities are of real concern to many concerned with climate policy.

Only when emission control investments are very long-lived and irreversible is there a stock effect associated with control capital—and that effect calls for a

---

[11] The fact that marginal damage is increasing reflects the fact that damage is not completely linear.

downward bias in control levels when learning is occurring rapidly, relative to the case of no learning or no uncertainty.

One interpretation of these results is that rapid rates of learning should cause today's societies to "go slow" on controlling greenhouse gas emissions. This is certainly one interpretation although go slow means undertaking some control of greenhouse gases, just not as much as in the case with no learning.

Another interpretation is that we should vigorously pursue emission control policies that are reversible, that do not involve large, long-lived sunk costs since irreversible emission control decisions unnecessarily tie our hands. To be specific, it might be appropriate to adopt temporary taxes on carbon in lieu of permanent taxes. With learning, our model suggests that a temporary (e.g., 5–10 years) tax on carbon might dominate a similar permanent tax on carbon. Of course we have not analyzed this fully; all we can say is that more flexibility in control may be desirable and a temporary tax is more likely to induce flexibility.

In any event, the results here should be qualified as arising from the specific model used and the specific nature of uncertainty (in damages) adopted in the analysis. Further research should definitely investigate other types of uncertainty.

APPENDIX: DETAILS ON STOCHASTIC GROWTH MODEL

The stochastic growth model is fairly completely described in the text. Parameter values are taken from and described more fully in [36], although there may be modest differences in the values of specific parameters due to our use of a different version of the DICE model.

The variables L and σ are parameters that vary with time. The population/labor supply (L) is 3.324 billion in 1965 and grows initially at a rate of 23.5% per decade, with the growth rate declining by 19.5% per decade (i.e., 19.5% of 23.5% is the decline). This leads to an asymptotic population of 11.09 billion. The uncontrolled greenhouse gas emissions–output ratio (σ) starts at 0.5368 in 1965, declining by 12.5% per decade thereafter.

The production function (Eq. (2c)) is

$$Y(t) = \left[1 - b_1 \mu(t)^{b_2}\right] A(t) K(t)^{\gamma} L(t)^{1-\gamma}, \tag{A-1}$$

where

$$\mu(t) = 1 - \frac{E(t)}{\sigma(t)Y(t)}. \tag{A-2}$$

Thus $\mu(t)$ is the emission control rate, defined by Eq. (A-2). The parameters b_1, b_2, and γ are 0.0686, 2.887, and 0.25, respectively, and $A(t)$ grows with time reflecting increases in total factor productivity. $A(1965) = 0.00852$ and grows initially at 20% per decade, with this growth rate declining by 11% per decade. The term in brackets in Eq. (A-1) reduces gross output by the cost of emission control.

The per capita damage function (Eq. (2d)) is given by

$$d(t) = \frac{\theta_1 T(t)^{\theta_2} Y(t)}{L(t)\left[1 + \theta_1 T(t)^{\theta_2}\right]}, \tag{A-3}$$

16   CHARLES D. KOLSTAD

where θ_1 and θ_2 take the values 0.001478 and 2, respectively.[12] This is equivalent to damage being quadratic in temperature with a 3°C temperature rise yielding a 1.3% decline in output.

The climate model (Eqs. (3b) and (3c)) is

$$T(t + 1) = T(t) + r_1\ln[M(t)/590] + r_2T(t) + r_3O(t) \qquad \text{(A-4)}$$

$$O(t + 1) = O(t) + r_4[T(t) - O(t)], \qquad \text{(A-5)}$$

where r_1, r_2, r_3, and r_4 take the values 1.3368, -0.4181, 0.09944, and 0.02. Values of T and O in 1965 are 0.2 and 0.1, respectively. Time (t) is in decades.

The CO_2 and capital stock adjustment equations ((2f) and (3a)) are completely described in the text except for the initial values of K and M which, for 1965, are 18.11 trillion U.S.\$ and 677 gigatons of carbon.

REFERENCES

1. K. J. Arrow and A. C. Fisher, Environmental preservation, uncertainty, and irreversibility, *Quart. J. Econom.* **88**, 312–319 (1974).
2. R. Balvers and T. Cosimano, Actively learning about demand and the dynamics of price adjustment, *Econom. J.* **100**, 882–898 (1990).
3. Jon Conrad, Quasi-option value and the expected value of information, *Quart. J. Econom.* **92**, 813–819 (1980).
4. M. L. Cropper, Regulating activities with catastrophic environmental effects, *J. Environ. Econom. Management* **3**, 1–15 (1976).
5. M. A. Cunha-e-sa, "Essays in Environmental Economics," Ph.D. Dissertation, Dept. of Economics, University of Illinois, Urbana, Illinois (1994).
6. R. C. D'Arge and K. C. Kogiku, Economic growth and the environment, *Rev. Econ. Stud.* **40**, 61–77 (1973).
7. M. A. H. Dempster, Introduction to stochastic programming, *in* "Stochastic Programming" (M. A. H. Dempster, Ed.). Academic Press, London (1980).
8. J. Edmonds and J. Reilly, Global energy and CO_2 to the year 2050, *Energy J.* **4**(3), 21–47 (1983).
9. Larry G. Epstein, Decision making and the temporal resolution of uncertainty, *Int. Econom. Rev.* **21** 269–283 (1980).
10. A. C. Fisher and W. M. Hanemann, Quasi-option value: some misconceptions dispelled, *J. Environ. Econom. Management* **14**, 183–190 (1987).
11. A. C. Fisher and W. M. Hanemann, Information and the dynamics of environmental protection: The concept of the critical period, *Scand. J. Econom.* **92**, 399–414 (1990).
12. B. A. Forster, Optimal consumption planning in a polluted environment, *Econ. Rec.* **49**, 534–545 (1973).
13. A. Myrick Freeman, The Quasi-option value of irreversible development, *J. Environ. Econom. Management* **11**, 292–294 (1984).
14. X. Freixas and J. J. Laffont, The irreversibility effect, *in* "Bayesian Models in Economic Theory" (M. Boyer and R. Khilstrom, Eds.). North-Holland, Amsterdam (1984).
15. S. Grossman and C. Shapiro, Optimal dynamic R & D programs, *Rand J.* **17** 581–593 (1986).
16. J. K. Hammitt, R. J. Lempert, and M. E. Schlesinger, A sequential-decision strategy for abating climate change, *Nature* **357**, 315–318 (1992).
17. Claude Henry, Option values in the economics of irreplaceable assets, *Rev. Econom. Stud. Symp.* 89–104 (1974).
18. R. A. Jones and J. M. Ostroy, Flexibility and uncertainty, *Rev. Econom. Stud.* **51**, 13–32 (1984).

[12] Equation (A-3) is somewhat convoluted because [36] adjusts gross output ($\bar{Y}$) by $\Omega = (1 - b_1\mu^{b2})/(1 + \theta_1T^{\theta2})$ to obtain net output (his Eq. III.A.11). Solving the identity $Y - Ld = \Omega\bar{Y}$ yields Eq. (A-3).

19. E. Keeler, M. Spence, and R. Zeckhauser, The optimal control of pollution, *J. Econom. Theory* **4**, 19–34 (1971).

20. C. D. Kolstad, George Bush vs Al Gore: Irreversibilities in greenhouse gas accumulation and emission control investment, *Energy Policy* **22**, 771–778 (1994).

21. C. D. Kolstad, Fundamental irreversibilities in stock externalities, *J. Public Economic.* forthcoming (1996).

22. Charles D. Kolstad, The timing of CO2 control in the face of uncertainty and learning, *in* "International Environmental Economics" (E. van Ireland, Ed.), Chap. 4. Elsevier, Amsterdam (1994).

23. Jean-Jacques Laffont, "The Economics of Uncertainty and Information" MIT Press, Cambridge, MA (1989).

24. R. J. Lempert, M. E. Schlesinger, and J. K. Hammitt, The impact of potential abrupt climate changes on near-term policy choices, *Climate Change* **26**, 351–376 (1994).

25. E. Malinvaud, First order certainty equivalence, *Econometrica* **37**, 706–718 (1969).

26. Deleted in proof.

27. Alan S. Manne, Robert Mendelsohn, and Richard Richels, MERGE: A model for evaluating regional and global effects of GHG reduction policies, *in* "Integrative Assessment of Mitigation, Impacts and Adaptation to Climate Change" (N. Nakicenovic, W. D. Nordhaus, R. Richels, and F. L. Toth, Eds.), IIASA Conference Proceedings CP-94-9, Laxenburg, Austria (1994).

28. A. S. Manne and R. G. Richels, Buying greenhouse insurance, *Energy Policy* **19**, 543–552 (1991).

29. A. S. Manne and R. G. Richels, "Buying Greenhouse Insurance: The Economic Costs of CO_2 Emission Limits." MIT Press, Cambridge, MA (1992).

30. J. Marshak and K. Miyasawa, Economic comparability of information systems, *Int. Econom. Rev.* **9**, 137–174 (1968).

31. J. R. Miller and F. Lad, Flexibility, learning and irreversibility in environmental decisions: A Bayesian approach, *J. Environ. Econom. Management* **11**, 161–172 (1984).

32. W. D. Nordhaus, Economic growth and climate: The case of carbon dioxide, *Amer. Econom. Rev.* (1977).

33. W. D. Nordhaus and G. W. Yohe, Future paths of energy and carbon dioxide emissions, *in* "Changing Climate" National Research Council Carbon Dioxide Assessment Committee. National Academy Press, Washington, DC (1983).

34. W. D. Nordhaus, To slow or now to slow: The economics of the greenhouse effect, *Econom. J.* (1991).

35. W. D. Nordhaus, An optimal transition path for controlling greenhouse gases, *Science* **258**, 1315–1319 (1992).

36. W. D. Nordhaus, "The 'DICE' Model: Background and Structure of a Dynamic Integrated Climate-Economy Model of the Economics of Global Warming," Cowles Foundation Discussion Paper 1009, New Haven, CT (Feb. 1992).

37. W. D. Nordhaus, Rolling the 'DICE': An optimal transition path for controlling greenhouse gases, *Resource Energy Econom.* **15**, 27–50 (1993).

38. W. D. Nordhaus, "Managing the Global Commons: The Economics of Climate Change" MIT Press, Cambridge, MA (1994).

39. Lars J. Olson, Environmental preservation with production, *J. Environ. Econom. Management* **18**, 88–96 (1990).

40. J. L. Paddock, D. R. Siegel, and J. L. Smith, Option valuation of claims on real assets: The case of offshore petroleum leases, *Quart. J. Econom.* **103**, 497–508 (1988).

41. S. C. Peck and T. J. Teisberg, CETA: A model for carbon emissions trajectory assessment, *Energy J.* **13**, 55–77 (1992).

42. S. C. Peck, H.-P. Chao, and T. J. Teisberg, Optimal control and learning strategies when environmental costs are cumulative, *in* "Proc., IFAC/IFORS/IAEE International Symposium on Energy Systems, Management and Economics, Oct. 25–27, 1989, Tokyo."

43. S. C. Peck and T. J. Teisberg, Global warming uncertainties and the value of information: An analysis using CETA, *Resource Energy Econom.* **15**, 71–97 (1993).

44. C. G. Plourde, A model of waste accumulation and disposal, *Can. J. Econom.* **5**, 119–125 (1972).

45. C. Plourde and D. Yeung, A model of industrial pollution in a stochastic environment, *J. Environ. Econom. Management* **16**, 97–105 (1989).

46. Frank Ramsey, A mathematical theory of saving, *Econom. J.* 1928.

47. Herbert Simon, Dynamic programming under uncertainty with a quadratic criterion function, *Econometrica* **24**, 74–81 (1956).
48. V. L. Smith, Dynamics of waste accumulation: Disposal versus recycling, *Quart. J. Econom.* **86** 600–616 (1972).
49. N. L. Stokey and R. E. Lucas, Jr., "Recursive Methods in Economic Dynamics." Harvard University Press, Cambridge, MA (1989).
50. Alistair Ulph and David Ulph, "Global Warming, Irreversibility and Learning," mimeo, University of London (November 1995).
51. W. K. Viscusi and R. Zeckhauser, Environmental policy choice under uncertainty, *J. Environ. Econom. Management* **3**, 97–112 (1976).
52. John P. Weyant, Costs of reducing global carbon emissions, *J. Econom. Perspect.* **7**(4), 27–46 (1993).

[16]

Discounting and distributional considerations in the context of global warming

Christian Azar [a,*], Thomas Sterner [b,1]

[a] *Institute of Physical Resource Theory, Chalmers University of Technology, Göteborg University, 412 96 Göteborg, Sweden*
[b] *Department of Economics, Göteborg University, Vasagatan 1, 411 80 Göteborg, Sweden*

Received 21 May 1995; accepted 6 May 1996

Abstract

The economics of global warming is reviewed with special emphasis on how the cost depends on the discount rate and on how costs in poor and rich regions are aggregated into a global cost estimate. Both of these factors depend on the assumptions made concerning the underlying utility and welfare functions. It is common to aggregate welfare gains and losses across generations and countries as if the utility of money were constant, but it is not. If we assume that a CO_2-equivalent doubling implies costs equal to 1.5% of the income in both high and low income countries, a pure rate of time preference equal to zero, and a utility function which is logarithmic in income, then the marginal cost of CO_2 emissions is estimated at 260–590 USD/ton C for a time horizon in the range 300–1000 years, an estimate which is large enough to justify significant reductions of CO_2 emissions on purely economic grounds. The estimate is approximately 50–100-times larger than the estimate made by Nordhaus in his DICE model and the difference is almost completely due to the choice of discount rate and the weight given to the costs in the developing world as well as a more accurate model of the carbon cycle. Finally, the sensitivity of the marginal cost estimate with respect to several parameters is analyzed.

Keywords: Climate change; Discounting; Pure rate of time preference; Distribution of income

1. Introduction

The existence of the greenhouse effect has been known for a very long time. Arrhenius (1896) calculated the effect of a doubling of the CO_2 concentration in the atmosphere and found that it would lead to an increase in the global mean temperature of approximately 6°C, an estimate somewhat higher than 1.5–4.5°C, the range that is now predicted with the help of advanced computer models. But it was not until 1988, following the Toronto Conference (Leggett, 1990), that the increasing emissions of greenhouse gases (GHG) became acknowledged as a major environmental problem by the United Nations and political leaders around the globe.

The UN Framework Convention on Climate Change was adopted at the UNCED conference in Rio de Janeiro 1992. Its ultimate objective is to

* Corresponding author. e-mail: frtca@fy.chalmers.se
1 e-mail: thomas.sterner@redcap.econ.gu.se

170 *C. Azar, T. Sterner / Ecological Economics 19 (1996) 169–184*

achieve a stabilization of greenhouse gas concentrations in the atmosphere at a level that would prevent dangerous anthropogenic interference with the climate system. Sweden introduced a carbon tax in the late eighties. Several countries have committed themselves not to increase emissions above their 1990 level. But even if this goal would be met globally, the atmospheric concentrations of CO_2 would continue to rise. In order to stabilize atmospheric concentrations at the present level by the year 2100, the accumulated emissions from 1990 to the end of the 21st century must not exceed some 300–430 Gton C (IPCC, 1995). This implies an annual average rate of carbon emissions equal to 2.7–3.9 Gton C/year which is equivalent to a 45–60% reduction of the present emissions. For the 22nd century even stronger reductions are needed in order to avoid a renewed increase of CO_2 in the atmosphere.

The demands for emission reductions and the decisions that have been made, have inspired several authors to study the economic costs and benefits of such policies. Nordhaus has published several studies (1982, 1991, 1993a), on the costs and benefits of GHG-emissions. Nordhaus's latest work (1993a), called the DICE-model, purports to determine an optimal emission path for GHGs.

Nordhaus concludes that only modest reductions of GHGs are motivated from an economic point of view. This result is strongly dependent on several assumptions. Nordhaus uses a pure rate of time preference equal to 3%/year, making impacts far into the future negligible, and a cost-damage function which ignores ethical issues such as the risk that millions of people will be far worse off than losing a few percent of their income. Nordhaus is also rather pessimistic about the possibilities for cost-effective CO_2-reductions through increased energy efficiency and improved renewable energy technologies. Finally, he treats climate change as a smooth and predictable process without risk for sudden catastrophic events.

Nordhaus's work has inspired several other studies of the economic impacts of global warming, e.g., Ayres and Walter (1991), Peck and Teisberg (1992), Fankhauser (1994, 1995), Haraden (1993), Cline (1992a,b), Parry (1993), Azar (1994a,1995) and Tol (1995).

Cline (1992a) analyses the costs and benefits of a program aiming to reduce the emissions of CO_2 to 4 Gton C/year, which is slightly more than half the present emissions. He finds a cost-benefit ratio that is larger than unity for certain sets of parameter values, and lower than unity for some others. Overall, he concludes that his analysis implies that the benefits of reducing GHG emissions exceed the costs "if policy makers are risk averse (...) or if one concentrates attention on high-damage cases (especially even a slim chance of an economic catastrophe)".

The consequences of the ever increasing use of fossil fuels are expected to have disastrous impacts for millions of people. In a cost-benefit analysis, their suffering, translated into a monetary cost, is compared to the monetary benefits of fossil fuel combustion. If the benefits exceed the costs it is concluded that no reductions in emissions are warranted. Such conclusions are highly controversial from an ethical point of view. Economists (e.g., Booth, 1994) and philosophers (e.g., Rawls, 1972) have argued that we should not be allowed to cause harm to others in order to increase our own consumption. It is not enough as in the simple cost-benefit analysis, to show that the winners *could* compensate the losers, rather, satisfactory compensation must actually be paid which, for various reasons may be complicated, expensive and sometimes impossible (see Spash (1994) for a thorough discussion).

In this paper, we analyze and identify three issues that are crucial for cost estimates of global warming: the retention of CO_2 in the atmosphere, the present value of future damages and the unequal distribution of income. In Section 2, a functional relationship between the economic costs of climate change, global mean temperature change and atmospheric CO_2 concentrations is discussed. We also discuss how the CO_2 concentration in the atmosphere is expected to change as a function of time. The method of discounting is given special consideration in Section 3, in which an expression for the marginal cost of CO_2-emissions is derived. In Section 4, we develop a method for taking into account the unequal distribution of income in the world when evaluating the costs of global warming. Numerical evaluations of our expressions are presented in Section 5, followed by a conclusion in Section 6.

C. Azar, T. Sterner / Ecological Economics 19 (1996) 169–184   171

2. The economic costs of the greenhouse effect

The marginal cost, MC_1, of a unit emission of CO_2 can be expressed as

$$MC_1 = \int_0^T G(t) \cdot \frac{\partial C(m_h)}{\partial m_h} V(t)\,dt, \qquad (1)$$

where index 1 indicates that only one group of income is considered, $G(t)$ is the fraction of a unit emission of CO_2 at present that remains in the atmosphere at time t, $C(m_h)$ is the damage function relating anthropogenic carbon levels in the atmosphere to global costs, m_h is the anthropogenic level of CO_2 in the atmosphere, $V(t)$ is the present value function, and T is the time horizon of study, i.e., the period over which the damage is assumed to remain.

The damage function, $C(m_h)$, relating the cost of climate change to the anthropogenic levels of CO_2 in the atmosphere is developed in Section 2.1. The expression for $G(t)$, is developed in Section 2.2. In Section 3, we develop a present value function, $V(t)$, appropriate for discounting costs occurring far into the future.

In this paper, we will not discuss the scientific basis for the greenhouse effect. The interested reader is referred to a number of consensus reports by the intergovernmental panel on climate change (IPCC, 1990, 1992, 1995). Instead, we move directly into the economic analysis.

2.1. A functional relationship between damages and the atmospheric CO_2-content

We assume that the damage function is given by [2]

$$C(k, m_h(t), Y(t)) = k \frac{m_h(t)}{m_p} Y(t) \qquad (2)$$

where C is the damage function, $Y(t)$ is the world income (WI) at time t, k is the fraction of WI that will be lost for a CO_2-equivalent doubling, m_h is the anthropogenic level of CO_2 in the atmosphere, and

[2] The greenhouse effect is caused by a number of different gases. Here we will only consider CO_2. It is, however, possible to further develop the analysis to include all greenhouse gases (see Fankhauser, 1994).

m_p is the *pre-industrial* level of CO_2 in the atmosphere. Total atmospheric contents of CO_2, $m_{tot}(t)$, is given by $m_{tot}(t) = m_p + m_h(t)$. Presently, $m_h(t) = 160$ Gton C, $m_p = 600$ Gton C and, hence, $m_{tot}(t) = 760$ Gton C.

Eq. (2) is probably the simplest functional form relating the damage of climate change to increases in the atmospheric contents of CO_2. It does not, for example, take into account the time delay between increases in atmospheric concentrations of greenhouse gases and thermal equilibrium, nor that the damage is likely to be dependent upon the rate of climatic change.

Although simple, this damage function has several advantages: First of all, it makes the analysis more transparent. Secondly, the introduction of more complexity does not increase the accuracy of the model, since uncertainties about the damage coefficient k are so great, and since there are almost no studies where the damage for other CO_2 concentrations in the atmosphere than a doubling is considered. Thirdly, the economic cost of climate change is likely to be a convex function of global average surface temperature change. This property is captured by the damage function defined by Eq. (2), since the temperature increase is a logarithmic function of atmospheric concentrations of CO_2. Hence the assumption of a linear relationship between damage and anthropogenic CO_2 concentrations is equivalent to assuming that damage is exponentially dependent upon the change in global average temperature.

A linear relationship between damage and anthropogenic CO_2 contents in the atmosphere has been used by Nordhaus (1991), Haraden (1993), Parry (1993) and Azar (1994a). In later work, Nordhaus (1993a) assumes that the damage is proportional to the square of the global average surface temperature change. Cline (1992a) assumes that damage is proportional to the temperature change raised to the power of 1.3 in his central case. For global average surface temperature increases below 6°C, the damage function assumed here fits well with the functional forms assumed by Cline and Nordhaus (Azar, 1995).

Nordhaus (1993a) uses $k = 1.33\%$ in his DICE-model. Cline (1992a) finds the cost for a temperature increase of 2.5°C, in the range 1–2% of the WI, and uses $k = 1.5\%$ as a central value. But both Cline's and Nordhaus's estimates are based on the U.S.

172 *C. Azar, T. Sterner / Ecological Economics 19 (1996) 169–184*

economy and then assumed to be valid for the global economy. Ayres and Walter (1991) estimate the global costs related to the expected sea level rise to lie in the range 2.1–2.4% of global income over the next fifty years. Only Fankhauser (1995) and Tol (1995) collect data from several regions of the world and estimate the cost of a CO_2-equivalent doubling at 1.4 and 1.9% of WI, respectively. [3]

It should be observed that these estimates for the costs of climate change could be criticized from several different points of view. They do for instance ignore difficult ethical dilemmas such as the miniaturization of losses of human lives and biological diversity. Both Fankhauser and Tol have received critique for using lower values for the loss of a statistical life in poor regions of the world (see, e.g., Ekins (1995), Meyer et al. (1995), a letter in Nature co-signed by 38 scientists, and Pearce (1995)). By weighting costs with (some) function of income, this problem can be resolved (see Section 4).

Furthermore, the estimates seem to imply a very low significance of the climate for human societies. Agriculture is only a few per cent of the economy in the industrial economies. Even a large reduction in harvests in one such (rich) country can be replaced by imports at a limited economic cost. This does not, however, for obvious reasons, generalize to the whole world.

We conclude that there are great uncertainties and ethical controversies involved in the cost estimates. We nevertheless follow others in assuming k to be equal to 1.5% of world income. Instead, the analysis focuses on how this cost estimate is affected when costs in poorer regions are weighted with income. The weight factors are developed in a framework where the marginal cost of CO_2 emissions is evaluated. It is shown that the discount rate and the weight factors are orders of magnitudes more important for the final estimate of the marginal cost of CO_2 emissions than the actual value of k.

2.1.1. Time perspective

In this paper we have assumed that the damage from climate change is proportional to the increase in the atmospheric concentration of greenhouse gases. In reality, damage from global warming will depend on the rate of climate change, the absolute magnitude of climate change, and how well and quickly human societies will adapt to the changing climate. One question of particular interest is how long damage from climate change will remain, given that the atmospheric concentrations of greenhouse gases are stabilized.

It takes approximately a millennium to remove 85% of the excess CO_2 from the atmosphere (Maier-Reimer and Hasselman, 1987). Thus, a unit emission of carbon emitted today will continue to cause climatic changes a thousand years into the future . However, it could be argued that costs associated with changing weather conditions (such as increased frequency of floods, droughts and hurricanes) are likely to decline once people have moved to places where weather conditions are not that adversely affected. But, since there are costs associated with migration, some people will remain in places with worsened weather conditions and the costs these people will bear must also be included.

Furthermore, large-scale migrations of people are likely to give rise to political and social conflicts which might be troublesome even far into the future. The historical roots important for understanding the conflicts in Palestine and former Yugoslavia date hundreds and sometimes even thousands of years back in time. Many conflicts in Africa and the Americas date back to the slave trade and the colonization which began several hundred years ago.

Irreversible damage includes losses of biological diversity, which will remain even if the atmospheric concentration of CO_2 would return to its pre-industrial value. In this paper we arbitrarily assume that Eq. (2) is valid 300–1000 years into the future and that no damage from climate change will occur after this period of time. This choice of time horizon may underestimate the cost of global warming since it neglects some irreversible aspects of climate change, e.g., the loss of biodiversity.

2.2. The carbon cycle

Several authors (e.g., Nordhaus, 1991, 1993a; Parry, 1993; Haraden, 1993; Azar, 1994a) have used

---

[3] All these estimates of the cost of a CO_2-equivalent doubling were originally calculated as fractions of gross world product.

C. Azar, T. Sterner / Ecological Economics 19 (1996) 169–184 173

the following model for the atmospheric retention of a unit emission of CO_2 at present:

$$G(t) = \beta e^{-\delta t}. \tag{3}$$

Here β is interpreted as the immediate retention ratio of a unit emission, and δ as the removal rate from the atmosphere. The values of β and δ are of importance to the cost analysis, but these parameter values cannot be determined uniquely since the removal rate of excess carbon from the atmosphere is much more complex than Eq. (3), see (IPCC, 1990).

Instead, we use a model for the carbon cycle developed by Maier-Reimer and Hasselman (1987), which we will refer to as the MRH-model. Since CO_2 is chemically stable in the atmosphere, its main sink is dissolution in the oceans. In the long run, an equilibrium between the atmosphere and the ocean will be established in which approximately 15% of the emitted carbon remains in the atmosphere. Note, however, that this fraction is not constant but increases with accumulated CO_2 emissions. Atmospheric CO_2 can also be absorbed by biomass (via photosynthesis) but this process will only constitute a net sink of carbon if the stock of biomass increases. There is evidence pointing to an increased growth rate and carbon storage as a result of increased atmospheric CO_2 concentration (the so-called CO_2 fertilization effect) but it is uncertain to which extent this will be true in the real world (see IPCC, 1995, for details). The MRH model does only take into account the atmosphere-ocean interaction, and the response function for a unit emission can be approximated by a sum of four exponentials and a constant term, i.e.,

$$G(t) = A_0 + \sum_j A_j e^{-t/\tau_j}, \quad A_0 + \sum_j A_j = 1. \tag{4}$$

The parameters A_j and t_j depend on the emission scenario of CO_2. The higher the accumulated emissions, the higher the fraction that remains in the atmosphere; the fraction of a unit emission that remains in the atmosphere when the atmosphere-ocean equilibrium is established, is as high as 30% for an emission scenario which stabilizes atmospheric concentrations at twice the pre-industrial level (Caldeira and Kasting, 1993). We use parameter values for the MRH-model that correspond to rather low accumulated emissions (a step function increase

of the pre-industrial atmospheric CO_2 concentration by a factor 1.25). We have, $A_0 = 0.131$, $A_1 = 0.201$, $A_2 = 0.321$, $A_3 = 0.249$, $A_4 = 0.098$, $\tau_1 = 363$ years, $\tau_2 = 73.6$, $\tau_3 = 17.3$ years and $\tau_4 = 1.9$ years (Maier-Reimer and Hasselman, 1987).

The more simple representation of the carbon cycle given by Eq. (3) could also be useful, but then the parameters β and δ should be determined by a least square fit to the MRH-model. Depending on the time perspective chosen, we get different values for the parameters β and δ. This aspect was investigated in Azar (1995) and we get $\beta \approx 0.4$ and $\delta \approx 0.001$ for a time horizon of a thousand years and $\beta \approx 0.56$ and $\delta \approx 0.003$ for a time horizon of 400 years. In his DICE-model, Nordhaus (1993a) puts $\beta = 0.64$ and $\delta = 0.008$ which is a reasonable approximation only for the first couple of centuries. However, over longer time horizons, Nordhaus's choice significantly underestimates the atmospheric retention of CO_2. This aspect is clearly shown in Fig. 1, where the retention ratio of CO_2 in the atmosphere for the model used by Nordhaus is compared with the full MRH-model.

It should be noted that a change in Nordhaus's choice of representation of the carbon cycle so that it more accurately reflects the long-term properties of the MRH-model would only marginally change the optimal emission rate in *his* model since the long-term aspects of the carbon cycle, and hence the

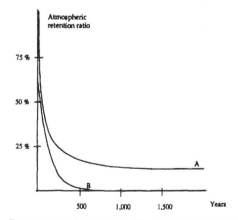

Fig. 1. Atmospheric retention of CO_2. Plot A represents the MRH-model and plot B Nordhaus's parameter values.

long-term costs of global warming, are anyway made negligible by his choice of discount rate. This aspect has also been stressed by Price (1995).

3. The choice of discount rate

The discount rate is most often taken to be constant in applied economic studies. This might be relevant on shorter time scales, but for longer time scales it is usually not. A constant discount rate should only be seen as a special case of the more general case where the discount rate is allowed to vary. This more general method of discounting has been discussed by Sterner (1994) and Azar (1995).

There are two different approaches to the choice of discount rate: one is based on the opportunity cost of capital (the marginal rate of return on investment) and the other is given by the social rate of time preference (SRTP). In an idealized economy, these two approaches yield the same discount rate, but in the real world a gap between the two exists. There are several reasons for this gap and they are analyzed at length in various references, e.g., Lind et al. (1982) and references therein. See also Arrow (1966), Bradford (1975) and Norgaard and Howarth (1991) for discounting in general, and Cline (1992a), Nordhaus (1994), Lind (1995) and Schelling (1995) for discounting in the context of climate change.

In this paper, we will base the discount rate on the social rate of time preference. It is composed of two components: the expectation that we will be richer in the future, and pure time preference. It is normally assumed that marginal utility is a decreasing function of consumption. This means that we get more utility for the first unit of consumption than the second, and so on. If income is expected to grow over time, the assumption of decreasing marginal utility implies that an additional unit of consumption $\Delta c(t)$ at time t is less worth than if it had been consumed today. The pure time preference is often rationalized in terms of impatience and uncertainty about the future existence of humankind.

These two reasons for discounting are made explicit in the so-called Ramsey rule,

$$r(t) = \gamma(c(t)) \frac{\dot{c}(t)}{c(t)} + \rho \tag{5}$$

where $c(t)$ is the per capita consumption, ρ is the pure rate of time preference [4] and γ is the negative of the elasticity of marginal utility of consumption, i.e.,

$$\gamma(c) = -U''(c)c/U'(c). \tag{6}$$

In the literature, γ is also referred to as the coefficient of relative inequality aversion and the coefficient of relative risk aversion. Thus, the higher the value for γ, the more risk and inequality averse we are. In Section 4, 5 we will vary γ in order to analyze the impact that this parameter has on the marginal cost of CO_2 emissions. It will be shown that the higher the value for this parameter, the less relevant are economic models of climate change that do not consider the global intragenerational distribution of income.

The term $\gamma g(t)$, where $g(t)$ is the relative per capita growth in consumption, could be referred to as *growth* discounting; we discount an income or a cost, not because of its position in time per se, but because we expect to be richer at the time when it occurs. The second reason for discounting, expressed by the term ρ, could be referred to as *time* or *utility* discounting, we discount a cost or an income solely because its position in time, no matter how rich or poor we are at that time.

The present value function is given by integration over time of Eq. (5). We get

$$V(t) = \exp\left\langle -\int_0^t [\gamma(c(\tau))\dot{c}(\tau)/c(\tau) + \rho]\,d\tau \right\rangle$$

$$= e^{-\rho t} \cdot \frac{U'(c(t))}{U'(c(0))}. \tag{7}$$

Thus if the economy stops growing, the only reason for discounting would be pure time preference, ρ. It should be noted that Eq. (7) is general enough to take into account possible reductions in per capita income in the future. If $\rho = 0$ and if we were to become poorer in the future (on a per capita basis), the present value function, $V(t)$, would be larger

---

[4] In the literature, ρ is often assumed constant over time despite the fact that there is no compelling reason why it should be constant, if it is not put equal to zero.

C. Azar, T. Sterner / Ecological Economics 19 (1996) 169–184   175

than unity, and this is equivalent to using a negative discount rate.

3.1. Constant relative risk aversion

Now, assume that the utility function is given by the so-called constant relative risk aversion (CRRA) functions, i.e.,

$$U(c(t)) = \begin{cases} (c(t))^{1-\gamma}/(1-\gamma) & \text{for} \quad \gamma > 0, \\ \ln(c(t)) & \text{for} \quad \gamma = 1. \end{cases}$$
(8)

Inserting Eq. (8) into Eq. (7) and assuming equal relative growth rates in WI and global consumption gives us the present value function as

$$V(t) = e^{-\rho t} \left(\frac{P(t)}{P(0)} \right)^{\gamma} \left(\frac{Y(0)}{Y(t)} \right)^{\gamma}.$$
(9)

Here $P(t)$ represent the global population at time t.

3.2. Numerical calculations

In Fig. 2, we have plotted the present value function for four different cases: in two of them, the discount rates are constant over time, and we get exponentially decaying present value functions; in the other two we have put the pure rate of time preference equal to zero and the present value function is declining solely because one is expected to get richer in the future (but with declining growth

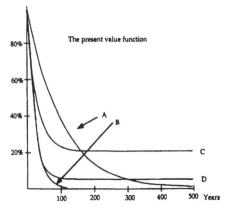

Fig. 2. The present value function. In plots A and B the discount rates are constant and equal to 1% per year and 5% per year, respectively. In plots C and D, we have assumed per capita consumption to grow logistically, and put the rate of time preference equal to zero. In both plot C and plot D the initial per capita growth rate in consumption is equal to 3% and the final per capita consumption is five times higher than the initial per capita consumption. The difference between plot C and plot D is explained by the different values for γ in plot C, $\gamma = 1$ and in plot D, $\gamma = 2$. The initial discount rate in case C is given by the per capita growth rate, i.e., 3%/year. The discount rate in case D is twice the discount rate in case C.

rates over time). Note the drastic impact that the two different methods of discounting have in the long run. This is extremely important for problems like global warming.

Another way to illustrate the effects of declining

Table 1
Share of first century in the value of a thousand years of constant costs

Growth pattern	Growth parameter [a]	Carrying capacity [a]	$\rho = 0\%$	$\rho = 0.1\%$	$\rho = 1.0\%$
Logistic (decline)	3%	0.5	8.6%	13%	58%
None	0	1	10%	15%	63%
Logistic	3%	2	13%	19%	70%
Logistic	3%	10	30%	40%	87%
Logistic	5%	10	24%	33%	85%
Logistic	3%	100	75%	82%	97%
Exponential	3%	∞	95%	95%	98%
Exponential	5%	∞	99%	99%	100%

[a] The logistic growth function is defined by Eq. (21). The growth parameter is given by a_γ and the carrying capacity is given by Y_∞. The carrying capacity is expressed as a factor of the present WI. Note that the growth parameter is not equal to the growth rate. The growth rate with a carrying capacity of twice the present income and a growth parameter of 3% will actually be 1.5%! The growth rate when the carrying capacity is half the present income is negative. In the calculations above, the marginal elasticity of utility γ is put equal to unity and the population growth is put equal to zero.

176   *C. Azar, T. Sterner / Ecological Economics 19 (1996) 169–184*

discount rates, is to calculate how we value the first century's costs as a fraction of total costs throughout the next thousand years. Table 1 summarizes the effect of choosing different carrying capacities (maximum values for WI) and growth parameters on the way we value the share of first century in a millennium of *constant* annual costs. The second row, third column, gives us a good starting point: With zero growth and zero rate of pure time preference we would simply value the first century at its share of the whole millennium: one tenth. If we combine this steady state with time preference then the share of our attention focused on the first century increases to 15% with 0.1%/year and all the way to 63% with 1%/year pure time preference. Thus a time preference of just 1%/year means that the first century is valued higher than the remaining nine centuries (which share a total of 37%).

Proceeding down through the table we see that the higher the final carrying capacity the greater the share in the present value accorded to the first century. The last two rows have exponential growth which can be seen as a special case of logistic growth but with an infinite carrying capacity. The results in these rows thus show the values obtained with 'ordinary' discounting at various rates (3, 3.1, 4, 5, 5.1 and 6%). They imply a virtual cut-off after a hundred years leaving no value to the last 9 centuries.

The very first row of Table 1 merits special mention: it illustrates the assumption that we have already overshot the Earth's carrying capacity and face a reduction in the scale of economic activity to half its present value. This is the situation in which the discounting logic works in reverse (negative effective discount rates). In this case we will get poorer in centuries to come and therefore a constant annual cost would be a greater problem in the distant than in the near future. For $\rho = 0$, the last 9 centuries of our millennium would thus account for more than their proportional share 91.4% while the first century would only account for 8.6%. As soon as we add pure time preference however we are back to the more customary habit of valuing the near future much higher than the distant one.

Finally, the attentive reader of Table 1 may ask why the figures of the 5th row are lower than those of the 4th. It might seem counterintuitive that higher

initial growth would give a lower share to the first century, contrary to our results for exponential growth (see rows 7–8) but is explained by the characteristics of logistic growth: the final level is the same (ten times the present) but with 5% it is attained faster so that in the first century there will be higher income levels. After two centuries income levels are practically the same. Thus the first century will be more heavily discounted relative to the rest with 5% than with 3% growth parameters.

3.3. Pure time preference

Individuals may have a pure time preference. An individual might for example prefer 100 USD today to 120 USD next year (even if the inflation rate would be zero). This can however not be taken as an argument that this individual's pure rate of time preference is 20% or more for all issues and all time periods. He or she might at the same time be very concerned about environmental impacts of radioactive waste that might occur hundreds of thousands of years from now. This can be taken as an argument that individual pure rates of time preference are not constant for different types of issues and for different time periods.

Rawls (1972) has argued that it is irrational for an individual to use a pure rate of time preference. But even if individuals would have a positive pure rate of time preference, it does not imply that society should have a positive pure rate of time preference. One reason is that the probability that each individual will die, is much higher than the probability that a whole society or the entire humankind will go extinct. Another is that individuals might be impatient whereas impatience on behalf of society as a whole is much more questionable.

The choice of pure time preference is a question of value judgements. At a societal level there is no good ethical justification for using a pure rate of time preference larger than zero. This position has been taken by several economists and philosophers, such as Sidgwick (1907), Ramsey (1928), Spash and d'Arge (1989), Broome (1992), Cline (1992a), Solow (1992), Eriksson (1994) and others.

Nordhaus (1993b) writes that "most economists and social philosophers find it hard to defend a pure rate of time preference above zero in the abstract, although the contingency of future generations has been used as a justification for discounting the distant future''. On the other hand, the contingency of future generations could only justify very low values for the pure rate of time preference.

Nevertheless, Nordhaus uses 3%/year in his DICE-model. He defends this value on the basis of the observed 'historical savings data and interests rates' (Nordhaus, 1992, p. 15). But, as discussed above, the fact that individual market behavior reveals values for the pure rate of time preference in the order of a couple of percent, cannot be translated into an argument for society to use a pure rate of time preference larger than zero.

Furthermore, the 'historical' records refer to a time period of a couple of decades. They might apply to the last century, but this has been a period of exceptional growth and is not suitable for forecasting rates over the next centuries, which is the time period relevant for the greenhouse effect.

Since the observed historical or the projected market interest rates consist of both pure time preference and the expectation that we will be richer in the future, the discount rate used in economic models of climate change should be lower than the projected market discount rate, if one believes that the pure rate of time preference should be put equal or close to zero.

The use of a lower discount rate than that observed, could be seen as a way of internalizing a market failure. Since future generations are not present in the market, their demand for various goods, including a stable climate, is not properly expressed. Thus putting the pure rate of time preference equal to zero when intergenerational matters are at stake, would be a way of getting prices right (for humanity, not just the present generation).

3.4. Pure rate of 'distance' preference – an analogy

The main argument for the use of a positive pure rate of time preference is that this is what individuals use in market transactions. In analogy, this argument could be used for the introduction of a pure rate of 'distance' preference since it is also true that individuals tend to care more for their relatives, their neighbors and their countrymen, than for people living in distant countries. A social planner would then define his global instantaneous welfare function by

$$W = \sum_i e^{-k_d x_i} U_i(c_i),$$ (10)

where x_i is the 'distance' (spatially, culturally or socially) to individual i and k_d is the rate of distance preference, i.e., the factor determining how much we should discount remote people's utilities per unit of distance. One can only imagine the reactions the discounting of distant people would have if it had been inserted into economic optimization models, for example models dealing with the cost of global climate change. The only value for k_d, the pure rate of 'distance' discounting, that everybody (now living) would agree on is zero. In the same manner, one could say that the only value for the pure rate of time preference, that everybody (now living plus unborn) can agree on is, once again, zero (Rawls, 1972). The sole reason why the discounting of future utility, but not distant utility, can prevail is that future generations are not around to claim their rights.

3.5. Conclusions

Now, we have developed the three functional relationships needed in order to calculate the marginal cost of CO_2 emissions. We insert Eqs. (2), (4) and (9) into (1) and get the following expression for the marginal cost of CO_2 emissions.

$$MC_1 = \frac{k}{m_p} \left(\frac{Y(0)}{P(0)} \right)^\gamma \int_0^T G(t) Y^{1-\gamma}(t) P^\gamma(t)$$
$$\times e^{-\rho t} dt.$$ (11)

We note that the cost is independent of the trajectory of CO_2 concentrations in the atmosphere, even if damage is assumed to be non-linear in temperature change. Furthermore, we note that for $\gamma = 1$, which corresponds to a logarithmic welfare function, the expression becomes independent of future growth scenarios. Eq. (11) is numerically evaluated in Section 5.

4. Considering the unequal distribution of income

In the analysis carried out so far, we have assumed that all citizens of the world are average citizens, in the sense that they are all equally rich

178 *C. Azar, T. Sterner / Ecological Economics 19 (1996) 169–184*

and that they will be affected equally by global warming. In reality, climate change will occur in a world where some countries are rich and others are poor. Furthermore, the poor countries are not only expected to suffer the most severe consequences of global warming, they are also, due to their lack of financial resources, less capable of coping with climate change.

In this section, we will therefore take unequal income distribution explicitly into consideration. This can be done in a fashion that is exactly analogous to the approach taken in Section 3, since we there used the fact that future generations are expected to be richer as an argument for discounting the value of costs that befall them. The reason is decreasing marginal utility of money and for the same reason we can argue that a given (say one dollar) cost which affects a poor person (in a poor country) should *be valued as a higher welfare cost than an equivalent cost affecting an average OECD citizen*. Note that even with optimistic growth scenarios the average Bengali citizen is likely to be poorer in 50 or even a 100 years than the average North American today so that conventional discounting of his/her future costs would not be valid.

Such weighting of costs is not necessary if those who will suffer the consequences of climate change, are compensated. But since it is likely that no compensation will be paid, [5] it is necessary to weight individual costs with respect to (individual) income to obtain some measure of the aggregate welfare loss. This is in principle recognized in welfare economics, but it is generally not done in the context of climate change. Two exceptions here are Ayres and Walter (1991) and d'Arge and Spash (1991).

Nordhaus (1994, p. 55) writes that a difficult issue in his own calculations is "the assumption that a dollar loss in a low-income country is the same as a dollar loss in a high-income country". Also Cline (1992a, p. 85) recognizes that this aspect is important, but without including it in the analysis. The methodology developed below is based on Azar (1994b).

---

[5] In many cases it will not even be possible to compensate victims of climate change. This aspect has been stressed by Spash (1994).

4.1. Formal approach

Here we develop the weight functions that will be used when aggregating the costs across different regions (with different income). We assume, for simplicity, that there are only two regions, one rich and one poor, and that the income in each region is equally distributed. The two groups will be denoted by r and p, respectively. Furthermore, we denote the population in each region by $P_r(t)$ and $P_p(t)$. The individuals in each group are identical, and the per capita income in each group is given by $y_r(t)$ and $y_p(t)$, respectively.

The aggregate welfare function, $W(t)$, can be written as a sum of the utility functions, $u(y(t))$, multiplied by the population in each region, viz.

$$W(t) = P_r(t)u(y_r(t)) + P_p(t)u(y_p(t)), \qquad (12)$$

Note, that the level of income in each region is the projected income when the impact of climate change has been taken into account. *Here we want to evaluate how global welfare will change if an additional unit of CO_2 is released to the atmosphere. This change in welfare will then be converted into monetary terms.*

Let $dC_r(t)$ and $dC_p(t)$ denote an infinitesimal damage at time t in region r and p, respectively, due to an infinitesimal emission of CO_2, dm_0, at present, $t = 0$. Then, the corresponding per capita damage in each region is given by $dC_r(t)/P_r(t)$ and $dC_p(t)/P_p(t)$, respectively, and we can express the marginal change in welfare at time t, as

$$\frac{dW(t)}{dm_0}$$

$$= -\left[\frac{dC_r(t)}{dm_0} u'(y_r(t)) + \frac{dC_p(t)}{dm_0} u'(y_p(t)) \right]. \qquad (13)$$

Now, we want to convert this expression for the loss of welfare into monetary terms. This can be done in several different ways. Here, we take the approach that Eq. (13) should be normalized by the marginal utility of income in the rich world at present. The main reason for this is that estimates of the costs of reducing the emissions are generally expressed in 'OECD-dollars', so our choice is necessary if we want to compare our results with studies of the cost of reducing the emissions that are borne by the industrial countries.

An alternative way of converting Eq. (13) into monetary terms would be to normalize it with the marginal utility of global average income. This approach was taken by Azar (1994b), and it implies that the costs in the rich world would be weighted with a factor lower than unity and, hence, significantly lower aggregate cost estimates would be obtained (a factor of 3^{γ}, given the distribution of income assumed below). However, this approach is less useful since the result of such a calculation would not be directly comparable to the costs of reducing the emissions in an industrialized country (since these costs are unweighted).

Dividing equation (13) with the marginal utility of income in the rich region at present, gives the present value of the weighted marginal cost at time t due to a unit emission at present, $V_C(t)$, as

$$V_C(t)$$
$$= \left[\frac{dC_r(t)}{dm_0} \frac{u'(y_r(t))}{u'(y_r(0))} + \frac{dC_p(t)}{dm_0} \frac{u'(y_p(t))}{u'(y_r(0))} \right] e^{-\rho t},$$
$$(14)$$

where the pure rate of time preference has been included for the sake of generality.

Eq. (14) can be rewritten as

$$V_C(t) = \frac{dC_r(t)}{dm_0} \frac{u'(y_r(t))}{u'(y_r(0))} e^{-\rho t}$$
$$+ \frac{u'(y_p(0))}{u'(y_r(0))} \left[\frac{dC_p(t)}{dm_0} \frac{u'(y_p(t))}{u'(y_p(0))} e^{-\rho t} \right],$$
$$(14')$$

where each term can be interpreted as the present value of the marginal cost at time t in each region and the factor in front of the bracket in the second term is the weight factor converting losses in the poor region into their 'rich world equivalents'.

Eq. (14) can also be rewritten as

$$V_C(t) = \left[\frac{dC_r(t)}{dm_0} + \frac{u'(y_p(t))}{u'(y_r(t))} \frac{dC_p(t)}{dm_0} \right]$$
$$\times \frac{u'(y_r(t))}{u'(y_r(0))} e^{-\rho t},$$
$$(14'')$$

where the term in the bracket is the weighted sum of the marginal cost in the two regions at time t, and the subsequent factor is the present value function in the rich world.

Note, that this method of weighting costs is general enough to take into account possible changes in the global distribution of income. Assume, for instance, that global income would become equally distributed when the damage from climate change will occur at time $t > t_1$, i.e., $y_r(t) = y_p(t)$ for $t > t_1$, then weighting would obviously be unnecessary. Costs could be calculated as the sum of the unweighted costs in the two regions and discounted by the present value function in the rich world, and this is exactly what one obtains from Eq. (14).

Now, integration over Eq. (14) yields the generalized marginal cost of CO_2 emissions, viz.,

$$MC_2 = \int_0^T V_C(t) \, dt$$
$$= \int_0^T \left[\frac{dC_r(t)}{dm_0} \frac{u'(y_r(t))}{u'(y_r(0))} \right.$$
$$\left. + \frac{dC_p(t)}{dm_0} \frac{u'(y_p(t))}{u'(y_r(0))} \right] e^{-\rho t} \, dt. \quad (15)$$

Here index 2 denotes that weighting has been done, and that two different groups of income have been included. Eq. (15) is easily generalized into N groups of income, and, since the distribution of income is highly skewed also within the rich and the poor countries, such a generalization would further increase the cost estimates.

We assume, in analogy with Eq. (2), that the marginal damage is proportional to the level of income and the fraction of a unit emission of CO_2 that remains in the atmosphere at time t, and we assume further, for illustrative purposes, that the proportionality factor is the same in each region, viz.

$$\frac{dC_i(t)}{dm_0} = \frac{k}{m_p} Y_i(t) \frac{dm_h(t)}{dm_0} = \frac{k}{m_p} Y_i(t) G(t),$$
$$(16)$$

where index $i = \{r, p\}$; Y_i represents the aggregate income in region r or p, respectively, and k is the fraction of aggregate income that is lost for a CO_2-equivalent doubling and it is assumed to be equal to 1.5%. The function $G(t)$ is defined by Eq. (4).

The assumption that the same fraction of income is lost in each region may imply an underestimate of the importance of the unequal distribution of income, since k is likely to be larger in poor countries, e.g., Bangladesh, than in richer countries, e.g., Sweden. The reason for expecting higher losses in poorer regions, at least as a fraction of total income, is that developing economies are more vulnerable to climate variability (e.g., a larger share of their economy is directly exposed to climatic events). However, even under the (optimistic) assumption that poorer countries will not be affected harder than richer countries, on a relative basis, it is shown that distributional considerations are important.

Assuming CRRA-utility functions (given by Eq. (8)) and inserting Eqs. (4) and (16) into Eq. (15), we get the generalized marginal cost of CO_2 emissions as

$$
MC_2 = \frac{k}{m_p} \left(\frac{Y_r(0)}{P_r(0)} \right)^\gamma \int_0^T G(t) e^{-\rho t}
$$
$$
\times \left[Y_r^{1-\gamma}(t) P_r^\gamma(t) + Y_p^{1-\gamma}(t) P_p^\gamma(t) \right] dt.
\tag{17}
$$

Finally, we note that if the per capita income in the two groups were identical, then Eq. (17) would be reduced to the case where the distribution of income has not been taken into account.

5. Scenarios, parameter values and results

We have chosen the following logistic growth scenarios for the world population and for WI:

$$
P(t) = \frac{P_\infty}{1 + [(P_\infty - P_0)/P_0] \cdot \exp(-a_p t)},
\tag{18}
$$

and

$$
Y(t) = \frac{Y_\infty}{1 + [(Y_\infty - Y_0)/Y_0] \cdot \exp(-a_Y t)}.
\tag{19}
$$

Here, a_p and a_Y are the growth rates for small populations and small WI, respectively, and P_∞ and Y_∞ are the global population and WI at infinite time, respectively, and P_0 and Y_0 the corresponding population and WI at the present time.

Parameter values for population growth are taken from Nordhaus's DICE-model: $a_p = 0.02$, $P_0 = 5.7$ billion and $P_\infty = 10.6$ billion people (Nordhaus, 1993a). For the gross world product (WI), we assume $Y(0) = 2 \cdot 10^{13}$ USD/year, $Y_\infty = 8 \cdot Y_0$ and $a_Y = 0.03$, which makes the initial growth rate in WI equal to 2.6%/year.

We assume that the populations in the rich group and in the poor group can be written as constant fractions of the total population, i.e., $P_r(t) = x_r P(t)$ and $P_p(t) = x_p P(t)$. The fractions x_r and x_p can be assumed constant without loss of generality, since we can always vary the income levels in the different groups. Here we put $x_r = 0.25$ and $x_p = 0.75$. Assume, further, that the total income in the different groups can be expressed as time dependent fractions of aggregate global income. We put $Y_r(t) = z_r(t) Y(t)$ and $Y_p(t) = z_p(t) Y(t)$.

We use three different scenarios for the global distribution of income (see Table 2). In the first, inequalities grow over time, in the second inequalities remain as they are today, and in the third scenario inequalities are reduced and eventually disappear.

Finally, we vary γ in the range $0 \le \gamma \le 3$. Empirical studies find γ centered in the range $1 \le \gamma \le 2$ (see, e.g., Blanchard and Fischer (1989) and Auerbach and Kotlikoff (1987)), but we include a wider

Table 2
Scenarios for the global distribution of income

Scenario	Income in the poor world	$z_p(t)$ [a]
A. Inequality increases	decreases from 25% to 15% of global income	$0.15 + 0.10e^{-0.01t}$
B. Inequality unchanged	remains constant at 25% of global income.	0.25.
C. Inequality decreases	increases from 25% to 75% of global income	$0.75 - 0.5e^{-0.02t}$

[a] Note that $z_r(t) = 1 - z_p(t)$. We have assumed that 75% of the global income is presently consumed by the richest fourth of the global population.

C. Azar, T. Sterner / Ecological Economics 19 (1996) 169–184 181

Table 3
The marginal cost of CO_2 emissions [a]

	The pure rate of time preference, ρ.			
	0%/year	0.1%/year	1%/year	3%/year
The marginal cost of CO_2 emissions, MC_1	85–200	75–140	32–33	13–13
The marginal cost of CO_2 emissions, MC_2	260–590	230–410	95–98	39–39

[a] In USD/ton C. The lower value in each box corresponds to a time horizon of 300 years, the upper value to a time horizon of 1000 years. In the first row, the distribution of income is not taken into account. In the second row, we have included this aspect, and assumed that the distribution of income remains constant over time, i.e., we have used scenario B. The calculations have been carried out for a logarithmic utility function, i.e., the negative of the elasticity of marginal utility, γ, is put equal to unity.

range for illustrative purposes. Cline (1992a) uses $\gamma = 1.5$ and Nordhaus (1993a) puts $\gamma = 1$. Values for the parameters $T = 300$ years, $\rho = 0$, $k = 1.5\%$, $m_p = 600$ Gton C and the fraction of a unit emission at present that remains in the atmosphere at time t, $G(t)$, are given and motivated earlier in the paper.

5.1. Results

In Fig. 3, we plot MC_1 and MC_2 as a function of γ for three different scenarios for the distribution of income (A, B and C, see Table 2). The curve for the marginal cost of CO_2 emissions in the case when no distribution of income has been taken into account is denoted by D.

The marginal cost of CO_2 emissions

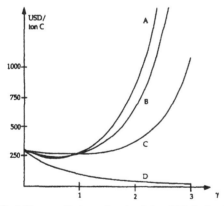

Fig. 3. The *generalized* cost of a unit emission of CO_2 is plotted as a function of γ in four cases. In plot A, B and C, the inequality situation is worsened, unchanged, and improved, respectively. In plot D, income distribution is not considered. The higher the value for γ, the higher is the discount rate, but also the inequality aversion.

We see that the marginal cost, MC_1, is a decreasing function of γ. This is due to the fact that higher values for γ imply higher discount rates. But we also see that when considering the global distribution of income in the calculations, higher values for γ will offset this dependence, since higher values for γ also imply a higher degree of inequality aversion.

Finally, we note that the cost estimates coincide for $\gamma = 0$ and this is explained by the fact that whenever $\gamma = 0$, which is equivalent to a utility function that is linear in income, the discount rate becomes zero and the weight factors equal to one. For a constant distribution of income (and the assumed values in case B), the ratio between MC_2 and MC_1 is given by $0.75 + 0.25 \cdot 9^\gamma$. For $\gamma = 1$, this means that our weighting procedure increases the total cost estimate by a factor of 3, which means that the cost of a CO_2 equivalent doubling could be expressed as 4.5% of WI.

One important implication for policy analysis is that the higher the value for γ, the less valid are the policy conclusions obtained from models where no distribution of income has been taken into account. [6]

5.2. Pure rate of time preference and the time horizon – a sensitivity check

The marginal cost of CO_2 emissions is also evaluated for different values of the pure rate of time

---

[6] In a comment to the critique that has been directed towards Nordhaus's use of a pure rate of time preference equal to 3%/year, Nordhaus (1993a) writes that while lowering the value of the pure rate of time preference and at the same time increasing the value of the coefficient of inequality aversion so as to keep the (initial) discount rate unchanged, only modest changes in the optimal policy occurs. This procedure is however questionable because of the observation above that the higher the value for γ, the more important it is to take into account the distribution of income.

182   *C. Azar, T. Sterner / Ecological Economics 19 (1996) 169–184*

preference (see Table 3). It is shown that the value of the pure rate of time preference is of crucial importance for the cost analysis.

It is clearly shown that the choice of time horizon becomes very important for low values for the pure rate of time preference, whereas it does not influence the cost analysis at all for $\rho = 3\%$/year. This means that more research should be put into evaluating the costs associated with the long-term consequences associated with climate change.

6. Conclusions

In this paper we have discussed some aspects of how to calculate the marginal cost of CO_2 emissions. This is such a large issue that it cannot in its entirety be covered in one paper. We have for instance not made any estimates of our own of the economic damage caused by increasing CO_2 levels in the atmosphere. On this point, we have accepted the conventional estimates in spite of the fact that they do not take into account the risk of truly catastrophic developments. We have instead concentrated on three issues: firstly, the retention of CO_2 in the atmosphere, secondly the method for discounting future costs and thirdly the unequal distribution of world income.

With regard to the retention of carbon in the atmosphere we note that the parameter values used by Nordhaus (1993a) imply that the atmospheric retention of an additional unit of carbon is practically negligible after a couple of hundred years which is not consistent with the ocean-atmospheric models of the carbon cycle. Instead, we use a model by Maier-Reimer and Hasselman (1987) which better captures the long-run aspects of the carbon cycle.

With respect to discounting we show that there is no rationale for a constant discount factor. Instead we decompose the discount rate into its two components: pure time preference and the results of economic growth. We argue that the pure time preference should be zero or very low and thus that economic growth is the main reason for discounting future costs and benefits. In the very long run with which we are dealing here, we expect the rate of economic growth to decline as the world economy reaches some level of sustainable activity (which

may be above or below the current level but is definitely not infinite which is the reason why exponential growth cannot go on forever). *Taken together these two factors imply that the discount rate will fall over time and we show that this will increase the aggregate cost of global warming very considerably.*

In Section 4, we discussed the impact of the unequal distribution of global income on the cost analysis. The world was divided into two regions, one rich and one poor, and we conservatively assumed the damage of climate change to be proportional to the income in each of the two regions. It was shown that the unequal distribution of income in the world has a considerable impact on the cost analysis. This conclusion is further reinforced if the damage proportionality factor is assumed to be higher in the poorer countries and if the world is divided into more than two regions (since that would capture the unequal distribution of income within the developing countries).

For a logarithmic utility function and a time horizon in the range 300 to 1000 years, we estimate the marginal cost of CO_2 emissions to lie in the range 260–590 USD/ton C, when costs occurring in the poor regions of the world are weighted by the inverse of income. These estimates are significantly higher than Nordhaus's estimate of 5 USD/ton C (Nordhaus, 1993a). This difference is almost entirely due to the fact that we have weighted costs in poorer regions so that they more properly reflect actual welfare losses in these regions, that we have put the pure rate of time preference equal to zero whereas Nordhaus uses a value of 3%/year (see Table 3), and a more accurate model of the carbon cycle.

The marginal cost of CO_2 emissions estimated in this paper is large enough to motivate strong reductions in the use of fossil fuels. Estimates of the marginal cost of CO_2 reduction vary greatly depending on the methodology of calculation (top-down versus bottom-up). Nordhaus (1993a) uses a top-down approach, which gives much higher estimates than the bottom-up approach, and estimates the marginal cost of CO_2 reduction to be zero initially and then to rise steadily to 200 USD/ton C for a reduction of 3 Gton C/year (which corresponds to around half of the present emissions). Much lower costs are reported by bottom-up modelers. See Grubb et al. (1993) and Wilson and Swisher (1993) for well-written surveys of the costs of reducing CO_2 emissions. Hence, even when comparing with the higher range estimates of the costs of reducing CO_2 emissions, our calculations show that economic considerations can motivate large reductions of the global emissions of CO_2.

Acknowledgements

We want to thank Olof Johansson for fruitful discussions and Dean Abrahamson, Karl-Erik Eriksson and Kristian Lindgren for careful reading of an earlier version of the manuscript. The financial support by the Bank of Sweden Tercentenary Foundation is gratefully acknowledged.

References

Arrhenius, S., 1896. On the influence of carbonic acid in the air upon the temperature of the ground. London Edinburgh Dublin. Phil. Mag. J. Sci., 5th Ser., April: 237–276.

Arrow, K.J., 1966. Discounting and Public Investment Criteria, In: ed. A.V. Kneese and S.C. Smith, Water Research. John Hopkins University Press, Baltimore, MD.

Auerbach, A.J. and Kotlikoff, J., 1987. Dynamic Fiscal Policy. Cambridge University Press, Cambridge.

Ayres, R.U. and Walter, J., 1991. The greenhouse effect: Damages, costs and abatement. Environm. Resource Econ., 1: 237–270.

Azar, C., 1994a. The marginal cost of CO_2 emissions. Energy Int. J., 19: 1255–1261.

Azar, C., 1994b. Economic theory and the greenhouse effect. Licentiate thesis. Institute of Physical Resource Theory, Chalmers University of Technology, Göteborg.

Azar, C., 1995. Long-term environmental problems. Economic measures and physical indicators. Ph.D. thesis. Institute of Physical Resource Theory, Chalmers University of Technology, Göteborg.

Booth, D.E., 1994. Ethics and the limits of environmental economics. Ecol. Econ., 9: 241–252.

Broome, J., 1992. Counting the Cost of Global Change. The White Horse Press, Cambridge.

Blanchard, O.J. and Fischer, S., 1989. Lectures on Macroeconomics. MIT Press, Cambridge, MA.

Bradford, D.F., 1975. Constraints on government investment opportunities and the choice of discount rate. Am. Econ. Rev., 65: 887–899.

Caldeira, A. and Kasting, B., 1993. Insensitivity of global warming potentials to carbon dioxide emission scenarios. Nature, 366: 251–253.

Cline, W.R., 1992a. The Economics of Global Warming. Institute of International Economics, Washington, DC.

Cline, W.R., 1992b. Optimal Carbon Emissions over Time: Experiments with the Nordhaus DICE-model. Institute of International Economics, Washington, DC.

d'Arge, R.C. and Spash, C., 1991. Economic strategies for mitigating the impacts of climate change on future generations, In: ed. R. Costanza, Ecological Economics – The Science and Management of Sustainability. Columbia University Press, New York, NY, pp. 367–383.

Ekins, P., 1995. Rethinking the costs related to global warming. A Survey of the issues. Environm. Resource Econ., 6: 231–277.

Eriksson, K.E., 1994. On discount, temporal justice, sustainability and limited foresight. Rich. Econ., 48: 341–355.

Fankhauser, S., 1994. The social costs of greenhouse gas emissions, an expected value approach. Energy J., 15: 157–184.

Fankhauser, S., 1995. Valuing Climate Change. The Economics of the Greenhouse. Earthscan, London.

Grubb, M., Edmonds, J., ten Brink, P. and Morrison, M., 1993. The cost of limiting fossil fuel CO_2 emissions: A survey and an analysis. Ann. Rev. Energy Environ., 18: 397–478.

Haraden, J., 1993. An updated shadow price for CO_2. Energy Int. J., 18: 303–307.

IPCC, 1990. Ed. J.T. Houghton, G.J. Jenkins and J.J. Ephraums, Climate Change: The IPCC Scientific Assessment. Cambridge University Press, Cambridge.

IPCC, 1992. Ed. J.T. Houghton, B.A. Callander and S.K. Varney, Climate Change 1992: The Supplementary Report to the IPCC Scientific Assessment. Cambridge University Press, Cambridge.

IPCC, 1995. Climate Change 1994. Radiative Forcing of the Climate Change and An Evalution of the IPCC IS92 Emission Scenarios. Cambridge University Press, Cambridge.

Leggett, J., 1990. The nature of the greenhouse threat, in: ed. J. Leggett, Global Warming: The Greenpeace Report. Oxford University Press, Oxford.

Lind, R.C. et al., 1982. Discounting for Time and Risk in Energy Policy. John Hopkins University Press, Baltimore, MD.

Lind, R.C, 1995. Intergenerational equity, discounting, and the role of cost-benefit analysis in evaluating global climate policy. Energy Policy, 23: 379–390.

Maier-Reimer, E. and Hasselman, K., 1987. Transport and storage of CO_2 in the ocean – An inorganic ocean-circulation carbon cycle model. Climate Dyn., 2: 63–90.

Meyer, A., et al., 1995. Economics of climate change. Nature, 378: 433.

Nordhaus, W.D., 1991. To slow or not to slow: The economics of the greenhouse effect. Econ. J., 101: 920–937.

Nordhaus, W.D., 1992. Explaining the 'DICE': Background paper on dynamic integrated model of climate change and the economy. Yale University, New Haven, CT.

Nordhaus, W.D., 1993a. Rolling the DICE: An optimal transition path for controlling greenhouse gases. Resource Energy Econ., 15: 27–50.

Nordhaus, W.D., 1993b. How much should we invest in preserving our current climate. In: ed. H. Giersch, Economic Progress and Environmental Concern. Springer Verlag, Berlin, pp. 255–299.

184   *C. Azar, T. Sterner / Ecological Economics 19 (1996) 169–184*

Nordhaus, W.D., 1994. Managing the Global Commons. The Economics of Climate Change. MIT Press, Cambridge, MA.

Norgaard, R. and Howarth, R.B., 1991. Sustainability and discounting the future. In: ed. R. Costanza, Ecological Economics – The Science and Management of Sustainability. Columbia University Press, New York, NY, pp. 88–101.

Parry, I.W.H., 1993. Some estimates of the insurance value against climate change from reducing greenhouse gas emissions. Resource Energy Econ., 15: 99–106.

Price, C., 1995. Emissions, Concentrations and disappearing CO_2. Resource Energy Econ., 17: 87–97.

Pearce, F., 1995. Price of life sends temperatures soaring. New Scientist, 1/4-1995.

Peck, S.C. and Teisberg, T.J., 1992, CETA: A model for carbon emissions trajectory assessment. Energy J., 13: 55–77.

Ramsey, F.P., 1928. A mathematical theory of saving. Econ. J., 138: 543–549.

Rawls, J., 1972. A Theory of Justice. Oxford University Press.

Schelling, T.C., 1995. Intergenerational discounting. Energy Policy, 23: 395–402.

Sidgwick, H., 1907. The Methods of Ethics. Macmillan, London.

Solow, R., 1992. An almost practical step towards sustainability. An invited lecture on the occasion of the fortieth anniversary of Resources for the Future, Washington, DC, 8 October.

Spash, C.L. and d'Arge, R.C., 1989. The greenhouse effect and intergenerational transfers. Energy Policy, 17: 88–96.

Spash, C.L., 1994. Double CO_2 and beyond: Benefits, costs and compensation. Ecol. Econ., 10: 27–36.

Sterner, T., 1994. Discounting in a world of limited growth. Environm. Resource Econ., 4: 527–534.

Tol, R.S.J., 1995. The damage cost of climate change toward more comprehensive calculations. Environm. Resource Econ., 5: 353–374.

Wilson, D. and Swisher, J., 1993. Exploring the gap: Top-down versus bottom-up analyses of the cost of mitigating global warming. Energy Policy, 21: 249–263.

[17]

Climate Change and the Representative Agent

RICHARD B. HOWARTH

Environmental Studies Program, Dartmouth College, Hanover, New Hampshire 03755, USA

Accepted 28 October 1998

Abstract. The artifice of an infinitely-lived representative agent is commonly invoked to balance the present costs and future benefits of climate stabilization policies. Since actual economies are populated by overlapping generations of finite-lived persons, this approach begs important questions of welfare aggregation. This paper compares the results of representative agent and overlapping generations models that are numerically calibrated based on standard assumptions regarding climate-economy interactions. Under two social choice rules – Pareto efficiency and classical utilitarianism – the models generate closely similar simulation results. In the absence of policies to redistribute income between present and future generations, efficient rates of carbon dioxide emissions abatement rise from 15 to 20% between the years 2000 and 2105. Under classical utilitarianism, in contrast, optimal control rates rise from 48 to 79% this same period.

Key words: climate change, overlapping generations models

JEL classification: D9, Q2

1. Introduction

Overlapping generations models have emerged in recent years as an important framework in the theory of environmental management (Burton 1993; Mourmouras 1993; Marini and Scaramozzino 1995). A broad range of policy issues – natural resource scarcity, biodiversity conservation, ozone depletion, and climate change – involve both long term horizons and an asymmetric distribution of costs and benefits between present and future society. Overlapping generations models clarify the conceptual issues that surround such problems by drawing a clear distinction between intertemporal efficiency and intergenerational fairness as criteria for social choice (Howarth and Norgaard 1995).

Substantial progress has been made in the analysis of numerically calibrated overlapping generations models (Auerbach and Kotlikoff 1987). Applied studies of global environmental change, however, remain strongly focused on the representative agent model pioneered by Frank Ramsey (1928). In Ramsey models, the utility or welfare of a fictional infinitely-lived agent is discounted relative to the present to obtain a compressed representation of individual choices and/or social preferences concerning the distribution of welfare between present and future generations.

The factors favoring the use of representative agent models in policy analysis are both historical and computational in nature. Historically, representative agent models played the dominant role in the development and pedagogy of the theory of economic growth. Overlapping generations models, in contrast, have generally been limited to the consideration of special topics that cannot, in principle, be addressed in models lacking age-structured populations (Blanchard and Fischer 1989, ch. 3). Computationally, representative agent models allow the great convenience of characterizing competitive equilibria using the streamlined methods of dynamic optimization. This practice is premised on the correspondence between efficient resource allocations and competitive equilibria that is central to welfare economics.

Despite their comparative familiarity and convenience, however, representative agent models are grounded on a transparently false depiction of human demographics. Since actual economies are characterized by successive cohorts of finite-lived persons, representative agent models are at best a heuristic device for describing the behavior of more complex systems. And since theoretical studies have shown that overlapping generations models can exhibit behavioral patterns that are qualitatively different from those generated by seemingly homologous representative agent specifications (Geanakoplos 1987), the use of representative agent models in policy analysis would seem to require careful justification.

One approach to this problem is to consider the conditions under which representative agent models provide an exact replication of the behavior of corresponding models with overlapping generations. Howarth (1996), for example, considers the links between representative agent and overlapping generations models in the analysis of climate stabilization policies. He finds that representative agent models may be used to describe optimal paths for aggregate economic variables (consumption, investment, and greenhouse gas emissions) if:

(1) Individuals are time-neutral with utility functions that are logarithmic in consumption

(2) Decision-makers seek to maximize a social welfare function in which the relative weights attached to the well-being of successive age cohorts decline geometrically from generation to generation.

Under these conditions, the utility discount rates of representative agent models capture the degree of altruism present decision-makers hold towards future generation.

A second approach is to show that representative agent and overlapping generations models yield closely similar numerical results in cases where exact correspondence theorems are generally invalid. This approach acknowledges the information losses that arise when aggregate models are used to simulate the behavior of heterogeneous agents (Kirman 1992). Such losses, however, are offset by the gains in simplicity and tractability associated with the representative agent framework. These approximation errors, if putatively small, might safely be ignored in the process of model building and interpretation.

Manne (1996) and Stephan et al. (1997) compare the performance of representative agent and overlapping generations models that are numerically calibrated to simulate climate–economy interactions in a competitive intertemporal economy. Manne characterizes the efficient policy choices that arise when rates of time preference are chosen to replicate expected rates of economic growth. Stephan et al. (1997), in contrast, examine the consequences of two policy regimes – a *laissez faire* baseline and a case where a 100% *ad valorem* tax is levelled against fossil fuels – in a setting where agents make myopic short-run decisions. Both studies conclude that representative agent and overlapping generations models yield similar results when calibrated to produce similar rates of capital accumulation.

The present analysis extends these results based on an overlapping generations model of climate change and the world economy constructed by Howarth (1998). The analysis confirms the finding that representative agent models may, under certain conditions, be used to guide environmental policy choices when such models are suitably calibrated and interpreted. In this setting, however, the pure rate of time preference as it arises in representative agent models has no natural interpretation. The appropriate choice of this parameter requires explicit appeals to the distinction between individual time preference and social preferences concerning intergenerational distribution as captured in overlapping generations models (Burton 1993).

Moreover, the analysis concludes that representative agent models provide only partial insights regarding the policies required to support optimal resource allocations as competitive equilibria. Although such models may be used to approximate the Pigouvian taxes necessary to internalize the social costs of greenhouse gas emissions, they shed no light on the policy instruments required to achieve an optimal distribution of welfare between present and future generations. These results suggest a continued role for overlapping generations models in the climate change policy debate.

2. The Model

The analysis begins with a summary of Howarth's (1998) overlapping generations model of the links between climatic systems and the global economy. This model, which represents the interplay between producer behavior, consumer behavior, and government policies in a competitive market setting, is numerically calibrated to match the core empirical generalizations of Nordhaus' (1994) *Managing the Global Commons*. Since Nordhaus' work is perhaps the best-known and most cited contribution to the literature on the economics of climate change, this approach ensures that the results described here are comparable with those of other studies. For a discussion and critique of Nordhaus' empirical analysis, see Howarth and Monahan (1996).

2.1. PRODUCTION POSSIBILITIES

An aggregate consumption-investment good is produced at a sequence of dates $t = 0, 1, \ldots, \bar{t}$. Time is measured in 35-year increments beginning in the year 2000. The time horizon is taken to be long but finite ($\bar{t} \rightarrow \infty$), capturing the prevailing notion that social and economic systems will one day be extinguished through a large asteroid collision or the eventual exhaustion of the sun.

Gross world output at date t (Y_t) is determined by inputs of capital (K_t) and labor (N_t) according to the Cobb–Douglas production function:

$$Y_t = A_t K_t^{0.25} N_t^{0.75}. \tag{1}$$

Output is measured in trillion dollars per period;[1] the capital stock is measured in trillion dollars with an initial value of $56 trillion; and labor inputs are indexed in terms of total human population, measured in billions of persons. The output elasticities attached to capital (0.25) and labor (0.75) capture the stylized fact that labor income accounts for some three-quarters of economic activity. In this specification, A_t is a parameter that captures changes in the level of total factor productivity over time. Production is divided between consummation (C_t), investment, and capital depreciation so that:

$$C_t + K_{t+1} = Y_t + (1 - 0.1)^{35} K_t. \tag{2}$$

The capital stock depreciates at the rate of 10%/year.

Total factor productivity is represented by the equation:

$$\begin{aligned} A_t = &\ (235 - 142(0.739)^t) \\ &* (1 - 0.0133(T_t/3)^2) \\ &* (1 - 0.0686(1 - E_t/E_{0t})^{2.89}). \end{aligned} \tag{3}$$

The first term in this expression captures exogenous technological change which, all else being equal, leads productivity to improve by 153% over the long term with an initial growth rate of 1.1%/year. In the second term, T_t represents the increase in mean global temperature relative to the preindustrial norm, measured in degrees Celsius. Climate change imposes damages on the world economy that are proportional to the square of the temperature increase caused by human activities. A 3 °C temperature change reduces gross output by 1.33%.

The final term in the total factor productivity equation captures the cost of efforts to control carbon dioxide emissions, the principal cause of human-induced climate change. In the absence of abatement measures, carbon dioxide emissions, measured in billion tons-carbon per period, increase in proportion to economic activity according to:

$$E_{0t} = (0.181 + 0.189(0.622)^t) Y_t. \tag{4}$$

The emissions/gross output ratio falls by 51% over the long run with an initial growth rate of -0.55%/year. In equation (3), E_t measures *actual* carbon dioxide emissions so that $1 - E_t/E_{0t}$ measures the rate of *emissions abatement* relative to uncontrolled levels. Emissions abatement is costly undertaking that reduces gross output by 0.93% for a 50% control rate. These costs rise to 6.86% of gross output with the total elimination of emissions.

The final step in the description of production possibilities involves the impact of current carbon dioxide emissions on future climatic conditions. The model assumes that the atmospheric stock of carbon dioxide, measured in billion tons-carbon, is determined by the recurrence relation:

$$Q_{t+1} - 590 = 0.64E_t + (1 - 0.00833)^{35}(Q_t - 590). \tag{5}$$

In this equation, 64% of carbon dioxide emissions remain in the atmosphere with the passage of one time period. The preindustrial carbon dioxide stock is 590 billion tons-carbon, while quantities in excess of this baseline level are removed from the atmosphere at the rate of 0.833%/year. The atmospheric stock of carbon dioxide in the year 2000 (the initial period of the analysis) is set equal to 784 billion tons-carbon.

The model assumes that carbon dioxide concentrations are related to changes in mean global temperature by the equation:

$$T_t = (5.92\log(Q_t/590) + F_t)/1.41. \tag{6}$$

In this expression, temperatures increase logarithmically with carbon dioxide concentrations, while a doubling of concentrations relative to preindustrial norm causes a 2.91 °C temperature increase in the absence of other factors. The parameter F_t captures the impacts of trace gases other than carbon dioxide – chlorofluorocarbons, methane, nitrous oxide, and water vapor – on aggregate climatic conditions. Because emissions of these gases are taken to be beyond the scope of policy intervention in this study, F_t (which is measured in W/m², a standard measure of radiative forcing) is specified by the exogenous relationship:

$$F_t = 1.42 - 0.764(0.523)^t. \tag{7}$$

Under these assumptions, non-CO_2 greenhouse gases generate a 0.47 °C increase in mean global temperature over the short run and a 1.0 °C increase in the further future.

2.2. PRODUCER BEHAVIOR

The model assumes that production decisions are managed by a set of competitive firms having common access to the technology described above. It is useful to note that equations (1)–(4) implicitly define a net production function $f(K_t, N_t, E_t, T_t, t)$ = $C_t + K_{t+1} - K_t$ that exhibits constant returns to scale in capital, labor, and carbon dioxide emissions. Firms take the state of environmental quality to be independent of their individual decisions but pay a unit tax v_t on carbon dioxide emissions. With the consumption good as numeraire, r_t as the interest rate or rental price of capital, and w_t as the wage rate, profit maximization yields the first-order conditions:

$$r_t = \frac{\partial f_t}{\partial K_t}, \quad w_t = \frac{\partial f_t}{\partial N_t}, \quad v_t = \frac{\partial f_t}{\partial E_t}. \tag{8}$$

Under competitive conditions, the price of each input is equated with its marginal productivity. Profits are zero because the production function exhibits constant returns to scale.

2.3. CONSUMER BEHAVIOR

The model represents consumer behavior through a sequence of overlapping generations in which individuals enjoy seventy-year life spans. At each date t, a cohort of:

$$n_t = 5.27 - 1.42(0.587)^t \tag{9}$$

billion persons is born whose lives stretch across periods t and $t + 1$. The total population at date t, which consists of individuals born at dates $t - 1$ ("the old") and t ("the young"), is thus:

$$N_t = n_{t-1} + n_t. \tag{10}$$

The total population in the year 2000 is set equal to 5.93 billion persons. These assumptions imply that population grows at an initial rate of 1.1%/year with long-run stabilization at 10.54 billion people.

Each individual is endowed with one unit of labor services in each period of his or her life that he or she supplies inelasticity to the production sector in exchange for wage income. Individuals hold no initial capital endowments but purchase capital goods in youth (k_{t+1}) that are rented out at the prevailing interest rate to augment consumption in old age. Defining c_{yt} as consumption in youth and c_{ot+1} as consumption in old age, a typical person's budget constraints take the form:

$$c_{yt} + k_{t+1} = w_t + \pi_{yt}. \tag{11}$$

$$c_{ot+1} = w_{t+1} + (1 + r_{t+1})k_{t+1} + \pi_{ot+1}. \tag{12}$$

In these equations, the terms π_{yt} and π_{ot+1} represent lump-sum income transfers that individuals receive from the government. The government uses these instruments to release the revenues raised by taxing carbon dioxide emissions and, possibly, to achieve a desirable distribution of welfare between generations.

Individual preferences are specified by the life-cycle utility function:

$$u_t = \log(c_{yt}) + \frac{1}{1+\rho}\log(c_{ot+1}). \tag{13}$$

Utility is logarithmic in consumption with a pure rate of time preference of $\rho = 0.29$, or 0.73%/year. This parameterization was chosen to match expected rates of economic growth (Nordhaus 1994) in a baseline simulation where savings-investment decisions were determined solely by market decisions in the absence of policies to redistribute income between generations.

The model assumes that consumers have perfect foresight concerning future prices and economic conditions. In this setting, utility maximization subject to equations (11) and (12) yields the first-order condition:

$$\frac{c_{ot+1}}{c_{yt}} = \frac{1 + r_{t+1}}{1 + \rho} \tag{14}$$

that is necessary and sufficient for an optimum. This equation implies that each individual's marginal rate of intertemporal substitution is equated with the gross return on capital investment, and is a standard result in models of economic growth.

2.4. GOVERNMENT POLICIES

The equations described above are sufficient to define an equilibrium path for the economy if aggregate consumption is equated with the sum of each individual's consumption ($C_t = n_t c_{yt} + n_{t-1} c_{ot}$), the aggregate capital stock is equated with the summed asset holdings of each old person ($K_t = n_{t-1} k_t$), and if government expenditures are equated with carbon tax revenues so that $n_t \pi_{yt} + n_{t-1} \pi_{ot} = v_t E_t$ at each point in time. The first two conditions are purely definitional, while the third may be relaxed to allow for government borrowing and lending without undue complication (Marini and Scaramozzino 1995). The balanced budget assumption, however, is useful for the purposes of this analysis and does not limit the generality of the results discussed here.

The "government" of this model represents an aggregate of worldwide political institutions as they relate to climate policy choices. Although the realities of this problem are interesting and complex and questions international cooperation loom large (Rose and Brandt 1993; Golombeck et al. 1995), attention is limited to the construction of two simple scenarios that highlight the basic behavior of the model.

In the first scenario – the *no transfers efficient path* – decision-makers aim to achieve a Pareto efficient resource allocation[2] by equating the marginal costs and benefits of carbon dioxide emissions while dividing carbon tax revenues in equal lump sums between all living persons. Under this assumption, $\pi_{yt} = \pi_{ot} = v_t E_t / N_t$, and the government does not impose net transfers of wealth between successive age cohorts. The distribution of well-being between generations is therefore wholly determined by market institutions, and is not derived from an explicit notion of welfare aggregation.

Howarth (1996) shows that a Pareto efficient resource allocation will prevail in this economy if carbon dioxide emissions tax are chosen according to:

$$v_t = -\sum_{t=1}^{\bar{i}-t} \frac{\partial f_{t+i}}{\partial T_{t+i}} \frac{\partial T_{t+i}}{\partial Q_{t+i}} \frac{\partial Q_{t+i}}{\partial E_t} \left(\prod_{j=1}^{i} \frac{1}{1 + r_{t+j}} \right). \tag{15}$$

This expression combines information on the marginal output loss caused by increased global temperatures ($-\partial f_{t+i}/\partial T_{t+i}$), the marginal impact of carbon dioxide *stocks* on the degree of temperature change ($\partial T_{t+i}/\partial Q_{t+i}$), and the marginal contribution of current carbon dioxide *emissions* to future atmospheric *stocks* ($\partial Q_{t+i}/\partial E_t$). In this equation, the efficient emissions tax is equated with the present value marginal costs that current emissions impose on the future economy. The social discount rate is set equal to the market rate of interest (r_t), which reflects both the marginal productivity of capital investment and the marginal time preference of each generation of consumers.

In the second scenario – the *utilitarian optimum* – decision-makers seek to maximize the summed utility of all present and future persons, or $\sum_{t=0}^{T} n_t u_t$, subject to the technical constraints of the model. While this social choice criterion is controversial – Manne (1995), for example, rejects this approach as "unrealistic," while Nordhaus (1994, p. 125, emphasis in original) claims that it rests on "a *hypothetical* view of how society should behave" that is seemingly at odds with actual policy choices – it constitutes a direct expression of Benthamite utilitarianism that has been specifically embraced by prominent contributors to the climate change literature (Broome 1992; Cline 1992). Although the merits of this debate are beyond the scope of this paper, the practical implications of the utilitarian framework for the model under consideration are of clear significance.

The utilitarian optimum is Pareto efficient and is therefore consistent with the Pigouvian tax rule equation (15). In contrast with the no transfer efficient path, however, supporting this allocation as a competitive equilibrium requires net transfers of wealth from present to future generations. In this context it is useful to define $\pi_{yt} - v_t E_t/N_t$ as the *net income transfer* received by a typical young person, or the lump-sum transfer she or he receives from the government in addition to his or her per capita share of carbon dioxide tax revenues.

2.5. THE REPRESENTATIVE AGENT

The purpose of this analysis is to compare the results of a numerically calibrated overlapping generations model of climate–economy interactions with those generated by a corresponding representative agent specification. Although representative agent models do not embody a realistic depiction of human demographics, proponents argue that they provide a reasonable approach to economic modelling because actual economies behave *as if* they were managed by a central planner who sought to maximize a particular objective function. This assertion constitutes a scientific hypothesis that is amenable to empirical test.

The representative agent model explored in this paper makes use of the intertemporal objective function employed by Nordhaus (1994):

$$U = \sum_{t=0}^{T} N_t \log(C_t/N_t)/(1+\delta)^t. \tag{16}$$

In this setting, a fictional agent weights the logarithm of per capita consumption by the total human population alive at each point in time. The argument of the objective function is discounted at the constant rate δ.

In contrast with the overlapping generations model, the mechanics of the representative agent approach are relatively straightforward. The objective function *U* is directly maximized subject to the technical constraints embodied in equations (1)–(7) and (9)–(10) without explicit attention to the choice problems confronting firms and consumers or the economic policies required to support optimal allocations as competitive equilibria. If a solution to this problem successfully mimics the competitive equilibrium that arises under a given policy scenario, then one may gauge the development of interest rates, wages, and carbon dioxide emissions taxes by calculating the marginal productivity of capital, labor, and carbon dioxide emissions according to equation (8).

It is important to note, however, that the representative agent framework suppresses information on the distribution of consumption between age cohorts and thus cannot, in general, be used to calculate the effective intergenerational transfers required to support a particular allocation as a competitive equilibrium. In the case of the no transfers efficient path, this problem is rendered moot by the *a priori* assumption that carbon dioxide tax revenues are divided equally between individuals. For the utilitarian optimum, in contrast, calculating π_{yt} requires specific information on capital investment and the per capita consumption of young persons at each point in time – variables that are defined only in relation to the parameters and behavioral relationships of the overlapping generations model.

Before proceeding to the results, it is necessary to discuss the calibration of the pure rates of time preference used to simulate the no transfers efficient path and the utilitarian optimum using the representative agent approach. According to Nordhaus (1994), a pure rate of time preference of 3%/year, or $\delta = 2.81$ per 35-year period, is required to match expected rates of economic growth and capital investment in a baseline competitive economy. The analysis employs Nordhaus' parameterization to investigate the merits of this claim.

To simulate the utilitarian optimum, in contrast, it is natural to set $\delta = 0$ so that equal weight is attached to the argument of the objective function at each point in time. Utilitarians, in fact, have explicitly called for the use of a zero rate of pure time preference in representative agent models of climate stabilization policy (Broome 1992; Cline 1992). The present analysis follows this recommendation for purposes of comparison.

3. Results

The results of the analysis are summarized in Tables I and II, which sketch the numerical simulations generated by both the overlapping generations and representative agent models for the years 2000, 2105, and 2350. Under the specified assumptions, each model run converges smoothly to a steady state with the passage of some ten generations, or 350 years. In each case, the economy remains at its steady state until it approaches the end of its planning horizon, when the remaining capital stock is consumed and the shadow price of carbon dioxide emissions falls towards zero (Howarth 1998). As is noted above, the short-run behavior of these

Table I. No transfers efficient path.

Year	Overlapping generations			Representative agent		
	2000	2105	≥2350	2000	2105	≥2350
Population (10^9 people)	5.9	9.7	10.5	5.9	9.7	10.5
Per capita consumption (1989 \$/person/yr)	⋅,092	10,402	15,059	4,085	10,429	15,055
Capital stock (10^{12} 1989 \$)	56	284	541	56	287	540
CO_2 emissions (10^9 tons-carbon/yr)	8.6	19.6	24.1	8.6	19.6	24.1
% emissions abatement	15	22	23	15	22	23
Mean temperature change (°C)	1.7	4.6	7.4	1.7	4.6	7.4
Interest rate (%/yr)	4.3	3.6	3.0	4.3	3.5	3.0
Wage income (1989 \$/person/yr)	3,462	8,491	12,248	3,462	8,515	12,244
Emission tax (1989 \$/ton-carbon)	15	51	69	15	51	69
Capital transfer to young (1989 \$/person/yr)	0	0	0	——undefined——		

Table II. Utiliarian optimum.

Year	Overlapping generations			Representative agent		
	2000	2105	≥2350	2000	2105	≥2350
Population (10^9 people)	5.9	9.7	10.5	5.9	9.7	10.5
Per capita consumption (1989 \$/person/yr)	3,161	11,684	18,053	3,140	11,680	18,053
Capital stock (10^{12} 1989 \$)	56	1,065	2,221	56	1,069	2,221
CO_2 emissions (10^9 tons-carbon/yr)	5.3	7.1	5.2	5.3	7.1	5.2
% emissions abatement	48	79	89	48	79	89
Mean temperature change (°C)	1.7	3.3	3.4	1.7	3.3	3.4
Interest rate (%/yr)	4.2	0.6	0	4.2	0.6	0
Wage income (1989 \$/person/yr)	3,364	11,356	17,611	3,364	11,392	17,611
Emission tax (1989 \$/ton-carbon)	131	570	900	131	571	900
Capital transfer to young (1989 \$/person/yr)	2,098	8,693	13,614	——undefined——		

simulations is insensitive to the precise length of the planning horizon, provided that the terminal date of the economy is far enough into the future ($\bar{t} \geq 50$) to allow for convergence to the steady states.

The principal finding of the analysis is readily apparent upon inspection of these tables. For both the no transfers efficient path and the utilitarian optimum, the representative agent specification provides a remarkably close approximation of the results derived using the overlapping generations model. The approximation errors introduced through use of the representative agent framework exceed 1% for only 5 out of 48 variables calculated by each model, and in no case does the difference between the models exceed 2%. From this one may conclude that the representative agent model provides an effective heuristic approach to simulating consumer preferences and social choices under the stipulated assumptions.

The results also shed light on the sensitivity of optimal climate change policies to the social norms and/or ethical values used to aggregate the present costs and distant future benefits of carbon dioxide emissions reductions. For the no transfers efficient path, carbon dioxide emissions increase from 8.6 to 24.1 billion tons-carbon/year between 2000 and 2350, with emissions abatement rates rising from 15% to 23% over this period. To implement this path as a competitive equilibrium, the government must tax emissions at a rate that grows from $15/ton-carbon in the short run to $69/ton-carbon in the further future. Both the efficient abatement rates and the accompanying emissions taxes are numerically comparable to those generated by other studies (Nordhaus 1994).

Since the no transfers efficient path entails relatively modest steps to control greenhouse gas emissions, this scenario allows for quite substantial increases in mean global temperature over the long-term future. Between 2000 and 2350, average temperatures rise by a full 5.7 °C. Although this perturbation may seem small when compared to interseasonal variations or to climatic differences between geographic regions, smaller changes have been associated with the coming and going of ice ages and all of their ensuing effects.

A very different set of policies emerges under the utilitarian optimum, where carbon dioxide emissions rise from 5.3 to 7.1 billion tons-carbon/year between 2000 and 2105 with a subsequent decline to 5.2 billion tons-carbon/year. Over the course of this simulation, the optimal rate of carbon dioxide emissions control rises smoothly from 48% to 89%, with an accompanying emissions tax that grows from $131/ton-carbon in 2000 to $900/ton-carbon in 2350. In comparison with the no transfers efficient path, the utilitarian optimum suggests substantially reduced greenhouse gas emissions and hence significantly reduced rates of climate change. Between 2000 and 2350, the net increase in mean global temperature is limited to 1.7 °C, or less than one-third the increase tolerated under the no transfers efficient path.

As is noted above, both the no transfers path and the utilitarian optimum are Pareto efficient competitive equilibria that equate the marginal cost and discounted future benefits of carbon dioxide emissions abatement. But while the rate of capital accumulation is determined solely by market institutions under the no transfer path, the utilitarian optimum entails aggressive policies to redistribute income from present to future generations. In Table II, the net income transfer that a typical young person receives from the government in addition to his or her per capita share of emissions tax revenues grows from $2,098/year in 2000 to $13,614/year in 2350. As a result, the utilitarian optimum leads consumption to decrease by 23% in the year 2000 but increase by 20% over the long run when compared with the no transfers efficient path.

In intuitive terms, the high rates of carbon dioxide emissions abatement that occur under the utilitarian optimum may be attributed to two interrelated factors. First, the intergenerational transfers that are implemented in this simulation lead to accelerated rates of capital accumulation and economic growth. Since the damages imposed by climate change are by assumption proportional to gross world output, increased economic activity augments the perceived costs of emissions. Second, the high rates of investment associated with the utilitarian optimum drive down interest rates in comparison with the no transfers path. Since the social discount rate is, under the assumptions of the model, appropriately equated with the market rate of interest (see Howarth and Norgaard 1995), the utilitarian optimum attaches comparatively more weight to future costs and benefits.

The difference between the two policy scenarios, then, cannot be reduced to a simple choice of discount rates in a model where all other variables are held constant. Instead, both discount rates and the perceived costs and benefits of policy alternatives are defined implicitly by the criteria through which the interests of present and future generations are mediated in social decision-making. In this setting, "optimal" policies cannot be identified without appeals to normative principles that are stronger than the well-grounded yet partial criterion of Pareto efficiency. The standard guidance of the Coase (1960) theorem that questions of efficient resource allocation and distributional fairness can be safely decoupled in environmental policy analysis breaks down when confronted with the facts surrounding climate change (Schmidt 1995). Indeed, the second-best policies that prevail when institutional constraints bar the achievement of an optimal income distribution may differ dramatically from those suggested by the efficiency criterion, a possibility confirmed in numerical simulations by Howarth (1998).

4. Conclusions

The analysis presented above points to two principal conclusions. First, representative agent models provide a close approximation of the aggregate behavior of more realistic (and more complex) overlapping generations specifications under the empirical assumptions and social choice rules considered in this paper. This finding confirms the earlier work of Manne (1996) and Stephan et al. (1997), providing reassurance concerning the use to aggregate models to represent the interests and preferences of decentralized agents in a market economy.

Second, optimal rates of greenhouse gas emissions control are dramatically sensitive to the criteria used to balance the interests of present and future generations. In the absence of policies to redistribute income between generations, only modest efforts to abate carbon dioxide emissions are justified by the standard criterion of economic efficiency. Under Benthamite utilitarianism, in contrast, optimal rates of emissions control rise from 48% in the short run to 89% in the long-term future. This result is consistent with the findings of other studies (Cline 1992; Chapman et al. 1995), pointing to the importance of ethical considerations in the climate change policy debate.

Although these results suggest that the simplification of representative agent models do not necessarily imply inaccuracy or imprecision, it is important to bear in mind the inherent limitations of such models in framing questions of social choice over intergenerational time scales. Under certain conditions – if utility is logarithmic in consumption, individuals are time-neutral, and the weight attached to the welfare of successive age cohorts declines geometrically from generation to generation – then the objective function employed in representative agent models may be understood as an exact depiction of social preferences (Howarth 1996).[3]

For the case considered here, however, these conditions are not satisfied, and the parameters of the objective function are chosen *ex post* to approximate the choices that arise under independently defined normative criteria.

The no transfers efficient path, for example, is defined by a commitment to two normative principles: (1) that climate change policies should achieve an efficient balance between the costs and benefits of greenhouse gas emissions abatement; and (2) that emissions tax revenues should be divided equally between all living persons. In the representative agent framework, in contrast, the distinction between the no transfers efficient path and the utilitarian optimum is ostensibly reduced to a choice of a single parameter: Should social decision-makers embrace the revealed pure rate of time preference of 3%/year? Or should they override private preference and employ a utility discount rate of zero? The question, framed in this way, misstates the nature of the underlying choice problem, as it attaches ethical significance to a parameter that is in this case artifactual.

Finally, although representative agent models may be used to approximate the behavior of aggregate economic variables – total consumption, capital investment, carbon dioxide emissions, and relative prices – they do not, in general, provide a complete characterization of the policies required to support a particular allocation as a competitive equilibrium. When decision-making aim to redistribute income between social groups or successive generations, detailed information on the economic status of each group is required to design the appropriate policy instruments. In the context of intergenerational social choice, questions of distributional fairness are most appropriately addressed using overlapping generations models. Such models are both comptuationally tractable and conceptually well-grounded, providing an analytical approach that avoids the ethical paradox of the representative agent.

Acknowledgement

This work was sponsored by the Global Change Research Assessment Program of the U.S. Department of Energy.

Notes

1. Monetary units are denominated in 1989 U.S. dollars throughout the analysis.
2. In overlapping generations models, a resource allocation is Pareto efficient if it is impossible to increase the life-cycle utility of one generation without rendering another generation worse off.
3. More generally, an anonymous referee suggests that competitive equilibria will maximize the weighted sum of each generation's life-cycle utility if utility is logarithmic in consumption and the welfare weights are set equal to each generation's share of total net wealth. In a similar vein, Manne (1996) uses dynamic optimization methods with endogenously determined welfare weights to find competitive equilibria in a numerically calibrated overlapping generations model.

References

Auerbach, A. J. and L. J. Kotlikoff (1987), *Dynamic Fiscal Policy*. New York: Cambridge University Press.

Blanchard, O. J. and S. Fischer (1989), *Lectures on Macroeconomics*. Cambridge, MA: MIT Press.

Broome, J. (1992), *Counting the Cost of Global Warming*. Cambridge: White Horse Press.

Burton, P. S. (1993), 'Intertemporal Preferences and Intergenerational Equity Considerations in Optimal Resource Harvesting', *Journal of Environmental Economics and Management* **24**, 119–132.

Chapman, D., V. Suri and S. G. Hall (1995), 'Rolling DICE for the Future of the Planet', *Contemporary Economic Policy* **13**, 1–9.

Cline, W. R. (1992), *The Economics of Global Warming*. Washington: Institute for International Economics.

Coase, R. H. (1960), 'The Problem of Social Cost', *Journal of Law and Economics* **3**, 1–44.

Geanakoplos, J. (1987), 'Overlapping Generations Model of General Equilibrium', in J. Eatwell, M. Milgate and P. Newman, eds., *The New Palgrave: General Equilibrium*. New York: Norton.

Golombek, R., C. Hagem and M. Hoel (1995), 'Efficient Incomplete International Climate Agreements', *Resource and Energy Economics* **17**, 25–46.

Howarth, R. B. (1996), 'Climate Change and Overlapping Generations', *Contemporary Economic Policy* **14**, 100–111.

Howarth, R. B. (1998), 'An Overlapping Generations Model of Climate-Economy Interactions', *Scandinavian Journal of Economics* **100**, 575–591.

Howarth, R. B. and P. A. Monahan (1996), 'Economics, Ethics, and Climate Policy: Framing the Debate', *Global Planetary Change* **11**, 187–199.

Howarth, R. B. and R. B. Norgaard (1995), 'Intergenerational Choices under Global Environmental Change', in D. W. Bromley, ed., *Handbook of Environmental Economics*. Oxford: Blackwell.

Kirman, A. P. (1992), 'Whom or What Does the Representative Individual Represent', *Journal of Economic Perspectives* **6**, 117–136.

Manne, A. S. (1995), 'The Rate of Time Preference: Implications for the Greenhouse Debate', *Energy Policy* **23**, 391–394.

Manne, A. S. (1996), 'Intergenerational Altruism, Discounting and the Greenhouse Debate', Department of Engineering Economic Systems and Operations Research, Stanford University.

Marini, G. and P. Scaramozzino (1995), 'Overlapping Generations and Environmental Control', *Journal of Environmental Economics and Management* **29**, 64–77.

Mourmouras, A. (1993), 'Conservationist Government Policies and Intergenerational Equity in an Overlapping Generations Model with Renewable Resources', *Journal of Public Economics* **51**, 249–268.

Nordhaus, W. D. (1994), *Managing the Global Commons*. Cambridge, MA: MIT Press.

Ramsey, F. (1928), 'A Mathematical Theory of Saving', *Economic Journal* **38**, 543–559.

Rose, A. and B. Stevens (1993), 'The Efficiency and Equity of Marketable Permits for CO_2 Emissions', *Resource and Energy Economics* **15**, 117–146.

Schmidt, A. A. (1995), 'The Environment and Property Rights Issues', in D. W. Bromley, ed., *Handbook of Environmental Economics*. Oxford: Blackwell.

Stephan, G., G. Müller-Fürstenberger and P. Previdoli (1997), 'Overlapping Generations or Infinitely-Lived Agents: Intergenerational Altruism and the Economics of Global Warming', *Environmental and Resource Economics* **10**, 27–40.

[18]

Intergenerational discounting

Thomas C Schelling

School of Public Affairs, University of Maryland, College Park, MD 20742, USA

A 'discount rate' for the consumption of future generations from current investments for their benefit is typically composed of two parts: 'time preference' and an allowance for the lower marginal utility of consumption due to higher average levels of consumption in the future. Time preference would be involved if one were postponing one's own consumption; it has little or nothing to do with income redistribution, which is what greenhouse abatement is about. A lower marginal utility of consumption is an anomaly in income redistribution: we rarely deliberately transfer consumption from the less to the more well-to-do. Time may serve as a kind of measure of distance; we may prefer beneficiaries who are closer in time, in geographical distance, in culture, surely in kinship. Perhaps to keep our thinking straight we should use a term like 'depreciation', rather than 'discounting'.

Keywords: Global warming; Intergenerational equity; Discounting

Economists who deal with very long-term policy issues, like greenhouse gas emissions over the next century or two, are nearly unanimous that future benefits that take the form of additions to future consumption need to be discounted to be commensurable with the consumption earlier forgone to produce those benefits. And there is a near consensus that the appropriate discount rate should be conceptualized as consisting of two components (Cline, 1992; Manne, this issue; Nordhaus, 1992; Fankhauser, 1993).

One is pure time preference and 'deals with the impatience of consumers and reflects their inborn preference of immediate over postponed consumption' (Fankhauser, 1993, p 13). The second reflects the changing marginal utility of consumption with the passage of time, and is decomposed into a rate of growth of consumption per capita and an elasticity of utility with respect to consumption. The two components, pure preference for early over later utility and declining utility with growing per capita consumption, are used to compare not only utility increments in the year, say, 2050 with costs incurred in 2000, but to compare utility increments in the year 2150 with increments in the year 2050.

I first discuss 'pure time preference' and then the relevance of the elasticity of utility with respect to income or consumption. But first, since I am going to argue that 'discounting' is not the appropriate concept for dealing with the benefits of reduced greenhouse gas emissions in

the distant future, I should clarify that I find traditional discounting perfectly appropriate for comparing costs and benefits of, say, hazardous-waste cleanup, as in the United States 'Superfund' program. In that kind of program discounting with appropriate rates of interest is crucial to determining which sites are worth cleaning up, how much they should be cleaned up, and when or in what order of priority they should be cleaned up. In that kind of program 'we' who pay the costs are saving and investing – foregoing some current consumption – in order to reap future benefits, along with our children and grandchildren. It makes sense to 'optimize' our investment portfolio by reference to appropriate discount rates. Global greenhouse gas abatement, I shall argue, is not like cleaning up our own land for our own benefit. *Costs* we incur for greenhouse gas abatement need to be discounted; *benefits* need an altogether different treatment.

Pure time preference

Alan Manne introduces his discussion of time preference with a quotation from Roy Harrod characterizing time preference as 'a polite expression for rapacity and the conquest of reason by passion'. I quoted Fankhauser above about 'impatience' and an inborn preference for immediate over postponed consumption. I am dubious about the ubiquity of that inborn impatience of consumers, at least for adults with decent levels of income, but my argument is that no kind of time preference pertinent to discounting the long-term costs and benefits of greenhouse gas abatement can have anything to do with the 'pure rate of time preference' defined in this fashion. That is because the alleged inborn preference for earlier rather than later consumption is exclusively concerned with the consumer's impatience with respect to his or her *own* consumption.

Alan Manne begins by asking us to 'consider an economy in which there is a single agent acting as producer, consumer, investor, and saver' (in this issue). An agent, it should be noticed, that is immortal. I suppose such an agent could have an inborn impatience about consumption. But greenhouse policy is not about saving for later consumption. It is about forgoing consumption in order that *somebody else* at a later time enjoy more consumption than would otherwise be available.

This assumption of the immortal agent, explicit in Manne, makes the issue one of 'optimization over time', one of maximizing the utilities of myriad heterogeneous peoples spread over continents and centuries as if they were all one family, all one 'agent'. It supposes that, whoever they are who pay for the investments that lead to increments in future consumption, they value increments in other people's utility *as if they were increments in their own utility*. It is this willingness to model all humankind as a single agent that makes optimization models attractive, feasible, and inappropriate.

The optimization models have no provision for redistributing current income. They redistribute only forward in time; contemporary Chinese get nothing from us, but future Chinese we treat as part of the family.

Introspectively I can find no impatience about an increment of consumption that may accrue to people whom I shall never know and who do not now exist, in the year 2150, compared with an increment closer in time, accruing to the people whom I shall never know, and who do not now exist, who might enjoy it instead in the year 2100, or closer still to the people in the year 2050.

I can imagine reasons – some of them may even appeal to me – for preferring a boost to consumption in 2025 to the same boost of consumption in 2075, but it is hard to see that it has anything to do with impatience and the inborn preference for immediate over postponed consumption. In 2025, my oldest son will be the age I am today and his brothers a little younger; with a little luck they will be alive and healthy and my grandchildren will be the ages that my children are today, and my great-grandchildren (whom I do not yet know) will have most of their lives ahead of them. Seventy-five years later they will all be strangers to me. My genes may be as plentiful in the population at the later date but they will be spread thinner. I probably would prefer the benefits to accrue to my own grandchildren rather than to

their grandchildren, but I must remind myself that my grandchildren's happiness may depend on their perceived prospects for their own grandchildren, and my 'time preference' becomes attenuated.

The point of all this is that we may have grounds for preferring utility increments to occur earlier rather than later to the descendants of people now alive, but this cannot have anything to do with the kind of time preference that Roy Harrod or Samuel Fankhauser were talking about, or Alan Manne or William Nordhaus.

Actually, time may serve as a kind of measure of 'distance'. The people who are going to be living in 2150 I may consider 'farther away' than the people who will be living in 2050. They will also be different in racial composition and geographical distribution from the people I most identify with. I observe that in redistributing income via transfer payments, in providing foreign aid, in contributing to charity etc, people are expected to differentiate, and do differentiate, among recipient peoples according to several kinds of distance or proximity. One is geographical: Americans are expected to be more interested in their own cities than in distant cities, their own country than distant countries. Another is political: East Coast Americans are more interested in the people of Los Angeles than in the people of Quebec. Another is cultural: some people are closer in language, religion, and other kinds of heritage. Sheer familiarity seems to matter, and of course kinship does. (Kinship distance has both horizontal and vertical dimensions; just as children are closer than grandchildren, children are closer than nieces and nephews. Time just happens to correlate with vertical distance.)

To be less interested in the welfare of East Africans than former Yugoslavians is less like 'discounting' than, perhaps, 'depreciating'. When we count future welfare less than our own we are depreciating generations that are distant in time, in familiarity, in culture, in kinship, and along other dimensions. (There is no reason to suppose that the depreciation would be exponential. Beyond certain distances there may be no further depreciation for time, culture, geography, race, or kinship.)

The crucial point is that these are not 'saving' decisions we are talking about, ie not decisions about postponing our consumption, but decisions about redistributing income – our income. To invest resources now in reduced greenhouse emissions is to transfer consumption from ourselves – whoever 'we' are who are making these sacrifices – for the benefit of people distant in the future. It is very much like making sacrifices now for people who are distant geographically or distant culturally. Deciding whether I care more about the people who will be alive in 2150 than the people who will be alive in 2050 is a little like deciding whether I care more about people in one continent than in another, or about English speaking people more than people who speak other languages, or about people who share my history and my culture more than people who do not. People do have preferences about whom to help; the preferences show up in charitable giving, in foreign aid, in immigration policy, in military intervention.

What we are talking about is very much like a foreign aid program, with some of the foreigners being our own descendants who live not on another continent but in another century.

William Cline half agrees with me. He, too, argues that impatience or 'myopia' 'may be a legitimate basis for a single individual's preferring consumption earlier rather than later in his lifetime' but is 'hardly a justifiable basis for making intergenerational comparisons' (Cline, 1992). He disagrees in believing that we should not prefer – except on marginal utility grounds, which I am about to discuss – our own consumption to the consumption of future people. I expect that, whether or not we should, we all do. If we do not, there is a most extraordinary anomaly: we greatly prefer our own consumption to that of distant contemporaries, or even quite close ones, but not to that of people distant in future time. It would be strange to forgo a per cent or two of GNP for 50 years for the benefit of Indians, Chinese, Indonesians and others who will be living 50 to 100 years from now – and probably much better off than today's Indians, Chinese, and Indonesians – and not a tenth of that amount to increase the consumption of contemporary Indians, Chinese, and Indonesians. At its peak, the Marshall Plan took about 1.5% of US GNP; it went to the foreigners 'closest' to the Americans in most respects; and it was recognized as a short-run emergency. Americans do nothing like that now for anybody alive, except other living Americans. Whether that is good or bad, I do not see why we should expect them so much to prefer to help the unborn.

Marginal utility

The other component of the proposed discount rate is the rate of change over time of the marginal utility of consumption. The argument for including that component must be that in transferring income, or redistributing income, an important goal is to maximize the integral over time of the aggregate utility of consumption. The expectation is that on average the marginal utility of global consumption will decline over time as a result of rising consumption per capita. Resources invested now out of our own incomes will benefit people in the future who are expected to be better off than we are – an unaccustomed direction for redistributing income!

Both within countries and among countries, we expect civilized governments to redistribute toward the poorer countries and toward the poorer elements of their own populations. Doing it that way probably, as Abba Lerner argued in *The Economics of Control* (1944) 50 years ago, increases total utility. But I doubt whether that is the only reason why people prefer to see income redistributed from rich to poor rather than the other way around.

The argument for transferring consumption from the poor to the rich, or from the decently well off to the much better off, would be that the resources transferred grow in the process, and grow so much that though the marginal utility of the recipient is lower than that of the donor, the magnitude that the gift achieves in transit more than compensates. (That the resources so invested 'grow' by forestalling decrements does not affect the argument.)

There is not much room for this idea in *contemporary* transfers. If a poor farmer has some poor soil and a richer farmer has rich soil somebody could argue that extracting seed from the poor farmer and giving it to the rich farmer will so enhance the resulting crop that the somewhat utility-satiated rich farmer will gain more utility than the poor farmer loses. But ordinarily that is just an argument for trade: the poor farmer is better off selling the seed to the rich farmer, and their joint utility is even higher. The ethical interest arises only if trade is not possible, as when we outfit somebody who will emigrate to the new world, become rich, and never be heard from again, or as we contemplate transferring consumption forward in time to people who have no way to reciprocate.

Arthur Okun introduced the 'leaky bucket' in his 1974 Godkin Lecture (1975). Transferring consumption from those who have plenty to those who do not typically entails inefficiency – some administrative costs, some deadweight losses due to tax avoidance or transfer seeking, some transfers going to unintended and undeserving recipients. His analogy was carrying water from where it was plentiful to where it was scarce in a leaky bucket. The 'big trade-off' was deciding how leaky the bucket can be before we judge the effort not worthwhile. Clearly if the bucket arrives dry the effort was a mistake; if the bucket arrives three-quarters full or one quarter, or even a sixteenth, somebody in charge has to consider what discount ratio or augmentation ratio is acceptable.

Somebody might – not many people will – use some elasticity to calculate the marginal utility of consumption (Okun's water) where it is scarce and where it is not and decide whether total utility goes up with the leaky-bucket transfer. Marginal utility is clearly pertinent, for those who understand it, but probably rarely decisive even for those who do understand it. Enough attention was paid to John Rawls's *Theory of Justice* (1971) by quite sophisticated people to somewhat dethrone utility maximization, at least to deny it exclusive status. And Rawls was talking about transferring from rich to poor.

Okun never got round to talking about the other bucket, the 'incubation bucket' in which the good things multiply in transit so that more arrives at the destination than was removed from the origin. The trade-off question here would be, what sacrifice of food where it is scarce would be worthwhile if, in being transported to where it was abundant, it grew handsomely. An alternative phrasing would be, recognizing the advantage of moving resources from where they are less fruitful to where they are more fruitful, how much do we want to 'discount' the greater fruitfulness when it accrues to people who already enjoy bountiful supply? And of course Okun, concerned with contemporary transfers, could not be interested: the market would take care of the efficiency problem, and nobody is interested in helping the rich at the expense of the poor.

The conclusion I reach is that 'optimization' models are inappropriate for dealing with very long-term public investments, especially when the beneficiaries will be spread over the planet. Optimization models imply that it is our own consumption that we are promoting in the future, and it is not. Not only do they incorporate an irrelevant 'time preference', they imply that we want to treat increments in other people's utility from consumption as if they were our own. I can see no acceptance of the principle that consumption should be so distributed (redistributed) as to maximize utility. No such contemporary redistribution has ever been witnessed; and it would be strange to feel a strong obligation to redistribute income from ourselves to others in the future, *valuing their utility from consumption as if it were our own*, and no corresponding obligation to contemporaries whose marginal utilities exceed our own and probably exceed those of their own descendants.

Depreciating the consumption of high-income future people makes sense; but the 'optimization' approach is based on the principle that if the material benefits we procure for those future high-income people are large enough to offset their reduced marginal utilities, we should procure those future utilities just as if those utilities were our own. Few citizens who understood this principle would ever vote for it.

I conclude that most of us will want to discount or depreciate heavily the extra consumption provided for (or conserved for) descendants of the current population, because they are likely to be better off as well as because they are distant and it is *our* hard-earned consumption that somebody is proposing we transfer forward in time.

The analogy, or at least a better analogy, than 'optimization of consumption over time', is transferring resources from North America and Western Europe to Africa or the Middle East, South or South-east Asia, China, Russia, or deserving peoples anywhere. It is an

aid program, not a savings program. There may be some reason for some people to prefer consumption increments that occur in 2075 over consumption increments that occur in 2125, just as there may be people who prefer consumption increments to occur in West Africa rather than East Africa, Russia than in Ukraine, or Boston rather than Los Angeles. And I have no quarrel with people who, when they are prepared to contribute large amounts to charity, indulge their own preferences about who the beneficiaries should be.

What should matter is your expectation about the course of per capita consumption over the next century or two. If both the developed and the developing worlds continue to grow in per capita consumption as they have done for the past 40 years, people in most countries are likely to be much better off in material welfare 50, 75 or 100 years from now than they are now. What we ought to feel we owe them is not the kind of ethical issue we have much practice with, because we are not used to thinking about making our own sacrifices, or imposing sacrifices on our contemporaries, for the benefit of people who are substantially better off.

The need to disaggregate

We must avoid a fallacy of composition here. If average per capita income rises in every country for the next 100 years, and if the poorer populations grow more rapidly than the wealthier populations, and if most of the economic sacrifices in the interest of carbon abatement are borne by the countries that can best afford it, the transfers will tend to be from the well-to-do people of Western Europe, North America, and Japan to the residents of what we now call the 'developing' countries, who should be far better off a century from now than they are now, but may not yet be as well off, during most of the intervening century, as we are now in Western Europe, North America, and Japan.

The significance of that point to me is that in deciding how to value consumption increments over the coming century or two, we need to disaggregate consumption according to the levels of per capita consumption at which they accrue. The optimization models err, on their own terms, in aggregating all future consumption and applying a uniform discount rate for declining marginal utility. Correctly, all increments in consumption should be valued at their own marginal utilities. In the optimization models, increments for poor people are discounted equally with increments for the rich; there is no adjustment for the fact that when Chinese per capita income has doubled, and Chinese marginal utility may have been halved – using the popular, but arbitrary, logarithmic utility function – Chinese marginal utility will still be many times that of the current populations most likely to pay for greenhouse abatement.

In neglecting to disaggregate, the optimization models make three assumptions in deriving a discount rate that are either dubious or wrong.

• They assume that elasticities of utility with respect to consumption are the same at all levels of consumption. (A logarithmic or power function meets that condition.) I count this one dubious.
• They assume that growth rates are uniform. Actually the optimization models themselves do not; on the contrary they recognize that China may develop much more rapidly than the currently advanced countries. But the discount-rate calculations use a single average growth rate.
• They assume that those who pay for abatement and those who benefit – or whose descendants benefit – are the same. Because all populations – all nations or regions – are assumed to enjoy increasing consumption per capita, and because investments in abatement precede benefits, the benefiting populations are assumed to have higher consumption levels and lower marginal utilities than the populations that finance the abatement.

I start from the premise that investments in greenhouse abatement, for the first 50 years, will be paid for by the countries that can afford it, ie the developed countries of Western Europe, North America, and Japan, and a few others. The beneficiaries of abatement will mainly be the descendants of those now living in the undeveloped countries, for several reasons explained below. Thus the consumption transfers will be from well-to-do countries that will mainly pay for abatement over the coming 50 years to the developing countries that, though probably better off progressively over the next 50 years, will have lower consumption levels 50 years from now than the current consumption levels of the developed countries. (I assume that benefits from abatement during the first 50 years will be negligible compared with benefits during the second 50 years.) Thus the consumption transfers, despite the hoped-for uniformly (not uniform) positive growth in GDP per capita everywhere, will be generally from rich to poor. That is, from lower marginal utility to higher marginal utility. The implications are startling, but first I should explain why the beneficiaries will be mainly the descendants of the populations now poor.

First, if the benefits of abatement were shared uniformly over the global population, they would accrue about 90% to the countries now considered undeveloped. The well-to-do are now about a fifth of the world's population; in 2075 the populations in countries now undeveloped are expected to be somewhere between

seven-eighths and eleven-twelfths of the global population. So those populations will comprise most of the beneficiaries. Second, the material productivity of the developed countries currently appears to be substantially immune to weather and climate; productivity of the outdoor-dependent or agriculture-dependent less-developed countries is potentially much more susceptible to adverse effects of climate change. So besides outnumbering the descendants of the currently developed countries, they can suffer greater greenhouse damage per capita. (Absolutely, the more developed could suffer more lost GDP per capita even though the damage might not be noticeable.) Finally, the currently developed countries enjoy GDP per capita 10 times or more that of the undeveloped; during the second half of the coming century they will probably still be ahead by a factor of four or more. So the marginal utility of consumption of the nine-tenths of the population will be several times that of the richer tenth. Thus the benefits in utility increments from material consumption will be overwhelmingly inherited by the descendants of those that are currently poor. (If Chinese per capita income increased at 4% per year for the next 50 years and 2% for the following 50 years, and US per capita income increased at 1% over the 100 years, Chinese per capita income would still be less than half the US level at the end of the century and the Chinese population will be many times larger than that of the USA. At those rates of improvement, the Chinese will be about up to the present US level, and we may be expected to lose interest in further increments.)

I said the implications are startling. One has already been mentioned: virtually all the benefits from enhanced consumption will accrue to countries that will not participate much in financing the abatement. The transfers will be from the currently rich to the descendants of the currently poor, who will, when the benefits begin to be felt, be much less poor than they are now but still poorer than the descendants of the currently rich and probably still significantly poorer than the abatement-financing countries are now.

Second, the implicit 'discount rate' based on marginal utility comparisons will be negative. The currently popular optimization models cannot show this negative rate, because GDP per capita is assumed to rise everywhere. But even if it does, disaggregating shows that the beneficiaries will be both poorer and more numerous than those who finance the increments in consumption. The assumed positive discount due to diminishing marginal utility is based on a 'fallacy of composition'.

Third, if GDP per capita continues to increase in most of the developing world, as I expect and as the optimization models assume, marginal utilities of the beneficiaries will be much higher during the first 50 years – before abatement benefits become significant – than in the second 50 years. This factor substantially tilts the advantage toward any direct investments in development that can raise living standards in the first and second generations (while reducing dependence on climate-susceptible economic activities) compared with investment in climate stabilization.

Even more drastic: if marginal utilities will be higher in the fifth decade than in the sixth, in the third than in the fourth, and in the first than in the second, today's undeveloped populations have stronger claims, on the basis of marginal utility, than the populations two or four generations in the future. Once we disaggregate the world's population by income level, it becomes logically absurd to ignore present needs and concentrate on the later decades of the coming century.

And that means that no framework for considering the benefits and costs of greenhouse abatement can isolate itself from the opportunity cost: direct investment in the economic improvement of the undeveloped countries. Abatement expenditures should have to compete with alternative ways of raising consumption-utility in the developing world.

A policy approach

Once we abandon the immortal-agent (optimization) approach, the two pertinent policy questions are:

- Do we want to help the future populations of China, Bangladesh, and Nigeria at our expense, because they are poor and will still be poor for some time?
- Assuming that we who pay for greenhouse abatement do not want to time-discount the consumption utility of poor countries, what mix of programs maximizes the integral of their consumption utility over time: greenhouse abatement, direct investment in their economic improvement, or direct subsidies to their consumption?

Nothing in this formulation can directly answer the question of *how much* to help the Chinese and the others. That remains a choice, not an analytical result. Just as there is no accepted formula for how much people want to help the Somalis, the Indians, the Chinese, or anybody else with current consumption, there is no formula that tells us how much people want to help with future consumption, whether with development aid or with greenhouse abatement. (I emphasize helping the poor; but there is likewise no analytical formula that could tell us how much to expect people to want to redistribute toward future Americans and Europeans.)

A different question is how to distribute Chinese and others' consumption over time when the marginal utility of their consumption is changing. The Chinese themselves may have a strong preference for current and

near-term consumption over the distant, more than diminishing marginal utility would prescribe. We then have to decide whether to depreciate future Chinese less than today's Chinese would depreciate them.

If we abandon optimization based on the immortal-agent image, what analytical procedure do we replace it with? A first approximation may be:

- Assess benefits as consumption increments country by country, or region by region (homogeneous with respect to per capita income), for *alternative levels* of greenhouse abatement.
- Identify a utility function (not chosen for its mathematical simplicity) by which to convert the consumption increments into commensurable 'utility' increments.
- Treat the results as a *menu* of what we get for our money when we invest *alternative* amounts of greenhouse abatement in the enhanced welfare of currently poor countries, not as an optimization that tells us how much to invest.
- Estimate the increments in consumption, and corresponding 'utilities', that could be procured in a sample of different countries with direct investment in infrastructure, industry, public health, education, research and development etc, to identify – for any level of aggregate contribution to future welfare – the efficient mix of investments in abatement and economic development. (We cannot allocate resources between greenhouse abatement and economic development country by country because greenhouse abatement is necessarily uniform in CO_2 concentration; we cannot give India public health and education, and Indonesia greenhouse abatement, on the basis of comparative advantage.)

The rate of interest

Optimization models often look to the market rate of interest – some rate, somewhere – to get a handle on an appropriate discount rate. What role does my analysis ascribe to the market rate of interest?

- The market rate of interest tells us nothing about how much people would like to contribute now to help others in the future.
- It tells us something about when those people would like to contribute: the earlier, the more it costs.
- It tells us little or nothing about what return we would get on public investment in poor countries that may be alternatives to greenhouse abatement.
- It tells us about an opportunity cost: instead of greenhouse abatement, or investment in development, we could invest commercially and dedicate the proceeds to somebody's future consumption.

The utility function approach

The discount-rate question should disappear. In its place is what utility function to use in valuing future increments in other people's consumption. This is a real question, not a matter of mathematical convenience. It is not a question economists have much practice with. The policy implications of such an approach are troublesome

The discounting procedure has a pseudo-familiarity; the analogy with saving-for-future-consumption has appeal. Everybody knows about interest rates, and they are genuinely pertinent to much national public investment. Marginal utilities from consumption are alien to most policy thinking. People usually understand the argument for redistributing from rich to poor, but no legislator ever thinks about whether the utility function is a power function, a logarithmic function, or a polynomial; whether there should be a universal utility function for all cultures and all times; whether material consumption is the only argument of the function, or anything of the sort.

My procedure (properly) gives no answer to the question, how much? An optimization model answers that question – incorrectly, but it gives an answer. Facing an optimization, a policy maker can say, 'I will do half that, no more', but at least the policy maker thinks he or she is doing half of something objectively arrived at. My procedure requires a *choice* of how much, with no benchmark.

It is hard to think about the future with my procedure and not be forced to think about the present. If marginal utilities of consumption are the correct target for investing in future welfare, they must be pertinent to today's welfare. But today's welfare vanishes from the greenhouse-optimization models because there is no greenhouse-abatement increment in current or near-term consumption. Hence the next point: greenhouse abatement, largely identified with energy policy, is insulated in optimization models from economic development. An answer to how much (and when) to abate is given in optimization models independently of what else is going on. When greenhouse abatement is identified as a mechanism for making income transfers to future generations, especially to those whose consumption levels are still comparatively low, it has to compete with transfers for investment in economic development. So there is not only an unanchored choice of how much to help, but a choice of what proportions through greenhouse abatement and direct assistance to development.

Carbon dioxide abatement is probably 'target efficient'. Poorer countries are probably more vulnerable to climate change than wealthier countries. But direct investments in public health, birth control, training and education, research, physical infrastructure, water resources etc, can also be directed to target populations, so the advantage may go either way.

I doubt whether developing countries would prefer to defer consumption increments to later generations, whether what is deferred comes out of their own resources or out of resources made available by wealthier countries. I would expect, if offered a choice of immediate development assistance or equivalent investments in carbon abatement, potential aid recipients would elect for the immediate. So if we, the developed, elect carbon abatement for their benefit, it is *our* choice of their descendants over themselves.

Whichever we choose, there is no reliable way we can constrain our own descendants' choices to continue or to discontinue what we began. We can invest in the consumption of future generations via carbon abatement or via direct investments; in 2050 they can discontinue the direct investments, or they can discontinue the carbon abatement. There may be institutional reasons for expecting discontinuance to be more likely with one approach or the other, but the preference is not self-evident.

A final word. This paper has been directed only at the valuation of future material consumption by individuals in GNP projections. That is what the optimization models assess. It has not examined the projections themselves, and it has omitted any reference to values other than those conventionally included in material consumption. It omits damages and benefits relating to nature, biodiversity, wildlife etc. It ignores environmental influences on public health, which are potentially important, for good or ill, in poor countries where the hazards remain more biological than chemical. It ignores the possibility that in developed countries the income elasticity of demand for environmental and recreational benefits may be high enough to bring developed-country benefits back into the picture. Any implications for greenhouse policy are limited accordingly.

References

Cline, W R (1992) *The Economics of Global Warming* Institute for International Economics, Washington, DC

Fankhauser, S (1993) *The Social Costs of Greenhouse Gas Emissions: An Expected Value Approach* Centre for Social and Economic Research on the Global Environment, University College and University of East Anglia, Norwich

Lerner, A P (1994) *The Economics of Control: Principles of Welfare Economics* Macmillan, New York

Nordhaus, W D (1992) 'An optimal transition path for controlling greenhouse gases' *Science* 258 1315–1319

Okun, A (1975) *Equality and Efficiency: The Big Trade-off* The Brookings Institution, Washington

Rawls, J (1971) *A Theory of Justice* Harvard University Press, Cambridge, MA

[19]

Economic and environmental choices in the stabilization of atmospheric CO₂ concentrations

T.M.L. Wigley*, R. Richels† & J.A. Edmonds‡

* University Corporation for Atmospheric Research, PO Box 3000, Boulder, Colorado 80307-3000, USA
† Electric Power Research Institute, PO Box 10412, Palo Alto, California 94303, USA
‡ Pacific Northwest Laboratory, 901 D Street, SW, Suite 900, Washington DC 20024-2115, USA

THE ultimate goal of the UN Framework Convention on Climate Change is to achieve "stabilization of greenhouse-gas concentrations...at a level that would prevent dangerous anthropogenic interference with the climate system". With the concentration targets yet to be determined, Working Group I of the Intergovernmental Panel on Climate Change developed a set of illustrative pathways for stabilizing the atmospheric CO₂ concentration at 350, 450, 550, 650 and 750 p.p.m.v. over the next few hundred years[1,2]. But no attempt was made to determine whether the implied emissions might constitute a realistic transition away from the current heavy dependence on fossil fuels. Here we devise new stabilization profiles that explicitly (albeit qualitatively) incorporate considerations of the global economic system, estimate the corresponding anthropogenic emissions requirements, and assess the significance of the profiles in terms of global-mean temperature and sea level changes. Our findings raise a number of important issues for those engaged in climate-change policy making, particularly with regard to the optimal timing of mitigation measures.

The IPCC Working Group I (WGI) concentration profiles (S350–S750; Fig. 1) were constructed under the following constraints: (1) prescribed initial (1990) concentration and rate of change of concentration; (2) a range of prescribed stabilization levels and attainment dates; and (3) the requirement that the implied emissions should not change too abruptly. Inverse calculations

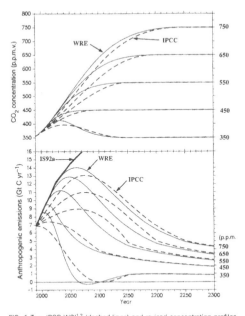

FIG. 1 Top, IPCC WGI[1,2] (dashed lines) and revised concentration profiles (WRE (this paper), solid lines) for stabilization of CO₂ at 350–750 p.p.m.v. Bottom, implied anthropogenic emissions using the model of Wigley[5]. IS92a is shown (thicker line) for comparison. Emissions were calculated following the procedure in ref. 1 in which the terrestrial biosphere sink is characterized solely by CO₂ fertilization of net primary productivity. The implications of using CO₂ fertilization as the sole terrestrial sink are discussed in ref. 4. The post-1990 inverse calculations were initialized by specifying a value for the 1980s-mean net deforestation (D_n80s). This determines the magnitude of the CO₂ fertilization factor. In the calculations in refs 1 and 2, D_n80s was taken as 1.6 Gt C yr⁻¹. This value has subsequently been revised downwards to 1.1 Gt C yr⁻¹ (ref. 2), the value used here. Other minor budget changes have been made to accord with most recent data.

were then used to determine the emission rates required to achieve stabilization via the specified pathways. These show that stabilization requires an eventual and sustained reduction of emissions to substantially below current levels. Furthermore, some have interpreted the results for the IPCC pathways to imply that an immediate reduction in emissions (relative to the central IPCC "existing policies" or "business as usual" emissions scenario, IS92a[3]) is required to achieve any of the stabilization targets.

The WGI analysis was not intended as a recommendation for policy, but it will be carefully scrutinized for its policy implications. Consequently, it is important to understand what the analysis does and does not tell us. The first conclusion of the IPCC analysis, that meeting any of the prescribed targets will require emissions to decline eventually to levels well below today's, is robust. One cannot conclude from the WGI results, however, that an immediate reduction in emissions is required if we are to stabilize concentrations at 750 p.p.m.v. or below. The WGI emissions results correspond to just one of a range of possible pathways toward a particular concentration target. Stabilization at the same level, via different concentration routes, would produce different emissions.

What therefore are appropriate criteria for selecting a concentration (and hence emissions) time-path? Some guidance is found in the Framework Convention itself. Article 3 states that "policies and measures to deal with climate change should be cost-effective so as to ensure global benefits at the lowest possible cost". Thus, if two paths were indistinguishable in terms of their environmental

implications, then the path with the lower mitigation (that is, emissions reduction) costs would be preferred. If two paths differed in terms of their environmental impacts, the issue becomes one of balancing benefits and costs. Here we examine alternative pathways for meeting the prescribed concentration targets. We then consider both the economic (costs) and environmental (benefits) implications of choosing one concentration trajectory over another.

In revising the IPCC WGI profiles, we add an additional constraint to the three noted above: that the resulting emissions trajectories initially track a 'business as usual' (BAU) path. This is an idealization of the assumption that the initial departure from BAU would be slow. We also assume that the higher the concentration target, the longer the adherence to BAU. This produces quite different concentration pathways, complementing the ones defined by IPCC WGI.

If we constrain emissions to follow BAU initially, the required concentration paths must depend on what we assume for this baseline scenario. We concentrate here on results for the central IPCC scenario (IS92a[3]). A higher baseline (such as IS92e or f) will lead to higher initial emissions. For a lower baseline such as IS92c, the task of stabilization of CO_2 concentrations at a level around 500 p.p.m.v. would require little action[4]. To derive the new profiles, we followed IS92a concentrations for 10–30 years and then fitted a smooth curve to the stabilization levels and dates used in ref. 1, using the same Padé approximant method. Figure 1 compares the new profiles with the WGI profiles. Further details are given in ref. 4.

The emissions implied by these new pathways (Fig. 1, lower panel) were obtained using the model of Wigley[5]. Although the precise values are model-specific, as shown by the inter-model comparison of Enting *et al.*[1], the qualitative character of the results and the relative differences in emissions due to concentration pathway differences are not.

The WGI analysis suggests that an immediate departure from the BAU path is required to meet all CO_2 concentration targets. Figure 1 shows that this is not so for concentration targets of 450 p.p.m.v. and above. Furthermore, for targets of 550 p.p.m.v. and above, the maximum rates of emissions decline are similar in both the new and WGI cases (but more prolonged in the former).

Figure 2 compares the old (WGI) and new results in more detail for the 550 p.p.m.v. stabilization case, and assesses the sensitivity of the results to the length of the interval over which BAU emissions are followed. The upper panel shows the WGI pathway and revised pathways following BAU for 10, 20 and 30 years (the 20-year case is that considered earlier). The emissions differences (middle panel) are striking in terms of the implied carbon intensity of the global energy system in the early decades of the next century. The different cumulative emissions pathways diverge initially and then become nearly parallel as one approaches and moves beyond the stabilization point (AD 2150 in this case). Cumulative emissions are noticeably higher in the cases that follow IS92a initially (a result that applies to all stabilization levels). This is because the products of early emissions have a longer time to be removed from the atmosphere, and because the associated higher concentrations give stronger oceanic and terrestrial sinks. Thus, later emissions reductions allow greater total CO_2 production, particularly for higher stabilization levels. These cumulative emissions differences, not considered by IPCC[2], may have important economic implications.

We now turn to how mitigation costs might vary with the choice of concentration profile. The rising emissions baseline that we use corresponds to an assumption that, in the absence of policy intervention, CO_2 emissions will continue to grow. This is consistent with the overwhelming majority of studies recently reviewed by the IPCC[6]. The implication is that stabilizing concentrations will entail some positive mitigation costs. A growing baseline, however, does not imply the absence of "no regrets" emissions reduction options (that is, with zero or negative mitigation costs). Such options are typically included in sizeable

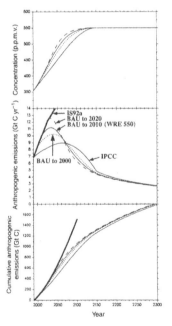

FIG. 2 Comparison of different concentration pathways (top panel) and implied emissions (middle) for stabilization of CO_2 levels at 550 p.p.m.v. in AD 2150. The pathways are: the original IPCC WGI S550 case[1]; the revised profile shown in Fig. 1 based on following BAU background emissions for 20 years, from 1990 to 2010 (WRE 550); and alternative revised profiles in which BAU is followed by 10 (BAU to 2000) or 30 years (BAU to 2020). The bottom panel shows the corresponding cumulative emissions. IS92a values are shown for comparison (thicker dashed lines).

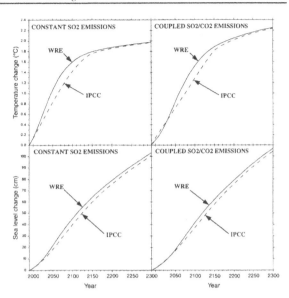

FIG. 3 Global-mean temperature (upper panels) and sea level changes (lower panels) for the S550 and WRE550 concentration stabilization pathways shown in Fig. 1. Results are from the models used in ref. 17, using the latest IPCC WGI estimate of the radiative forcing to 1990 and best-guess values of the climate sensitivity and ice-melt model parameters. Sea level changes include the contributions from oceanic thermal expansion, and ice melt from the world's glaciers and small ice caps, Greenland, and Antarctica. For the left panels, SO_2 emissions are held constant at their 1990 level. For the right panels, the effects of changes in anthropogenic SO_2 emissions (S) are added, with these changes directly coupled to those of fossil CO_2 emissions (F; values from Fig. 1) using $S = [S(1990)/F(1990)]F$. In both cases, the effects of non-CO_2 greenhouse-gases are accounted for by scaling CO_2 forcing by 1.33, the mean scaling for the IS92 emissions scenarios (compare ref. 21).

quantities in most economic analyses[7,8]. A growing baseline only means that economically competitive low-carbon alternatives are in insufficient supply to arrest future growth in carbon emissions. Conversely, if one were to assume that there are ample no-cost options to produce a falling emissions baseline, stabilization would entail little if any mitigation costs[9].

Several analysts have studied how mitigation costs might vary with the timing of the emissions reductions. For example, Nordhaus[10] and Manne and Richels[11] have identified cost-effective mitigation strategies for meeting a range of concentration targets. These studies show that to maintain cost-effectiveness, emissions tend to adhere to BAU the higher the concentration target (as assumed *a priori* here). Richels and Edmonds[12], in examining alternative emissions reduction pathways for stabilization at 500 p.p.m.v., found that the pathway can be just as important as the concentration stabilization level in determining the ultimate cost. Pathways involving modest reductions below a BAU scenario in the early years followed by sharper reductions later on were found to be less expensive than those involving substantial reductions in the short term. A similar conclusion can be found in Kosobud *et al.*[13].

Viewing the stabilization issue as a carbon budget allocation problem helps explain why concentration pathways with higher near-term emissions have lower overall mitigation costs. Because cumulative emissions are approximately independent of the concentration pathway, for each stabilization level there is, roughly, a fixed allowable amount of CO_2 to be released. The basic choice is, therefore, how this budget is to be allocated over time. From this perspective, the reasons for drawing more heavily on the budget in the early years are: (1) *Positive marginal productivity of capital.* With the economy yielding a positive return on capital[14], the further in the future an economic burden (here, emissions reduction) lies, the smaller is the set of resources that must be set aside today to finance the burden. (2) *Capital stock.* Stock for energy production and use is typically long-lived (for example, power plant, housing and transport). The current system is configured based upon a set of expectations about the future. Unanticipated changes will be costly. Time is therefore needed to reoptimize the capital stock. (3) *Technical progress.* There is ample evidence for past and potential future improvements in the efficiency of energy

supply, transformation and end-use technologies. Thus, the availability of low-carbon substitutes will probably improve and their costs reduce over time. In addition, as the emissions budget will be somewhat larger (that is, greater cumulative emissions) for pathways with higher emissions earlier, dependence on higher-cost, carbon-free alternatives is reduced.

We must stress that, even from the narrow perspective of a cost-effectiveness analysis, our results should not be interpreted as suggesting a "do nothing" or "wait and see" policy. First, all stabilization pathways still require future capital stock to be less carbon intensive than under a BAU scenario. As most energy production and use technologies are long-lived, this has implications for current investment decisions. Second, new supply options typically take many years to enter the market place. To ensure sufficient quantities of low-cost, low-carbon substitutes in the future requires a sustained commitment to research, development and demonstration today. Third, any available "no regrets" measures for reducing emissions should be adopted immediately. Last, it is clear from Fig. 1 that one cannot go on deferring emissions reductions indefinitely, and that the need for substantial reductions of emissions is sooner the lower the concentration target.

It is, of course, also important to examine the environmental consequences of selecting one concentration or emissions trajectory over another. This is because different concentration pathways imply, not only different emissions reduction costs, but also different benefits in terms of averted environmental impacts. In benefit-cost analyses of climate change policy options, it is common to use global-mean temperature and sea level rise as coarse indicators of the extent of climate impacts[14,15]. We therefore calculate how these indicators are affected by differences in the pathways to stabilization at an atmospheric CO_2 concentration of 550 p.p.m.v., based on the model of Wigley and Raper[16,17]. We first consider the direct effects of greenhouse-gas concentration changes, and then how these results may be modified by SO_2 emissions. All results use the central IPCC-recommended estimate of climate sensitivity[18] (2.5 °C equilibrium global-mean warming for a doubling of atmospheric CO_2 levels) and best-guess ice-melt model parameters[17].

Figure 3 (left panels) shows that, if greenhouse gases alone are considered, both temperature change and sea level rise would be noticeably affected by the choice of pathway towards stabilization at 550 p.p.m.v. These results, however, depend critically on how SO_2 emissions are assumed to change in the future. For the greenhouse-gas-alone case, we have assumed these emissions to remain constant at their 1990 level. As an alternative, we also consider a case where SO_2 emissions are closely coupled to fossil-fuel-derived CO_2 emissions. This case is consistent with the IPCC (IS92) emissions scenarios, except for IS92d, out to at least 2050 (ref. 3). It could occur if developing countries were less successful than developed countries in decoupling SO_2 and CO_2 emissions. In global-mean terms, SO_2/CO_2 emissions coupling leads to compensation between the reduced warming from reduced CO_2 emissions and an increased warming due to reduced SO_2 emissions[19,20].

To demonstrate the significance of this link, we give a specific example. This example is not meant to provide quantitative information on environmental impacts (which, for climate change, cannot be achieved through global-mean temperature alone), but to draw attention to aerosol influences as a critical factor in assessing the benefit–cost balance. Figure 3 compares global-mean temperature and sea level results for constant SO_2 emissions (left panels) with those for directly coupled CO_2 and SO_2 emissions (right panels). With SO_2 coupling, the lower-emissions case (S550) actually has warmer temperatures out to around 2040. This is because the much shorter lifetime of aerosols leads to a more rapid radiative forcing response to SO_2 emissions changes than to CO_2 emissions changes, allowing the former to dominate initially (compare refs 19,20). For sea level, coupling has a similar but less marked effect.

The market (for example, agriculture, timber and fisheries) and non-market (for example, biodiversity, environmental quality and human health) implications of these results are unclear: do pathway-related differentials up to $\sim 0.2\,°C$ in global-mean temperature and 4 cm in global-mean sea level change translate into significantly higher damages and, if so, are these large enough to offset the reduced cost of a more economical transition away from fossil fuels? The answer depends on the regional details associated with these changes, and the sensitivities of impact categories to changes in important climate variables. Both aspects are highly uncertain. Nevertheless, it is clear that the choice of emissions path requires the consideration of both costs and benefits. □

Received 30 May; accepted 8 December 1995.

1. Enting, I. G., Wigley, T. M. L. & Heimann, M. *Future Emissions and Concentrations of Carbon Dioxide: Key Ocean/Atmosphere/Land Analyses* (Division of Atmospheric Res., CSIRO, Australia, 1994).
2. Schimel, D. S. et al. in *Climate Change 1994: Radiative Forcing of Climate Change and an Evaluation of the IPCC IS92 Emissions Scenarios* (eds Houghton, J. T. et al.) 35–71 (Cambridge Univ. Press, 1995).
3. Leggett, J. A., Pepper, W. J. & Swart, R. J. in *Climate Change, 1992. The Supplementary Report to the IPCC Scientific Assessment* (eds Houghton, J. T., Callander, B. A. & Varney, S. K.) 69–95 (Cambridge Univ. Press, 1992).
4. Wigley, T. M. L. in *The Global Carbon Cycle* (eds Wigley, T. M. L. & Schimel, D. S.) (Cambridge Univ. Press, in the press).
5. Wigley, T. M. L. *Tellus* 45B, 409–425 (1993).
6. IPCC Working Group III in *Climate Change 1994: Radiative Forcing of Climate Change and an Evaluation of the IPCC IS92 Emissions Scenarios* (eds Houghton, J. T. et al.) 233–304 (Cambridge Univ. Press, 1995).
7. Dean, A. & Hoeller, P. *Costs of Reducing CO_2 Emissions* (OECD Economic Studies No. 19, OECD, Paris, 1992).
8. Energy Modeling Forum *Reducing Global Carbon Emissions–Costs and Policy Options* (EMF 12, Stanford Univ., Stanford, CA, 1993).
9. Goldemberg, J., Johansson, T. B., Reddy, A. & Williams, R. *Energy for a Sustainable World* (Wiley-Eastern Report, New Delhi, India & World Resources Institute, Washington, DC, 1987).
10. Nordhaus, W. D. *The Efficient Use of Energy Resources* (Yale Univ. Press, New Haven, CT, 1979).
11. Manne, A. & Richels, R. *The Greenhouse Debate—Economic Efficiency, Burden Sharing and Hedging Strategies* (Working Paper, Stanford Univ., Stanford, CA, 1995); *Energy J.* (in the press).
12. Richels, R. & Edmonds, J. A. in *Integrative Assessment of Mitigation, Impacts, and Adaptation to Climate Change* (eds Nakicenovic, N., Nordhaus, W. D., Richels, R. & Toth, F. L.) 341–352 (International Institute for Applied Systems Analysis, Laxenburg, Austria, 1994); *Energy Policy* (in the press).
13. Kosobud, R., Daly, T., South, D. & Quinn, K. *Energy J.* 19, 213–232 (1994).
14. Nordhaus, W. D. *Managing the Global Commons: The Economics of Climate Change* (MIT Press, Cambridge, MA, 1994).
15. Fankhauser, S. *Valuing Climate Change* (Earthscan, London, 1995).
16. Wigley, T. M. L. & Raper, S. C. B. *Nature* 357, 293–300 (1992).
17. Raper, S. C. B., Wigley, T. M. L. & Warrick, R. A. in *Rising Sea Level and Subsiding Coastal Areas* (ed. Milliman, J. D.) (Kluwer Academic, Dordrecht, The Netherlands, in the press).
18. Mitchell, J. F. B., Manabe, S., Tokioka, T. & Meleshko, V. in *Climate Change. The IPCC Scientific Assessment* (eds Houghton, J. T., Jenkins, G. J. & Ephraums, J. J.) 131–172 (Cambridge Univ. Press, 1990).
19. Wigley, T. M. L. *Nature* 349, 503–506 (1991).
20. Edmonds, J. A., Wise, M. & MacCracken, C. *Advanced Energy Technologies and Climate Change: An Analysis Using the Global Change Assessment Model (GCAM)* (PNL-9798, UC-402, Pacific Northwest Lab., Richland, WA, 1994).
21. Wigley, T. M. L. *Geophys. Res. Lett.* 22, 45–48 (1995).

ACKNOWLEDGMENTS. We thank the following for useful discussions: B. Bolin, H. Dowlatabadi, M. Grubb, E. Haites, A. Manne, R. Moss, W. Nordhaus, L. Pitelka, S. Smith, J. Weyant and L. Williams. The views expressed here, however, are solely those of the authors. This work was supported by the US Department of Energy and the Electric Power Research Institute.

[20]

Decoupling China's Carbon Emissions Increase from Economic Growth: An Economic Analysis and Policy Implications

ZHONGXIANG ZHANG *

Research Program, East-West Center, Honolulu, Hawaii

Summary. — As the world's second largest carbon emitter, China has long been criticized as a "free-rider" benefiting from other countries' efforts to reduce greenhouse gas emissions but not taking responsibility for its own emissions. China has been singled out as one of the major targets at the subsequent negotiations after the Kyoto meeting. By analyzing the historical contributions of interfuel switching, energy conservation, economic growth and population expansion to China's CO_2 emissions during 1980–97, this article clearly demonstrates that the above criticism is unjustified. Moreover, given the fact that the role of China is an issue of perennial concern at the international climate change negotiations, the article envisions some efforts and commitments that could be expected from China until its per capita income catches up with the level of middle-developed countries. By emphasizing the win-win strategies, these efforts and commitments are unlikely to jeopardize China's economic development and, at the same time, would give the country more leverage at the international climate change negotiations subsequent to the Buenos Aires meeting. © 2000 Elsevier Science Ltd. All rights reserved.

Key words — China, energy, carbon dioxide emissions, CGE model, environmental policy, climate change

1. INTRODUCTION

China is the world's most populous country and largest coal producer and consumer. At present, it contributes 13.5% of global carbon dioxide (CO_2) emissions, which makes it the world's second largest emitter of CO_2, after the United States, according to the World Energy Council (see Table 1). China's share in global CO_2 emissions is expected to increase and is likely to exceed that of the United States by 2020, if the current trend of economic development in China continues (World Bank, 1994; Energy Information Administration, 1999). In the face of a potentially serious global climate change problem, Annex I countries [1] finally committed themselves to legally binding emissions targets and timetables for reducing their greenhouse gas emissions in December 1997, at a meeting in Kyoto, Japan. Under the Kyoto Protocol to the United Nations Framework Convention on Climate Change (UNFCCC), these industrialized countries together must reduce their emissions of six greenhouse gases by at least 5% below 1990 levels over the commitment period 2008–2012, with the European Union (EU), the United States and Japan required to reduce their emissions of such gases by 8%, 7% and 6% respectively (UNFCCC, 1997). The Protocol will become effective once it is ratified by at least 55 parties whose CO_2 emissions represent at least 55% of the total from Annex I countries in the year 1990.

Since China has made no concrete commitments, it has been criticized as a "free-rider" benefiting from other countries' efforts to abate greenhouse gas emissions but not taking responsibilities of its own. This article is devoted to examining whether the above criticism holds up by analyzing the historical contributions of interfuel switching, energy conservation, economic growth and population

* I would like to thank Jose Goldemberg, Thomas B. Johansson, Walter Reid and two anonymous referees for useful discussions and comments on an earlier version of the article. The views expressed here are those of the author. The author bears sole responsibility for any errors and omissions that may remain Final revision accepted: 6 August 1999.

Table 1. *Shares of global CO_2 emissions and world population, 1996*[a]

	Share of global CO_2 emissions (%)	Share of the world population (%)
USA	25.0	4.7
EU-15	14.7	6.5
China	13.5	21.5
CIS Republics	10.2	5.0
Japan	5.6	2.2
India	3.6	16.3
Canada	2.1	0.5
Australia	1.3	0.3

[a] *Source*: Jefferson (1997).

expansion to China's CO_2 emissions during 1980–97. Such an analysis clearly indicates that China has made a significant contribution to reducing global CO_2 emissions, although none of these carbon savings has resulted from conscious domestic climate mitigation policies. Moreover, given the fact that the role of China is an issue of perennial concern at the international climate change negotiations, the article envisions some plausible strategies that China might take subsequent to the Buenos Aires meeting.

2. HISTORICAL EVOLUTION OF CO_2 EMISSIONS IN CHINA

With more than 1.2 billion people, China is home to about 21.5% of the world's population (see Table 1) and has a large and rapidly growing economy, making the country an important player on the world's stage. Since launching its open-door policy and economic reform in late 1978, China has experienced spectacular economic growth, with its gross domestic product (GDP) increasing at the average annual rate of about 10% over 1978–97. Along with the rapid economic development, energy consumption rose from 571.4 million tons of coal equivalent (Mtce) in 1978 to 1440.0 Mtce in 1997. Currently, China consumes almost 1,400 million tons of coal a year, leading the world in both production and consumption of coal. As indicated in Figure 1, coal has accounted for about 75% of the total energy consumption over the past years. This share has remained stable after having increased from 70% in 1976, indicating that coal has fuelled much of China's economic

growth over the past two decades. Although China surpassed Russia to become the world's second largest energy producer and user in 1993, China's current per capita energy consumption of 1.165 tons of coal equivalent (tce) is about half the world's average, or only about 1/12th of that of the United States (see Table 3).

Accompanying the growth in fossil fuel use, China's CO_2 emissions have grown rapidly. The corresponding CO_2 emissions from fossil fuels in China over 1980–97 have been calculated based on fossil fuel consumption and by using the CO_2 emission coefficients given in Table 2 that are measured in tons of carbon per ton of coal equivalent (tC/tce) and are generally considered suitable for China. As shown in Table 3, the total CO_2 emissions in China rose from 358.60 million tons of carbon (MtC) in 1980 to 847.25 MtC in 1997, with an average annual growth rate of 5.2%. China thus ranks as the world's second largest CO_2 emitter only behind the United States. But on a per capita basis, China's CO_2 emissions of 0.685 tC in 1997 (see Table 3) were very low, only about half the world average.

The breakdown of CO_2 emissions by fuel is shown in Figure 2. Because of the coal-dominant structure of Chinese energy consumption, it is not surprising that coal predominates, accounting for 81.3% of the total emissions in 1997. This share has remained almost unchanged over the past two decades.

3. THE CONTRIBUTIONS OF CO_2 EMISSIONS IN CHINA

Let us now examine the contributions of interfuel switching, energy conservation, economic growth and population expansion to China's CO_2 emissions over the past 17 years.

CO_2 emissions can be decomposed as follows: [2]

$$C = \left(\frac{C}{FEC} \right) \cdot \left(\frac{FEC}{TEC} \right) \cdot \left(\frac{TEC}{GDP} \right) \cdot \left(\frac{GDP}{POP} \right) \cdot POP,$$

where C is the amount of CO_2 emissions, FEC is the total carbon-based fossil fuel consumption, TEC is the total commercial energy consumption, GDP is the gross domestic product, and POP is the population.

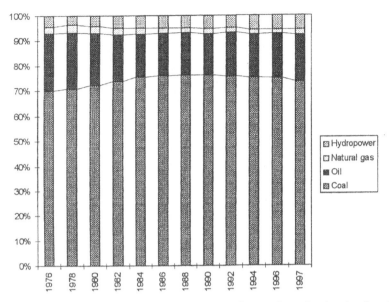

Figure 1. *Composition of energy consumption in China, 1976–97. Sources: Drawn based on data from the State Statistical Bureau (1992, 1998).*

Table 2. *CO_2 emission coefficients for China*[a]

Fuels	tC/tce
Coal	0.651
Oil	0.543
Natural gas	0.404
Hydropower, nuclear power and renewables	0

[a] *Source:* Energy Research Institute (1991).

Taking logs and differences over time yields:

$$\Delta \log C = \Delta \log(C/FEC) + \Delta \log(FEC/TEC)$$
$$+ \Delta \log(TEC/GDP)$$
$$+ \Delta \log(GDP/POP) + \Delta \log(POP).$$

This is a perfect decomposition method because it gives no residual on the right-hand side. In other words, the sum of the five terms on the right-hand side of the above equation is exactly equal to the term on the left-hand side. This can be illustrated as follows. Subtracting the five terms on the right-hand side from the term on the left-hand side, we have

$$\Delta \log C - (\Delta \log(C/FEC) + \Delta \log(FEC/TEC)$$
$$+ \Delta \log(TEC/GDP) + \Delta \log(GDP/POP)$$
$$+ \Delta \log(POP))$$

$$= \Delta \log C - (\Delta \log C - \Delta \log FEC + \Delta \log FEC$$
$$- \Delta \log TEC + \Delta \log TEC - \Delta \log GDP$$
$$+ \Delta \log GDP - \Delta \log POP + \Delta \log POP)$$
$$= \Delta \log C - \Delta \log C = 0.$$

Now let us explain what is meant by the five terms on the right-hand side of the above identity. The first term on the right-hand side shows the effect of changes in the composition of carbon-based fossil fuels on emissions, and the second term indicates the contribution of the penetration of carbon-free fuels $(1 - FEC/TEC)$ to a reduction in emissions (if the share of carbon-free fuels $(1 - FEC/TEC)$ is increased, the CO_2 emissions can be effectively reduced). These two terms therefore capture the contribution of interfuel substitution to the changes in emissions, as explained below: fuels vary considerably in their relative CO_2 emissions. Specific CO_2 emission from burning coal is 1.6 times that from natural gas and 1.2 times that from oil (see Table 2). Hydropower, nuclear energy and renewables do not produce CO_2 emissions. In this regard, increased use of carbon-free energy sources, along with substitution of natural gas for the more pollution-producing coal and oil, would clearly reduce CO_2 emissions. The third term shows the effect

Table 3. *Determining factors for CO$_2$ emissions in China*[a]

Year	POP (million)	C (MtC)	GDP[b]	TEC (Mtce)	FEC (Mtce)	GDP/POP (US$)[c]	TEC/GDP[d]	FEC/TEC	C/FEC (tC/tce)	TEC/POP (tce)	C/POP (tC)	C/GDP[e]
1980	987.05	358.60	3011.87	602.75	578.70	305	2.001	0.960	0.620	0.611	0.363	1.191
1981	1000.72	352.63	3170.25	594.47	567.66	317	1.875	0.955	0.621	0.594	0.352	1.112
1982	1016.54	367.82	3455.86	620.67	590.51	340	1.796	0.951	0.623	0.611	0.362	1.064
1983	1030.08	390.39	3832.34	660.40	625.66	372	1.723	0.947	0.624	0.641	0.379	1.019
1984	1043.57	421.41	4413.94	709.04	674.23	423	1.606	0.951	0.625	0.679	0.404	0.955
1985	1058.51	456.58	5008.53	766.82	729.63	473	1.531	0.952	0.626	0.724	0.431	0.912
1986	1075.07	482.01	5452.52	808.50	770.42	507	1.483	0.953	0.626	0.752	0.448	0.884
1987	1093.00	517.32	6083.45	866.32	826.12	557	1.424	0.954	0.626	0.793	0.473	0.850
1988	1110.26	554.98	6768.91	929.97	886.08	610	1.374	0.953	0.626	0.838	0.500	0.820
1989	1127.04	577.37	7044.13	969.34	921.94	625	1.376	0.951	0.626	0.860	0.512	0.820
1990	1143.33	586.87	7314.16	987.03	936.40	640	1.349	0.949	0.627	0.863	0.513	0.802
1991	1158.23	618.90	7986.64	1037.83	988.01	690	1.299	0.952	0.626	0.896	0.534	0.775
1992	1171.71	650.12	9123.88	1091.70	1038.21	779	1.197	0.951	0.626	0.932	0.555	0.713
1993	1185.17	687.61	10354.59	1159.93	1099.61	874	1.120	0.948	0.625	0.979	0.580	0.664
1994	1198.50	724.65	11665.79	1227.37	1157.41	973	1.052	0.943	0.626	1.024	0.605	0.621
1995	1211.21	771.24	12891.31	1311.76	1231.74	1064	1.018	0.939	0.626	1.083	0.637	0.598
1996	1223.89	820.71	14127.21	1389.48	1313.06	1154	0.984	0.945	0.625	1.135	0.671	0.581
1997	1236.26	847.25	15370.91	1440.00	1357.92	1243	0.937	0.943	0.624	1.165	0.685	0.551

[a] *Sources*: Calculated based on data from the State Statistical Bureau (1992, 1998).
[b] Measured in 100 million US$ at 1980 prices and at the average exchange rate 1 US$ = 1.5 Chinese yuan.
[c] At 1980 prices.
[d] Measured in tce per thousand US$ at 1980 prices.
[e] Measured in tC per thousand US$ at 1980 prices.

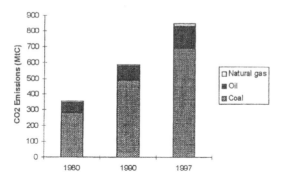

Figure 2. *China's CO_2 emissions by fuel.*

of changes in the aggregate energy intensity on emissions, and the last two terms show the effect on emissions due to growth in income per capita and population respectively. Needless to say, this identity is in a form suitable for analyzing the historical contributions of interfuel switching, energy conservation, economic growth, and population expansion to CO_2 emissions by examining the relevant time-series data.

Table 4 shows the results of this analysis for 1980–97, based on data given in Table 3. It quantifies the historical contribution to CO_2 emissions each factor has made. Population data, GDP values and commercial energy consumption of various types have been taken from the State Statistical Bureau (1992, 1998). The corresponding CO_2 emissions associated with the fossil fuel consumption have been calculated above. Part of the data in Table 3 is presented in Figure 3, after normalization to the year 1980.

The results in Table 4 and Figure 3 clearly indicate the relative importance of each factor in terms of its contribution to CO_2 emissions growth. Given that China has been the most rapidly expanding economy over the past 17 years, it is not surprising that economic growth measured in per capita GDP was overwhelming. This factor alone resulted in an increase of 799.13 MtC. During the corresponding period,

through its strict family planning program, China experienced a very low rate of population growth in comparison with other countries at China's income level, which in turn contributed to a smaller increase in China's CO_2 emissions than would otherwise have been the case. [3] As a result, population expansion was responsible for an increase of 128.39 MtC, an increase in emissions considered to be modest given its population size. In addition, the change in fossil fuel mix contributed to an increase in emissions (3.93 MtC), but its role was very limited because the share of coal use in total commercial energy consumption increased only slightly during the period.

By contrast, a reduction in energy intensity tended to push CO_2 emissions down. Since the early 1980s, the Chinese government has been placing great emphasis on energy conservation and has formulated and implemented approximately 30 energy conservation laws concerning the administrative, legislative, economic and technological aspects of energy conservation. After years of preparation, China's Energy Conservation Law was enacted on November 1, 1997 and came into force on January 1, 1998. In order to efficiently use energy, China has significantly reduced subsidies for energy consumption, with coal subsidy rates falling from 61% in 1984 to 37% in 1990 and to 29% in 1995, and petroleum subsidy rates falling from

Table 4. *Breakdown of the contributions to CO_2 emissions growth, 1980–97 (MtC)[a]*

Due to change in fossil fuel carbon intensity	Due to penetration of carbon free fuel	Due to change in energy intensity	Due to economic growth	Due to population expansion	Total change in CO_2 emissions
+3.93	−10.48	−432.32	+799.13	+128.39	+488.65

[a] A positive sign indicates an increase; a negative sign indicates a decline.

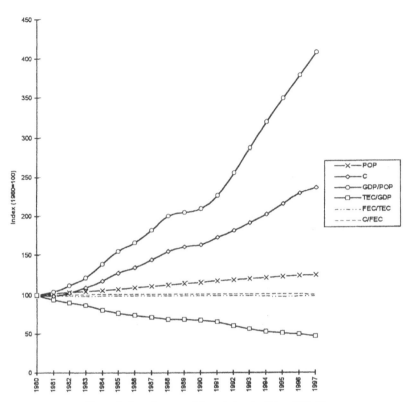

Figure 3. *Contribution to CO_2 emissions in China, 1980–97.*

55% in 1990 to 2% in 1995 (Kosmo, 1987; World Bank, 1997a). Currently, coal prices are largely decided by the market and vary significantly, depending on the destination of the coal. [4] Energy pricing reforms may have already proceeded to the point where the bottlenecks to more adoption of efficiency measures have less to do with energy prices than other factors (Sinton, Levine & Wang, 1998). Along with the economic reforms that, among other achievements, have spurred investment in more energy efficient production technologies (World Bank, 1997b), the Chinese government has also played a crucial role both in promoting a shift of economic structure toward less energy-intensive services (see Table 5) and a shift of product mix toward high value-added products, and in encouraging imports of energy-intensive products. [5] Furthermore, efforts have been made toward implementing nationwide energy conservation programs. For example, state capital construction loans for efficiency

are at an interest rate 30% lower than commercial loans, and state technological renovation loans for efficiency are with 50% of the interest subsidized (Sinton *et al.*, 1998). The creation of over 200 energy conservation technology service centers throughout the country, which have worked most closely with the end-users of the efficient technologies, devices and practices that the government has sought to promote, has been extremely valuable. In the power industry, efforts have been made toward developing large-size, coal-fired power plants. In 1987, only 11 power stations had an unit capacity of 1 gigawatt (GW) and above. The combined capacity of these power stations was about 15 GW, accounting for one-seventh of the country's total. By 1994, there were 34 power stations with a unit capacity of 1 GW and above, with a combined capacity of 43 GW, accounting for 21.4% of the country's total (SETC, 1996). In the meantime, the share of generating units having a capacity of

Table 5. *The composition of GDP in China, Japan and the United States (percentage of GDP)*[a]

	China			Japan	United States
	1980	1990	1997	1995	1995
Agriculture	30.1	27.1	18.7	2	2
Industry	48.5	41.6	49.2	38	26
Services	21.4	31.3	32.1	60	72

[a] *Sources*: State Statistical Bureau (1998) and World Bank (1997c).

100 MW and above increased from 32.5% in 1984 to 57.2% in 1994 (MOEP, 1985; SETC, 1996). Along with these large units commissioned into operation, the average generation efficiency of thermal power increased from 28.5% in 1984 to 29.7% in 1994. Given the sheer size of the Chinese power industry, even these small efficiency improvements translate into large coal savings when multiplied by tens of GW of capacity installed.

Clearly, it is by implementing these policies and measures that great progress in decoupling China's GDP growth from energy consumption has been made, with an annual growth of 10.06% for the former but only 5.26% for the latter during 1980–97. This achievement corresponds to an income elasticity of energy consumption of 0.52 and to an annual saving rate of 4.37%. [6] The fact that most developing countries at China's income level have the income elasticity of energy consumption well above one (see Table 6) clearly indicates that China's achievement is rarely accomplished in countries at this level of development (IEA, 1998). [7] As a result, a reduction of 432.32 MtC was achieved. In other words, without the above policies and measures toward energy conservation, China's CO_2 emissions in 1997 would have been 432.32 MtC higher, or more than 50% higher, than its actual emissions.

In addition to energy conservation, the penetration of carbon-free fuels contributed to a small reduction in CO_2 emissions (−10.48 MtC). This is mainly due to the underdevelopment of hydropower, and partly because the development of nuclear power in China is still at the start-up stage.

From the preceding analysis, it follows that China has made a significant contribution to reducing global CO_2 emissions, although none of these carbon savings has resulted from conscious domestic climate mitigation policies. Unfortunately, China's contribution has been too little appreciated. While China's achievements in this area are impressive, we might ask how the OECD countries have performed in this regard. They accounted for 50.3% of global CO_2 emissions in 1996 compared with 49.6% in 1990 (Jefferson, 1997) and promised at the Earth Summit in June 1992 to individually or jointly stabilize emissions of CO_2 and other greenhouse gases at their 1990 levels by 2000. As shown in Table 7, the total CO_2 emissions in the OECD countries rose by 7.8% over 1990–96. On their current trends, CO_2 emissions in the United States and EU-15 (the 15-member countries of the European Union) would be 13% and 8% above the promised targets in 2000 respectively (Jefferson, 1997; Reid & Goldemberg, 1997). Therefore, it is fair to say that, with few exceptions, few OECD countries are likely to meet their voluntary commitments to stabilizing CO_2 emissions at their 1990 levels by 2000.

Table 6. *Growth rates of GDP and energy consumption, and the income elasticity of energy consumption among different economies, 1980–94*[a]

	Annual growth of GDP (%)	Annual growth of energy consumption (%)	Income elasticity of energy consumption
Low-income economies[b]	2.5	3.3	1.32
China	11.0	4.5	0.41
India	5.2	6.3	1.21
Upper-middle-income economies	2.5	3.9	1.56
High-income economies	2.8	1.1	0.39

[a] *Source*: Calculated based on data from the World Bank (1996).
[b] Excluding China and India.

Table 7. *Changes in CO₂ emissions from fossil fuel among selected countries and regions (%)[a,b]*

	1990–96	1995–96
OECD[c]	+7.8	+2.6
EU-15	+0.9	+2.3
Denmark	+41.0	+20.6
Germany	−7.8	+2.1
Netherlands	+10.0	+2.6
United Kingdom	−1.0	+2.9
United States	+8.4	+3.3
Canada	+5.5	+1.6
Japan	+14.3	+1.8
Australia	+9.5	+2.2
New Zealand	+10.7	+4.0
Norway	+14.5	+7.3
CIS and C&E Europe	−31.0	−2.6
Developing countries	+32.0	+5.1
World	+6.4	+2.7

[a] A positive sign indicates an increase; a negative sign indicates a decline.
[b] *Source*: Jefferson (1997).
[c] Excluding Mexico, Korea, Hungary and Poland.

4. WHAT CAN BE EXPECTED FROM CHINA AT THE CLIMATE CHANGE NEGOTIATIONS SUBSEQUENT TO BUENOS AIRES?

Of course, the above discussion is not to justify no further action by China. Indeed, faced with both the mounting pressure from the United States and the new post-Kyoto negotiating environment, and given the global characteristics of climate change and China's importance as a source of future CO₂ emissions in line with its industrialization and urbanization, China must take further responsibility.

(a) *The changed negotiating environment*

Prior to Kyoto, developing counties' demand for US leadership in emissions reduction and the EU proposal for a 15% cut in emissions of a basket of three greenhouse gases below 1990 levels by 2010 put collective pressure on the United States, which leads the world in greenhouse gas emissions. Now the United States has made legally binding commitments at Kyoto. The Kyoto target is seen as insufficient but yet not unreasonable given that the US economy would not be unduly disrupted. [8] Now the ball has kicked into China's court. The United States has made it clear that bringing key developing countries, including China, on board has been and will continue to be its focus of international climate change negotiations.

According to some US senators, it will be countries like China, India and Mexico that will decide whether the United States will ratify the Kyoto Protocol. It is therefore conceivable that the pressure will mount for China to make some kind of commitment at the negotiations subsequent to Buenos Aires. The world's media will undoubtedly bring attention to China's nonparticipation, which will be seen as holding up the ratification of the Protocol by the US Senate and possibly even be blamed for "blowing up" subsequent negotiations aimed at dealing with developing countries' commitments.

While preparing for greater and greater pressure from the United States, China should take the following non-US factors into account in developing its post-Kyoto climate negotiation strategies.

First, although the group of 77 and China managed to block the US proposal for allowing a developing country to commit voluntarily to reductions in greenhouse gas emissions at Kyoto, the United States had partial success in weakening the position of the group. As might be expected, the United States will continue to apply the "divide and rule" tactic by getting at least a few to accept obligations they are not required to undertake and then putting pressure on the rest of the developing countries to do the same, exploiting the fact that developing countries such as Argentina have already determined to take on voluntary commitments. Given the fact that developing countries are a more diverse and heterogeneous group than Annex I countries, and that their interests in the climate change debate are heterogeneous and occasionally competing, it might be very difficult to prevent some countries in the group—particularly those countries with a relatively high per capita income and that perceive the greatest potential gain from emissions trading—from being drawn into making commitments of their own at the negotiations subsequent to Buenos Aires.

Second, after the first commitment period 2008–2012, China will surpass the United States as the world's largest greenhouse gas emitter, due mainly to its sheer size of population and partly to its rapid economic growth and continued heavy reliance on coal. While it will still take another couple of decades for cumulative greenhouse gas emissions from China to exceed those of the United States, Western media and some US senators could deliberately misguide the general public's attention and then shift the attack from the United States to China.

Third, although in accordance with the principle of common but differentiated responsibilities Annex I countries should take the lead in reducing their greenhouse gas emissions and providing adequate technology transfer and financing to non-Annex I countries, broadening commitments to include all countries in the long term is necessary and unavoidable in order to achieve the UNFCCC's ultimate objective of stabilizing greenhouse gas concentrations in the atmosphere at a level that would prevent dangerous anthropogenic interference with the climate system.

(b) *China's strategies at the climate change negotiations subsequent to Buenos Aires*

Faced with a different situation from that at Kyoto, China should rethink its strategies at the international climate change negotiations subsequent to Buenos Aires. On the one hand, China should make more efforts to communicate to the industrialized world the substantial contributions it has already made to limiting greenhouse gas emissions. China has cut its energy consumption per unit of output in half since 1980, indicating that if the energy intensity were the same now as in 1980, China would consume twice as much energy, and produce twice as much CO_2 emissions as it now does. Unfortunately, this achievement is not widely known or appreciated outside of China: outsiders know that the Chinese economy is booming, but they are not as cognizant of China's very impressive improvement in energy efficiency. Therefore, efforts toward effective communication about what has been achieved in China to the outside world will help to correct the distorted picture that had been painted.

On the other hand, while insisting on its legitimate demand for industrialized countries to provide adequate technology transfer and financing, and demanding that emissions targets beyond the first commitment period be set for Annex I countries at the subsequent negotiations over new additional developing countries' commitments, China could propose and direct negotiations, rather than just react and respond. In proposing its voluntary efforts and commitments, China should bear in mind that demanding "equal per capita entitlements" is politically unrealistic for the time span we are considering, although it is perfectly justified on

grounds that all human beings are born equal and that the atmosphere is a global common. On the other hand, the US demand for imposing a cap on China's future emissions is absolutely unacceptable for China, at least until its per capita income catches up with the level of middle-developed countries. For these reasons, I put aside the proposal for either "equal per capita entitlements" or an absolute cap on national emissions. I envision the following six proposals that could be put on the table as China's plausible negotiation position, which are each described in the order of their stringentness.

First, China could regard its active participation in the Clean Development Mechanism (CDM) under the Kyoto Protocol as "meaningful participation." If appropriate rules and guidelines for the CDM are defined, what then are the potential areas in China's interest? It is usually acknowledged that the success of the CDM premises an effective understanding of local (host country) development aspirations and the use of the CDM to push ahead with efforts to achieve these aspirations. Thus, in order to enhance their possibility of success, there is the need to make due consideration of local objectives and local conditions in designing the CDM projects. Considering that China is more concerned with local pollutants, such as SO_2, NOx and particulates from coal burning, and regards them as its own environmental priorities, it is expected that the most potential areas of interest to China are related to those activities and options aimed at: (i) improving the efficiency of energy use, particularly at energy-intensive energy sectors (for example, iron and steel industry, chemical industry, building materials industry, and power industry) and devices (for example, industrial boilers); (ii) pushing efficient use of coal through increasing proportion of raw coal washed; popularizing domestic use of coal briquette; substitution of direct burning of coal by electricity through development of large-size, high-temperature and high-pressure efficient coal-fired power plants; expanding district heating systems and developing co-generation; increased penetration of town gas into urban households; and through development and diffusion of environmentally sound coal technologies; (iii) speeding up the development of hydropower and nuclear power; and (iv) developing renewables (Zhang, 1997b).

Second, just as Article 3.2 of the Kyoto Protocol requires Annex I countries to "have made demonstrable progress" in achieving their commitments by 2005, China could commit to demonstrable efforts toward slowing its greenhouse gas emissions growth at some point between the first commitment period and 2020. Securing the undefined "demonstrable progress" regarding China's efforts is the best option that China should fight for at the international climate change negotiations subsequent to Buenos Aires.

Third, if the above commitment is not considered "meaningful," China could go a little further to make voluntary commitments to specific policies and measures to limit greenhouse gas emissions at some point between the first commitment period and 2020. Policies and measures might need to be developed to demonstrate explicitly whether China has made adequate efforts. Such policies and measures might include abolishing energy subsidies, improving the efficiency of energy use, promoting renewable energies, and increasing the research and development (R&D) spending on developing environmentally sound coal technologies.

China should resort to all means of securing either of the above deals. If all the attempts prove unsuccessful, China might resort to the last three options.

Fourth, China could make a voluntary commitment to total energy consumption or total greenhouse gas emissions per unit of GDP at some point around or beyond 2020. In my view, carbon intensity of the economy is preferred to energy intensity of the economy (i.e., total energy consumption per unit of GDP) because all the efforts toward shifting away from high-carbon energy are awarded by the former. Such a commitment would still allow China to grow economically while improving the environment. It reflects a basic element of the UNFCCC, which has recognized the developing countries' need for further development and economic growth. The industrialized countries have no reason or right to argue against it. To do so would contradict their claim that asking China's involvement in combating global climate change is not intended to limit its capacity to industrialize, reduce poverty and raise its standard of living. Even if the Chinese government has claimed that China will continue its efforts toward improving energy efficiency and minimizing further degradation of the environment in any event, it would be wise to propose an explicit value for carbon intensity of the Chinese economy as a

starting point for negotiations. In this regard, there is a pressing need for comprehensive analysis and quantification of the economic implications of climate change for China. For a long time, the Chinese government has claimed that asking China to take action would seriously harm China's economic development. Until now, however, inside of China there has been no single comprehensive study indicating the economic effects of possible future carbon limits for China, for example, in terms of foregone national income, although there have been some such studies done outside of China (e.g., Zhang, 1997a, 1998). Findings that show that China would be the region hardest hit by carbon limits can help to convince the world of the Chinese government's claim. Such information can be used to China's advantage in bargaining a possible targeted carbon intensity with other countries, as well.

The fifth option would be for China to commit voluntarily to an emissions cap on a particular sector at some point around or beyond 2020. Taking on such a commitment, although already burdensome for China, could raise the concern about the carbon leakage from the sector to those sectors whose emissions are not capped.

This leads to the final option that China could offer: a combination of a targeted carbon intensity level with an emissions cap on a particular sector at some point around or beyond 2020. China ultimately cannot afford to go beyond it until its per capita income catches up with the level of middle-developed countries.

It should be pointed out that before legally binding commitments become applicable to Annex I countries, they have a grace period of 16 years starting from the Earth Summit in June 1992 when Annex I countries promised individually or jointly to stabilize emissions of CO_2 and other greenhouse gases at their 1990 levels by the end of this century to the beginning of the first commitment period in 2008. Therefore, China could demand a grace period before either of the last three commitments becomes legally binding. Even without the precedent for Annex I countries, China's demand is by no means without foundation. For example, the Montreal Protocol on Substances that Deplete the Ozone Layer grants developing countries a grace period of 10 years (Zhang, 1997a). Moreover, China could insist that accession of developing countries and burden sharing be based on ability to pay. As such, a country is expected to take on emissions limitation commitments once it exceeds a threshold level of per capita income. On the one hand, this approach would avoid the costing negotiations for accession of developing countries on an individual basis. On the other hand, the approach would bind China and other developing countries, thus giving China more clout in the final bargaining in determining a threshold level.

5. CONCLUSIONS

In the face of a potentially serious global climate change problem, the industrialized countries finally committed themselves to binding legally emissions targets and timetables for reducing their greenhouse gas emissions in December 1997 in Kyoto. Since China has made no concrete commitments, it has been criticized as a "free-rider." By examining the historical evolution of China's CO_2 emissions during 1980–97, however, and analyzing the historical contributions of interfuel switching, energy conservation, economic growth and population expansion to CO_2 emissions, we have shown that such criticism is without foundation. Indeed, China has made a significant contribution to reducing global CO_2 emissions. By implementing a series of policies and measures toward energy conservation, China has cut its energy consumption per unit of output in half since 1980. In other words, without these efforts, China's CO_2 emissions in 1997 would have been 432.32 MtC higher, or more than 50% higher, than its actual emissions. Given the fact that most developing countries at China's income level have the income elasticity of energy consumption well above one (see Table 6), this makes China's achievement unique in the developing world, and surpasses that of the OECD countries, most of which will fail to honor their promises at the Earth Summit to stabilizing CO_2 emissions at their 1990 levels by 2000. Clearly, in order to correct a much distorted picture that has been painted of China, there is a pressing need for China to communicate effectively its achievements to the outside world.

Of course, this is not to justify in action by China. Indeed, faced with both the mounting pressure from the United States and the new post-Kyoto negotiating environment, and given the global characteristics of climate change and China's importance as a source of future CO_2 emissions in line with its industrialization and urbanization, China cannot come away without taking due responsibilities. Indeed, taking responsibility for combating global climate change should be in China's interest on the following grounds.

First, because climate-sensitive sectors such as agriculture still account for a much larger proportion of GDP in China than in the developed countries (see Table 5), China is even more vulnerable but less able to adapt to climate change than the developed countries. Therefore, a broad commitment to global efforts toward limiting greenhouse gas emissions would reduce the potential damage from climate change in China itself. After all, it is not only the developed countries whose climate will change if greenhouse gas emissions are not reduced.

Second, energy is relatively scarce in China, with per capita energy endowments far below the world average (see Table 8). Although energy consumption per unit of output in China has been cut in half since 1980, its major industries continue to use energy far more intensively than in industrialized countries (see Table 9). By making the above commitments, China will be pushed to use its scarce energy resources more efficiently.

Third, driven by the threat of further degradation of the environment [9] and the harmful economic effects of energy shortages, China is already determined to push energy conservation and enhanced energy efficiency in general and more efficient coal usage in particular. Although it is taking such drastic domestic efforts on its own, China badly needs assistance and economic and technical cooperation with the developed countries, because of the huge amounts of capital and technical expertise required. In this regard, the CDM, if designed appropriately, could provide an opportunity for China to get increased access to more advanced energy efficiency and pollution control technologies and additional funding.

On the other hand, economic development remains a priority for China. For this reason, any demand for imposing a cap on its future emissions is unacceptable for China, at least until its per capita income catches up with the level of middle-developed countries. Realistic efforts and commitments that could be expected from China range from attempts to slow its greenhouse gas emissions growth at some point between the first commitment period and 2020, to a commitment to a combination of a targeted carbon intensity level with an emissions cap on a

Table 8. *Proved reserves and utilization rates of fossil fuels in China, 1997*[a]

Resources	Proved reserves	R/P ratio[b] (years)		Per capita proved reserves[c]	
	China	China	World	China	World
Coal	114.5 billion tons	82	219	95	182
% world total	11.10%				
Oil	3.3 billion tons	21	41	3	25
% world total	2.30%				
Natural gas	1.16 trillion cubic meters	52	64	967	25517
% world total	0.80%				

[a] *Sources*: Calculated based on data from the British Petroleum (1998) and World Bank (1997c).
[b] *R/P* ratio stands for the lifetime of proved reserves at 1997 rates of production.
[c] Measured in tons for coal and oil, and in cubic meters for natural gas and based on population in 1995.

Table 9. *A comparison of unit energy consumption for selected energy-intensive users*[a]

	1980 China	1994 China	Advanced level abroad
Comparable energy consumption per ton of steel (tce/t)	1.30	1.03[b]	0.6 (Italy)
Energy consumption per ton of synthetic ammonia (tce/t)			1.2
Large plants	1.45	1.34[b]	
Small plants	2.90	2.09	
Energy consumption per ton of cement clinker (kgce/t)	206.5	175.3	108.4 (Japan)
Net coal consumption of coal-fired plants (gce/kWh)	448	413	327 (ex-USSR)
Thermal efficiency of industrial boilers (%)		60–70	80–85

[a] *Source*: Zhang (1997a).
[b] In 1990.

particular sector around or beyond 2020. With their focus on the win-win strategies, such efforts and commitments are unlikely to jeopardize severely Chinese economic development and, at the same time, would give China more leverage at the international climate change negotiations subsequent to Buenos Aires. Though aimed at limiting greenhouse gas emissions, they will also contribute to the reduction of local pollutants and thus will be beneficial to a more sustainable development of the Chinese economy as well as to the global climate.

NOTES

1. Annex I countries refer to the Organisation for Economic Co-operation and Development (OECD) member countries and countries with economies in transition. These countries have committed themselves to legally binding greenhouse gas emissions targets.

2. This is a concrete form of the so-called Ehrlich equation $I = PAT$, where I represents the adverse environmental impact, P is the population, A is the consumption per capita, and T is the amount of resources required by environmentally damaging technology for producing one unit of consumption (Ehrlich & Ehrlich, 1990). It is used as a proxy for a determinant of environmental impact.

3. During 1980–97, the annual average growth rate of population in China was 1.33%. In contrast, the corresponding figure for low-income economies (excluding China) during 1980–95 was 2.35%, and the world average was 1.66% (World Bank, 1997c).

4. For example, the nine-mouth price of Datong mixed coal was 128 yuan per ton in June 1994. The same coal retailed for 230 yuan per ton in Shanghai, 262 yuan per ton in Nanjing, 280 yuan per ton in Guangzhou, and 340 yuan per ton in Xiamen (SETC, 1996).

5. About 10% of the total energy savings during 1981–88 were attributed to imports of energy-intensive products (Zhang, 1997a).

6. The income elasticity of energy consumption is defined as the change in energy consumption divided by the change in economic growth.

7. As shown in Table 6, the income elasticity of energy consumpin China is quite low by international standards. In addition to energy conservation, there are other two possible explanations for this. First, the growth of energy consumption is underestimated relative to the GDP growth. In other words, the GDP growth rate is overestimated. It has been widely argued that China's statistical authorities underestimate China's GDP level and thus overestimate the GDP growth rate. Using a measurement technique closer to Western national accounting practice, Maddison (1997), for example, re-estimates China's GDP. He found that during 1952–78 China's GDP grew at an average annual rate of 4.4%, in comparison with the official rate of 6%. For 1978–94, his estimate for the GDP growth rate is 7.4%, whereas the official growth figure is 9.8%. Second, quantitative restrictions have kept energy consumption from rising as would otherwise have occurred. Drawing on the analysis of

rationing by Neary and Roberts (1980), the quantitative restrictions act like an implicit energy tax levied at rates varying with use and fuel. Generally speaking, households face a higher implicit tax than industrial users, and oil and natural gas are taxed at a higher rate than coal.

8. As indicated in Table 7, the US CO_2 emissions in 1996 were already 8.4% above 1990 levels. To meet the Kyoto commitments requires the United States to cut its greenhouse gas emissions by up to 30% from its business-as-usual levels during 2008–2012 (Energy Information Administration, 1999). This is not tremendous but not trivial either.

9. Existing estimates for the economic costs of China's environmental degradation vary, depending on the comprehensiveness of the estimates. For example, using the measure of willingness to pay, the World Bank (1997b) has estimated that air and water pollution cost China about 8% of its GDP, around $54 billion annually, while Smil (1996) puts China's environmental damages between 5.5% and 9.8% of its GNP.

REFERENCES

British Petroleum (1998). *BP statistical review of world energy 1998*. BP: London.

Ehrlich, P., & Ehrlich, A. (1990). *The population explosion*. New York: Touchstone.

Energy Information Administration (1999). International energy outlook 1999. DOE/EIA-0484(99), Department of Energy, Washington, DC.

Energy Research Institute (1991). CO_2 emissions from fossil fuel combustion and reduction countermeasures in China. Beijing: State Planning Commission.

IEA (1998). *World energy outlook 1998*. Paris: International Energy Agency (IEA).

Jefferson, M. (1997). Potential climate change: carbon dioxide emissions 1990–96. *World Energy Council Journal*, 76–82.

Kosmo, M. (1987). *Money to burn? The high costs of energy subsidies*. Washington, DC: World Resources Institute.

Maddison, A. (1997). *Measuring Chinese economic growth and levels of performance*. Paris: Organisation for Economic Co-operation and Development.

MOEP (1985). *Electric power industry in China 1984–85*. Beijing: Ministry of Electric Power (MOEP).

Neary, J. P., & Roberts, K. W. S. (1980). The theory of household behaviour under rationing. *European Economic Review, 13*, 25–42.

Reid, W., & Goldemberg, J. (1997). Are developing countries already doing as much as industrialised countries to slow climate change? *Climate Notes*. Washington, DC: World Resources Institute.

SETC (1996). *China energy Annual Review 1996*. Beijing: State Economic and Trade Commission (SETC).

Sinton, J. E., Levine, M. D., & Wang, Q. Y. (1998). Energy efficiency in China: accomplishments and challenges. *Energy Policy, 26* (11), 813–829.

Smil, V. (1996). *Environmental problems in China: estimates of economic costs*. Honolulu: East–West Center.

State Statistical Bureau (1992). *Energy statistical yearbook of China 1991*. Beijing: State Statistical Publishing House.

State Statistical Bureau (1998). *A statistical survey of China 1998*. Beijing: State Statistical Publishing House.

UNFCCC (1997). Kyoto Protocol to the United Nations Framework Convention on Climate Change (UNFCCC). FCCC/CP/1997/L.7/Add.1, Bonn.

World Bank (1994). *China: Issues and options in greenhouse gas emissions control*. Washington, DC: World Bank.

World Bank (1996). *World Development Report 1996*. New York: Oxford University Press.

World Bank (1997a). *Expanding the measure of wealth: indicators of environmentally sustainable development*. Washington, DC: World bank.

World Bank (1997b). *Clear water, blue skies: China's environment in the new century*. Washington, DC.

World Bank (1997c). *World Development Report 1997*. New York: Oxford University Press.

Zhang, Z. X. (1997a). *The economics of energy policy in China: implications for global climate change*. New Horizons in Environmental Economics Series. Edward Elgar, England.

Zhang, Z. X. (1997b). Operationalization and priority of joint implementation projects. *Intereconomics (Review of International Trade and Development),32* (6), 280–292.

Zhang, Z. X. (1998). Macroeconomic effects of CO_2 emission limits: a computable general equilibrium analysis for China. *Journal of Policy Modeling, 20* (2), 213–250.

[21]

Modeling non-CO_2 greenhouse gas abatement

Robert C. Hyman, John M. Reilly, Mustafa H. Babiker, Ardoin De Masin and Henry D. Jacoby

Joint Program on the Science and Policy of Global Change, Massachusetts Institute of Technology, MIT Building E40-428, 77 Massachesetts Avenue, Cambridge, MA 02139-4367, USA

E-mail: rhyman@alum.mit.edu

Although emissions of CO_2 are the largest anthropogenic contributor to the risks of climate change, other substances are important in the formulation of a cost-effective response. To provide improved facilities for addressing their role, we develop an approach for endogenizing control of these other greenhouse gases within a computable general equilibrium (CGE) model of the world economy. The calculation is consistent with underlying economic production theory. For parameterization it is able to draw on marginal abatement cost (MAC) functions for these gases based on detailed technological descriptions of control options. We apply the method to the gases identified in the Kyoto Protocol: methane (CH_4), nitrous oxide (N_2O), sulfur hexaflouride (SF_6), the perflourocarbons (PFCs), and the hydrofluorocarbons (HFCs). Complete and consistent estimates are provided of the costs of meeting greenhouse-gas reduction targets with a focus on "what" flexibility – i.e., the ability to abate the most cost-effective mix of gases in any period. We find that non-CO_2 gases are a crucial component of a cost-effective policy. Because of their high GWPs under current international agreements they would contribute a substantial share of early abatement.

1. Introduction

Human activities are contributing a complex mix of greenhouse gases (GHGs) to the atmosphere, perturbing the radiation balance of the Earth and very likely modifying its climate. Carbon dioxide (CO_2) from fossil fuel burning and human land use change is the most important single anthropogenic influence. Also of critical importance, however, are emissions of non-CO_2 gases including methane (CH_4) and nitrous oxide (N_2O) that are naturally present in the atmosphere, and a group of industrial gases including perfluorocarbons (PFCs), hydrofluorocarbons (HFCs), and sulfur hexafluoride (SF_6). Taken together with the already banned chlorofluorocarbons (CFCs), they are of significance roughly equivalent to CO_2 [17]. To effectively limit climate change, and to do so in a cost-effective manner, climate policies need to deal with all of them.

Previous studies have explored the degree to which abatement opportunities among these non-CO_2 GHGs could substantially reduce the cost of meeting an emissions target. The savings found, compared with a CO_2-only policy, were more than proportional to the emission contribution of these non-CO_2 sources [7,11,15,16]. At the time most of these earlier studies were done, however, the non-CO_2 gases had not been fully incorporated within the underlying analytic models.[1] Instead, exogenous marginal abatement curve (MAC) functions for these gases were combined with economic model results for fossil carbon emissions (e.g., [7,16]).

An important disadvantage of analysis using exogenous MAC functions is their inability to capture many of the interactions that would result from a GHG constraint. For instance, there are spillover effects of the control of one gas

onto emissions of others that are not easily captured using an exogenous abatement curve approach. Gases such as CH_4, N_2O, and SF_6 will be affected by a carbon restriction because some of their emissions sources are closely tied to energy production and use. Methane is emitted from energy transport activities and N_2O is produced in fossil fuel combustion. Reduced electricity production that might result from restrictions on fossil fuels would reduce SF_6 emissions because of its use in electrical switchgear. Also omitted are effects on prices of exports and imports of energy and other goods, and the terms of trade, and on investment in and depletion of fossil fuel resources. Endogenizing abatement of GHGs within a CGE model, which includes these mechanisms, allows the interactions between controls of different gases to be consistently assessed.

A further issue concerns welfare analysis. Economic costs estimated as areas under a MAC function are not consistent with the equivalent variation measure of welfare most commonly used in assessing policy costs in CGE models. Explicit representation of these abatement opportunities within the CGE production structure allows consistent costing of controls applied across several gases, and ensures comparability among studies using different analytical models.

In section 2 we describe an approach for incorporating non-CO_2 GHGs in a CGE model, along with a method for estimating the necessary parameters. Functions representing the abatement costs of these gases are fit to results from detailed, bottom-up studies of cost. Avoiding the often shrill debate between "top-down" and "bottom-up" models of energy, the approach allows the assessment to be consistent with partial-equilibrium bottom-up studies while taking account of the economy-wide interactions that any control action will stimulate. The analytic approach is introduced using CH_4 as an example. In section 3 we describe its im-

---

[1] Manne and Richels [11] introduced abatement costs as an endogenous component of their model, but did not consider the industrial gases (HFCs, PFCs, and SF_6).

plementation in the MIT EPPA model [3] and extension to all the non-CO$_2$ gases. Section 4 presents a sample calculation, showing the relative importance of the non-CO$_2$ gases among countries and as function of time and stringency of policy. The differences in results from this all-gas CGE approach, as compared with analysis using MAC curves, is explored in section 5. Section 6 concludes with thoughts about next steps in multi-gas policy and its assessment.

2. Representing the non-CO$_2$ gases in a CGE model

2.1. Alternative formulations of emissions control

The common approach to modeling the control of CO$_2$ from fossil energy combustion is, in general, not applicable to the other GHGs. Modeling CO$_2$ control is simplified by the fact that it is emitted in fixed proportions with the burning of oil, coal, and natural gas. The modeled activity of energy-using sectors – like agriculture, industrial production or provision of household services – may involve a number of energy inputs, some of them from fossil sources. Abatement of CO$_2$ emissions results from some combination of changed demands for energy services, increased efficiency in their use, or substitution among energy sources. However achieved, reduction of CO$_2$ emissions is synonymous with lower overall fossil fuel use or a shift to less carbon-intensive sources.[2] In a CGE model, these emissions can be estimated in proportion to the activity levels of the coal, oil and gas industries.

Emissions of the other GHGs cannot, in general, be tied in fixed proportions to activity in the sectors that produce them, because actions can be taken to reduce emissions per unit of activity. Given this fact, there are a number of avenues for endogenizing pollution control that are consistent with production theory and the restrictions of CGE modeling. One is to create a clean-up sector that removes the pollution, using capital, labor, and other inputs. In such an approach, emitting sectors would purchase abatement services from the clean-up sector and this clean-up service would be another input into the production of, for example, agriculture, coal mining, or natural gas distribution. Such an approach would provide flexibility to represent the factor shares of the clean-up activity. Adequate representation of available opportunities would, however, require many clean-up sectors because (to take just one example) the technology for abating CH$_4$ emissions from agriculture, coal-mining, and landfills all differ from one another.

A second approach would be to create an alternative production process that is "cleaner" than conventional technology, and that includes a cost structure reflecting the extra cost. For example, an agricultural production function might

be added that produces agricultural goods but with less CH$_4$ than existing agricultural practice. Production from the alternative activity would cost more than the conventional one, the premium in cost reflecting the additional inputs needed to reduce emissions. Again, the limit to this approach is that there are many alternative production activities that produce different levels of each of the GHGs, so many different production functions would have to be created to represent the ways that production costs and emissions might change under different combinations of GHG control. Failure to introduce a wide range of combinations for each gas and sector of origin would give the unrealistic "bang–bang" solutions characteristic of this type of activity analysis.

We have chosen a simpler approach, modeling the GHG directly as an input into the production function. We thus are able to compactly introduce GHG control by introducing such an input for each GHG in each sector from which the gas is emitted. As shown below, we then require only an emissions coefficient and an elasticity of substitution between the GHG and other inputs.[3]

2.2. Details of implementation

Representing emissions as an input is common in analytical general equilibrium models of pollution control (e.g., [4,6]). A couple of practical considerations arise, however, in using this approach in CGE modeling. Many CGE models, including the one applied here, use Constant Elasticity of Substitution (CES) production functions, and a feature of this family of relations is that each input must always have a non-zero cost share. In economic terms, the actual input of GHG disposal is the cost of controlling emissions. If there is no such control under current conditions then the cost share becomes zero, which is inconsistent with the "necessary input" feature of CES functions. We overcome this problem by positing a very low initial price ($1/ton of carbon equivalent) for each GHG. In fact, this procedure is not particularly unrealistic because for many of these gases there is currently a small incentive to collect or recycle the gas [17]. Introducing a small initial cost requires rebalancing the social accounting matrix underlying the model [3], but because these costs are a very small percentage of any production sector ($\ll$1%) this correction does not introduce significant changes in the base year conditions.

A second limitation of the CES structure is that it constrains the elasticity of substitution to be identical between all pairs of inputs. To overcome this restriction a nested production structure is usually imposed, and with sufficient layers in the nest any degree of flexibility can be achieved in the representation of elasticities between individual input pairs.[4]

---

[2] An exception is carbon sequestration technologies that, at a cost, divert the carbon from the fuel or the smokestack to some form of storage, and thus change the relationship between fuel use and carbon. For an approach that can be used to model sequestration parallel the approaches discussed here see [13].

[3] In fact, this approach would not be that dissimilar from CGE modeling of CO$_2$ control if, instead of evaluating the fossil fuel input as energy, it was treated as a carbon (disposal) input. With this change in treatment the ability to gradually substitute away from carbon use would represented by an elasticity of substitution between carbon and other inputs, but this is just the set of elasticities of substitution that describe the demand for fuels and energy.

[4] For the details of the nesting structure of the model applied here, see [3].

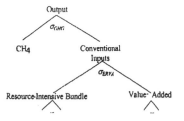

Figure 1. The agriculture production structure with methane as input to production.

The practical task in modeling the non-CO$_2$ gases is to decide how to structure the GHG nest while avoiding needless complexity. We have chosen to place these GHGs at the top of the nest, as illustrated in figure 1 for the CH$_4$ emitted from agricultural production. This formulation implies, other things equal, that a rise in the price of the GHG (as a result of a tighter emissions constraint) leads to a substitution away from it by means of a proportional increase in the use of all other inputs.

Detailed data on technological options for controlling other GHGs might be developed that suggest a different set of input usage than implied by this assumption. In practice, it is difficult to make a close translation between inputs as represented in engineering studies and as estimated and represented in production functions. The distinction between capital and material inputs is blurred, and engineering studies typically do not allocate management, insurance, bookkeeping, and other such overhead expenses to a small add-on emissions control technology. Thus it is not clear exactly how to allocate such expenses in a consistent way in the conversion to a more elaborate production function format. Moreover, what is often available is a single engineering cost estimate that refers to a single technology. So, even if a true representation of a particular technology could be constructed, it might not apply at different levels of abatement. Thus, locating GHG disposal at the top of the nest, and the implications of doing so, represent in our judgment a good first approximation of input demand resulting from emissions control.

A third practical task is the estimation of the elasticity of substitution, σ_{GHG} in figure 1. Here we make use of the observation that, once we have represented emissions as an input in the production function, the supply of abatement opportunities (often described as a marginal abatement curve or MAC), is the inverse of the input demand function for emissions. Such MAC functions are often developed as a summary description of detailed process models that evaluate abatement options (e.g., [5,19,20]). The input demand function can be derived directly from the CES production function, and the demand elasticity is directly related to the substitution elasticity. We can thus fit an inverse input demand function to a MAC and estimate an elasticity of substitution that fits the underlying bottom-up data.

The mathematics of this relationship, using CH$_4$ as an example, is as follows. A constant elasticity of substitution

(CES) function is of the form:

$$P_o = \left[\theta[P_{i1}]^{1-\sigma} + (1 - \theta)[P_{i2}]^{1-\sigma}\right]^{1/(1-\sigma)}, \quad (1)$$

where

P_o = Price of the output of the CH$_4$-emitting sector,

P_{i1} = Price of CH$_4$,

P_{i2} = Price of all óther inputs to the production process, itself the result of the sector production nest representing these inputs,

θ = CH$_4$ input share,

σ = Substitution elasticity between CH$_4$ and the other input aggregate.

By differentiating this function with respect to P_{i1}, the unit demand function (i.e., the quantity of methane demanded to produce one unit of output) is obtained. If X_1 is the input quantity of methane, this unit demand function is

$$X_1 = \theta \left[\frac{P_o}{P_{i1}}\right]^{\sigma}. \quad (2)$$

The price elasticity of demand can be derived by taking the derivative of (2) with respect to P_{i1}:

$$\frac{\partial X_1}{\partial P_{i1}} = -\frac{\theta\sigma}{P_{i1}}\left(\frac{P_o}{P_{i1}}\right)^{\sigma} + \frac{\theta\sigma}{P_o}\left(\frac{P_o}{P_{i1}}\right)^{\sigma}. \quad (3)$$

To derive the elasticity of input demand ε_{di}, we multiply expression (3) by P_{i1}/X_1 and substitute for X_1 from above, yielding

$$\varepsilon_{di} = \frac{\partial X_1/X_1}{\partial P_{i1}/P_i} = -\sigma\left(1 - \frac{P_i}{P_o}\right). \quad (4)$$

If we let α equal the cost share of methane in production costs, i.e.

$$\alpha = \frac{P_i}{P_o}, \quad (5)$$

we can rearrange terms to see that the elasticity of substitution σ is equal to:

$$\sigma = -\frac{\varepsilon_{di}}{1 - \alpha}. \quad (6)$$

In fact, control costs for methane are a small share of total production costs, especially for the level of aggregation typical in CGE models so that $1 - \alpha$ is essentially equal to one. Therefore, the substitution elasticity is virtually the same as the price elasticity of demand. Methane marginal abatement curves can be thus generated by the following equation

$$Abatement = 1 - X_1 = 1 - \theta\left[\frac{P_o}{P_{i1}}\right]^{\sigma}, \quad (7)$$

where σ is estimated to match a MAC from detailed bottom-up studies. In this form, baseline emissions are assumed to be equal to 1.0, so that abatement is expressed here as a percentage of baseline emissions. For our purposes, we may

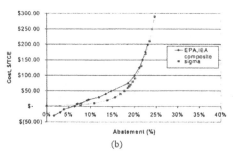

(a)   (b)

Figure 2. Comparison of EPPA parameterization with methane MAC curve. (a) Agriculture MAC for China. (b) Agriculture MAC for the US. Source: bottom-up abatement curves were derived by combining data from IEA [9,10] and US EPA [19]. For details, see [8].

substitute into equation (7) the values $\theta = 1.0$ (i.e., baseline emissions = 100%) and that $P_o = 1$ (the initial price index for output for that sector), yielding:

$$Abatement = 1 - \left[\frac{1}{P_{GHG}}\right]^\sigma, \qquad (8)$$

where $P_{i1} = P_{GHG}$ is the emissions price applied to CH₄ in this case. Note that the choice of this function imposes a key restriction on the functions. "Abatement" can never be less than zero, which rules out explicit representation of "no regrets" options.[5]

Two sample applications of this approach are shown in figure 2, which presents the underlying engineering estimate of the MACs for the abatement of CH₄ emissions from the agriculture sectors of China and the US, along with the σ_{GHG} approximation.

The first part of the engineering estimate shows that some negative cost (beneficial) or no-regrets options are estimated to be available: the cost of abatement is more than covered by the sales value of the gas. Bottom-up results of this form present two choices for constructing the approximation. One approach is to accept non-adoption of apparent no-regrets options as evidence that they are not economic, and shift up the MAC so that all portions of the curve are above the horizontal axis, as shown with the dashed line MAC in figure 3. A second approach is to include the no regrets "abatement" in the reference scenario, assuming that it will occur in the absence of a climate policy. The relevant portion of the MAC, then, is only that part that crosses the $0/tCe axis, the part to the right of the vertical dotted line in figure 3.

[5] As previously noted, a $1/MtCe is assigned to the base level of emissions because all inputs are necessary inputs in a CES, so that their use can only approach (but not equal) zero as the price becomes very low. Viewed as an inverse demand for abatement, zero is the base level of emissions, and this occurs at $1/MtCe. Computationally, we include code to provide that, if a policy solution yields an equilibrium price less than $1, emissions do not exceed the reference emissions. Such a result can occur, for example, in a situation where there is hot air in the carbon market and there is inter-gas trading but no international trading. Without code to detect and avoid this condition, emissions can be much higher than in the reference, suggesting negative abatement.

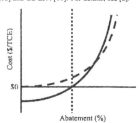

Figure 3. Negative cost abatement opportunities.

In the simulations discussed below we have adopted the first approach, and chosen an elasticity value that, we argue, overcomes some of the biases that often exist in bottom-up studies. It is often difficult in these types of studies to fully allocate a variety of overhead and transactions costs that are involved in such mitigation efforts (for instance, an agricultural emissions reduction option might require farmer education and government outreach programs to help farmers realize the benefits of methane mitigation). These studies may also underestimate the rate of return a firm requires to undertake a relatively small investment – e.g., when there are other higher-return activities to which scarce management and financial resources will be devoted. And, it can also be difficult to identify all of the various site- or enterprise-specific conditions that may add to abatement costs. Cost evidence from already operating facilities, for example, may reflect the fact that these sites had the most favorable economic conditions. On the other hand, to the extent bottom-up studies focus mostly on existing technologies that seem feasible today, they can under-represent the options available at higher prices.

In the examples shown in figure 2 the underlying engineering analysis foresaw no way to achieve more than about a 25 to 30% reduction from reference emissions levels. However, if the carbon-equivalent prices actually rise to $50, $100 and higher, so that market participants actually faced these prices, there would be strong incentives to search out and develop options not currently foreseen in engineering studies. The US EPA [19,20] estimates, that are in part the basis for our work, are described by their authors as

R.C. Hyman et al. / Non-CO₂ gas abatement   179

conservative, including only those technological options that have been demonstrated so that the costs can be confidently assessed.

We did not econometrically fit the estimate, but instead chose a value for σ and compared that to the bottom-up MAC, to allow us to judgmentally adjust the fit. The non-negativity requirement of the CES meant that our estimates assume that the no regrets portion of the curve is an underestimate of the full cost of abating these emissions, and that there are positive, albeit small costs at these levels of abatement. At higher costs, our estimates allow a somewhat greater potential to abate than in the bottom-up MACs, for the reasons discussed above. Figure 2 illustrates the approximate nature of our fits.

3. Implementation in the MIT EPPA model

We apply the method above to the MIT Emissions Prediction and Policy Analysis (EPPA) model [3]. This model simulates the world economy in order to produce scenarios of anthropogenic greenhouse gas emissions and to analyze the economic impact of climate change policies. It is part of a larger Integrated Global System model of human–climate interaction [14]. EPPA is a recursive dynamic multi-regional general equilibrium model. It is built on a comprehensive energy-economy data set that accommodates a consistent representation of energy markets in physical units as well as detailed accounts of regional production and bilateral trade flows. The base year for the model is 1995, and it is solved recursively through time at 5-year intervals. The model has 12 regions, eight commodity groupings, and a consumption sector, as shown in table 1. Nested constant elasticity of substitution (CES) functions are used to describe technologies and preferences, as noted earlier.

A first step in introducing GHGs into the EPPA structure is to identify those sectors responsible for emissions. Table 2 shows each GHG source and the responsible economic sector in EPPA. A second step is the development of an inventory of GHG emissions by region and sector and determination of the time path of emissions factors. Earlier

versions of EPPA [3] included such an inventory and future emissions projections, and the development of these data is described by Mayer et al. [12]. Uncertainties in the inventories and in future projections, comparisons with the IPCC's SRES projections [18], and the climatic implications of future emissions uncertainty using the EPPA model have been explored elsewhere [21].

The limitation of the version of EPPA described in Babiker et al. [3] was that, because emissions were introduced as Leontief (fixed coefficient) inputs, the model could not be used to accurately cost abatement opportunities of these gases. The critical new element introduced here is implementation of the cost function approach shown above, which was developed first by Hyman [8] in application to CH_4. To develop estimates for all the non-CO_2 gases, we draw on earlier work that developed exogenous marginal abatement curves for CH_4, N_2O, SF_6, PFCs, and HFCs. The underlying sources of information are the US EPA [20], the IEA [10], and engineering estimates developed in consultation with industry as described in [15]. The earlier work constructed a single aggregate MAC for each country/region but we are now able to make use of the disaggregated sectoral detail. Thus, even though we use the same basic technological data for different regions of the world, the actual regional abatement opportunities vary considerably depending on the emissions levels of each gas from each activity.

In addition, the coefficients for CH_4 and N_2O vary by region for agriculture (table 3). While the EPPA model includes only an aggregate agriculture sector, we are able to reflect differences in the make-up of the agriculture sector as it affects abatement costs by choice of the elasticity of substitution for CH_4. In particular, the underlying data provide different abatement opportunities for rice production, manure disposal, and enteric fermentation by livestock. In general, CH_4 is produced from manure only when it is kept under anaerobic conditions in manure pits. This manure handling practice occurs mainly in the United States and other developed countries. The relatively higher elasticity of substitution for these regions thus reflects the fact that a share of the methane emitted from these regions is from manure handling and there are technologies to collect this methane.

Table 1
Regions and sectors in EPPA.

Regions in EPPA		Sectors in EPPA	
Annex B		*Non-Energy Production Sectors*	
USA	United States	AGRIC	Agriculture
JPN	Japan	ENINT	Energy-intensive industries
EU	European Union (1995 members)	OTHIND	Other industries and services
OOE	Other OECD	*Energy Production Sectors*	
FSU	Former Soviet Union	OIL	Crude oil production
EET	Eastern Europe	GAS	Natural gas production
Non-Annex B		COAL	Coal production
CHN	China	REFOIL	Refined oil production
IND	India	ELEC	Electricity production
EEX	Energy Exporting LDCs	*Consumption*	
BRA	Brazil	CONS	Household consumption
DAE	Dynamic Asian Economies		
ROW	Rest of World		

Table 2
Non-CO$_2$ gas sources and EPPA activities.

Gas and source	EPPA representation	
	Activity	Sector
CH$_4$		
Coal seams	Coal production	COAL
Petroleum production	Oil production	OIL
Transmissions and distribution losses	Gas consumption	GAS
Landfill, wastewater gas	Household consumption	CONS
Industrial sewage, paper and chemicals	Energy intensive production	ENINT
Industrial sewage, food processing	Other industry production	OTHINT
Rice, enteric fermentation, manure management, agr. waste, savannah, and deforestation burning	Agriculture production	AGRIC
N$_2$O		
Adipic and nitric acid production	Energy intensive industry	ENINT
Refined oil products combustion	Refined oil consumption in all sectors	REFOIL
Coal combustion	Coal consumption in all sectors	COAL
Agr. soils, manure management, agr. waste, savannah, and deforestation burning	Agriculture production	AGRIC
HFCs		
Air conditioning, foam blowing, other	Other industry production	OTHIND
PFCs		
Semi-conductor production, solvent use, other	Other industry production	OTHIND
Aluminum smelting	Energy intensive industry production	ENINT
SF$_6$		
Electrical switchgear	Electricity production	ELEC
Magnesium production	Energy intensive industry production	ENINT

Table 3
Elasticities of substitution for CH$_4$ and N$_2$O with other inputs.

Sector	Region	σ_{CH_4}	σ_{N_2O}
AGRIC	USA	0.05	0.04
	JPN	0.08	0.04
	EU	0.07	0.04
	OOE	0.04	0.04
	FSU	0.05	0.04
	EET	0.08	0.04
	CHN	0.07	0.02
	IND	0.04	0.02
	EEX	0.02	0.02
	BRA	0.02	0.02
	DAE	0.07	0.02
	ROW	0.03	0.02
ENINT	All regions	0.11	1.0
OTHIND	All regions	0.11	–
REFOIL	All regions	0.15	0.0
GAS	All regions	0.15	–
COAL	All regions	0.30	0.0
Final Demand	All regions	0.11	–

Table 4
Elasticities of substitution for PFCs, HFCs, and SF$_6$ with other inputs.

Sector	Region	σ_{PFC}	σ_{HFC}	σ_{SF_6}
ENINT	All regions	0.30	–	0.3
OTHIND	All regions	0.30	0.15	–
ELEC	All regions	–	–	0.3

(–) Not applicable.

On the other hand, the technological data we used did not present practical means for abating methane from enteric fermentation. As this is a particularly large share of CH$_4$ emissions from agriculture in developing countries, the low elasticity of substitution reflects the inability to abate these, at least as represented in the analyses on which we based our estimates.

Abatement opportunities for N$_2$O are based on earlier work [15]. The underlying estimates were from econometri-cally estimated elasticities of demand for nitrogen fertilizer, which tend to show relatively limited price response. For developed regions, an initial low-cost abatement opportunity was identified to reflect evidence that, through soil testing and better crediting of nitrogen from manure and other organic sources, the amount of inorganic nitrogen applied could be reduced without a substantial yield penalty. Developing countries tend not to apply excess nitrogen, and in many developing country areas nitrogen may be a limiting nutrient so that soil testing would likely indicate that more rather than less nitrogen should be applied. Elasticities of substitution for PFCs, HFCs, and SF$_6$ with other inputs are given in table 4.

3.1. National cost curves for the US and China

The economic results of including other gases in the EPPA model can be illustrated by deriving a national cost curve from the model. Such a relation can be estimated by simulating the model numerous times with progressively tighter emissions constraints. The simulations were derived assuming a cap and trade system, with trading among gases,

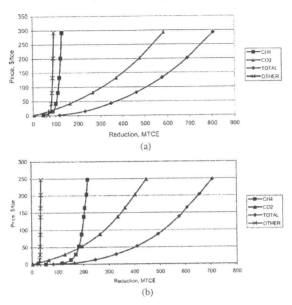

Figure 4. National cost curves for the USA (a) and for China (b).

using 100-year Global Warming Potential (GWP) indices. The results for the USA and China are plotted in figure 4. The "All-Gas" curve is, in effect, a MAC for the nation assuming an efficient policy, which is the horizontal sum of the reductions achieved for each contributing gas: CO_2, CH_4, and a single curve aggregating all of the others. Such a national MAC derived from the EPPA model represents the underlying bottom-up technology studies as captured by the choice of σ for each sector and each gas, as well as all of the economic interactions among sectors.

These summary MACs allow a direct comparison of the relative contribution of different gases at different carbon prices. Taking the US as an example, at low prices a large percentage of any reduction is achieved from the non-CO_2 gases. Even though CO_2 accounts for about 80% of US total GHG emissions when weighted using 100-year GWPs, economically efficient levels of abatement of CH_4 alone, and separately the combination of the other gases (N_2O, SF_6, PFCs, and HFCs), are greater than the abatement potential of CO_2 when carbon prices are less than about $25/tCe. At about $25/tCe, the CH_4 and other non-CO_2 gas curves cross the CO_2 abatement curve, indicating that at higher prices the contribution of CO_2 abatement becomes more important.

Two phenomena are responsible for the disproportionate contribution of non-CO_2 abatement at low prices. First, in carbon-equivalent terms many of these gases see much larger incentives for reduction of emissions at low carbon-equivalent prices than does CO_2 because of the differences in radiative forcing (and lifetime) as represented in Global Warming Potentials (GWP). Consider methane that is vented

from a coal mine, for example. It could be captured and sold to a natural gas pipeline, say at a price of $3 per thousand cubic feet (MCF). In the absence of any charge on emissions, the $3 price would be the firm's incentive to abate the methane. Now assume an emissions penalty of $50 per ton of carbon-equivalent. If the mine-owner is charged only for the carbon dioxide that will be released when the methane is ultimately burned, the incentive to abate rises by about $0.70 per MCF, for a total incentive of $3.70. If, however, the methane is penalized for its carbon-equivalent radiative effect, as defined by its GWP, the incentive rises to over $8.00 per MCF. The incentives for controlling emissions of the industrial gases and nitrous oxide are still stronger, because their radiative potency is so much greater than either methane or carbon dioxide. For example, sulfur hexafluoride sells for around $10 per pound but with a GWP of 23,900 a carbon-equivalent price of $50 per ton would translate into a penalty for emitting the gas of $150 per pound, 15 times the product's selling price. The $50 carbon charge equals $0.17/gallon of gasoline given the carbon contained in it. At a price of $1.50 per gallon this is only an 11% increase.

The second factor is that some reduction of these gases is realized as a byproduct of CO_2 reduction, as noted earlier. Other interactions, such as feedbacks of CH_4 reduction on CO_2-emitting activities, are present but are orders-of-magnitude smaller. So, for example, at a price of $50 per ton carbon-equivalent (tCe) the non-CO_2 gases would be responsible for over half of the total reduction, as can be determined from figure 4 by noting where ~ $50 per tCe price would cross the CO_2 and non-CO_2 abatement curves.

At higher prices, the CO$_2$ abatement comes to dominate other gases. In part this shift reflects the simple fact that for the US, non-CO$_2$ gases are less than 20% of GWP-weighted emissions, so even if all emissions were abated there is only so much they can contribute. It also reflects the underlying technological estimates as reflected in figure 2, that show limits on non-CO$_2$ abatement potential, particularly from agricultural sources.

A similar pattern holds for China. There, CH$_4$ is a larger component of emissions, and the other non-CO$_2$ gases are considerably less important. The industrial gases (HFCs, PFCs, and SF$_6$) are not big contributors to China's emissions, so there is little abatement potential. Emissions of N$_2$O come mainly from fertilizer and manure management, where our estimates show very limited abatement potential. On the other hand, CH$_4$ from coal mines is an important emissions source that can be abated at low cost. And, we included IEA estimates of abatement costs from paddy rice, another important source of CH$_4$ emissions from China. Together, however, all non-CO$_2$ gases account for somewhat more than 50% of abatement at a price of $50 per tCe.

4. A sample application

To demonstrate the application of this all-gas analysis we construct a simple policy, applied uniformly across all countries. It is assumed that reductions in all gas emissions, weighted by the IPCC GWPs, are reduced by either 10% or 20% below year-2000 levels, and maintained at these levels through 2040. No emissions permit trading is allowed among countries. Within countries, however, two cases are constructed. One assumes policies that will yield a common marginal cost across the gases by imposing a total GWP-weighted GHG cap with inter-gas trading. The other does not adopt this efficient pricing approach, but imposes proportional reductions on each gas.

4.1. The relative role of the non-CO$_2$ gases

Table 5 shows the percentage of the carbon-equivalent reduction that is realized from the non-CO$_2$ gases, assuming that intergas trading is allowed. Again taking the US as the first example, two aspects of the results are worth special note. First, the less stringent the constraint, the greater the relative role of the non-CO$_2$ gases. So, in 2010 they account for 36% of reductions under a national cut of 10% below the 2000 level, but only 29% of a 20% cut. This result could

be anticipated from the shape of the US cost function in figure 4. By the same token, as the US economy grows over time the stringency of any target reduction increases, so at a 10% target the relative role of the non-CO$_2$ gases falls from 36% in 2010 to 24% in 2040. With a tightening target rather than a constant one, the reduction in relative role would be still greater. Put another way, these gases (some with very high GWPs) are a crucial part of a cost-effective policy in the near term, but over time (and with tightening targets) they are driven out of the economy, so the burden of control falls ever more heavily on CO$_2$.

Results for China show a similar pattern, with the total contribution of non-CO$_2$ gases somewhat higher than in the US. With a 10% reduction below 2000, non-CO$_2$ gases account for 43% of an efficient abatement policy in China in 2010, falling to 30% by 2040.

4.2. The importance of multi-gas coordination

Up to this point in the discussion, and particularly in figure 4 and table 5, we have assumed a cost-efficient reduction in all gases in each country. The assumption can be thought of as implying an all-gas constraint with free trading across gases within a domestic economy. How great a difference does it makes whether such a cost-effective policy is pursued? One way to consider the economic importance of this flexibility is to compare the cost-effective (equal marginal cost) approach with a policy that applies the agreed national percentage reduction individually to each of the gases, allowing no trade among them. This analysis is meant to be indicative only and should not be interpreted as the value of a trading system versus a command and control system, which involves far greater complexities.[6]

The result is shown in figure 5. Starting with a counterfactual of no trading among gases, the figure shows the percent reduction in GDP loss achieved by a change to the efficient policy. Again the 10% and 20% reduction targets

Table 5
Percentage of stated reduction from non-CO$_2$ gases.

Country	% Reduction	Time period			
		2010	2020	2030	2040
USA	10	36	31	28	24
	20	29	26	26	24
China	10	43	34	31	30
	20	38	32	30	29

[6] For example, our analysis assumes that marginal cost is equalized across the various sources of each gas (e.g., equalization of the marginal cost of CH$_4$ reduction in agriculture with CH$_4$ reduction from land fills and coal mining, and for that matter, equalization of costs across every coal mine and every livestock producer). The advantages to trading would be much greater if we set the target sector-by-sector and gas-by-gas, or if we compared it to a command and control system where targets were set for each producing source with no explicit mechanism by which marginal costs were equalized. Of course proportional reduction in all gases is just one particular constraint. If a country really wished to pursue gas-by-gas, sector-by-sector or source-by-source targets it might hope to set those targets based on an assessment of the comparative ease of abating among different sources, and therefore avoid truly costly mistakes in setting caps. The value of trading then depends on how well a country is able to make such an assessment, its willingness to make reduction assignments on that basis, and its ability to adjust those assignments as conditions change. The comparison here is thus indicative of the differential abatement potential across gases, in economic terms, rather than the value of trading per se, which depends on how close one is able to set caps to the solution a trading system would generate. Existence of other economic distortions can also affect the economic benefits of a trading system. One can often do better than placing economically ideal policies, like a cap and trade system, on top of markets that are heavily distorted (see [2,4]).

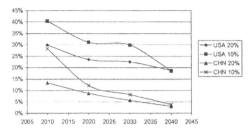

Figure 5. Percentage reduction in GDP loss with shift to trading.

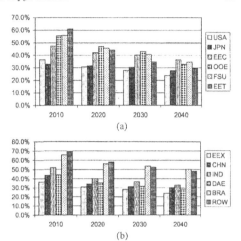

Figure 6. Percent reduction from non-CO_2 gases for a 10% total GHG reduction from 2000 (a) Annex B, (b) non-Annex B.

are shown, using the US and China as examples. Several insights may be drawn from these results. First, for both countries, and over all periods, the gain from trading is greater under the less restrictive target. This result is simply a reflection of the fact that the non-CO_2 gases play a greater role under a looser constraint, so handling them in an efficient manner makes a greater difference. Similarly, as the constraints tighten with time and economic growth, and the relative role of the non-CO_2 gases diminishes, the saving from an efficient policy, in relation to the proportional reductions, is diminished.

The implication of these results is that, in a climate regime where the stringency of control is expected to increase with time, efficient handling of the non-CO_2 gases is of particular importance in the first few decades of control, essentially because their control allows postponement of the more expensive reductions in CO_2 emissions.[7] The difference between the US and China reflects the fact that a proportional reduction in gases is closer to the cost-effective solution in China than in the US. While this is the simple explanation, it reflects many factors and so it is not possible to generalize this result, for example, as a difference between developed and developing countries. Among the reasons for the difference between the US and China is the fact that a larger share of CH_4 emissions in the US is from easier-to-abate sources like landfills, concentrated livestock manure, and coal mines – whereas a significant share of China's CH_4 emissions is from harder-to-abate sources like ruminant animals and rice production. And, the easier-to-abate industrial gases are important in the US but not in China. On the other side, however, non-CO_2 GHGs are just 17% of total US GHG emissions but, by our estimate in 2010, they are 30% of China's emissions. More generally, differential growth in total GHGs among regions, and differential growth among gases and sectors will interact with the comparative ease of abatement of different gases from different sectors to determine just how much gain there is in moving from a proportional reduction to cost-effective trading.

---

[7] This decline in importance over time may be less than estimated here if the non-CO_2 abatement curves are unduly pessimistic about evolving technologies to abate some sources of GHGs. Agricultural CH_4 abatement is particularly limited by the assumption that ruminant livestock emissions cannot be abated.

4.3. Regional contributions of non-CO_2 gases to a cost effective climate policy

While we focused on the US and China as an example to illustrate some key results, the policy of a 10% reduction below 2000 was enforced in all regions in the EPPA model. We plot the percentage contribution of the non-CO_2 gases to a cost effective policy implemented in each region for Annex B countries (figure 6a) and the developing country regions (figure 6b). As before, there is trading among gases so that the GWP-weighted marginal cost of abatement is equal across gases but there is no trading across regions. We make no claims to the likelihood, reasonableness, or equity of this policy. While it is a cost-effective solution within a country/region, the fact that marginal costs are not equated across regions means that it is not globally cost-effective. The policy represented here, with identical constraints in each region, was chosen to show the importance of the non-CO_2 gases without the confounding effects of widely varying constraints.

As can be seen from figures 6a and 6b, reductions in the non-CO_2 GHGs contribute at least 34% to a cost-effective policy in all regions in 2010, if the goal of such a policy is to achieve total GHG reductions of 10% below 2000. For some regions, the contribution of non-CO_2 GHGs is as much as 65 to 70% (e.g., Brazil and the ROW region). As for China and the US, the contribution declines over time, again reflecting gradual tightening of the constraint with growth, and the general shape of the abatement curves for non-CO_2 GHGs. The different contributions across regions in table 6 reflect underlying differences in the relative contributions of different GHGs. Countries with higher contributions from the non-CO_2 GHGs in the reference forecasts also tend to have a higher contribution of them in a cost-effective abatement strategy. This is not strictly the case, however, because it

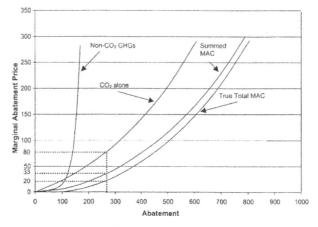

Figure 7. Effects of endogenizing GHG abatement.

Table 6
Percentage of reference GHG emissions from non-CO_2 gases.

	USA	JPN	EU	OOE	EEX	CHN	FSU	IND	EET	DAE	BRA	ROW
2000	17	10	20	36	39	31	32	56	39	30	61	58
2010	17	12	20	35	39	30	29	50	36	29	59	57
2020	18	13	21	34	40	29	28	45	34	29	58	55
2030	18	14	22	34	41	29	27	40	32	28	58	53
2040	17	15	22	31	41	30	26	37	30	27	57	51

depends on the sources of non-CO_2 gases, and the abatement potential of fossil emissions as well. For many of the non-Annex B countries a much greater share of the non-CO_2 gases come from hard-to-abate agricultural sources whereas in developed countries more of the non-CO_2 gases come from easier to abate landfill or coal mining, or from industrial gases.

For example, EPPA's EEX region contains most of Africa and most of its non-CO_2 gases are CH_4 from ruminant livestock or N_2O from soils. Both of these sources are represented as having limited abatement potential (see the low elasticities of substitution in table 3). Thus, in contrast to many other regions where the non-CO_2 gas contribution to a cost-effective policy is more than proportional to their contribution to emission, the 40% abatement contribution of non-CO_2 gases is just about proportional to their contribution to total emissions in EEX. This is similarly the case for India. On the other hand, the 35% contribution of non-CO_2 gases to Japanese abatement is 3½ times their contribution to reference emissions because a disproportionate share are from easier to control industrial sources rather than agriculture.

5. How important is endogenous representation of GHGs?

As discussed in section 1, there are several reasons for including all GHGs in a single model rather than running

separate models. We consider three issues where we are able to quantify the benefits of endogenous representation of abatement as compared with the use of exogenous abatement curves. These are: (1) market equilibrium effects in GHG permit markets – i.e., changes in the carbon price because of abatement of other GHGs, (2) interaction effects among policies directed at GHGs – for example, a policy directed toward CO_2 might indirectly affect emissions of CH_4, N_2O or SF_6 through their effects on coal mining, fossil fuel combustion, or electricity production, and (3) consistent cost accounting – how the integrated area under an exogenous abatement curve compares with the standard welfare concept applied in CGE modeling. We consider these issues, again with US and China as examples.

To consider the first two issues above we construct two new marginal abatement curves (MACs), one for the non-CO_2 GHGs and one for CO_2. In contrast to the curves represented in figure 4 that were derived by jointly constraining all gases at the same time, the new set of MACs were constructed by separately constraining the model to control first only the non-CO_2 gases, and then only CO_2, so that any interaction effect is eliminated.[8] We then add these together to create a total "Summed MAC". These are shown in figure 7 along with the GHG MAC from figure 4 now labeled as the "True Total MAC".

Our first concern, with the permit market equilibrium, arises because non-CO_2 GHGs have been a secondary consideration in climate policy. Thus one way that analysis of abatement potential has proceeded is to use a carbon price estimate from energy models that consider only CO_2 abatement, on the assumption that the abatement contribution of any one of these non-CO_2 sources was too small to have a

---

[8] Hyman [8] showed that constraints on the non-CO_2 gases by themselves had virtually no economy-wide interaction effect, so this method of deriving a total non-CO_2 abatement curve is essentially equivalent to summing together individual abatement curves for each gas and sector without running the model at all.

measurable effect on the market clearing price of GHGs. To illustrate, consider a 275 MtCe GHG constraint that, when evaluated using a CO_2-only MAC from EPPA, results in a market price for permits of \$80/tCe. This is shown in figure 7 by following the vertical dashed line that starts at 275 MtCE to the CO_2 MAC and then horizontally to the price axis. However, we can determine from figure 7 that, for a total constraint of 275 MtCe, and using the True Total MAC, that the market price would fall to \$20.

To date the common method of avoiding this error and bringing the non-CO_2 gases into a CGE analysis has been to construct an exogenous MAC for these sources, and then sum with a CGE-generated MAC for CO_2. This procedure yields the Summed MAC in figure 7, and it falls afoul of our second concern above: omissions of interaction effects. Comparison of the Summed MAC, with the True Total MAC in figure 7 reveals that the policies have a synergistic effect – more total abatement is achieved at every price when the policies are implemented together than if each is imposed separately. Rather than the true \$20 marginal cost for a 275 MtCe constraint, the Summed MAC procedure would yield \$33/tCe, a 65% overestimate.

The third benefit of endogenous abatement is consistent costing of abatement options. The cost concept most commonly derived from CGE models is lost welfare measured as equivalent variation – the amount of income that would be needed to make consumers just as well off as without the abatement. Using exogenous MACs the cost is approximated by integrating underneath the MAC up to the equilibrium price. This latter procedure is familiar in partial equilibrium analyses. In such studies all of the inputs are assumed to have fixed prices – unaffected by demand and supply changes caused by the abatement activity. In an economy without distortions, and assuming that the abatement activity was small relative to the economy (so that prices were not affected) these costs would represent the real resource cost. Such MACs can also be constructed from complex partial or general equilibrium models, as we have done, in which case the feedbacks in the model are incorporated, although the integrated area under an abatement curve does not have an immediate interpretation in terms of the standard equivalent variation measure of welfare.

To consider what difference the cost accounting makes, we evaluated costs in three ways. Again we use the US and China as examples, applying our constraints at 10 and 20 percent below 2000 with a focus on 2010 (table 7). The three are: (1) welfare measured as equivalent variation, (2) integrated costs under the Summed MAC in figure 7, and (3) integrated costs under the True Total MAC in figure 7. As shown in table 7, the cost estimates using the Summed MAC

Table 7
Alternative cost measures, billions of 1995 \$US.

Cost measure	USA	CHN
Welfare loss	9.7	12.5
Summed MAC	28.6	20.4
True MAC	21.9	16.4

exceed the cost derived from the True Total MAC by about 30% for the US and about 25% for China. We take this as our measure of the possible error of not endogenously treating non-CO_2 GHG abatement.[9] Neither of these is a good approximation of the preferred measure, welfare loss. Even the True Total MAC overstates the US cost by greater than a factor of two, and China's cost by about 30%.

The reason for the difference among these estimates is to be found in the price changes that the integrated MAC cannot reflect. Since the welfare loss concept measures the income that would be required to make consumers as well off as before the policy change, it includes consideration of consumers' willingness to substitute among goods given new prices, whereas the MAC measures do not take this substitution into account. This factor alone suggests that the welfare cost will be less than that from an integrated MAC. In addition, one of the price effects that has proven to be important in the welfare estimates is the shift in the terms of trade (the price of domestic versus international goods). As has been shown elsewhere [1], one effect of carbon policy is to depress the producer prices of fossil energy. Large energy importers like the US gain from these depressed prices and this effect is fully reflected in the welfare measure. Since China relies to a greater extent than the US on its domestic energy resources it is not surprising that the welfare cost measure in China is larger, in relation to the integrated MAC measure, than in the US. China has less offsetting gain from lower fuel import costs.

Another issue shown to be of importance in CGE cost estimation is the extent of existing distortions in the economy [2]. When distortions exist the market prices of inputs may not reflect their true resource cost. For example, subsidies lead to production above the efficient level whereas taxes depress production of a sector below the efficient level. The true resource cost of inputs drawn from subsidized sectors is less than the market price because drawing resources from those sectors has the benefit of bringing the level of production closer to the efficient level. The price of resources drawn from a taxed sector will under represent their true resource cost because the production level of the sector is falling further below the efficient level. Depending, then, on where resources are drawn from, their market prices may be above or below the true resource cost.

6. Summary and conclusions

A growing body of work has shown for developed countries that non-CO_2 GHG abatement can make a contribution to a cost effective policy that is disproportionate to their contribution to emissions. We find similar results. For the US, Japan, and the EU non-CO_2 GHGs contribute less than 20% of GWP-weighted emissions in our 2010 reference forecast, but their contribution toward a cost-effective emissions control policy is on the order of twice that percentage. We find

---

[9] Reilly et al. [16] iterated between a CGE model and exogenous MAC for non-CO_2 GHGs to approximate this interaction effect.

that this is not generally the case for developing country regions. For these regions, the non-CO_2 GHG gases are a larger share of emissions, but they are often emitted from hard-to-abate sources such as ruminant livestock and rice production. They turn out to contribute a large share to a cost effective combination of GHG reductions but that contribution is closer in proportion to their contribution to emissions.

We also find that the contribution of non-CO_2 GHG abatement falls as policies become more stringent, and that this trend holds for all regions. It reflects the relative shape of the CO_2 and non-CO_2 abatement cost curves and the obvious fact that, with an ever-tightening total GHG constraint, CO_2 emissions must eventually be cut more deeply. The non-CO_2 GHGs can, however, serve a crucial role in a cost-effective transition.

A key objective of this paper is methodological – to develop and demonstrate a method for incorporating non-CO_2 GHG abatement endogenously within a CGE model. The benefits of endogenous treatment of the non-CO_2 GHGs are several. These include accounting for permit market equilibrium, synergisms between CO_2 and non-CO_2 GHG policies, and consistent cost accounting. Because non-CO_2 GHGs can make a big contribution to reductions it is not analytically defensible to take a partial equilibrium approach to estimating their contribution – i.e., taking as given a carbon price from an energy model. In the example we considered, the market equilibrium price fell by 75% and the estimated non-CO_2 GHG contribution fell by 25% compared with the partial equilibrium estimate. We also found that there are strong synergisms between CO_2 and non-CO_2 GHG abatement efforts. In the cases we examined, failure to account for these effects leads to a significant overestimate of the CO_2 price. Finally, we showed that integrated costs under exogenous marginal abatement curves, even when constructed from a CGE model, are not directly comparable to the welfare concepts usually drawn from CGE models and widely used to measure the cost of CO_2 policies.

Given these differences, analysts seeking to compare various costs that might exist in the literature must avoid comparing apples and oranges – numbers described as GHG policy costs but measuring very dissimilar cost concepts. Because much of the CO_2 abatement cost literature has relied on CGE model-based estimates of costs, it is important to compare non-CO_2 GHGs on the same footing. It is thus an important step forward to be able to include all GHGs within CGE modeling frameworks.

References

[1] M. Babiker, J.M. Reilly and H.D. Jacoby, The Kyoto Protocol and developing countries, Energy Policy 28 (2000) 525–536.

[2] M.H. Babiker, G. Metcalf and J. Reilly, Tax distortions and climate policy, Journal of Environmental and Economic Management (forthcoming).

[3] M.H. Babiker, J.M. Reilly, M. Mayer, R.S. Eckaus, I. Sue Wing and R.C. Hyman, The MIT Emissions Prediction and Policy Analysis (EPPA) model: Revisions, sensitivities, and comparisons of results, MIT Joint Program on the Science and Policy of Global Change, Report 71 (2001).

[4] M. Babiker, L. Viguier, J. Reilly, A.D. Ellerman and P. Criqui, The welfare costs of hybrid carbon policies in the European Union, Environmental Modeling and Assessment (2002) submitted.

[5] M.A. Brown, M.D. Levine, J.P. Romm, A.H. Rosenfeld and J.G. Koomey, Engineering-economic studies of energy technologies to reduce greenhouse gas emissions: Opportunities and challenges, Annual Review of Energy (1998) 287–385.

[6] D. Fullerton and G.E. Metcalf, Environmental controls, scarcity rents, and pre-existing distortions, Journal of Public Economics 80(2) (2001) 249–267.

[7] K. Hayhoe, A. Jain, H. Pitcher, C. MacCracken, M. Gibbs, D. Wuebbles, R. Harvey and D. Kruger, Costs of multigreenhouse gas reduction targets for the USA, Science 286 (1999) 675–677.

[8] R.C. Hyman, A More Cost-Effective Strategy for Reducing Greenhouse Gas Emissions: Modeling the Impact of Methane Abatement Opportunities, Master's Thesis (Massachusetts Institute of Technology, Cambridge, MA, 2001).

[9] IEA [International Energy Agency], Abatement of methane emissions, IEA Greenhouse Gas R&D Programme, Cheltenham, UK (1998).

[10] IEA [International Energy Agency], Technologies for the abatement of methane emissions, IEA Greenhouse Gas R&D Programme, Cheltenham, UK (1999).

[11] A. Manne and R. Richels, An alternative approach to establishing trade-offs among greenhouse gases, Nature 410 (2001) 675–677.

[12] M. Mayer, R. Hyman, J. Harnisch and J. Reilly, Emissions inventories and time-trends for GHGs and other pollutants, Technical Note 1, MIT Joint Program on the Science and Policy of Global Change (2000).

[13] J.R. McFarland, H.J. Herzog and J. Reilly, Economic modeling of the global adoption of carbon capture and sequestration technologies, Sixth International Conference on Greenhouse Gas Control Technologies (GHGT-6), Kyoto (October 2002).

[14] R. Prinn, H. Jacoby, A. Sokolov, C. Wang, X. Xiao, Z. Yang, R. Eckhaus, P. Stone, D. Ellerman, J. Melillo, J. Fitzmaurice, D. Kicklighter, G. Holian and Y. Liu, Integrated global system model for climate policy assessment: Feedbacks and sensitivity studies, Climatic Change 41(3/4) (1999) 469–546.

[15] J. Reilly, M. Mayer and J. Harnisch, Multiple gas control under the Kyoto Agreement, joint program on the science and policy of global change, Environmental Modeling and Assessment (forthcoming).

[16] J. Reilly, R. Prinn, J. Harnisch, J. Fitzmaurice, H. Jacoby, D. Kicklighter, J. Melillo, P. Stone, A. Sokolov and C. Wang, Multi-gas assessment of the Kyoto Protocol, Nature 401 (1999) 549–555.

[17] J. Reilly, H.D. Jacoby and R. Prinn, Multi-Gas Contributors to Global Climate Change: Climate Impacts and Mitigation Costs of non-CO₂ Gases (Pew Center for Climate Change, Arlington, VA, 2003).

[18] N. Nakićenović and R. Swart, eds., Special Report on Emissions Scenarios (World Meteorological Organization, Geneva, 2000).

[19] US EPA [US Environmental Protection Agency], US methane emissions 1990–2020: Inventories, projections, and opportunities for reductions, Office of Air and Radiation, Washington, DC (1999).

[20] US EPA [US Environmental Protection Agency], U.S. high GWP gas emissions 1990–2020: Inventories, projections, and opportunities for reductions, Report No. EPA-000-F-97-000, US Environmental Protection Agency, Washington, DC (June 2001).

[21] M.D. Webster, M. Babiker, M. Mayer, J.M. Reilly, J. Harnisch, R. Hyman, M.C. Sarofim and C. Wang, Uncertainty in emissions projections for climate models, Atmospheric Environment 36 (2002) 3659–3670.

[22]

Climate Change and Forest Sinks: Factors Affecting the Costs of Carbon Sequestration[1]

Richard G. Newell

Resources for the Future, Washington, DC 20036

and

Robert N. Stavins[2]

*John F. Kennedy School of Government, Harvard University, Cambridge, Massachusetts 02138;
and Resources for the Future, Washington, DC 20036*

Received September 11, 1998; revised May 4, 1999; published online August 10, 2000

The possibility of encouraging the growth of forests as a means of sequestering carbon dioxide has received considerable attention, partly because of evidence that this can be a relatively inexpensive means of combating climate change. But how sensitive are such estimates to specific conditions? We examine the sensitivity of carbon sequestration costs to changes in critical factors, including the nature of management and deforestation regimes, silvicultural species, relative prices, and discount rates. © 2000 Academic Press

1. INTRODUCTION

The Kyoto Protocol to the United Nations Framework Convention on Climate Change [37] establishes the principle that carbon sequestration can be used by participating nations to help meet their respective net emission reduction targets for carbon dioxide (CO_2) and other greenhouse gases.[3] Several studies have found that growing trees to sequester carbon could provide relatively low-cost net

---

[1] Valuable comments on previous versions of this paper were provided by Lawrence Goulder, William Nordhaus, Andrew Plantinga, Kenneth Richards, Roger Sedjo, two anonymous referees, an associate editor, and participants in seminars at the Universities of California at Los Angeles and Santa Barbara, Maryland, Michigan, and Texas, Harvard, Stanford, and Yale Universities, Resources for the Future, and the National Bureau of Economic Research. The authors alone are responsible for any errors.

[2] Address correspondence to: Professor Robert N. Stavins, John F. Kennedy School of Government, Harvard University, 79 John F. Kennedy St., Cambridge, MA 02138, phone: 617-495-1820, Fax: 617-496-3783. E-mail: robert_stavins@harvard.edu

[3] After fossil-fuel combustion, deforestation is the second largest source of carbon dioxide emissions to the atmosphere. Estimates of annual global emissions from deforestation range from 0.6 to 2.8 billion tons, compared with slightly less than 6.0 billion tons annually from fossil-fuel combustion, cement manufacturing, and natural gas flaring, combined [10, 31]. There are three pathways along which carbon sequestration is of relevance for atmospheric concentrations of carbon dioxide: carbon storage in biological ecosystems, carbon storage in durable wood products, and substitution of biomass fuels for fossil fuels [24]. The analysis in this paper considers the first two pathways. For further discussion, see Parks et al. [18].

212   NEWELL AND STAVINS

emission reductions for a number of countries [3], including the United States [1, 4, 19, 20, 23, 33].[4]

When and if the United States chooses to ratify the Kyoto Protocol and/or subsequent international agreements, it will be necessary to decide whether carbon sequestration policies—such as those that promote forestation[5] and discourage deforestation—should be part of the domestic portfolio of compliance activities. The potential cost-effectiveness of carbon sequestration activities will presumably be a major criterion, and so it is important to ask what factors affect the costs of such programs. We examine the sensitivity of sequestration costs to changes in key factors, including the nature of the management regimes, silvicultural species, relative prices, and discount rates.

Our analytical model takes account of current silvicultural understanding of the intertemporal linkages between deforestation and carbon emissions, on the one hand, and between forestation and carbon sequestration, on the other. Furthermore, our analysis uses a methodology whereby econometric estimates of the costs of carbon sequestration are derived from observations of landowners' actual behavior when confronted with the opportunity costs of alternative land uses [33]. This is in contrast with "engineering" or "least cost" approaches used to estimate the costs of carbon sequestration, of which even the best are unlikely to capture important elements of landowner behavior, such as the effects of irreversible investment under uncertainty, non-pecuniary returns from land use, liquidity constraints, decision making inertia, and other costs and benefits of land use of which the analyst is unaware.[6]

In summary, we find, first, that the costs of carbon sequestration can be greater if trees are periodically harvested, rather than permanently established. Second, higher discount rates imply higher marginal costs and non-monotonic changes in the amount of carbon sequestered. Third, higher agricultural prices lead to higher marginal costs or reduced sequestration. Fourth, retarded deforestation can sequester carbon at substantially lower costs than increased forestation. These results depend in part on the time profile of sequestration and the amount of carbon

---

[4] There is a range of estimates of the relevant marginal cost function. These various estimates are compared by Stavins [33], whose own estimates are significantly greater than the others for more ambitious sequestration programs.

[5] Distinctions are sometimes made in the forestry literature between "afforestation" and "reforestation," where the former refers to changes from non-forest to forest production on lands that have not been forested during the preceding 50 years or more, and the latter refers to changes to forest production on lands that have more recently been deforested [11]. In our analysis, there is no reason to make this distinction, and so we simply refer to any change *to* forest use as "forestation." This is in contrast to a change *from* forest use of land—"deforestation."

[6] The simplest of previous analyses derived single point estimates of average costs associated with particular sequestration levels [8, 13, 14, 27, 29], sometimes assuming that the opportunity costs of land are zero [7, 16, 38, 39]. "Engineering/costing models" have constructed marginal cost schedules by adopting land rental rates or purchase costs derived from surveys for representative types or locations of land, and then sorting these in ascending order of cost [15, 23]. Simulation models include a model of lost profits due to removing land from agricultural production [19], a mathematical programming model of the agricultural sector and the timber market [1, 2], a related model incorporating the effects of agricultural price support programs [4], and a dynamic simulation model of forestry [35]. An analysis by Plantinga [20] adopts land-use elasticities from an econometric study to estimate sequestration costs, an approach similar in some respects to the methodology used here. For surveys of the literature, see Richards and Stokes [24] and Sedjo et al. [28, 30].

released upon harvest, both of which may vary by species, geographic location, and management regime, and are subject to scientific uncertainty.

In Section 2 of the paper, we describe the analytical model; in Section 3, we carry out simulations for various scenarios and thereby examine the sensitivity of the marginal cost of carbon sequestration; and in Section 4, we offer some conclusions.

2. ANALYTICAL MODEL

We draw upon econometrically estimated parameters of a structural model of land use, layer upon it a model of the relationships that link changes in alternative land uses with changes in the time paths of CO_2 emission and sequestration, and examine the sensitivity of carbon sequestration costs to key underlying factors. Our analysis focuses on the empirically relevant land-use options of forest and farm.[7]

2.1. *A Structural, Empirical Model of Land Use*

In previous work with a different policy motivation, Stavins and Jaffe [34] developed a dynamic optimization model of a landowner's decision of whether to keep land in its status quo use or convert it to serve another purpose.[8] Landowners are assumed to observe current and past values of economic, hydrologic, and climatic factors relevant to decisions regarding the use of their lands for forestry or agricultural production and on this basis form expectations of future values of respective variables. Given this information, landowners attempt to maximize the expected long-term economic return to the set of productive activities that can be carried out on their land. They face ongoing decisions of whether to keep land in its current state—either forested or agricultural use—or to convert the land to the other state. Relevant factors a landowner would be expected to consider include: typical agricultural and forestry revenues for the area, the quality of a specific land parcel for agricultural production, agricultural costs of production, and the cost of converting land from a forested state to use as cropland. Thus, we anticipate that a risk-neutral landowner will seek to maximize the present discounted value of the stream of expected future returns.

We summarize the formal statement of the landowner's problem in the Appendix, where the application of control theoretic methods yields a pair of necessary conditions for changes in land use. The first necessary condition implies that a parcel of cropland should be converted to forestry use if the present value of expected net forest revenue exceeds the present value of expected net agricultural revenue. Stated formally, forestation (conversion of agricultural cropland to forest) occurs if a parcel is cropland and if

$$\left(F_{it} - D_{it} - A_{it} \cdot q_{ijt} + M_{it} \right) > 0, \tag{1}$$

---

[7] In both industrialized nations and in developing countries, nearly all deforestation is associated with conversion to agricultural use [11].

[8] A detailed description of the dynamic optimization model and the derivation of the econometrically estimatable model is found in Stavins and Jaffe [34], while Stavins [32] provides an illustration of the use of the model for environmental simulation.

where i indexes counties, j indexes individual land parcels, and t indexes time; upper case letters are stocks or present values; lower case letters are flows; F is forest net revenue, equal to the expected present value of annual net income from forestry per acre (i.e., stumpage value); D is the expected present value of the income loss (when converting to forest) due to delay of first harvest for one rotation period; A is the expected present value of the future stream of typical agricultural revenues per acre; q is a parcel-specific index of feasibility of agricultural production, including effects of soil quality and soil moisture; and M is the expected cost of agricultural production per acre, expressed as the present value of an infinite future stream.

On the other hand, a forested parcel should be converted to cropland if the present value of expected net agricultural revenue exceeds the present value of expected net forest revenue plus the cost of conversion. That is, deforestation occurs if a parcel is forested and if

$$\left(A_{it} \cdot q_{ijt} - M_{it} - C_{it}^{\alpha P_{it}} - \left(F_{it} - W_{it} \right) \right) > 0, \qquad (2)$$

where C is the average cost of conversion per acre, P is the Palmer hydrological drought index, and W_{it} is the windfall of net revenue per acre from a one-time clear cut of forest (prior to conversion to agricultural use).

Inequalities (1) and (2) imply that all land in a county (of given quality) will be in the same use in the steady state. In reality, counties are observed to be a mix of forest and farmland. Although this may partly reflect deviations from the steady state, it is due largely to the *heterogeneity* of land, particularly regarding its suitability for agriculture. As shown in Stavins and Jaffe [34], such unobserved heterogeneity can be parameterized within an econometrically estimatable model so that the individual necessary conditions for land-use changes aggregate into a single-equation model, in which the parameters of the basic benefit–cost relationships and of the underlying, unobserved heterogeneity can be estimated simultaneously.

The complete model yields a set of econometrically estimatable equations, as shown in the Appendix. Using panel data for 36 counties, comprising approximately 13 million acres of land, in Arkansas, Louisiana, and Mississippi, during the period 1935–1984, the parameters of the complete model were estimated with nonlinear least squares procedures [34]. Table I provides descriptive statistics of the major variables used in the simulation analysis.

2.2. *A Dynamic Simulation Model of Future Land Use*

Our initial step in moving from an estimated model of historical land use to a model of carbon sequestration involves introducing relevant silvicultural elements into the necessary conditions previously derived. There are three principal silvicultural dimensions to be considered: symmetries and asymmetries between forestation and deforestation, alternative species for forestation, and alternative manage-

TABLE I

Descriptive Statistics[a]

Variable	Mean	Standard deviation	Minimum	Maximum
Gross agricultural revenue ($/acre/year)	259.04	44.58	184.77	376.03
Agricultural production cost ($/acre/year)	220.39	52.03	143.61	359.81
Forest revenue[b] ($/acre/year)				
Mixed stand	19.29	7.45	6.71	38.36
Pine stand	58.96	23.38	19.92	118.24
Tree-farm establishment cost ($/acre)	92.00	0.00	92.00	92.00
Conversion cost ($/acre)[c]	27.71	0.00	27.71	27.71
Carbon sequestration due to forestation[d] (tons/acre)				
Natural regrowth of mixed stand, periodically harvested	43.36	0.00	43.36	43.36
Natural regrowth of mixed stand, no harvest	50.59	0.00	50.59	50.59
Pine plantation, periodically harvested	41.05	0.00	41.05	41.05
Pine plantation, no harvest	49.99	0.00	49.99	49.99
Carbon emissions due to deforestation[e] (tons/acre)	51.83	0.00	51.83	51.83
Interest rate[f]	5%	0.00	5%	5%

[a]The sample is of 36 counties in Arkansas, Louisiana, and Mississippi, located within the Lower Mississippi Alluvial Plain. All monetary amounts are in 1990 dollars; means are unweighted county averages.

[b]Gross forest revenue minus harvesting costs; an annuity of stumpage values.

[c]The historical analysis uses actual conversion costs, varying by year.

[d]Present-value equivalent of life-cycle sequestration.

[e]Present-value equivalent of life-cycle emissions.

[f]The historical analysis uses actual, real interest rates; simulations of future scenarios use the 5% real rate.

ment regimes. Two of the equations from the land use model need to be adjusted for this purpose,

$$q_{it}^y = \left[\frac{F_{it} - D_{it} + M_{it}}{A_{it}} \right] \tag{3}$$

$$q_{it}^x = \left[\frac{F_{it} - W_{it} + M_{it}}{A_{it} - C_{it}^{\alpha P_{it}}} \right], \tag{4}$$

where, for each county i at time t, q^y is the threshold value of land quality (i.e., suitability for agriculture) below which the incentive for forestation manifests itself, and q^x is the threshold value of land quality above which the incentive for deforestation manifests itself.

First, we note that Eqs. (3) and (4) already exhibit two significant asymmetries between forestation and deforestation. Forestation produces a supply of timber (and an associated forest-revenue stream) only with some delay, since the first harvest subsequent to establishment occurs at the completion of the first rotation, while deforestation involves an immediate, one-time revenue windfall from cutting of the stand, net of a loss of future revenues from continued forest production. Additionally, under actual management practices during the sample period of historical analysis, costs were associated with converting forestland to agricultural cropland, but no costs were involved with essentially abandoning cropland and allowing it to return to a forested state. For the simulations associated with carbon sequestration policies, however, we need to allow for the possibility of "tree farming," that is, intensive management of the forest, which brings with it significant costs of establishment.

Second, there is the choice of species. In the econometric analysis, only mixed stands[9] were considered to reflect historical reality, but in the carbon-sequestration context it is important to consider the possibility of both mixed stands and tree farms (plantations of pure pine). We develop revenue streams for both, based upon observed practice in the region.[10]

The third silvicultural dimension is the choice of management regime. The historical analysis assumed that all forests were periodically harvested for their timber. For purposes of carbon sequestration, however, we should consider not only such conventional management regimes, but also the possibility of establishing "permanent stands" that are never harvested. These three silvicultural considerations lead to the respecification of Eq. (3),

$$q_{its}^y = \left[\frac{F_{its} - D_{its} + M_{it} - K_{it}}{A_{it}} \right], \qquad (5)$$

where subscript s indicates species and K is the cost associated with establishing a pine-based tree farm.[11] For the case of permanent (unharvested) stands, F and D are set equal to zero. Combining variable values associated with these silvicultural dimensions into logical sets yields four scenarios to be investigated: natural regrowth of a mixed stand, with and without periodic harvesting, and establishment of a pine plantation, with and without periodic harvesting.

2.3. *Generating a Forest Supply Function*

Next, we introduce some policy-inspired modifications to develop a forest supply function. First, note that dynamic simulations of fitted values of the model, employing current/expected values of all variables (including prices), will generate

---

[9] Mixed stands of appropriate shares of various species of hardwoods and softwoods, specific to each county and time period, were included in the data used for econometric estimation. The calculated revenue streams draw upon price data for both sawlogs and pulpwood in proportion to use, based upon 55-year rotations.

[10] The tree-farm revenue streams represent a mix of 80% loblolly pine and 20% slash pine, based upon practice in the area [5]. We use a rotation length of 45 years for loblolly and 30 years for slash pine, also reflecting standard practice [15].

[11] Forest establishment costs include the costs of planting (purchase of seedlings, site preparation, and transplanting), post-planting treatments, and care required to ensure establishment [15]. We adopt a value of $92/acre ($1990), based upon estimates by Richards et al. [23] for converted cropland in the Delta (three-state) region.

baseline predictions of future forestation and/or deforestation [32].[12] These results constitute our baseline for policy analysis. Second, we can simulate what land-use changes would be forthcoming with changed values of specific variables. In general, we can examine the consequences of public policies that affect the economic incentives faced by landowners. The difference in forestation/deforestation between the first (baseline) and the second (counterfactual) simulation is the predicted impact of a given policy.

In order to generate a representation of the forest supply function, several types of policies can be considered. A payment (subsidy) could be offered for every acre of (agricultural) land that is newly forested. But this would provide an incentive for landowners to cut down existing forests simply to replant in a later year in exchange for the government payment. On the other hand, a tax could be levied on each acre of land that is deforested. But such an approach would provide no added incentive for forestation of land that is not currently in that state. One solution is to think of a two-part policy that combines a subsidy on the flow of newly forested land with a tax on the flow of (new) deforestation. As a first approximation, the two price instruments can be set equal, although this is not necessarily most efficient.

We simulate this policy by treating the subsidy as an increment to forest revenues in the forestation part of the model (Eq. (4)) and treating the tax payment as an increment to conversion or production costs in the deforestation part of the model (Eq. (5)). Letting Z represent the subsidy and tax, the threshold equations ((3) and (4)) for forestation and deforestation, respectively, become

$$q_{its}^y = \left[\frac{(F_{its} - D_{its} + Z_{it}) + M_{it} - K_{it}}{A_{it}} \right] \tag{6}$$

$$q_{its}^x = \left[\frac{F_{its} - W_{its} + (M_{it} + Z_{it})}{A_{it} - C_{it}^{\alpha P_{it}}} \right]. \tag{7}$$

Thus, a dynamic simulation based upon Eqs. (6) and (7) in conjunction with the other equations of the model (see the Appendix), in which the variable Z is set equal to zero, will generate a baseline quantity of forestation/deforestation over a given time period. By carrying out simulations for various values of Z over the period and subtracting the results of each from the baseline results, we can trace out a forest acreage supply function, with marginal cost per acre (Z) arrayed in a schedule with total change in acreage over the time period, relative to the baseline.[13]

---

[12] Statistical tests, reported in Stavins and Jaffe [34], indicate a high degree of structural (and parametric) stability of the model over the 50-year time period of estimation. It is therefore possible to carry out future factual and counter-factual simulations. Extrapolations of historical trends would imply future increases in the relative price of timber to agricultural crops, but extrapolations of historical trends of relative yields would favor agriculture. Not knowing what the future will bring, the baseline simulations employ constant values of all variables, including real prices and yields. Nevertheless, the baseline simulations exhibit changes in land use over time, both because of the partial-adjustment nature of the model and because modifications of silvicultural practices are assumed for both baseline and policy simulations, as is explained later.

[13] This is a partial-equilibrium analysis of a 36-county region. If a national analysis were being carried out, it would be necessary to allow for price endogeneity, i.e., allow for land-use changes induced by changes in Z to affect agricultural and forest product prices. On this, see Stavins [33].

It might be argued that since the policy intervention we model is a tax/subsidy on land use, not on carbon emissions and sequestration, it does not lead to the true minimum carbon-sequestration marginal cost function. This may seem to be a valid criticism in the narrowest analytic sense, but it is not valid in a realistic policy context. It would be virtually impossible to levy a tax on carbon emissions or a subsidy on sequestration, because the costs of administering such policy interventions would be prohibitive. Looked at this way, such an instrument would likely be *more* costly per unit of carbon sequestered than would the deforestation tax/forestation subsidy policy considered here.[14]

2.4. *Computing the Marginal Cost of Carbon Sequestration*

For any parcel of land, there are several types of comparisons that could be made between the time-paths of carbon emissions/sequestration in a baseline and a policy simulation. First, we can consider a parcel that is continually in cropland in both simulations, in which case it exhibits zero net carbon sequestration/emission over the long run in both, and so the policy impact is also zero.[15] Second, a parcel may continually be in a forested state in both simulations, in which case it sequesters carbon in both simulations, but net sequestration due to the policy intervention is again zero. Third, a parcel may be in agricultural use in the baseline, but forestation takes place in the policy simulation in year t; here, net carbon sequestration due to the policy intervention will be the time-path of annual sequestration that commences in year t. Fourth, a parcel may be in a forested state in the baseline, but deforestation takes place in the policy simulation in year t; then the net carbon emissions due to the policy intervention will be the time-path of annual *emissions* that commence in year t, assuming durable wood products are produced from merchantable timber.

Carbon-Sequestration Time Profiles

The next step, conceptually, is to link specific time paths of carbon sequestration (and emissions) with forestation and deforestation. Scientific understanding of these linkages is evolving; we draw upon recent biological models and employ a set of temporal carbon yield curves based on Moulton and Richards [15] and Richards et al. [23].[16] Figure 1 provides a pictorial representation of one example of the time-path of carbon sequestration and emission linked with a specific forest management regime. In the example, the time profile of cumulative carbon

---

[14] This is not to suggest that a uniform tax/subsidy would be the first-best policy. A more efficient but still practical policy instrument might well involve a non-uniform tax/subsidy, set in accordance with regional and other factors.

[15] With constant relative prices in the baseline, the time-path of policy-induced changes in land use in the model is always such that individual counties are characterized by increases or decreases in forested acreage, *relative to the baseline*, but never both.

[16] Nordhaus [17] and Richards et al. [23] also use carbon yield curves, while many other sequestration cost studies have used point estimates of average flows.

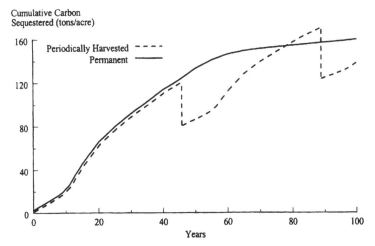

Source: Based on data from Moulton and Richards (1990) and Richards (1994).

FIG. 1. Time profile of carbon sequestration (Loblolly pine in delta states region).

sequestration is for establishing a new loblolly pine plantation. Carbon sequestration occurs in four components of the forest: trees, understory vegetation, forest floor, and soil.[17] When a plantation is managed as a permanent stand, cumulative sequestration increases monotonically, with the magnitude of annual increments declining so that an equilibrium quantity of sequestration is essentially reached within 100 years, as material decay comes into balance with natural growth.

The figure also shows the sequestration path for a stand that is periodically harvested. In this case, carbon accrues at the same rate as in a permanent stand until the first harvest, when carbon is released as a result of harvesting, processing, and manufacturing of derivative products.[18] Much of the carbon sequestered in wood products is also released to the atmosphere, although this occurs with

---

[17] Although shares vary greatly among forest types, reference points are: tree carbon contains about 80% of ecosystem carbon, soil carbon about 15%, forest litter 3%, and the understory 2% [23]. Variation in these shares is significant; for some species, soil carbon accounts for nearly 50% of total forest carbon.

[18] Our calculations of releases from the understory, forest floor, soil, and non-merchantable timber are based upon Moulton and Richards [15] and Richards et al. [23]. The share of total forest carbon that actually ends up in merchantable wood varies considerably by species. A reasonable reference point is about 40%. Much of the remaining 60% is released at the time of harvest and in the manufacturing process (in both cases through combustion), the major exception being soil carbon, which exhibits much slower decay.

considerable delay as wood products decay.[19] In this scenario, the forest is replanted and the process begins again.[20]

Although the carbon yield curve with harvesting in Fig. 1 eventually moves above the yield curve for a "permanent" stand, this need not be case. It depends upon the share of carbon that is initially sequestered in wood products and upon those products' decay rates (plus the decay rate of soil carbon). With zero decay rates, the peaks in the harvesting yield curve would increase monotonically, but with positive decay rates the locus of the peaks approaches a steady-state quantity of sequestration, because eventually decay in the stock of carbon stored in existing wood products offsets the amount of new carbon sequestered through tree growth. That steady-state quantity can, in theory, lie above or below the level associated with the equilibrium level of the "permanent" yield curve.[21]

Discounting Carbon Costs and Benefits

Recognizing the intertemporal nature of net carbon sequestration raises a question: how can we associate a number—the marginal cost of carbon sequestration—with diverse units of carbon that are sequestered in different years over long time horizons? Previous sequestration studies have used a variety of methods to calculate costs in terms of dollars per ton, the desired units for a cost-effectiveness comparison. These approaches have been classified as "flow summation," "mean carbon storage," and "levelization" [24].

The "flow summation" approach is the simplest: the present value of costs is divided by the total tons of carbon sequestered, regardless of when sequestration occurs. This summary statistic fails to take into account the time profile of sequestration, and second, the measure is very sensitive to the length of the time horizon selected for calculation (in the case of periodic-harvesting scenarios). Furthermore, assuming that not only costs but also benefits of sequestration are to be discounted over time, this approach implies that marginal benefits of sequestra-

---

[19] As Sedjo et al. [30] point out, examinations of the long-term effects of timber growth on carbon sequestration are "highly dependent upon the assumptions of the life-cycle of the wood products" (p. 23). Harmon et al. [9] found this to be the case in their scientific review. The two critical parameters are the assumed length of the life-cycle of wood products and the assumed share of timber biomass that goes into long-lived wood products. Drawing upon the work of Row [25], Row and Phelps [26], and Turner et al. [36], we develop a time-path of gradual decay of wood products over time, based upon an appropriately weighted average of pulpwood, sawlog, hardwood, and softwood estimates from Plantinga and Birdsey [21]. The final profile is such that one year following harvest, 83% of the carbon in wood products remains sequestered; this percentage falls to 76% after 10 years, and 25% after 100 years (and is assumed to be constant thereafter). At an interest rate of 5%, the present-value equivalent sequestration is approximately 75%, identical to that assumed by Nordhaus [17].

[20] Another potential scenario, which we do not consider, is that harvested wood is used for fuel. If this is to produce electricity or liquid fuels such as methanol, thereby substituting for fossil-fuel use, then there would be two additional effects to consider: (1) the net impact on atmospheric CO_2 emissions of each unit of forestation would be significantly enhanced, and (2) the demand for wood would be increased, which would matter in a general-equilibrium setting. On the other hand, the general-equilibrium effects of bringing a new source of wood to the market would also need to be considered.

[21] There has been a significant amount of debate within the scientific community about the relative superiority of these two regimes in terms of their carbon-sequestration potential. Harmon et al. [9] find that old growth forests are superior to periodic harvesting approaches in their ability to sequester carbon, but Kershaw et al. [12] demonstrate that this is dependent upon specific circumstances.

CLIMATE CHANGE AND FOREST SINKS 221

tion are increasing exponentially over time at the discount rate. A similar summary statistic is based upon "mean carbon storage." In this case, the present value of costs is divided by the numerical average of annual carbon storage. This statistic suffers from the same problems as the first.

The third alternative—"levelization"—seems most reasonable: the discounted present value of costs is divided by the discounted present value of tons sequestered. Alternatively (and equivalently), an annuity of present value costs is divided by an annuity of present value tons. This is the approach we use. It may be thought of as assuming that the marginal damages associated with additional units of atmospheric carbon are constant and that benefits (avoided damages) and costs are to be discounted at the same rate. Note that such an assumption of constant marginal benefits is approximately correct if damages are essentially proportional to the rate of climate change, which many studies have asserted.[22]

Specifically, we define the present values (in year t) of the time-paths of carbon sequestration and carbon emissions associated with forestation or deforestation occurring in year t as Ω_t^S and Ω_t^E, respectively. Thus, the total, present-value equivalent net carbon sequestration/emissions associated with any baseline or policy simulation are calculated as

$$PV(SEQ) = \sum_{i=1}^{36} \left[\sum_{t=0}^{90} \left(FORCH_{it}^a \cdot D_{it}^a \cdot \Omega_t^S - FORCH_{it}^c \cdot D_{it}^c \cdot \Omega_t^E \right) \cdot (1 + r)^{-t} \right],$$
(8)

where

$$\Omega_t^S = \sum_{h=t}^{90} CS_h \cdot (1 + r)^{t-h}$$
(9)

$$\Omega_t^E = \sum_{h=t}^{90} CE_h \cdot (1 + r)^{t-h},$$
(10)

and where $FORCH^a$ and $FORCH^c$ are forestation and deforestation, respectively, as a share of total county area (see the Appendix for formulae), D^a and D^c are dummy variables for forestation and deforestation, respectively, and CS_h and CE_h are, respectively, annual incremental carbon sequestration and carbon emissions per acre under individual scenarios.

We develop the constituent carbon yield curves for various forest species, location, and management conditions, and initially use a 5% discount rate. The present-value equivalent carbon-sequestration measure associated with natural

---

[22] If the marginal damages of carbon emissions were expected to change at some rate g over time, an appropriate modification of the levelization procedure could entail reducing the discount rate for carbon by the rate g. For monotonically increasing sequestration time profiles this modification would raise the present-value tons of carbon and lower the marginal cost of carbon sequestration if marginal damages were growing over time (i.e., $g > 0$); it would do the opposite if damages were expected to fall. For non-monotonic sequestration paths, such as those involving periodic harvesting, the effect depends on the specific shape of the path; $g > 0$ could in principle raise or lower present-value carbon. For the scenarios we investigate, such a modification—which is equivalent to lowering the discount rate (for $g > 0$)—also raises the present-value carbon for the harvesting scenarios, but not by as much as for the non-harvesting scenarios.

regrowth of a mixed stand is 43.36 tons if periodically harvested and 50.59 tons if permanent; for a pine plantation the values are 41.05 if periodically harvested and 49.99 tons if permanent.[23] Additionally, we calculate present-value carbon emission measures for deforestation with sale of merchantable timber (51.83 tons). These values are also reported in Tables I and IV. As described above, these values depend on the time profile of sequestration and the amount of carbon released upon harvest, both of which may vary by species, geographic location, and management regime, and are subject to scientific uncertainty. Silvicultural scenarios with more rapid carbon accumulation and less emissions upon harvest will exhibit higher carbon present values and thus lower costs of carbon sequestration per ton.

Since we derive marginal costs on an annual per acre basis using the tax/subsidy scheme, Z, we first convert present value tons of carbon to an equivalent annuity, $AV(SEQ)$, as

$$AV(SEQ) = \frac{PV(SEQ)}{PVFAC(r)}, \tag{11}$$

where $PVFAC$ is a present-value factor used to annualize the present value at rate r. We then divide the carbon-sequestration annuity by the total acreage of forestation, $TFORCH$, relative to the baseline in order to place it on a per acre basis. Lastly, we compute the marginal cost per ton of carbon sequestration MC for each scenario by dividing marginal cost per acre per year by the per acre carbon-sequestration annuity:

$$MC = \frac{Z}{\left(\dfrac{AV(SEQ)}{TFORCH} \right)}. \tag{12}$$

As discussed below, Table II illustrates this computation for a periodically harvested pine plantation.

3. THE COSTS OF CARBON SEQUESTRATION

The results of dynamic land-use simulations for the 90-year period from 1990 to 2080 constitute the fundamental inputs into the final carbon simulation model consisting of Eqs. (8), (9), and (10).[24] A 90-year period was used to allow at least

[23] The yield curves provided in Fig. 1 are simply examples for one species, loblolly pine. The growth curves that underlie respective yield curves are themselves a function, partly, of precipitation and temperature, both of which are presumably affected in the long run by atmospheric concentrations of CO_2 and induced climate change [6]. We ignore this endogeneity to climate change in estimating sequestration costs, as have all previous studies. Likewise, all studies have ignored potential economic endogeneity of relevant variables to climate change. The mixed-stand carbon paths are weighted averages from hardwood and pine constituents, assuming 55% hardwoods and 45% southern pine [5]. The assumed density of carbon in merchantable hardwoods is from Moulton and Richards [15] for Delta state hardwoods. In the case of softwoods (pines), density and assumed rotation length are for loblolly pine and slash pine [15], weighted as 80% and 20%, respectively, of total softwoods. Carbon-sequestration patterns and merchantable wood volumes for pine are based on Richards et al. [23] for cropland in the Delta region.

[24] In a prior step, the econometrically estimated parameters were used with newly available data for 1989 to simulate total forested acreage per county in 1989, the base year for the simulations.

TABLE II

Land Change and Carbon-Sequestration Costs and Quantities,
Periodically Harvested Pine Plantation

Marginal cost per acre ($/acre/year) Z	Forestation relative to baseline (1,000's acres) TFORCH	Average cost per acre ($/acre/year)	Annualized carbon sequestration relative to baseline (1,000's tons/year) AV(SEQ)	Marginal cost of carbon sequestration ($/ton) $MC = Z/[AV(SEQ)/TFORCH]$	Average cost of carbon sequestration ($/ton)
0	0	0.00	0	0.00	0.00
10	518	10.00	784	6.61	6.61
20	1,057	15.10	1,600	13.21	9.97
30	1,615	20.25	2,445	19.82	13.38
40	2,192	25.45	3,319	26.42	16.81
50	2,787	30.69	4,219	33.03	20.27
60	3,398	35.96	5,145	39.63	23.76
70	3,893	41.27	5,895	46.24	27.26
80	4,224	46.60	6,395	52.84	30.78
90	4,455	51.95	6,745	59.45	34.31
100	4,653	57.32	7,045	66.05	37.86
200	6,579	105.63	9,961	135.97	69.77
300	7,484	129.15	11,332	202.03	85.31
400	7,897	142.25	11,957	268.05	93.96
500	8,212	155.98	12,434	334.11	103.03
600	8,470	169.22	12,825	400.18	111.77
700	8,689	182.74	13,156	466.22	120.71
800	8,874	195.72	13,437	532.20	129.28
900	9.038	208.21	13,685	598.31	137.53
1,000	9,178	219.53	13,897	664.35	145.01

Notes: Variable symbols are given at the bottom of certain headings to illustrate how figures were computed (see Section 2.3). Discount rate is 5%; baseline forestation is 52,000 acres; baseline carbon sequestration is 4.6 million tons.

one rotation of each forest species; given the consequences of discounting, the results are not fundamentally affected by the length of the period of analysis once that period exceeds 50 years or so. Different time-paths of annual carbon increments, CS_h and CE_h, and different cost and revenue streams of forestation and deforestation are associated with each of the four scenarios to be examined.

As previously described, simulations are employed to trace out the supply curve of net carbon sequestration, in which the marginal costs of carbon sequestration, measured in dollars per ton, are arrayed in a schedule with net annualized[25] carbon sequestration (relative to the baseline). Table II provides the results for one scenario, a periodically harvested pine plantation, with the sale of merchantable timber when/if deforestation occurs. We focus initially on this scenario and provide detailed results for it, by way of example. The relatively attractive forest revenues associated with this management regime result in a small amount of net forestation taking place in the baseline simulation, a gain of about 52 thousand

[25] As explained above, both dollars of costs and tons of sequestration (and emission) are discounted. Hence, annual sequestration refers to an annuity that is equivalent to a respective present value for a given discount rate.

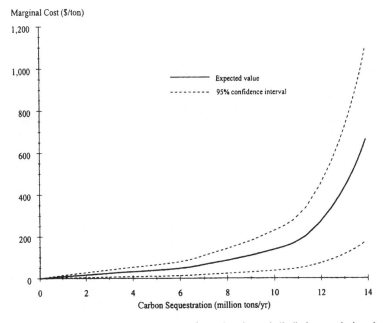

FIG. 2. Marginal cost of carbon sequestration (scenario #3—periodically harvested pine plantation).

acres (over the 90-year study period). Baseline net carbon sequestration is approximately 4.6 million tons annually. As can be seen in Table II and Fig. 2, the marginal costs of carbon sequestration increase approximately linearly until these costs are about $66 per ton, where annual sequestration relative to the baseline has reached about 7 million tons. This level of sequestration is associated with a land-use tax/subsidy of $100 per acre and net forestation relative to baseline of 4.7 million acres.

Beyond this point, marginal costs increasingly depart from a linear trend. Beyond about $200 per ton, they turn steeply upward. Indeed, the marginal cost function appears to be nearly asymptotic to a sequestration level of about 15 to 16 million tons annually (Figure 2).[26] This is not surprising. Such an implicit limit would be associated in the model with net forestation of about 10.5 million acres,

---

[26] Although the assumption of exogenous prices becomes less tenable as land-use impacts become more severe, it is nevertheless true that the relevant agricultural prices (and to a lesser degree, stumpage values) are determined on national and international markets of which the study region represents only a trivial share. In any event, however, the reliability of the model's predictions decreases as we move further outside the range of the data on which the underlying econometric parameters were estimated.

TABLE III

Costs of Carbon Sequestration for Alternative Silvicultural Scenarios
for 5 Million Tons of Sequestration above Baseline

	Alternative silvicultural scenarios			
Species regime	Natural regrowth of mixed stand		Pine plantation	
Management regime	Periodic harvest	No harvest	Periodic harvest	No harvest
Scenario	#1	#2	#3	#4
Baseline change in forestation (1,000 acres)	−259	−297	52	−69
Baseline carbon sequestration (1,000 tons)	4,005	3,931	4,578	4,368
Marginal cost per acre ($/acre/year)	55.80	49.20	58.40	49.10
Forestation relative to baseline (1,000 acres)	3,074	2,662	3,301	2,710
Average cost per acre ($/acre/year)	33.80	30.31	35.12	30.23
Forestation carbon sequestration (tons/acre)	43.36	50.59	41.05	49.99
Deforestation carbon emissions (tons/acre)	51.83	51.83	51.83	51.83
Annualized carbon sequestration (1,000 tons/year)	5,000	5,000	5,000	5,000
Marginal cost of carbon sequestration ($/ton)	34.33	26.30	38.57	26.61
Average cost of carbon sequestration ($/ton)	20.79	16.20	23.20	16.38

Note: Discount rate is 5%.

for a total forested area of 13 million acres, just shy of the total area of the 36 counties of the study region.[27]

3.1. *Alternative Silvicultural Scenarios*

Simulated costs of carbon sequestration are summarized in Table III for four scenarios. In scenario #1, all forestation is assumed to be through natural regrowth of mixed stands that are periodically harvested. The more modest forest revenues associated with this management regime (relative to the pine plantation) result in net deforestation taking place in the baseline simulation, a loss of about 260 thousand acres. The marginal cost of carbon sequestration is about $34 when 5 million tons are sequestered annually.

---

[27] An advantage of our revealed-preference approach, compared with the usual engineering approaches, is that because the simulation model's parameters are econometrically estimated, those parameters have associated with them not only estimated values (coefficients), but also estimated standard errors. Hence, we can provide a richer description of the marginal cost function through the use of stochastic (Monte Carlo) simulations, drawing upon the relevant variance–covariance matrix. Based upon these simulations, Fig. 2 provides not only a set of point estimates of the marginal cost function, but also the 95% confidence interval around that function. There is also uncertainty associated with a number of the variables employed in the analysis. Hence, the figure probably presents an under-estimate of the true error bounds.

If we modify the previous scenario to eliminate periodic harvesting (thus setting the forest revenue stream for *new* forests equal to zero), deforestation increases somewhat in the baseline (scenario #2, Table III).[28] The timber revenue stream in scenario #1 was forestalling some conversion of forest to agriculture; with the elimination of this revenue stream in scenario #2, deforestation increases. On its own, preventing periodic harvesting of timber would tend to increase the marginal costs of carbon sequestration, since the net opportunity costs associated with an agriculture/forestry change increase. Indeed, this modest loss of expected revenue (about 13%) does cause a modest decrease in the total amount of induced forestation that occurs relative to the case with harvesting (scenario #1). But the time-path of carbon sequestration without harvesting is sufficiently favorable to overcome this effect, so that the marginal costs of sequestration are actually *less* in the no-harvest cases than in those cases where periodic harvesting is permitted. For example, the marginal cost of carbon sequestration is now only $26 (compared with $34 in the presence of periodic harvesting) when 5 million tons are sequestered annually.

The picture changes somewhat when we allow for tree farms of pure pine to be established as the regime of forestation. Now the economic incentives that exist in the baseline actually cause little or no deforestation to occur. Potential annual revenues from forestry are significantly greater than in the case of mixed stands, but up-front plantation establishment costs partially mitigate this effect. Overall, a given land-use tax/subsidy brings about greater net forestation in the pure pine case, but this effect is overwhelmed by the differences in carbon-sequestration potential, and so the periodic pine scenario (#3) exhibits *greater* marginal seques-tration costs than the periodic mixed-stand case (scenario #1). The difference in carbon sequestration is being driven by the fact that retarded deforestation is responsible for a considerable part of the net carbon sequestration (relative to baseline) for the mixed stands, but in the pine plantation case, we find that all of the carbon sequestration in scenario #3 is due to forestation (which in present-value equivalent terms provides substantially less carbon saved per acre). Scenario #4, the pine plantation without periodic harvesting, provides an intermediate case, which yields results quite similar to the related mixed-stand scenario (#2), because the absence of periodic harvesting eliminates one of the major economic differ-ences and the carbon yield curves themselves are similar.

3.2. *Discount Rates*

Because of the long time horizons employed in the analysis, it is natural to ask about the sensitivity of the results to the assumed discount rate (5%). Changing the discount rate has two types of effects on the simulations. First, many of the economic variables take on new values. One example is the trade-off between foregone future forest revenues F and the immediate windfall of revenue from

---

[28] Note that the alternative scenarios imply alternative parameter values for each pair of baseline and counter-factual simulations. What is critical for our marginal cost calculations is that any pair of baseline and counter-factual simulations employs identical assumptions (parameter values), with the exception, of course, of Z_{it}, the tax/subsidy that generates the counter-factuals and leads to our marginal cost estimates.

TABLE IV

Present-Value Equivalent Carbon Sequestration and Emissions
with Alternative Discount Rates

Carbon sequestration and emissions	Alternative discount rates			
	2.5%	5.0%	7.5%	10.0%
Present-value equivalent carbon sequestration (tons per acre)				
Natural regrowth of mixed stand				
Periodic harvest (scenario #1)	61.90	43.36	30.63	22.72
No periodic harvest (scenario #2)	91.48	50.59	32.85	23.52
Pine plantation				
Periodic harvest (scenario #3)	54.66	41.05	30.76	23.75
No periodic harvest (scenario #4)	80.68	49.99	34.33	25.25
Present-value equivalent carbon emissions (tons per acre)				
Deforestation	54.28	51.83	50.99	50.55

carrying, W. Second, the present-value equivalent tons per acre of sequestration are affected by changing discount rates (Table IV).[29]

In Table V, we examine the impact of changing discount rates on three output variables: marginal sequestration costs, induced forestation, and induced carbon sequestration. The sensitivity analysis is carried out for two pine-plantation scenarios—periodically harvested (#3) and no periodic harvests (#4). First, we find that as the discount rate increases (from 2.5% to 10%), marginal sequestration costs increase monotonically, as expected. The simplest explanation of this effect is that the present-value equivalent sequestration decreases with increased interest rates. The magnitude of the impact is similar to that reported by [23], who found that raising the discount rate in their analysis from 3 to 7% nearly doubled marginal costs.

Next, we find that as the discount rate increases, the forestation caused by a given ($50/acre) subsidy/tax increases. This is also as anticipated, since the up-front subsidy/tax becomes more important, relative to discounted future flows of net revenue, with the increased discount rate. Finally, and most interesting, as the discount rate increases, the impact on induced carbon sequestration is not monotonic: at first increasing interest rates increase induced sequestration, but then they have the opposite effect, decreasing carbon sequestration. The explanation is that there are two factors at work here: land-use changes and the present-value equivalent of carbon sequestration per acre. At first, the land-use effect is dominant, and so with higher interest rates, we find more induced forestation and so more sequestration, but then the effect of smaller present values of carbon sequestration per acre becomes dominant, and so carbon sequestration begins to decrease with higher discount rates. The effect is particularly dramatic in scenario

---

[29] The rotation period may also be responsive to changes in the discount rate. The extent of the response will depend on the range of discount rates analyzed and the sensitivity of stumpage values to changes in rotation period. While the effect can, in principle, be substantial, it is not for the species and range of discount rates we analyze, and the ultimate effect on annualized carbon yields and sequestration costs is very small.

TABLE V

Discount Rate Sensitivity of the Cost and Quantity
of Carbon Sequestration, Pine Plantation

Carbon sequestration and forestation costs and quantities	Alternative discount rates			
	2.5%	5.0%	7.5%	10.0%
Marginal cost of sequestration ($/ton) (Sequestration = 5 million tons/year)				
Periodic harvest (scenario #3)	33	39	58	92
No periodic harvest (scenario #4)	18	27	46	81
Forestation relative to baseline (1,000 acres) (Subsidy/tax = $50/acre)				
Periodic harvest (scenario #3)	1,467	2,787	4,368	6,131
No periodic harvest (scenario #4)	1,453	2,763	4,336	6.092
Carbon sequestration relative to baseline (1,000 tons/year) (subsidy/tax = $50/acre)				
Periodic harvest (scenario #3)	3,271	4,219	4,302	3,928
No periodic harvest (scenario #4)	4,460	5,099	4,832	4,242

#4, where there is no periodic harvesting, since the fall in present-value carbon equivalents is greatest in that case.

3.3. *The Economic Environment*

It is of particular interest to ask what would happen to the estimated quantities of carbon sequestration and marginal costs if there were significant changes in the economic environment. The baseline simulation with recent price data reflects the reality currently being experienced in the study area—minimal, although not trivial, deforestation. In contrast to this, other parts of the United States—such as New England and the Middle Atlantic states—began to experience positive net rates of forestation as early as the middle of the 19th century. Such background patterns of land-use changes are potentially important. By modifying the assumed level of agricultural product prices in the analysis, we can produce baseline simulations with significant amounts of forestation or deforestation occurring (in the absence of policy intervention), and then investigate the consequences of policy interventions in these new dynamic contexts. We focus here on sensitivity analysis for the periodically harvested pine plantation scenario.

Thus, we change agricultural product prices (in both the baseline and policy simulations) and observe what happens to net forestation and sequestration. As can be seen in Table VI, increasing agricultural prices produces baseline simulations with significant deforestation. What are the impacts of such price changes on carbon sequestration *relative to baseline* at a given level of policy intervention, such as a land-use subsidy/tax of $50 per acre? Not surprisingly, we find that induced sequestration decreases monotonically as the background agricultural product price level increases. The change, however, is by no means linear. The context of low agricultural prices (30% below the base case) increases induced sequestration by 80%, whereas the high price context (30% above the base case) decreases induced sequestration by only 25%.

TABLE VI

Sensitivity of Results to Agricultural Prices,
Periodically Harvested Pine Plantation

Carbon sequestration and forestation costs and quantities	Departures from base case agricultural product prices						
	−30%	−20%	−10%	Base case	+10%	+20%	+30%
Baseline forestation/deforestation (1,000 acres)	5,968	3,317	1,430	52	−977	−1,758	−2,362
Marginal cost of carbon sequestration ($/ton) (Sequestration = 5 million tons/yr)	21.93	26.88	32.44	37.91	38.87	39.60	40.94
Carbon sequestration relative to baseline (1,000 tons/year) (subsidy/tax = $50/acre)	7,656	6,212	5,094	4,219	3,914	3,669	3,183

Note: Discount rate is 5%.

The same non-linear impact is seen when we observe the effect of agricultural price changes on the marginal costs of sequestration, again in Table VI. Marginal sequestration costs increase monotonically as we increase the background context of agricultural prices. This is as expected, since the opportunity cost of the land increases. Once again, the change is far from linear; decreases in agricultural prices have a much greater impact than do increases. This happens because higher agricultural product prices result in a substantial amount of deforestation in the baseline. As a result, the effect of a given tax/subsidy—in the context of high agricultural prices—is not only to increase forestation, but also to *retard deforestation*. And the carbon consequences of a unit of retarded deforestation (51.83 tons per acre from Table II) are significantly greater than those associated with a unit of forestation (41.05 tons per acre from Table II), in terms of present-value equivalents. The increased "carbon efficiency" of the policy intervention in the context of a high level of background deforestation thus reduces the marginal costs of sequestration below what they otherwise would be in the context of high agricultural prices.

4. CONCLUSIONS

When and if the United States chooses to ratify the Kyoto Protocol or subsequent international agreements, it will be necessary to decide whether carbon sequestration policies should be part of the domestic portfolio of U.S. compliance activities. For this reason, we have examined the sensitivity of sequestration costs to changes in key factors, including the nature of the management and deforestation regimes, silvicultural species, relative prices, and discount rates.

What conclusions can be drawn from these quantitative results? First, there is the somewhat surprising finding that marginal sequestration costs can be greater for cases with periodic harvesting of timber. Despite the fact that opportunity costs for landowners are less, the more favorable sequestration pattern provided by permanent stands can counteract and overwhelm this effect.[30]

---

[30] A consistent set of assumptions is employed in the baseline and policy simulations underlying each scenario. This means that comparisons across scenarios typically involve different amounts of deforestation (or forestation) in respective baselines.

Second, changing the discount rate has two types of effects: many of the economic variables take on new values, and the present-value equivalent tons per acre of sequestration are affected. As the discount rate increases, the *marginal costs* of sequestration increase monotonically, because the present-value equivalent sequestration decreases. But as the discount rate increases, the impact on the *quantity* of induced carbon sequestration is not monotonic, because two factors work in opposite directions: forestation increases, but the present-value equivalent of carbon sequestration per acre decreases.

Third, background patterns of land-use changes are potentially important, a reality that we investigated by varying the baseline level of agricultural product prices. We found that induced sequestration decreases monotonically and non-linearly as the background agricultural product price level increases. Likewise, marginal sequestration costs increase monotonically and non-linearly as agricultural prices increase because the opportunity cost of the land increases.

Fourth and finally, there is the striking asymmetry between the marginal costs of carbon sequestration through forestation and those through retarded deforestation. This provides another argument for focusing carbon-sequestration efforts in areas of relatively high rates of deforestation, such as in tropical forests. In addition to the fact that these areas are more efficient engines of carbon storage than temperate forests and in addition to the lower opportunity costs of land that we would ordinarily anticipate to be associated with such areas, there is the additional reality that in an intertemporal economic context, retarded deforestation provides carbon conservation at much lower marginal costs than does forestation of the same area.[31] Of course this would have to be considered alongside other conditions present in any particular context, such as institutional concerns pertaining to administrative feasibility and the strength of property rights.

For many countries, carbon sequestration through forestation or retarded deforestation may be a cost-effective approach to contributing to reduced global atmospheric concentrations of CO_2. This seems most likely to be true for developing nations, although even for highly industrialized countries such as the United States, carbon sequestration through land-use changes could arguably be part of a cost-effective portfolio of short-term strategies [33]. Whether and to what degree "forestry instruments" belong in individual nations' global climate policy portfolios will depend upon geographic, institutional, and economic characteristics of countries and key local characteristics of forestry and land-use practices [22]. The investigation reported in this paper represents one step along the way to such comprehensive analysis.

APPENDIX: THE DYNAMIC OPTIMIZATION PROBLEM

A risk-neutral landowner will seek to maximize the present discounted value of the stream of expected future returns,

$$
\max_{\{g_{ijt}, v_{ijt}\}} \int_0^\infty \Big[(A_{it} q_{ijt} - M_{it})(g_{ijt} - v_{ijt}) - C_{it}^{\alpha P_{it}} g_{ijt} \\
+ f_{it} S_{ijt} + W_{it} g_{ijt} - D_{it} v_{ijt} \Big] e^{-r_t t} \, dt
$$

[31] Additionally, many would argue that the non-climate change benefits of retarding tropical deforestation typically exceed those of increased forestation in temperate zones, because of the preservation of biological diversity in these exceptionally rich ecologies.

$$subject\ to: \quad \dot{S}_{ijt} = v_{ijt} - g_{ijt}$$

$$0 \le g_{ijt} \le \bar{g}_{ijt}$$

$$0 \le v_{ijt} \le \bar{v}_{ijt},$$

where I indexes counties, j indexes individual land parcels, and t indexes time; upper case letters are stocks or present values and lower case letters are flows.[32] The variables are:

A_{it} discounted present value of the future stream of typical expected agricultural revenues per acre in county I and time t;

q_{ijt} parcel-specific index of feasibility of agricultural production, including effects of soil quality and soil moisture;

g_{ijt} acres of land converted from forested to agricultural use (deforestation);

v_{ijt} acres of cropland returned to a forested condition (forestation);

M_{it} expected cost of agricultural production per acre, expressed as the discounted present value of an infinite future stream;

C_{it} average cost of conversion per acre;

P_{it} the Palmer hydrological drought index and α is a parameter to be estimated, to allow precipitation and soil moisture to influence conversion costs;

f_{it} expected annual net income from forestry per acre (annuity of stumpage value);

S_{ijt} stock (acres) of forest;

r_t real interest rate;

W_{it} windfall of net revenue per acre from clear cut of forest, prior to conversion to agriculture;

D_{it} expected present discounted value of loss of income (when converting to forest) due to gradual regrowth of forest (first harvest of forest does not occur until the year $t + R$, where R is the exogenously determined rotation length);

$\bar{g}_{ijt}$ maximum feasible rate of deforestation, defined such that

$$\int_t^{t+\Delta} \left[\bar{g}_{ij\tau} \right] d\tau = S_{ijt}$$

for arbitrarily small interval, Δ, over which $\bar{g}_{ij\tau}$ is constant; and

$\bar{v}_{ijt}$ maximum feasible rate of forestation, defined such that

$$\int_t^{t+\Delta} \left[\bar{v}_{ij\tau} \right] d\tau = T_{ijt} - S_{ijt}$$

for arbitrarily small interval, Δ, over which $\bar{v}_{ij\tau}$ is constant.

The application of control theoretic methods yields a pair of necessary conditions for changes in land use [34]. Forestation (conversion of agricultural cropland to forest) occurs if a parcel is cropland and if

$$\left(F_{it} - D_{it} - A_{it} \cdot q_{ijt} + M_{it} \right) > 0, \tag{A1}$$

---

[32] This specification implies that all prices and costs are exogenously determined in broader national or international markets, a reasonable assumption in the present application.

where F is forest net revenue, equal to f_{it}/r_t. On the other hand, deforestation occurs if a parcel is forested and if

$$\left(A_{it} \cdot q_{ijt} - M_{it} - C_{it}^{\alpha P_{it}} - (F_{it} - W_{it}) \right) > 0. \tag{A2}$$

These inequalities imply that all land in a county will be in the same use in the steady state. In reality, counties are observed to be a mix of forest and farmland, due largely to the *heterogeneity* of land. If conversion costs are allowed to be heterogeneous across land parcels (within counties) and flood-control projects affect conversion costs as well as agricultural feasibility (yields), then the conversion cost term in the first equation in the Appendix (i.e., the objective function) is multiplied by q_{ijt}. As shown in [34], such unobserved heterogeneity can be parameterized within an econometrically estimatable model so that the *individual* necessary conditions for land-use changes aggregate into a single-equation model, in which the parameters of the basic benefit–cost relationships and of the underlying, unobserved heterogeneity can be estimated simultaneously. The complete model yields the following set of econometrically estimatable equations:

$$FORCH_{it} = FORCH_{it}^a \cdot D_{it}^a - FORCH_{it}^c \cdot D_{it}^c + \lambda_i + \phi_{it}$$

$$FORCH_{it}^a = \gamma_a \cdot \left[d_{it} \cdot \left[F\left[\frac{\log(q_{it}^y) - \mu(1 + \beta_2 E_{it})}{\sigma(1 + \beta_3 E_{it})} \right] \right] + (1 - d_{it}) - \left[\frac{S}{T} \right]_{i,t-1} \right]$$

$$FORCH_{it}^c = \gamma_c \cdot \left[d_{it} \cdot \left[1 - F\left[\frac{\log(q_{it}^x) - \mu(1 + \beta_2 E_{it})}{\sigma(1 + \beta_3 E_{it})} \right] \right] + \left[\frac{S}{T} \right]_{i,t-1} - 1 \right]$$

$$d_{it} = \left[\frac{1}{1 + e^{-(N_i + \beta_1 E_{it})}} \right]$$

$$q_{it}^y = \left[\frac{F_{it} - D_{it} + M_{it}}{A_{it}} \right] \tag{A3}$$

$$q_{it}^x = \left[\frac{F_{it} - W_{it} + M_{it}}{A_{it} - C_{it}^{\alpha P_{it}}} \right], \tag{A4}$$

where all Greek letters are parameters that can be estimated econometrically;[33]

FORCH   change in forest land as a share of total county area;
FORCH^a   forestation (abandonment of cropland) as a share of total county area;
FORCH^c   deforestation (conversion of forest) as a share of total county area;
D^a and D^c dummy variables for forestation and deforestation, respectively;
ϕ an independent (but not necessarily homoscedastic) error term;

---

[33] The econometrically estimatable coefficients have the following interpretations: λ_i is a county-level fixed-effect parameter; γ_a and γ_c are partial adjustment coefficients for forestation and deforestation; μ is the mean of the unobserved land-quality distribution; σ is the standard deviation of that distribution; α is the effect of weather on conversion costs; β_1 is the effect of government flood-control programs on agricultural feasibility; β_2 is the effect of these programs on the heterogeneity mean; and β_3 is the effect of programs on the standard deviation.

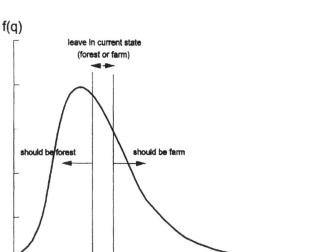

FIG. 3. The distribution of land quality and economic thresholds of forestation and deforestation.

d	probability that agricultural production is feasible;
q^y	threshold value of (unobserved) land quality (suitability for agriculture) below which the incentive for forestation manifests itself;
q^x	threshold value of land quality above which the incentive for deforestation manifests itself; E is an index of the share of a county that has been artificially protected from flooding by Federal programs (by time t);
E	index of share of county artificially protected from periodic flooding;
S	stock (acres) of forest;
F	cumulative, standard normal distribution function;
T	total county area; and
N	share of a county that is naturally protected from periodic flooding.

A simplified, pictorial representation of the model is provided in Fig. 3. The skewed distribution in the figure represents the parameterized lognormal distribution of unobserved land quality; and q_{it}^y and q_{it}^x are the forestation and deforestation thresholds, respectively. Note that each is a (different) function of the benefits and costs of forest production relative to agricultural production. The asymmetries between Eqs. (3) and (4) cause the separation between the two thresholds (where economic signals suggest to leave land in its existing state, whether that be forest or farm). Thus, if expected forest revenues increase, both thresholds shift to the right and we would anticipate that some quantity of farmland would be converted to forest uses. Likewise, an increase in expected agricultural prices means a shift of the two thresholds to the left, and consequent deforestation.

REFERENCES

1. R. M. Adams, D. M. Adams, J. M. Callaway, C. Chang, and B. A. McCarl, Sequestering carbon on agricultural land: Social cost and impacts on timber markets, *Contemp. Policy Issues* 11, 76–87 (1993).
2. R. Alig, D. Adams, B. McCarl, J. M. Callaway, and S. Winnett, Assessing effects of mitigation strategies for global climate change with an intertemporal model of the U.S. forest and agricultural sectors, *Environ. Resour. Econom.* 9, 259–274 (1997).
3. J. P. Bruce, H. Lee, and E. F. Haites, "Climate Change 1995: Economic and Social Dimensions of Climate Change," contribution of Working Group III to the Second Assessment Report of the Intergovernmental Panel on Climate Change, Cambridge Univ. Press, New York (1996).
4. J. M. Callaway and B. McCarl, The economic consequences of substituting carbon payments for crop subsidies in U.S. agriculture, *Environ. Resour. Econom.* 7, 15–43 (1996).
5. R. Daniels, personal communication, Mississippi State University, Agricultural Extension Service, Starkville, MS (1994).
6. R. K. Dixon, S. Brown, R. A. Houghton, A. M. Solomon, M. C. Trexler, and J. Wisniewski, Carbon pools and flux of global forest ecosystems, *Science* 263, 185–190 (1994).
7. R. K. Dixon, J. K. Winjum, K. J. Andrasko, J. J. Lee, and P. E. Schroeder, Integrated land-use systems: Assessment of promising agroforest and alternative land-use practices to enhance carbon conservation and sequestration, *Climatic Change* 27, 71–92 (1994).
8. D. J. Dudek and A. LeBlanc, Offsetting new CO_2 emissions: A rational first greenhouse policy step, *Contemp. Policy Issues* 8, 29–42 (1990).
9. M. E. Harmon, W. K. Farrell, and J. F. Franklin, Effects on carbon storage of conversion of old-growth forest to young forests, *Science* 247, 699–702 (1990).
10. R. A. Houghton, Tropical deforestation and atmospheric carbon dioxide, *Climatic Change* 19, 99–118 (1991).
11. C. J. Jepma, M. Asaduzzaman, I. Mintzer, S. Maya, and M. Al-Moneef, "A Generic Assessment of Response Options," Draft, Intergovernmental Panel on Climate Change, Report of Working Group III. Geneva, Switzerland (January 20, 1995).
12. J. A. Kershaw, C. D. Oliver, and T. M. Hinckley, Effect of harvest of old growth douglas-fir stands and subsequent management on carbon dioxide levels in the atmosphere, *J. Sustainable Forestry* 1, 61–77 (1993).
13. G. Marland, "The Prospect of Solving the CO_2 Problem through Global Reforestation," DOE/NBB-0082, U.S. Department of Energy, Washington, DC (1988).
14. O. Masera, M. R. Bellon, and G. Segura, Forestry options for sequestering carbon in Mexico: Comparative economic analysis of three case studies, *presented at* Terrestrial Carbon Sequestration: An Economic Synthesis Workshop, Bergendal, Sweden, May 15–19 (1995).
15. R. J. Moulton and K. R. Richards, "Costs of Sequestering Carbon Through Tree Planting and Forest Management in The United States," GTR WO-58, U.S. Department of Agriculture, Forest Service, Washington, DC (1990).
16. New York State Energy Office, "Analysis of Carbon Reduction in New York State," Albany (1993).
17. W. D. Nordhaus, The cost of slowing climate change: A survey, *Energy J.* 12, No. 1, 37–65 (1991).
18. P. J. Parks, D. O. Hall, B. Kriström, O. R. Masera, R. J. Moulton, A. J. Plantinga, J. N. Swisher, and J. K. Winjum, An economic approach to planting trees for carbon storage, *in* "Economics of Carbon Sequestration in Forestry" (R. A. Sedjo, R. N. Sampson, and J. Wisniewski, Eds.), CRC Press, Boca Raton, FL (1997).
19. P. J. Parks and I. W. Hardie, Least-cost forest carbon reserves: Cost-effective subsidies to convert marginal agricultural land to forests, *Land Econom.* 71, 122–136 (1995).
20. A. J. Plantinga, The costs of carbon sequestration in forests: A positive analysis, *presented at* Terrestrial Carbon Sequestration: An Economic Synthesis Workshop, Bergendal, Sweden, May 15–19 (1995).
21. A. J. Plantinga and R. A. Birdsey, Carbon fluxes resulting from U.S. private timberland management, *Climatic Change* 23, 37–53 (1993).
22. K. R. Richards, R. Alig, J. D. Kinsman, M. Palo, and B. Sohngen, Consideration of country and forestry/land-use characteristics in choosing forestry instruments to achieve climate mitigation goals, *in* "Economics of Carbon Sequestration in Forestry" (R. A. Sedjo, R. N. Sampson, and J. Wisniewski, Eds.), CRC Press, Boca Raton, FL (1997).

23. K. R. Richards, R. J. Moulton, and R. A. Birdsey, Costs of creating carbon sinks in the U.S., *Energy Conservation Management* **34**, 905–912 (1993).

24. K. R. Richards and C. Stokes, "Regional Studies of Carbon Sequestration: A Review and Critique," Mimeo, Pacific Northwest Laboratory, Washington, DC (June 1995).

25. C. Row, HARVCARB: Modeling forest management and the carbon balance, *presented at* the Western Forest Economics Meeting, Welches, Oregon, May 4–6 (1992).

26. C. Row and R. B. Phelps, Tracing the flow of carbon through the U.S. forest products sector, *in* "Proceedings of the 19th World Congress of the International Union of Forest Research Organizations, Montreal, Canada, August 5" (1990).

27. E. S. Rubin, R. N. Cooper, R. A. Frosch, T. H. Lee, G. Marland, A. H. Rosenfeld, and D. D. Stine, Realistic mitigation options for global warming, *Science* **257**, 148–149, 261–266 (1992).

28. R. A. Sedjo, R. N. Sampson, and J. Wisniewski (Eds.), "Economics of Carbon Sequestration in Forestry," CRC Press, Boca Raton, FL (1997).

29. R. A. Sedjo and A. M. Solomon, Climate and forests, *in* "Greenhouse Warming: Abatement and Adaptation" (N. J. Rosenberg, W. E. Easterling III, P. R. Crosson, and J. Darmstadter, Eds.), Resources for the Future, Washington, DC (1989).

30. R. A. Sedjo, J. Wisniewski, A. Sample, and J. D. Kinsman, "Managing Carbon via Forestry: Assessment of Some Economic Studies," Discussion Paper 95-06, Resources for the Future, Washington, DC (November 1995).

31. T. M. Smith, W. P. Cramer, R. K. Dixon, R. Leemans, R. P. Nelson, and A. M. Solomon, The global terrestrial carbon cycle, *Water Air Soil Pollution* **70**, 19–37 (1993).

32. R. N. Stavins, Alternative renewable resource strategies: A simulation of optimal use, *J. Environ. Econom. Management* **19**, 143–159 (1990).

33. R. N. Stavins, The costs of carbon sequestration: A revealed-preference approach, *Amer. Econom. Rev.* **89**, 994–1009 (1999).

34. R. N. Stavins and A. B. Jaffe, Unintended impacts of public investments on private decisions: The depletion of forested wetlands, *Amer. Econom. Rev.* **80**, 337–352 (1990).

35. S. Swinehart, "Afforestation as a Method of Carbon Sequestration: A Cost–Benefit Analysis," Ph.D. dissertation, Department of Operations Research/Engineering-Economic Systems, Stanford University, Stanford, CA (1996).

36. D. P. Turner, J. Lee, G. J. Koperper, and J. R. Barker (Eds.), "The Forest Sector Carbon Budget of the United States: Carbon Pools and Flux Under Alternative Policy Assumptions," U.S. Environmental Protection Agency, Corvallis, OR (1993).

37. United Nations General Assembly, "United Nations Framework Convention on Climate Change," A/AC.237/18 (Part II)/Add.I and A/AC.237/18 (Part II/Add.1/Corr.1), New York (1997).

38. G. C. Van Kooten, L. Arthur, and W. Wilson, Potential to sequester carbon in Canadian forests: Some economic considerations, *Canad. Public Policy* **18**, 127–138 (1992).

39. J. K. Winjum, R. K. Dixon, and P. E. Schroeder, Estimation of the global potential of forest and agroforest management practices to sequester carbon, *Water Air Soil Pollution* **62**, 213–227 (1992).

[23]

AN ECONOMETRIC ANALYSIS OF THE COSTS OF SEQUESTERING CARBON IN FORESTS

ANDREW J. PLANTINGA, THOMAS MAULDIN, AND DOUGLAS J. MILLER

The Kyoto Protocol and the U.S. Climate Change Plan recognize afforestation as a potential means of reducing atmospheric CO_2 concentrations. To examine the cost-effectiveness of afforestation, we use econometric land use models to estimate the marginal costs of carbon sequestration in Maine, South Carolina, and Wisconsin. Our findings include the following: (a) earlier studies of afforestation programs tend to underestimate carbon sequestration costs, (b) afforestation still appears to be a relatively low-cost approach to reducing CO_2 concentrations, (c) Wisconsin offers the lowest-cost opportunties for carbon sequestration, and (d) projected population changes have the largest effect on costs in South Carolina.

Key words: afforestation, carbon, climate change, econometric models, land-use change.

The Kyoto Protocol, adopted by a majority of the world's nations at the Third Conference of the Parties of the Framework Convention on Climate Change in Kyoto, Japan, in December 1997, sets specific targets for the reduction of greenhouse gases. Currently, the United States is proposing to reduce greenhouse gas emissions to 1990 levels between 2008 and 2012 and achieve further reductions below 1990 levels during the following five-year period. Many approaches can be used to achieve these targets, including improving energy efficiency and switching to fuels with lower carbon content (U.S. Office of Technology Assessment). Another possibility, which is given explicit recognition in the Kyoto Protocol and the U.S. Climate Change Action Plan (Clinton and Gore), is to offset emissions of CO_2 by planting trees.

Trees and other vegetation sequester carbon in the biomass and soils of forests through the photosynthetic conversion of CO_2 to carbon (Birdsey). Since forest land stores more carbon than land in other uses such as agriculture, afforestation—the conversion of nonforest land to forest—achieves a net reduction in atmospheric CO_2 concentrations. Previous studies have shown that afforestation can offset a substantial portion of the CO_2 emitted annually in the United States (Marland, Lashof and Tirpak). However, while afforestation may be a feasible approach, the decision to pursue an afforestation strategy should be based at least partly on the costs of afforestation relative to the costs of other approaches. The purpose of this article is to use econometric models of land use shares to estimate the marginal costs of afforestation programs in three U.S. states.

Most earlier studies of the costs of sequestering carbon in forests begin by identifying agricultural lands capable of supporting trees and agricultural returns from these lands, typically measured by prevailing agricultural rents in a region (e.g., Moulton and Richards, Parks and Hardie). Agricultural rents are assumed to represent the opportunity costs of enrolling land in an afforestation program, and all qualifying lands are assumed to be enrolled. The costs of carbon sequestration are calculated by converting the area of enrolled land to carbon storage units. The fundamental assumption underlying this approach (as well as the methods used in related studies by Adams et al. and Alig et al.) is that landowners will enroll land in a carbon sequestration program if compensated for the specified agricultural returns.

A shortcoming of these analyses is that they do not account for a number of factors that

Andrew Plantinga and Thomas Mauldin are, respectively, assistant professor and former graduate student, Department of Resource Economics and Policy, University of Maine, and Douglas Miller is assistant professor, Department of Economics, Iowa State University.

The authors would like to thank Ralph Alig and two anonymous referees for constructive comments. This research was partially supported by the USDA Forest Service, Pacific Northwest Station, and USDA National Research Initiative Competitive Grants Program (Grant No. 9703946). Maine Agricultural and Forest Experiment Station Publication No. 2312.

can potentially influence land enrollment decisions. For instance, afforestation may be irreversible to some degree due to high costs of converting forest land back to agricultural use. This may give rise to an option value associated with keeping land in agriculture (Dixit and Pindyck), increasing the payments required by landowners to enroll land. In addition, agricultural landowners may have little familiarity with forestry and therefore may face the costs of acquiring the skills and knowledge needed to manage forest land. Finally, enrollment decisions may be influenced by private, nonmarket benefits derived by the landowner, such as recreation. Stavins and Jaffe find evidence that landowners do not make immediate and complete adjustments in land use allocations in response to changing economic conditions.

Plantinga (1997) and Stavins take an alternative approach to measuring carbon sequestration costs. In these studies, the opportunity costs of enrollment are derived from econometric-based estimates of the shares of land devoted to forestry and agriculture. Thus, the costs of simulated afforestation programs are based on observations of actual decisions by landowners facing returns to alternative uses. In principle, econometric models can account for the additional factors influencing land enrollment decisions discussed above and, thus, econometric-based estimates may more accurately measure the costs of carbon sequestration. The cost estimates in Plantinga (1997) and Stavins suggest that earlier analyses have understated the costs of afforestation programs.

In this study, we use econometric land use models to simulate carbon sequestration programs in Maine, South Carolina, and Wisconsin. Our analysis extends the work of Plantinga (1997) and Stavins in a number of important ways. First, we apply an identical methodology in the three states, enabling us to make regional cost comparisons.[1] The state-level perspective is appropriate given that states are currently developing CO_2 mitigation strategies (referred to as Climate Change Action Plans) under directives from the U.S. Environmental Protection Agency. Second, we model the effects of projected population increases. Carbon sequestration programs will require a long-term commitment of land to

forest; yet, over time, increases in population are likely to divert land from agriculture, increasing the opportunity costs of land enrollment and, thus, the costs of carbon sequestration. Finally, we examine alternative program designs, including programs that minimize the costs of land enrollment and permit timber harvesting.

This article is organized as follows. First, we discuss the carbon flows associated with forest stands and the methods we use to quantify carbon flows. The next section presents the methodology used to model land use shares, followed by a presentation of the results for three states. This is followed by a section describing the approach used to simulate carbon sequestration programs and a discussion of the simulation results. A final section presents conclusions.

Carbon Sequestration in Forests

Carbon is stored in forests when trees and other plants convert CO_2 to carbon through photosynthesis. Carbon in forests can be divided into four components: carbon in trees, soils, floor litter, and understory vegetation (Birdsey). Carbon is stored in the biomass of trees and understory plants and builds up in soils and floor litter through leaf and root abscission. Following stand establishment, the total volume of carbon in the forest increases until trees reach maturity. After this time, forest carbon will be roughly in equilibrium as old trees die, creating gaps in the canopy and opportunities for younger trees to grow (Plantinga and Birdsey 1994).

Timber harvesting disrupts the positive flows of CO_2 to the forest. Within roughly a decade following the harvest, a substantial portion of the forest carbon is converted back to CO_2 (Heath et al.). This includes most of the carbon in the litter and understory vegetation and some of the carbon in trees (e.g., nonmerchantable parts of the trees such as branches).[2] The merchantable portion of trees is processed into primary wood products such as lumber and paper, which typically releases additional CO_2 (e.g., wood waste is burned for energy). Additional carbon is converted to CO_2 when primary products are processed

---

[1] Plantinga (1997) examines a fourteen-county region of Wisconsin and Stavins considers thirty-six counties along the Mississippi River in Arkansas, Louisiana, and Mississippi.

[2] For example, these components account for approximately 29% of the carbon in a thirty-year-old southern pine stand in the southeastern United States and 30% of the carbon in a sixty-five-year-old maple-beech stand in the Lake States region.

814 November 1999 Amer. J. Agr. Econ.

into end-use products and end-use products are disposed. However, carbon may remain fixed in end-use products (e.g., lumber used in home construction) and landfills for decades and even centuries following a harvest.[3]

In our simulations of carbon sequestration programs, we examine scenarios with and without timber harvesting. In both cases, we follow Stavins and Nordhaus and express carbon flows over the course of the program in present value terms. An alternative approach commonly used in carbon sequestration studies (e.g., Moulton and Richards, Parks and Hardie) is to express carbon storage as the mean annual flow over the course of a timber rotation. This approach ignores the time profile of sequestration and may be sensitive to the length of the time horizon (Stavins). Another advantage of the discounting approach is that it yields a carbon measure comparable to our present value cost measure, allowing us to normalize costs on units of carbon sequestered. Cost per unit carbon estimates may then be compared to the costs of reducing emissions using alternative strategies such as fuel switching. Richards analyzes a range of methods for measuring carbon flows. He demonstrates that discounting carbon flows is appropriate if real marginal benefits from carbon sequestration (i.e., marginal damages avoided from reducing CO_2 concentrations) are constant over time.

To illustrate our approach, the present value of carbon flows in a southern pine stand in the southeastern United States is 30.3 (short) tons per acre, assuming a sixty-year time horizon, no harvesting, and a 5% discount rate.[4] If the forest is harvested and replanted in year 30, the present value of flows is 23.7 tons per acre.[5] In our simulations, we evaluate sixty-year programs since extending the time horizon has little impact on the present value of carbon flows. Allowing for an additional cycle of harvesting and growth out to year 90 reduces the present value of flows by only 0.6 tons per acre. Additional cycles have a small effect on the present value measure because

discounting reduces the value of distant future flows and CO_2 released by a harvest is offset by subsequent forest growth.

Econometric Models of Land Use

Land use share models have been widely analyzed in the past decade (Lichtenberg, Stavins and Jaffe, Parks and Kramer, Wu and Segerson, Plantinga 1996, Hardie and Parks, Miller and Plantinga). For this application, we follow the standard approach of estimating logistic share equations. The first step in this procedure is to derive optimal land allocation rules from the solution to an individual land manager's profit-maximization problem. Static formulations are found in Lichtenberg, Wu and Segerson, and Hardie and Parks, and dynamic models are presented in Stavins and Jaffe, Orazem and Miranowski, Parks, and Plantinga (1996). We are concerned with the landowner's decision to allocate land to forest and agriculture. Since forest and agricultural land yield returns with different periodicity, we consider an optimal dynamic allocation rule. As in Plantinga (1996) and Stavins and Jaffe, landowners allocate land to the use providing the greatest present discounted value of profits.

Following Miller and Plantinga, we aggregate the optimal allocations by individual landowners to derive the observed share of land in county i in use k in time t, denoted $y_k(t, i)$. The observed shares are an additive function of the expected share ($p_k(t, i)$) and a composite error term related to sampling errors and exogenous shocks affecting land use allocations ($\epsilon_k(t, i)$). The expected land use shares are a function of county-level economic-decision and land-quality variables ($\mathbf{X}(t, i)$). We specify

$$(1) \quad p_k(t, i) = \frac{e^{\boldsymbol{\beta}_k' \mathbf{X}(t,i)}}{\sum_{s=1}^{K} e^{\boldsymbol{\beta}_s' \mathbf{X}(t,i)}}$$

for $k = 1, \ldots, K$ where $\boldsymbol{\beta}_k$ is a vector of unobserved parameters. The logistic specification restricts the expected shares to the unit interval and ensures that they sum to one. As well, the logarithm of the observed shares normalized on $y_1(t, i)$ yields

$$(2) \quad \ln(y_k(t, i)/y_1(t, i)) = \boldsymbol{\beta}_k' \mathbf{X}(t, i) - \boldsymbol{\beta}_1' \mathbf{X}(t, i)$$

for $k = 2, \ldots, K$. The model is identified if

---

[3] As reported in Plantinga and Birdsey (1993), approximately 57% of the carbon in the merchantable portion of softwood sawtimber trees in the southern United States survives the initial processing stage. Fifty years following the harvest, 39% of the carbon remains in products and landfills. Percentages are similar for other regions.

[4] This value is for a forest stand established through artificial regeneration (i.e., planting) on cropland with site index exceeding 79 feet. Our data on carbon flows in forest stands are from Birdsey.

[5] We use the disposition percentages in table 3 of Plantinga and Birdsey (1993) to calculate the postharvest flows of carbon in solid wood products and landfills.

we normalize the parameters by setting $\beta_1 = 0$ and can be consistently estimated by least squares provided the number of observations exceeds the number of unknown parameters in β_k.

Estimation Results for Three U.S. States

We estimate land use share models for Maine, South Carolina, and Wisconsin. These states represent a broad range of current land use patterns, physiographic conditions, and apparent opportunities for afforestation. Maine is heavily forested and, thus, has little agricultural land available for conversion. In contrast, South Carolina and Wisconsin have large amounts of agricultural land. South Carolina has a longer growing season than Maine and Wisconsin and suitable conditions for growing valuable southern pine species. For these reasons, the U.S. South has been regarded as providing the best opportunities for carbon sequestration through afforestation (Marland, Sedjo and Solomon). On average, Maine has poorer land quality than South Carolina and Wisconsin. These states have similar average land characteristics, though there is greater variation in land quality in Wisconsin than in South Carolina.

We model private forest and agricultural land (cropland and pasture) in Maine, South Carolina, and the southern two-thirds of Wisconsin. We focus on southern Wisconsin since much of the land in northern Wisconsin is publicly owned and little is in agricultural use. Private forest and agricultural land account for between 80% and 93% of the total land area in the three study areas. We assemble county data on land areas at different points in time and, normalizing on total land area, form land use shares $y_k(i, t)$, where k indexes forest ($k = 1$) and agricultural ($k = 2$) uses and i and t index counties and time, respectively.[6] Total land area equals the area of all land in the county except publicly owned forest (e.g., National Forest land) and major parklands. We assume that the area of land in these uses is determined by factors exogenous to our model. The use of cross-sectional data is required because we have limited time-series information on forest area. In our models, we primarily measure spatial variation in land use arising from spatial differences in land rents. As discussed below, rents vary across space due to differences in forest species composition and cropping patterns. A third category (urban/other land) is defined as all land not classified as private forest, agricultural land, and publicly owned forest and parks (i.e., $y_3(i, t) = 1 - y_1(i, t) - y_2(i, t)$). This category includes developed land in urban, suburban, and rural areas, and other unclassified land.

We measure rents from forestry ($R_1(i, t)$) as the present discounted value of a stream of real timber revenues per acre. Revenue streams are calculated separately for major forest species in each state using species-specific stumpage prices, timber yield curves, and rotation lengths.[7] County-level forest rent measures are constructed as the weighted average of species-specific rents where weights are based on species composition within counties. According to U.S. Forest Service inventories, intensively managed forests are a negligible portion of private forests in the states examined and, thus, we ignore timber management costs.

Agricultural rents ($R_2(i, t)$) equal the present discounted value of the stream of real annual per acre net revenues from crop and pasture land. Net revenues for each county are a weighted average of revenues (price times yield) less variable production costs for major crop and pasture uses where weights correspond to county-level agricultural land shares.[8] We assume that fixed costs for agricultural production (e.g., machinery) are constant across crops and fixed costs for holding land (e.g., property taxes) are constant across land use alternatives. We assume that the effects of fixed costs on land use decisions are measured, along with other constant factors, in the intercept terms included in each model.

Ideally, we would formally model factors such as option values and private, nonmarket benefits referred to in the first section. How-

---

[6] We collect data for all sixteen counties in Maine for the years 1971, 1982, and 1995, all forty-six South Carolina counties (1986 and 1993), and forty-nine counties in the southern two-thirds of Wisconsin (1983 and 1996). Observations of forest area are from periodic U.S. Forest Service Forest Inventory and Analysis surveys, and agricultural data are from the Census of Agriculture.

[7] Stumpage prices are from Maine Forest Service, Wisconsin Department of Natural Resources, and Timber-Mart South. Timber yields are from Birdsey and rotation lengths correspond to the optimal rotation length for a 5% discount rate. A 5% rate is also used to calculate the present value of the timber and agricultural revenue streams.
[8] Crop prices and yields are from each state's Agricultural Statistics Service. Cost data are from farm budgets prepared by state Agricultural Extension Services.

816 *November 1999* *Amer. J. Agr. Econ.*

ever, the necessary data are unavailable.[9] Instead, we note that the model coefficients on the rent variables implicitly account for these effects. If, for instance, there are significant option values associated with conversion to forest or high costs for farmers to acquire forest management skills, landowners should be unresponsive to relative increases in forest rents. Alternatively, landowners may be more responsive to forest rent increases if they derive substantial nonmarket benefits from forests. The coefficients on the rent variables are assumed to approximate the sum of these effects.

In many empirical land use analyses (e.g., Wu and Segerson, Hardie and Parks), population measures are used to account for the allocation of land to nonrural uses such as development. As in the cited studies, we use population density ($PD(i, t)$) to explain the share of land devoted to urban/other uses. The aggregate land use shares also are a function of composite land quality measures. For instance, if a county has a large amount of high-quality land best suited for crop production, then the agricultural share in the county will be higher, all else equal. We include measures of the average Land Capability Class (LCC) rating ($Q_1(i)$) and the percentage of total land in LCC I and II ($Q_2(i)$).[10] The second variable controls for the presence of high-quality agricultural land and accounts, to some degree, for within-county variation in land quality. The land quality variables are assumed to be constant over time. In the three models, we include a constant term (C) and intercept shifters ($D(t)$) for each time period except the last. In the Maine model, we include a variable ($TT(i)$) measuring the travel time (the fastest route over major roads) from the center of counties to Portsmouth, New Hampshire. Almost all agricultural and wood products produced in Maine are transported south through Portsmouth and to markets beyond, and we use $TT(i)$ as a measure of transportation costs.

For each state, we estimate models with $\ln(y_2/y_1)$ and $\ln(y_3/y_1)$ specified as linear functions of the independent variables described above. Given that the logistic transformation

(1) is used largely due to convenience, we conduct Ramsey's RESET test (see pp. 195–96 in Davidson and MacKinnon) to evaluate the log-linear specification (2). In all cases, we fail to reject the null hypothesis of linearity at the 5% level. Further, the model (2) is known to have a heteroskedastic error structure due to the logarithmic transformation. Although other authors use weighted least squares to adjust for the induced heteroskedasticity, we note that the aggregate land use data do not directly conform to the grouped data sampling process (e.g., see the discussion in Maddala, p. 29). For this reason, we use White's test to evaluate the null hypothesis of homoskedasticity under a general alternative hypothesis (see p. 561, Davidson and MacKinnon). In all models, we fail to reject the null hypothesis of homoskedasticity at the 5% level.

Under this specification, the two log-share equations include the same set of regressors for each state and time period. Thus, the least squares estimator applied separately to each equation is identical to the seemingly unrelated regression (SUR) estimator, and we do not have to make an explicit adjustment for cross-equation correlation. Due to the spatial separation between states and temporal separation between time periods, we do not adjust for cross-regional or temporal correlation among the equations. Finally, we test the null hypothesis of no differences in the model parameters over time, and the tests fail to reject the null in all cases. Consequently, many of the econometric features commonly found in land use models do not have a significant influence on our models, and the unknown parameters of equation (2) may be estimated with a relatively straightforward and uncomplicated procedure.

To a large degree, the empirical results conform with prior expectations (table 1). The estimated coefficients can be interpreted as the percentage change in the share ratio y_k/y_1 for a one-unit change in the independent variable. In the $\ln(y_2/y_1)$ equations, the coefficients on forest and agricultural rents are negative and positive, respectively, and all except one are significantly different from zero at the 5% level. All else equal, an increase in the forest rent decreases the share of agricultural land relative to the forest share. An increase in the agricultural rent has the opposite effect. In the $\ln(y_3/y_1)$ equations, the forest rent coefficients are negative, as expected, but none are significantly different from zero. This is a plau-

---

[9] Moreover, techniques for incorporating the implications of option value theory into econometric models are in their infancy. See Dixit and Pindyck for a review of studies and Schatzki for an application in the context of land use.

[10] The LCC rating system is described in U.S. Department of Agriculture. Land quality measures based on LCC data are used in land use studies by Wu and Segerson, Plantinga (1996), Hardie and Parks, and Miller and Plantinga.

Table 1. Estimation Results for Land Use Share Models

Parameter	Maine $\ln(y_2/y_1)$	Maine $\ln(y_3/y_1)$	South Carolina $\ln(y_2/y_1)$	South Carolina $\ln(y_3/y_1)$	Wisconsin $\ln(y_2/y_1)$	Wisconsin $\ln(y_3/y_1)$
Rents						
R_1	−0.04	−0.03	−0.01	−0.0002	−0.02	−0.01
	(−1.65)	(−1.43)	(−6.68)	(−0.27)	(−3.49)	(−1.21)
R_2	0.0003	−0.0003	0.001	0.0003	0.001	0.0002
	(2.68)	(−2.57)	(4.14)	(1.35)	(5.27)	(0.82)
Other						
PD	0.002	0.002	−0.27	2.66	0.06	1.90
	(0.96)	(1.78)	(−0.70)	(6.95)	(0.18)	(5.48)
C	1.37	0.42	−0.97	−1.49	0.29	3.96
	(0.95)	(0.36)	(−1.19)	(−1.87)	(0.27)	(3.20)
$D(71)$	−0.09	−0.04				
	(−0.42)	(−0.25)				
$D(82)$	0.20	−0.09				
	(1.20)	(−0.66)				
$D(83)$					0.15	−0.03
					(1.50)	(−0.29)
$D(86)$			0.21	0.09		
			(2.07)	(0.92)		
TT	−0.20	−0.02				
	(−1.97)	(−0.21)				
Land Quality						
Q_1	−0.74	−0.29	−0.15	−0.01	−0.47	−1.09
	(−3.67)	(−1.78)	(−1.02)	(−0.05)	(−2.50)	(−5.12)
Q_2	2.18	1.73	1.25	−1.08	0.54	−1.53
	(0.90)	(0.88)	(1.72)	(−1.52)	(0.77)	(−1.92)
$\bar{R}^2$	0.70	0.59	0.53	0.44	0.72	0.72

Note: Subscripts on share and rent variables refer to forest ($k = 1$), agricultural ($k = 2$), and urban/other land ($k = 3$) and *t*-ratios are in parentheses.

sible result since forest rents are unlikely to influence the allocation of land to urban and other uses. The effect of agricultural rents on the urban/other to forest ratio are ambiguous a priori, and most of the estimated coefficients are not significantly different from zero.

As expected, the coefficients on population density are positive in the $\ln(y_3/y_1)$ equations and all are significantly different from zero at the 5% level. Population density does not have a significant effect on the ratio of agricultural to forest land. Counties with higher average LCC ratings (Q_1), corresponding to lower average land quality, tend to have less agricultural land relative to forest land (i.e., lower values of y_2/y_1). Conversely, counties with larger shares of high-quality agricultural land (Q_2) tend to have higher agricultural to forest-share ratios, though the coefficients on Q_2 are not significantly different from zero in the Maine and Wisconsin models. The effects of Q_1 and Q_2 on $\ln(y_3/y_1)$ are ambiguous a priori and many of the coefficients are not significantly different from zero. Finally, counties

in Maine with higher transportation costs tend to have less agricultural land relative to forest.

Simulation of Carbon Sequestration Programs

Estimates of the land use shares in equation (1) are the basis for our simulations of carbon sequestration programs. The basic approach is to simulate the effects of forest subsidies by increasing the forest rent variables. This implies increases in forest area and, in turn, increases in carbon sequestration. Each subsidy level is associated with a change in carbon stored, measured by the carbon flows following afforestation of agricultural land. We assume that in the absence of afforestation, net carbon sequestration on agricultural lands is zero and, further, that conversion to forest entails no loss of carbon from agricultural soils.

Our carbon sequestration program is modeled on the Conservation Reserve Program

818   *November 1999*   *Amer. J. Agr. Econ.*

Table 2. Summary of Carbon Sequestration Scenarios

Scenario	Baseline	Harvesting	Payments
Scenario 1	Population constant at 1995 levels	no	uniform
Scenario 2	Population constant at 1995 levels	yes	uniform
Scenario 3	Projected population	no	variable
Scenario 4	Projected population	yes	uniform

(CRP), a U.S. Department of Agriculture program that pays landowners to retire marginal cropland. Land is enrolled for a period of ten years and landowners are required to convert their land to forest. All cropland and pasture is qualified for enrollment. However, similar to the CRP, which limits enrollment to 25% of the cropland in a county, we limit enrollment to 25% of a state's agricultural land. The CRP enrollment limits are imposed to limit supply-related impacts on agricultural markets. Since agricultural commodity and timber prices are assumed to be exogenous in our simulations, we impose similar enrollment limits. While there are many possible ways to design the program, we have adopted the basic structure of the CRP because we feel it provides a reasonable starting point for the analysis of carbon sequestration programs.

Our carbon sequestration program begins in 2000 and operates for sixty years. Landowners enroll land at the start of each decade in exchange for fixed annual payments plus the cost of establishing trees on agricultural land. Establishment costs are provided for land first entering the program, but not for reenrolled land (or reforested land in scenario 2). The ten-year stream of discounted payments augments the rents received from forest land, and landowners increase the share of land allocated to forest.[11] The payments to the landowner represent the opportunity cost of enrollment (i.e., returns to agricultural production). For a range of payments, we simulate increases in forest acreage[12] and calculate the total carbon sequestration costs as the present value of establishment costs and payments over the sixty-year program horizon.

Following the procedure discussed above, we calculate the flows of carbon associated with land entering and leaving the program and, for each payment level, the total cost per ton of carbon sequestered (equal to the ratio of present value costs to present value carbon flows). A marginal cost schedule is then constructed by arraying unit changes in total costs with total carbon sequestered.

We consider four scenarios in order to test the sensitivity of our results to varying assumptions regarding the structure of carbon sequestration programs (table 2). For scenarios 1 and 2, we assume all variables except forest rents remain constant at 1995 levels during the program. These scenarios allow us to gauge the effects of projected population changes considered in scenarios 3 and 4. Baseline projections of forest, agricultural, and urban/other land areas are generated by setting payments for afforestation to zero throughout the program. In scenarios 1 and 2, baseline projections are simply the 1995 acreages (the first column of table 3) since population (and all other variables) are assumed to remain constant. For scenarios 3 and 4, we generate baseline projections for each county in the three states that incorporate Department of Commerce population projections.[13] State-level population and baseline area projections are presented in table 3. In all states, increases in urban/other land and declines or little change in forest and agricultural acreages are projected. In our simulations, urban/other land is restricted to remain at baseline values to ensure that only agricultural land is enrolled in the program.

In scenario 1, the same payment is offered statewide, as opposed to offering different payments in each county (see below). A uniform payment minimizes the costs of enrolling a given area of land since it equates marginal enrollment costs across counties. Scenario 1 assumes no timber harvesting. To

---

[11] In the econometric model we do not include timber management costs in the forest rent measure. Accordingly, tree establishment costs are excluded when we simulate landowner responses to enrollment payments. However, establishment costs (from Moulton and Richards) are added to the costs of the carbon sequestration program.

[12] Enrolled land is assumed to have the same composition of forest species as found in the corresponding county in the last year of the econometric analysis. We do not consider the establishment of single-species forest plantations. Stavins finds similar cost per ton of carbon figures for mixed-species forests and plantations. Plantations tend to sequester more carbon but are also more expensive to establish.

[13] We allocate projected state population changes to counties based on each county's share of the state population change from 1980 to 1990.

Table 3. Baseline Area Projections with Projected Population Changes

	mid 1990s	2000	2010	2020	2030	2040	2050
Maine							
Population	1,279	1,308	1,377	1,433	1,445	1,460	1,475
Forest land	16,954	16,946	16,928	16,913	16,909	16,905	16,901
Agricultural land	551	552	554	555	556	556	557
Urban/other land	2,349	2,255	2,272	2,285	2,288	2,292	2,295
South Carolina							
Population	3,596	3,990	4,287	4,664	5,040	5,391	5,759
Forest land	12,316	12,190	12,021	11,850	11,672	11,503	11,321
Agricultural land	2,814	2,805	2,759	2,713	2,668	2,625	2,581
Urban/other land	4,114	4,276	4,491	4,708	4,931	5,143	5,368
Wisconsin (southern counties)							
Population	3,577	3,869	4,248	4,654	5,068	5,495	5,937
Forest land	5,689	5,658	5,618	5,575	5,533	5,490	5,447
Agricultural land	10,229	10,139	10,020	9,892	9,764	9,635	9,508
Urban/other land	5,055	5,176	5,335	5,506	5,677	5,848	6,018

Note: State populations are measured in thousands and land areas are measured in thousand acres. Population projections are the medium projections in U.S. Department of Commerce.

identify the effects of timber harvesting on the costs of carbon sequestration, scenario 2 replicates scenario 1 but accounts for timber harvesting at optimal rotations lengths for a 5% discount rate. In scenario 2, revenues from timber harvesting reduce the payments required by landowners to enroll land in the program. However, timber harvesting also reduces the total carbon sequestered (see discussion in the second section). Because population is assumed to remain constant in scenarios 1 and 2, the payment offered in the first decade of the program will enroll the same amount of land in subsequent decades.

Scenarios 3 and 4 incorporate projected increases in population. Increases in population divert land from agriculture to urban/other uses and this increases the payments needed to enroll a given amount of agricultural land. The objective of the scenario 3 is long-term enrollment. Payment levels are set to ensure that land enrolled during the first decade of the program is enrolled throughout the entire program. In this case, payments must vary across counties to accommodate different changes in population density at the county level. For instance, payments required to keep land enrolled in a county undergoing rapid population growth may need to be higher than those in a county with stable population. The advantage of long-term enrollment is that land does not leave the program, thereby avoiding losses of carbon associated with land conversion. The potential disadvantage is that it may be expensive relative to programs that reduce

enrollment costs by allowing high-cost land to leave the program.

Scenario 4 explores this approach by using a uniform statewide payment to minimize enrollment costs.[14] Thus, in contrast to scenario 3, enrolled land may leave the program if the level of the statewide payment is insufficient. In particular, in counties experiencing rapid population growth, land may exit the program and be converted to urban/other use. We assume the forest land is harvested upon leaving the program. In addition, we allow new land to be enrolled in less-expensive counties to replace the acres exiting the program. While this approach has the advantage of minimizing enrollment costs, it has the disadvantage that carbon storage is reduced when land is removed from the program. Furthermore, additional enrollment costs are incurred when new land is enrolled.

The results of our simulations are summarized in marginal cost curves for Maine, South Carolina, and Wisconsin (figures 1, 2, and 3). In Maine and Wisconsin, scenario 1 has the lowest costs and scenario 2 has the highest costs. At the highest carbon sequestration levels, corresponding to enrollment of 25% of each state's agricultural land, marginal costs range from $95 to $120 per ton of carbon

---

[14] Ideally, a program would minimize the costs of carbon sequestration, rather than land enrollment. However, given the spatial heterogeneity in forest species composition and associated sequestration rates, such a program would be extremely complex and, as Stavins suggests, prohibitively expensive to administer.

820   November 1999   Amer. J. Agr. Econ.

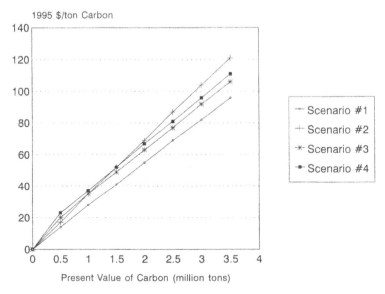

Figure 1.   Marginal costs of carbon sequestration in Maine

in Maine and $75 to $95 per ton of carbon in Wisconsin. The higher costs for scenario 2 reflect the reduction in carbon sequestration that results from harvesting. For instance, in Maine, the statewide average present value of carbon flows is 25.4 tons per acre with no harvesting (scenario 1) and 22.6 tons per acre with harvesting (scenario 2). In Wisconsin, the average values are 24.3 and 21.3 tons per acre, respectively. The present value of payments is lower in scenario 2 because landowners receive revenues from timber har-

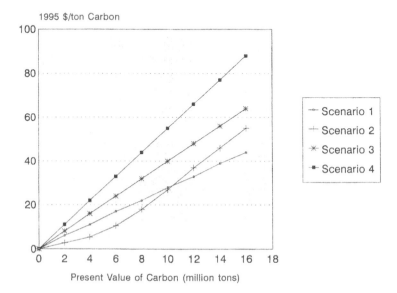

Figure 2.   Marginal costs of carbon sequestration in South Carolina

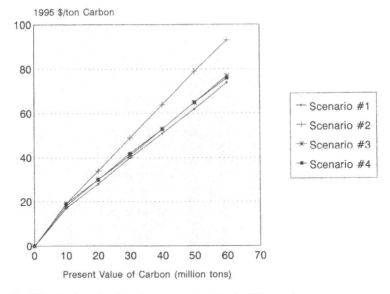

Figure 3.   Marginal costs of carbon sequestration in Wisconsin

vesting. However, the reduction in payments does not offset the loss of carbon, leading to higher costs in scenario 2.

In South Carolina, scenarios 1 and 2 have similar costs as well as the lowest costs compared to the other scenarios. At the highest sequestration level, costs range from $45 to $55 per ton carbon. The average present value of carbon flows is 22.9 tons per acre in scenario 1 and 18.3 tons per acre in scenario 2. In contrast to Maine and Wisconsin, the reduction in payments in scenario 2 offsets carbon losses from harvesting so that per ton costs are similar to those in scenario 1. Timber revenues are higher in South Carolina than in Maine and Wisconsin due to the presence of valuable southern pine species.

Projected changes in urban/other land increase carbon sequestration costs in scenario 3 relative to scenario 1. However, in none of the states are the effects dramatic. At the highest sequestration levels, marginal costs rise by about $10 per ton in Maine, $20 per ton in South Carolina, and $5 per ton in Wisconsin. In Maine, the population is projected to increase by only 200,000 people, which has little effect on current land use shares. In South Carolina and Wisconsin, considerably greater increases in population are projected (2.2 and 2.4 million people, respectively), but this has a fairly small effect on the area of agricultural

land, reducing it by approximately 230,000 acres in South Carolina and 720,000 acres in Wisconsin. As the agricultural land base declines, it becomes increasingly expensive to bring additional agricultural land into the program. However, in our simulations, projected declines in agricultural land area are not large enough to affect the present value of costs greatly. Similar results were obtained with the high population projections by the U.S. Department of Commerce.

Costs in scenario 4 are slightly higher than those in scenario 3, except in Wisconsin where the costs are virtually identical. Per acre payments are lower in scenario 4 because the highest-cost land leaves the program. However, additional establishment costs are paid for newly enrolled land and this results in higher total enrollment costs for scenario 4. As well, scenario 4 has lower carbon storage due to losses of carbon from land leaving the program. In summary, harvesting (scenario 2) has the largest effect on costs in Maine and Wisconsin, while population increases (scenarios 3 and 4) have little impact. In South Carolina, costs are most affected by population increases.

Finally, we compare the costs of the programs in the three states (figure 4). Relative to South Carolina and Wisconsin, an afforestation program in Maine would be extreme-

822 *November 1999*   *Amer. J. Agr. Econ.*

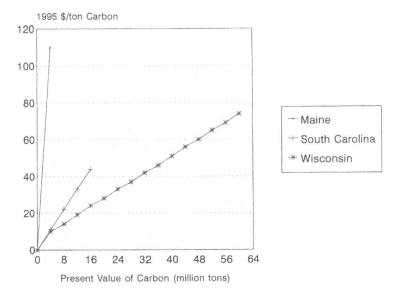

Figure 4. Marginal costs of carbon sequestration in Maine, South Carolina, and Wisconsin (scenario 1)

ly expensive and would sequester relatively little carbon. Compared to South Carolina, an afforestation program in Wisconsin would be cheaper and would sequester about four times as much carbon. The difference in costs between Maine and Wisconsin is primarily related to differences in the opportunity costs of agricultural land. Similar amounts of carbon are sequestered on forest land in South Carolina and Wisconsin; yet, it is substantially cheaper to enroll agricultural land in Wisconsin and, thus, per ton carbon sequestration costs are lower.

Conclusions

In this study, we estimate the costs of reducing CO_2 concentrations through afforestation. We find that marginal costs per metric ton of carbon rise from $0 to between $95 and $120 in Maine, $45 and $90 in South Carolina, and $75 and $95 in Wisconsin. The costs of afforestation programs we considered compare favorably to costs of alternative mitigation approaches. For instance, National Academy of Sciences (NAS) reports average cost estimates ranging from approximately $100 to $900 per ton for substitution of alternative fuels for coal. The U.S. Office of Technology Assess-

ment (OTA) average cost estimates for co-generation, increased residential energy efficiency, and fuel switching range from about $200 to $2,000 per ton. Our highest average cost estimates for afforestation are approximately $60 per ton in Maine (scenario 2), $45 per ton in South Carolina (scenario 4), and $48 per ton in Wisconsin (scenario 2), estimates significantly below the NAS and OTA figures.[15] It bears mention that the NAS and OTA studies also report savings (i.e., negative costs) from a variety of programs involving increased fuel efficiency, though Jaffe and Stavins estimate significant positive costs for these approaches.

While our results provide further evidence that afforestation is a cost-effective strategy for offsetting CO_2 emissions, our cost estimates are higher than those found in most earlier analyses (e.g., Moulton and Richards, Adams et al., Parks and Hardie, Alig et al.).[16]

---

[15] Comparison of average cost estimates is hampered by differences across studies in the total reduction of CO_2 emissions. The NAS and OTA estimates correspond to programs that achieve greater total CO_2 reductions than our programs. Our conclusion that afforestation is cheaper than other approaches holds if we take the scale of the programs as given.

[16] It is easiest to compare costs with Moulton and Richards (MR) since MR report cost estimates on a state-by-state basis. The other studies report national cost estimates, precluding direct cost comparisons. However, we note that the cost estimates in these analyses

For instance, Moulton and Richards (MR) assume that 667,000, 1,472,000, and 11,232,000 acres of agricultural land (cropland and pasture) will be enrolled in Maine, South Carolina, and Wisconsin at average annual payments of $72, $65, and $51 per acre, respectively.[17] Our land use models predict that at these payment levels only 28%, 90%, and 27% of the MR acreage for Maine, South Carolina, and Wisconsin, respectively, will be enrolled. Assuming a linear extrapolation of our marginal cost curves, we estimate that to achieve the MR acreage targets, payments would be have to be approximately 4 times higher in Maine and Wisconsin and 1.1 times higher in South Carolina. These results are consistent with the other econometric analyses of carbon sequestration programs (Plantinga 1997, Stavins) and indicate the importance of deriving cost estimates from observed landowner behavior. Apparently, landowners are less willing, or require greater incentives, to convert land to forest than had been assumed in earlier studies.

Our results suggest that program structure has a moderate effect on costs. In South Carolina and Wisconsin, harvesting increases marginal costs by at most $10 and $20 per ton of carbon, respectively. Harvesting has a larger effect on costs in Maine. Because total enrollment costs are high in Maine, reductions in carbon sequestration have a large effect on the cost per ton of carbon (marginal costs increase by as much as $25). In all states, there are relatively small differences in costs between scenario 1, which assumes constant population, and scenario 3, which incorporates population projections. Population increases do not significantly reduce the agricultural land base and, therefore, carbon sequestration costs are not greatly affected. Finally, we find that programs that minimize enrollment costs tend to be more expensive than programs that involve long-term land enrollment. Enrollment cost savings from allowing expensive land to leave the program are more than offset by losses of carbon from land conversion and additional establishment costs.

---

are similar to the national-level estimates in MR. For instance, the Adams et al. estimates are slightly above the MR estimates except at the highest enrollment level.

[17] Regional wet cropland acreage (table 2, column 7 in MR) is allocated to states by applying each state's proportion of erodible cropland (table 2, column 2 in MR). The reported payments are for cropland. MR assume lower payments are needed to enroll pasture, implying that our enrollment estimates (see below) are somewhat overstated.

Our analysis permits comparisons of carbon sequestration costs in different U.S. regions. Much attention has focused on afforestation programs in the southern United States (Marland, Sedjo and Solomon), in part because of suitable conditions in the South for fast-growing tree species. However, for the states we examined, we find lower costs and greater potential for carbon storage in the northern Midwest than in the south. Carbon sequestration rates are comparable in the two states, but opportunity costs of agricultural land are lower in Wisconsin. The high costs for Maine suggest that there are limited opportunities for carbon sequestration programs in the heavily forested northeastern states. Lastly, as noted in the introduction, states are in the process of developing greenhouse gas emissions inventories and identifying strategies for reducing emissions. Our results suggest that there are large differences in carbon sequestration costs among states. Therefore, an efficient national afforestation program should be designed to enroll land in states with the lowest carbon sequestration costs.

*[Received June 1998;
accepted February 1999.]*

References

Adams, R., D. Adams, J. Callaway, C. Chang, and B. McCarl. "Sequestering Carbon on Agricultural Land: Social Cost and Impacts on Timber Markets." *Contemp. Policy Issues* 11(January 1993):76–87.

Alig, R., D. Adams, B. McCarl, J. Callaway, and S. Winnett. "Assessing the Effects of Global Change Mitigation Strategies with an Intertemporal Model of the U.S. Forest and Agricultural Sectors." *Environ. Resour. Econ.* 9(April 1997):259–74.

Birdsey, R.A. *Carbon Storage and Accumulation in United States Forest Ecosystems.* Washington DC: U.S. Department of Agriculture, Forest Service, Gen. Tech. Rep. WO-59, August 1992.

Clinton, W., and A. Gore. *The Climate Change Action Plan.* Washington DC: White House Office of Environmental Policy, 1993.

Davidson, R., and J.G. MacKinnon. *Estimation and Inference in Econometrics.* New York: Oxford University Press, 1993.

Dixit, A.K., and R.S. Pindyck. *Investment Under Uncertainty.* Princeton NJ: Princeton University Press, 1994.

824 *November 1999* *Amer. J. Agr. Econ.*

Hardie, I.W., and P.J. Parks. "Land Use with Heterogeneous Quality: An Application of an Area Base Model." *Amer. J. Agr. Econ.* 77(May 1997):299–310.

Heath, L.S., R.A. Birdsey, C. Row, and A.J. Plantinga. "Carbon Pools and Fluxes in U.S. Forest Products." *NATO ASI Series,* Vol. 1, no. 40(1996):271–78.

Jaffe, A.B., and R.N. Stavins. "Dynamic Incentives of Environmental Regulations: The Effects of Alternative Policy Instruments on Technology Diffusion." *J. Environ. Econ. Manage.* 29(November 1995):S43–S63.

Lashof, T., and D. Tirpak, eds. *Policy Options for Stabilizing Global Change: Report to Congress.* Washington DC: U.S. Environmental Protection Agency, 1989.

Lichtenberg, E. "Land Quality, Irrigation Development, and Cropping Patterns in the Northern High Plains." *Amer. J. Agr. Econ.* 71(February 1989):187–94.

Maddala, G.S. *Limited Dependent and Qualitative Variables in Econometrics.* New York: Cambridge University Press, 1983.

Marland, G. *The Prospect of Solving the CO_2 Problem through Global Reforestation.* Washington DC: U.S. Department of Energy, Office of Energy Research, DOE/NBB-0082, 1988.

Miller, D.J., and A.J. Plantinga. "Modeling Land Use Decisions with Aggregate Data." *Amer. J. Agr. Econ.* 81(February 1999):180–94.

Moulton, R., and K. Richards. "Costs of Sequestering Carbon through Tree Planting and Forest Management in the U.S." Washington DC: U.S. Department of Agriculture, Forest Service, Gen. Tech. Rep. WO-58, December 1990.

National Academy of Sciences. *Policy Implications of Greenhouse Warming: Mitigation, Adaptation, and the Science Base.* Washington DC: National Academy Press, 1992.

Nordhaus, W.D. "The Cost of Slowing Climate Change: A Survey." *Energy J.* 12(1991):37–65.

Orazem, P., and J. Miranowski. "A Dynamic Model of Acreage Allocation with General and Crop-Specific Soil Capital." *Amer. J. Agr. Econ.* 76(August 1994):385–95.

Parks, P.J. and I.W. Hardie. "Least-Cost Forest Carbon Reserves: Cost-Effective Subsidies to Convert Marginal Agricultural Land to Forests." *Land Econ.* 71(February 1995): 122–36.

Parks, P.J., and R.A. Kramer. "A Policy Simulation of the Wetlands Reserve Program." *J. Environ. Econ. Manage.* 28(March 1995): 223–40.

Plantinga, A.J. "The Cost of Carbon Sequestration in Forests: A Positive Analysis." *Critical Rev. Environ. Sci. and Tech.* 27(November 1997):S269–S278.

———. "The Effect of Agricultural Policies on Land Use and Environmental Quality." *Amer. J. Agr. Econ.* 78(November 1996): 1082–91.

Plantinga, A.J., and R.A. Birdsey. "Carbon Fluxes Resulting from U.S. Private Timberland Management." *Climatic Change* 23(January 1993):37–53.

———. "Optimal Forest Stand Management When Benefits are Derived from Carbon." *Natural Resour. Model.* 8(Fall 1994):373–87.

Richards, K.R. "The Time Value of Carbon in Bottom-Up Studies." *Critical Rev. Environ. Sci. and Tech.* 27(November 1997):S279–S292.

Schatzki, S.T. "A Theoretical and Empirical Examination of Land Use Change Under Uncertainty." PhD dissertation, Harvard University, 1998.

Sedjo, R.A., and A.M. Solomon. "Climate and Forests." *Greenhouse Warming: Abatement and Adaptation.* Norman J. Rosenberg, William E. Easterling III, Pierre R. Crosson, and Joel Darmstadter, eds., pp. 105–19. Washington DC: Resources for the Future, 1989.

Stavins, R. "The Costs of Carbon Sequestration: A Revealed-Preference Approach." *Amer. Econ. Rev.,* in press.

Stavins, R., and A. Jaffe. "Unintended Impacts of Public Investment on Private Decisions: The Depletion of Forest Wetlands." *Amer. Econ. Rev.*(June 1990):337–52.

U.S. Department of Agriculture. *Land Capability Classification.* SCS Agric. Handbook 210, Washington DC, 1973.

U.S. Department of Commerce. *Bureau of Economic Analysis Regional Projections to 2045.* Vol. 1, *States.* Washington DC, 1995.

U.S. Environmental Protection Agency. *State Workbook: Methodologies for Estimating Greenhouse Gas Emissions.* Washington DC, 1995.

U.S. Office of Technology Assessment. *Changing by Degrees: Steps to Reduce Greenhouse Gases.* Washington DC, 1991.

Wu, J., and K. Segerson. "The Impact of Policies and Land Characteristics on Potential Groundwater Pollution in Wisconsin." *Amer. J. Agr. Econ.* 77(November 1995):1033–47.

Part III
Policy Design for GHG Mitigation

[24]

A second-best evaluation of eight policy instruments to reduce carbon emissions

Ian W.H. Parry [a,*], Roberton C. Williams III [b]

[a] Resources for the Future, 1616 P Street, Washington, DC 20036, USA
[b] Department of Economics, Stanford University, Stanford, CA 94305, USA

Received 20 March 1998; received in revised form 10 May 1998; accepted 1 June 1998

Abstract

This paper uses a numerical general equilibrium model to compare the costs of alternative policies for reducing carbon emissions in a second-best setting with a distortionary tax on labor. We examine a carbon tax, two energy taxes, and both narrow-based and broad-based emissions permits and performance standards. The presence of pre-existing tax distortions raises the costs of all these policies, and can affect their relative cost rankings. In fact, the superiority of emissions taxes and emissions permits over other instruments can hinge on whether these policies generate revenues that are used to reduce other distortionary taxes. © 1999 Elsevier Science B.V. All rights reserved.

JEL classification: L51; H21; D58

Keywords: Carbon abatement policies; Relative costs; Pre-existing taxes; General equilibrium welfare effects

1. Introduction

The continued accumulation of heat-trapping gases in the atmosphere raises the prospect of future global warming and associated changes in climate. There are enormous uncertainties surrounding the potential nature, extent and effects of future climate change. Global warming may turn out to be a very serious problem,

348   I.W.H. Parry, R.C. Williams III / Resource and Energy Economics 21 (1999) 347–373

or it may not. Given the risks involved, most governments deem it prudent to begin steps for reducing emissions of carbon dioxide (CO_2), the most important heat-trapping gas. At the 1997 United Nations conference in Kyoto, Japan, developed countries pledged to reduce CO_2 emissions to around 5% below their 1990 levels by 2008–2012. Given the current dependency on fossil fuels, these steps are likely to involve significant economic costs. Clearly, it is important—not only for its own sake but also to enhance the likelihood of a lasting international agreement—to understand the nature of these costs and how they might be minimized by choice of the appropriate policy instrument.

In the past, economists have strongly advocated the use of broad-based emissions taxes and tradable emissions permits over other types of policy instruments to protect the environment.[1] These other policy instruments include 'command and control' policies (such as emissions limits per unit of output and mandated energy-saving technologies), indirect environmental taxes (such as taxes on energy use rather than on emissions) and narrowly focused policies that do not cover all sources of emissions in the economy. In partial equilibrium models, these other instruments involve various sources of inefficiency, and therefore achieve a given amount of emissions reduction at greater economic cost than emissions taxes and emissions permits.[2]

However, the results from several recent studies cast some doubt on the conventional wisdom about relative cost-effectiveness. These studies have re-examined the issue of instrument choice in a second-best setting, using general equilibrium models that incorporate pre-existing tax distortions in the labor market.[3] Parry (1997) and Goulder et al. (1997) find that the introduction of an emissions tax, or emissions permits, exacerbates the efficiency costs of pre-existing labor tax distortions. This is because these policies raise the costs to firms of producing output and this typically leads to a (slight) reduction in the overall level of employment in the economy. Taking into account this 'tax-interaction effect' significantly raises the costs of both policies.[4] However, in the case of the emissions tax, much of this added cost may be offset by an efficiency gain from a 'revenue-recycling effect' if the revenues are used to reduce other distortionary taxes.

Parry et al. (1999) apply a similar analysis in the specific context of carbon abatement. Under their central estimates, they find that non-auctioned carbon

[1] See, for example, Cropper and Oates (1992) and Oates and Portney (1992).

[2] See, for example, Spulber (1985) and Tietenberg (1985).

[3] An earlier, closely related literature examined the effects of substituting environmental taxes for other distortionary taxes (see, for example, Sandmo, 1975; Bovenberg and de Mooij, 1994, and the surveys by Goulder, 1995 and Oates, 1995).

[4] A similar result has emerged in other contexts. For example, Browning (1997) finds that the welfare costs of monopoly pricing in the US are several times larger, when allowance is made for the impact of reduced production on compounding labor tax distortions.

I.W.H. Parry, R.C. Williams III / Resource and Energy Economics 21 (1999) 347–373   349

emissions permits (or quotas) reduce welfare in their model, unless the environmental benefits from reducing carbon emissions exceed a threshold of US$18 per ton. Some studies estimate benefits of below US$18 per ton (for example, Nordhaus, 1991, 1994), although there is considerable uncertainty and controversy surrounding the estimates. In contrast, Parry et al. (1999) find that a carbon tax with revenues used to reduce distortionary taxes can significantly increase welfare as long as environmental benefits per ton are positive. [5] Thus, generating the revenue-recycling effect could be a necessary condition for carbon abatement policies to improve overall welfare.

Goulder et al. (1999) analyze a broader class of policy instruments using a model (initially calibrated for NO_x emissions). They compare emissions taxes and emission permits with a performance standard (limiting emissions per unit of output), a technology mandate, and a tax on fuel (rather than emissions) in a second-best setting with distortionary factor taxes. They find that pre-existing taxes can crucially affect the relative costs of different policies. In particular, emissions permits may only generate significant cost savings over technology mandates, performance standards and fuels taxes, if the permits are auctioned and the revenues used to reduce pre-existing tax distortions. They also demonstrate that the relative cost discrepancies between policies varies considerably with the extent of pollution abatement. [6]

Of course, from a public finance perspective, it has long been recognized that the presence of pre-existing distortions in the economy changes the welfare impacts of a new regulatory tax. The contribution of the recent literature in environmental economics is to indicate the likely direction, and potential magnitude, of this welfare change under plausible parameter values. Recent studies also illustrate how second-best considerations affect the welfare impacts of non-tax regulatory policies.

This paper has two purposes. It aims first to synthesize this recent literature and draw out the policy lessons in the specific context of carbon abatement, and second, to examine a richer set of policy instruments, including certain narrowly focused policies that have been proposed for curbing carbon emissions. We analyze the costs and overall welfare impacts of eight policy options for reducing US carbon emissions. These are a tax on the carbon content of fossil fuels, a BTU tax, a gasoline tax, a broad-based and narrow-based (specific to electricity) emissions quota, a quota requiring an equal proportionate emissions reduction

---

[5] If carbon quotas are auctioned, with the revenues used to cut distortionary taxes, then the welfare impacts of this policy are equivalent to those of the carbon tax in their analysis. To date, pollution quotas, such as those to reduce sulfur and CFC emissions, have been grandfathered rather than auctioned.

[6] Earlier, Fullerton and Metcalf (1997) showed that the cost of reducing pollution by an incremental amount could be lower under a command and control policy than under emissions permits in the presence of distortionary taxes.

across all industries, and both broad-based and narrow-based (specific to electric utilities) performance standards. [7] We use a numerical general equilibrium model that allows for pre-existing tax distortions in the labor market, and which is calibrated to the U.S. economy.

We find that pre-existing taxes substantially raise the cost of all three of the quota policies when quotas are given out free to existing firms. This increase in cost results because the policies generate a costly tax-interaction effect, but no direct revenue-recycling effect. [8] The proportionate increase in cost can differ significantly across the policies. Indeed, for modest reductions in emissions, the overall costs of the narrow-based emissions quota are actually less than under the broad quota. This is because the tax-interaction effect is relatively weaker under the narrow quota, and this can more than compensate for the relative inefficiency of this policy in a first-best setting. For each quota policy to increase welfare, marginal environmental benefits must exceed a strictly positive threshold level.

Pre-existing taxes raise the cost of all the tax instruments by around 30%, if revenues from these taxes are used to reduce the distortionary labor tax. All these instruments can potentially increase welfare so long as marginal benefits from reducing carbon are positive. Even the gasoline tax, which only affects a minor share of emissions sources, can be less costly than the broad carbon emissions quota, at modest levels of abatement. However, these results change substantially if revenues from the tax instruments are used to finance (lump sum) transfers to households, and hence forgo the efficiency gain from revenue recycling. In this case, the cost of the carbon tax is equal to that of the broad carbon emissions quota, and the gasoline and BTU taxes are more costly.

For performance standards that limit emissions per unit of output, the proportionate increase in costs due to pre-existing taxes is roughly the same as under the revenue-neutral tax policies. In other words, the tax-interaction effect is relatively weaker under these policies and this compensates for the fact that they do not generate a revenue-recycling effect. Indeed, this means that the overall costs of performance standards can be less than under a carbon emissions quota despite the first-best cost disadvantage of performance standards.

These results, and those of earlier studies, raise concerns about the efficiency costs of carbon quotas. They suggest that using carbon quotas to achieve emissions reduction targets may result in significantly higher costs than other policy instruments. Indeed, under some scenarios for environmental benefits, other policy instruments can potentially increase welfare while carbon permits reduce welfare.

---

[7] Somewhat surprisingly, there has been little economic modeling to compare these policy instruments in the context of carbon abatement, even in models that ignore pre-existing taxes. Most studies have focused on carbon taxes and/or carbon emissions quotas.

[8] A minor fraction of the quota rents do accrue to the government through corporate and personal income taxes. Consequently, emissions quotas do produce an indirect revenue-recycling effect in our analysis, but it is small relative to that under an emissions tax.

I.W.H. Parry, R.C. Williams III / Resource and Energy Economics 21 (1999) 347–373 351

These efficiency drawbacks of carbon quotas would be offset if the quotas were auctioned and the revenues used to reduce other distortionary taxes. Policy makers may be reluctant to auction carbon quotas for a range of reasons, including opposition from affected industries. However, our results suggest that the decision not to auction quotas comes at a substantial welfare cost.

Our analysis abstracts from a number of factors that can importantly influence the overall welfare impacts of carbon abatement policies. For example, our model is static and thus does not capture technological innovation and capital accumulation over time. We also abstract from heterogeneity in abatement costs among firms within (though not between) industries, which is likely to play down the relative costs of performance standards. Thus, this is far from a fully comprehensive evaluation of policy instruments. Nonetheless, our analysis does underscore the importance of incorporating pre-existing tax distortions in more complex models, and illustrates how second-best considerations can affect the relative costs of a variety of different abatement policies. Our results also provide a useful benchmark for gauging the empirical significance of future extensions to the model, such as allowing for capital accumulation.

The Section 2 describes the model, which is solved by numerical simulation. [9] Section 3 presents the empirical results and sensitivity analysis. Section 4 offers conclusions and discusses some limitations to the analysis.

2. The model

This section describes the model structure, the various carbon abatement policies examined, and the calibration of the model.

2.1. Model description

2.1.1. Household behavior

We assume a static, closed economy, representative agent model. Households have preferences over two consumption goods, C_I and C_N, and leisure (or non-market) time. C_I represents aggregate consumption produced by relatively energy-intensive industries and C_N represents an aggregate of all other (non-energy-intensive) consumption. Households allocate their time endowment $(\bar{L})$ between labor supply (L) and leisure $(l = \bar{L} - L)$. Emissions of carbon (e) reduce

---

[9] Several earlier studies have included simple analytical models that derive the tax-interaction and revenue-recycling effects of different environmental policy instruments in the presence of pre-existing taxes. For models utilizing a utility-maximizing framework, see Goulder et al. (1997, 1999) and for a diagrammatic exposition, see Parry (1997).

352   I.W.H. Parry, R.C. Williams III / Resource and Energy Economics 21 (1999) 347–373

utility. [10] Utility takes the following nested constant elasticity of substitution (CES) structure:

$$U = U(l, C_{\mathrm{N}}, C_{\mathrm{N}}, e) = \left(\alpha_l l^{\rho_u} + \alpha_F C^{\rho_u} \right)^{\frac{1}{\rho_u}} + \phi(e) \tag{1}$$

where

$$C = \left(\alpha_{C_{\mathrm{I}}} C_{\mathrm{I}}^{\rho_c} + \alpha_{C_{\mathrm{N}}} C_{\mathrm{N}}^{\rho_c} \right)^{\frac{1}{\rho_c}}$$

$\phi' < 0$ and the αs and ρs are parameters. ρ_u is related to the elasticity of substitution between consumption and leisure (σ_u) as follows: $\rho_u = (\sigma_u - 1)/\sigma_u$. ρ_c is related to the elasticity between consumption goods (σ_c) in the same manner. There are two separability assumptions underlying this formulation. First, utility is separable in emissions, implying that changes in emissions per se do not affect household choices over consumption and leisure. [11] Second, preferences over consumption goods and leisure are weakly separable. Along with the homothetic property of CES functions, this implies that consumption goods are equal substitutes for leisure (Deaton, 1981). [12]

The government levies a tax at the rate t_L on labor income and provides a (real) lump sum transfer to households of G. It also regulates carbon emissions through a range of different policies that are discussed below. In the case of a quota, the quota rents (π) accrue to households (who own firms). We assume rents are also taxed at the rate t_L. [13] Thus, the household budget constraint is given by:

$$p_{C_{\mathrm{I}}} C_{\mathrm{I}} + p_{C_{\mathrm{N}}} C_{\mathrm{N}} = (1 - t_L)\{p_L L + \pi\} + p_C G \tag{2}$$

where $p_{C_{\mathrm{I}}}$ and $p_{C_{\mathrm{N}}}$ denote market prices for the two consumption goods and p_C is the general price level. This expression equates expenditure on goods with the sum of after-tax labor and rent income and the government transfer (expressed in nominal terms). Households choose their consumption of goods and leisure to maximize utility (1) subject to the constraint (2).

---

[10] This represents the present discounted utility loss due to changes in future global climate caused by additions to the current concentration of CO_2 in the atmosphere.

[11] That is, there are no feedback effects on labor supply from changes in environmental quality. For more discussion of this issue, see de Mooij (1998) and Williams (1998).

[12] We think this is a reasonable benchmark assumption because there is no empirical evidence to suggest that energy-intensive consumption goods are relatively stronger or weaker substitutes for leisure than non-energy-intensive consumption goods. If energy-intensive consumption were a relatively strong (weak) leisure substitute, this would strengthen (weaken) the tax-interaction effect discussed below.

[13] The effective rate of tax on labor and non-labor income is approximately the same (see, for example, Lucas, 1990).

I.W.H. Parry, R.C. Williams III / Resource and Energy Economics 21 (1999) 347–373   353

2.1.2. Firm behavior

There are seven intermediate goods industries in the model, in addition to the two final goods industries producing C_I and C_N. Three fossil fuels are produced —coal (F_C), petroleum (F_P) and natural gas (F_N)—and the combustion of these fuels produces carbon emissions in the form of CO_2. Coal is the most carbon-intensive fuel per unit of energy and natural gas the least. The remaining intermediate goods are electricity (E), transport (T), an aggregate of other energy-intensive intermediate goods (I), such as metal processing, and an aggregate of non-energy-intensive intermediate goods (N), such as services and agricultural production. All of the intermediate goods and labor are used as inputs in the production of intermediate goods. Final goods are produced using only intermediate goods as inputs. This model structure allows for a variety of different channels for reducing carbon emissions. Within the fossil fuel industries, production can be shifted away from coal to petroleum and natural gas. Within intermediate goods industries, production can be shifted to the non-energy-intensive sector. Finally, households can substitute towards non-energy-intensive consumption and leisure. Note that carbon emissions are released when fossil fuels are used (that is, combusted) as inputs, rather than when they are produced, and in this sense a highly disproportionate share of emissions comes from the electricity and transportation sectors.

We assume that firms within an industry are homogenous and behave competitively in both input and output markets. The production functions for each industry have the following nested CES form:

$$X_j = \left[\left(\sum_i \alpha_{i,m} X_{i,m}^{\rho_{jM}} \right)^{\frac{\rho_j}{\rho_{jM}}} + \left(\sum_i \alpha_{i,m} X_{i,m}^{\rho_{jG}} \right)^{\frac{\rho_j}{\rho_{GM}}} + \alpha_{i,L} X_{i,L}^{\rho_i} \right]^{\frac{1}{\rho_j}}$$

$$m = \{T,I,N\}, \ g = \{F_N,F_C,F_P,E\}, \ j = \{F_N,F_C,F_P,E,T,I,N,C_I,C_N\} \quad (3)$$

where X is output and the ρs and the αs are parameters. ρ is related to the elasticity of substitution between factors in production in the same manner as in the utility function. This formulation separates fossil fuels and electricity from other intermediate goods and from labor. This enables us to allow for easier substitution between fuel inputs than between fuel and non-fuel inputs. The CES form implies constant returns to scale, so supply curves are perfectly elastic for given input prices.

Aggregate carbon emissions are given by:

$$e = \beta_{FN} X_{FN} + \beta_{FC} X_{FC} + \beta_{FP} X_{FP} \quad (4)$$

where β_j is carbon emissions per unit of fossil fuel j. Thus, emissions are proportional to fuel use—there are currently no economically viable end-of-pipe abatement technologies for scrubbing emissions before they enter the

354   *I.W.H. Parry, R.C. Williams III / Resource and Energy Economics 21 (1999) 347–373*

atmosphere. [14] We assume that firms and households do not internalize any of the external costs from carbon emissions.

2.1.3. Government policy

The government reduces carbon emissions using one of eight possible policy instruments. Some of these instruments are 'broad' in the sense that they affect all potential sources of emissions. Others are 'narrow' and only affect emissions from specific industries. The policy instruments are the following.

2.1.3.1. Carbon tax. This is a tax levied on the carbon content of each of the three fossil fuels. It is equivalent to a tax on carbon emissions, given the proportionality between emissions and fuel use. This tax covers all potential sources of emissions. [15]

2.1.3.2. Carbon quota (or emissions permits). This policy restricts the total quantity of carbon emissions. Quotas are tradable, which enables marginal abatement costs across industries to be equated. We assume the quotas are given out free to firms, and therefore that quota rents are retained by the private sector. If instead, the government were to auction the quotas, this policy would be equivalent to the carbon tax in our model. This is because it would raise the same amount of revenue for the government and provide the same incentives for firms and households.

2.1.3.3. BTU tax. This policy taxes fuels in proportion to implied energy content rather than carbon content. Like the carbon tax, the BTU tax covers all potential emissions sources. However, it implies a lower tax on coal and a higher tax on natural gas, because energy per unit of carbon is relatively low for coal and relatively high for gas. [16]

2.1.3.4. Gasoline tax. We model this policy as a tax on petroleum input into transportation. This is a narrow tax, as it does not cover carbon emissions from

---

[14] This means there is no efficiency advantage from imposing regulations on users—as opposed to producers—of fossil fuels. In contrast, in the case of sulfur emissions, electric utilities can install 'scrubbers' to capture part of the emissions from burning coal before they escape into the atmosphere. If sulfur regulations were imposed on coal producers this would not provide incentives for coal users—the electric utilities—to install scrubbers, and therefore would involve some inefficiency.

[15] Variations of the carbon tax have been implemented in several countries, for example, Sweden and Holland.

[16] A version of the BTU tax was proposed in 1993, but was eventually removed from the budget deal and replaced by a slight increase in the federal gasoline tax. The European Union has proposed a similar tax on energy as part of a package of measures to reduce carbon emissions.

I.W.H. Parry, R.C. Williams III / Resource and Energy Economics 21 (1999) 347–373 355

coal and natural gas, or emissions from petroleum use in other industries. Emissions from the transport sector initially account for around a quarter of total carbon emissions in our analysis. [17]

2.1.3.5. Narrow carbon quota. This policy limits carbon emissions from the electricity sector only. [18] Initially, these emissions are around a third of total carbon emissions. Again, the quotas are given out free to firms rather than auctioned.

2.1.3.6. Uniform quota. Some industry groups have argued that it is only 'fair' that all industries should reduce emissions by the same amount. We consider a quota policy where all industries are required to reduce emissions in the same proportion. Under this policy, carbon quotas are tradable among firms within the same industry but not among firms in different industries. The policy covers all potential emissions sources, but the pattern of emissions reductions across industries differs from that under the carbon tax and broad carbon quota. This is because equalizing the proportionate emissions reduction across industries will not generally equalize marginal abatement costs across industries.

2.1.3.7. Narrow performance standard. A performance standard restricts the allowable emissions rate per unit of production. We consider a narrow policy that limits carbon emissions per unit of electricity output only. [19]

2.1.3.8. Idealized performance standard. We also consider a broad performance standard imposed on all industries. We refer to this as an ideal policy, since it would be difficult to implement in practice. [20] Thus, our cost estimates represent lower bound estimates for a broader-based performance standard. Our purpose in

---

[17] Our 'gasoline tax' really represents a more general tax on all petroleum-based fuels used in transportation, which also include, for example, jet and diesel fuels.

[18] It has been argued that this policy would be relatively easy to implement, since electric utilities have experience with the sulfur trading program.

[19] This policy is equivalent in its effects (given our homogeneous firm setting) to a tax on carbon emissions from electric utilities with the revenues recycled as a subsidy per unit of electricity output (Bovenberg and Goulder, 1998). This type of tax/subsidy policy has been proposed as a means to reduce industry opposition to taxes on carbon emissions.

[20] For example, it may be difficult to cover all emissions sources because many different types of 'downstream' industries use fossil fuels. Nonetheless, it seems plausible that a performance standard could be applied to transportation in addition to electricity, and these two industries account for around 60% of total carbon emissions. In transportation the standard could limit carbon emissions per vehicle mile in the same way that existing regulations limit emissions per mile for carbon monoxide, nitrogen oxides and hydrocarbons. Our idealized policy also assumes that different standards are set so as to equalize marginal abatement costs across industries. This may be difficult to approximate in practice.

356   *I.W.H. Parry, R.C. Williams III / Resource and Energy Economics 21 (1999) 347–373*

analyzing this policy is to examine whether pre-existing taxes are likely to affect the costs of broader-based performance standards in the same way that they affect the costs of the narrow-based performance standard.

The government budget constraint is:

$$p_C G = t_L p_L L + R. \tag{5}$$

This equation equates nominal government spending with tax revenues, which consist of labor tax revenues plus R, revenue from abatement policies. R is direct tax revenues under the tax instruments and indirect revenues from the taxation of rents $(t_L \pi)$ under the quota instruments. It equals zero under the performance standards. We assume the government budget must always balance.

2.1.4. The tax-interaction and revenue-recycling effects

To the extent that the above policy instruments raise the costs of producing output, they will increase the relative price of consumption goods and reduce the real household wage. In turn, this reduces labor supply and produces an efficiency loss through the 'tax-interaction effect' (Parry, 1997; Goulder et al., 1997). This efficiency loss arises because the labor tax drives a wedge between the gross wage paid by firms, which equals the value marginal product of labor, and the net wage received by households, which equals the marginal opportunity cost of labor supply in terms of forgone leisure time. The impact of carbon abatement policies on the economy-wide labor supply is likely to be small. Nonetheless, the efficiency loss per unit reduction in labor supply is 'large' because taxes drive a substantial wedge between the gross and net wage. As a result, the efficiency loss from the tax-interaction effect may still be substantial relative to the first-best (or partial equilibrium) costs of carbon abatement policies.

A controversial issue is how to value the additional revenues raised by the tax policy instruments, and the indirect revenues raised from the partial taxation of rents created by quotas. We consider two cases that span the range of possibilities in our model. In our benchmark case, real government spending is held constant and the rate of income tax is adjusted to maintain budget balance. Thus, the revenues raised by carbon abatement policies produce an efficiency gain from the reduction in the rate of pre-existing distortionary tax—the so-called 'revenue-recycling effect' (Goulder, 1995). We also consider a case where the revenue consequences of abatement policies are neutralized by adjusting the lump sum transfer. In this case, there is no efficiency gain from raising revenue. [21] Thus, we

---

[21] Roughly speaking, this may represent the case when the revenues finance additional transfer payments (such as pensions), additional public spending that is a close substitute for private spending (such as health care and education), or increases in income tax deductions for dependents.

I.W.H. Parry, R.C. Williams III / Resource and Energy Economics 21 (1999) 347–373   357

can clearly illustrate the efficiency gains to be had from using revenues to cut other taxes. [22]

2.1.5. Equilibrium conditions

For a given set of preference, production and government parameters, the model is solved numerically by finding a vector of goods prices and the price of labor such that: (a) the demand for all goods equals the supply; (b) the demand for and supply of labor are equal; (c) the household and government budget constraints are satisfied; and (d) carbon emissions equal a particular target level.

2.2. Model calibration

Roughly speaking, the σ (or ρ) parameters are calibrated to existing estimates of the relevant elasticity and the α parameters to observed output and input ratios. The σ parameters are most important for determining the relative costs of different carbon abatement policies. Here we discuss the parameter values used in the benchmark simulations (the results from alternative parameter values are reported in Section 3.5). Our data set is summarized in Table 1.

An important parameter is the consumption/leisure substitution elasticity σ_U. We choose this, along with the labor time endowment, to imply uncompensated and compensated labor supply elasticities of 0.15 and 0.4, respectively (this gives $\sigma_U = 0.96$). These are roughly central estimates from the literature, and are meant to capture the effects of changes in the real wage on average hours worked, the labor force participation rate and effort on the job. [23] We assume a pre-existing tax rate on labor of 40%. [24] These parameters imply that the efficiency loss from raising taxes to increase the lump sum transfer by a dollar is 30 cents. This is broadly consistent with other studies (for example, Browning, 1987; Ballard et al., 1985).

---

[22] In a dynamic setting, additional revenues might be used to reduce the government budget deficit. This produces a potential efficiency gain by permitting a reduction in future tax rates. The revenues may also be used to increase spending on public goods. This produces an efficiency gain (loss) if households value the extra spending at more (less) than the dollar amount of the spending. For a public choice perspective on how governments may spend new sources of revenues, see Becker and Mulligan (1997).

[23] See, for example, the survey by Russek (1994). We use a slightly higher value for the compensated elasticity since the studies in his survey do not capture effort effects.

[24] Other studies use similar values (for example, Browning, 1987; Lucas, 1990). The sum of federal income, state income, payroll and consumption taxes amounts to around 36% of net national product. This average rate is relevant for the labor force participation decision. The marginal tax rate, which affects average hours worked and effort on the job, is higher because of various deductions. A recent paper by Browning (1994) suggests that the 'wedge' in the labor market may be significantly larger than 40% because of various non-tax distortions, such as regulations on businesses. To the extent that this is the case, our analysis may underestimate the tax-interaction and revenue-recycling effects.

Table 1
Benchmark data for the numerical model

(A) Input–output flows (in millions of 1990 US dollars per year except as otherwise noted)

	F_C	F_P	F_N	E	T	I	N	C_I	C_N	l	Total input value
F_C	2990	63	0.1	19866	9.2	2928	1595	744	15		28209
F_P	455	56404	9703	8717	134273	7256	38742	22959	7863		286371
F_N	48	26973	22893	5931	326	13138	23999	70786	311		164404
E	963	2848	888	56	5268	19613	89299	63685	59		182678
T	2833	8976	1823	7703	85615	31418	175737	324546	3072		641725
I	1374	22585	15842	1288	3675	242415	531839	419	8540		827977
N	6612	34141	16242	40270	181477	161624	4674494	328666	3479102		8922627
L	12933	134382	97014	98847	231081	349586	3386924	811805	3498962	2394871	6705638
Total output value	28209	286371	164404	182678	641725	827977	8922627				
e	68	210	76	478	358	113	191	232	22		1749

(B) Parameter values

	Elasticity of substitution among energy, labor and materials	Elasticity of substitution in energy (fuels and electricity) nest (σ_E)	Elasticity of substitution in materials nest (σ_M)
F_C	1.70	0.16	0.53
F_P	0.53	0.20	0.20
F_N	0.73	0.89	0.20
E	0.76	0.20	0.95
T	0.54	0.20	0.20
I	0.43	0.82	0.27
N	0.48	0.53	1.51
C_I	0.53	0.59	0.26
C_N	0.85	0.97	0.76

$\sigma_C = 0.52$, $\sigma_U = 0.96$ (elasticities of substitution between final goods and between consumption and leisure, respectively).

I.W.H. Parry, R.C. Williams III / Resource and Energy Economics 21 (1999) 347–373 359

The elasticities of substitution in the inner and outer nests of the production functions are calculated based on estimates by McKibbin and Wilcoxen (1995). These elasticities are given in Table 1B. The carbon content of the three fossil fuels (β) is calculated by dividing the recorded carbon emissions for each fuel by the quantity of fuel combusted in 1990, using data from the *Annual Energy Outlook*. The α parameters are calibrated such that the model generates our benchmark data set in Table 1A, in the absence of emissions regulation, given the production and consumption elasticities and the initial labor tax. This data shows the value of output from, and the value of inputs into, each of the nine industries in our model. It was obtained by consolidating data from the *Survey of Current Business* and scaling up to 2000, our base year, assuming annual growth rates of 2.6% for all flows.

Below, we refer to our benchmark case with the income tax as the 'second-best' case. We also consider a 'first-best' case in which the pre-existing income tax is set to zero, and lump sum transfers from (to) households neutralize any revenue consequences of abatement policies. We compare the policy instruments on the basis of costs for a given level of abatement and consider emissions reductions of up to 25% of baseline levels.

3. Results

This section discusses the empirical results from the model. In the first three subsections, we present graphs comparing the marginal cost of emissions reduction under each policy instrument, without the labor tax, and with the labor tax under our two alternative assumptions concerning the recycling of revenues. We also include a summary table that ranks the different policies according to the total costs at 5% and at 25% emissions reduction. Section 3.4 examines how pre-existing taxes can affect the welfare potential of the policy instruments under different scenarios for environmental benefits. As illustrated in Section 3.5, our quantitative results are somewhat sensitive to alternative parameter values. Thus, the qualitative nature of our findings are perhaps more important the specific point estimates.

3.1. Costs of policy instruments in a first-best setting

Fig. 1 shows the marginal cost of reducing emissions under each policy instrument, assuming a first-best setting with no labor tax. Marginal costs are expressed in dollars for the last ton of carbon reduced. All marginal cost curves have a zero intercept because, in the absence of regulation, firms are not charged for their carbon emissions and therefore produce emissions until the marginal product of emissions is zero. Several important facts about the first-best costs of the various policies are evident in Fig. 1.

360   *I.W.H. Parry, R.C. Williams III / Resource and Energy Economics 21 (1999) 347–373*

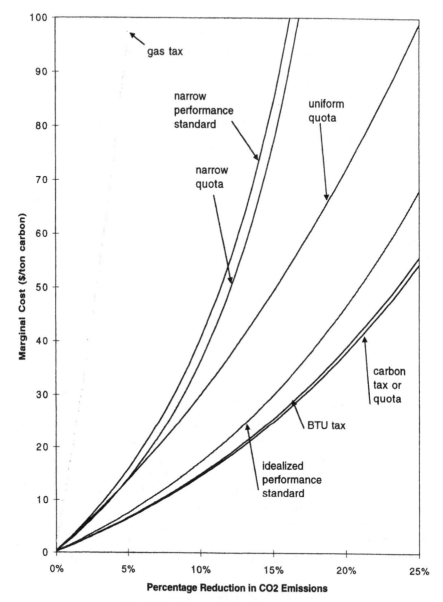

Fig. 1. First-best costs of emissions reduction.

The carbon tax and the carbon quota have the same marginal cost curve and are the least costly instruments. This is because they cover all potential sources of emissions, induce an equalization of marginal abatement costs across all industries, and give the appropriate incentives for firms to reduce production of energy-intensive goods. The marginal cost curve under each policy is increasing,

I.W.H. Parry, R.C. Williams III / Resource and Energy Economics 21 (1999) 347–373 361

reflecting the increasing difficulty of reducing emissions by substitution between fossil fuels or between energy-intensive and non-energy intensive production.

Fig. 1 also shows that the cost differences between broad and narrow based policies are typically much more important than the differences in costs between different broad based policies, or between different narrow based policies. Marginal costs under the BTU tax exceed those under the carbon tax. This is because the BTU tax does not induce an equalization of marginal abatement costs across different industries; instead the marginal costs of abating carbon by reducing natural gas use exceed those for reducing coal use. The idealized performance standard is also somewhat more costly than the carbon tax. The difference between these instruments has to do with whether firms are charged for their remaining emissions or not. Firms can reduce emissions by reducing output of energy-intensive goods (the 'output substitution effect'), or by reducing emissions per unit of output by substituting away from carbon-intensive inputs in production (the 'input substitution effect'). [25] Under the performance standard firms are not charged for their remaining emissions per unit of output, leading to an inefficiently weak output substitution effect. In contrast, under the carbon tax, firms pay a direct charge for emissions, and hence the marginal private costs of producing output are larger. [26] However, empirically, these cost differences between the carbon tax, BTU tax and the idealized performance standard are relatively small. [27]

Similarly, the narrow performance standard is only slightly more costly than the narrow emissions quota. However, the marginal costs of these policies are roughly three times as large as the broad-based policies discussed above. This is because the narrow policies only cover around 30% of emissions sources. The gasoline tax is substantially more costly than the other narrow policies, both because it is a much narrower tax and because it is difficult to substitute other fuels for gasoline in the transportation sector. In contrast, there exist much greater possibilities for substituting other inputs for coal in the production of electricity to reduce carbon emissions. Marginal costs for the uniform emissions quota are significantly greater than for the other broad policies, although they are still well below those for the narrow-based policies. The uniform quota forces the same proportionate emissions reduction across all sectors. This is a relatively costly policy because the marginal costs of emissions abatement are so much higher for transportation than for

---

[25] For more discussion of these effects, see Goulder et al. (1999).

[26] Under the carbon quota, firms effectively pay for remaining emissions, either by purchasing quotas from other firms or by using their own quotas instead of selling them to other firms.

[27] Only a small fraction of emissions reductions under the carbon tax come from output substitution. Therefore, the weaker output substitution effect under the performance standard causes the costs of these policies to differ only slightly. Similarly, while the BTU tax encourages overuse of coal and underuse of natural gas, this has only a small effect, so the BTU tax is only slightly more costly than the carbon tax.

362   I.W.H. Parry, R.C. Williams III / Resource and Energy Economics 21 (1999) 347–373

Table 2
Total costs of emissions reduction by policy (as a percent of GDP)

| | Percent emissions reduction | | | |
| | First-best case | | Second-best case | |
	5	25	5	25
Carbon tax	0.006	0.203	0.008	0.279
BTU tax	0.006	0.207	0.008	0.282
Gas tax	0.084	4.106	0.112	4.995
Broad quota	0.006	0.203	0.058	0.610
Narrow quota	0.012	0.838	0.046	1.321
Uniform quota	0.013	0.391	0.122	1.129
Ideal performance standard	0.007	0.250	0.009	0.341
Narrow performance standard	0.014	0.914	0.019	1.228

electricity. In contrast, the other broad policy instruments allow a disproportionate amount of emissions reduction to come from electricity.

Table 2 summarizes the costs of the different policies, showing the total costs under each policy instrument for a 5 and 25% reduction in carbon emissions, expressed relative to the costs of the carbon tax. The gasoline tax is roughly 15 times as costly as the carbon tax and carbon quota, while the narrow quota and narrow performance standard are around two to four times as costly. In contrast, the BTU tax is only slightly more costly, and the broad performance standard around 25% more costly. The table also shows that the relative cost discrepancies between policy instruments are not particularly sensitive to the level of emissions reduction.

3.2. Costs of policy instruments in a second-best setting with revenue-recycling

We now explore how the above results are affected by second-best considerations. Fig. 2 shows the marginal costs of the policy instruments when the initial labor income tax is 40% and when any revenue consequences of the policies are offset by adjusting the income tax rate. Changes in labor supply now have efficiency consequences, since the tax creates a wedge between the marginal social benefit and marginal social cost of labor.

There are two notable results concerning the quota policies. First, the efficiency loss from the tax-interaction effect causes a substantial upward shift in the marginal cost curves under all three policies, compared with the first-best case shown in Fig. 1. The marginal cost curves have positive intercepts because an incremental emissions reduction now causes a first-order (or non-incremental) efficiency loss in the labor market. This stems from the incremental reduction in labor supply following the increase in product prices and consequent fall in the real household wage.

I.W.H. Parry, R.C. Williams III / Resource and Energy Economics 21 (1999) 347–373   363

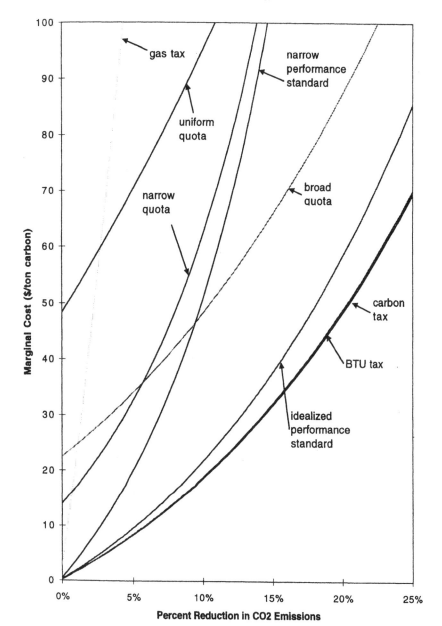

Fig. 2. Second-best costs of emission reduction.

The second result is that the marginal cost of the narrow quota lies below that of the broad quota for low levels of emissions reduction. This is surprising because in a first-best setting marginal costs are always substantially greater under the narrow-based quota. However, the tax-interaction effect is relatively weaker under the narrow quota than under the broad quota. The tax-interaction effect depends on the increase in the (share-weighted) average price of consumption goods, which equals the increase in output price for the affected industries multiplied by the share of this output in total consumption. Although the narrow-based quota has a larger impact on product prices in the affected industries, output from these industries is a smaller share in the total value of consumption than under the broad quota. For modest emissions reductions, this smaller tax-interaction effect under the narrower policy dominates the first-best advantage of the broader policy. [28]

In contrast to the quota policies, the marginal cost curves for the three tax instruments still have zero intercepts. This is because these policies produce a revenue-recycling effect that exactly offsets the tax-interaction effect for the initial incremental reduction in emissions. [29] However, the marginal cost curves have steeper slopes than the corresponding curves in Fig. 1. That is, for a non-incremental emissions reduction, the tax-interaction effect dominates the revenue-recycling effect and there is a net efficiency loss from interactions with the tax system. These policies replace revenues from the broad-based labor tax with revenues from a relatively narrow-based tax on carbon, gasoline or energy. Ignoring the environmental benefits, the narrow-based taxes are more distortionary than the labor tax because they are easier for firms and households to avoid. [30]

The marginal costs for the performance standards also have zero intercepts. At first glance, this is a surprising result because they do not generate a revenue-recycling effect to counteract the tax-interaction effect. However, the tax-interaction effect is weaker (relative to the first-best costs of the policy) under each of these policies than under the tax or quota policies. This is because there is no charge for remaining emissions per unit of final output. Thus, the increase in (marginal) costs of producing final output and the increase in product prices are relatively smaller. [31]

As indicated in Table 2, pre-existing taxes raise the total costs of emissions reduction under the three quota policies by around 270–880% at a 5% emissions reduction and by 60–200% at a 25% emissions reduction, relative to their total costs in a first-best setting. For the three tax instruments, pre-existing taxes raise

---

[28] This result has an intriguing policy implication. Previously, economists have argued that carbon trading programs should cover as many emissions sources as possible. However, some emissions sources, such as those from the forestry sector or from small scale metal processing, may be very costly to administer. The above result suggests that to reduce emissions by a modest amount by a non-auctioned quota, even if there were no administrative costs, it might actually be less efficient to cover all emissions sources.

[29] The quota policies do produce an indirect revenue recycling benefit through the partial taxation of quota rents. For the broad carbon quota, this amounts to 40% of the revenue recycling effect under the carbon tax.

[30] If energy-intensive consumption were a stronger (weaker) substitute for leisure than non energy-intensive consumption, the marginal cost curves would have positive (negative) intercepts.

[31] For more discussion on this, see Goulder et al. (1999).

I.W.H. Parry, R.C. Williams III / Resource and Energy Economics 21 (1999) 347–373 365

total costs by 35% at all levels of emissions abatement; and for the performance standards the increase in cost is also 35%. Thus, the cost discrepancies between the tax policies and the performance standards are increased in the same proportion by the pre-existing tax.

Allowing for second-best considerations overturns a number of the key results that emerged from the first-best analysis.

(i) The equivalence of the carbon tax and quota breaks down dramatically. Since the quota generates only a weak revenue-recycling effect, it is over seven times as costly as the carbon tax at a 5% emissions reduction and more than twice as costly at a 25% emissions reduction.

(ii) The tradable carbon quota can be considerably more costly than the performance standard or a quota that does not allow trades between industries (the uniform quota).

(iii) The largest cost discrepancies are no longer necessarily between broad- and narrow-based policies. Substantial cost discrepancies also arise between policies that generate a relatively large tax-interaction effect (the carbon quota) and policies that generate a relatively small tax interaction effect (for example, the broad performance standard) or offset the tax-interaction effect with a substantial revenue-recycling effect (for example, the carbon and BTU taxes).

(iv) The relative cost differences between policy instruments now depend importantly on the level of emissions abatement. Indeed, for incremental abatement the carbon quota is infinitely more costly than the carbon tax. This reflects the positive intercept of the marginal cost curve under the quota and the zero intercept under the tax. [32]

3.3. Costs of policy instruments in a second-best setting with no revenue recycling

Fig. 3 shows the marginal cost curves when the revenues raised by a given policy instrument (direct revenues under the tax policies and indirect revenues from the taxation of rents under the quota policies) are returned to households as lump sum transfers. This raises the cost of the tax and quota policies above the levels shown in Fig. 2, because this change eliminates the beneficial revenue recycling effect. A striking result is that now the performance standard—particularly the idealized version—can easily be the most cost-effective policy. That is, a command and control policy beats both the carbon tax and the carbon quota! This

---

[32] We caution the reader that the results in this figure come from a relatively simple and aggregated model. For example, the relative cost advantage of the BTU tax over the gasoline tax can be significantly weaker in a dynamic model that incorporates taxes on capital. This is because capital is overtaxed relative to labor from an efficiency perspective, and capital effectively bears more of the burden of the BTU tax than the gasoline tax (see Bovenberg and Goulder, 1997).

366   *I.W.H. Parry, R.C. Williams III / Resource and Energy Economics 21 (1999) 347–373*

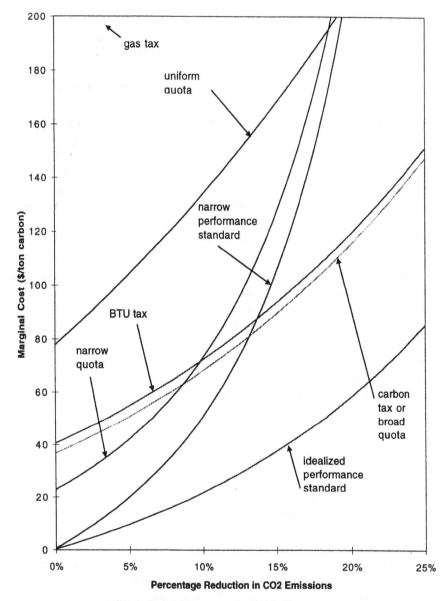

Fig. 3. Costs with tax revenues returned lump sum.

result arises because the tax-interaction effect is relatively weak under performance standards. [33] Fig. 3 clearly underscores the point that the efficiency case for

---

[33] Again, we emphasize that our analysis does not capture the additional inefficiency under a
performance standard that can result from heterogeneous abatement costs among firms within industries.

I.W.H. Parry, R.C. Williams III / Resource and Energy Economics 21 (1999) 347–373   367

using the tax policy instruments requires more than just raising revenue. The revenues must also be used to cut rates of other distortionary taxes.

3.4. Welfare potential of policy instruments

We now consider how the potential welfare gain from the different policy instruments is affected by pre-existing taxes. To do this requires some assumptions about the benefits from carbon abatement. We assume the marginal benefits from abatement are approximately constant over the range of abatement under consideration. [34] Using median parameter values, benefit estimates are typically around US$5 to US$20 per ton of carbon reduced (Nordhaus, 1991, 1994). However, these estimates are highly uncertain. Under more extreme scenarios for climate change and/or lower discount rates, benefit estimates can easily be several times larger. [35] We consider benefit scenarios ranging from US$0 to 150 per ton.

3.4.1. First-best case

The horizontal axis in Fig. 4 shows marginal benefits from reducing carbon emissions ranging from US$0 to 150 per ton. The vertical axis shows the maximum potential welfare gain from each policy instrument for the given values of marginal benefits, in the first-best case with no labor tax. The maximum welfare potential is obtained by first calculating the optimal emissions reduction (where marginal benefit equals marginal abatement cost in Fig. 1) and then the difference between total benefits and total costs at this level of abatement.

All policy instruments can potentially improve welfare as long as environmental benefits per ton are positive, since the marginal cost curves in Fig. 1 all have zero intercepts. However, the welfare potential of the instruments differs substantially, due to differences in abatement costs. For example, the welfare potential of the narrow performance standard is only around 50% of that for the carbon tax and carbon quota.

3.4.2. Second-best case

Fig. 5 shows the corresponding maximum welfare curves in the second-best case, assuming revenues raised by the policy instruments are used to reduce the labor tax. All the curves are lower than the respective curves in Fig. 4, since pre-existing taxes raise abatement costs under each policy. Pre-existing taxes

---

[34] This seems reasonable since potential climate change depends on the future stock of CO_2 in the atmosphere and current global CO_2 emissions—let alone US emissions—only have small impacts on future stock levels (see Pizer, 1997).

[35] The Nordhaus estimates may be on the low side because they exclude some factors that are difficult to quantify. These include the possibility of non-linearities in the climate system leading to catastrophic climate changes, ecosystem impacts and potentially adverse effects on the distribution of world income.

368   I.W.H. Parry, R.C. Williams III / Resource and Energy Economics 21 (1999) 347–373

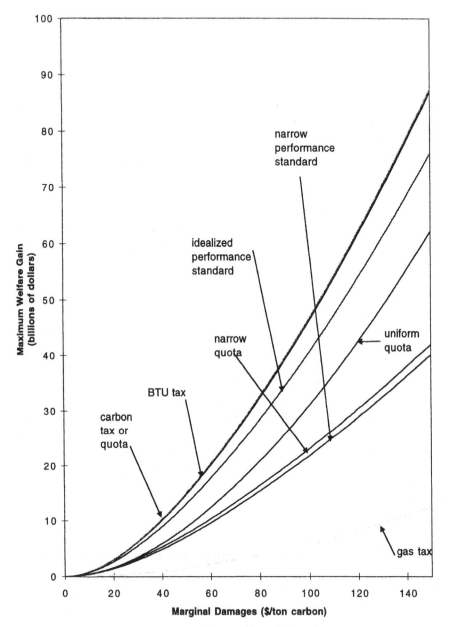

Fig. 4. First-best maximum welfare gain by policy.

dramatically reduce the welfare potential of the quota policies. These policies cannot improve welfare—that is, the intercepts of the marginal cost curves lie above marginal environmental benefits—if marginal benefits are below US$14 per ton for the narrow carbon quota, US$23 per ton for the broad carbon quota and

I.W.H. Parry, R.C. Williams III / Resource and Energy Economics 21 (1999) 347–373 369

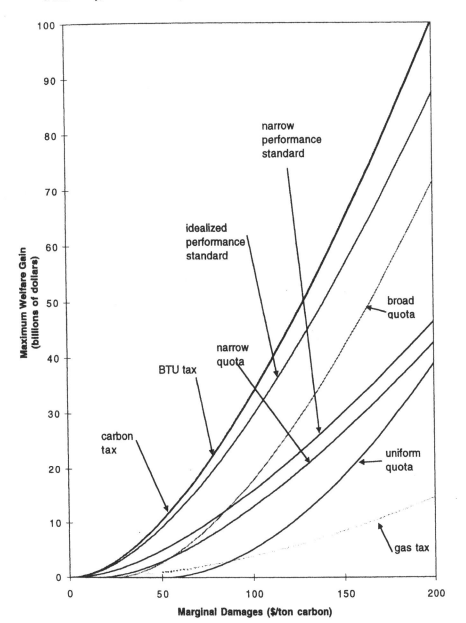

Fig. 5. Second-best maximum welfare gain by policy.

US$48 for the uniform quota. Even if we assume marginal benefits are as large as, say, US$75 per ton, the welfare potential of the carbon quota is still only 30% of that for the quota in the first-best case. Under plausible scenarios for marginal benefits, the welfare potential of certain policy instruments that are inefficient in a first-best sense—including performance standards, the narrow carbon quota and the revenue-neutral gas and BTU taxes—can exceed that of the broad carbon quota. The potential welfare gain is greatest under the revenue-neutral carbon tax. Even so, the welfare potential of this policy in a second-best setting is still significantly lower—by around 30%.

3.5. Sensitivity analysis

The above results are based on central estimates for parameter values. We now discuss how the costs of policies are affected by alternative assumptions about important parameters. [36] In each case, we consider marginal costs at emissions reductions of 5 and 25% under the carbon tax, broad carbon quota and idealized performance standard. The results are summarized in Table 3.

In the second row, we vary the uncompensated labor supply elasticity between 0 and 0.3 (holding the compensated elasticity constant) and in the third row we vary the compensated labor supply elasticity between 0.2 and 0.6 (holding the uncompensated elasticity constant). Higher elasticities imply a greater degree of substitution between consumption and leisure, and this strengthens the tax-interaction effect. As a result, the costs of the quota are sensitive to varying these elasticities. The costs of the performance standard are less sensitive, since the tax-interaction effect is relatively weaker under this policy. A larger consumption-leisure elasticity also implies a larger revenue-recycling effect, and hence the costs of the carbon tax are also less sensitive to these elasticities.

A higher initial labor tax clearly increases the welfare loss from the tax-interaction effect and welfare gain from the revenue-recycling effect. Therefore, it raises the costs of all the carbon abatement policies, and has a disproportionate effect on the cost of the carbon quota, because the sum of the two second-best effects is largest for this policy. There is less uncertainty over the effective tax on labor in the US than certain other parameters in our model. A plausible range is probably 35–45%, and our cost estimates are only modestly sensitive to these alternative values. In the fourth row, we vary the labor tax between 20 and 60% to provide a feel for the possible importance of the tax-interaction effect in other countries that might have much lower or much higher labor taxes. For example, increasing the tax rate from 40 to 60% roughly doubles the costs of the carbon tax and performance standard. However, it nearly quadruples the cost of the carbon quota!

Finally, in the fifth row, we assume there is no taxation of quota rents, or equivalently that revenue from taxing quota rents is returned to households in lump sum transfers. This eliminates the partial revenue-recycling effect under the

---

[36] The relative—though not absolute—costs of the policies are not particularly sensitive to alternative assumptions about production elasticities, the elasticity of substitution between goods in the utility function, and the size of fossil fuel industries relative to GDP.

I.W.H. Parry, R.C. Williams III / Resource and Energy Economics 21 (1999) 347–373   371

Table 3
Sensitivity analysis (marginal cost of emissions reduction by policy

	Percent emissions reduction					
	Carbon tax		Carbon quota		Ideal performance standard	
	5	25	5	25	5	25
(1) Central case	8.3	69.4	34.0	113.9	9.5	85.4
(2) Uncompensated labor supply elasticity = 0.0–0.3	7.5–9.3	63.0–77.3	30.7–38.2	103.9–129.3	8.6–10.7	77.8–95.0
(3) Compensated labor supply elasticity = 0.2–0.6	8.3–8.3	69.3–69.5	21.4–46.4	92.8–136.1	9.5–9.5	85.3–85.7
(4) Labor tax = 0.2–0.6	7.0–17.2	59.3–143	15.2–132	73.2–391	8.0–19.8	73.2–176
(5) No taxation of quota rents	n/a	n/a	50.8	147.5	n/a	n/a

carbon quota and significantly raises the overall costs of the quota. In this case the quota is equivalent to a carbon tax with lump sum replacement of revenues.

4. Conclusion

This paper has examined the implications of pre-existing tax distortions in the labor market for the costs and overall welfare impacts of a variety of policy options to reduce US carbon emissions. These policies include a carbon tax, two energy taxes, and both narrow-based and broad-based emissions permits and performance standards. The presence of pre-existing tax distortions raises the costs of all these policies, and can affect their relative cost rankings. In fact, the superiority of emissions taxes and emissions permits over other instruments can hinge on whether these policies generate revenues that can be used to reduce other distortionary taxes.

There are a number of potentially important limitations to our analysis. First, the analysis does not capture efficiency impacts arising from the interactions between carbon abatement policies and other pollutants within the energy sector (such as sulfur and nitrogen oxide emissions), and pre-existing regulations on these emissions. To the extent that carbon abatement policies indirectly reduce the quantity of these pollutants they will produce environmental benefits, but they will also exacerbate the costs of the pre-existing regulations. [37] Second, our analysis does not capture heterogeneity in abatement costs among firms within industries.

---

[37] Boyd et al. (1995) estimate the indirect benefits from reducing other pollutants. However, their analysis does not take into account pre-existing regulations on these pollutants.

372   *I.W.H. Parry, R.C. Williams III / Resource and Energy Economics 21 (1999) 347–373*

This tends to understate the costs of the performance standards relative to the costs of other policy instruments. Third, the model is static and therefore does not incorporate the impacts of carbon abatement policies on the capital market, which is also distorted by taxes. As illustrated by Bovenberg and Goulder (1997), policies that effectively raise (lower) the overall burden of taxation on capital relative to labor produce an additional efficiency loss (gain) since capital is already 'over-taxed' relative to labor. Nor does our model capture the effects of abatement policies on technological innovation. If the amount of R&D into cleaner technologies is inefficiently low, [38] then to the extent that carbon abatement policies create incentives for such R&D they may induce an important source of welfare gain.

Acknowledgements

We thank Mike Toman for helpful comments on an earlier draft. We are also grateful to the Environmental Protection Agency for financial support (grant number R 825313-01-0).

References

Ballard, C.L., Shoven, J.B., Whalley, J., 1985. General equilibrium computations of the marginal welfare cost of taxes in the United States. American Economic Review 75, 128–138.

Becker, G.S., Mulligan, C.B., 1997. Efficient taxes, efficient spending, and big government. Working paper, University of Chicago.

Bovenberg, A.L., de Mooij, R.A., 1994. Environmental levies and distortionary taxation. American Economic Review 84, 1085–1089.

Bovenberg, A.L., Goulder, L.H., 1997. Costs of environmentally-motivated taxes in the presence of other taxes: general equilibrium analyses. National Tax Journal 50, 59–88.

Bovenberg, A.L., Goulder, L.H., 1998. Environmental taxation. In: Auerbach, A., Feldstein, M. (Eds.), Handbook of Public Economics, 2nd edn. North-Holland, Amsterdam (forthcoming).

Boyd, R., Krutilla, K., Viscusi, W.K., 1995. Energy taxation as a policy instrument to reduce CO_2 emissions: a net benefit analysis. Journal of Environment and Management 29, 1–24.

Browning, E.K., 1987. On the marginal welfare cost of taxation. American Economic Review 77, 11–23.

Browning, E.K., 1994. The non-tax wedge. Journal of Public Economics 53, 419–433.

Browning, E.K., 1997. A neglected welfare cost of monopoly—and most other product market distortions. Journal of Public Economics 66, 127–144.

Cropper, M.L., Oates, W.E., 1992. Environmental economics: a survey. Journal of Economic Literature 30, 675–740.

---

[38] The level of R&D can be suboptimal when innovators do not receive compensation for the environmental benefits from new technologies, or when they cannot appropriate all the spillover benefits to other firms from innovations.

de Mooij, R.A., 1998. The double dividend in the case of environment-economy interaction. Working paper, Research Center for Economic Policy, Holland.

Deaton, A., 1981. Optimal taxes and the structure of preferences. Econometrica 49, 1245–1259.

Fullerton, D.G., Metcalf, 1997. Environmental controls, scarcity rents, and pre-existing distortions. NBER working paper No. 6091.

Goulder, L.H., 1995. Environmental taxation and the 'double dividend': a reader's guide. International Tax and Public Finance 2, 157–183.

Goulder, L.H., Parry, I.W.H., Burtraw, D., 1997. Revenue-raising vs. other approaches to environmental protection: the critical significance of pre-existing tax distortions. Rand Journal of Economics 28, 708–731.

Goulder, L.H., Parry, I.W.H., Williams, R.C., III, Burtraw, D., 1999. The cost-effectiveness of alternative instruments for environmental protection in a second-best setting. Journal of Public Economics (in press).

Lucas, R.E., 1990. Supply-side economics: an analytical review. Oxford Economic Papers 42, 293–316.

McKibbin, W., Wilcoxen, P., 1995. The theoretical and empirical structure of *G*-cubed. Brookings Institution, Washington, DC (unpublished manuscript).

Nordhaus, W.D., 1991. To slow or not to slow: the economics of the Greenhouse Effect. The Economic Journal 101, 920–937.

Nordhaus, W.D., 1994. Managing the Global Commons: The Economics of Climate Change. MIT Press, Cambridge.

Oates, W.E., 1995. Green taxes: can we protect the environment and improve the tax system at the same time?. Southern Economic Journal 61, 914–922.

Oates, W.E., Portney, P.R., 1992. Economic incentives and the containment of global warming. Eastern Economic Journal 18, 85–98.

Parry, I.W.H., 1997. Environmental taxes and quotas in the presence of distorting taxes in factor markets. Resource and Energy Economics 19, 203–220.

Parry, I.W.H., Williams, R.C. III, Goulder, L.H., 1999. When can carbon abatement policies increase welfare? The fundamental role of distorted factor markets. Journal of Environmental Economics and Management 37, 52–84.

Pizer, W.A., 1997. Prices vs. quantities revisited: the case of climate change. Discussion paper no. 98-02, Resources for the Future, Washington, DC.

Russek, F., 1994. Taxes and labor supply. Working paper, Congressional Budget Office, Washington, DC.

Sandmo, A., 1975. Optimal taxation in the presence of externalities. Swedish Journal of Economics 77, 86–98.

Spulber, D.F., 1985. Efficient regulation and long run optimality. Journal of Environmental Economics and Management 12, 103–116.

Tietenberg, T.H., 1985. Emissions trading: An exercise in reforming pollution policy. Resources for the Future, Washington, DC.

Williams, R.C., III, 1998. The impact of pre-existing taxes on the benefits of regulations affecting health or productivity. Working paper, Stanford University.

[25]

Combining price and quantity controls to mitigate global climate change

William A. Pizer*

Resources for the Future, 1616 P Street NW, Washington, DC 20036, USA

Received 14 July 1999; received in revised form 18 December 2000; accepted 21 March 2001

Abstract

Uncertainty about compliance costs causes otherwise equivalent price and quantity controls to behave differently and leads to divergent welfare consequences. Although most of the debate on global climate change policy has focused on quantity controls due to their political appeal, this paper argues that price controls are more efficient. Simulations based on a stochastic computable general equilibrium model indicate that the expected welfare gain from the optimal price policy is five times higher than the expected gain from the optimal quantity policy. An alternative hybrid policy combines both the political appeal of quantity controls with the efficiency of prices, using an initial distribution of tradeable permits to set a quantitative target, but allowing additional permits to be purchased at a fixed "trigger" price. Even sub-optimal hybrid policies offer dramatic efficiency improvements over otherwise standard quantity controls. For example, a $50 trigger price per ton of carbon converts the $3 trillion expected loss associated with a simple 1990 emission target to a $150 billion gain. These results suggest that a hybrid policy is an attractive alternative to either a pure price or quantity system.

Keywords: Climate change; Decision-making under uncertainty; Price and quantity controls; General equilibrium modeling

JEL classification: Q28; D81; C68

410   W.A. Pizer / Journal of Public Economics 85 (2002) 409–434

1. Introduction

Seminal work by Weitzman (1974) drew attention to the fact that, in regulated markets, uncertainty about costs leads to a potentially important efficiency distinction between otherwise equivalent price and quantity controls. Despite this well-known observation and its relevance for climate change policy, most of the debate concerning the use of taxes and emission permits to control greenhouse gases (GHGs) has centered on political, legal and revenue concerns.[1] This paper responds to this important omission by examining the efficiency properties of permit and tax policies to mitigate global climate change.[2]

The basic distinction among policy instruments arises because taxes fix the marginal cost of abatement at a specified tax level (assuming optimal firm behavior). With uncertainty about costs, this generates a range of possible abatement levels and emission outcomes. In contrast, a permit system precisely limits emissions but leads to a range of potential cost outcomes. When coupled with a model of the benefits associated with emission reduction, this divergence in emission and cost outcomes creates a distinction in the expected welfare associated with each policy.

In the case of climate change, part of the cost uncertainty arises due to uncertainty about the level of future baseline emissions. The Intergovernmental Panel on Climate Change (1992; hereafter IPCC) gives a range of CO_2 emission levels in 2010 of between 9.2 and 13.1 gigatons carbon (GtC).[3] This requires a uniform + 15% adjustment to IPCC forecasts of carbon emissions. See p. 71 in Nordhaus (1994b). The cost of attaining a particular target, say the 1990 emission level of 8.5 GtC, will obviously fluctuate depending on the level of future uncontrolled emissions.

In addition to the baseline, however, there is considerable uncertainty about the cost of reducing emissions below the baseline. A study by Nordhaus (1993) reports that a $30/ton carbon (tC) tax might reduce emissions anywhere from 10 to 40%. While some models predict that a $300/tC would virtually eliminate emissions, other models require a tax in excess of $400/tC.[4] This wide range of

---

[1] See Wiener (1998), McKibbin and Wilcoxen (1997) and Goulder et al. (1997).

[2] Earlier work by the author (Pizer, 1999) focused on the effect of uncertainty on the level of control, measured by a control rate or emission tax. That paper compared price and control rate policies, but did not consider fixed emission limits. Recent work by Newell and Pizer (1998) and Hoel and Karp (1998) considers the theory of price and quantity regulation applied to pollution such as greenhouse gas emissions that accumulate in the environment.

[3] The actual range is 8.1–11.4 GtC. However, we include the carbon equivalent of CFC emissions in our discussions of controllable greenhouse gas/carbon emissions in order to parallel the treatment in Nordhaus (1994b) and Pizer (1999).

[4] A recent report by the Energy Information Administration (1998) indicates similar marginal costs ranging from $50 to $400/tC to achieve comparable reductions in emissions based on different models. Weyand and Hill (1999) suggest even higher costs.

W.A. Pizer / Journal of Public Economics 85 (2002) 409–434 411

reduction estimates only compounds the uncertainty about baselines to generate extreme uncertainty about the cost of a particular emission target 10–15 years in the future.

Motivated by the policy implications of these large uncertainties, this paper uses a modified version of the Nordhaus (1994b) DICE model in order to analyze alternative policies under uncertainty. In particular, the model incorporates uncertainty about a wide range of model parameters developed in both Nordhaus (1994b) and Pizer (1996). The simulations are then sped up using a technique presented in Pizer (1999) that greatly facilitates computation. Details concerning costs and benefits are discussed in the next section while additional detail can be found in Pizer (1999) and Nordhaus (1994b).

Two sets of simulations are emphasized. The first set focuses on the choice of policy in the year 2010 only. By examining estimated marginal cost and benefit schedules in this single period, we can directly apply Weitzman's original intuition. Such an analysis reveals the consequences of very short-term policy decisions, showing that the optimal price policy (a tax of $7.50/tC) yields expected social benefits of $2.5 billion in net present value versus the optimal quantity policy (a 13 GtC permit scheme) yielding only $0.3 billion.

The single-period experiments are followed by simulations of the optimal price and quantity policies over a 100-year horizon. These longer-term policy simulations indicate that an optimal permit path would similarly begin with a 13 GtC target in 2010, but rise gradually over time to about 45 GtC by 2100 in order to accomodate economic growth. This policy generates $69 billion in expected net benefits versus a no policy, business-as-usual alternative. Meanwhile, the optimal tax policy starts at $7/tC in 2010 and rises to about $55/tC by 2100. In contrast, this policy generates $337 billion in expected net benefits – five times the gain of the optimal permit policy.

Since these results are driven by untestable assumptions about the consequences of climate change, an obvious question is whether they are sensitive to increasingly non-linear climate effects. Indeed, the presence of a significant threshold can reverse the preference for taxes. Specifically, when damages rise from 1% to 9% as the mean global temperature rises from 3 to 4 degrees above historic levels, this is sufficient to encourage the use of quantity-based regulations over a 50-year policy horizon.

Finally, a combined hybrid policy is proposed as an alternative to both the pure tax and permit approaches Roberts and Spence (1976); Weitzman (1978); and McKibbin and Wilcoxen (1997). Such a mechanism would involve an initial distribution of tradeable permits, with additional permits available from the government at a specified "trigger" price. This system turns out to be only slightly more efficient than a pure tax system. However, it achieves this efficiency while preserving the political appeal of permits: the ability to flexibly distribute the rents associated with emission rights. More importantly for current policy discussions, sub-optimal hybrid policies based on an aggressive target and high trigger price lead to better welfare outcomes than a pure quantity-based policy with the same target. Both the improved flexibility and better welfare outcomes make the hybrid policy an attractive alternative to either permits or taxes alone.

2. Background

2.1. Weitzman–Roberts–Spence

The analysis presented in Weitzman (1974) concerns the choice of a policy instrument to regulate a market where either political considerations or market failure require government intervention. A price (tax) or quantity (permit) instrument is at the government's disposal and the question posed by Weitzman is which of the two leads to the best welfare outcome, measured as net social surplus.[5] Importantly, the policy must be fixed *before* any uncertainty is resolved and cannot be revised.[6]

Weitzman's basic result was that price instruments would be favored when the marginal benefit schedule was relatively flat and quantity instruments would be favored when the marginal cost schedule was relatively flat. In particular, he derived an expression for the relative welfare advantage of prices over quantities:

$$\Delta = \frac{\sigma^2}{2c_2^2}(c_2 - b_2) \tag{1}$$

where σ^2 is the variance of the shocks to the marginal cost schedule, c_2 is the slope of the marginal cost schedule and b_2 is the slope of the marginal benefit schedule.[7] Based on this expression, the price instrument is preferred when benefits are relatively flat ($\Delta > 0$ when $b_2 < c_2$) and the quantity instrument is preferred when benefits are relatively steep ($\Delta < 0$ when $b_2 > c_2$). More recently, Hoel and Karp (1998) and Newell and Pizer (1998) have demonstrated that Eqs. (1) continues to hold when benefits are related to the stock of accumulated output, rather than the annual flow, after adjusting b_2 to account for discounting, decay, growth, and the potential correlation of cost shocks over time.

Not long after Weitzman's original article, several authors proposed a hybrid policy in place of pure price or quantity controls (Weitzman, 1978; Roberts and

---

[5]Here and throughout it is assumed that the quantity instrument is an *efficient* quantity instrument; e.g. a tradeable permit system with negligible transaction costs.

[6]Laffont (1977) provides a careful description of the information structure assumed in policy choice problems formulated in the Weitzman tradition.

[7]The parameter b_2 is actually minus the slope since the schedule of total benefits is usually concave. This result is derived for the case of linear marginal costs and benefits, where uncertainty enters as small shifts to each curve (therefore the slopes b_2 and c_2 are known with certainty). The uncertainty about costs is assumed to be independent of any uncertainty about benefits. See Stavins (1996).

W.A. Pizer / Journal of Public Economics 85 (2002) 409–434   413

Spence, 1976). A hybrid policy gives producers the choice of either obtaining a permit in the marketplace or purchasing a permit from the government at a specified trigger price.[8] Such a policy operates like a permit scheme with uncertain costs and fixed emissions as long as the marginal cost, reflected by the permit price, remains below the trigger. When the trigger price is reached, however, control costs are capped and emissions become uncertain, as in a tax scheme. By setting the trigger price high enough or the number of permits low enough, the hybrid policy can mimic either a pure quantity or pure price mechanism, respectively. Since it encompasses both tax and permit mechanisms as special cases, the hybrid policy will always perform at least as well as either pure policy.[9]

Policymakers and economists often focus on many considerations other than the partial equilibrium welfare concerns highlighted by the Weitzman–Roberts–Spence analysis (Stavins, 1989; Goulder et al., 1997; and Parry and Williams, 1999). In the United States, experience with quantity-based permit systems for both national SO_x and regional NO_x pollution control has created political support for market-based quantity controls – especially when valuable permits are provided gratis to those bearing the most concentrated cost burden. At the same time, popular opposition to taxes of any kind makes the prospect for pure price-based regulations rather grim.[10] Yet, a hybrid system with welfare properties nearly identical to (or better than) a pure price-based mechanism retains virtually all the politically desirable characteristics of a permit system.[11] Since this paper indicates that price-based or hybrid mechanisms produce five-times the welfare gain associated with quantity controls, it suggests an opportunity for significant and feasible policy improvement.

2.2. Costs of climate change mitigation

In order to compare price- and quantity-based policies to mitigate climate change, we need a dynamic model of mitigation costs, benefits, and uncertainty. To this end, we make use of the model developed in Pizer (1999), which involves a stochastic extension to the deterministic climate–economy model presented in Nordhaus (1994b). Based on the previous discussion of Weitzman–Roberts–Spence, we focus our attention on the model's characterization of costs, benefits and uncertainty, leaving the more interested reader to consult earlier work.

The global cost of climate change mitigation is typically measured as the

---

[8] A hybrid policy may also involve a price floor at which the government offers to buy back permits. However, this type of subsidy program creates dynamic inefficiencies. See Chapter 14 of Baumol and Oates (1988).

[9] Such policies have been proposed in the climate change arena by McKibbin and Wilcoxen (1997), McKibbin (2000) and Kopp et al. (2000).

[10] See Pearce (1991) for a discussion of the pros and cons of carbon taxes.

[11] The one feature it does not share is an absolute cap on emissions. This is, however, somewhat illusory since even an absolute cap can be relaxed in the face of future political pressure.

reduction in consumable output associated with a particular emission level of greenhouse gases. This cost calculation is conveniently viewed in two steps: (1) calculation of the required emission reduction, expressed as a fraction of gross emissions; and (2) calculation of the fractional reduction in global output required to achieve that fractional emission reduction.[12] The first part of the calculation is determined by growth forecasts of population, productivity, and the carbon intensity of production (because carbon dioxide is the primary anthropogenic greenhouse gas). None of these trends are known with certainty and are therefore assigned probability distributions based on Nordhaus (1994b), Nordhaus and Popp (1997), and Pizer (1996).

Fig. 1 shows the resulting distribution of CO_2 emission forecasts used in this paper, along with the 1992 IPCC future emission scenarios for comparison. The

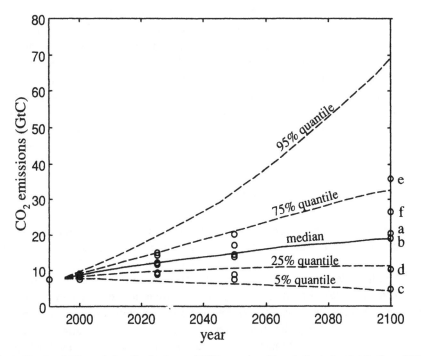

Fig. 1. Simulated CO_2 emission distribution vs. IPCC scenarios. Lines indicate the distribution of CO_2 emission paths generated by the model. Circles (O) indicate 1992 IPCC CO_2 emission scenarios (p. 12 IPCC 1992; pp. 101–112, Pepper et al., 1992) adjusted to include controllable CFC's (see p. 71 Nordhaus (1994b)): letters in right margin refer to individual IPCC scenarios.

---

[12]There is a third step – converting the fractional loss of global output into an actual dollar loss. However, we really care about utility, not the level of output or consumption. Assuming roughly logarithmic utility (so $du = (1/c)dc$), fractional losses are a reasonable focal point since changes in utility are more closely related to fractional (versus level) changes in consumption.

W.A. Pizer / Journal of Public Economics 85 (2002) 409–434   415

IPCC forecasts tend to fall between the 5th and 75th quantiles of our simulations. This is consistent with more recent analysis suggesting a wider range of possibilities than those contained in the 1992 scenarios (IPCC, 2000).[13]

The second part of the cost calculation – relating fractional reductions in greenhouse gases to fractional reductions in world output – is based on a survey of studies first summarized in Nordhaus (1993). These studies compute costs by various means, including engineering assessments, econometric estimation, and mathematical programming. The relationship and range of estimates are approximated in Nordhaus (1994b) by a power rule,

fractional reduction in global output

$$= b_1(\text{fractional reduction in GHG emissions})^{2.887} \tag{2}$$

Nordhaus (1994b) considers a range of values for b_1: 0.027, 0.034, 0.069, 0.080 and 0.133, with the best guess being 0.069. These values imply that a 20% reduction global emissions would require 0.026%, 0.033%, 0.066%, 0.077% and 0.128% reductions in global output, respectively. Here and in Pizer (1999), these values are assumed to occur with equal probability, independent of other uncertainty in the model (including the emission levels shown in Fig. 1).

There are two subtle assumptions embedded in Eqs. (2) that bear mentioning. First, the relation assumes that marginal costs are increasingly steep as additional reductions are undertaken, and second, the choice of emission level is an annual decision involving an annual cost function. Both of these points are important in this analysis because they affect the slope of marginal costs, in turn affecting the difference in expected welfare between taxes and permits.

The assumption of increasing marginal costs would seem innocuous based on the fact that one input – the uncontrolled emission level – is fixed. However, it has been argued that once non-marginal changes in production technologies are considered, costs could fall (Lovins, 1996). This relates to the second point: Over time the stock of both human and physical capital could evolve in a less carbon intensive direction, making emission choice a multi-period – rather than single-period – decision.[14] Both effects suggest a preference for price controls when regulation is focused on the near term, possibly switching to a preference for quantity controls when regulation is flexibly applied over a long horizon (e.g., with banking and borrowing).[15]

---

[13]The 1992 scenarios were specifically criticized for ignoring the possibility that developing country income converges to developed country income (per capita), which would lead to higher uncontrolled emission forecasts.

[14]This touches on the issue of endogenous technological change; see Grübler and Messner (1998); and Goulder and Mathai (2000).

[15]If emissions can eventually be reduced at substantially lower costs, it suggests that the long-run marginal cost curve is flatter than the short-run marginal cost curve, favoring quantity controls applied over a sufficiently long horizon; see Eqs. (1).

2.3. Benefits of climate change mitigation

In contrast to mitigation costs, which are rooted in the economically familiar areas of aggregate energy use and fuel substitution, mitigation benefits are determined by long-term climate changes and the economic impacts associated with those changes. With only limited historical experience concerning climatic changes and especially their economic consequences, this is understandably the most subjective and uncertain area of climate–economy modeling.[16] Nordhaus (1994a) found that scientists' opinions on the possible damages from climate change range from 0% up to a 50% loss of global output.

A simple model of climate dynamics coupled with a damage function based on the square of the change in global mean temperature drives our mitigation benefits. Economic activity determines a baseline, uncontrolled emission level for carbon dioxide. Mitigation activities reduce current emissions below the baseline. Each ton of unmitigated carbon dioxide generates a rise in the global mean temperature that peaks about 40 years after it is emitted, then dissipates slowly with a half-life of about 60 years. The initial 40-year delay arises because the global mean temperature equilibrates gradually in response to higher levels of accumulated carbon dioxide as the earth's atmosphere traps more solar radiation.[17] The subsequent decline follows the gradual decay of carbon dioxide and other greenhouse gases in the atmosphere. A one-time 100 million ton increase in emissions (roughly 1% of annual global emissions in 1990) generates a peak temperature rise of about 2/10,000 of one degree Celsius using best-guess parameter values. Uncertainty in the climate model could double or halve this estimated temperature increase.[18]

The economic consequences of climate change depend on these increases in global mean temperature. Following Nordhaus (1994b) and Pizer (1999), we specify a quadratic damage function with

$$\text{fractional reduction in output due to climate damages} = D_0 \cdot (T/3)^2 \qquad (3)$$

where T is the change in temperature relative to a pre-industrialization baseline

---

[16]Current atmospheric CO_2 concentrations of 368 ppm are higher than in any period over the past 400,000 years, which ranged 200–300 ppm (Petit et al., 1999). Some work has used cross-sectional variation in climate to estimate economic consequences of climate changes such as temperature and precipitation (Mendelsohn et al., 1994). While instructive, these analyses ignore the difference between regional and global climate changes – analogous to the difference between partial and general equilibrium – as well as changes in storm patterns and extreme weather behavior.

[17]As temperatures rise the earth radiates more heat into space, counteracting the increased retention of solar radiation due to higher levels of greenhouse gases. Eventually the earth reaches a new greenhouse gas/temperature equilibrium.

[18]There is uncertainty about both the amount of emitted CO_2 that is rapidly absorbed by oceans (atmospheric retention rate) as well as the temperature change resulting from changes in atmospheric CO_2 (climate sensitivity).

(circa 1860) and D_0 is a parameter describing the global output reduction associated with a 3° temperature increase. Nordhaus (1994b) focuses on a best-guess value of 0.013 for D_0 with a sensitivity analysis including values of zero, 0.004, 0.013, 0.016 and 0.032. Pizer (1999) assumes these five values occur with equal probability and independently of other uncertainty in the model.

The main weakness of this model of mitigation benefits is its failure to capture possibly abrupt temperature changes and/or economic consequences related to both the level and rate of change in greenhouse gas concentrations. The thermohaline circulation of the North Atlantic Ocean, for example, warms Northern Europe by as much as 10 degrees Celsius and could collapse as a result of increased greenhouse gas emissions (Broecker, 1997; Stocker and Andreas, 1997). Such a collapse would lead to more dramatic consequences than those predicted by this model. In Section 4 we consider relaxing the quadratic functional form in Eqs. (3) to address this possibility of more abrupt climate effects.

2.4. Economic behavior

These models of costs and benefits are dynamically linked via a simple one-sector stochastic growth model (Pizer, 1999). A representative agent chooses between consumption and savings each period based on the expected return to capital, which itself depends on population, the capital stock, and productivity. Productivity includes the negative consequences of both mitigation costs and climate damages. In this way, current mitigation costs and climate damages influence both current and, through investment, future consumption and output. Of course, mitigation activities also reduce greenhouse gas emissions and future climate damages.

We compute the optimal savings level each period based on a linearized steady-state decision rule (Campbell, 1994). This allows us to simulate the economic and climate outcomes quite rapidly for a single random draw of model parameters and stochastic shocks over a 250-year horizon. We then use eight thousand random draws to approximate the range of uncertain outcomes.

Mitigation costs and controlled (actual) emissions are computed separately in each period and for each state of nature based on the specified carbon tax or permit policy. The uncontrolled emission level and global output gross of climate mitigation are both determined by state variables at the beginning of each period. Under a permit policy, Eqs. (2) can be used to directly compute mitigation costs, where fractional reductions equal one minus the ratio of permits to uncontrolled emissions. In the case of a tax policy, Eqs. (2) can be differentiated to yield a marginal cost expression that, when set equal to the tax rate, can be solved for the fractional emission reduction. This reduction can then be substituted into the original relation to yield mitigation costs. With separate calculations in each state of nature, this procedure highlights how tax policies fix marginal costs and lead to

418   *W.A. Pizer / Journal of Public Economics 85 (2002) 409–434*

uncertain emissions while permit policies fix emissions and lead to uncertain marginal costs.

The welfare effects of a particular policy are computed in terms of discounted utility for each state of nature. Discounted utility is then valued in a particular base year using the marginal utility of consumption in that year. Dollars in the base year can be averaged across states of nature to yield expected welfare. Additional details concerning the model specification, simulation, and welfare calculations can be found in Pizer (1999).

3. Simulation results

Given the long-term nature of climate change, a policy to reduce greenhouse gas emissions inevitably involves decisions spanning many decades. In the first part of this Section, however, we consider the expected welfare consequences of choosing price or quantity controls for GHG emissions in a single year, 2010. By focusing on a single year in the near future, we can address the difference between alternate price/quantity controls now, without becoming mired in the question of longer-term policy. In addition, focusing on a single year allows us to easily visualize the policy in quantity/price space. While the policy is implemented in a single period, the measurement of costs and benefits includes consequences over a 250-year horizon.

The second part of this section considers price and quantity policies spanning many periods. The policies are open-loop: There are no revisions to future policies as we learn about uncertain outcomes. Although such feedback is both desirable and more realistic, it would require a simplification of either the model or the specification of uncertainty.[19] With our motivating interest in instrument choice under uncertainty – and not learning – this is an undesirable trade-off.

Based on the idea that policies are often fixed for long periods of time, we use these open-loop policies to provide an alternate bound on the welfare difference associated with the choice between price and quantity controls. A policy optimization over many periods also allows us to see whether the choice of policy in the future influences the optimal near-term policy choice. The remainder of the paper then considers the sensitivity of these results to key damage damage assumptions as well as hybrid policies that combine price and quantity controls.

3.1. Marginal costs and benefits

We begin by computing schedules of mitigation costs and benefits in 2010. The benefits schedule is computed using 100 distinct simulations that fix emissions at

---

[19]See Kelly and Kolstad (1999) who consider closed-loop policies in a similar model focused on learning.

W.A. Pizer / Journal of Public Economics 85 (2002) 409–434   419

intervals of 0.1 GtC over the range 5–15 GtC in the year 2010, leaving emission levels in other periods unchanged. By "turning off" the mitigation costs associated with the fixed emission level and comparing welfare to the base case where 2010 emissions are left unchanged, we can compute the gross benefit of a particular emission level (e.g., gross of costs).

The cost schedule is computed by repeating these simulations with mitigation costs turned on. This produces estimates of the net benefits. By subtracting these net benefits from the aforementioned gross benefits, we produce estimates of cost. Both schedules can be converted to marginal ($/tC) measures by dividing the change in benefits and costs associated with an incremental 0.1 GtC reduction, measured in $billions, by 0.1 GtC.

These two calculations result in a distribution of marginal benefits and marginal costs at each simulated emission level. Fig. 2 summarizes these distributions by showing both the mean marginal cost and marginal benefit at each level of emissions along with the 5% and 95% quantiles based on 8,000 states of nature (note that the 5% marginal benefit quantile overlaps the x-axis). Keeping in mind that 1990 GHG emissions were around 8.5 GtC, this figure indicates that achieving 1990 emission levels in 2010 would involve a marginal cost of between zero and

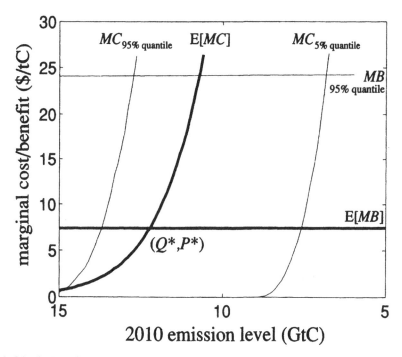

Fig. 2. Distribution of marginal costs and benefits in 2010. (The 5% quantile of marginal benefits overlaps the x-axis.).

420   *W.A. Pizer / Journal of Public Economics 85 (2002) 409–434*

in excess of $30/tC[20] – far more than even the 95% quantile of marginal benefits. This large variation occurs for two reasons: Marginal costs are assumed to rise steeply given the specified cost function in Eqs. (2), and baseline emissions in 2010 are not known with certainty as highlighted in Fig. 1. Realizations of marginal costs in this figure are essentially a collection of fairly steep curves whose horizontal intercept is unknown.

This figure indicates that marginal benefits, in contrast, are relatively constant though unknown. Considering the description of climate damages in the previous section, this may not come as a surprise. First, climate damage is presumed to be a gradual phenomenon with little consequence for small temperature changes, reflected in the quadratic damage function given in Eqs. (3) coupled with small values of D_0. Second, damages depend on the accumulated *stock* of GHGs in the atmosphere and not the annual *flow*.[21] Emissions in any single year, such as the 8.5 GtC emitted in 1990, represent a small fraction of the extra 190 GtC accumulated since the beginning of industrialization. This damage relation contrasts with traditional pollutants, such as particulates, SO_x, NO_x, etc., whose damages depend on the annual emission level because they dissipate rapidly in the environment.

The scale of Fig. 2 masks the fact that marginal mitigation benefits/emission damages actually fall from $7.45 to $7.37 as emissions rise from 5 to 15 GtC. This is surprising because we generally assume convex damages: As we pollute the environment, there ought to be increasingly dire consequences from each additional ton. In the case of climate change, however, a key physical relationship connects the logarithm of atmospheric greenhouse gas concentrations to the change in temperature.[22] That is, there is some fixed (but unknown) temperature change associated with each doubling of the level of carbon dioxide and other GHGs in the atmosphere – thus as we emit more, the marginal temperature change is actually less. This feature coupled with quadratic damages due to temperature change guarantees a very flat and slightly concave benefit/damage relation. We revisit this assumption in Section 4.

3.2. Comparative advantage of prices over quantities

Under the assumptions made by Weitzman, the optimal permit level is simply the emission level where expected marginal benefits equal expected marginal costs and the optimal tax level is similarly the expected marginal benefit at that intersection. Thus $P^* = \$7.50$ and $Q^* = 12$ GtC indicate the optimal tax and permit policies in 2010 for controlling GHG emissions based on a Weitzman analysis. Calculating the slopes at the intersection, $B'' = 0$ and $C'' = 5.4 \$/(tC \cdot$

---

[20]The actual 95% marginal cost quantile at 8.5 GtC is $180/tC.

[21]More specifically, temperature change depends on the GHG stock and damages depend on temperature change.

[22]See Eq. (2.9) in Nordhaus (1994b).

W.A. Pizer / Journal of Public Economics 85 (2002) 409–434 421

GtC), and setting σ^2 equal to the variance of marginal costs at the optimum, 270 ($/tC)^2, allows a rough calculation of the welfare gain of taxes over permits using Eqs. (1):

$$\Delta = \frac{270 \; (\$/tC)^2}{2 \cdot (5.4 \; \$/(tC \cdot GtC))^2}(5.4 - 0 \; \$/(tC \cdot GtC)) \approx \$25 \text{billion}.$$

Discounting this to 1995 (the base year of the model) with a 6% discount rate suggests a gain of $10 billion from using taxes instead of permits – just in the year 2010.

This analysis based on Fig. 2 provides important intuition and a rough approximation of the welfare consequences of taxes and permits. However, it ignores important failures of the Weitzman assumptions in the current exercise. Costs are not quadratic and the quantity control is not binding in all cases.[23] In order to overcome these limitations, we now turn to the direct evaluation of social welfare.

Numerically maximizing expected welfare over the range of possible price and quantity controls in 2010, we find that the optimal price policy is a $7.50/tC tax, yielding a $2.5 billion gain, and the optimal quantity policy is a 13 GtC emission limit, yielding a $0.3 billion gain.[24] The positive gain associated with price controls is quite robust: Taxes of up to $20/tC (almost three times the optimal level) continue to generate positive expected benefits. In contrast, quantitative targets below 12 GtC have negative expected benefits. A policy set at 8.5 GtC – the emission level in 1990 and 20% below the median emission estimate in 2010 – yields a expected net loss of $10 billion.

The difference between optimal policies based on these direct simulations, $2.2 billion, is considerably less than the estimated value based on Fig. 2, $10 billion. While the Weitzman approach provides good qualitative intuition about the relative advantage of price- and quantity-based policies, the violation of key assumptions clearly limits its quantitative application in this setting.[25]

3.3. Optimal policy paths

Up to this point the analysis has focused on the costs and benefits of different policies in a single year. The problem of climate change, however, is spread out over decades if not centuries. Policies to combat climate change may remain in

---

[23]Uncontrolled emissions in 2010 are less than $Q^* = 12$ GtC in many of the simulated outcomes; see Figs. 1 and 2.

[24]When optimizing over quantity controls, we require that emissions be at or below the specified quantity target in all states of nature (emissions will fall below the quantity target if uncontrolled emissions are low).

[25]See Yohe (1978) and Watson and Ridker (1984) for further discussion.

place for a long time. Further, it is not obvious whether the results comparing different instruments in a single year are appropriate for a multi-period analysis. In particular, policies in future periods may influence the choice of policy in 2010.

We now consider optimal policy *paths* for both taxes and permits. To compute optimal policies, these paths are parameterized with six values describing the tax or permit level in 2010 (the first year of implementation), 2020, 2040, 2070, 2110 and 2160. Policies in intervening years are based on smooth interpolations,[26] except the level in 2160 which is allowed to be discontinuous and is held fixed through the end of the simulation (2245). The length of the simulation as well as the spacing of the policy parameters were chosen to emphasize policy evaluation in the 2000–2100 period and especially the early 2000–2050 period.

Fig. 3 shows the optimized permit and tax policies over 2000–2100. In the top panel, we see the optimal quantity limit on global greenhouse gas emissions. Interestingly, the optimal permit level of 13 GtC in 2010 is roughly the same as the optimal permit level determined in the one-period analysis. There are two explanations. First, given the large initial stock of GHGs in 1995 (190 GtC above the pre-industrialization level), emission reductions do not substantially affect the GHG stock for many years. Second, as we noted in the previous section, the marginal benefits are flat over a wide range of stock levels. Thus, future policies are unlikely to affect the value of discounted marginal benefits today both because marginal benefits are flat and, even if they were not flat, significant changes in the stock level will not occur for many years, leading us to discount the value of those changes in present value terms.

A second observation is that a proposal to reduce emissions to their 1990 levels (roughly 8.5 GtC) and to then maintain (or further reduce) that level in the future is far below the optimal permit level in these simulations, a point emphasized in Nordhaus' original analysis. In particular, the optimal permit level rises in the future to accomodate growth in population and productivity. While it is more useful to focus on the near-term policy implications – specifically the fact that they are essentially independent of future manipulations of the GHG stock – this second point shows that our historical experience with growth and technology coupled with our current climate damage assumptions is inconsistent with stabilizing long-term GHG emissions.

Finally, we note that when the optimal permit policy is implemented it improves welfare on average by $69 billion discounted to 1995 (total discounted benefits minus total discounted costs). This can be compared to annual global output in 1995 of $24 trillion.

The bottom panel of Fig. 3 shows the path of carbon taxes that maximize expected welfare. The initial tax of $7.35 is close to, but slightly lower than, the tax computed in the one-period analysis. Unlike the optimal permit policy which

---

[26]Policies are interpolated to 10-year intervals using a cubic spline; annual policies are linearly interpolated from the 10-year values.

W.A. Pizer / Journal of Public Economics 85 (2002) 409–434 423

Optimal Permit Policy

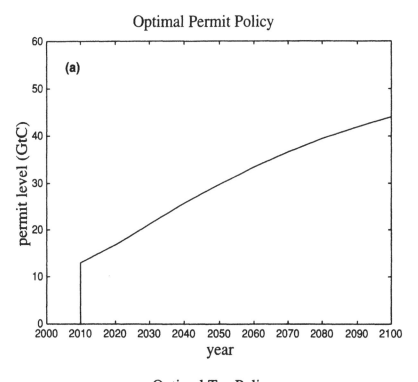

Optimal Tax Policy

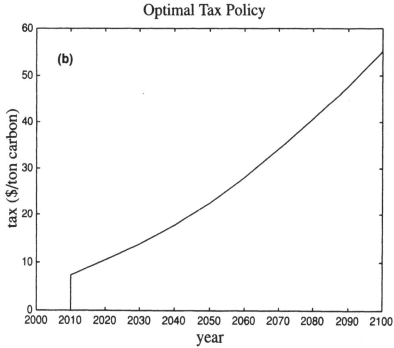

Fig. 3. Optimized permit and tax policies over time.

424   W.A. Pizer / Journal of Public Economics 85 (2002) 409–434

relaxes over time in order to accomodate growth, the optimal tax policy becomes *more stringent* in the future. This occurs because a given tax encourages proportional reductions – if the economy doubles and the tax remains the same, emissions will double. Although some increase in emissions is desirable as the economy grows, a proportional increase is not. Therefore the optimal tax must increase in stringency at the same time an optimal permit system must be relaxed. When this optimal tax policy is imposed, it improves welfare on average by $338 billion. Compared to the $69 billion gain under the optimal permit instrument, this represents an expected improvement that is *five times higher*.

4. Catastrophic damages

We have noted that the efficiency gains associated with price-based regulation follow largely from underlying assumptions about climate behavior and the likely economic consequences. Let us now consider how the results change if these assumptions are relaxed. There are at least two rationales for considering this possibility: The climate might behave in a more dramatic, non-linear way than specified by Schneider and Thompson (1981) and subsequently used by Nordhaus (1994b) and Pizer (1999). Alternately, the economic consequences of climate change – with which we have little experience – might be more convex than suggested by a quadratic damage function.[27]

For transparency we focus on the latter possibility, that damages are increasingly convex, and consider the impact of changing the exponent in Eqs. (3). Specifically, we consider a modified damage function of the form

$$\text{fractional reduction in GDP due to damages} = D_0 \times (T/3)^{d_1} \tag{3a}$$

where d_1 is allowed to take on values 2–12. Note that by writing the damage function such that $(T/3)$ is raised to the exponent d_1, the "kink" in the damage function is fixed at 3 degrees and D_0 continues to reflect the damage associated with this amount of warming.[28]

It turns out that one additional modification is necessary to conduct the sensitivity analysis. Earlier, it was noted that the choice of policy in 2010 was relatively insensitive to whether or not mitigation policies were implemented in future years. This allowed us to consider isolated price and quantity controls in 2010 without worrying about what occurred in the future. It also allowed us to consider policies over a 50- or 100-year horizon without worrying that the 250-year simulation horizon would be too short to produce sensible results. This

---

[27]For a more general discussion of catastrophic damages, see Gjerde et al. (1999).

[28]It is possible to treat the kink as unknown, but this only smooths out the non-linearity. Sensitivity analysis in this direction does not qualitatively alter the price/quantity comparison.

W.A. Pizer / Journal of Public Economics 85 (2002) 409–434 425

ability to focus on near-term policies is lost when damages acquire catastrophic proportions. The choice of current policy depends on how well we avoid catastrophes in the future. In the absense of future controls, for example, it becomes desirable to increase emissions now in order to create short-term damages that reduce the capital stock and thereby reduce emissions in the future indirectly – a rather perverse result. Even when future controls are included, welfare estimates become sensitive to the simulation horizon and to minute policy changes hundreds of years in the future, obscuring the effect of near-term policies.

In order to continue our focus on the near-term distinction between price and quantity controls, we hold future policy constant in a sensible way across all of our policy simulations. Specifically, emissions after 2060 are costlessly reduced to 6 GtC, a level that avoids any catastrophes in the distant future if prudent policies are pursued in the near term.[29] The elimination of mitigation costs after 2060 leads us to a slightly different comparison of prices and quantities under the benchmark assumption of quadratic damages discussed previously: Prices generate a $138 billion expected gain while quantity controls generate only $20 billion. Compared to the analysis in Section 3.3 this raises the relative advantage (price gain ÷ quantity gain) from a factor of five to a factor of seven.[30]

Fig. 4 shows how this difference between prices and quantities varies as the damages become increasingly non-linear ($d_1 > 2$). In the top panel, indicating the expected welfare difference between prices and quantities, Δ in Eqs. (1), we see that prices continue to be preferred until the non-linearity becomes quite large. This crossover occurs when $d_1 \approx 7$. With this degree of non-linearity, best-guess damages rise from 1% of global output with 3 degrees of warming to 9% with 4 degrees of warming.[31] A second observation in the left panel is that initially the comparative advantage of prices over quantities increases in absolute terms as marginal damages become steeper, apparently violating Weitzman's Eqs. (1). That is, as d_1 in Eqs. (3a) rises from two to three, the marginal benefit slope b_2 in Eqs. (1) presumably rises as well – which should reduce Δ. Such a conclusion is mistaken, however, as both σ^2 and c_2 (the variance of cost shocks and slope of marginal costs) in Eqs. (1) may be changing along with the marginal benefit slope as d_1 rises.

---

[29]Of course, one could argue that the most important effect of near-term policy should be its influence on future emissions and mitigation costs, not current emissions. However, such an effect is arguably more dependent on the aggressiveness of mitigation policy than the choice of policy instrument. Since this paper is tightly focused on the issue of instrument choice, and since such connections between current and future policy are probably more complex than the current model allows, our emphasis on near-term emission reductions and mitigation costs remains a sensible starting point.

[30]This should not come as a surprise since we are now more focused on the near term and the ratio for a single year discussed in Section 3.1 is more than a factor eight ($2.5B ÷ $0.3B).

[31]The actual damage function is $1 - (1 + D_0(T/3)^{d_1})^{-1}$; see Nordhaus (1994b). The distinction between this expression and Eqs. (3a) is only important at high damage levels.

Relative Advantage (absolute difference)

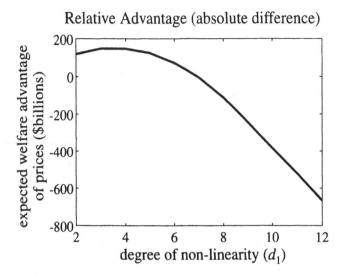

Relative Advantage (% of quantity gain)

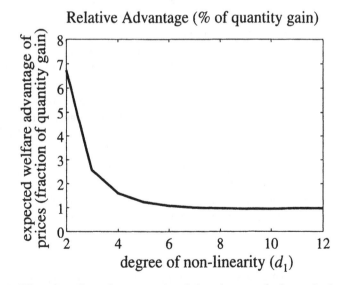

Fig. 4. Effect of non-linear damages on the relative advantage of price mechanisms.

In the bottom panel, another pattern arises. When we consider the ratio of welfare gains under prices and quantities, that is,

$$\frac{\text{expected welfare with optimal price controls} - \text{expected welfare without any mitigation}}{\text{expected welfare with optimal quantity controls} - \text{expected welfare without any mitigation}}$$

that ratio may be much larger than one but never falls noticeably below one.[32] In

---

[32]The smallest value of this ratio is about 0.95 when $d_1 = 9$.

other words, when $d_1 = 12$ the $600 billion dollar advantage associated with quantity controls, shown in the left panel, pales in comparison to the roughly *$34 trillion dollar* expected welfare gain associated with either policy, generating a ratio near one in the bottom panel. However, when $d_1 = 2$ the $118 billion dollar difference is quite large compared to the $20 billion dollar gain associated with the optimal quantity policy. Here, the ratio of the gains associated with a price price policy is almost a factor of seven times larger than the gains associated with a quantity policy.

Why is the gain from an optimal quantity policy never more than a few percent higher than the gain from an optimal price policy? Quantity controls are only preferred when marginal damages are quite steep. In this case, the gains from any policy to drastically reduce emissions – even an inefficient one – will be large. Although price controls will necessarily over-control in some cases in order to guarantee adequate control in others, this inefficiency will be small relative to the gain from reduced damages. In the extreme, sufficiently high prices will induce 100% abatement and will be equivalent to a quantitative ban on emissions.[33]

When we look more closely at the simulations, we see that this is indeed the case. In the absence of any policy, the likelihood that temperatures rise by more than 4 degrees by 2100 exceeds 9%. In the presence of catastrophic damages ($d_1 = 12$) optimal price and quantity controls both reduce emissions in such a way that the temperature increase never exceeds 4 degrees – roughly the point where the catastrophic consequences begin. Fig. 5 shows the actual policy choices. In terms of quantity controls, the optimal policy involves an emission limit of 10 GtC from 2010 through 2060. In terms of price controls, it involves a tax that begins at about $15 per ton in 2010 and rises to more than $500 per ton by 2060. These are considerably more aggressive than the policies based on quadratic damages.

5. Hybrid policies

As pointed out in Section 2.1, a hybrid permit policy – where an initial quantity target is coupled with a trigger price at which additional, above-target, permits are sold – will perform at least as well as either a pure tax or permit scheme (which are counted as special cases). We now explore the extent to which this is true for climate change mitigation policies and then consider the welfare consequences of certain suboptimal policies.

5.1. Optimal hybrid policies

We return to the case of quadratic climate damages and begin with the choice of

---

[33] An important distinction between the real world and the stylized world of Weitzman (1974) is that real cost shocks are not arbitrarily large; we can impose price policies that for all practical purposes guarantee a certain level of emissions.

428 *W.A. Pizer / Journal of Public Economics 85 (2002) 409–434*

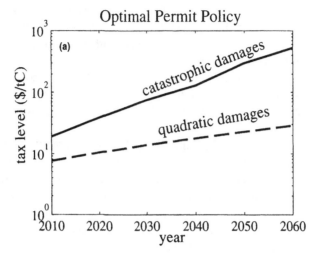

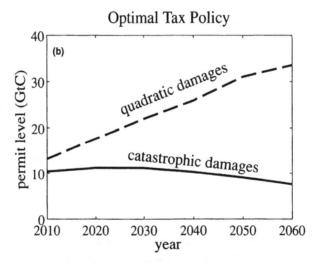

Fig. 5. Optimal policies with quadratic and catastrophic damages.

policy in 2010. A hybrid policy in the year 2010 can be represented by an arbitrary point in a two-dimensional plane, where one dimension is the initial quantity target and the other dimension is the trigger price. Picking any point in that plane, we can use our climate–economy model to compute the expected welfare gain of the policy represented by that point. Repeating the process over a grid of quantity target/trigger price combinations, we can create a surface summarizing the welfare gains associated with those policies. Fig. 6 plots this surface for initial permit levels of between zero and 15 GtC and trigger prices of between zero and 25 $/tC.

The proper way to read Fig. 6 is to note that for a grid of emission targets (0–15

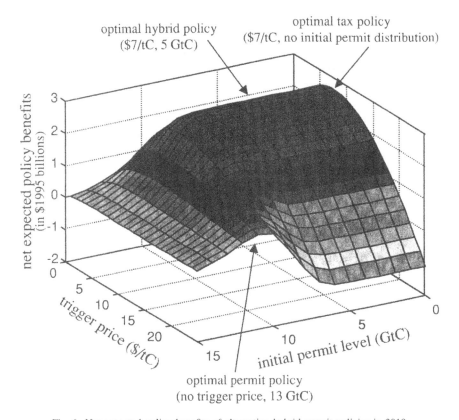

Fig. 6. Net expected policy benefits of alternative hybrid permit policies in 2010.

GtC) and trigger prices (0–$25/tC), the expected welfare gain relative to business as usual (no policy) is plotted on the z-axis in net present value terms. For low permit levels (< 5 GtC; back right edge of figure), the policy is essentially a tax and the surface traces out, from front to back, the welfare gain associated with a pure price policy. Similarly, for high trigger prices ($25/tC; front right edge of figure), the surface roughly traces, from left to right, the welfare gain associated with a pure quantity policy.

The global optimum, a 5 GtC target and $7/tC trigger price, yields a welfare gain that is imperceptibly higher than the $2.5 billion gain achieved with a straight tax of $7.50/tC.[34] More importantly, however, it performs considerably better than even the best pure permit policy. Relative to sub-optimal permit policies – such as

---

[34]Such a policy is remarkably close to the proposal suggested by McKibbin and Wilcoxen (1997). They advocated 1990 emission levels as the permit volume coupled with a $10/ton C trigger. 1990 global controllable GHG emissions were 8.5 GtC.

430   *W.A. Pizer / Journal of Public Economics 85 (2002) 409–434*

a 1990 emission level with its noted $10 billion expected loss – *any* of the policies depicted in Fig. 6 perform better, with none losing more than $1 billion.

When we consider the path of optimal hybrid policies in the future, it turns out that the path of the optimal trigger price is nearly identical to the path of the optimal tax level shown in the bottom panel of Fig. 3. As long as the quantity target is low enough (roughly 10 GtC) to ensure that the trigger price is reached most of the time, the specific value of the target is unimportant. This result, that expected welfare is maximized regardless of the quantitative target as long as we couple the target with a well-chosen trigger price, may be particularly useful in the context of the ongoing debate over both domestic and international climate policy.

In particular, there has been a consistent emphasis on quantity-based regulatory schemes in the US and abroad for a variety of political reasons. Permit systems, for example, allow a flexible distribution of the rents associated with emission rights. By avoiding the label of a "tax," permits also escape the negative associations many people have with income and property taxes. Yet, these same quantity-based schemes eventually meet with considerable resistance over the potential cost of mitigation. This analysis suggests that such resistence is well-founded: The risk of high mitigation costs significantly raises the expected burden of quantity-based regulation, even if the best-guess burden is low.

Not only does this risk raise the expected burden of quantity-based regulation, it also threatens to become a self-fulfilling prophesy. If firms and other private agents remain skeptical that a domestic or international policy will remain in force in the face of high costs, for example, they may defer mitigation action, delay innovative research and maintain less efficient, out-dated capital equipment. Such action could, in turn, lead to exactly the high cost outcome that forces governments to reformulate the policy.

Without abandoning many of desirable features associated with a permit mechanism, however, a hybrid policy transparently reduces if not eliminates the risk of high costs, making it a promising policy option.

5.2. Sub-optimal policies

Recognizing that real-world policies usually deviate from the optimal programs proposed by economists, it is useful to ask how well certain sub-optimal policies perform. In particular, the 1997 Kyoto Protocol seeks a quantitative limit on emissions that is slightly below 1990 emission levels.[35] The previous section suggests that a cap on the global permit price via a hybrid mechanism could offer substantial welfare improvements over the pure quantity target.[36]

---

[35]This limit, however, only applies to developed countries. Allowance for both GHG sinks as well as unintentional reductions in Eastern Europe also affects the target.

[36]As delegates continue to work out important provisions of the treaty – including the definition of "compliance" – there are a number of proposals that incorporate price-like, hybrid features.

Table 1

Trigger price ($/tC)[a]	Expected welfare gain
5	181
10	237
20	272
30	256
50	146
70	− 14
100	− 287
150	− 739
no trigger price	− 3359

Net benefits of hybrid policies with 1990 emission targets; (expected net present value in 1995 $billions; policies begin in 2010)

[a] Both the trigger price and target are fixed from 2010 forward.

Table 1 shows the effect of different trigger prices on a policy that otherwise limits global emissions to 1990 levels beginning in 2010 and continuing through the end of the simulation. Not surprisingly, the "no trigger price" option (e.g., a true quantity policy) entails the greatest losses, on the order of $3 trillion in net present value. This is analogous to the results in the single-period simulations where we noted that low quantity targets generated large welfare losses.[37] Surprisingly, trigger prices as high as $50/tC still generate positive welfare gains even though the optimal hybrid trigger price (identical to the optimal tax level shown in the bottom panel of Fig. 3) remains significantly below $50/tC for the next 100 years.

A second observation from Table 1 is that even as the trigger price approaches $100/tC, the expected welfare loss remains an order of magnitude lower than the pure permit approach. At $100/tC, the expected loss is around $300 billion – versus $3 trillion using permits alone. Even with a tax of $250/tC (not shown), the expected loss is cut in half. This highlights the role of a trigger price as a "safety valve" for adverse cost outcomes.[38] In 2010, there is barely a one-in-four chance that additional permits will be sold at a trigger price of $100/tC. Yet, the expected loss is reduced by a factor of ten. Regardless of whether one is confident about the exact welfare outcomes presented in this paper, the potential for a hybrid permit policy to reduce extremely adverse cost outcomes should be clear.

---

[37]E.g., the $10 billion loss associated with a target of 1990 emissions in 2010.

[38]One could also imagine there is an implicit safety valve in any permit system – that policy will be revised if it turns out to be too expensive. While such an approach suffers from the credibility issue noted earlier, it does avoid the immense welfare losses associated with an unrevised permit policy (I thank Lans Bovenberg for making this point).

6. Conclusion

Discussions of alternative tax and permit mechanisms for combating climate change have generally ignored the fact that the costs are highly uncertain. Such uncertainty can lead to large efficiency differences between the two policies. This paper has explored this question in the context of an integrated climate–economy model capable of simulating thousands of uncertain states of nature.

The resulting welfare analysis indicates that taxes are much more efficient than permits for controlling GHG emissions – by a factor of *five to one* ($337 billion versus $69 billion in net benefits). This derives from the relatively flat marginal benefit curve associated with emission reductions. Relatively flat marginal benefits are partially a product of the assumed quadratic damage function and partially a generic feature of stock pollutants like GHGs. An alternative assumption of abrupt and catastrophic damages – with damages rising from 1% to 9% as temperatures increase from 3 to 4 degrees – is sufficient to reverse the preference for price controls. Under these conditions, however, both price and quantity controls produce enormous welfare gains relative to the absence of any policy, dwarfing the difference between them.

In addition to pure tax and permit systems, this paper explored the possibility of a hybrid permit system. The hybrid policy involves an initial allocation of permits followed by the subsequent sale of additional permits at a fixed trigger price if costs are unexpectedly high. The optimal hybrid policy offers an imperceptible welfare improvement over the optimal tax policy. Yet it achieves this efficiency while maintaining the potential to flexibly distribute the rents associated with emission rights. Viewed as a modification to an aggressive permit policy, it leads to significant welfare gains even when the trigger price is above the optimal level. Finally, a hybrid policy offers a more predictable – and therefore credible – alternative to an aggressive quantity target where unexpectedly high costs could lead to policy revisions or even abandonment. Such credibility enhances the likelihood that firms will move ahead with investments to reduce control costs. Taken together, the improved flexibility, welfare outcomes, and credibility make the hybrid policy an appealing alternative to either permit or tax policies alone.

Acknowledgements

Financial support from the National Science Foundation (Grant SBR-9711607) and the Environmental Protection Agency (Cooperative Agreement CR825715) is gratefully acknowledged. Lans Bovenberg, Gary Chamberlain, Lawrence Goulder, Dale Jorgenson, Charles Kolstad, Raymond Kopp, Richard Morganstern, Richard Newell, Robert Stavins and three anonymous referees provided valuable comments on earlier drafts. Peter Nelson provided excellent research assistance. The author alone is responsible for all remaining errors.

References

Baumol, W.J., Oates (, W.E., 1988. The Theory of Environmental Policy, 2nd Edition. Cambridge University Press, Cambridge, UK.

Broecker, W.S., 1997. Thermohaline circulation, the Achilles heel of our climate system: Will man-made CO_2 upset the current balance? Science 278, 1582–1588.

Campbell, J.Y., 1994. Inspecting the mechanism: An analytical approach to the stochastic growth model. Journal of Monetary Economics 33 (3), 463–506.

Energy Information Administration (1998). Impacts of the Kyoto protocol on US energy markets and economic activity.

Gjerde, J., Grepperud, S., Kverndokk, S., 1999. Optimal climate policy under the possibility of a catastrophe. Resource and Energy Economics 21 (3–4), 289–317.

Goulder, L., Parry, I.W., Burtraw, D., 1997. Revenue-raising vs. other approaches to environmental protection: The critical significance of pre-existing tax distortions. RAND Journal of Economics 28, 708–731.

Goulder, L.H., Mathai, K., 2000. Optimal CO_2 abatement in the presence of induced technological change. Journal of Environmental Economics and Management 39 (1), 1–38.

Grübler, A., Messner, S., 1998. Technological change and the timing of mitigation measures. Energy Economics 20 (5–6), 495–512.

Hoel, M. and L. Karp, 1998. Taxes versus quotas for a stock pollutant. Working paper, University of Oslo and University of California at Berkeley.

Intergovernmental Panel on Climate Change, 1992. Climate Change 1992: The Supplemental Report to the IPCC Scientific Assessment. Cambridge University Press, Cambridge.

Intergovernmental Panel on Climate Change, 2000. Special Report on Emission Scenarios. Cambridge University Press, Cambridge.

Kelly, D.L., Kolstad, C.D., 1999. Bayesian learning, growth, and pollution. Journal of Economic Dynamics and Control 23 (4), 491–518.

Kopp, R., Morgenstern, R., Pizer, W., Toman (, M., 2000. A proposal for credible early action in US climate policy. In: Brockmann, K., Stonzik, M. (Eds.), Flexible Mechanisms for Efficient Climate Policy: Cost Saving Policies and Business Opportunities. Physica-Verlag, Heidelberg.

Laffont, J.-J., 1977. More on prices vs. quantities. Review of Economic Studies 44 (177-182), 1.

Lovins, A., 1996. Negawatts: Twelve transitions, eight improvements, and one distraction. Energy Policy 24 (4), 331–344.

McKibbin, W.J., 2000. Moving beyond Kyoto. Brookings Policy Brief No. 66, The Brookings Institution.

McKibbin, W.J., Wilcoxen, P.J., 1997. A better way to show global climate change. Brookings Policy Brief No. 17, The Brookings Institution.

Mendelsohn, R., Nordhaus, W., Shaw, D., 1994. The impact of global warming on agriculture: A Ricardian analysis. American Economic Review 84 (4), 753–771.

Newell, R., Pizer, W., 1998. Regulating stock externalities under uncertainty. Discussion Paper 99-09, Resources for the Future.

Nordhaus, W.D., 1993. The cost of slowing climate change. Energy Journal 12 (1), 37–65.

Nordhaus, W.D., 1994a. Expert opinion on climate change. American Scientist 82 (1), 45–51.

Nordhaus, W.D., 1994b. Managing the Global Commons. MIT Press, Cambridge.

Nordhaus, W.D., Popp, D., 1997. What is the value of scientific knowledge? An application to global warming using the PRICE model. Energy Journal 18 (1), 1–45.

Parry, I.W., Williams, R.C., 1999. A second-best evaluation of eight policy instruments to reduce carbon emissions. Resource and Energy Economics 21, 347–373.

Pearce, D.W., 1991. The role of carbon taxes in adjusting to global warming. Economic Journal 101, 938–948.

Pepper, W., Leggett, J., Swart, R., Wasson, J., Edmonds, J., Mintzer (, I., 1992. Emission scenarios for the IPCC: An update; assumptions, methodology and results. Detailed documentation in support of Chapter A3 In: Houghton, J.T., Callander, B.A., Varney, S.K. (Eds.), Climate Change 1992: The Supplementary Report to the IPCC Scientific Assessment. Cambridge University Press, Cambridge.

Petit, J. et al., 1999. Climate and atmospheric history of the past 420,000 years from the Vostok ice core, Antarctica. Nature 399, 429–436.

Pizer, W.A., 1996. Modeling long-term policy under uncertainty. Ph.D. thesis, Harvard University.

Pizer, W.A., 1999. The optimal choice of policy in the presence of uncertainty. Resource and Energy Economics 21, 255–287.

Roberts, M.J., Spence, M., 1976. Effluent charges and licenses under uncertainty. Journal of Public Economics 5, 193–208.

Schneider, S., Thompson, S., 1981. Atmospheric CO_2 and climate: Importance of the transient response. Journal of Geophysical Research 86, 3135–3147.

Stavins, R.N., 1989. Harnessing market forces to protect the environment. Environment 31(1), 5–7, 28–35.

Stavins, R.N., 1996. Correlated uncertainty and policy instrument choice. Journal of Environmental Economics and Management 30 (2), 218–232.

Stocker, T.F., Andreas, S., 1997. Influence of CO_2 emission rates on the stability of the thermohaline circulation. Nature 388, 862–865.

Watson, W.D., Ridker, R.G., 1984. Losses from effluent taxes and quotas under uncertainty. Journal of Environmental Economics and Management 11, 310–326.

Weitzman, M.L., 1974. Prices vs. quantities. Review of Economic Studies 41 (4), 477–491.

Weitzman, M.L., 1978. Optimal rewards for economic regulation. American Economic Review 68 (4), 683–691.

Weyand, J., Hill, J., 1999. Introduction and overview. Energy Journal Special Issue, vii–xliv.

Wiener, J.B., 1998. Global environmental regulation: Instrument choice in legal context. Yale Law Journal 677, 108.

Yohe, G., 1978. Towards a general comparison of price controls and quantity controls under uncertainty. Review of Economic Studies 45, 229–238.

[26]

Technologies, energy systems and the timing of CO_2 emissions abatement

An overview of economic issues

Michael Grubb

Energy and Environmental Programme, Royal Institute of International Affairs, 10 St James's Square, London SW1Y 4LE, UK

This paper provides an overview of economic issues involved in timing limitations on CO_2 emissions from energy systems. It highlights issues relating to technology availability, development and diffusion, and the inertia of energy systems, as being particularly important. The paper sets this in the context of wider uncertainties surrounding the problem and briefly considers other aspects relevant to timing. The paper is stimulated by the debate in the USA about optimal abatement paths, in particular recent claims that it would be economically preferable to defer such abatement action, in favour of measures that support technology development but do not affect emission trends for many years. This paper categorizes the various economic issues involved and concludes that for each economic argument that has been advanced to justify deferring emission constraints, there are countervailing economic arguments that could be used in support of rapid near term emissions abatement. Rational policy lies between these extremes. A policy of deferring all emissions abatement exposes economic systems and industries, as well as the environment, to significantly greater costs and risks than those arising from a more balanced approach. Furthermore the modelling studies that have been used to justify deferring emissions abatement do so because they embody the economic factors favourable to delay and largely neglect the countervailing issues, to the point where their results have little relevance to the overall problem of timing emissions abatement. © 1997 Elsevier Science Ltd. All rights reserved

Keywords: CO_2 emissions; Abatement; Optimal pathways

Climate change poses one of the biggest dilemmas for energy policy, both within governments and within industries. Among the core issues to be considered are those surrounding the timing of emission constraints: given all the uncertainties and the very long time horizon of the climate change problem and of energy systems, how much effort should be put into limiting emissions at present. This paper attempts to set out the range of economic issues that need to be considered in making a comprehensive assessment of the timing issue relating to CO_2 emission limitations and draws a number of qualitative conclusions.

The formal Objective of the UN Framework Convention on Climate Change includes 'stabilization of greenhouse gas concentrations at a level that would prevent dangerous anthropogenic interference with the climate system'. Although the Objective and the later Convention text also contains references to the importance of limiting rates of change and the need for an approach which adjusts to the accumulation of knowledge,[1] the emphasis upon long-term stabilization has led to various analyses looking at emission pathways under fixed objectives for stabilizing concentrations. Analysis has focused upon CO_2 as the single most important gas in terms both of its projected contribution to the problem and the potential economic implications of control.

The IPCC Second Assessment Report illustrates that various different emission pathways can be followed to-

---

[1] 'The ultimate Objective of this Convention .. is to achieve ..stabilisation of greenhouse gas concentrations at a level that would prevent dangerous anthropogenic interference with the climate system. Such stabilisation should be achieved within a time frame sufficient to allow ecosystems to adapt naturally, to ensure that food prodution is not threatened and to enable economic development to proceed in a sustainable manner'. UN Framework Convention on Climate Change, Article 2: Objective.

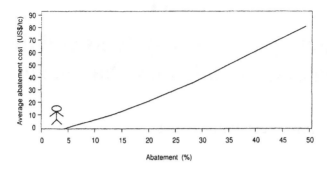

Figure 1 Technology menus and development: current situation technology portfolio (How far to go along the curve?)

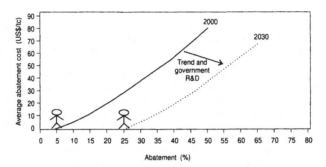

Figure 2 Technology menus and development: exogenous technology development (autonomous and government R&D) (Do R&D then sprint?)

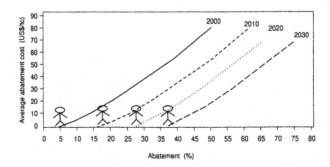

Figure 3 Technology menus and development: exogenous plus induced technology development (autonomous and R&D and market) (Start walking and see)

wards stabilization, including (for higher concentrations) pathways in which emission constraints are deferred by periods of years to decades (Houghton *et al.*, 1996). A paper by Wigley *et al.* (1996, hereafter the WRE paper) presents this carbon cycle modelling analysis, and has attracted widespread attention for its suggestion that pathways in which abatement is deferred would be economically preferable.[2] This was justified in part by reference to economic modelling studies that used resource allocation/equilibrium models, which are discussed below.

The WRE paper states that four main reasons justify the belief that deferring CO_2 emissions abatement may be economically preferable: technical progress; capital stock considerations; positive marginal product of capital (discounting); and greater absorption of CO_2 emissions emitted earlier. This paper explores the economic issues surrounding the optimal timing of CO_2 constraints, structuring the issues similarly but setting each in a broader context, as follows.

This paper first explores technical change and emphasizes that it is part of a broader set of issues surrounding the availability and evolution of energy technologies and systems and the way in which such systems respond to different inducements or pressures. I show that assumptions concerning these processes, many of which fall outside the purview of global economic modelling studies, have a powerful impact on the timing problem.

Capital stock is similarly but one aspect of a broader set of issues surrounding the inertia of complex, interrelated and capital intensive systems such as energy. The analysis here emphasizes that capital stock investment and turnover are continuous processes and that inertia increases the costs of rapid action whether now or in the future. The appropriate trade-offs and implications for timing being determined by the characteristic timescales involved and tentative modelling are presented to give some insight into this.

I then turn to consider the limitations of analysis framed in terms of optimal trajectories towards pre-set stabilization goals, emphasizing that the whole exercise must be set in a framework of uncertainty and learning and demonstrating that recognizing this can have radical implications for the issues of optimal timing.

This in turn highlights the limitations of focusing solely upon long-term stabilization as an external constraint. I therefore extend the discussion to include more explitly issues of climate impacts including rates of change and illustrates that such impacts need to be considered explicitly to give a balanced insight into the influence of discounting and the carbon cycle upon optimal emission trajectories.

Finally, a note on economic modelling is presented and the strength and weaknesses of the different modelling approaches so far employed. Conclusions then seek to bring together the insights of the analysis.

Technical change

Technical change is key to finding low-cost solutions to the climate problem. Given the combined pressures of population and economic growth, the radical relative reductions in CO_2 emissions that would be required to stabilization the atmosphere in the next century can only be achieve at low cost if technologies for much greater efficiency and carbon-free supplies can be improved substantially.

Technical change can have an important influence on issues of timing abatement. If technical change acts to make abatement cheaper in the future, then *ceteris paribus* it would apparently be cheaper to wait until such cost reductions occur before embarking upon much abatement. It is indeed clear that widespread and premature deployment of technologies that are inadequately developed and whose costs will decline, may well be more costly than deferring such deployment and for little benefit.

Overall however the issue of technical change is much more complex than this suggests and four kinds of issues need to be clarified.

The continuum of abatement options

The first is that there are a wide range of options and technologies for limiting emissions, at varying cost levels and with different prospects for cost reductions. Even when we have exhausted 'no regrets' options that can be implemented at no costs, there are a wide range of options, including many cheap ones such as incremental improvements in building insulation, car and appliance efficiency etc.[3] The IPCC s Working Group II report details a huge range of such options.

An economic representation of this is illustrated in Figures 1–3, which shows an estimate of the 'abatement cost curve' for CO_2 reductions derived by Nordhaus from a number of (mostly top-down) studies (Nordhaus, 1991). Clearly even after all 'negative cost' options have been utilized, some additional reductions can be achieved at very modest costs, as one would expect; with a fixed cost curve, the cost then rises steadily as greater reductions are sought.

Over time, technology development can be expected to lower technology costs and thus move the curve to the right. The argument that technology development will reduce abatement costs in the future appears to have been interpreted as an argument for deferring emissions abatement in general, i.e. waiting at the origin while governments pursue sufficient new R&D and then moving rapidly to exploit a wide range of technologies once there has been 'enough' (in some unspecified sense) development. It may be characterized as a 'do R&D, then sprint' approach.

---

[2]See Wigley *et al.* (1996). Tom Wigley, the lead author of the WRE paper, has objected to economic critiques of the WRE paper on the grounds that it is primarily a scientific paper and contains no economic modelling. This paper refers the WRE analysis in this context only because the paper does contain central economic assertions and it is these that have received considerable policy and political attention, and these assertions do unfortunately downplay or neglect many of the issues addressed in this paper, as do the modelling studies to which the WRE paper refers in its brief economic discussion. Some of the countervailing issues are indeed noted later in the WRE paper as caveats requiring further consideration, which this paper seeks to provide.

[3]The extent of negative-cost and low-cost options is actually a very important question in the context of the WRE paper, since its conclusions are claimed to be policy relevant and are stated in terms of near-term emission levels. Some studies claim that most OECD countries could at least stabilize emissions in the near term by implementing such low-cost measures; the Working Group II report of the IPCC's Second Assessment Report lists a plethora of such options.

Alternatively, one could move steadily along the curve but remain in the region of fairly low (but non-zero) abatement costs. If and as technology development shifts the curve to the right, more options will become available at modest cost (if we find that we are starting to climb too far up the cost curve, so that it is getting expensive, then it should always be possible to ease off while development continues). This could be termed a steady walk approach and it is not obvious that it involves much higher costs than waiting – depending upon how ambitiously one moves up the curve.

Induced technology development

The above discussion assumes that all technological development occurs independently of emission abatement efforts. This reflects an idea of technology development as an exogenous process – the idea that technology development occurs independently of market conditions. This would apply, for example, to the extent that technology development represents an automatic accumulation of knowledge, or is fostered primarily by government R&D.

In fact, the idea that new technologies develop autonomously, or arise primarily because governments pay to develop them, is an idea that economists who work on technology issues abandoned decades ago. More than thirty years ago, Arrow (1962) noted that much knowledge is acquired through learning by doing and explored the economic consequences of this; see also some of the reviews in Dasgupta and Stoneman (1987). Government R&D can help but most effective technology development and dissemination is done by the private sector in the pursuit of markets. In other words, much technology development is induced by market circumstances – market experience leads to cost reductions and expectations about future market opportunities determine how industries deploy their R&D efforts.

This is not surprising, since in fact corporate R&D swamps that by governments in most countries. The energy sector in the 1980s provided powerful examples of the fact that technology development depends powerfully upon market conditions. The cost of offshore oil platforms fell greatly as companies sought to keep operations economic in the face of declining oil prices. The costs of wind energy fell threefold over the 1980s as an artificial market was created in California and then steadily tightened, and has continued to do so as supports have shifted to European markets. Even gas turbine/combined cycle stations started their major developments as natural gas and electricity system conditions emerged to make a market available (for a detailed account of some of these developments see Grubb and Walker, 1992).

In these circumstances, it is in steering the markets that governments may have the biggest impact on technology development (though government R&D can also play an important role for technologies still in an early stage of development). This can also be illustrated with reference to Figure 3. Induced technology development implies that the act of moving steadily along the curve helps to push the

curve further to the right. In other words, abatement efforts generate market opportunities, cash flows and expectations that enable industries to orient their efforts and learning in the direction of lower carbon technologies. Hence, on this model, action itself generates cheaper technological options arising out of accumulating experience.[4] In this case, deferring emission reductions simply delays or slows down the generation of options that can address the problem at low cost.

Therefore, conclusions about how technology development affects optimal timing hinges critically upon the assumptions made about how technology develops. The evidence suggests that an important role needs to be accorded to the potential for inducing technology development through actions that affect energy markets. Various policies can affect energy markets and provide appropriate stimuli, but abatement itself is probably the most direct and broad-ranging. Notably, policies that act to constrain CO_2 emissions will tend to create incentives in energy markets to turn the bulk of corporate energy R&D away from improving fossil fuel technologies towards developing and deploying lower carbon technologies.

Technology clustering and lock-in

A third important issue in technology development is that of clustering, and related effects of 'lock-in and 'lock-out . Studies of the economics of technology development have demonstrated that technological development tends to be strongly biased towards existing modes (see for example Nakicenovic and Grubler, 1991). Industries that have a large market share in any particular technology can spend large R&D and other resources trying to make incremental improvements to those technologies to protect their existing position, and try in various ways to discourage the emergence of new options with which small competitors might threaten their pre-eminence.

Furthermore, no industry exists in isolation but is, rather, part of a very extensive network, dependent upon infrastructure, supplier relationships and consumer outlets, as well as interrelated technologies. Consequently, technological trends have an evolutionary character, with interrelated lines of development and deployment. On the grand scale, 'Kondriatev waves' of interrelated technological developments (such as the internal combustion engine combined with petroleum extraction and refining technologies and distributional infrastructure) have been proposed. On a smaller scale, a whole disciplinary approach of morphological analysis has been developed to explore the interrated evolution of particular technological strands (e.g. with de-

---

[4]Note that one objection that has been raised to this is the fact that stimulating innovation in one sector (e.g., energy) may reduce innovation in another sector, so that there is no 'free lunch'. In fact, the evidence for this is rather slim; it is not all obvious that challenges in one sector do in general cause them to draw 'innovation resources' from elsewhere, though the possibility deserves further empirical study. However, the broader argument about the implications of adaptability does not hinge upon this issue; it simply asserts that the ability to innovate and develop alternate systems gives us some freedom in how to orient developments in our economic systems with respect to environmental impacts.

tailed studies of ferrous metal technologies) (Nakicenovic and Grubler, 1991).

Such factors give rise to phenomena of technological 'lock-in' and 'lock-out'. For example, as the steam turbine began to dominate electricity supply, R&D expenditure became focused upon making marginal improvements in their performance. Conversely, the technology of refrigeration using hydrocarbons that developed in Central Europe in the 1930s withered as CFC refrigeration developed, and has only very recently been revived, with little intervening development until the pressure of the CFC phaseout.

Because of such phenomena, it can be very difficult for new technologies to be adequately developed and brought into the market quickly. Thus, establishing market share takes time and appears to be a very important prerequisite for adequate technological development, because such development depends on cumulative corporate R&D and the parallel evolution of a series of interrelated industries.

On all three counts therefore – tehnology availability, technology development processes and technology clustering – understanding the economics of technology evolution is extremely important to climate change policy. A rounded understanding suggests strongly that developing markets for low carbon options, for example by emission reduction programmes, is a very important part of fostering the developments required to achieve low cost, long term reductions.

Adaptability in energy systems

Put together, these various features of induced technology development, technology clustering etc. form a basis for expecting that energy systems are to an important degree adaptable – over time, they can and have developed to accommodate various constraints. This is hardly surprising given the issues set out above and this evidence is complemented by analyses of responses to the oil shocks (e.g. in Japan) and by international comparisons that show just how different energy systems can be, as summarized in Grubb *et al.* (1995).

In that paper we show that if appropriate technology and systems development is indeed induced by emission constraints, it stands the argument about waiting for cost reductions on its head. Rather it becomes optimal to act earlier with steady pressure, so as to stimulate the necessary technological and systemic developments. This is hardly surprising; it is all indication that complex technological systems evolve, but that they may need significant pressures to evolve in different directions, for example in the direction of minimising particular external environmental impacts that have previously not affected corporate investment and R&D decisions.

Similar insights are developed in an analysis by Hourcade (1993), who discusses the 'flexibility' of the French energy economy in terms of different development paths. His study models explicitly the role of policy in accelerating paper technology diffusion and develops scenarios that differ widely in CO₂ emission but not long-run costs.

The World Energy Council also offers insight on such issues and their implications; one of the Recommendations of the Tokyo World Energy Congress Statement urges 'governments, business decision-makers and energy consumers' to 'start taking action now to adapt to the needs of our long term future ... the next two or three decades represent the key period of opportunity for a transition to a more sustainable path of development for the long term. Research done and action taken now will begin the shift of direction required of 'minimum regrets' action' (World Energy Council, 1995).

To explore the implications further however we first need to consider another aspect of energy systems, namely investment cycles and inertia.

Capital stock turnover and inertia

Capital stock turnover

The fact that 'time is needed to reoptimize the capital stock' has been advanced as a second reason for deferring abatement. Certainly, a major change takes time, if it is to be done without high cost. But capital stock is continually being restructured, as existing stock is refurbished or retired and new stock is created to replace this as well as to meet demand growth or changes in demand structure.[5] New capital investment is thus continually occurring.

A key to economically efficient abatement is thus to seek to make new capital stock less carbon intensive than it otherwise would be. This, obviously, involves a steady departure of emissions from the 'business as usual' trajectory, starting as soon as climate change is recognized to be a potentially serious problem (a point that may reasonably be identified with the publication of the IPCC's First Assessment Report in 1990).

The economic importance of getting this right is itself apparent from the scenarios in the WRE paper. For stabilization at 550 ppm of CO₂, their 'deferred abatement' case shows the new pathway as involving emissions rising over the next 40 years from the current level of just under 7 GtC pa to a peak about 4 GtC pa higher, before dropping by about 2 GtC pa over the subsequent 40 years (and even faster thereafter). Thus the delay scenario involves constructing an additional 4 GtC pa of capital stock over and above that anyway required for replacement. In total, WRE's central deferred scenario thus means investing in at least as much new CO₂ based capital stock over the next few decades as is embodied in the world's entire energy systems today. Then to meet their target, the additional stock must be replaced by carbon free sources over the subsequent decades.

This highlights that capital stock is continually being created and replaced. Altering such new investments may be an opportunity for relatively low-cost abatement efforts.

---

[5]Frequently the oldest capital stock is also the least efficient, with rising maintenance costs. The net costs of retiring such stock rather than refurbishing it for a longer (polluting) life may be small and may indeed result in net gain when other factors are considered. When the costs are finely balanced the economic issues are similar to those involved in new investment to meet demand growth.

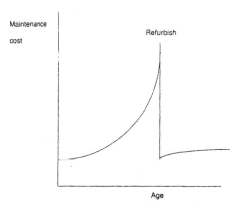

Figure 4 Timing of refurbishment decision

Lowering the carbon intensity of new investments implies a steady departure of emissions from business-as-usual trends. Furthermore, this is not simply a matter of new investments and replacement of existing stock at the end of its 'lifetime'. Aging capital stock generally incurs rising maintenance costs, and the relevant decision is when to undertake investment to avoid this (Figure 4): either retiring the plant or undertaking major refurbishment. Particularly concerning old and relatively inefficient coal-fired power stations that are common in many industrialized coutnries, climate change should influence the decision towards earlier retirement or conversion to gas-fired plant – again implying a continuous departure of emissions from the business-as-usual trends.

Especially when coupled with uncertainties about the actual objective (see below), this has powerful industrial implications. Inappropriate delay in constraining emissions is not in the interests of industry, but is against it. It increases the exposure of industry to the risk that new, carbon-intensive investments will have to be prematurely retired, at large cost and dislocation compared with the costs of avoiding such investments in the first place (e.g. coal power plants or mines left 'stranded', or frontier oil exploration and development left without sufficient high price markets when they mature).

The World Energy Council, in the conclusions to the Tokyo World Energy Congress (WEC, 1995), recognized this in stating that 'action postponed will be opportunity lost, guaranteeing that when action can no longer be avoided the ensuing costs will be higher; dislocations more severe; and the effects much less predictable, than if appropriate actions are taken today'.

Inertia

Since scenarios that defer action to limit greenhouse gas emissions generally imply more rapid subsequent abatement (if the same ultimate goal is to be achieved), adequate understanding of inertia in energy systems is essential to analysing timing issues.

The existing structure of capital stock in energy producing sectors, discussed above, is one source of inertia. However, such 'first order capital stock issues – the structure of power generation facilities, petroleum refineries etc – represents only a component of the issue. Considering only these first-order components appears to suggest that most of the stock has a lifetime of 30–40 years, suggesting possibilities for almost complete transitions over such a period at low cost, if adequate alternatives are available.

In fact the situation is far more complex. Some causes of CO₂ emissions lie in even more fixed structures such as poor building construction, urban sprawl etc. Thus town planning today, for example, could have implications for abatement potential and costs at the end of the next century.

The discussion above points to deeper sources of inertia. Further emissions growth involves expansion of a huge complex of interdependent infrastructure and industries dependent ultimately upon emitting CO₂. Certain transport and urban developments – infrastructure that may substantively last throughout the next century – carry with them a whole structure of personal and business location consequences; upon which the infrastructure in turn comes to depend. Coal fired power stations carry with them a complex network of delivery systems, usually stretching back through rail and/or port facilities right back to the decisions and investment surrounding coal mines for the next century. The costs of escaping from such interdependent systems rapidly is likely to be far higher than more gradual, steady transitions and avoiding such construction in the first place (to the extent that adequate alternatives are available) is likely to be cheaper still.

This obviously relates to the phenomena of technology clustering, lock-in and lock-out discussed above. Established industries invest to protect their comparative advantage and draw upon clusters of technologies surrounding them. New entrants and even fundamental shifts are of course possible – but they take a long time to evolve and be deployed on a large scale. Hourcade's study develops the concept more explicitly with reference to European transport in terms of 'bifurcations' – different paths that, once followed, are costly to escape from (Hourcade, 1993).

The issue is thus far deeper than one of just understanding capital stock replacement. It involves basic questions about the inertia in socio-economic and political systems. Scenarios that involve a period of substantial emissions growth followed by rapid changes in trajectory towards reductions could involve economic dislocation far beyond issues of capital stock. Labour forces trained for carbon intensive operations would have to be made redundant and/or retrained, the network of industries based around growing fossil fuel consumption and carbon based infrastructure would have to be thrown into reverse, reformed and remodeled etc. Each new investment in carbon intensive stock may make the transition towards a low carbon system that little bit more difficult and slower.

Inertia also relates closely to questions of uncertainty and precaution. This is discussed more fully below, but Figure 5 highlights the need to think carefully about the inertia

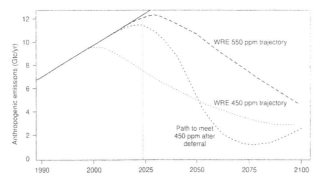

Figure 5 Potential impact of deferring emissions abatement given uncertain stabilization target

of the system. It sketches the changes that would be required if we were to follow until 2020 the 'deferred abatement trajectory set out in the WRE paper for a 550 ppm limit, but then find that we have to stay within a 450 ppm limit.[6] Within the space of 30 years, we would then have to dismantle or transform more than two thirds of the world s carbon based infrastructure – more carbon intensive stock than exists in the whole of the world s energy systems today.[7] It would furthermore require not only faster, but much deeper action – car free cities, for example, rather than the low emission, high efficiency vehicles that might be consistent with a smoother abatement trajectory.

Implications of inertia for abatement paths and the cost of delay

A full systems analysis of the costs of having to make such relatively abrupt and deep changes has yet to be done. But general insights into the influence of inertia on optimal trajectories and abatement efforts can be explored using the DIAM model (Chapuis *et al.*, 1997), adapted to analyse explicitly the influence of inertia on optimal pathways under a

stabilization constraint, as summarized in the appendix and applied more fully elsewhere (HaDuong *et al.*, 1997).

Abatement costs in the model depend upon both the degree of abatement (departure from reference case) and the rate of abatement (being quadratic in both).

By introducing a term that depends on the *rate* of abatement, the model captures inertia in the system. For determining optimal pathways and relative costs under a stabilization constraint, only the ratio c_h/c_a needs to be specified, not the absolute values. Its square root $T_c = (c_h/c_a)^{1/2}$ is a duration that we can interpret as the 'characteristic time' for changes in the global energy system. If we interpret T_c as the exponential half life time of equipment, then it is related to the annual depreciation rate of capital δ by $T_c = (\ln 2)/\delta$.

What timescales might be appropriate? In reality, energy systems are characterized by a mix of capital stock of varying lifetime and many other sources of inertia. Some components have a stock life of only a few years, but the majority of energy related investment is in manufacturing plant (typical lifetime 10–30 years), power stations (30–50 years), building stock (lifetime 20–200 years) and transport/urban planning infrastructure (40–200 years). Other sources of inertia include the timescale for new sources to develop and penetrate substantially; it has for exemple been shown that new energy sources can take 50 years to penetrate from 1% to 50% of their ultimate potential (Andere *et al.*, 1991). As a central value we take T_c = 50 years.

Figure 6 shows that given this, for a stabilization limit of 550 ppm CO_2 – which even on a 'business as usual' trajectory would not be reached until towards the end of the next century – expenditure on the optimal trajectory only starts to rise significantly in the second quarter of the next century and the cost of deferring action until 2020 is slight. For a ceiling of 450 ppm, however, which would otherwise be reached in the second quarter of the next century, significant expenditure is already optimal and a sharp jump in expenditure is required after a delay to 2020 as the system has rapidly to change direction, with much higher overall costs.

[6]The 450 ppm and 550 ppm trajectories are estimated from the graphs in CURE, and the transition is estimated on the basis of equilibrating the areas of excess emissions against the later deficit, with some allowance for the greater absorption of the earlier emissions. The IMAGE model, which contains a full carbon cycle model, has been applied to consider different trajectories of stabilisation at 450 ppm. Results indicate that delaying abatement until 2025 would then require rather more drastic subsequent abatement than is depicted in Figure 5: the concentration unavoidably overshoots 450 ppm and emissions in their projections go below zero in the period 2075–2100 in order to try and bring concentrations back towards 450 ppm (Alcamo, 1996). Thus, Figure 5 may understate the degree of reduction required after a delay to stay within such a limit.
[7]Quite apart from the economic and social costs of waiting and then forcing a rapid transition, in reality it is doubtful whether governments, after putting off action for another couple of decades, could or would impose such drastic changes of direction. This in turn is a reflection of the high welfare costs associated with rapid contractions in any given industry, probably much greater than measured in GDP terms. The political feasibility of such scenarios is thus doubtful; starting off on such a trajectory in reality would probably not deliver the objective claimed.

166 *Technologies, energy systems and CO_2 emissions abatement: M. Grubb*

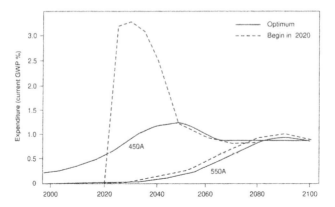

Figure 6 Expenditure over time for stabilization of CO_2 concentratios at 450 and 550 ppm, with (dashed) lines and without (solid lines) abatement deferred until 2020.[a]

[a]Unit is percentage of 1990 world gross product, calibrated so that the total cost is comparable to that in Nordhaus (1993). However, the relative shape of emission and expenditure paths are independent of the scale of the abatement costs.

This reflects behaviour that should be obvious, but which appears to have been neglected in the analytic debate to date. Stripped of other considerations, we can with little cost defer abatement action until we get to within a certain distance from the date at which the stabilization ceiling would be breached on a 'business as usual' trajectory. Expenditure then needs to rise steadily, to force the system to change direction. To put it simply, in a framework of aiming for a fixed stabilization ceiling, discounting ensures that most expenditure is deferred until it is rendered unavoidable by the inertial characteristics of the system. It follows also that conclusions about the merits and costs of deferring abatement in this framework depend heavily assumptions about the inertia of the system and a largely arbitrary selection of the stabilization ceiling. Note that different results would be obtained in a cost/benefit framework, in which emission reductions would incur an explicit benefit, or when uncertainty is considered (see below).

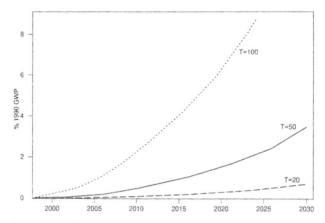

Figure 7 cost of deferring emissions abatement under 500 ppm limit[a]

[a]The figure shows the additional abatement expendiutre incurred, as a function of the time for which abatement is deferred. After the delay period, emission trajectories are optimized as before. Reults are shown for each of three 'characteristic times' of stock turnover analysed in Figure 1. The model does not represent induced technological development.

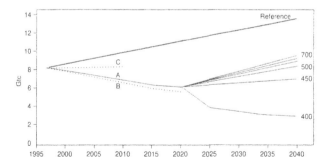

Figure 8 Optimal emssion paths when the stabilization constraint is stochastic[a]

[a]Objectives are specified according to the uncertainty structures specified in Table 1. The pathway minimizes the exected value of abatement expenditure, using dynamic programming under stochastic constraint. System characteristic response time $T = 50$ years in all cases. Optimal paths after resolution of uncertainty are shown only for case A.

Figure 7 shows how the inertia related cost of deferring action depends upon the length of deferral and the inertial timescale of the system, for a stabilization ceiling of 500 ppm CO_2. This level might otherwise be reached during the third quarter of the next century on 'business as usual' emissions growth and given the influences of other greenhouse gases it almost certainly corresponds to a change greater than the 'CO_2 equivalent doubling' benchmark used for most studies of the long-term impact of climate change. For the central inertial case ($T_c = 50$), the costs of deferring abatement beyond the early years of the next century start to rise steadily. In addition, we consider cases with $T_c = 20$ and 100 years respectively, to explore the impact of differing assumptions concerning the inertia of the system. The cost of deferral rises sharply as the inertia of the system is increased. Inertia is not a reason for deferring abatement, as many have claimed. It is precisely the opposite.

The impact of uncertain stabilization objectives

To consider the policy implications of such issues requires more careful consideration of the real policy challenge. Recent studies[8] have analysed the long-term objective of stabilizing atmospheric concentrations at a pre-specified level and discussed paths towards this objective as a fixed constraint. This may be an interesting exercise, but it is one that is only weakly related to the problem we face.

The real problem we face is characterized by concern about potential impacts of a highly uncertain nature and magnitude. The Climate Change Convention establishes an aim ultimately of stabilizing the atmosphere, but we do not know at what level it needs to be stabilized, or how the in-

terim impacts on climate change and consequent human impacts may be related to the rate at which the atmosphere changes (the Convention Objective also refers to rates of change). I consider the economic implications of stabilization uncertainties and physical impacts in turn.

A common misconception is that by analysing a number of different scenarios, we have analysed uncertainty. This is not the case at all. We are not in a position to choose an appropriate stabilization objective, indeed it would be highly irrational to choose a single objective and stick with it for the next 100 years without reference to what we learn. It would also be contrary to the Convention, which emphasizes the need to adjust policy in the light of accumulating knowledge. We have to develop policy in the full recognition of uncertainties and the expectation of learning more.

This brings the question of inertia to the fore even more. If we delay action in the belief that we are aiming at a 500 ppm target, for example, then after a couple of decades it may simply be too late to be able to stabilize at 400 ppm however urgent the problem then turns out to be; and as illustrated above even stabilization at 450 ppm might by then involve radical changes of direction that could prove economically very disruptive.

Of course the issue of uncertainty cuts both ways. If we act on the assumption of aiming at a lower level, but after a while conclude that we can safely go to higher levels, conversely we may have incurred more costs than needed. But the costs of excessive caution against excessive optimism may be highly asymmetric (within limits). Steady sustained pressure to limit emissions cannot expose us either economically or environmentally to the scale of risks that may be incurred by a long delay, if there is a real possibility that a low stabilization level may prove necessary. The risk of over reacting – excessive abatement – seems comparable only if we embark upon drastic and very costly abatement programmes that later prove unnecessary.

[8]See Houghton *et al.* (1996) and note 2, see also the section on economic modelling which follows in this paper.

Table 1 Probability distributions and resolution date for the stabilization constraint (%)

	Resolution date	Mean	400	450	500	550	600	650	700
A	2020	550	2.5	10	20	35	20	10	2.5
B	2020	500	10	20	40	20	10	0	0
C	2010	550	2.5	10	20	35	20	10	2.5

The fundamental importance uncertainty in this regard is illustrated in Figure 8, which shows results from running the DIAM model in the following way. The stabilization limit is expressed stochastically i.e. as a range of possible outcomes. The central case (case A in Table 1) assumes that the most probable outcome, and the mean of the whole distribution, is a requirement to stay within a 550 ppm limit, roughly equivalent to doubling pre-industrial CO_2 concentrations neglecting the additional impact of other gases. But this constraint is not certain: the possible range spans from 400–700 ppm. The extremes only have a 2.5% (1 in 40) probability, but as illustrated by the results in Figure 8 the lower levels have a huge influence on the optimal path. The costs of ignoring such a possibility and then being forced into drastic action are so high that it proves economically more prudent to bring down global emissions more steadily until uncertainties are resolved.

The sensitivity studies using different assumptions summarized in Table 1, show that adopting different assumptions in terms of the mean outcome (case B) has little influence: it is the possibility of low levels being required, combined with the inertia in the system, that drives the strongly precautionary approach. What does enable a somewhat more relaxed strategy is earlier resolution of the uncertainties, as illustrated by case C.

Obviously the specific results are sensitive to the assumptions, particularly those relating to the lower possible stabilization levels, the timescale over which the uncertainties are resolved and the inertia of the system. But the qualitative insight appears undeniable and again we find that economic reality turns popular perception on its head. In systems with high inertia, uncertainty is not a reason for delay, but quite the opposite. The best initial path is a complex balance of such risks but an appropriate balance clearly does not involve following 'business and usual' emissions while waiting for evidence to accumulate.

Limitations of stabilization analysis: impact costs, time preferences and the rate of atmospheric change

One important objection to the above approach is that it is unrealistic to suppose that the stabilization constraint is really a hard constraint. In the real world, if we carried on with current emission trends and then discovered the climate problem to be more serious than previously envisaged, there would still be limits to the degree of abatement costs and rates of abatement that would be considered acceptable. At this point we recognize that abatement strategy is bound at some level to reflect judgement about the costs

or risks that cannot be captured only in terms of a stabilization constraint.

Thus a reasonable appraisal of the economic issues involved in timing emissions abatement ultimately cannot avoid the need to consider the actual impacts of climate change. These are of course fraught with uncertainty. However, several qualitative considerations indicate that considering impact costs leads to different time profiles than optimization under a fixed (or perhaps even a stochastic) stabilization constraint.

First is a very simple observation. Assuming that less extensive changes to the atmosphere involve lower adverse impacts, early action carries a benefit associated with enabling lower stabilization levels to be achieved. Analysis of fixed pathways under a stabilization constraint – in which there is zero benefit to doing better than the specified constraint – does not reflect this.

Second, consideration of the damages expected from climate change, whether they are large or small, brings a new element into consideration of time discounting. The argument that discounting makes it cheaper to defer the costs of abatement applies conversely to impacts: avoiding damages earlier also has a greater present economic value. Deferring emissions abatement defers abatement costs, but it brings impact costs nearer. So even neglecting all other considerations, the implications of time discounting for the overall policy problem are not as clear cut as is implied in studies that consider only the question of stabilization without reference to damages.

In physical terms the time paths of impacts may be expected to differ according to the time path of emissions (as the WRE paper is careful to note; it presents calculations of how global average temperature and sea level change varies between scenarios). One particular feature of this is however worth highlighting. One proxy index of climate change impacts may be the rate at which radiative forcing in the atmosphere (which ultimately drives average temperature) changes.[9] The question of rates of change may be particularly important given the tendency of some complex systems to become more unstable when subject to high rates of change; and given the inertia of human societies. Thus more rapid radiative and temperature change seems likely to bring more rapid, and perhaps more volatile, climatic change; and human societies are likely to have greater difficulty in adapting to such changes than if they occurred more slowly and smoothly.

---

[9]Note that the rate of radiative change has no direct impacts in itself, but represents a driving force that emerges as subsequent temperature and other changes.

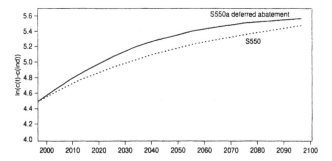

Figure 9 Impact of derferred abatement on radiative change[a]

[a]The figure compares the radiative forcing associated with CO_2 emissions (as indexed by the log of CO_2 concentration relative to pre-industrial concentrations) in the IPCC 550 ppm stabilization profile against the profile arising from the WRE secnario with abatement delayed until 2010 (550a). Although they converge on the same concentration, the average rate of change in the first 50 years of the next century is about 30% higher for the case with delayed abatement.

Source: Wigley and Schimel (1993).

Because the radiative impact of CO_2 is approximately logarithmic with concentration, the rate of radiative change in most scenarios is greatest at present and in the near future. Figure 9 shows how deferring abatement until 2010 and following the WRE 550a (deferred) trajectory, greatly extends the period of high rates of radiative change from CO_2, as compared with the original IPCC stabilization trajectory in which abatement begins in 1990.[10] Averaged over the period 2000–50, the average rate of change is about 30% higher than in the IPCC trajectory for the same ultimate stabilization limit.

This is reflected in projections of temperature change. The WRE paper shows that deferring emissions abatement implies a more rapid temperature change through the middle of the next century and then a rather abrupt transition as the stabilization ceiling is approached. For their central case, averaged over the next 50 years, the rate of temperature change appears to be more than 20% higher than is the case without deferral of emissions abatement.

The Dutch IMAGE model has also been used to explore the implications of deferred abatement under a 450 ppm ceiling. Compared to the original IPCC scenario for stabilization at 450 ppm, the scenario in which abatement is delayed until 2025 (followed by rapid reductions) leads to a 40% higher rate of global average temperature change over the first half of the next century and a higher overall peak

temperature later in the century. Other indicators that are substantially affected througout the next century by delayed action include maize yields and natural vegetation change (Alcamo, 1996).

We do not know the extent to which the physical and human impacts of climate change depend upon the rate of radiative and temperature change, but it is clearly something that needs to be factored into consideration of emission paths and deserves further analysis urgently.

A brief note on economic modelling

The discussion so far has not discussed specific results from the major economic models that have been used to underpin claims about the economic desirability of deferring abatement. The WRE paper cites results from Manne and Richels (1995) (MERGE model), Richels and Edmonds (1995) (Edmonds and Reilly model) and Kosubud *et al.* (1994) (Argonne National Lab). The models involved are all general equilibrium models, like the OECD GREEN model and the Australian MEGABARE model. In their results, costs are indeed minimized by pathways that involve little or no abatement for years or decades (depending on the target set).

The strength of such models is their ability to model the theoretically optimal allocation of resources at a given point in time, given assumptions about the resources available, technology costs and various constraints. Unfortunately such a framework is very weak in both the dimensions of inertia and technology development discussed above – the key dimensions required for analysis of technological and systems aspects of the timing issue. Most such models do reflect capital stock turnover, but only first-order issues of energy production stock; they do not contain

[10]If emissions are assumed to have been growing steadily and continue to do so, then the rate of radiative change would already be declining from its peak. Given a more realistic representation of CO_2 emissions over the past 20 years (i.e. the very slow growth in global emissions following the oil shocks, followed by large reductions in the CEITs), but with resumed global growth from the mid-1990s, the rate of radiative change may approach its maximum in the coming years and delaying abatement would increase the maximum rate of change as well as extending it.

170 *Technologies, energy systems and CO_2 emissions abatement: M. Grubb*

Table 2 Balancing the economic issues

Issue	Favouring deferral	Favouring early abatement
Technology development	Exogenous technical change implies cheaper to focus on R&D and wait for improvements	Low cost measures may have substantial impact on trajectories Endogenous (market induced) change will accelerate development of low-cost solutions Clustering effects highlight importance of getting on lower emission trajectories
Capital stock and inertia	Deferral avoids action now that could (if rapid enough) force premature retirement/disutilization of current stock	Exploit natural stock turnover by influencing new investments Reduces maximum rate of reduction and associated transitional scrapping and disequilibria Reduces risk from uncertainties in stabilization constraint and hence risk of being forced into very rapid changes
Discounting	Reduces the present value of abatement costs	Reduces impacts and (*ceteris paribus*) reudces their present value
Carbon cycle and radiative change	More early emissons absorbed, thus enabling higher total carbon emissions under a given stabilization constraint	Reduces high rates of radiative and termperature change over coming decades (except for sources with high aerosol emissions) Enables lower stabilization levels to be achieved

representation of energy-consuming stock such as building or road infrastructure, nor do they capture linkages between different parts of the supply system (such as mines, ports and power stations). Because they assume that the economy is in a state of full, equilibrium resource allocation, and do not model the inertia associated with interdependence among different economic sectors, they only capture a fraction of the full costs associated with imposing rapid changes. Attempts by the author to mimic the dynamic behaviour of MERGE using the DIAM model suggests that its results correspond to an inertial time constant T_c, as defined above, well under 20 years. Such rates of response defy credibility.

The modelling of capital stock in MERGE appears to be no less sophisticated than most other general equilibrium models, and in many respects is probably more so. In short such models do not, and cannot in any of their current incarnations, capture the full inertia of energy systems or of new investments. Thus they simply do not provide realistic insight into the full economic and welfare costs of making more rapid changes of direction and steeper abatement after a period of delay.

In addition, these models all assume that technology development is exogenous, i.e. the costs of different options, and the rate of cost reductions, are external to the market conditions assumed in the model. None of the models cited embody mechanisms by which emission constraints can stimulate corporate R&D, learning by doing, or other behaviour that may reduce the costs of lower carbon technology; nor do they capture issues of technology clustering or wider adaptative responses.

Consequently, the economic modelling studies which have been widely referred to in the context of justifying delays in emissions abatement cannot be considered to give reliable insight into the timing issue. And, as noted above, most of these studies focus on the question of time paths to fixed, pre-set stabilization constraint, which for the reasons discussed above is only weakly related to the actual policy problem.

Other studies, using different approaches, indicate just how much results can differ. Even neglecting issues of dynamics, cost–benefit studies indicate that some significant abatement action would be optimal now and that the appropriate level of control is increased when uncertainty is taken into account. Nordhaus (1991, 1995) estimates modest initial control, Cline (1992) calls for stronger action, but neither suggests it is optimal to defer action and both recognize that the appropriate level of control is increased when uncertainty is taken into account (Nordhaus, 1995; Cline, 1992). Grubb et al. (1995) extend such frameworks and show that if the energy system has high inertia but is in the long run highly adaptive, then the costs of delaying abatement may be many times higher than when these factors are ignored or assumed to be negligible.

More recently, the Dutch RIVM group have introduced a model which focuses explicitly on issues of technology development and diffusion, including induced technical change, and the inertia of energy systems (de Vries and Janssen, 1996). As would be expected from the discussion in this paper, their results do differ radically from those of general equilibrium models. They conclude that even under a relatively relaxed 550 ppm target, delay leads to higher costs and that 'the delayed response strategy of 'wait and see' is probably a risky one'. Early emission reduction measures 'are found to be efficient because they not only stimulate alternatives but also stimulate price-induced [and long-lasting] energy conservation investments'.

Conclusions

The discussion in this paper highlights many issues that need to be considered in addressing the optimal timing of CO_2 emission limitations.

The analysis of energy technology and systems issues illustrates their complexity. The fact that energy technology development may make large emission reductions cheaper in the future needs to be assessed against other factors: the diversity of options currently available; the fact that such technology development may actually be induced by abatement action; and the interacting nature of technology and systems development. To the extent that energy systems have a broader capacity to adapt given time, all this implies that countervailing economic benefits may flow from earlier action.

Furthermore, energy systems are characterized by continuous slow stock turnover combined with tremendous inertia to rapid change. Incremental changes towards greater efficiency and lower carbon options in the course of stock replacement and expansion may consequently be much cheaper than continuing to construct new carbon intensive capital stock, since that that stock may be exposed to the risk of requiring more rapid reductions later on.

This assumes particular importance when the high uncertainties about the damages from climate change are recognized. The fact that we cannot know at present the concentration at which the atmosphere should be stabilized makes the question of inertia extremely important, because of the potentially very high industrial and economic costs if the initial response proves to be much too relaxed. Consideration of impacts, and particularly rates of change in the first half of the next century, highlights the need to consider the benefits that may come from earlier action, in terms of reducing rates of change, alongside considerations of aiming at a fixed stabilization ceiling.

These various economic issues are summarized in Table 2. Some favour deferral, some rapid action. Clearly, focusing only on the economic factors that favouring deferral leads one to the conclusion that this will be cheaper. Conversely, focusing only on the economic and other reasons for early action, without reference to the factors that could make rapid action now more expensive, will lead one to conclude that we should take rapid and perhaps drastic abatement action.

Economics is about making trade-offs. Neither of the above extremes represents a balanced approach, or a balanced conclusion. The problem requires serious analysis of many complex dimensions, but I would suggest that it should be possible for most analysts to agree on the following minimal conclusions.

(1) Economic issues surrounding the optimal timing of greenhouse gas emissions abatement are complex, with some factors favouring deferral and others favouring strong early reductions in emissions.

(2) Questions of technology and systems availability and development are very important, and must recognize the wide spectrum of technologies both currently and potentially available and the spectrum of processes by which such technologies may be developed and incorporated in energy systems.

(3) In an equilibrium framework, considering only exogenous technology development and first-order capital

stock turnover under a pre-set stabilization constraint (as in most models) favours deferring emission reductions. Focusing only on an opposite mix of issues favours rapid and drastic abatement. Neither represents a balanced assessment of the policy problem.

(4) A balanced assessment would recommend avoiding large-scale deployment of technologies that are immature and costly, but would favour steady abatement efforts to exploit at least low cost measures, to deter new carbon intensive investments (including major refurbishments), and to stimulate development and diffusion of lower carbon technologies, practices and infrastructure through market incentives as well as government R&D.

Thus given acceptance of the basic climate problem, from any credible economic perspective some abatement action is justified now.[11] The question of just how much will doubtless be a topic of modelling wars for many years to come. For to go much beyond the general conclusions set out here, much more research and model application of technology and systems development and deployment processes, in a context of high uncertainty, among other things, is required.

Acknowledgements

This paper is based upon a presentation first prepared for a workshop organized and hosted by the Centre for Global Change at Maryland Workshop. I am grateful to Irvin Mintzer and others at the centre for the invitation to participate, and to all at the workshop for stimulating discussion. The underlying analysis was stimulated by the claims in the WRE paper and associated debates in the IPCC Working Group III and I am indebted to the WRE authors for this provocation, particularly Richard Richels who has responded thoughtfully to the various criticisms raised. I am indebted to my co-authors in developing and applying the DIAM model: Minh Ha Duong, Jean-Charles Hourcade, and Thierry Chapuis, for their key role in developing the model and the associated ideas and results shown in Figures 6–8. Finally, I am indebted to Jane Chapman for preparing the other diagrams, and to her, Matthew Tickle and all others at RIIA's Energy and Environmental Programme who have borne well the excessive distraction and strains of addressing this issue fully as a side activity from my main responsibilities at the Institute.

References

Alcamo, J. (1996) Results presented at 3rd International Workshop on the IMAGE 2 Model. Delft, The Netherlands. 15–16 February.

Andere, J., Haefele, W., Nakicenovic, N. and McDonald, A. (1991). *Energy in a Finite World*. Ballinger, Cambridge, MA

Arrow, K. J. (1962). The economic implications of learning-by-doing. *Review of Economic Studies* 29 155–173.

Chapuis, T., HaDuong, M. and Grubb, M. (1997). DIAM: a model for studying the dynamics of inertia and adaptability in the climate change issue. Submitted to *Energy Economics*.

Cline, W. R. (1992). *The Economics of Global Warming*. Institute for International Economics, Washington, DC.

[11]Strictly, the only condition that appears to be required is the assumption that higher rates and degrees of atmospheric change increase the risk of adverse impacts.

Dasgupta, P. and Stoneman. P. (1987). *Economic Policy and Technological Performance* Cambridge University Press

Grubb, M and Walker. J (1992) *Emerging Energy Technologies: Impacts and Policy Implications.* Royal Institute of International Affairs. London

Grubb, M., Chapuis, T. and HaDuong, M. (1995). The economics of changing course. *Energy Policy* 23 (4) 1–14.

HaDuong, M., Grubb. M. and Hourcade, J. C. (1997). Optimal emission paths towards CO₂ stabilisation and the cost of deferring abatement: the influence of uncertainty and inertia. Submitted to *Nature*.

Houghton, J. T. *et al.* (eds) (1996). *Climate Change 1995.* Contribution of Working Group I to the Second Assessment Report of the Intergovernmental Panel on Climate Change, Cambridge University Press.

Hourcade, J. C. (1993). Modelling long-run scenarios: methodology lessons from a prospective study on a low CO₂ intensive country. *Energy Policy* 21 (3) 309.

Kosubud, R., Daly. T., South, D. and Quinn, K. (1994). Tradable cumulative CO₂ permits and global warming control. *The Energy Journal* 15 (2) 213–232.

Manne, A. and Richels, R. (1995). The grenhouse debate: economic efficiency. burden-sharing and hedging strategies. *The Energy Journal* 16 (4).

Nakicenovic, N. and Grubler, A. (eds) (1991). *Diffusion of Technologies and Social Behaviour* Springer-Verlag, Berlin/Heidelberg

Nordhaus, W. D. (1991) 'The cost of slowing climate change: a survey' *The Energy Journal* 12 (1) 37–65

Nordhaus, W. D. (1995). *Managing the Global Commons: The Economics of Climate Change.* MIT Press.

Richels, R. and Edmonds, J. (1995). The costs of stabilizing atmospheric CO₂ concentrations. *Energy Policy* 23 (4/5) 373–378.

de Vries, B. and Janssen. M. (1996). *Global Energy Futures: An Integrated Perspective with the TIME Model.* GLOBO report series No. 17, RIVM, Bilthoven

Wigley, T. (1993). Stabilisation of CO2 concentration levels. In Wigley, T. and Schimel. D. (eds), *The Global Carbon Cycle.* CUP.

Wigley, T., Richels. R. and Edmonds, J. (1996). Economic and environmental choices in the stabilization of atmospheric CO₂ concentrations. *Nature* 379 240–243.

World Energy Council (1995). *Energy for our Common World: What will the Future Ask of Us?* Conclusions and Recommendations of the 16th WEC Congress, Tokyo, London

Appendix

Development of the DIAM model for analysing inertia and optimal pathways under stabilization constraints

The results displayed in Figures 3, 4 and 5 of this paper are derived from the DIAM model, a numeric economic optimization model that is derived from the analytic framework set out in Grubb *et al.* (1995) and described fully in Chapuis *et al.* (1997). As compared with previous versions, the model used here is given an improved carbon cycle representation, we adapt the cost structure to clarify the role of inertia and to include autonomous technical improvements, and the benefits of reducing the CO₂ concentration are excluded: optimization is adapted specifically to analyse emission time-paths under a concentration ceiling, as follows. This version of the model and its results are described more fully in HaDuong *et al.* (1997).

CO₂ accumulation in the atmosphere is represented by including explicitly a carbon response function, derived from the Wigley carbon cycle model. Emissions in the absence of any abatement are based on the IPCC central reference scenario IS92a, but smoothed to avoid confusing short-term variations in the underlying growth rate to give a reference case with 2% pa linear growth in CO₂ emissions. We extend this linear trend up to 2100 and assume that this represents the optimum trajectory in the absence of constraints: there are no free emission reductions, all deviations from the reference are assumed to incur a cost. After 2100, reference emissions are constant for one century, they then decrease linearly to zero to 2300.

Emissions from changes in land use $E^{ref\ landuse}_t$ are exogenous, they correspond to the IS92a scenario. Fossil emissions $E^{ref\ fossil}_t = E^{ref\ total}_t - E^{ref\ landuse}_t$ are controlled by a control parameter $\varepsilon(t)$, so that emissions at time t are given by:

$$E_t = E^{ref\ landuse}_t + E^{ref\ fossil}_t (1 - \varepsilon_t)$$

The mitigation costs at time t are a quadratic function of both the degree of abatement $\varepsilon(t)$ and the rate of abatement $\varepsilon'(t)$, with the general form:

$$C^{abatement}_t = \left[c_{level}\varepsilon_t^2 + c_{rate}(\varepsilon_t - \varepsilon_{t-1})^2 \right] \frac{E^{ref}_t}{E^{ref}_{t0}} \frac{1}{(1+d)^t}$$

Thus, the abatement costs are the sum of a recurring loss that depends upon the level of abatement, and a transitory cost that depends on the rate of abatement. The second, rate dependent term reflects the inertia in the system, which includes the costs associated with forcing changes in the mix and utilization of existing capital stock. Both cost components are scaled according to the size of the reference energy system E^{ref}_t/E^{ref}_{t0}. To reflect the influence of autonomous technical progress in reducing future abatement costs, that WRE highlight as one of the factors that could make it cheaper to defer abatement, we make the scale of costs decline at a rate $d = 1\%$ pa.

The DIAM model finds the emissions pathway that minimizes the discounted total costs of abatement within the stabilization constraint specified, integrated from 1997 to the year 2300 at a discount rate of 3% pa. Though the pathway is independent of the scaling in c_{level} and c_{rate} (degree 1 homogeneity) for presenting numeric results on expenditure we set $c_{level} = 4$ such that a constant abatement of 50% of 1990 emissions incurs an annual loss of 1% of 1990 GWP, roughly in line with the estimates derived by Nordhaus (1991). Inertial costs add to this; this version of the model does not take any account of the role of induced technical change or other factors that may reduce abatement costs.

The ratio of the two components, c_{rate}/c_{level}; this defines the relative importance of inertia in the system. We can relate this to a characteristic timescale as described in the text.

[27]

Energy-Efficiency Investments and Public Policy

Adam B. Jaffe* and Robert N. Stavins**

Concern about carbon dioxide as a greenhouse gas has focused renewed attention on energy conservation because fossil fuel combustion is a major source of CO_2 emissions. Since it is generally acknowledged that energy use could be significantly reduced through broader adoption of existing technologies, policy makers need to know how effective various policy instruments might be in accelerating the diffusion of these technologies. We examine the factors that determine the rate of diffusion, focusing on (i) potential market failures: information problems, principal-agent slippage, and unobserved costs, and (ii) explanations that do not represent market failures: private information costs, high discount rates, and heterogeneity among potential adopters. Through a series of simulations we explore how alternative policy instruments—both economic incentives and more conventional, direct regulations—could hasten the diffusion of energy-conserving technologies.

INTRODUCTION

The role new technologies can play in solving a wide range of environmental and natural resource problems is receiving increasing attention from policy makers.[1] Concern about carbon dioxide (CO_2) as a greenhouse gas has focused particular attention on the role of energy-conserving technologies.

The Energy Journal, Vol. 15, No. 2. Copyright ® 1994 by the IAEE. All rights reserved.

* Department of Economics, Harvard University; and National Bureau of Economic Research.

** John F. Kennedy School of Government, Harvard University; and Resources for the Future.

1. A prominent spokesman for this perspective has been U.S. Vice President Al Gore. See Gore (1992). Activity within the Congress has also been significant. For example, Senate Bill S-978, introduced by Senator Max Baucus—the Chairman of the Senate Environment and Public Works Committee—would create a National Environmental Technology Panel under the White House Office of Science and Technology Policy to unify the efforts of the ten Federal agencies that spent $4 billion on environmental technology development in 1992. It would also establish an EPA Bureau of Environmentally Sustainable Technologies to channel Federal funds to support "green technology" development. Five other pending bills contain similar goals.

Since the largest anthropogenic source of CO_2 emissions is combustion of fossil fuels for energy generation, reductions in energy use could constitute a powerful option for reducing the risk of global climate change. It is widely acknowledged that energy use could be significantly reduced through broader adoption of existing technologies, and it is almost as widely accepted that much unadopted technology is cost-effective at current prices.[2]

In this paper, we examine two inextricably linked questions: what factors determine the rate of adoption of energy-conserving technologies; and what types of public policy can accelerate their diffusion. Our analysis reflects two contexts in which energy-conservation adoption decisions occur. One setting *prompts* a decision about *whether or not* to incorporate an energy-conserving technology at a specified time. In the second context, a decision must be made not only *whether* to adopt such a technology but also *when* to do so.

INVESTING IN ENERGY-EFFICIENCY TECHNOLOGIES

There appear to exist a number of proven technologies that engineering calculations show to be cost-effective at current prices but that are not widely used. Frequently cited examples include compact fluorescent light bulbs, improved insulation materials, and energy-efficient appliances (Norberg-Bohm 1990). From an economic perspective, there are two fundamental categories of potential explanations of this seemingly anomalous behavior: (1) market failures may cause what appears to be non-optimizing behavior; and (2) there may be reasons why the observed behavior is indeed privately optimal, despite engineers' calculations.

Market-Failure Explanations

Several sources of potential market failure may affect energy-conserving technology adoption rates. One of these is lack of information. It is costly for people to learn of an innovation's existence, and to learn enough to know if it is profitable and how to use it. Because information has public-good attributes, it may be under provided by the market. Further, if others' use of a technology is an important source of information, adoption creates positive externalities because it generates information that is valuable to others.

Principal-agent problems are another possible source of market failure. These failures can arise when energy-efficiency decisions are made by parties other than those who pay the bills. If the builder of a new house cannot credibly represent its energy-conserving features to potential buyers, the sale

---

2. See, for example, Carlsmith, Chandler, McMahon, and Santino (1990) and Shama (1983).

price may not fully reflect efficiency attributes. Similarly, a landlord may not be able to recover the total value of energy-efficiency investments where renters pay fuel bills. Conversely, in some situations, renters may have to make investments but landlords pay for fuel (Fisher and Rothkopf 1989).

Finally, consumers may face "artificially low" energy prices that explain their disinterest in conservation. First, electricity and natural gas are typically priced on an average-cost basis that may not reflect the incremental cost of new energy supplies. Second, electricity is highly subsidized in some parts of the country. Third, uninternalized environmental externalities may be associated with the use of energy from particular sources.

Non-Market-Failure Explanations

The second category of "economic explanations" of low adoption rates consists generally of the view that engineers are ignoring or at least underestimating certain costs of adoption. Beyond the tautological validity of such a claim, there are reasons to give it credence. Learning about the new technology is one aspect of cost. Although the pure information-creation part of this cost has public-good aspects and therefore fits into the market failure category, there is also a purely private part of the cost that relates to information acquisition and absorption. It is by no means costless to learn how a generic technological improvement fits into one's own home or firm or to learn about reliable suppliers.[3] Even after basic information about a technology has been generated and disseminated, the purchase price of the new product is no more than a lower bound on its adoption cost.

An alternative explanation of low adoption rates is that users have relatively high implicit discount rates.[4] As will be discussed further below, the empirical observation that consumers make decisions *as if* they had very high discount rates could mean either that principal/agent problems or other market failures exist, or that they truly have high discount rates. Sutherland (1991) and Hassett and Metcalf (1992) argue that truly high discount rates may, in fact, be

3. Some have argued that not only costly information acquisition but also *biased* estimates of likely energy savings play a role. Consumers may not believe experts' assessments of the benefits of new technologies. On the other hand, the bias may go in the opposite direction, since some studies indicate that consumers systematically overestimate energy savings associated with some types of new technologies (Stern 1986).

4. Hausman (1979) estimated that consumers used average implicit discount rates of 20 percent for purchasing room air conditioners with substantial variation by income class; and Dubin and McFadden (1984) found average implicit discount rates of 20 percent for space-heating and water-heating investments, again with significant variation by income. In a comment on Hausman (1979), Gately (1980) estimated discount rates of 45 to 300 percent for refrigerators. Likewise, Ruderman, Levine, and McMahon (1987) found personal implicit discount rates as low as 20 percent and as high as 800 percent for heating and cooling equipment and for residential appliances.

appropriate, because these investments are irreversible and there is much uncertainty about their payback, given that future energy prices are highly uncertain, and energy life-cycle savings in any particular application can only be estimated.[5] To the extent that consumers' true discount rates are high for these reasons, this would not represent a market failure.

Finally, even if a given technology is profitable on *average*, it will not be profitable for some individuals or firms. If the relevant population is heterogeneous with respect to the amount of energy they use, for example, even a technology that looks very good for the average user will be unattractive for a portion of the population. Hence, we can also interpret the engineer's cost-effectiveness calculations to mean that the technology is profitable for the mean household or firm.

As a necessary precondition for our policy analysis, we go on to explore both these market and nonmarket failures in light of the two classes of energy-efficiency investments noted above. The first group, requiring a decision about *whether* to incorporate a technology at a given time, may include construction of new industrial, commercial, or residential structures or expansions or other modifications of existing establishments. By way of example, we will discuss the question of whether to incorporate a potential energy-saving technology in the construction of a new home. The second group, requiring "*whether*-and-*when* determinations," includes retrofit decisions in various types of structures; here, our discussion will focus on the adoption decision faced by an individual considering the installation of an energy-saving technology in an existing home.

STATIC ADOPTION DECISIONS

Here we consider a builder who has the option of incorporating a new technology into the design of a house at a specified time, taking as given other design features of the house. We allow for the factors noted in the preceding section, as follows: (1) Houses may be heterogeneous in their energy use. (2) The housing market may discount energy savings because builders cannot represent them credibly. (3) The prevalence of the practice among builders in the area as well as the builder's own experience with the technology may affect incremental adoption costs. (4) Regulation may affect the decision by modifying

---

5. Stoft (1993) attempts to use the CAPM model of Sutherland to estimate how high consumer discount rates should be, and finds that this mechanism does not explain implicit discount rates as high as have typically been found by researchers. This analysis does not, however, incorporate the mechanism modelled by Hassett and Metcalf.

the cost of the new technology.[6] (5) Tax credits or other subsidies may be associated with the use or adoption of energy-conserving technologies.

The builder's decision may be modeled as an attempt to maximize the sum of the base selling price of the house (in the absence of the energy-saving technology) and the present discounted value of the expected energy savings if the technology is adopted (that is, the capitalized value of the installed technology), minus the costs of adoption.[7] These may include costs associated with up-front purchase and installation, the implicit or explicit cost effects of regulation, and learning effects due to previous use by this builder or current use by other builders in the area.

Not surprisingly, such an optimization problem yields a necessary condition for technology adoption that compares the overall cost of adoption with the expected increase in the selling price of the house.[8] In particular, the technology should be employed at time of construction, T, if:

$$\delta \cdot (1 - w) \cdot G(k_{ijT}, \mu_{ijT}) + \gamma D_{iT} > L(C_{iT}, S_{ijT}, v_{iT}) - X_{iT} \qquad (1)$$

where $\delta =$ discount ($0 \leq \delta < 1$) or premium ($\delta > 1$) applied by market to value of energy savings;

$w =$ index of average quantity of energy used by the technology relative to energy consumption if the technology were not employed ($0 < w \leq 1$);

$k_{ijT} =$ vector of current and expected future values of observable characteristics of home j (for example, size, type of heating plant), and region i (price of fuel, climate, average income and education);

$\mu_{ijT} =$ unobserved factor affecting energy use;

$G(\cdot) =$ function that relates elements of k_{ijT} to expected discounted present value of fuel expenditures;

6. Our interpretation is that regulation requires the use of the technology, creating an explicit or implicit penalty for not using it. Alternatively, regulation may merely encourage use of the technology by, for example, setting an overall energy budget for the house.

7. This approach is fully deterministic, but as our previous discussion of potential explanations of the gradual diffusion of energy-efficiency technologies suggests, uncertainty may play a significant role. It is possible to focus instead on that dimension of the diffusion process. See, for example: Hassett and Metcalf (1992); and Howarth and Anderson (1992).

8. The optimization problem and its basic solution is provided in Appendix A. For a detailed description of the model and its solution, see Jaffe and Stavins (1994).

$\gamma =$ parameter that captures the average perceived monetary equivalent cost of ignoring regulation, presumably a function of the nature of the regulations, the magnitude of penalties, perceived probabilities of enforcement, and likely stigma;[9]

$D_{iT} =$ dummy variable set to unity if jurisdiction i has regulation in year T requiring that the technology be installed;

$C_{iT} =$ engineering estimate of purchase and installation cost of adoption of the technology;

$S_{ijT} =$ cumulative stock of houses built previously by builder that incorporate the technology;

$v_{iT} =$ fraction of newly constructed homes in jurisdiction i that incorporate the technology;

$L(\cdot) =$ function that generates the "effective cost" of installation from the engineering cost and the prevalence of use of the technology; and

$X_{iT} =$ subsidy or tax credit in jurisdiction i for adopting the technology.

This inequality indicates that the builder will use the technology if the valuation placed by the market on the savings in expected energy costs plus the implicit or explicit value of complying with regulations (if any) exceeds the "cost of installation." The cost of installation includes the purchase and installation cost and the cost of learning about the technology. It may be reduced by a government subsidy.

By specifying reasonable functional forms for the $G(\cdot)$ and $L(\cdot)$ functions, rearranging the adoption condition in the form of a benefit/cost ratio, and taking logarithms of both sides of the resulting expression, we have:[10]

---

9. See Russell, Harrington, and Vaughan (1986).
10. For a discussion of functional forms and complete derivation, see Jaffe and Stavins (1994).

$$\log(\delta) + \log(1 - w) + \beta_1 \log\left[\int_T^\infty (P_{it})e^{-rt}dt\right] + \sum_{m=2}^M \left[\beta_m \log(k_{ijT}^m)\right]$$

$$- \log\left[(C_{iT})^{\alpha_1} \cdot (v_{iT})^{\alpha_2} \cdot (\frac{S_{ijT}}{\alpha_3})^{\alpha_4} - \gamma D_{iT} - X_{iT}\right] + \log(\mu_{ijT}) \geq 0 \tag{2}$$

where P_{it} =   price of fuel;

β_m =   set of parameters associated with the k_{ijT}^m observable
characteristics;

e =   base of natural logarithms; and

r =   real market rate of interest.

Equation (2) illustrates how a variety of factors can affect the diffusion of energy-efficiency technologies. First of all, principal-agent problems associated with the builder-homeowner relationship will have an unambiguously negative impact. If principal-agent slack exists, the parameter δ will be greater than zero but less than unity, and so $\log(\delta)$ in equation (2) will be negative. Ideally, it would be desirable to model explicitly the information problems that create principal/agent slack in the new-home market. This would be necessary, for example, in order to quantify the effect on energy efficiency of policy interventions such as mandatory energy-efficiency audits. This effort would only be worthwhile, however, if the parameters of the richer model could be estimated empirically. Because information itself is unobserved, we do not believe that this is possible. For this reason, we use the simpler formulation where the parameter δ is a placeholder for the more complex phenomenon.

Equation (2) also shows that adoption will be more likely the higher future energy prices are expected to be, and will be lower the higher is the discount rate r that individuals apply to expected energy savings. To clarify further the relationship among principal/agent slack (captured by δ), the discount rate r, and expected future prices, we assume for simplicity that consumers expect that the future price of energy will be some constant value P_i', and we then rearrange equation (2), solving out the present discounted value price term:

$$\log(\delta) + \beta_1\log(P_i') - \beta_1\log(r) \geq \log\left[(C_{iT})^{\alpha_1} \cdot (v_{iT})^{\alpha_2} \cdot (\frac{S_{ijT}}{\alpha_3})^{\alpha_4} - \gamma D_{iT} - X_{iT}\right]$$

$$- \log(1 - w) - \sum_{m=2}^{M}\left[\beta_m \log(k_{ijT}^m)\right] - \log(\mu_{ijT}) \tag{3}$$

Equation (3) shows that the effects of δ, P_i', and r are indistinguishable from each other. If we could measure r and P_i', then we could use equation (3) (together with assumptions about the distribution of μ_{ijT}) to estimate δ. In practice, we cannot measure either of these. So instead what is typically done is to ignore the principal/agent issue (i.e. set δ to unity), assume that P_i' is equal to the current price, and then *estimate* the discount rate from some version of equation (3). What is typically found is that r is relatively high. But what equation (3) shows is that this result can mean any of three different things. It could mean that δ is less than unity; it could mean that P_i' is less than assumed by the researcher; or it could mean that consumers truly utilize a high discount rate to evaluate these investments. There is simply no way, based only on observed purchase decisions, to disentangle these three phenomena.

Returning to equation (2), the term behind the summation sign shows that climatic departures from temperate conditions (increases in heating and/or cooling degree days) will encourage adoption, *ceteris paribus*. Other factors affecting energy use, such as income or education, could also matter. The second line of equation (2) demonstrates that decreases in adoption costs will accelerate technology diffusion. Such decreases could be due to: changes in the direct costs of equipment purchase and installation (C_{iT}); changes in "effective costs of adoption" associated with *learning* (inversely correlated in our model with the prevalence of installation of the technology within the region, v_{iT}); and the builder's own cumulative experience with the technology (S_{ijT}). Depending on the magnitude of the parameter (α_2), there may be a dynamic externality in which increased adoption today fosters future adoption by increasing v_{it}.

Finally, direct regulations—such as building codes—can directly and positively affect adoption by decreasing expected costs (γ),[11] and government programs in the form of subsidies or tax credits (X_{iT}) can directly reduce costs and thereby spur diffusion.

---

11. The magnitude of this impact is clearly an empirical matter. See, for example: Jaffe and Stavins (1993a, 1993b). In another strand of this research, we investigate the empirical implications of this model by specifying appropriate functional forms, and estimating parameters econometrically with data on the diffusion of thermal insulation in new residential construction in the United States over the period 1979-1988 (Jaffe and Stavins 1993b).

DYNAMIC ADOPTION DECISIONS

In this second case, we consider a homeowner who is thinking about injecting blown insulation into exterior walls. To minimize expected costs,[12] he or she must decide *at what time* (if any) to perform the retrofit installation.[13] Because the technology may be significantly less costly in the future, this is not simply a yes-no decision like the one faced by the builder.

The costs that the homeowner wishes to minimize consist of three elements—the present discounted value of annual energy costs from the present to the time that the energy-saving technology is adopted; the present value of annual energy costs after the adoption; and the present value of the one-time cost of adoption. This dynamic optimization problem[14] yields a necessary condition that adoption is predicted to occur at time T such that:

$$(1 - \delta \cdot w) \, g \, (k_{ijT}, \mu_{ijT}) + \gamma D_{iT} \geq r \cdot \left[L(C_{iT}, V_{iT}) - X_{iT} \right]$$

$$- \left[\frac{\partial L}{\partial C_{iT}} \right] \cdot \left[\frac{dC_{iT}}{dT} \right] - \left[\frac{\partial L}{\partial V_{iT}} \right] \cdot \left[\frac{dV_{iT}}{dT} \right] + \left[\frac{dX_{iT}}{dT} \right] \tag{4}$$

where $g(\cdot)$ is a function that relates elements of k_{ijT} to annual fuel expenditures; V_{iT} is the fraction of retrofit candidates in jurisdiction i that have adopted the technology by time T; and all other variables are as defined previously.

The left-hand side of equation (4) indicates that higher annual energy costs can encourage adoption, as can the effectiveness of the technology[15] and the existence of relevant regulations. The first term on the right-hand side of the equation indicates that higher adoption costs (whether direct or indirect) and higher interest rates discourage installation, and that government subsidies can encourage adoption. Finally, the presence of the last set of terms—the time derivative of adoption cost—indicates that adoption is discouraged by

---

12. It is also possible that energy conservation enters directly in some people's utility functions. Further, note that if the homeowner is not risk-neutral, the riskiness of the investment can be captured by appropriate adjustment of the interest rate. In this regard, Hassett and Metcalf (1992) examine the effect of uncertainty on the retrofit decision. By focusing on utility-maximization instead of cost-minimization, we could also investigate the possibility that the optimal consumption of energy services (for example, the thermostat setting) would change if the house became more energy-efficient.

13. Because retrofitting an existing building is typically much more expensive than incorporating a new technology at the time of construction, our analysis of new construction ignored the possibility that the retrofit option affects the initial installation optimization problem.

14. The model is presented and solved in Appendix B. A more complete version is found in Jaffe and Stavins (1994).

15. Note that $1 - \delta w$ is the expected proportion of energy saved.

expectations of decreased effective costs of adoption in the future. Thus, even if the current savings in energy costs are greater than the yearly annuity of adoption costs, it can pay to wait *if* those adoption costs are expected to fall over time at a sufficiently rapid rate.

By adopting appropriate functional forms for $g(\cdot)$ and $L(\cdot)$ in the retrofit context, we have:

$$
\left[(1 - \delta \cdot w) \cdot P_{iT} \cdot \sum_{m=2}^{M} \beta_m k_{ijT}^m \right] + \gamma D_{iT} - r \cdot \left[\alpha_3 + \alpha_1 C_{iT} + \alpha_2 V_{iT} - X_{iT} \right]
$$
$$
+ \alpha_1 \left[\frac{dC_{iT}}{dT} \right] + \alpha_2 \left[\frac{dV_{iT}}{dT} \right] - \left[\frac{dX_{iT}}{dT} \right] + \mu_{ijT} \geq 0
\tag{5}
$$

Equation (5) is a statement about the *current* rate of energy savings; it does not involve present values of future streams, in contrast with equation (2) in the new construction case. On the other hand, it does include the time rate of change of adoption costs, which brings into play current expectations of future adoption costs. Put more concretely, to the extent that one expects that compact fluorescent light bulbs are getting cheaper or easier to find or easier to install, one might wait until next year to purchase and install them even if they are currently economical.[16]

Adoption decisions in the retrofit case are thus made on the basis of current energy prices without concern for the future paths of energy prices. However, equation (5) does indicate that interest rates still matter, since it is the annuity of adoption costs that is critical. Higher implicit discount rates (r) will tend to retard adoption. As in the new-construction case, adoption will be slowed by artificially low energy prices (P_{iT}). Climatic departures from temperate conditions will encourage adoption, as will other factors that increase energy use. The existence of relevant regulations can encourage adoption as well.

The second bracketed term on the first line of equation (5) implies that high adoption costs will unambiguously discourage adoption, whether they are associated with: direct costs of equipment purchase and installation (C_{iT}); changes in effective costs of adoption associated with *learning* (inversely correlated with cumulative adoption in the area, V_{iT}); or government programs in the form of subsidies or tax credits (X_{iT}).

---

16. Thus the model produces a potential nonmarket-failure explanation of gradual diffusion, beyond those suggested above.

Despite the irrelevance of future energy price paths, equation (5) reminds us that the current time rate of change of adoption costs does matter. In particular, it can pay to wait if purchase or installation costs, or both, are falling, even though *current* net benefits of adoption are positive. Likewise, if adoption is taking place very fast and information about the technology is thus increasing rapidly, it can pay to wait since $\alpha_2 < 0$. Finally, if government subsidies or tax credits are increasing fast enough over time, one may choose to wait for the higher subsidy at a later date even though the current benefit-cost picture is otherwise positive.

THE ROLE OF PUBLIC POLICY

Either conventional command-and-control regulatory policies or incentive-based economic instruments can be used to influence the rate of technological diffusion. Which policy instruments will be best will depend in well-defined ways upon the relative importance of the various causes of the gradual diffusion of those technologies. If the diffusion process is relatively unaffected by economic forces, then the economist's standard argument that some sort of market mechanism is the best way to internalize the social costs of CO_2 emissions, for example, would presumably carry much less weight than otherwise. If people are not using technologies that are cost-effective at today's prices, should we rely on carbon taxes or other policies that would raise the cost of energy use? We would be more likely to achieve success, the argument goes, with regulatory mandates requiring the use of particular technologies.

Some of the factors we have identified as influencing the rate of diffusion suggest a role for government intervention, but others should *not* be taken as meriting policy responses. In particular, the nonmarket failures may help to explain the gradual diffusion, but they *do not* argue for government intervention.[17] Falling into this category are high discount rates,[18] the individual costs of absorbing and adapting to a new technology, heterogeneity of potential adopters, and the "dynamic wait-and-see" conditions that emerge in the retrofit case. The other major set of factors we have examined—the market failures—not

17. More rapid diffusion is not necessarily better; in other words, the socially optimal rate of diffusion is not instantaneous. To the degree that a "gradual" diffusion rate is partially explained by market failures, however, that diffusion rate can be said to be sub-optimal. In such case, appropriate government actions can be employed to correct for the market-failure and thus to accelerate the diffusion process.

18. To the extent that high *implicit* discount rates reflect market failures such as principal/agent problems, they might provide evidence in favor of a need for policy intervention. To the extent, however, that consumers are not choosing efficient technologies because they truly have high discount rates for these kinds of investments, this would not merit a policy response.

54 / The Energy Journal

only help explain gradual diffusion but also provide a set of potential justifications for government intervention.

The evaluation of policies intended to influence energy-efficiency technology adoption decisions requires simulations that emulate the dynamic nature of the respective decision processes. For illustrative purposes, we develop a simulation model of aggregate technological diffusion in the new-home construction case, based on equation (2). To simplify our analysis, we assume that μ (an unobserved factor influencing energy use) has a logistic distribution and is independent of other house-specific variables. Therefore, the fraction of homes in year T that will incorporate the technology is the probability that condition (2) holds, which is equal to the logistic cumulative probability function evaluated at the left-hand side of equation (2), or:

$$v_T = \frac{1}{1 + e^{-A_T}} \tag{6}$$

where v_T is the fraction of newly constructed homes in year T that use the technology, and A_T is the left-hand side of equation (2).[19]

Using this simulation model, we graph in Figure 1 a base-case (no new policy) diffusion path for the time period 1978-1988. We chose to simulate this particular time interval because it encompasses a significant turning point in real energy prices. The resulting nonmonotonic diffusion curve is typical of some energy-efficiency technologies in new homes during this period.[20] With the help of the simulation model, simple differential calculus, or simpler inspection of the behavioral relationships, we can now explore the likely consequences of alternative public policies.

---

19. Given the assumption of independence of μ and the other variables, those variables in equation (2) that vary across i and/or j are evaluated at their means. To keep things simple for the policy analysis, we drop the term with S_{ijT} from the learning function; i.e., we set α_4 in equation (2) equal to zero. Otherwise it would be necessary to simulate multiple builder decisions simultaneously. Also, for the simulation model, we replace v_{iT} by the previous period's value, $v_{i,T-1}$; and we adopt simple static expectations on prices, so that P_{ij} is replaced by P_{iT}.

20. In fact, our base-case parameter and variable values reflect actual data for triple-pane windows, and the simulated diffusion curve is similar to the observed diffusion path of that technology in the United States. The shape of the diffusion path is partly a consequence of the related path of expected, real energy prices, and is related to the decreasing use of triple-pane windows during the second half of the timer period (Jaffe and Stavins 1993a).

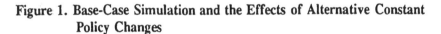

Figure 1. Base-Case Simulation and the Effects of Alternative Constant Policy Changes

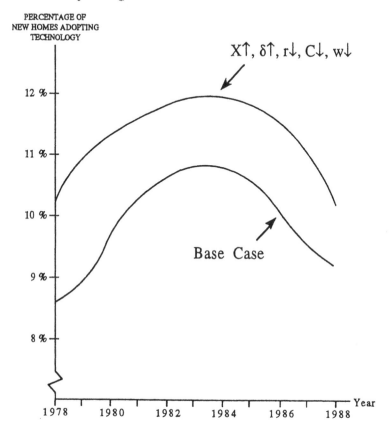

First, the public-good aspect of incomplete information can suggest a number of policy responses, depending upon the nature of the incomplete information. Where uncertainty surrounds the potential benefits of energy-conservation technologies in new construction, our analysis suggests that government could establish standards for energy audits and disclosure requirements for new buildings, thereby increasing δ. Graphically, this shifts the diffusion path in Figure 1 upward. Likewise, public information campaigns about the potential benefits and costs of adopting new technologies could be effective in the new construction case ($\delta\uparrow$, $\alpha_1\downarrow$, $r\uparrow$) and the retrofit case ($\alpha_3\downarrow$, $r\downarrow$).[21] Focusing on the attributes of the technologies themselves, product

21. As with increases in δ, so too with decreases in the (constant) interest rate,(r); the effect is to shift the diffusion path upward while retaining its basic (nonmonotonic) shape.

labeling requirements, or guidelines could be effective for new construction ($\alpha_1\downarrow$, $\delta\uparrow$) and retrofitting ($\alpha_3\downarrow$, $\delta\uparrow$).

Concern about principal-agent problems has led in the past to legislative proposals requiring the U.S. Department of Energy to develop a *voluntary* home energy rating system that would provide consumers with better information on the efficiency of prospective homes ($\delta\uparrow$). Standards for audits and disclosure would have the same basic result.

The appropriate policy response to artificially low energy prices will depend, of course, upon the reason for the problematic pricing. One approach would be to increase energy prices ($P_{it}\uparrow$) in those markets where they are currently subsidized. In this same context, the existence of uninternalized environmental externalities associated with particular sources of energy clearly calls for those externalities to be internalized, through pollution taxes, tradeable permit systems, or other economic instruments ($P_{it}\uparrow$), or through conventional command-and-control regulations ($D_{iT}\uparrow$).

It is frequently asserted that free-rider problems will lead to less than the socially optimal amount of research and development by private firms. To the extent that this is true in the energy-efficiency technology area, government support for technological research and development may be called for. In our analysis, this could translate into decreases in the purchase and installation costs of new technologies ($C_{iT}\downarrow$) and/or increases in the effectiveness (engineering efficiency) of those technologies ($w\downarrow$). Further, since adoption behavior can itself result in positive externalities if others' use of a technology is an important source of valuable information, there is an argument in favor of government employing "adoption subsidies" or tax credits ($X_{iT}\uparrow$).[22]

As indicated, some energy-efficiency technologies used in new home construction—such as triple-pane windows—have exhibited nonmonotonic diffusion paths. What policies could have been used to foster a monotonically increasing diffusion path in the face of falling real energy prices? First of all, if adoption costs had been falling sufficiently rapidly over time, the depressing incentive effects of falling energy prices would have been reversed. Indeed, various hypothetical time paths of falling adoption costs (C_{iT}) produce diffusion paths in which the "negative effect" of falling energy prices after 1983 is overcome. Depending upon the rate at which adoption costs fall, the diffusion path of the technology can take on a constantly rising pattern or a classical sigmoid shape (Figure 2).

---

22. In the new-home construction case, simulations of decreases in the purchase and installation costs of new technologies (C_{iT}), increases in those technologies' engineering efficiency ($1-w$), and increases in adoption subsidies or tax credits (X_{iT}) exhibit the same effect: upward shifts of the nonmonotonic diffusion path (see Figure 1).

Figure 2. The Effect of Decreasing Adoption Costs on Technological Diffusion

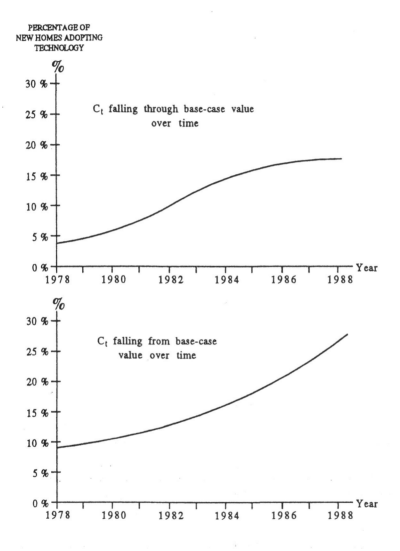

PERCENTAGE OF
NEW HOMES ADOPTING
TECHNOLOGY

Besides supporting technological research and development efforts to bring down adoption costs, C_{iT}, how else might government policy be employed to counteract the post-1983 price effects and maintain adoption rates, or even push them to continually higher levels? First, government support of research and development—an approach that is favorably viewed by the present Administration for a host of environmental and resource problems—can have the

Figure 3. The Effect of Increasing Engineering-Efficiency on Technological Diffusion

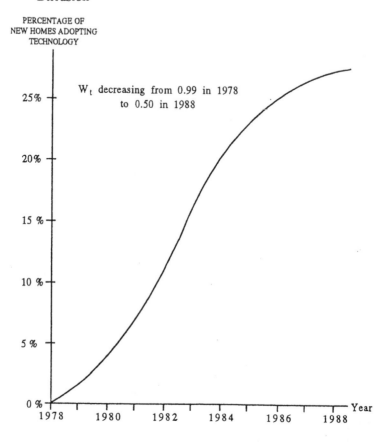

effect not only of decreasing option costs but also on increasing the efficiency of available technologies ($w\downarrow$). Figure 3 shows that as w falls over time from an initial value of 0.99 (indicating virtually no efficiency advantage) to 0.50 (indicating that the technology cuts energy demand by 50 percent), annual adoption increases monotonicly in an essentially sigmoid path from zero to 30 percent of newly constructed homes.

Other dynamic government policies could be employed to compensate for falling energy prices. For example, a *continuously increasing* subsidy (X_{iT}) of sufficient magnitude could be used to maintain adoption rates at their peak level (again, in the face of falling energy prices). Indeed, subsidies of various magnitudes can be employed to have essentially whatever effect is desired. At one extreme, a constant subsidy set equal to the basic engineering cost of the technology results in a 100 percent rate of adoption after only eight years (the delay resulting from the effect of learning on effective costs of adoption).

Figure 4. The Effect of a One-Time Increase in Regulatory Stringency on the Annual Rate of Technological Diffusion

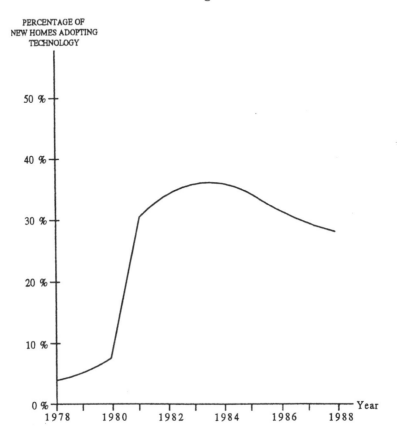

The obvious alternative to a subsidy on the technology (or a tax on energy prices) is a conventional regulatory approach, such as the use of building codes in the new-construction context. Although regulations can—in theory—have the desired effect, our analysis indicates that a one-time change in regulatory stringency should not be expected to lead automatically to an increasing or even a constant level of annual adoption. Figure 4 represents a situation in which a command-and-control regulation is initiated in the year 1981. As expected, adoption increases dramatically in that year and then continues to increase at a much slower rate to the peak year of 1983. Subsequent to that time, however, the effects of falling energy prices dominate, and we find the rate of diffusion falling gradually despite the constant level of regulation. Conventional regulations, like market-based instruments, can be effective, but neither are likely to be a panacea in the face of strong, contrary forces in the economy.

CONCLUSIONS

Understanding the causes of the gradual diffusion of energy-conserving technologies is key to identifying appropriate policy responses. One set of causes, which we have labelled the "nonmarket-failure" causes—private information costs, high discount rates, and heterogeneity among potential adopters—do not provide legitimate justifications for government intervention. On the other hand, a fairly large number of potential market-failure explanations —information problems, principal-agent slippage, and unobserved costs—can provide solid arguments for government action. While our analysis indicates how alternative policy instruments—both economic incentives and direct regulations—can hasten the diffusion of energy-conserving technologies, the selection of appropriate policy instruments will depend upon the relative importance of the various underlying explanations of the gradual diffusion of energy-efficiency technologies.

APPENDIX A

In the new construction case, we focus on a simple discrete technology for purposes of explication, although the model can be generalized to represent multi-valued discrete or continuous technological choices, such as installation of insulation of various "R-values" in exterior walls. In our example, the builder's problem is:

$$
\max_{\{I\}} \pi_{ijT} = B + \left[I \cdot \delta \cdot (1 - w) \cdot \int_{T}^{\infty} g(k_{ijt}, \mu_{ijt}) \cdot e^{-rt} dt \right] \tag{A1}
$$

$$
- I \cdot \left[L(C_{iT}, S_{ijT}, v_{iT}) - \gamma D_{iT} - X_{iT} \right]
$$

where uppercase letters represent stocks or present values; lowercase letters represent flows; and Greek letters represent parameters (except for π and μ, as indicated below). The variables are:

π_{ijT} = profit associated with adopting the technology in constructing house j in geographic area (and political jurisdiction) i at time T;

I = indicator of choice to adopt the technology ($I = 1$ if the technology is used and 0 otherwise);

$B =$ base selling price of the house without the technology;

$\delta =$ discount $(0 \le \delta < 1)$ or premium $(\delta > 1)$ applied by market to value of energy savings;

$w =$ index of average quantity of energy used by the technology relative to energy consumption if the technology were not employed $(0 < w \le 1)$;

$k_{ijt} =$ vector of current and expected future values of observable characteristics of the home (for example, size, type of heating plant), and region (price of fuel, climate, average income and education);

$\mu_{ijt} =$ unobserved factor affecting energy use;

$g(\cdot) =$ function that relates elements of k_{ijt} to annual fuel expenditures;

$e =$ base of natural logarithms;

$r =$ real market rate of interest;

$C_{iT} =$ engineering estimate of cost of adoption of the technology;

$S_{ijT} =$ cumulative stock of houses built by builder that incorporate technology;

$v_{iT} =$ fraction of newly constructed homes in jurisdiction i that incorporate the technology;

$L(\cdot) =$ function that generates the "effective cost" of installation from the engineering cost and the prevalence of use of the technology;

$D_{iT} =$ dummy variable set to unity if jurisdiction i has regulation in year T requiring that the technology be installed;

$\gamma =$ parameter that captures the average perceived monetary equivalent cost of ignoring regulation, presumably a function of the nature of the regulations, the magnitude of penalties, perceived probabilities of enforcement, and likely stigma; and

$X_{iT} =$ subsidy or tax credit in jurisdiction i for adopting the technology.

This optimization problem yields a necessary condition for technology adoption that compares the overall cost of adoption with the expected increase in the selling price of the house. We derive the necessary condition for adoption by denoting the expected discounted present value of the function $g(\cdot)$ as $G(\cdot)$. Thus, the technology should be employed if:

$$\delta \cdot (1 - w) \cdot G(k_{ijT}, \mu_{ijT}) + \gamma D_{iT} > L(C_{iT}, S_{ijT}, v_{iT}) - X_{iT} \qquad \text{(A2)}$$

APPENDIX B

In the retrofit case, the costs that the homeowner wishes to minimize consist of three elements—the present discounted value (PV) of annual energy costs from the present to the time that the energy-saving technology is adopted; the PV of annual energy costs after the adoption; and the PV of the one-time cost of adoption:

$$\min_{\{T\}} \quad PV(T) = \int_0^T g(k_{ijt}, \mu_{ijt}) \cdot e^{-rt} dt \quad + \quad w \cdot \int_T^\infty g(k_{ijt}, \mu_{ijt}) \cdot e^{-rt} dt \qquad \text{(B1)}$$

$$+ \quad [L(C_{iT}, V_{iT}) - X_{iT}] \cdot e^{-rT} \quad + \quad \gamma \cdot \int_0^T D_{it} \cdot e^{-rt} dt$$

$$\text{subject to} \quad T \geq 0$$

where T is the time of adoption (installation); V_{iT} is the fraction of retrofit candidates in jurisdiction i that have adopted the technology by time T; and all other variables are as defined previously. Although interventions such as regulations are typically not utilized in this retrofit context, we allow for their impact here because in other possible applications—such as industrial pollution control—they can be designed either to affect all sources (thus requiring retrofitting at existing sources) or only new sources.[1]

The formulation of installation cost differs slightly in the retrofit case from the new construction case. Since the homeowner will not usually have previous experience with the technology, we take the effective cost to depend only on the engineering cost and the local prevalence of the technology. Given the nature of the retrofit situation, we take this prevalence to be represented by the fraction of the stock that has been retrofitted, rather than the current retrofit rate.

First-order conditions for maximizing $PV(T)$ in equation (B1) subject to the constraint of equation (B2) can be expressed in a condensed form in which adoption should occur in year T if:[2]

$$\frac{\partial PV(T)}{\partial T} \geq 0 \quad \text{and adoption hos not yet occured.} \quad \text{(B3)}$$

By evaluating the inequality condition in equation (B3), dividing by e^{-rT}, and rearranging terms, we have the following equation, in which adoption is predicted to occur at time T such that:

$$(1 - \delta \cdot w)\, g\,(k_{ijT}, \mu_{ijT}) + \gamma D_{iT} \geq r \cdot \left[L(C_{iT}, V_{iT}) - X_{iT} \right]$$

$$- \left[\frac{\partial L}{\partial C_{iT}} \right] \cdot \left[\frac{dC_{iT}}{dT} \right] - \left[\frac{\partial L}{\partial V_{iT}} \right] \cdot \left[\frac{dV_{iT}}{dT} \right] + \left[\frac{dX_{iT}}{dT} \right] \quad \text{(B4)}$$

---

1. The effect of regulation enters into the objective function as the final term in the second line of equation (B1). Thus, we are viewing regulations as an additional cost to be minimized, where this cost is equal to the "effective penalty" of noncompliance from the present time to the date of adoption (and compliance). Alternatively, the limits of the integral in the regulation term could be the time of adoption (T) and infinity, in which case the term would be subtracted instead of added. Then we would be viewing the effect of regulation as providing a benefit (an "avoided cost") to the adopter from the time of adoption onward. These two specifications of the impact of regulations are equivalent.

2. Sufficiency depends upon the satisfaction of second-order conditions, discussed in Jaffe and Stavins (1994).

64 / The Energy Journal

ACKNOWLEDGMENTS

This paper is part of an ongoing research project on the diffusion of energy-conserving technology. We thank Harvey Brooks, Trudy Cameron, James Hines, Maryellen Kelley, Sharon Oster, Ariel Pakes, Alex Pfaff, Peter Wilcoxen, Richard Zeckhauser, and participants in seminars at the National Bureau of Economic Research, and Princeton, Cornell, Stanford, and Harvard Universities for helpful comments on earlier work of the project. Research assistance by Jesse Gordon, editorial assistance by Toni Jean Rosenberg, comments from two anonymous referees, and funding from the U.S. Environmental Protection Agency are gratefully acknowledged.

REFERENCES

Carlsmith, Roger, W. Chandler, J. McMahon, and D. Santino (1990). *Energy Efficiency: How Far Can We Go?* Oak Ridge, Tennessee: Oak Ridge National Laboratory.

Dubin, Jeffrey A. and Daniel L. McFadden (1984). "An Econometric Analysis of Residential Electric Appliance Holdings and Consumption." *Econometrica* 52(2):345-362.

Fisher, Anthony, and Michael Rothkopf (1989). "Market Failure and Energy Policy." *Energy Policy* 17(4):397-406.

Gately, Dermot (1980). "Individual Discount Rates and the Purchase and Utilization of Energy-Using Durables: Comment." *Bell Journal of Economics* 11(1):373.

Gore, Senator Al (1992). *Earth in the Balance: Ecology and the Human Spirit*. New York: Houghton Mifflin Company.

Hassett, Kevin A. and Gilbert E. Metcalf (1992). "Energy Tax Credits and Residential Conservation Investment." Working Paper No. 4020. Cambridge, Massachusetts: National Bureau of Economic Research.

Hausman, Jerry A (1979). "Individual Discount Rates and the Purchase and Utilization of Energy-Using Durables." *The Bell Journal of Economics* 10(1):33-54.

Howarth, Richard B., and Bo Anderson (1993). "Market Barriers to Energy Efficiency." *Energy Economics* 15(4): 262-275.

Jaffe, Adam B., and Robert N. Stavins (1993a). "The Diffusion of Energy Conserving Windows: The Effect of Economic Incentives and Building Codes." Paper presented at the annual meeting of the American Economic Association, Anaheim, California.

Jaffe, Adam B., and Robert N. Stavins (1993b). "Prices, Regulation, and Energy Conservation." Paper presented at the Conference on Market Approaches to Environmental Protection, Stanford University.

Jaffe, Adam B., and Robert N. Stavins (1994). "The Energy Paradox and the Diffusion of Conservation Technology." *Resource and Energy Economics*, forthcoming.

Norberg-Bohm, Vicky (1990). "Potential for Carbon Dioxide Emissions Reductions in Buildings." *Global Environmental Policy Project Discussion Paper*. Cambridge, Massachusetts: Energy and Environmental Policy Center, John F. Kennedy School of Government, Harvard University.

Ruderman, Henry, Mark D. Levine, and James E. McMahon (1987). "The Behavior of the Market for Energy Efficiency in Residential Appliances Including Heating and Cooling Equipment." *The Energy Journal* 8(1):101-124.

Russell, Clifford S., Winston Harrington, and William J. Vaughan (1986). *Enforcing Pollution Control Laws*. Washington, D.C.: Resources for the Future.

Shama, Avraham (1983). "Energy Conservation in U.S. Buildings, Solving the High Potential/Low Adoption Paradox from a Behavioral Perspective." *Energy Policy* 11(2):148-167.

Stern, Paul C (1986). "Blind Spots in Policy Analysis: What Economics Doesn't Say About Energy Use." *Journal of Policy Analysis and Management* 5(2):200-227.

Stoft, Steven (1993). "Appliance Standards and the Welfare of Poor Families." *The Energy Journal* 14(4):123-128.

Sutherland, Ronald (1991). "Market Barriers to Energy-Efficiency Investments." *The Energy Journal* 12(3):15-34.

[28]

P.R. Shukla

The Modelling of Policy Options for Greenhouse Gas Mitigation in India

Greenhouse gas (GHG) emissions in India have important implications for global climate change. Emission trajectory and mitigation policies for India are analyzed using two models, a bottom-up energy systems optimization model (MARKAL) and a top-down macroeconomic model (Second Generation Model (SGM)). MARKAL is used to analyze technologies, peak electricity demand, carbon taxes, and a range of different policy scenarios. Carbon taxes and emissions permits are analyzed using SGM. In the reference scenario, energy use and carbon emissions increase nearly fourfold between 1995 and 2035. The analysis indicates that investment in infrastructure can substantially lower energy intensity and carbon intensity. A high carbon tax induces the substitution of natural gas and renewable energy for coal, and also causes a significant decrease in gross national product and consumption. The limitations of present models for analyzing mitigation policies for developing countries are discussed. Improvements for realistic representation of developing country dynamics and a policy agenda for GHG mitigation studies in developing countries are proposed.

INTRODUCTION

A least-cost response to global climate change in developing countries presents a variety of challenges and opportunities. Although current emissions from developing countries account for only one-third of global anthropogenic greenhouse gas (GHG) emissions, their future share of emissions will be much higher. GHG mitigation in developing countries is therefore crucial for the stabilization of atmospheric greenhouse gas concentrations at a level that would prevent dangerous anthropogenic interference with the climate system (1).

Within developing countries, there are a large number of low-cost mitigation opportunities such as the promotion of energy efficiency, a less carbon-intensive fuel mix, and renewable energy technologies. Unlike developed countries, in which previous infrastructure investments and consumption practices have locked the economy into a high energy and high emissions path, developing countries can make decisions that promote low energy and carbon intensities. The conventional development path can be leapfrogged by making decisions that encourage patterns of development that can be sustained by low resource use. While such development is desirable, market forces alone may not induce investments along this development path. On the contrary, the competition in global markets often compels developing countries to shift their investments away from a long-term goal of sustainability, which can be regarded as an impediment to economic progress and a hindrance to the competitiveness of national industries. In their formulation of GHG mitigation strategies, developing countries must resolve the conflict between their immediate economic goals and their long-term goal of developing sustainably.

MODELLING PARADIGMS

GHG mitigation requires an understanding of the complex and dynamic interactions among energy, environment, and economy. Models that have been used to capture these interactions are commonly classified as one of two types: bottom-up or top-down. Bottom-up models specify technologies, resources, and demands in detail. Top-down models have higher sectoral aggregation, but better characterization of impacts on economic growth, price feedbacks, and trade (2). Most top-down models are based on an equilibrium framework and assume the economy to be in competitive equilibrium resulting from optimal decisions made by consumers, producers, and the government.

The model dichotomy also reflects two different paradigms. Bottom-up models follow the optimistic "engineering paradigm", whereas top-down models reflect the pessimism of the "economic paradigm". Bottom-up models presume the existence of an efficiency gap. Opportunities such as "no regret" improvements in energy efficiency are identified to make energy services efficient. The existence of an efficiency gap is explained by identifying myriad barriers to efficiency. The pessimism of top-down models originates from the assumption that the present technology mix is the end-product of an efficiently performing market. Recent model developments have attempted to bridge the gap between the two modelling approaches (3), but with limited success (4).

Gaps in the Modelling of Developing Countries

Numerous GHG policy studies have been performed in developing countries (5, 6). Most use bottom-up models. Top-down studies of developing countries are rare (7). The present models express the economic dynamics of developing countries in the image of developed market economies. Developing country realities such as underdevel-

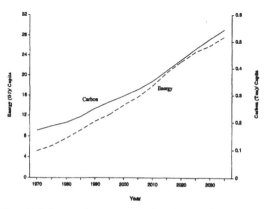

Figure 1. In India, per capita energy consumption and carbon emissions (including biomass) have been rising, and will continue to rise in the future unless strong mitigation efforts are made. Biomass is assumed to be carbon neutral. The data points from 1995 onwards are from the MARKAL reference scenario.

Climate Change

oped markets, vast informal and traditional sectors, predominant government monopolies, restrictions on trade, and multifarious barriers to competition are inadequately modelled. Consequently, estimation of future GHG emissions and policy prescriptions for their mitigation are distorted.

Both model types need considerable refinement, adaptation, and extension to provide realistic and insightful analysis of mitigation policies for developing countries (8). An adequate modelling framework for developing countries should include: the traditional and informal sectors; developmental priorities beyond economic efficiency, including equity; development alternatives with substantial investment in infrastructure; research and development; institutional arrangements that can alter development patterns; and strategies for influencing consumer behavior.

INDIA: ENERGY AND ENVIRONMENT PROFILE

India is a fast-growing developing economy. Its population of 900 mill. will grow to 1400 mill. by 2025 (9). Three quarters of India's population live in rural areas under a traditional economy. Agriculture's share of the gross national product (GNP) remains around 30% (10). In 1991, per capita income was USD 350 (USD 1150 with purchasing power parity) (11). Although per capita energy consumption and carbon emissions are increasing (Fig. 1), they remain well below the global average. Until 1990, government policies followed a mixed-economy model. Both agriculture and consumer industries were developed in the private sector. Energy, infrastructure, and heavy industry were in the government domain. The prices of energy, essential commodities, and services were regulated. Currency was not convertible. Since 1991, the Indian government has initiated market-oriented reforms. Although these reforms have influenced industries and external trade, their impact on rural and traditional economies has been marginal.

Economic development in India has followed an energy-intensive and carbon-intensive path. Domestic coal is the primary energy source for electricity and industry. Oil consumption has increased rapidly to meet growing transport demand. The domestic oil supply has not met the national demand, leading to growing oil imports. Noncommercial biomass contributes more than 25% of energy. The growing population and limited supply of clean fuels in rural areas, and the inability of the rural masses to buy commercial fuels, has resulted in a rural energy

crisis. Unsustainable use of forest biomass by industry and an increasing demand for land has contributed to severe deforestation. Of the anthropogenic carbon emissions, 40% are attributed to changes in land use (12). Substantial use of fossil fuel has led to poor air quality in most Indian cities. Because biomass use is decentralized, its impact on outdoor air quality is low except during the winter months in urban areas. However, the extensive use of biomass fuels for domestic cooking causes severe indoor air pollution (13) and has a significant impact on the health of women and children.

GHG MITIGATION ANALYSIS WITH THE MARKAL MODEL

MARKAL is an energy systems model ideally suited for techno-economic analysis (14). It is driven by exogenously forecasted activity levels for different economic sectors. Technologies are used to signify the input and output relationships among sectoral demands, energy demands, and energy resources. The costs of technologies and resources are specified exogenously. GHG emissions are accounted for as by-products of the energy-consuming technologies used to meet the demand from economic sectors. The model is formulated as a linear program in order to minimize discounted total energy and environmental costs over the planning horizon, while meeting energy needs and other constraints. Linear formulation facilitates the handling of the large number of variables and constraints (more than 5000 and 4000, respectively, for Indian MARKAL) that are required for a detailed bottom-up analysis.

Indian MARKAL: The Reference Scenario

Indian MARKAL is set up for a 40-yr period (1995 to 2035). The reference scenario assumes a 4.5% average annual growth rate in GNP. The growth rate ranges from 6% in the early years to 2.5% in later years. The economy is divided into two segments: modern and traditional. The transition of traditional activities into the modern economy is accounted for by adjusting future demand in the end-use sectors. Demand is disaggregated into 40 sectors and is forecasted for each sector using a logistic function (15) that follows an s-curve pattern. This is realistic for developing economies that are currently experiencing high economic growth but will stabilize at a lower growth rate in the future. Electricity demand is specified separately for daily peak and off-peak hours. An 8% annual discount rate is used.

Technology representation is detailed; 600 present and future technologies, including 90 electricity-generating technologies, are included. The cost of a service delivered by a technology and fuel combination varies by location because of differences in capital costs, natural causes such as the quality of a coal mine or wind pattern, and economic conditions such as the type of institutional arrangements (16). Fuel and technologies are modelled with heterogenous costs to allow realistic competition. Energy consumption and fuel mix for the reference scenario are shown in Figure 2. Analyses of different scenarios and comparison with the reference scenario are discussed below.

Growth Scenarios

The high-growth and low-growth scenarios assume average annual GNP growth rates of 5% and 4%, respectively,

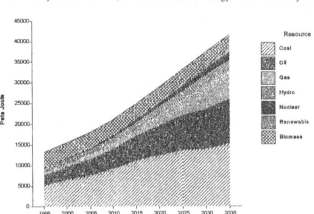

Figure 2. Energy consumption for the reference scenario increases threefold over four decades. Coal continues to dominate the energy supply. Shares of natural gas and oil increase significantly.

compared to 4.5% for the reference scenario. Sectoral demand in the growth scenarios is estimated from demand in the reference scenario and the elasticity of demand with GNP. Both energy intensity and carbon intensity decline over time in the growth scenarios (Figs 3 and 4). Of the reductions in future energy and carbon intensity 90% result from technology improvements, while a change in fuel mix accounts for the remaining 10%.

Energy intensity declined after 1980 due to the decreasing share of traditional biomass fuels in the total energy mix, the increasing shares of petroleum products and natural gas, and the penetration of energy-efficient technologies. Carbon intensity continued to increase until 1990, however, due to the decline in the share of hydropower (which is carbon free) in the electricity sector, the decline in the share of biomass fuels (which are assumed to be carbon neutral), and a rapid increase in the use of coal. Since 1990, carbon intensity has been declining as a result of the relatively higher rate of penetration of petroleum products and natural gas and further improvements in energy efficiency. As can be seen in Figure 3, energy intensity also began to decline at a faster rate after 1990.

In the low-growth scenario, both energy and carbon intensity decline initially as the share of domestic energy from gas and hydropower increases. Both the energy and carbon intensity in the high-growth scenario are greater than the intensities in the reference scenario, but the gap narrows in later years. Initially, high growth is fueled by domestic coal as well as imported oil and gas. In later years, penetration of gas increases as domestic coal becomes more expensive. Evidently, higher growth would require robust mitigation actions such as investments in infrastructure and energy efficiency, promotion of clean coal and renewable technologies, and a carbon tax.

Carbon Tax Scenarios

Five carbon tax scenarios are analyzed (Table 1). The carbon tax scenarios range from a no tax scenario, to a stabilization tax scenario in which the tax is the amount necessary to stabilize the atmospheric GHG concentration over the long-term (17). Compared to the no tax scenario, carbon emissions under the stabilization tax decline by 25% (Fig. 5). Successively higher tax levels lead to lower emissions, but marginal mitigation gains are low at higher tax levels. The implementation of a carbon tax reduces emissions by promoting a change in fuel mix, wherein coal is replaced by gas and, to a lesser extent, by hydro and renewable energy. Coal demand declines drastically under higher carbon taxes (Fig. 6).

Penetration of Renewable Energy

Supported by government programs in India, several renewable energy technologies have penetrated decentralized and rural ap-

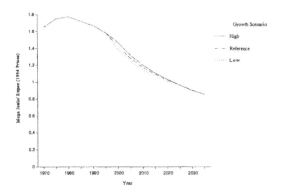

Figure 3. Energy intensity peaked in 1980. Future growth rate does not affect energy intensity. It will decline under any growth scenario.

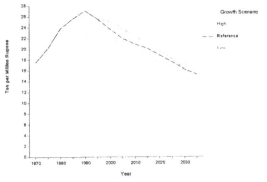

Figure 4. Carbon intensity peaked in 1990. It will decline in the future under any growth scenario.

plications as well as centralized electricity generation. An analysis of renewable electricity-generating technologies (Fig. 7) suggests that several of the technologies have competitive potential. The penetration of renewable technologies is vitally influenced by a carbon tax. Wind power and small hydropower have much potential within the next decade. These technologies are at a takeoff stage and can penetrate rapidly if a level playing field is provided by taxing fossil fuels. A stabilization tax would accelerate the penetration of wind power by four times (to 4750 MW) in 2005 relative to the no tax scenario. The penetration of small hydropower would receive a similar boost as a result of the stabilization tax. The present cost of solar photovoltaic (PV)

Table 1. Carbon tax scenarios (USD per ton of carbon), 1995 to 2035.

Scenario	1995	2000	2005	2010	2015	2020	2025	2030	2035
Stabilization tax	11.96	26.99	40.00	59.99	79.00	99.00	120.04	143.57	162.00
High tax	7.50	20.24	30.00	44.99	59.25	74.25	90.03	107.68	121.50
Medium tax	0.00	5.00	20.00	29.99	39.50	49.50	60.02	71.78	81.00
Reference	0.00	0.00	10.00	15.00	19.75	24.75	30.01	35.89	40.50
No tax	0.00	0.00	0.00	0.00	0.00	0.00	0.00	0.00	0.00

Ambio Vol. 25 No. 4, June 1996

power is too high. A stabilization tax and the declining cost of PV technologies make them competitive after the year 2010. A higher carbon tax accelerates the penetration of all renewable technologies. For example, under the no tax regime, PV technology takes off after the year 2030; under the stabilization tax regime, PV technology takes off two decades earlier. Interestingly, each successively higher tax level advances the take-off of PV penetration by about five years.

Infrastructure Scenarios

The four infrastructure scenarios analyzed are: *i*) a transport scenario, shifting traffic from road to rail; *ii*) a clean coal scenario, with additional coal washing capacity; *iii*) an electricity transmission and distribution (T&D) scenario aimed at reducing losses and extending electricity reach to rural areas; and *iv*) a demand-side management (DSM) scenario with efficient electricity use and peak load measures. Simultaneous implementation of these scenarios lowers energy and carbon intensities by 10%. The infrastructure scenarios assume only modest institutional changes and investments; they do not include more far-reaching alternatives such as relocating activities, changing consumption behavior, substituting communication for transportion, or mandating the use of renewable technologies. Although difficult to implement, such far-reaching changes could lead to an economy with very low energy and carbon intensities.

Transport Scenario: Transport is among the fastest-growing sectors. Between 1990 and 2030, passenger travel (in person km) is projected to increase more than ninefold; freight travel (in ton km) is projected to increase approximately sevenfold. In the past two decades, road transport's share of freight movement increased from 35% to 56% while its share of passenger movement increased from 59% to 77% (18). A rapid increase in road traffic has contributed to rapidly declining standards of road safety and an increase in urban pollution. Rail capacity in India is constrained by limited track length, slow electrification of tracks, and inadequate locomotive supply and wagon capacity. Excess demand exists for freight and passenger movement by rail. The transport scenario assumes that, over a decade, the investment in rail capacity will shift 25% of road movement to

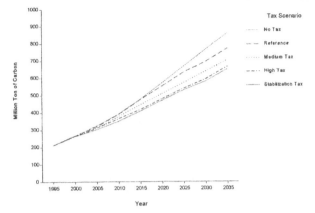

Figure 5. Carbon emissions under different tax scenarios. In the reference scenario, carbon emissions increase fourfold over 40 years. Higher taxes reduce emissions because gas and some renewable energy are substituted for coal.

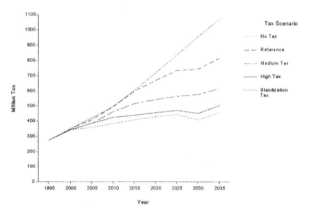

Figure 6. Carbon taxes have dramatic effects on coal consumption. If no tax is applied, coal consumption in 2035 exceeds one thousand million tons. Under the stabilization tax, coal consumption declines to 400 million tons.

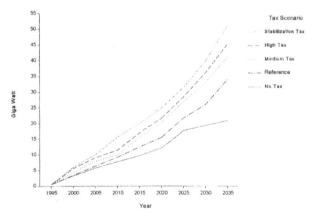

Figure 7. Higher carbon taxes accelerate the penetration of renewable technologies for electricity production. In 2035, renewable power capacity under the stabilization tax is more than twice as high as in the no tax scenario.

rail and investment in road infrastructure will enhance efficiency by 5%. These infrastructure improvements translate into 2% energy savings and 0.5% savings in carbon emissions in 2035. There are additional benefits such as reduced oil consumption (Fig. 8) and better air quality in cities due to lower traffic.

Clean Coal Scenario: Coal-washing capacity has stagnated at about 10% for the last two decades. Indian coal has a high ash content (35%). Associated problems such as ash disposal, particulate and sulfur dioxide emissions, and excess transport burden can be mitigated by coal washing. Washed coal has better combustion efficiency and lower weight for the same energy content. The clean coal scenario assumes that 15% of coal produced in the year 2000 and 50% of that produced in year 2035 will be washed, compared to 10% for the reference scenario. In 2035, ash disposal and sulfur dioxide emissions decline by one-third, freight transport demand on railways declines by 3%, and energy use and carbon emissions decline by 1%.

Electricity T&D Scenario: Two deficiencies of the electricity T&D network in India are high losses and inadequate reach in rural areas. High T&D losses translate into direct system inefficiency. Inadequate reach and disruptions in electricity supply during peak load hours induce energy and economic inefficiencies and, at the same time, adversely affect social development. Two direct energy consequences of poor rural electrification are the inefficient use of kerosene for lighting and diesel engines for irrigation. The electricity T&D scenario assumes investment in efficient T&D technologies, extension of the rural electrification network, and adequate electricity supply to rural areas. These investments reduce energy and carbon intensities through savings in electricity, diesel, and kerosene. The long-term impact on India of the electricity T&D scenario is a reduction of 3.8% in energy intensity and 2.7% in carbon intensity in year 2035.

DSM and Peak Electricity Scenario: Demand-side management of electricity use refers to a broad range of strategies for influencing the consumption behavior of energy users in terms of quantity and timing of energy use. Electricity planning in India has focused on the supply side. Within the integrated least-cost energy planning framework, many DSM options are less expensive than investment in new power plants. In addition, DSM conserves energy resources and reduces emissions. A central problem of electric power planning in India is meeting the peak demand. At present, there is a 19% shortage in electric power capacity for meeting peak demand (19). This causes frequent power shut-downs, which lower economic productivity as well as quality of life. DSM strategies also influence users to shift their time of electricity use away from peak load hours. Implementation of DSM will require creating institutions, financing users to replace inefficient appliances, enforcing equipment standards, reforming electricity pricing to include economic and social costs, and establishing differential tariffs for peak and nonpeak hours. Analysis of DSM measures with the MARKAL model shows a 9% reduction in electricity generation and 15% decline in electric power capacity in the year 2035, relative to the reference scenario. These translate into a decline of 4% in energy intensity and 5% in carbon intensity.

GHG MITIGATION ANALYSIS WITH SGM

The Second Generation Model (SGM) used for top-down analysis is a computable general equilibrium model (20) calibrated for 1985. Our analysis spans 45 yrs, from 1985 to 2030. The economy is represented by nine producing sectors (including

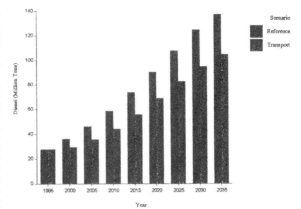

Figure 8. Diesel consumption increases fivefold over 40 years in the reference scenario. Improvement in transport infrastructure and shifting 25% of road traffic to rail will reduce diesel consumption by 25%.

seven energy sectors), four final-demand sectors, and three factors of production. Each sector has several subsectors that represent different technologies or fuel grades. For example, there are six subsectors for the electricity sector. There are 20 subsectors in total and each produces a homogenous good. Production relations are represented by constant elasticity of substitution functions. Technological change is assumed to be "Hicks Neutral" and is exogenously introduced as change in total factor productivity. Technological progress also results from selection of new technologies. Economic growth occurs through enhanced factor supply and improved productivity (e.g., technological progress).

Investment in a sector (or subsector) in each period depends on the savings in the economy and expected profit in the sector. Investment allocation is determined by a logit function. Capital is assumed to be the "putty-clay" type; that is, once the investment occurs, the technology cannot be changed. Capital is modelled using a vintage approach and investments operate for life or until they cover operating expenses. Data are required for the 1985 input-output table, past capital investment pattern, energy flows in the economy at subsector and technology level, reserves of resources, land supply, and current emissions. The labor supply is estimated using a separate demographic model. Both renewable and natural resources are explicitly treated. Only commercial energy sources are considered. Traditional biomass fuels are ignored since national accounts and official input-output data do not include their value.

The Reference Scenario

The reference scenario's carbon tax trajectory for SGM is identical to the trajectory for the MARKAL reference case (Table 1). The carbon tax is modelled as an additive tax per ton of carbon content in fossil fuels. Revenue from the carbon tax is recycled to households by adding to income. In SGM, the carbon tax alters the macroeconomy. Demand and supply respond to endogenous price changes and the economy moves to a new equilibrium state. In MARKAL, demands from economic activities are inelastic to the price of servicing the demand, and energy supply and costs are exogenous. Thus, in MARKAL, the carbon tax influences the energy and emissions only through changes in technology investments and fuel mix.

The SGM reference scenario predicts annual growth rates of 3.5% for GNP and 3% each for energy use and carbon emis-

Ambio Vol. 25 No. 4, June 1996

sion between 1990 and 2030. Coal and oil are projected to be the dominant fuels. Coal is the primary source of electricity. Strict comparability between SGM and MARKAL is not possible due to differences in model specifications and assumptions. SGM ignores the traditional biomass fuels that are accounted for in MARKAL. Unlike MARKAL, where it is exogenous, the growth rate of the economy is endogenous to SGM. In addition, the different perspectives of top-down and bottom-up models discussed earlier are pertinent. Keeping these caveats in mind, it is interesting to compare the results of the two models.

The GNP growth rate predicted by the SGM reference case is lower (3.5%) than the growth rate predicted for the low-growth case in MARKAL (4%). To compare the results of the two models, a new MARKAL scenario was developed with a 3.5% annual growth in GNP. This scenario is identical to the MARKAL reference scenario in all respects, except for the end-use demands which are adjusted to the 3.5% growth rate. After correcting for biomass fuels, which are ignored in SGM, the aggregate energy and carbon intensities in the new scenario are 20% lower than in the SGM reference scenario. In both cases, coal dominates the energy supply. SGM restricts gas imports to maintain the trade balance endogenously. Gas consumption and penetration of renewables are higher in the new MARKAL scenario than in the SGM reference scenario. In SGM, in the year 2030, a carbon tax causes 0.1% GNP loss annually and 0.4% consumption loss compared to a no carbon tax future. The no tax scenario in SGM has 25% higher energy- and carbon-intensity than the reference scenario.

Mitigation Scenarios

Top-down models are highly suitable for analyzing the effects of economic instruments such as taxes, subsidies, emission quotas, and permits. Carbon taxes alter the cost structure of fossil fuels. Two mitigation scenarios are analyzed using SGM. Carbon emissions in the SGM reference scenario are three times higher in 2030 than in 1990. The 1 X mitigation scenario assumes the application of a carbon tax to stabilize future carbon emissions at the 1990 level. The 2 X scenario assumes that carbon emissions stabilize at twice the 1990 level. SGM computes the optimal carbon tax trajectory for achieving each mitigation scenario (Fig. 9). The tax level required for achieving the 2 X scenario is 25% higher than the reference scenario after 2025. The carbon tax induces stronger response in SGM than in MARKAL. In SGM, the tax results in inputs to existing technologies rather than energy; investment in technologies that are not carbon intensive; and price-induced losses in consumption and GNP (Fig. 10). In MARKAL, the tax influence is limited and stems only from future technology investments.

The carbon tax that is necessary to achieve the 1 X scenario is very high. Meeting such a low-emission target requires considerable adjustments in the economy, such as totally phasing out coal-based electric power by 2010, and large investments in nuclear, renewable, and energy-efficient technologies. Emissions are also reduced as a result of substituting other inputs in production and consuming sectors throughout the economy for fossil energy; this substitution leads to an annual 6% loss in GNP and an annual 14% loss in consumption in the year 2030 (Fig. 10).

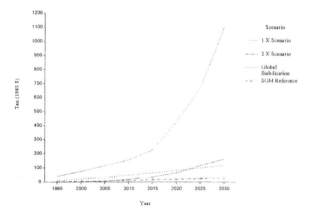

Figure 9. The carbon tax necessary to stabilize emissions at 1990 levels (1 X scenario) is very high. Emissions under the global stabilization tax will be twice the 1990 level.

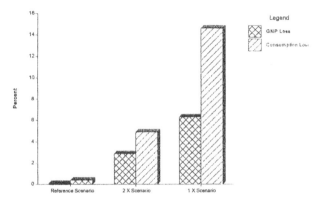

Figure 10. Higher mitigation targets for India will cause a significant reduction in annual GNP and consumption. In this figure, losses are indicated for the year 2030.

The tax trajectory for stabilizing India's emissions at the 1990 level is very high compared to the tax trajectory for stabilizing global carbon emissions. The global stabilization tax trajectory is in fact closer to the 2 X scenario (Fig. 9). Reduction of emissions in India to the 2 X level is thus beneficial within a global greenhouse regime, but further mitigation is too expensive. Reduction to the 2 X level, however, is in itself a substantial gain. India's participation in the global greenhouse protocol thus has mutual advantages.

Emissions Trading: Permit Scenarios

The use of tradable permits is a much discussed instrument for achieving greenhouse gas mitigation efficiently. Permits are created to match a global emission target. Each country is allocated permits based on an agreed-upon allocation scheme. A country can sell excess permits if its emissions are below the allocation. Otherwise, permits must be purchased from the global permits market to cover excess emissions. The suitability of alternate allocation schemes, in terms of satisfying the principles of equity, efficiency, and widest participation, is a subject of considerable debate (21, 22). Due to its large population and low per capita emissions, the alternate allocation schemes have significantly different equity implications for India. SGM was used to analyze two extremely different types of permit allocation schemes: a "Grandfathered Emission" scheme in which each country is allocated permits for emissions equal to 1990 emissions within that country, and an "Equal per Capita Emission" scheme in which each country is allocated permits for a share of global emissions that is equal to its share of the global population.

A global protocol for stabilizing greenhouse gas concentrations will specify the annual GHG emission trajectory over a long-term horizon, and the total global tradable permits released in a given period will correspond to this annual emission trajectory. Each nation will be allocated permits according to the agreed-upon allocation scheme. Under the tradable permits regime, the price of a permit in the global market will be equal to the marginal cost of mitigation. India will be a net buyer of permits under the "Grandfathered Emission" scheme and a net seller under the "Per Capita Emission" scheme. For the stabilization policy, the permit price will follow the stabilization tax trajectory (Table 1). Under these schemes, the net gain (loss) for a nation is the sum of the GNP loss from the global carbon tax and the gain (loss) from selling (buying) permits. Under these allocation schemes, India's net loss or gain will be very high (Fig. 11). For example, under the "Grandfathered Emission" scheme, India's net annual loss is USD 50 bill. (1985 dollars) in the year 2030, 5% of India's projected GNP for that year. The net annual gain under the "Equal per Capita Emission" scheme is USD 57 bill. in the year 2030. India, therefore, has a strong motivation for participating in the global negotiations of the protocol for the initial allocation of permits.

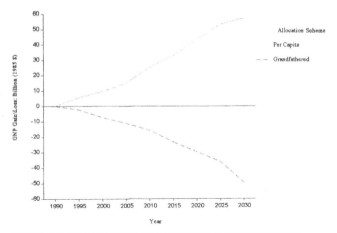

Figure 11. India gains substantially under schemes that allocate permits in proportion to population. Schemes using previous emissions for allocation will cause substantial losses. India's stake in the permit negotiations is very high.

Modelling Insights and Observations

The two mitigation policy studies for India suggest that: *i*) the choice of a model paradigm is crucial for this type of policy analysis; *ii*) model results can be reconciled by making comparable assumptions; and *iii*) policy analysis is enriched by comparing consistent top-down and bottom-up model scenarios. Although the policy analysis from the two studies provides valuable insights, the structure and perspective of models treat India like a developed market economy and thus impose serious conceptual and practical limitations. Model results remain questionable because of weak and incomplete representation of reality; policy prescriptions lack conviction; and the often observed skepticism of policy makers towards formal models is amplified.

DEVELOPING COUNTRY DYNAMICS

Developing countries are dual economies where the modern industrial sector co-exists with a vast informal and traditional economy. The traditional economy accounts for up to 70% of GNP and includes most rural markets and the urban periphery (23). The traditional economy is nonmonetized and has weak market linkages that restrict the flow of finances across regions and sectors. Personalized transactions and informal contracts are made to circumvent imperfect information (24) and the institutional gap. Informal financing dominates the credit submarkets catering to small, poor, and risky borrowers and also competes with and complements the formal financing in other submarkets (25).

The informal sector includes economic activities that are deliberately under-reported in national accounts (26). For example, in India, the income from undeclared sources was estimated at 50.7% of GNP in 1987 (27). The informal sector's share in employment was 50% in Calcutta in 1971 and 45% in Jakarta in 1976 (28). Informal credit accounts for up to two-thirds of total credit in Bangladesh and China and two-fifths in India (29). Interest rates in the traditional and informal sectors tend to be very high and hinder the penetration of efficient technologies.

Developing country dynamics include the processes that govern the transition of the traditional and informal economy into a modern industrial economy. These processes alter the institutions, technology, investment, land use, capabilities, income, behavior of producers, government policies, and consumer preferences.

Development Process and Paradoxes

The development process reveals numerous paradoxes. The co-existence of diverse technology vintages, inefficient use of traditional biomass energy, and great resistance to penetration of efficiency measures are some paradoxes that have tormented energy and environmental policy makers. The explanation of these paradoxes is rooted in transitional dynamics. For example, contrary to conventional technology assessment that emphasize the trade-off between capital cost and fuel cost, the decisive factor for the penetration of efficient technologies in the traditional sector is the value of labor. Because labor is abundant and lacks monetized value (30), it is substituted for capital and commercial energy at every opportunity. Traditional biomass fuels are collected or home-grown, and have value only in use. Substituting technology for biomass fuels is resisted as long as biomass resources are accessible and labor is abundant; thus, energy-efficient technologies and commercial fuels fail to penetrate. Ironically, technological inefficiency emerges not as a cause, but as a result of underdevelopment that is characterized by inadequate employment and exchange opportunities.

Poor infrastructure and institutional arrangements breed new paradoxes. It is a paradox that poor people in developing countries use more expensive and yet unclean fuels. For example, kerosene is used extensively for lighting by the poor. Per unit of light delivery (in lumens), kerosene is 20 times more expensive than tube light in India. In addition, kerosene use is cumbersome and polluting. This paradox is the result of poor access to infrastructure (poor rural electrification) and institutions. Inefficiency is rooted in underdevelopment. Such paradoxes reflect the duality of transitional processes in the development phase. These paradoxes are not cases of market failure. On the contrary, they point to the fact that the market dynamics presumed by models are nonexistent.

POLICY MODELLING FOR DEVELOPING COUNTRIES

Most of the models used for GHG mitigation studies have originated in developed countries. They presume the existence of institutions, interconnected and global markets, competition among producers, and perfect information. When applying these models to the economies of developing countries, analysts most often model developing economies in the image of developed market economies. As a result, the development process is overlooked, an entire epoch is ignored, and policy prescriptions become unrealistic. Model dynamics and policy analysis must be altered to reflect developing country realities. Some of the crucial aspects needing explicit representation in mitigation modelling are described below.

Dual Economy

In the traditional and modern sectors of the economy, production, consumption, investment, market relations, resources, technologies, and institutional structure differ significantly. For example, rice production in modern agriculture is capital- and energy-intensive whereas, in traditional agriculture, it is labor-intensive (31). Representation of the traditional sector requires explicit inclusion of nonmarket activities, local resources, subsistence behavior, biomass energy, excess labor, multiple and high discount rates, and technological stagnation. Unpaid tasks, such as biomass collection, need to be valued and added to national accounts. Other important issues to be considered include representation of labor supply, rural to urban migration, changing consumer preferences, shifts in government policy, technological progress in both sectors, and transactions between the two sectors.

Disequilibrium and Distortions

Commodity and factor markets are assumed by the models to be in equilibrium. However, this is not true for developing countries. Energy markets perpetually experience excess demand. Energy supply and infrastructure are often controlled by government monopolies, and there are myriad barriers to competition and restrictions on international trade that distort the market response. In India in 1994, for example, the electricity sector had excess peak power demand of 19%. Estimation of parameters, such as the price elasticity of demand, using equilibrium assumptions tend to be misleading. Poor data availability and reliability also distort the representation of reality.

Biomass: The Missing Fuel

Biomass contributes 35% of energy in developing nations (32). Most biomass is home-grown or collected by family labor. Under sustainable production and use, the biomass fuels are carbon neutral. But their present use pattern is unsustainable and adds to deforestation and consequently to the carbon flux. Fourteen million hectares of land were deforested globally in 1989, with the net effect of adding 1.4 gigatons to the atmospheric carbon flux (33). Traditional biomass use is very inefficient. The energy efficiency of traditional cook stoves is only 8%. Policies regulating biomass use in developing countries can offer vital opportunities for least-cost global GHG mitigation. Yet, the traditional use of biomass continues to be inadequately represented in most bottom-up studies; and biomass use is totally ignored by top-down models because its economic value is not accounted

for in national statistics.

Biomass is used to meet the cooking energy needs of most rural households and half of the urban households in India. Biomass collection requires the work of many people, mainly women. Collection time, about three hours per household daily, is increasing due to depletion of village woodlots. Biomass does not acquire monetary value because it is collected by unpaid labor and is not traded. Eight billion person days are spent annually for biomass collection in India. This is equivalent to full-time employment for 30 mill. persons, 11% of India's total employment. Valued at minimum wage, biomass is worth 150 bill. Rupees or 2% of India's GNP in 1994. Its kerosene equivalence is more than 20 mill. tons. Biomass acquires implicit value either from the opportunity cost of labor used for its collection or the price equivalent of a substitute fuel, which in India is kerosene. Policies that enhance the value of labor, such as employment generation, women's development, education, and minimum wage can therefore alter biomass use. Pricing policies for kerosene would also affect the use of biomass energy.

Kerosene Subsidy in India

Kerosene is highly subsidized in India and is used by low-income and rural households for cooking and illumination. Typical top-down model analysis usually recommends removal of the kerosene subsidy because any tax or subsidy is treated by the model as a distortion which, if corrected, enhances the gross domestic product. Although the income elasticity of biomass energy is negative, its elasticity to the price of kerosene is positive (34). Reduction of the kerosene subsidy would thus increase biomass use as well as its negative environmental impacts, deforestation and indoor air pollution. Both deforestation and indoor air pollution are detrimental to the quality of life of the poor, especially women. In this context, the kerosene subsidy is an environmental and developmental instrument rather than an energy policy intervention and has a positive impact on GHG mitigation.

Choosing a Development Path

The United Nations Framework Convention on Climate Change appropriately recommends, and reminds us, in its statement of objective that policies for stabilizing GHG concentrations should enable economic development to proceed in a sustainable manner (1). Choice of a development path has crucial implications for the future resource use pattern and the energy and GHG intensities of a nation. In the past, a lop-sided emphasis on economic efficiency led to extremely resource-intensive development in industrialized countries. This path is now unsustainable. Most developing countries are prepared to make major investment decisions in the coming decades. They can shift to a much less resource-intensive trajectory by investing in infrastructure such as rail and communication, renewable resources, location planning to promote lower logistical costs, education of consumers, and by investing in people. Superior technological and developmental alternatives provide developing countries with a window of opportunity for leapfrogging developed countries in terms of sustainable development.

GHG mitigation studies for developing countries should focus on analysis of alternative policies that transform the development pattern rather than incremental and isolated project-level interventions. Although market dynamics ensure economically efficient choices, they often reject choices that are superior in terms of other criteria such as equity, conservation of resources, preservation of environment, biodiversity, and cultural diversity. Present models need to be adapted so that they include these additional criteria. In their consideration of GHG mitigation strategies, developing countries will benefit by explicitly considering developmental choices such as investment in education, demographic measures, institutions, infrastructure, employment, consumer education, sustainable agriculture, land use planning, and decentralization.

CONCLUSION

The participation of developing countries in GHG protocol has global benefits. Numerous low-cost mitigation opportunities exist in developing countries. New investments in infrastructure and institutions open a window of opportunity for developing countries to switch to a development path that is not resource-intensive. The conventional development pattern is both energy and carbon intensive. Mitigation gains will be substantive if the development path chosen for the future is not energy or emission intensive. For India, conventional development with no carbon tax and little investment in mitigation will increase carbon emissions nearly fourfold between 1995 and 2035. In addition to a carbon tax, other mitigation policies such as investment in infrastructure and institutions will be necessary to achieve substantial mitigation. A carbon tax to stabilize India's emissions at the 1990 level will cause a 14% loss in consumption and a 6% loss in GNP in the year 2035. Developmental actions will achieve similar mitigation at lower costs.

Present mitigation models lack realistic representation of developing country dynamics. Mitigation policy analysis for developing countries will improve if activities in the traditional and informal sectors are accounted for, disequilibrium and distortions are explicitly treated, traditional biomass energy is included, and innovative policy options are emphasized. Present models emphasize only economic efficiency. Other objectives such as equity and sustainability require consideration. Climate change modelling has made notable advances in recent years. Integrated assessment models provide a unified framework for evolving mitigation and adaptation policies (35). Modelling frameworks linking climate change policies with sustainable development (36) are also proposed. Notwithstanding these advances, model dynamics are still governed by a developed country perspective. Reorientation of model dynamics and perspective to address developing country realities are refinements needing immediate attention.

Developing countries have a large stake in decisions regarding global GHG protocol. Under different GHG allowance schemes, India's loss or gain can be equivalent to 5% of its GNP. An equitable and just policy regime will encourage wide participation of developing countries in GHG mitigation endeavors. Stabilization of GHG concentrations calls for a quantum change in future emissions. The problem of climate change is a challenge as well as an opportunity to move the global economy towards sustainable development. Challenges posed by climate change are too serious to be ignored. But the opportunity it has offered the global community to shift the development pattern towards a sustainable path will prove too costly, if missed. It is a test of our ability to resolve truly global problems, many more of which will be forthcoming as developing economies are integrated into the global economic system in the next century.

References

1. UNEP/WMO. 1992. *United Nations Framework Convention on Climate-Text*. UNEP/WMO Unit on Climate Change, Geneva, 5 pp.
2. Hourcade, J.C. 1993. Modelling long-run scenarios: methodology lessons from a prospective study on a low CO_2 intensity country. *Energy Policy 21*, 309–325.
3. Grubb M., Edmonds, J., Brink, P. ten and Morrison, M. 1993. The costs of limiting fossil-fuel CO_2 emissions: a survey and analysis. *Ann. Rev. Energy Environ. 18*, 397–478.
4. Wilson, D. and Swisher, J. 1993. Exploring the gap: top-down versus bottom-up analyses of the cost of mitigating global warming. *Energy Policy 21*, 249–63.
5. Sathaye, J. and Christensen, J. (eds). 1994. Methods for the economic evaluation of greenhouse gas mitigation options. Special Issue. *Energy Policy 22*.
6. UNEP Collaborating Center on Energy and Environment. 1993. *UNEP Greenhouse Gas Abatement Costing Studies: Analysis of Abatement Costing Issues and Preparation of a Methodology to Undertake National Greenhouse Gas Abatement Costing Studies (Phase Two, Part 2, Country Summaries)*. Risø National Laboratory, Denmark.
7. Dean, A. and Hoeller, P. 1992. *Costs of Reducing CO_2 Emissions: Evidence from Six Global Models*. OECD Economic Studies 19.
8. Shukla, P.R. 1995. Greenhouse gas models and abatement costs for developing nations: a critical assessment, *Energy Policy 7*, 1–11.
9. World Resources Institute. 1995. *World Resources 1994-95: A Guide to the Global Environment*. Oxford University Press, Delhi.
10. Center for Monitoring Indian Economy. 1994. *Basic Statistics Relating to Indian Economy*. Bombay.
11. United Nations Development Program. 1994. *Human Development Report*. Oxford University Press, Delhi, 133 pp.
12. World Resources Institute. 1992. *World Resources 1992-93: A Guide to the Global Environment*. Oxford University Press, New York.
13. Smith, K. R. 1987. *Biofuels, Air Pollution and Health: A Global Review*. Plenum Publishing Corporation, New York.
14. Berger, C, Haurie, A. and Loulou, R. 1987. *Modeling Long Range Energy/Technology Choices: The MARKAL Approach*. Report. GERAD, Montreal.
15. Edmonds, J. and Reilly, J. 1983. A long-term global energy-economic model of carbon dioxide release from fossil fuel use. *Energy Econ. 5*, 74–88.
16. Clarke J.F. and Edmonds J.A. 1993. Modelling energy technologies in a competitive market. *Energy Econ.*, 123–129.
17. Edmonds, J., Barns, D., Wise, M. and Ton, M. 1992. *Carbon Coalitions: The Cost of Effectiveness of Energy Agreements to Alter Trajectories of Atmospheric Carbon Dioxide Emissions*. Report. Prepared for the US Office of Technology Assessment and PNL Global Studies Program.
18. Tata Energy Research Institute. 1995. *TERI Energy Data Directory and Yearbook*, New Delhi.
19. Center for Monitoring Indian Economy. 1994. *Current Energy Scene in India*. Bombay.
20. Edmonds, J.A., Pitcher, H.M., Baron, R. and Wise, M.A. 1992. Modelling future greenhouse gas emissions: The second generation model description. *Proc. UN Univ. Conf. Global Climate Change*. Tokyo.
21. Rose, A. 1990. Reducing conflict in global warming policy: The potential of equity as a unifying principle. *Energy Policy*, 927–935.
22. Kverndokk, S. 1995. Tradeable CO_2 emission permits: initial distribution as a justice problem. *Environ. Values*, 129–148.
23. Jagannathan, V.N. 1987. *Informal Markets in Developing Countries*. Oxford University Press, New York.
24. Clifford, G. 1978. The bazaar economy, information and change in peasant marketing. *Am. Econ. Rev. 68*, 28–32.
25. Ghate, P.B. 1992. Interaction between the formal and informal finance sectors: The Asian experience. *World Development 20*, 859–872.
26. Feige, E.L. 1990. Defining and estimating underground and informal economies: The new institutional economics approach. *World Development 18*, 989–1002.
27. Gupta, S. 1992. *Black Income In India*. Sage Publications, New Delhi.
28. Sethuraman, S.V. 1981. *The Urban Informal Sector in Developing Countries: Employment, Poverty and Environment*. ILO, Geneva.
29. Montiel, P., Agenos, P.R. and Haque N. 1993. *Informal Financial Markets in Developing Countries: A Macroeconomic Analysis*. Blackwell, Oxford UK and Cambridge USA.
30. Bose, S.A. 1993. *Money, Energy and Welfare: The State and the Households in India's Rural Electrification Policy*. Oxford University Press, Delhi.
31. Moulik T.K., Dholakia B.H. and Shukla P.R. 1990. Energy demand forecast for agriculture in India. *Economic and Political Weekly XXV*, A165–175.
32. Hall, D.O. 1991. Biomass energy. *Energy Policy 19*, 711–737.
33. Rosillo-Calle, F. and Hall, D.O. 1992. Biomass energy, forests and global warming. *Energy Policy 20*, 124–136.
34. Walker, I.O. and Birol, F. 1992. Analysing the cost of an OPEC environmental tax to the developing countries. *Energy Policy 20*, 559–567.
35. Dowlatabadi, H. and Morgan M.G. 1993. A model framework for integrated assessment of the climate problem. *Energy Policy 21*, 209–221.
36. Rotmans, J., van Asselt, M.B.A., de Bruin A.J., den Ellen, M.G.J., de Greef, J., Hilderink, H., Hockstra, A.Y., Janssen, M.A., Koster, H.W., Martens, W.J.M., Niessen, L.W. and de Vries, H.J.M. 1994. *Global Change and Sustainable Development: A Modelling Perspective for the Next Decade*. RIVM. Report No. 461502004. Bilthoven, The Netherlands.
37. The author gratefully acknowledges the Shastri Indo-Canadian Institute for supporting the MARKAL model analysis and Battelle, Pacific Northwest Laboratories, for supporting the Second Generation Model analysis. The following people made this paper possible and are much appreciated: Jae Edmonds, Jean Charles Hourcade, Richard Loulou, Karen Fisher-Vanden, and Amit Kanudia. The author alone, however, is responsible for the paper's contents.

P.R. Shukla is a professor and is Chairman of the Public Systems Group at the Indian Institute of Management (IIMA), Ahmedabad, India. After obtaining his PhD from Stanford University, he joined IIMA in 1979. He has been a consultant to the Government of India on energy and greenhouse gas policy models. He has worked with several international research teams on climate change modelling and policy analysis. He was a member of the global team at Battelle, Pacific Northwest Laboratory, Washington D.C., and developed the SGM application for India. He is working with CIRED, Paris, on the extension of the IMACLIM-NEXUS model to developing countries. He is a chief co-investigator of a joint research project sponsored by Shastri Indo-Canadian Institute in partnership with McGill University, Montreal for assessing the future energy and environment policies for India. He is a lead author of the IPCC's Second Assessment Report on Climate Change. His research interests include modelling and analysis of long-term energy and climate change policies for developing countries and implications of international trade and environmental policies for developing countries. His address: Indian Institute of Management, Ahmedabad, India 380015.

[29]

POLITICAL ECONOMY OF THE KYOTO PROTOCOL

SCOTT BARRETT
London Business School[1]

The Kyoto Protocol, negotiated in December 1997, is the first international treaty to limit emissions of green-house gases. But Kyoto does not mark the conclusion to international cooperation on climate change. It is really just a beginning. This paper shows that, in the aggregate, the benefits of undertaking the Kyoto reductions should exceed the corresponding costs—provided these are achieved cost-effectively. But, although Kyoto seeks to promote cost-effectiveness, it may yet prove very costly. Moreover, the agreement may not even achieve the reductions that it promises, either because emissions will relocate to the countries that are not required to stay within Kyoto-prescribed ceilings or because ''paper' trades will be promoted by the protocol's mecha-nisms. More fundamentally, Kyoto does not deter non-compliance, and it only weakly deters non-participation. These flaws need to be mended, but the nature of the problem makes that an especially difficult task.

I. INTRODUCTION

The Kyoto Protocol, negotiated in December 1997, is a climate change treaty with a difference. Unlike the Framework Convention on Climate Change that preceded it, the Kyoto Protocol incorporates targets and timetables—that is, ceilings on the emissions of greenhouse gases and dates by which these ceilings must be met. And though global emissions will continue to rise, even if the protocol is implemented to the letter, the reduction from a business-as-usual emissions bench-mark may be close to being opti-mal in the sense of balancing the global marginal costs and benefits of abatement. Assuming full participation and cost-effective implementation, a recent study by the Clinton Administration esti-

[1] This paper began to form in my mind at the NBER–Yale Global Change Workshop in Snowmass, Colorado, where I was able to learn from, and put my questions to, some of the leading economists working on this issue. I am grateful to all the participants for sharing their ideas, and especially to Charles Kolstad, William Nordhaus, and Robert Stavins for inviting me to participate in the workshop. I am also grateful to Wilfred Beckerman, Dieter Helm, Tim Jenkinson, Chris Riley, Stephen Smith, Robert Stavins, Peter Zapfel, and an anonymous referee for helpful comments on an earlier draft. David Pearce also provided helpful comments at a seminar presentation.

S. Barrett

mated the marginal cost of meeting the Kyoto targets to range from \$14 to \$23/ton (Clinton Administration, 1998). Most estimates of the global marginal damage of greenhouse gas emissions are of a similar magnitude (see IPCC, 1996, ch. 6), and so it would seem that the Kyoto Protocol is a near ideal outcome for the world.

But this is only if the assumptions behind the Clinton Administration's estimates are correct: that participation in the agreement will be full and implementation cost-effective. A number of features of the Protocol will promote cost-effective implementation, including provisions for trading in the entitlements to emit greenhouse gases. However, though the details of the flexible mechanisms incorporated in Kyoto have yet to be worked out, implementation may turn out to be very costly, not least because participation is unlikely to be full. The marginal cost of implementing Kyoto could be ten times the estimates noted above. Moreover, the reduction in emissions effected by Kyoto could be less than the amount promised because of 'trade leakage'. Indeed, since leakage will be greater the greater are the between-country differences in marginal costs, the same forces causing costs to be higher will cause benefits to be lower. The Kyoto Protocol may turn out not to be such a good deal after all.

Worse, the agreement may not even be sustainable, and not just because high implementation costs could impel the parties to renegotiate the treaty. For another potential problem stalks Kyoto: compliance enforcement and free-rider deterrence. The Protocol defers discussion of enforcement to a future meeting of the parties, but it is sensible to ask: what would happen if in, say, 10 years' time, one of the parties to the agreement announces that it will not be able to comply with it? Or suppose, instead, that a party announces that it will withdraw from the agreement, because the costs of meeting it are too steep. What will prevent such a withdrawal? The treaty, at least in its present form, offers little protection from such deviations. And this is not just a problem for the future. Countries can reason backwards. If future deviations cannot be prevented, why should a country invest in abatement measures today?

Even this may not be the worst of the Protocol's problems. It is possible, maybe even likely, that the

agreement will never enter into force. In July 1997, the United States Senate voted 95–0 in favour of a non-binding resolution urging the President of the United States not to negotiate an agreement that required that only the industrial countries reduce their greenhouse-gas emissions or that would result in serious harm to the US economy, where by 'serious harm' the Senate meant, in the words of Senator Robert Byrd, a co-author of the resolution, 'capital flight and a loss of jobs in the United States'. This is important because the Senate must ratify (by a two-thirds majority) any treaty that is to be binding on the United States, and an effective climate-change treaty is sure to require US participation. There are many reasons for this, but perhaps the most obvious is that United States is the world's largest emitter. Its emissions are about 50 per cent higher than the entire emissions of the European Union.

The Clinton Administration previously endorsed the principle that the industrial countries should reduce their emissions first, and could not easily reverse out of this promise in Kyoto. And nor was Europe keen on relaxing the so-called Berlin Mandate. So the agreement reached in Kyoto clashed with the Senate's recommendation that developing countries reduce their emissions (whether implementation of the Protocol will be costly to the United States is a question requiring some analysis, and I shall return to it later). Of course, the Senate could have been bluffing, perhaps in the hope that its resolution would give President Clinton an edge in the Kyoto negotiations. Indeed, during the debate on the resolution, Senator Byrd said that the resolution would 'add strength to our US negotiating team'. But just after the negotiations ended in Kyoto, a number of senators asked that the treaty come to the Senate floor for ratification so that they could reject it. President Clinton has since said that he would not send the treaty to the Senate without 'meaningful participation from key developing countries'.

If the United States does not ratify the treaty, it is possible that the agreement will still come into force. To enter into law, and therefore to become binding on the countries that are parties to it (but not other countries), the Protocol must be ratified by at least 55 countries, responsible for at least 55 per cent of the total carbon-dioxide emissions of the so-called 'Annex I' countries (the industrial countries listed in

Table 1
Status of the Kyoto Protocol

Annex I countries	CO_2 emissions 1990 (gigagrams)	Share of Annex I 1990 emissions (%)	Kyoto target 2008–12 (% relative to 1990 or alternative base year)	Projected emissions 2000
United States	4,957,022	36.00	93	104
European Union*	3,288,667	24.05	92	103
Austria*	59,200	0.43	92	111
Belgium*	114,410	0.84	92	n.a.
Denmark*	52,025	0.38	92	103
Finland*	53,900	0.39	92	131
France*	366,536	2.68	92	109
Germany*	1,014,155	7.42	92	90
Greece*	82,100	0.60	92	115
Ireland*	30,719	0.22	92	120
Italy*	428,941	3.14	92	113
Luxembourg*	11,343	0.08	92	67
Netherlands*	167,600	1.23	92	92
Portugal*	42,148	0.31	92	129
Spain*	227,322	1.66	92	122
Sweden*	61,256	0.45	92	104
UK*	577,012	4.22	92	102
Australia*	288,965	2.11	108	115
Canada*	462,643	3.38	94	110
Iceland	2,172	0.02	110	105
Japan*	1,155,000	8.45	94	104
New Zealand*	25,476	0.19	100	116
Norway*	35,514	0.26	101	111
Switzerland*	45,070	0.33	92	97
Liechtenstein	208	n.a.	92	118
Monaco	n.a.	n.a.	92	n.a.
Economies in Transition	3,364,259	24.60	103	81
Alternative base year	3,531,476	—	98	77
Bulgaria* 1990	82,990	0.61	107	84
1988	96,878	—	92	72
Czech Republic	165,792	1.21	92	82
Estonia	37,797	0.28	92	54
Hungary 1990	71,673	0.52	110	96
1985–7	83,676	—	94	82
Latvia	22,976	0.17	92	74
Lithuania*	n.a.	n.a.	92	n.a.
Poland* 1990	414,930	3.03	108	96
1988	478,880	—	94	83
Romania 1990	171,103	1.25	107	n.a.
1989	198,479	–	92	n.a.
Russian Federation	2,388,720	17.47	100	83
Ukraine	n.a.	n.a.	100	n.a.
Slovakia	58,278	0.43	92	84

S. Barrett

Table 1 (continued)

Annex I countries	CO$_2$ emissions 1990 (gigagrams)	Share of Annex I 1990 emissions (%)	Kyoto target 2008–12 (% relative to 1990 or alternative base year)	Projected emissions 2000
Croatia	n.a.	n.a.	95	n.a.
Slovenia	n.a.	n.a.	92	n.a.
Total 1990	13,675,067	100	95	98
Total base	13,842,284	—	94	97

Notes: Two Annex I countries (Belarus and Turkey) are excluded from the table, as they are not included in Annex B of the Kyoto Protocol. Four other countries (Liechtenstein, Monaco, Croatia, and Slovenia) are included in Annex B but not in Annex I. *Indicates that the country is a signatory to the Kyoto Protocol, as of 23 October 1998. CO$_2$ emissions exclude land-use change and forestry.
Source: All data are from the web page of the Climate Change Secretariat, http://www.unfcc.de.

the original Framework Convention) in 1990. As shown in Table 1, the United States accounts for only 36 per cent of Annex I emissions. So, if enough of the countries making up the balance of Annex I emissions ratify the agreement, Kyoto will still enter the canon of climate law.

As of October 1998, 59 countries had signed the Protocol, including the 15 member states of the European Union and nine other Annex I countries (signatories are identified in Table 1 by an asterisk). These signatories make up just over 42 per cent of total Annex I emissions, and so the minimum participation required by the treaty would seem to be within easy reach. But putting a signature on a treaty does not obligate a country to ratify and, as of October 1998, only one country has ratified the Kyoto Protocol (though this in itself signifies nothing as the treaty was only recently negotiated): the small island state, Fiji.

Ratification by the current signatories is not inevitable. If the USA does not ratify the agreement, the other Annex I countries will benefit less from participating; these countries will have to undertake the emission reductions prescribed by the treaty (and shown in column 3 of Table 1) without the benefit of substantial US abatement. It is even possible that non-participation by the USA will *increase* the cost to these countries of keeping within their Kyoto limits, because of the treaty's

trading arrangements (explained later in the paper). It thus seems likely that many Annex I countries will await US ratification before serving the Kyoto Protocol up to their own parliaments. This means that, if the USA does not ratify the agreement, then it may not enter into force.[2]

Why should countries negotiate a treaty that could leave them worse off, or that may never even enter into international law? The scenario seems unlikely, but it is entirely in keeping with the history of climate-change policy. As described in section II, countries have previously announced their intention to keep within self-imposed emission ceilings—and then failed to meet them. Moreover, the Kyoto Protocol is not unique in the annals of international cooperation. The Law of the Sea Convention, negotiated in 1982, did not enter into force until 1994—and participation by the major maritime powers, including the United States and United Kingdom, had to await negotiation of a side agreement which effectively rewrote key provisions in the original treaty.

Of course, predicting whether Kyoto will endure, or whether it will achieve much if implemented, depends on many details. It depends, especially, on assumptions about how the important concepts in the agreement will be interpreted, about the institutions that will be developed to support it, about costs of taking action, and about the future evolution of the treaty. All these details are uncertain. They

[2] Just as it is hard to imagine a Gulf War coalition forming without the support of the United States, so it is hard to see how an effective climate-change regime could develop without American backing.

23

OXFORD REVIEW OF ECONOMIC POLICY, VOL. 14, NO. 4

are discussed in my analysis of the agreement in section III.

In the long run, whether or not Kyoto enters into law will not matter very much. If the Protocol fails to become law, countries will attempt to renegotiate the agreement. If Kyoto does enter into law but later collapses for whatever reason, a new agreement can always be negotiated. Even if Kyoto succeeds—if it enters into law and is implemented to the last detail—a string of amendments will need to be negotiated, to say what must be done after 2012. Kyoto is really just the start of a long process, and it must be remembered that climate change is a very long-run problem. What will matter most in the future is whether countries perceive that substantial mitigation is justified, and whether the international system can muster the cooperation needed to sustain this effort. I turn to these fundamental issues in section IV. The final section of the paper pulls these different analyses together and revisits the theme of this introduction.

II. GETTING TO KYOTO

(i) Preliminaries

The so-called greenhouse gases include not only carbon dioxide (CO_2), but also methane, nitrous oxide, fluorocarbons (including hydrofluorocarbons and perfluorocarbons), tropospheric ozone (precursors of which include nitrogen oxides, non-methane hydrocarbons, and carbon monoxide), and sulphur hexafluoride.[3] However, CO_2 accounts for the bulk of aggregate warming potential and, mainly for this reason, the policy debate has focused on the extent to which emissions of this gas should be limited. In 1988, a semi-political conference held in Toronto recommended that, as a first step, CO_2 emissions should be reduced 20 per cent from the 1988 level by 2005. This so-called 'Toronto target' was arbitrary, but the idea that countries should commit to meeting a target for emission reduction (as opposed to, say, a carbon tax or a technology standard) has

endured. It is perhaps the most important feature of the Kyoto Protocol.

In the same year that this conference was held, the Intergovernmental Panel on Climate Change (IPCC) was formed, at the request of the UN General Assembly. The IPCC was asked to report on what was known and not known about climate change, on the potential impacts of climate change, and on what could be done to forestall and adapt to climate change. The IPCC's first assessment report, published in 1990, concluded that 'emissions resulting from human activities are substantially increasing the atmospheric concentrations of the greenhouse gases ... [and] will enhance the greenhouse effect, resulting on average in an additional warming of the Earth's surface' (IPCC, 1990, p. 1). The report calculated that 'the long-lived gases [including CO_2] would require immediate reductions in emissions from human activities of over 60 per cent to stabilize their concentrations at today's levels', and it predicted that, under the 'Business-as-Usual' scenario, global mean temperature would rise by between 0.2°C and 0.5°C, and mean global sea level would rise by between 3 and 10cm, per decade during the next century. Rather ominously, the IPCC noted that 'the complexity of the system means that we cannot rule out surprises'.

(ii) Unilateral Pledges

Following publication of the IPCC's 1990 report, a number of OECD countries announced intentions to reduce their CO_2 emissions.[4] Some pledged to meet the Toronto target (Austria, Denmark, Italy, Luxembourg; New Zealand pledged that it would do so by 2000 rather than 2005). Some set a goal of stabilizing their CO_2 emissions at the 1989 level by 2000 (Norway) or at the 1990 level by 2000 (Finland, Switzerland, United Kingdom) or to reduce emissions 3–5 per cent by 2000 (The Netherlands). Germany, helped by unification, set the most ambitious target: to reduce CO_2 emissions 25–30 per cent from the 1987 level by 2005. Australia pledged to reduce its emissions of all greenhouse gases not

---

[3] Other halocarbons, including chlorofluorocarbons (CFCs) and hydrochlorofluorocarbons (HCFCs), are also potentially important from the policy perspective, but are being controlled by the Montreal Protocol and its associated amendments. Moreover, it is now known that the direct warming effect of these gases is partly offset by a cooling effect caused by the reduction in stratospheric ozone.

[4] The International Energy Agency (1992) has compiled a comprehensive listing of climate-change policies, and I am drawing here from this report.

controlled under the Montreal Protocol (that is, excluding CFCs and HCFCs), while other countries (Canada and the United States among them) set a target of stabilizing the emissions of all greenhouse gases, including those covered by the Montreal Protocol. France and Japan pledged to stabilize their CO_2 emissions at the 1990 level by 2000 but only on a per-capita basis (allowing emissions to increase as population increased). Spain, a relatively poor OECD member, set the goal of limiting its growth in CO_2 emissions to 25 per cent. Finally, some countries merely promised to play a part in achieving a collective target. In October 1990 the European Community (EC) announced its intention to stabilize Community-wide emissions at the 1990 level by 2000, a target to which all its member states were collectively bound. Members of the European Free Trade Association, including Iceland and Sweden, were in turn bound by a separate agreement jointly to meet the EC target.

All this may give the impression that much was being done, but the reality was different. Few countries put into place policies that would contribute to their targets being met, and there seemed little need to do so. For some of these targets were intended merely as goals, while others were conditional on other countries taking similar action (this was true of Britain, for example, under the Thatcher government). Though New Zealand set for itself an ambitious goal of reducing its CO_2 emissions 20 per cent from the 1990 level by 2000, it simultaneously insisted that any policy adopted should have a net benefit for New Zealand. Several countries claimed to be 'committed' to achieving a particular emission ceiling, but none truly was committed. If a country learned later that its interests would be badly served by meeting its target, then there would be nothing to stop it from failing to meet it. Indeed, it would be hard to argue that a country would even be morally bound to meet a target which it had set for itself, especially when other countries were at the same time failing to meet *their* targets.

The EC's climate policy was especially important, partly because of the Community's relatively large share of global emissions and partly because of the way the Community's target was framed. When the target was agreed in 1990, no decision was made as to how it would be met, and as it was a collective target, no country was individually responsible for

meeting it. A collective policy for meeting the target was needed. The European Commission proposed meeting the target by means of an energy conservation programme coupled with a fiscal measure, a carbon tax. The tax, which was to be set at a rate equivalent to $3 per barrel of oil, rising over time to $10 per barrel, would probably have been enough to meet the stabilization target (see Barrett, 1992). But in May 1992, shortly before the Rio Earth Summit convened, the Community announced a number of modifications to the original tax proposal.

The first of these was to supplement the carbon tax with an energy tax (the combined tax would be equivalent to the per-barrel tax noted above). Ostensibly, the intention was not just to reduce carbon-dioxide emissions but also to conserve energy. But the real reason was to dilute the advantage that a pure carbon tax would give nuclear energy and countries with high shares of nuclear electricity generation (such as Belgium and France). A second modification was to exempt the main energy-using industries from having to pay the tax. This was to stop these industries from suffering a 'competitive disadvantage', relative to non-EC countries. The final modification was to make implementation of the EC tax conditional on other OECD countries (especially the United States and Japan) adopting the same tax. As the chances of this were nil, this meant that Europe was not prepared to implement the policy needed to achieve its own target.

(iii) To Rio

The Community's policy was being mapped out just as negotiations on the Framework Convention on Climate Change were coming to a close. Throughout these negotiations, Europe tried to persuade the United States to fix a date for stabilizing its CO_2 emissions. The United States refused, however, and the final text of the Framework Convention, which was signed by over 150 countries at the Rio Earth Summit in June 1992, did not commit any signatories to meeting specific targets and timetables (contrary to reports one often reads in the newspapers). Article 4 says that developed country parties recognize 'that the return by the end of the present decade to earlier levels of anthropogenic emissions of carbon dioxide and other greenhouse gases' would be desirable. It also says that these parties should devise policies 'with the aim of returning individually or jointly to their 1990 levels of these anthropogenic emissions'. But in contrast to the Kyoto Protocol, no country was required by the Framework Convention to meet any particular target by any particular date. Indeed, it was precisely for this reason that this agreement was ratified by so many countries and came into force so quickly (in December 1993).

(iv) After Rio

The IPCC revised its earlier predictions in 1995, partly to take account of the effect of aerosols on radiative forcing. Aerosols are tiny airborne particles, released when fossil fuels are burned, and result in a local cooling effect (unlike some greenhouse gases, which can persist in the atmosphere for decades, even centuries, aerosols have an atmospheric lifetime of about a week). Once aerosols were included in the climate models, the IPCC predicted more modest change: an increase in global mean temperature of about 0.14–0.28°C per decade, as compared with an increase of 0.16–0.36°C per decade when the effects of greenhouse gases alone were considered. Aerosols were also predicted to limit mean sea level rise to about 2–8cm per decade.

Though inclusion of aerosols lowered slightly the predicted consequence of climate change, it also increased confidence in the estimates of climate models. When aerosols were included, the predicted changes accorded better with the historical record. Partly for this reason, the IPCC (1995, p. 22) was able to warn that, 'the balance of evidence suggests that there is a discernible human influence on global climate'. Still, even today the science of climate change is riddled with uncertainties: about the extent and timing of climate change; about regional variations; about whether small changes in atmospheric concentrations could, beyond some point, trigger a discontinuous change in some important climate feature.

(v) From Berlin to Kyoto

At the first Conference of the Parties to the Framework Convention, held in Berlin in 1995, the industrialized parties agreed to negotiate emission limits within specified time frames, such as 2005, 2010,

and 2020. These quantitative ceilings were to be included in a new protocol that might be ready for signing by the end of 1997. Importantly, developing countries were not expected to limit their emissions. It was this differential treatment of industrialized and developing nations in the so-called 'Berlin mandate' that the US Senate later objected to and that ultimately came to be embodied in the Kyoto Protocol.

It is as well to recall, however, that at this time most countries had still not devised, let alone implemented, effective policies for meeting the targets they had set unilaterally years before. Some countries, including Norway and Finland, conceded that they did not expect to meet their targets (Grubb, 1995), despite having imposed hefty carbon taxes. The few countries that did expect to meet their targets were only able to do so for reasons of fortuitous circumstance (in Britain, the 'dash for gas'; in Germany, unification), not determined policy. Most importantly, the European Union (EU) signally failed to devise a policy sure of meeting its 'commitment' to stabilize emissions at the 1990 level. In a letter to the chairman of the European Parliament's environment committee, leaked on the eve of the Berlin conference, Jacques Santer, the President of the European Commission, conceded that 'a single tax . . . applicable in all member states [was] no longer conceivable'.[5] At the same time, the Commission had not developed an alternative collective policy for meeting the EU's target. Evidence supplied to the European Commission suggested that at most three of the EU's 15 member states would stabilize their own CO_2 emissions at the 1990 level by 2000.[6] And, yet, when Europe's diplomats headed for Kyoto, they were hoping to tighten up on the earlier targets, to secure an agreement that would reduce emissions (of the three main gases, carbon dioxide, methane, and nitrous oxide) 7.5 per cent by 2005 and 15 per cent by 2010.

III. ANALYSIS OF THE KYOTO AGREEMENT

As noted in the Introduction, the Kyoto Protocol specifies maximum emission levels for the so-called Annex I countries (see Table 1), and dates by which

[5] *The European*, 17–23 March 1995, p. 1.
[6] *Ibid.*

these ceilings (calculated relative to 1990 emission levels) must be met. Just as significant, the emissions of developing countries are entirely unconstrained by the protocol. These twin features fulfil the promise made at the First Conference of the Parties in Berlin in 1995, and in this sense made Kyoto a success. Ultimately, however, whether Kyoto succeeds will depend on how it becomes implemented, and especially on whether implementation can be made cost-effective.

A variety of so-called 'flexible mechanisms' are built into Kyoto, and they have the *potential* of supporting a cost-effective final allocation of climate-change mitigation. It is hard to say, however, to what extent this potential will be realized. The data are sketchy in places and analyses of some features of the agreement have not yet been undertaken. Much will also depend on how the flexible mechanisms take shape and how countries devise their own policies. We can say something about certain bench-mark cases, and problem areas can be pointed out. But that is about as far as our analysis can go. It happens, however, that this is enough to support the warning that introduced this paper.

(i) Cost Implications of the Emission Limits

Suppose that the limits negotiated in Kyoto were met exactly, with no potential for arbitrage across countries. That is, suppose that the EU kept its emissions to 92 per cent of its 1990 level, that the USA limited its emissions to 93 per cent of its 1990 level, that China emitted as much as it pleased, and so on. Then the marginal cost of climate-change mitigation would vary from country to country. It would be zero in China, where emissions were unconstrained (and growing rapidly), and high in Europe and the United States. How high? According to one study (Nordhaus and Boyer, 1998), the marginal cost of implementing the individual targets in the protocol could be $125 per ton of carbon by around 2010. Another study (Manne and Richels, 1998) predicts that marginal costs could be $240 per ton of carbon in 2010. This difference in marginal cost ($0 in the developing countries compared to $125 or $240 in the OECD countries) in turn implies that the total cost of achieving any given emission ceiling will be excessive. Shifting just one ton of abatement from the OECD countries to the developing countries would save the world at least $100,

perhaps much more. Shifting more abatement would save even more money (though of course the marginal cost saving will fall as more abatement is shifted). Total costs will, of course, be minimized where the marginal cost of abatement is everywhere equal.

As noted earlier, estimates prepared by the Clinton Administration suggest that a cost-effective agreement—that is, an agreement which reduced global emissions by the same amount as required by the Kyoto Protocol, but which did so by distributing the burden of abatement such that marginal costs were everywhere equal—could lower marginal costs to around $14–23 per ton, about one-tenth the level that would be needed to implement the individual emission ceilings in the protocol. This is a huge difference, and one that is reflected also in other studies. For example, Nordhaus and Boyer (1998) estimate the marginal cost of a cost-effective Kyoto Protocol to be $11/ton in 2010. Manne and Richels (1998) obtain a much higher figure—$70/ton in 2010—but one that is still low in comparison with their estimate of marginal costs when the Kyoto Protocol targets are met exactly.

Estimates of reductions in total costs are of a similar relative magnitude. According to the Clinton Administration's analysis, the total cost to the USA of implementing Kyoto could be just $7–12 billion per year, if the agreement is implemented cost-effectively, but perhaps ten times as large otherwise. Manne and Richels (1998) predict that cost-effective implementation of Kyoto would cost the USA around $20 billion or 0.25 per cent of GDP in 2010, but perhaps four times as much if implemented without trading. (Would this cause 'serious harm' to the US economy? Ask the Senate.) Nordhaus and Boyer (1998) estimate that the total cost of implementing Kyoto without trading (in present value terms) would be about seven times the cost-effective level.

But this is to compare extremes. As detailed below, the Kyoto Protocol offers a number of mechanisms intended to lower total implementation costs. As also explained, these mechanisms will not work perfectly, and so will not mimic the cost-effective outcome. The costs of implementing Kyoto are likely to lie somewhere between the bench-marks given above.

OXFORD REVIEW OF ECONOMIC POLICY, VOL. 14, NO. 4

Note, however, that we cannot even be sure of this. For example, the estimates of marginal and total costs given above assume that domestic implementation by every nation is cost-effective—that the marginal costs of abatement are everywhere equal *within* each country. This is unlikely to happen. It is certainly not a feature of most environmental policies that have been adopted in the past. The carbon taxes adopted by most Nordic countries, for example, vary by sector, with households having to pay more than industry (partly out of a concern for trade leakage). Until we know the policies that countries will develop to meet their targets—and these have not been spelled out yet—we will not know how costly it will be to meet the Kyoto targets.

(ii) Flexible and Market Mechanisms

Net emissions targets

The extent of climate change will depend on atmospheric concentrations (though with a lag) of greenhouse gases, and changes in these concentrations depend on the removal of CO_2 from the atmosphere as well as gross emissions. CO_2 removal depends in turn on land use: growing trees absorb carbon from the atmosphere; the standing forest stores carbon (if burned, trees release carbon back into the atmosphere). So if trees are planted and the standing forest is prevented from being burned, concentrations will fall (all else being equal), and these activities should be encouraged just as emissions are discouraged. The emission limits specified in the Kyoto Protocol do this. They allow deductions for 'removals by sinks resulting from direct human-induced land-use change and forestry activities, limited to afforestation, reforestation and deforestation since 1990'. In other words, the Kyoto targets limit *net* emissions.[7]

Will including carbon sinks reduce the costs of meeting the Kyoto limits substantially? The Clinton Administration's (1998, p. 24) analysis suggests that it could. 'Promoting afforestation and reforestation,' the report maintains, 'may reduce atmos-

pheric concentrations of CO_2 at much lower costs than reducing emissions of greenhouse gases resulting from industrial activity.' At the margin, assuming that only abatement of gross emissions is undertaken, this must surely be right. However, Stavins (1998*b*) finds that the marginal cost of carbon sequestration rises steeply—more steeply than marginal gross abatement costs for the United States. So the aggregate cost savings from carbon sequestration may not be all that large.

Measurement problems are also bound to be rife. The Protocol insists that the changes in net emissions be 'measured as verifiable changes in carbon stocks', but such changes cannot be measured with the same precision as the carbon emissions resulting from fossil fuel consumption. And how is one to interpret whether an action constitutes a 'direct human-induced land-use change'? Would the recent fires in Indonesia count? Settling these matters is a subject of ongoing negotiations.

Comprehensive emissions targets

The Protocol's net emission limits apply to a bundle of greenhouse gases and not just carbon dioxide. The other gases include methane, nitrous oxide, hydrofluorocarbons, perfluorocarbons, and sulphur hexafluoride.[8] These are bundled up with carbon dioxide into an aggregate measure, with the weights attached to individual gases reflecting their 'global warming potentials'. Abatement of a ton of nitrous oxide, for example, is equivalent to abatement of around 315 tons of carbon.

This 'comprehensive approach' to climate change mitigation was championed by the Bush Administration, and is to be welcomed. In allowing for trade-offs between different types of gases, the total cost to climate-change mitigation will be lowered.

By how much will this mechanism lower costs? I have not seen any estimates, though in a statement before the US House of Representatives,[9] Janet Yellen of the Council of Economic Advisers noted

---

[7] To be precise, the Protocol allows sinks to play a role in capping emissions. It does not include carbon sinks in the emissions baseline, with one exception. If a country's carbon sinks were a net source of greenhouse-gas emissions in 1990, then its net emissions from sinks must be incorporated into the baseline.

[8] Note that the European Union and Japan sought to limit just three gases. It was the USA that insisted on including all six gases.

[9] Janet Yellen, Statement before the US House of Representatives Committee on Government Reform and Oversight, Subcommittee on National Economic Growth, Natural Resources, and Regulatory Affairs, 19 May 1998, http://www.state.gov/ www/policy_remarks/1998/980519_yellen_climate.html.

S. Barrett

that 'a strategy of reducing non-CO_2 greenhouse gas emissions by a greater percent than CO_2 emissions could lower emissions permit prices (that is, marginal costs) by as much as 10 per cent'.

'Banking'

Kyoto does not require that the emission ceilings shown in Table 1 be met every year; it requires only that they be met by each Annex I party on average over the 5-year period, 2008–12. Moreover, parties are allowed to carry forward additional reductions to a future control period. That is, if a country reduces its emissions by more than required in the first control period (2008–12), it can 'bank' or carry forward the surplus to the next control period. Finally, certified emission reductions, carried out under the Clean Development Mechanism (CDM; see below) from 2000 to 2007 can also be carried forward to the first commitment period, 2008–12. This allows Annex I countries to benefit from taking early action through the CDM.

These provisions could be helpful, but they do not go far enough. In particular, Kyoto does not allow parties to shift emission reductions toward the future—that is, to 'borrow' future emission reductions. Of course, if abatement is shifted forward, the benefits of the abatement in present value terms will fall. But costs may fall much more. If abatement is rushed (and it will be under the Kyoto timetable), some of the existing capital stock will have to be scrapped before its useful life is up. It would be cheaper if emission reductions could be effected by incremental investments. Manne and Richels (1998) estimate substantial savings to a gradual transition to the Kyoto targets, with marginal costs being reduced by a factor of ten or more in 2010.

Emissions trading

Perhaps the most important flexible mechanism in the Kyoto agreement is the provision for trading among the Annex I countries. According to the Clinton Administration's (1998) analysis, this provision could lower the marginal cost of implementing Kyoto by 72 per cent, and lower the total cost of implementation by 57 per cent, compared with the bench-mark of meeting the national targets unilaterally. Nordhaus and Boyer (1998) obtain a similar result. By their calculations, the present value total cost of implementing Kyoto would be reduced 45 per cent by Annex I trading.

Whether savings like these will ever be realized will depend on how the institutions supporting trading develop. If the trading arrangements allow a market to develop which provides ready price discovery and low transactions costs, then the bulk of these gains will be realized. Otherwise just a fraction, perhaps a small fraction, of these gains will be pocketed.

Europe has thus far been suspicious of the concept, believing it to be a ploy for letting the United States evade its responsibilities. This is a gross misunderstanding of the problem. As noted before, *where* abatement takes place is of no relevance to the climate. Absolutely nothing can be gained by making the United States or any other country pay more than is necessary for abatement. Indeed, it is not even obvious that the USA would gain disproportionately from trading. Calculations by McKibbin *et al.* (1998) show that Europe would gain more from trading than the United States.

'Hot air' trading

One reason that trading among the Annex I countries would lower marginal and total costs is that the economies in transition are allowed by Article 3 to choose an alternative base year to 1990 (subject to some restrictions). As shown in Table 1, Bulgaria has chosen 1988 as a base year; Hungary, the average of 1985–7; Poland, 1988; and Romania, 1989. The effect is to create a surplus of emission entitlements that may not be exhausted by economic growth in these countries, even by 2010. Russia must retain its 1990 base year, but it will still have a huge surplus by the year 2000, if the projections shown in Table 1 prove correct (unfortunately, projections to 2008–12 are not available).

As long as these emission ceilings do not bite, marginal abatement costs in the economies in transition will be zero without Annex I trading. Trading, however, will lower costs for all the Annex I countries for two reasons: first, by redistributing abatement within the Annex I group of countries, such that marginal costs are everywhere equal; and second, by relaxing the total constraint on Annex I emissions.

To see the importance of this second effect, consider the consequences of trading within a US–Russian umbrella. In the year 2000, the estimates in

OXFORD REVIEW OF ECONOMIC POLICY, VOL. 14, NO. 4

Table 1 suggest that emissions in the USA could not exceed $0.93 \times 4,957,022 = 4,610,030$ gigagrams without trading. If the estimates in the table are to be believed, Russia will easily stay within its limits, emitting only $0.83 \times 2,388,720 = 1,982,638$ gigagrams of CO_2 in 2000. Hence, without trading, total emissions for both countries would not exceed $4,610,030 + 1,982,638 = 6,592,668$ gigagrams. But Russia is allowed to emit up to $2,388,720$ gigagrams of CO_2 in 2000. So total allowed emissions for both countries under a trading regime are $4,610,030 + 2,388,720 = 6,998,750$ gigagrams. Trading thus eases the total constraint on the two countries by $6,998,750 - 6,592,668 = 406,082$ gigagrams in 2000. For reasons that should be obvious, this difference in aggregate emissions between the trading and no-trading cases is sometimes referred to as 'hot air'.

As noted at the bottom of Table 1, the Kyoto emission constraints are expected to bind in the aggregate, even by the year 2000. Annex I emissions are projected to be 97 per cent of the adjusted base-year emissions, whereas Kyoto requires that they be 94 per cent of this level. However, the 'hot air' released by trading does ease the aggregate emissions constraint for Annex I emissions. Annex I trading lowers costs partly by lowering total abatement.

Note, however, that though the 'hot air' provision appears to be a loophole, had it not been created—had the economies in transition been given tighter emissions constraints—it is likely that the other Annex I countries would have insisted that their own emission constraints be relaxed. For in reducing the amount of 'hot air', the costs to the other Annex I countries of fulfilling *their* commitments would increase. When seen in the context of the negotiations, a bigger problem with the 'hot air' provision may be that it gave away something for nothing.

Of course, the economies in transition could be justified in putting their resources somewhere other than in climate-change mitigation (many of these countries are poorer than some non-Annex I countries). But the other Annex I countries have given these economies *more* than was needed to make their participation incentive compatible. This is not just a matter of redistributing the gains from cooperation. Had less been given away, the incentives for the other Annex I countries to participate in the

agreement would have increased, whereas the European economies in transition would still have had an incentive to participate, so long as their incentive compatibility constraints were satisfied.

Joint implementation

The Kyoto Protocol also allows 'joint implementation' (JI) trades among the Annex I countries. These are bilateral project-based, rather than market-based, trades, in which one country receives 'emission reduction units' for undertaking projects in another country that reduce net emissions.

JI trades must be individually negotiated, and so will entail transactions costs. These costs will likely be high because of the elusive nature of the commodity being traded. JI projects must provide 'a reduction in emissions by sources, or an enhancement of removals by sinks, that is *additional* to any that would otherwise occur' (emphasis added). Calculating this additional reduction will not be easy, because of course one is not able to observe the emissions profile that would have been realized had the trade not taken place. This must instead be inferred. Costly analyses will thus need to be undertaken. Experience with the emissions trading programme in the United States suggests that where transactions costs are high, bilateral trading will be limited.

Clean development mechanism

The JI concept is extended to include non-Annex I countries through the CDM. This allows Annex I countries to meet their emission ceilings by undertaking projects in developing countries that provide 'additional' and 'certified' emission reductions. The CDM is potentially of huge significance, for it provides the only means within the Kyoto framework of shifting abatement toward the non-Annex I countries.

But the CDM has a number of problems. One is that it is not obvious whether the CDM would be limited to emission reductions or whether it can include sequestration projects. The provisions for JI explicitly allow sequestration projects to be included, but the CDM article is silent on this question.

An even more important difference is that one of the parties to a CDM transaction will not have its emissions capped. Potentially, therefore, the CDM

30

could produce only 'paper' emission reductions. Moreover, as Stavins (1998a) warns, it is likely that the least beneficial CDM projects will be adversely selected by this mechanism. Indeed, the problem is doubly worrying. Not only do developing countries have incentives to offer projects that would have been undertaken anyway, but the Annex I countries have incentives also to select these projects, if they can be acquired at lower cost (this is just another manifestation of the free-rider problem).

It will therefore be a matter of interest not only to the parties engaging in a CDM transaction but also to all other parties whether a transaction really will provide 'reductions in emissions that are additional to any that would occur in the absence of the certified project activity'. And it is for this reason, in contrast to the JI provisions, that the emission reductions resulting from a CDM transaction must be 'certified by operational entities to be designated by the Conference of the Parties'.

Though necessary, certification will be costly, and the countries carrying out CDM trades will have to pay for certification (as noted in the Protocol, 'a share of the proceeds from certified project activities [will be] used to cover administrative expenses'). Moreover, Kyoto insists that a share of the proceeds from CDM trades also be used 'to assist developing country Parties that are particularly vulnerable to the adverse effects of climate change to meet the costs of adaptation'. This sounds like a tax. If CDM transactions are taxed, and if transactions costs are high, the volume of CDM trades will be very low.

There is no way of knowing by how much costs will be reduced by the CDM, not least because the important details have yet to be negotiated. In her statement to the US House of Representatives, however, Janet Yellen offered a guess:

The CDM cannot realistically be expected to yield all the gains of binding targets for developing countries, but it might shave costs by roughly another 20 to 25 per cent from the reduced costs that result from trading among Annex I countries.

As suggested by this statement, CDM transactions costs could have been reduced considerably had the Kyoto diplomats succeeded in negotiating emission limits for the developing countries. The issue is not whether these countries should pay to participate.

Most poor countries would have every incentive to walk away from an agreement that required them to dig into their pockets, and few people would blame them for doing so. But if developing countries had agreed to be bound by targets, then they would be able to trade with the Annex I countries and— subject to appropriate choice of their emission ceilings—be virtually sure of being better off. An earlier draft of the Protocol allowed developing countries to choose, at any time and on a voluntary basis, a level of emissions control that was appropriate to their circumstances, but the provision was subsequently expunged, apparently at the insistence of China and India (see Jacoby et al., 1998). Since inclusion of developing countries in some manner is vital, the matter is sure to be on the agenda of future meetings of the parties.

'Supplemental' trading

A further problem is that JI, CDM, and emissions-trading transactions are intended to be 'supplemental' to domestic actions, a constraint reaffirmed by the G8 group of countries meeting in April 1998. According to a *Financial Times* article (6 April 1998) on the G8 summit, the virtue in this constraint is that it will prevent the leading industrial nations (plus Russia) from being able 'to evade painful domestic reductions in greenhouse gas emissions'.

This is a twisted logic. It cannot be good for the environment. If anything, the restriction on trading, in elevating between-country differences in marginal costs, will harm the environment by magnifying the leakage problem. And it cannot be sure to make developing countries any better off either.

Whether this constraint will ever bite, however, is another unknown, for the parties have not defined what 'supplemental' means. If the notion is interpreted as being qualitative, then it will easily be satisfied, for even with unconstrained trading every Annex I country will undertake *some* abatement at home. More serious would be an arbitrary, quantitative limit on trading. Unfortunately, there is some support for such a cap, especially in Europe. The European Parliament adopted a resolution in September 1998 calling for 'an agreement to have a quantitative ceiling on the use of flexibility mechanisms to ensure that the majority of emissions reductions are met domestically'.

OXFORD REVIEW OF ECONOMIC POLICY, VOL. 14, NO. 4

Table 2
European Union Burden-sharing Agreement

Member state	National target (%)
Austria	−13
Belgium	−7.5
Denmark	−21
Finland	0
France	0
Germany	−21
Greece	+25
Ireland	+13
Italy	−6.5
Luxembourg	−28
Netherlands	−6
Portugal	+27
Spain	+15
Sweden	+4
United Kingdom	−12.5
Total EU	**−8**

'Bubbles' and 'umbrellas'

Article 4 of the Protocol allows parties to negotiate a side agreement, in which they pledge to fulfil their Kyoto ceilings jointly. This provision was important in that it made it possible for the European Union to negotiate on behalf of its 15 member states in Kyoto. The emission ceiling shown in Table 1 for the European Union is thus an aggregate ceiling. The European side agreement, establishing emission ceilings for individual member states, was negotiated in September 1998 and resulted in the burden-sharing agreement shown in Table 2.

Under the terms of the Kyoto agreement, Europe is thus treated as a 'bubble' (in the jargon of the US emissions-trading programme). As long as the total target for Europe is achieved, each member state is considered also to be in compliance. However, should the total target not be met, each member state is held individually accountable for meeting the targets it accepted in the side agreement.

Note that the concept need not be confined to Europe. A number of countries (Australia, Canada, Japan, New Zealand, Russia, Ukraine, and the United States) have discussed setting up an 'um-brella' group of trading countries under this article, and it is likely that international trading will begin in this way.

(iii) Non-permanent Emission Caps

Another concern about the emission limits in the Kyoto Protocol is that they are not permanent (as are the limits in the Montreal Protocol and the US sulphur-dioxide trading programme, for example). Emission limits for subsequent control periods will be established by future conferences and codified in future amendments; negotiations of the second round of limits (that is, those that apply beginning in 2013) are required to begin by 2005, but Kyoto has nothing more to say about these limits.

This matters because many actions to reduce emissions involve investments with very long lifetimes. Whether these investments will be worth making will depend on the magnitude of future limits. If one believes that future limits will be very tight, then long-term carbon-saving investments will appear more attractive today. If one believes that future limits will be slack, then costly carbon-saving investments will not pass the required hurdle.

Strategy may also intrude. If a country invested more in abatement than needed just to meet its target in the 2008–12 period, then this may only increase the emission reduction that it would have to meet in the next period. The reason is that, once the costs of the investment have been sunk, the costs to this country of reducing its emissions in the next period will be lower; its bargaining position will therefore have been compromised. Turning this argument around, a country might be able to negotiate an easier target for the next control period if it invested less in reducing its abatement costs in the first control period.

But it is easy to overstate this problem. Suppose Kyoto *had* imposed permanent emission ceilings. Then a different problem would arise: the parties to the protocol would question the credibility of the ceilings, knowing that the limits could always be renegotiated. If the countries believed that the future ceilings were too tight, they would 'under-invest' in abatement. Of course, once they had done so, the costs of meeting the original limits would be higher, and the case for lowering these ceilings would therefore be strengthened. The belief that the initial limits were 'too tight' would be self-fulfilling.

(iv) Arbitrary Emission Limits

Nordhaus and Boyer (1998, p. 17) question Kyoto's choice of emission limits, noting that they do not relate to 'a particular goal for concentrations, temperature, or damages'. The targets certainly should take account of damages (see especially section V); at the very least they should provide a benefit (measured in terms of the damages avoided by the mitigation) that exceeds the cost of meeting the targets. But they should not take direct account of concentrations or temperature (even though these will be linked to damages).

One reason for this is that it is very hard to say by how much emissions should be limited. For example, though the Framework Convention requires that concentrations be stabilized at 'a level that would prevent dangerous anthropogenic interference with the climate system', no one knows what this level is.

But there is a deeper reason, too. For suppose that such a level could be identified. Then, if parties to the agreement pledged to ensure that this level was not exceeded, every party would have a strong incentive to withdraw from the agreement (or not to accede to it in the first place). The reason is that, if a party withdrew and increased its emissions, the remaining parties would have to reduce their emissions to ensure that the aggregate concentration target continued to be met. In a sense, the withdrawal would be rewarded. Similarly, if a country acceded to the agreement, the burden of meeting the aggregate target would be spread more widely, and, as a consequence, the original signatories would presumably be allowed to reduce their abatement levels—at the expense of the additional party having to increase its abatement. Accession would essentially be punished. An aggregate target thus exacerbates any incentives that may already exist for countries to free ride. That Kyoto does not specify an aggregate target is a virtue.

So, how should the targets reflect damages? Obviously, if the concern were with limiting total damages, then the effect would be the same as just described. However, suppose parties to the agreement were concerned only with maximizing their own collective pay-off (the difference between their total benefit and cost of mitigation). Then the incentives would be better aligned. If a country withdrew from the agreement, the remaining parties would reduce their abatement (since the aggregate marginal damage for the parties to the agreement would fall with the withdrawal); the withdrawal would be punished. If a country acceded, the countries that were already parties to the agreement would increase their abatement (since the aggregate marginal damage for parties would increase); the accession would be rewarded.[10]

(v) Quantities vs Prices

Setting quantitative targets may seem to be the obvious remedy, and it has been at the forefront of negotiations ever since the Toronto conference. But it has problems.[11] One problem is that the link between actions and outcomes, as measured in

---

[10] This is the basic mechanism underlying the self-enforcing agreements studied in Barrett (1994).
[11] Hahn (1998) summarizes a number of alternative prescriptions. See also Nordhaus (1998).

OXFORD REVIEW OF ECONOMIC POLICY, VOL. 14, NO. 4

emissions relative to an historical base year, is tenuous. Carbon-dioxide emissions were 7 per cent lower in Britain in 1995 compared with 1990, even though Britain has not adopted a radical policy for reducing emissions. Similarly, emissions in Germany fell 12 per cent between 1990 and 1995. Emissions in Bulgaria, the Czech Republic, Estonia, Hungary, Latvia, and Slovakia fell by even more— by up to 50 per cent over this same period, without any of these countries adopting radical climate change mitigation policies. By contrast, emissions in all the countries that imposed carbon taxes in the early 1990s (Denmark, Finland, The Netherlands, Norway, and Sweden) were 4–15 per cent *higher* in 1995 than in 1990.

Another problem is uncertainty. There is, of course, great uncertainty about the magnitude of climate-change damages. But there is uncertainty also about the costs of climate-change mitigation, and in a seminal paper Weitzman (1974) showed that the latter kind of uncertainty can have important implications for the choice of policy instrument (emission limit versus carbon tax). If a quantitative limit were fixed, marginal costs would be uncertain. If a tax were fixed, emission reductions would be uncertain. Weitzman showed that the tax is superior if the marginal cost curve is steep relative to the marginal benefit curve. Essentially, the tax ensures that marginal costs and benefits do not differ by much.

Pizer (1998) has calculated that taxes would be much more efficient than quantity limits for climate-change mitigation (in his simulations, the net benefits to using the tax are five times the estimate for a quantity control). A combination of policies can do even better (Roberts and Spence, 1976), though Pizer (1998) finds that a hybrid policy is unlikely to improve much on the pure tax scheme in the case of climate change. The essential point is that, even if the Kyoto targets were met cost-effectively, an alternative policy that leaned more in the direction of controlling marginal costs directly (carbon taxes) would be even better.

(vi) Leakage

Because participation in the Kyoto Protocol is not full, there is a potential for 'leakage'. As the Annex I countries reduce their emissions, comparative advantage in the greenhouse-gas-intensive industries will shift towards the non-Annex I countries. This trade effect will be reinforced by the workings of the energy market; as demand for the carbon-intensive fuels in the Annex I countries falls, world prices for these fuels will fall, and consumption in the non-Annex I countries will therefore increase. Consequently, emissions outside the Annex I countries will increase; the environmental benefits of the agreement will be reduced. Potentially, if leakage is strong enough, the agreement would only succeed in redistributing global emissions. The effort to negotiate and implement the agreement would have been wasted.

How significant a problem is 'leakage'? The Clinton Administration (1998, p. 72) maintains that, with cost-effective implementation, the Protocol 'would likely have little impact on competitiveness'. Maybe so. But if implementation is not cost-effective—and as I have already explained it could be far from this mark—then the consequences could be different. Bernstein *et al.* (1998) find that leakage could be significant: for every 100 tons of carbon abated by the Annex I countries, non-Annex I emissions could rise 5–10 tons (global emissions would thus fall by only 90–95 tons). Manne and Richels (1998) and Nordhaus and Boyer (1998) also predict significant levels of leakage.

These levels may not appear high, but they will certainly be politically visible.[12] Leakage would damage particular industries, and these will surely lobby for protection. The Senate resolution drew attention to the problem, and the proposed EC carbon tax was modified partly to take account of the concerns voiced by the energy-intensive industries about a possible loss in 'competitiveness'. It is no surprise that unilateral carbon taxes within countries vary by sector, with industry—and especially the energy-intensive export industries—always paying the lowest amount. When the EU burden-sharing rule was being negotiated, a number of countries (Austria, Denmark, The Netherlands, Spain, and Finland) wanted to make meeting the national targets conditional on the introduction of EU-wide emissions-control measures. These countries were concerned that, as they reduced emis-

---

[12] Previous studies have shown that leakage could be more substantial (IPCC, 1996, ch. 11).

sions, perhaps by imposing steep carbon taxes at home, output in the sectors most highly taxed would shift elsewhere within the Union. The Danish minister said that, though he accepted that Denmark's –21 per cent target was unconditional, Denmark would only be able to achieve –17 per cent without EU-wide measures being adopted.[13]

This links up with a point made in the Introduction: that concerns about leakage provide another reason for wanting to encourage trading. In reducing the between-country difference in marginal costs, trading reduces leakage. Trading therefore lowers costs *and* increases benefits.

IV. COMPLIANCE ENFORCEMENT AND FREE-RIDER DETERRENCE

Assume the best: that enough countries ratify Kyoto that it comes into force and that the flexible mechanisms in Kyoto allow abatement to be cost-effective. Then we can ask: Will the parties to Kyoto actually comply with the agreement? Will they stay within the limits prescribed by Tables 1 and 2?

It is a remarkable fact that non-compliance with international agreements is extremely rare. And, when it does occur, the reason is usually that the deviant was for some reason unable to comply, rather than that it chose not to comply.

But why do parties comply? One reason is that they are expected to by customary of international law. And it is obvious why custom demands compliance. If states could not be relied upon to act as they said they would act, then what would be the point of entering into agreements?

But does this mean that compliance is not a problem? If it does, then it should not matter that the Kyoto Protocol does not (yet) include any provisions for punishing non-compliance. As Chayes and Chayes (1995, pp. 32–3) note, the authority to impose sanctions 'is rarely granted by treaty, rarely used when granted, and likely to be ineffective when used'. So Kyoto's failure to enforce compliance by sanctions may be an irrelevance.

However, the facts are open to a different interpretation: that

both the high rate of compliance and relative absence of enforcement threats are due not so much to the irrelevance of enforcement as to the fact that states are avoiding deep cooperation—and the benefits it holds whenever a prisoners' dilemma situation exists—because they are unwilling or unable to pay the costs of enforcement (Downs *et al.*, 1996, p. 387).

This last interpretation may seem cynical and unconvincing. After all, as we have seen, Kyoto does strive to sustain 'deep' cooperation—a treaty that imposes a cost measured as a fraction of GDP can hardly be described as 'shallow'. But, then again, Kyoto has not even entered into force yet, let alone been implemented. So we cannot really choose between these different theories.

Indeed, it would not even be sensible to choose between them because neither quite gets to the heart of the matter. The Chayeses consider the need to enforce compliance as being independent of the need to deter free-riding—something that they dismiss as being of little practical importance. Downs *et al.*, by contrast, conflate the two problems. Compliance enforcement and free-rider deterrence are related problems and should be analysed jointly.

It is important to note that customary law does *not* require that states be parties to a treaty. Sovereignty means that countries are free to choose to participate in a treaty or not as they please (Barrett, 1990). So if free-riding is to be deterred—if participation in a treaty is to be full—then some kind of treaty-based mechanism must provide the right incentive. It must correct for the harmful incentives that otherwise condemn countries to the fate of the famous prisoners' dilemma.

Suppose that an agreement exists, that it consists of a certain number of parties, and that it requires that these parties undertake some action. The required action (climate-change mitigation) is costly to the parties that undertake it, but provides a benefit that is shared by parties and non-parties alike (climate-change mitigation is a public good). So each party will have an incentive to withdraw from the agree-

---

[13] 'EU States Agree Kyoto Emissions Limits', *ENDS Environment Daily*, 17 June 1998, http://www.ends.co.uk/subscribers/envdaily/articles/98061701.html.

OXFORD REVIEW OF ECONOMIC POLICY, VOL. 14, NO. 4

ment, for in doing so each can gain more from avoiding steep mitigation costs than it loses from its own small slice of greenhouse-gas abatement.

If a party is to be deterred from withdrawing—which it is entitled to do under international law[14]—then it will need to be punished for withdrawing, and punished severely. It will be up to the other parties to the agreement to impose the punishment, but they may be reluctant to do so. The reason is that it is very hard to punish a deviant without also harming oneself. For example, suppose the punishment is that, in the event of one country withdrawing (and therefore cutting its abatement substantially), the other parties reduce their mitigation. Then the countries called upon to impose the punishment will be shooting themselves in the foot, so to speak. The punishment may not be credible.

Let us suppose, however, that a credible punishment can be found to deter some level of free-riding. Then it can be shown that the same punishment can be relied upon to enforce compliance (deter non-compliance); see Barrett (1998a). The reason is intuitive. Suppose a party contemplates 'cheating' on the agreement, perhaps by reducing its emissions by less than required by the agreement. To be deterred from cheating, it must face a punishment, and the punishment must be sufficiently severe that the country is made better off by not cheating. The larger the deviation from compliance, the larger must be the punishment which deters non-compliance. But the larger the required punishment, the larger will be the harm self-inflicted on the countries asked to impose it. If a punishment becomes too large it will cease to be credible and non-compliance will not be deterred.

Recall, however, that I have assumed that there exists a credible punishment that can deter (further) withdrawals from the agreement. The worst harm that a signatory could do by not complying would be for it to choose an emission profile that matched

what it would do if it withdrew from the agreement. Hence, if every signatory is deterred from withdrawing, each also is deterred from not complying. The binding constraint on international cooperation is free-rider deterrence, not compliance enforcement. Once free-riding can be deterred, compliance can be enforced free of charge.

The example of the Montreal Protocol is relevant here. This agreement, which is phasing out the use of ozone-depleting chemicals world wide, is among the great successes of international cooperation. It is also often held up to be a model for future agreements. Like Kyoto, the Montreal Protocol did not initially incorporate a mechanism for punishing non-compliance; choice of such a mechanism was to be deferred to a future meeting of the parties. So failure by Kyoto to include a mechanism for enforcement might seem not to matter. However, there is a big difference between the two treaties. The Montreal Protocol *did* offer incentives for countries to participate in the form of a trade sanction between parties and non-parties in the substances controlled by the treaty and in products containing these substances. And this device has succeeded in making participation in the Montreal Protocol virtually full.[15] It has also been invoked to enforce compliance with the agreement.[16] When seen in this light, compliance enforcement is a problem for Kyoto because the agreement does not employ a mechanism to deter free-riding.

Actually, the minimum participation clause may provide some assistance in deterring free-riding. You can think of it this way. Suppose more than 55 countries have ratified the treaty, and Annex I participation falls just a tiny bit short of the 55 per cent minimum required for entry into force. Then, if one more Annex I country ratifies, and so makes the minimum participation clause bind on all parties, it will have a non-marginal effect on the behaviour of others—the other Annex I parties will now have to fulfil their obligations under the treaty. This might

---

[14] The Kyoto Protocol allows a party to withdraw 3 years after the Protocol has entered into force for a party, upon giving 1 year's notice.

[15] A provision was also made for controlling trade in products made using these substances, but this was never implemented.

[16] The biggest challenge to the Montreal Protocol came when Russia declared that it would not be able to comply by 1996. The Implementation Committee threatened to invoke sanctions—and the combination of this threat and the sweetener of financial assistance was enough to compel Russia into preparing a plan for eventual compliance. The carrot of financial assistance was justified, by the way, since the original Montreal Protocol was negotiated by the Soviet Union in 1987, before its collapse. See Barrett (1998b).

just provide the incentive for the marginal ratification, and push the treaty over the minimum participation threshold.[17]

However, this trick is not sure to work—and even if it did succeed, it provides absolutely no incentive for *successive* accessions to the treaty. To see this, notice that the next country to ratify will not alter the behaviour of the existing parties one little bit. So why should it accede? The Kyoto Protocol does not provide any incentives for more than the minimum of participation. This is in sharp contrast to Montreal, which provides ample incentives for full participation.

Let us suppose, however, that Kyoto's minimum participation level is met and that the agreement enters into force. Could full implementation then be relied upon? The answer is not obvious. Suppose just one country foresees that it will fail to comply. Then it could withdraw from the agreement, upon giving sufficient notice, and so avoid having to deviate from the custom of compliance. Of course, its withdrawal would be penalized if it brought about the collapse of the agreement, as required by the minimum participation clause. But the other parties may not want the agreement to collapse, even taking as given this country's withdrawal, perhaps because, having previously sunk money into abatement investments, the cost of sticking with the agreement would be low. But if this is true—if a country cannot expect to be punished for deviating, then every party would have an incentive not to try very hard to comply with the agreement.

A more likely scenario is that a number of countries will wait to undertake substantial investments in abatement until others have already done so. The risk is that, with everyone behaving in this way, the policies and investments needed to implement Kyoto will not be made. The Protocol seems to have anticipated this problem, for it requires that every Annex I party demonstrate progress in achieving its target by 2005. But this will not suffice. If enough of these parties have made little progress, then none can be singled out for having acted unusually. Anyway, if no penalties can be applied, a lack of progress by all parties, or a large enough number of parties, would only provide a reason for renegotiat-

ing the agreement. To compound these problems, delay in implementing Kyoto will raise the costs of sticking to the Kyoto timetable, and so increase the incentives not to stick to this timetable.

The solution to all these problems may seem obvious: invoke the kind of sanctions used by the Montreal Protocol. However, production of every good has implications for greenhouse-gas emissions. Should *all* trade between parties and non-parties be banned? The threat to do so would almost certainly not be credible. Should trade in a select range of products be banned? That might be credible, but it might also threaten the stability of the multilateral trading arrangements. The answers are not obvious. But perhaps the questions should be asked (I was told that the subject never came up in Kyoto).

V. SUMMARY

If there is one lesson to draw from this analysis it is this: the Kyoto Protocol must produce for its parties a favourable benefit–cost ratio or else it will either never enter into law or it will collapse.

As I noted in the opening paragraph of this paper, the overall reductions in emissions contained within Kyoto probably could provide a benefit–cost ratio for the world in excess of one. However, actually realizing this potential gain will not be easy. The overall level of abatement prescribed by Kyoto would have to be achieved cost-effectively—and this will require that abatement be undertaken in non-Annex I countries. Participation by the non-Annex I countries could potentially be achieved through the Clean Development Mechanism, but this would be sufficient only under the most favourable of assumptions. It seems more likely that emission caps would also need to be negotiated for the developing countries. Let me repeat here that this does *not* imply that the non-Annex I countries would need to pay for this abatement themselves. The reason for broadening participation is not to redistribute costs so much as to lower the total bill. There is an important precedent for this. The Montreal Protocol capped emissions of ozone-depleting substances in developing countries, and these countries did not have to pay to stay within these limits;

[17] This is what I call a 'linchpin' equilibrium. See Barrett (1998a).

OXFORD REVIEW OF ECONOMIC POLICY, VOL. 14, NO. 4

the 'incremental costs' of their compliance were paid for by the industrialized countries.

Achieving a favourable benefit–cost ratio implies not just that costs must be kept low, but also that benefits must be kept high. As noted earlier, lowering implementation costs will actually raise benefits by lowering leakage. But there is another problem: one way of lowering costs is to approve CDM transactions that may not ultimately yield reductions in net emissions (so-called paper trades). Shaving costs in this way would ultimately ruin the agreement. This is yet another reason why Kyoto should be revised to include emission caps for the developing countries.

If these requirements can be met (and that is a big if), then the US Senate's objections would fall away, and the Kyoto Protocol could then enter into force. The problems of non-compliance and free-riding would at the same time be eased. If the costs of participation were lowered (and the benefits increased), then the incentives to deviate in these ways would be reduced.

However, these incentives to deviate would not be eliminated by cost-effective abatement. Achieving a favourable benefit–cost ratio is only a necessary condition for achieving global cooperation; it is not sufficient (Barrett, 1994, 1998*a*). And it is not obvious how the required sanctions could be made credible. So Kyoto has two mountains to climb. The first—achieving a favourable benefit–cost ratio—is challenge enough. The second—deterring free-

riding and non-compliance—has not yet come into view, but it may prove the harder climb.

POST SCRIPT

After this paper was written, the parties to the Framework Convention met in Buenos Aires (in November 1998). The issues raised in this paper were not resolved at this meeting, but a Plan of Action was agreed, with deadlines for finalizing the Protocol's flexible mechanisms. For the first time, the issue of how compliance should be enforced was raised, though to my knowledge no mechanism for enforcing compliance was proposed. At the meeting, the United States became the 60th country to sign the Kyoto agreement. Another small island state, Antigua and Barbuda, became the second to ratify it. Argentina, which hosted the meeting, announced its intention to adopt an emission limit voluntarily, and Kazakhstan said that it would join the group of Annex I countries and accept, in the words of the press release, a 'legally binding target' (adding more 'hot air'?).

These developments are to be welcomed, but the fundamental problems raised in this paper remain. The press release issued at the start of the Buenos Aires talks concluded by noting that the agreement would not become legally binding until the minimum participation requirements had been met. 'It is hoped,' the statement reads, 'that this will happen in 2001.' It is regrettable that we cannot anticipate with more confidence an event of such importance.

REFERENCES

Barrett, S. (1990), 'The Problem of Global Environmental Cooperation', *Oxford Review of Economic Policy*, 6(1), 68–79.

— (1992), 'Reaching a CO_2 Emission Limitation Agreement for the Community: Implications for Equity and Cost-Effectiveness', *European Economy*, Special Edition No. 1, 3–24.

— (1994), 'Self-Enforcing International Environmental Agreements', *Oxford Economic Papers*, 46, 878–94.

— (1998*a*), 'A Theory of Full International Cooperation', *Journal of Theoretical Politics*, forthcoming.

— (1998*b*), 'Montreal vs. Kyoto: International Cooperation and the Global Environment', in I. Kaul, I. Grunberg, and M. A. Stern (eds), *Global Public Goods: International Cooperation in the 21st Century*, New York, Oxford University Press, forthcoming.

Bernstein, P. M., Montgomery, W. D., and Rutherford, T. F. (1998), 'Trade Impacts of Climate Policies: The MS-MRT Model', paper prepared for the Yale–NBER Workshop on International Trade and Climate Policy, Snowmass, CO, 12 August.

Chayes, A. and Chayes, A. H. (1995), *The New Sovereignty*, Cambridge, MA, Harvard University Press.

S. Barrett

Clinton Administration (1998), 'The Kyoto Protocol and the President's Policies to Address Climate Change: Administration Economic Analysis', White House, Washington, DC, July.

Downs, G. W., Rocke, D. M., and Barsoom, P. N. (1996), 'Is the Good News About Compliance Good News About Cooperation?', *International Organization*, 50, 379–406.

Grubb, M. (1995), 'The Berlin Climate Conference: Outcome and Implications', Briefing Paper No. 21, London, Royal Institute of International Affairs.

Hahn, R. W. (1998), *The Economics and Politics of Climate Change*, Washington, DC, American Enterprise Institute for Public Policy Research.

International Energy Agency (1992), *Climate Change Policy Initiatives*, Paris, OECD.

IPCC (1990), *Climate Change: The IPCC Scientific Assessment.*

— (1995), *IPCC Second Assessment· Climate Change 1995*, WMO and UNEP.

— (1996), *Climate Change 1995: Economic and Social Dimensions of Climate Change*, Cambridge, Cambridge University Press.

Jacoby, H. D., Prinn, R. G., and Schmalensee, R. (1998), 'Kyoto's Unfinished Business', *Foreign Affairs*, July/August.

McKibbin, W. J., Shackleton, R., and Wilcoxen, P. J. (1998), 'What to Expect from an International System of Tradable Permits for Carbon Emissions', mimeo.

Manne, A. S., and Richels, R. G. (1998), 'The Kyoto Protocol: A Cost-Effective Strategy for Meeting Environmental Objectives?', mimeo.

Nordhaus, W. D. (1998), 'Is the Kyoto Protocol a Dead Duck? Are There Any Live Ducks Around? Comparison of Alternative Global Tradable Emissions Regimes', mimeo, Department of Economics, Yale University.

— Boyer, J. G. (1998), 'Requiem for Kyoto: An Economic Analysis of the Kyoto Protocol', paper prepared for the Energy Modeling Forum meeting, Snowmass, Colorado, 10–11 August.

Pizer, W. A. (1998), 'Prices vs. Quantities Revisited: The Case of Climate Change', Resources for the Future Discussion Paper 98–02.

Roberts, M. J., and Spence, M. (1976), 'Effluent Charges and Licenses Under Uncertainty', *Journal of Environmental Economics and Management*, 5, 193–208.

Stavins, R. N. (1998a), 'What Can We Learn from the Grand Policy Experiment? Lessons from SO_2 Allowance Trading', *Journal of Economic Perspectives*, 12, 69–88.

— (1998b), 'The Costs of Carbon Sequestration: A Revealed-Preference Approach', *American Economic Review*, forthcoming.

Weitzman, M. L. (1974), 'Prices vs. Quantities', *Review of Economic Studies*, 41, 477–91.

39

[30]

International Equity and Differentiation in Global Warming Policy

An Application to Tradeable Emission Permits

ADAM ROSE[1], BRANDT STEVENS[2], JAE EDMONDS[3] and
MARSHALL WISE[3]
[1]*Department of Energy, Environmental, and Mineral Economics, The Pennsylvania State University, University Park, PA 16802, USA;* [2]*Demand Analysis Office, California Energy Commission, Sacramento, CA 95814, USA;* [3]*Pacific Northwest Laboratory, Washington, DC 20024, USA*

Accepted 10 February 1998

Abstract. One of the major obstacles to reaching a comprehensive agreement on global warming is the setting of greenhouse gas emission reduction targets for individual countries. Long-standing tensions between industrialized and developing countries have raised the issue of *equity* in burden-sharing. Moreover, individual industrialized nations have pleaded special circumstances and have sought *differentiation* in their obligations. This paper analyzes alternative rules for distributing tradable carbon dioxide emissions permits. A non-linear programming model, which distinguishes between allocation-based and outcome-based rules, is used to analyze the relative welfare outcomes. The model is applied to the world body of nations and yields several important policy implications.

Key words: global warming, tradeable permits, equity, non-linear programming

JEL classification: Q25, Q28

1. Introduction

Any successful policy to deal with global warming must have several attractive features. Given the potentially immense sums that may have to be spent on abatement, it is important that the policy be *efficient* or, at least, cost-effective. Given the likely differences in both costs and benefits across countries, it would be desirable that the policy be *equitable*, or fair.[1]

Equity considerations are usually accorded a secondary role in economic policy-making, but, in the case of global warming, they may be crucial. First, no supra-national institution can force a greenhouse gas (GHG) agreement; hence, it will depend on voluntary compliance. Second, appeals to global economic efficiency alone will not be sufficient to rally countries together, given the wide disparities in their current welfare and in welfare changes implied by efficient policies. Thus, over and above its normative role in policy-making, equity might serve a positive role as a unifying principle that facilitates a greenhouse warming agreement. A global problem requires a global solution and hence as many participants as possible, but the public good nature of GHG abatement means it is prone to free rider problems. Many analysts of the issue have concluded that greater cooperation is likely to be forthcoming if the policy process, implementation decision, and outcomes are perceived to be fair (see, e.g., Morrisette and Plantinga, 1991; Bohm and Larsen, 1994; IPCC, 1996).

A marketable permits, or entitlements, approach to greenhouse gas mitigation has several attractive features (see, e.g., Barrett et al., 1992). Following Coase (1960), a marketable permits scheme will be cost-effective irrespective of how the permits are distributed. Thus, we are not faced with a disincentive or other problem that leads to an efficiency-equity tradeoff. The same is true of a global carbon tax and the lump sum redistribution of its revenues.

One significant problem arises with respect to equity, however. Unlike efficiency, no universal consensus exists on the best definition at either the interpersonal or international level. Compounding the problem, many policy pronouncements are based on ambiguous or erroneous definitions of equity, and incomplete assessments of their welfare implications.

The purpose of this paper is to analyze alternative distributional rules for global warming policy. We present several equity principles, as well as other approaches to sharing costs and benefits, and discuss their transformation into operational rules for distributing tradeable greenhouse gas emission permits. Next we formulate a non-linear programming model and analyze the implications of the various criteria in terms of relative burden-sharing.

Note that our simulations are performed for a disaggregation of the world economy into nine regions, and that we assume *all* regions are considering commitments to mitigate GHGs. This differs from the outcome of the Conference of the Parties to the Framework Convention on Climate Change held in Kyoto, Japan, in December 1997 (COP-3), where only Annex I countries (a combination of 34 OECD and the Eastern European countries) committed to targets and timetables for GHG mitigation during the first phase of an international accord (FCCC, 1997).[2] Attention now focuses on how to induce commitments from developing countries to mitigate GHGs. These nations have, however, frequently expressed concerns about the fairness of an international agreement, often in relationship to their own limited resources and a long history of cumulative emissions by industrialized countries (see, e.g., Agarwal and Narain, 1991). Thus, an analysis of direct interactions between industrialized and developing countries that incorporates transfers and addresses equity issues in a comprehensive manner is especially timely.

2. Review of the Literature

This paper builds on several recent studies on "burden-sharing" in global warming policy. Most of these studies have offered rather limited concepts of "equitable" allocations, and instead have focused on "acceptable," "pragmatic," or "coalition-forming" rules for distributing permits. We use the term "differentiation" to include these various alternatives to formal equity.[3]

Larsen and Shah (1994) analyzed several rules for allocating permits among major countries of the world in reference to returning to 1987 CO_2 emission levels in the Year 2000. Their empirical analysis was confined to the costs of mitigation, though they implicitly addressed benefits by assuming OECD countries have a positive willingness to pay for mitigation and developing countries have a negative willingness to pay. Also, they assumed that all countries have the same mitigation cost function. Larsen and Shah focused on allocations they believed provided participation incentives, without providing much discussion of the conceptual justification for the alternatives. Their emphasis was on "acceptable" allocations, defined as those involving zero costs of participation for poorer countries. Implicitly, this notion of "acceptability" is akin to Pareto improvement, in which policies are supported if no one is made worse off as a result. A crude notion of equity enters into the analysis, however, since the group of industrialized countries is expected to suffer positive costs, while avoiding imposing any costs on developing countries. No justification is given for the alternative cost-imposing rules on industrialized countries – allocations according to GDP, population, and a combination of the two.

Bohm and Larsen (1994) examined a mitigation target of reducing CO_2 emissions twenty percent below 1990 levels in the year 2010 for only Europe and the former Soviet Union. They note that "Participation in such a regime is expected to hinge on fairness of the distributional consequences" (p. 219). They stipulate initial allocations that lead to an equalization of net costs "per GDP" as fair in the short run, and initial allocations that are based on population as fair in the long run. They also refer to these as "objective criteria." Moreover, they analyze cases in which the costs for the poorer countries are specified as not exceeding zero. The authors show that European countries can save as much as eighty-five percent on their mitigation costs if they engage in a treaty that allows for permit trading with the countries of Eastern Europe and the former Soviet Union.

Edmonds et al. (1995) performed an analysis for nine world regions to limit emissions to 1990 levels over a time horizon with four milestone periods culminating in the Year 2050. Their analysis is based on the Edmonds-Reilly-Barns model (see Edmonds et al., 1986), which combines aspects of a carbon cycle model and an energy-CO_2 emissions model (including technological change). They examine a variety of trading regimes with carbon permit allocation based on several criteria: population, GDP, and historical emissions ("grandfathering"), as well as an alternative requirement to impose "no harm" on non-Annex I nations by mitigation efforts. They find that commonly proposed fairness criteria such as population, GDP, and historical emissions correspond poorly to allocations that leave non-Annex I nations "unharmed." They also examine the cost sensitivity from delaying mitigation actions and from technology development and dissemination. As in other studies, they find that flexibility in individual country mitigation levels significantly reduces emissions mitigation costs as does technology development and dissemination.

Richels et al. (1996) follow up on the Edmonds study by using four major energy-economy models representing both bottom-up and top-down approaches to apply the previous burden-sharing formulas to an examination of the impacts on various world regions, with a specific separation of OECD countries. They first examine a rather stringent emission reduction requirement of twenty percent below 1990 levels by various target dates, and find that the flexibility offered by a system of permits (as well as a relaxation of yearly timing requirements of emission reductions) could reduce global costs by more than eighty percent. In addition, their analysis indicates that because of international trade effects, non-OECD countries would still likely suffer negative impacts even when they are not required to mitigate GHGs.

Rose and Stevens (1993) performed an analysis of several explicit equity criteria in distributing emission permits to meet a twenty percent reduction for projected Year 2000 CO_2 emission levels by eight major (though not comprehensive) regions of the world, with cost and benefit functions adapted from Nordhaus (1993). The authors did not present a formal model of permit distributions, nor did they distinguish between "allocation-based" and "outcome-based" criteria as does the present paper. In addition, though some underpinnings of the equity criteria were presented, on further inspection some of the criteria are arbitrary and others suffer from the problem of "partition dependence" to be discussed below. One interesting finding for the select few but philosophically distinct criteria simulated was that the welfare outcomes of their implementation did not differ much.

Still another approach to permit allocation is provided by Barrett (1992), who examined the problem in game-theoretic framework using stylized data in a four-region setting for the U.S., China, the Soviet Union, and the Rest of the World. Most of the criteria utilized were based on self-interest, though a Kantian imperative (falling in-between self-interest and the altruism inherent in most equity criteria) was also analyzed.

Thus, all of the aforementioned papers have several limitations.[4] Most of these are overcome in the current analysis, which includes:

- A set of major world regions covering the entire globe.
- An extended time horizon.
- The specification of an explicit model that is sufficiently general to cover all types of distributions (allocation-based, process-based, outcome-based), is applicable to both cost-effectiveness and optimality analysis, and to both permits and carbon taxes.
- Differential cost functions between regions.
- Applicability to a range of distribution criteria, beyond those involving equity, to include acceptability criteria and "differentiation" in general.

- Examination of several subtleties associated with burden-sharing criteria, including arbitrariness and partition dependence.

Still, our empirical analysis does not incorporate benefits associated with greenhouse gas mitigation, though the model is sufficiently general to do so. Also, the model is not fully dynamic, though it can be reformulated into a dynamic linear programming version as well.

3. International Equity and Differentiation Criteria

The equity principles and differentiation analyzed in this paper, a general operational rule emanating from each, and a corresponding rule applicable to the allocation of marketable permits for CO_2 emissions are presented in Table I. The reader is referred to Rose (1992) for a discussion of conceptual underpinnings of each of the criteria.[5] Note that, although the discussion below is presented in the context of marketable permits, the criteria apply equivalently to redistributing carbon tax revenues (see, e.g., Pezzey, 1992; Rose and Stevens, 1998).

An important distinction is whether a given equity criterion applies to the *process* by which a criterion is chosen, the *initial allocation* of permits, or to the *final outcome* of the implementation of the policy instrument, i.e., to net welfare impacts following trading and greenhouse gas mitigation. For example, the Sovereignty criterion refers to the right to emit GHGs, so it applies directly to permit allocations, while Horizontal Equity applies to welfare changes, i.e., outcomes. Other criteria do not have any pre-determined rules at either end (e.g., Consensus Equity and Market Justice) but apply more to the manner in which decisions are made (see, e.g., Rayner and Malone, 1997). We can thus divide the criteria into three categories as denoted in Table I.

Outcome-based criteria are more in keeping with the "welfarist" orientation of equity in terms of much of traditional Welfare Economics. However, some equity concepts are based on inherent rights (e.g., Egalitarian) that tie them to initial allocations. Others relate to the fairness of the process of allocating/trading the rights, though emphasis on the process begs the question of what rule will be chosen and what its equity implications are. In the case of global warming, the allocation stage is more immediate and more certain than the final outcome, and hence might receive more attention, but this would be shortsighted. At the same time, concerns about the eventual outcome are compounded by actual or perceived uncertainties about potential benefits, economic and emissions growth rates, permit prices, and, the competitiveness of the permits market. Still, these considerations are too important to ignore, and improving knowledge of them will enable all nations to make more informed judgments about bottom-line impacts.[6]

A number of other rules for sharing the benefits and costs of global warming policy, several of which were discussed in the previous section, are summarized in Table II. Below, we briefly discuss several major examples and show that, despite the use of more pragmatic labeling as, for example, "acceptable" criteria,

Table I. Alternative equity criteria for global warming policy

Criterion	Basic Definition	General Operational Rule	Operational Rule for CO_2 Permits
Allocation-Based			
Sovereignty	All nations have an equal right to pollute and to be protected from pollution	Cut back emissions in a proportional manner across all nations	Distribute permits in proportion to emissions
Egalitarian	All people have an equal right to pollute or to be protected from pollution	Allow emissions in proportion to population	Distribute permits in proportion to population
Ability to Pay	Mitigation costs should vary directly with national economic well-being	Equalize abatement costs across nations (gross cost of abatement as proportion of GDP equal for each nation)[a]	Distribute permits to equalize abatement costs (gross cost of abatement as proportion of GDP equal for each nation)[a]
Outcome-Based			
Horizontal	All nations should be treated equally	Equalize net welfare change across nations (net gain or loss as proportion of GDP equal for each nation)[b]	Distribute permits to equalize net welfare change (net gain or loss as proportion of GDP equal for each nation)[b]
Vertical	Welfare gains should vary inversely with national economic well-being; welfare losses should vary directly with GDP	Progressively share net welfare change across nations (net gain (loss) proportions inversely (directly) correlated with per capita GDP)[b]	Progressively distribute permits (net gain (loss) proportions inversely (directly) correlated with per capita GDP)[b]
Compensation	No nation should be made worse off	Compensate net losing nations	Distribute permits so no nation suffers a net loss of welfare
Process-Based			
Rawls' Maximin	The welfare of the worst-off nations should be maximized	Maximize the net benefit to the poorest nations	Distribute largest proportion of net welfare gain to poorest nations
Consensus	The international negotiation process is fair	Seek a political solution promoting stability	Distribute permits in a manner that satisfies the (power weighted) majority of nations
Market Justice	The market is fair	Make greater use of markets	Distribute permits to highest bidder

[a] Gross cost refers to abatement cost only and does not include benefits or permit transactions. [b] Net welfare change (gain or loss) is equal to the sum of mitigation benefits − abatement costs + permit sales revenues − permit purchase costs.

Table II. Alternative differentiation rules for global warming policy

Criterion	Basic Definition	Operational Rule for CO_2 Permits	Link to Equity
Grandfathering	Nations have inherent right to emit	Distribute permits equivalent to baseline year emission (or proportion thereof)	Equivalent to Sovereignty
No Purchase	Poor nations should not have to buy permits	Distribute permits to poor countries equal to their baseline emissions in each year	Roughly equivalent to Rawlsian
Income Gap	The gap between rich and poor nations should not widen	Distribute permits so as to maintain the gap between rich and poor nations	Equivalent to Horizontal
No Harm	Some nations should not incur costs	Distribute permits so as to avoid costs to some nations	Roughly equivalent to Vertical
Kantian	Each nation chooses an abatement level as large as the abatement level it would like others to undertake	Distribute permits in proportion to emissions following negotiation	Equivalent to Sovereignty plus elements of Consensus
GDP	Richer nations require more permits	Distribute permits in direct proportion to GDP	Similar to Consensus
Ad Hoc	Some nations have special considerations	Distribute permits to take special considerations into account	Depends on circumstances

most of these rules either embody some aspect of equity or can be modeled in a mathematically equivalent manner.

Grandfathering is equivalent to Sovereignty if applied across the board. Typically, however, it is formulated with countries partitioned into groups, often favoring developing countries. This is the case of many policy analyses associated with the Berlin Mandate, which suggest that these countries can be usefully brought into a global permit market scheme, even if they do not have mitigation targets, by granting them permits equivalent to their gross emissions (thereby promoting global efficiency by capitalizing on low cost mitigation options). The "No Purchase" criterion is then a special case of Grandfathering as currently under discussion.

The "No Harm" rule would be equivalent to Compensation[7] if it were applied to all nations, but typically it is also applied to the partition of developing countries. thus, it is roughly equivalent to Vertical Equity (we say roughly, because it is not a pure proportioning, but rather a bifurcation with all developing countries treated equally). It also begs the question of how the "harm" should be distributed across industrialized countries.

The rule to "Limit the Income Gap" between rich and poor nations simply translates into Horizontal Equity if the gap is stated in proportional terms and translates into Vertical Equity if in absolute monetary terms (below we will further distinguish total and per capita versions of these criteria). That is, burdens that are an equal proportion of GDP will maintain the overall GDP proportions among countries. For absolute disparities, the explanation of the role of Vertical Equity is more complicated. If one considers both costs and benefits of greenhouse gas mitigation, and global net benefits are positive, then equal absolute improvements in net welfare will be consistent with Vertical Equity and will also maintain absolute disparities. Ironically, when benefits are not considered, and the outcome is measured in terms of net costs, maintaining absolute income disparities would require that cost changes be equal for all countries, though this would mean they would be a smaller proportion of GDP for wealthy countries than for poor ones – a clear violation of most equity principles.

The Kantian imperative involves a type of pragmatic altruism embodied in the Golden Rule. Barrett (1992) has found that it yields results close to the Nash equilibrium, but effectively it implies equal proportional cutbacks in emissions among all nations as in the case of Sovereignty equity.

The GDP criterion violates all principles of altruism, as it would favor wealthy countries. If we take a cynical view of the policy-making process and suggest that more wealthy countries will have greater clout in the determination of final welfare distribution, then it is similar to our definition of Consensus equity, which is based on process considerations, but is proxied by initial (allocation) conditions.

Several analysts claim that objective criteria exist. From a normative standpoint, only a "No Harm" criterion applied to all countries would qualify, since it is consistent with the concept of Pareto improvement. From a positive economic standpoint, other analysts have suggested that some criteria are more likely to be acceptable than others to a majority of nations, and are therefore more likely to lead to global agreement. However, their acceptability seems to be more dependent on notions of equity than some natural or inherent characteristics (e.g., most of the acceptability criteria call for some favorable treatment for developing countries). Even the numerous "differentiation" proposals now on the table are either a matter of individual country self-interest or appeals to fairness, while trying to avoid the use of the latter term. Thus, as with most other areas of economics, there are few criteria free of value judgments.[8]

4. Model Specification

The model framework we use to examine the international welfare implications of alternative distributional criteria is nonlinear programming. Actually, two versions of the model are needed to perform the analysis given the operational distinctions between allocation-based and outcome-based criteria. In the former, we set the permit allocations for each country according to the equity criterion being simulated and solve for permit trades and net benefits or net costs (when benefits are not evaluated). In the latter case, we set the net benefit or net cost levels for each country according to the equity criterion being simulated and solve for the initial permit allocations and permit trades.

To facilitate the exposition, we will present the models in a cost-effectiveness context. This also reflects the current state of most of the serious policy pronouncements on the issue, given the difficulty of identifying an optimal level of emission reductions (in terms of maximizing net benefits). In effect, we take a global target of emission reductions as given and minimize the cost of achieving it across countries. Thus, the objective function of our model can be specified as:

$$\text{minimize } TC = \sum_{i=1}^{n} \left[\frac{(1 - R_i) \cdot \ln(1 - R_i) + R_i}{\alpha_i} \right] \cdot E_i \tag{1}$$

where

$TC \equiv$ total global abatement cost (endogenous)

$R_i \equiv$ percentage abatement for country i (endogenous) $0 \leq R_i \leq 1$

$E_i \equiv$ gross (unabated) CO_2 emission (in tons) for country i (exogenous)

$\alpha_i \equiv$ slope parameter of abatement cost function for country i (exogenous)

Our illustrative abatement cost function yields a marginal cost function of the form: $-\ln(1 - R_i)/\alpha_i$. For positive α_i, the function exhibits positive and increasing marginal cost as percentage abatement increases, consistent with theoretical expectations and empirical findings on diminishing returns for pollution control.

A. ALLOCATION-BASED MODEL

For allocation–based criteria, we minimize the sum of global abatement costs, TC, subject to the following constraints:

$$(1 - R_i)E_i - P_i \leq \bar{P}_i \qquad i = 1 \ldots n \tag{2a}$$

$$\sum_{i=1}^{n} P_i = 0 \tag{2b}$$

where

$\bar{P}_i \equiv$ permit allocation (in tons) for country i (exogenous)
$P_i \equiv$ permit purchases or sales (in tons) for country i (exogenous)
and other variables are as previously defined.

Equation (2a) enables us to examine the consequences of alternative permit allocations on mitigation levels and costs. The constraint requires that each country's initial stock of permits, as designated by a permit distribution criterion (equity-based or otherwise), be greater than or equal to its gross annual CO_2 emissions minus emissions abated minus emission permits bought or sold. Suppose, for example, that a treaty is based on the Sovereignty criterion requiring abatement of each country's emissions equal to 20%; this defines a permit distribution of 80% of each country's gross emissions, E_i. Relative marginal abatement costs would determine each country's decision to add additional permits to its stock and abate less than 20% or to sell permits from its stock and abate more than 20% of initial emissions.

In equation (2a), we specify individual permit allocations, $\bar{P}_i$, and the model solves for the individual country abatement percentage, R_i, and permit trades, P_i, so as to minimize the sum of global abatement costs. The model equalizes the marginal abatement costs of all nations at a level equal to the equilibrium permit price, which it calculates as well. Equation (2b) requires permit purchases to equal permit sales (negative values of P_i).

Major features of the solution to this problem (and the outcome-based model below) are invariant to the permit distribution. Consistent with the Coase Theorem, different distributions of a fixed, global permit supply should not affect the global permit price, the ith country's optimal percentage abatement nor each country's post-trading stock of permits.[9] Alternative initial distributions of permits do affect the number of permits bought and sold by each country and individual country net benefits. All of these considerations will be illustrated by the analysis below.

B. OUTCOME-BASED MODEL

In order to examine the implications of equity criteria that distinguish between alternative *welfare outcomes*, we must solve an alternative model with the following constraints (again minimizing total costs of abatement, as denoted in equation (1):

$$\left[\frac{R \cdot \ln R - R}{\beta_i}\right] \cdot G - \left[\frac{(1 - R_i) \cdot \ln(1 - R_i) + R_i}{\alpha_i}\right] . \tag{3a}$$

$$E_i + \lambda P_i = NB_i \qquad i = 1 \ldots n$$

$$\bar{P}_i + R_i \cdot E_i + P_i \geq E_i \qquad i = 1 \ldots n \tag{3b}$$

$$\sum_{i=1}^{n} \bar{P}_i = (1 - R) \sum_{i=1}^{n} E_i \tag{3c}$$

$$\sum_{i=1}^{n} P_i = 0 \tag{2b}$$

where

$R \quad \equiv$ percentage global abatement (exogenous)
$G \quad \equiv$ global emissions (exogenous)
$\lambda \quad \equiv$ equilibrium (shadow) price of permits (endogenous)
$NB_i \equiv$ level of net benefit (welfare change) for country i (exogenous)
$\beta_i \quad \equiv$ slope parameter of benefit function for country i (exogenous)
and the other variables are as previously defined, though $\bar{P}_i$ is now endogenous.

The first constraint refers to the specification of the net benefit for each country, with the constants on the right-hand side determined by the equity criterion to be modeled.[10] For example, the Horizontal Equity criterion requires that the constraint be the same proportion of GDP for all countries. Our illustrative total benefit function yields the marginal benefit function: $\ln R/\beta_i$. For negative values of β_i, marginal benefits are positive but decreasing as the global percentage abatement increases, consistent with theoretical expectations and empirical findings of declining marginal benefits from pollution control.

Equation (3b) is a rearrangement of equation (2a) to reflect a difference in endogenous and exogenous variables, and requires that each country's initial permit stock (solved for endogenously in this case) plus abatement level plus permit purchases or sales be greater than or equal to annual gross CO_2 emissions for each country. The equilibrium permit price (dual variable λ), is related to equation (3b), as well as to equation (2a). Equation (3c) ensures the number of permits allocated is consistent with the global optimum or cost-effectiveness target. The model solves for the benefits, costs, abatement percentages, emission levels, permit trades, and permit assignments for each country.[11] This model formulation is consistent with the properties of the Coase Theorem as well.[12]

Table III combines the discussion of this section and the previous one. It contains the mathematical specification of equity criteria as constraints of our programming

Table III. Constraint specification for non-linear programming models

Permit distribution criterion	Allocation or outcome constraint[a,b]
Sovereignty	$\bar{P}_i = (1 - R)E_i$
Egalitarian	$\bar{P}_i = \frac{Pop_i}{Pop}\bar{P}$
Ability to Pay[b]	$\frac{\bar{P}_i}{\bar{P}_j} = \left(\frac{GDP_j^*}{GDP_i^*}\right)^\gamma \quad \gamma > 1; GDP_j^* > GDP_i^*$
Horizontal Equity (total population reference base)	$NB_i = \alpha GDP_i \quad \text{where } \alpha = \frac{NB}{GDP} = \frac{NB_i}{GDP_i}$
Horizontal Equity (per capita GDP reference base)	$NB_i = \beta_i NB \quad \text{where } \beta_i = \frac{Pop_i}{Pop}$
Vertical Equity[d]	$\frac{NB_i/GDP_i}{NB_j/GDP_j} = \left(\frac{GDP_j^*}{GDP_i^*}\right)^\gamma \quad \gamma > 1; GDP_j^* > GDP_i^*$
Compensation[e]	$NB_i \geq 0$
Consensus	$NB_i = \delta\left(\frac{Pop_i}{Pop}\right) + (1 - \delta)\left(\frac{GDP_i}{GDP}\right) \quad 0 \leq \delta \leq 1$
Market Justice[e]	$\bar{P}_i = 0; \quad \lambda P_i \geq 0$

[a] Symbols are defined in text (symbols without subscripts represent totals summed over individual countries, i).
[b] Criteria are specified in terms of the most general case, where benefits of mitigation are included. Modifications are needed for some cases that include only costs.
[c] $GDP_i^* \equiv GDP_i/Pop_i$
[d] For cases where only net costs, NC, are considered (i.e., benefits are omitted):
$\frac{NC_j/GDP_j}{NC_i/GDP_i} = \left(\frac{GDP_j^*}{GDP_i^*}\right)^\gamma$.
[e] For a further discussion, see endnote 13.

model. We contend that most other distribution criteria can be specified in a similar, if not equivalent, manner.[13]

5. Simulation Results

Our simulations are based on an adaptation of the Berlin Mandate analysis of Edmonds et al. (1995) and Richels et al. (1996). These analyses call for a return to Year 1990 baseline emission levels globally by the Year 2000, reduction of emissions by 20% below 1990 levels by the Year 2010, and a stabilization of emissions at that level through the Year 2050. Although these targets are set globally, the entire mitigation cost burden is, however, to be borne by OECD countries. We utilize the individual country emission projections and global mitigation requirement of the Berlin Mandate analyses as a starting point, but apply alternative burden-sharing criteria that extend to *all* nations, though grouped into nine major world regions.

Note that the criteria we simulate have been chosen to illustrate several important policy-making considerations, and our analysis should not be taken as any special endorsement of them over other criteria.[14]

The basic data we used are contained in Appendix Table A. The table also presents the equilibrium permit price and global emission reduction requirements for milestone years. The reason the global emission reductions do not increase over the time horizon is the tapering off of gross emissions because of slow downs in population and economic growth, as well as autonomous energy efficiency improvements (AEEI).

The data in Appendix Table A, mitigation cost estimates, and optimal trading analyses are based on the MiniCAM 2.0 model as described in Edmonds et al. (1996a). We employ the anthropogenic emissions component of the model, which is a combination of the original Edmonds-Reilly-Barns model (Edmonds and Reilly, 1985; Reilly et al., 1987; Edmonds and Barns, 1992) and the agriculture-land-use module (Edmonds et al., 1996). The MiniCAM 2.0 model is a long-term, global, recursive, energy-agriculture-land-use-economy model with 11 regions, solving at 15-year time steps, for the period 1990 to 2095, and endogenously clearing global energy, agriculture, and land-use markets in an internally consistent manner. The model produces outputs of GNP, energy production, transformation, and distribution; agricultural, livestock, forest, and commercial biomass energy production, and land allocation, and computes emissions of greenhouse related gases including: CO_2, CO, CH_4, N_2O, NO_x, and SO_2, by region and year. Reference case emissions reflect the central case developed by the Intergovernmental Panel on Climate Change (IPCC), IS92a (Leggett et al., 1992), which employed a version of the Edmonds-Reilly-Barns model.

Annual greenhouse related emissions depend on a suite of factors operating through supply and demand functions, including population, technology, factor productivity, and policy instruments. In permit trading regimes, we assume a global market for permits whose cost is borne by the purchaser and whose revenues are received by the seller. We explore a carbon emission market explicitly, ignoring in this paper the additional complexity of a comprehensive approach to greenhouse emission trading. The model's decision-makers undertake mitigation efforts up to the point at which marginal costs become equal to the permit price. Total direct cost is computed as the integral over all incremental mitigation efforts. Net costs are computed, as per Edmonds et al. (1995), as the sum of transfer payments associated with permit sales and purchases plus direct mitigation costs.

Countries having marginal mitigation costs greater than or equal to the world market price of permits will buy permits, and some countries having mitigation costs less than this price will sell them.

SOVEREIGNTY EQUITY

To simulate the Sovereignty criterion, we allocate permits at the level of 1 minus the abatement percentage (as listed in Appendix Table A) times each country's gross CO_2 emissions. The results are presented in Table IV. For example, for the Year 2005, the cost of CO_2 abatement for each world region after trading is listed in the first data column. Eastern Europe and the Former Soviet Union (EEFSU) incur the highest equilibrium mitigation costs, with the global total being $30.6 billion; still, this figure is several billion dollars less than the cost of an inflexible quota system (see also Rose and Stevens, 1993, 1998). The emission trading associated with this permit distribution rule is presented in column 2, where positive entries denote purchases and negative entries (subtractions from costs) denote sales. Note that purchases and sales cancel out so that the sum of the trading column is $0.0, and the net costs are equal to the total optimal mitigation cost level of $30.6 billion. Under this criterion, the U.S., Canada and Western Europe, and the Middle East are buyers, and all other countries are sellers. On net (column 3), the U.S. suffers the greatest cost impact – $8.2 billion on an annual basis – though China suffers the largest burden in relation to GDP (0.33%). The global present discounted value for the entire 15-year period (2005–2019) is $150.3 billion, as presented in column 4.

The situation changes for the beginning of the second time period, the Year 2020, as indicated in the second partition of Table IV. Most notable is the large increase in equilibrium abatement cost for the EEFSU and the fact that developing regions such as Latin America and Africa are permit buyers. Total equilibrium mitigation costs rise to $40.9 billion in the Year 2020, and again the U.S. incurs the largest cost burden in absolute terms. Also, net costs are greater for all nine regions in the Year 2020 than in 2005.

Due to technological advances, global equilibrium mitigation costs decrease in the Year 2035 relative to the Year 2020. However, these costs increase significantly for the EEFSU because technological advances are more slowly forthcoming in this region. As shown in the third partition of Table IV, in the year 2035, Canada and Western Europe now become permit sellers, since their emissions have reduced significantly and their mitigation costs have as well. In this last milestone year of the analysis, the largest cost burden falls on the EEFSU and China, followed by the U.S. As in other years, the net burden is lowest for the Middle East, Latin America, and "Other" OECD countries. Note also the steady rise in the mitigation cost burden for Africa over the three time periods due to its projected economic growth and slower potential to lower mitigation costs. The world total present discounted value of mitigation costs for the period 2035–2049 are lower than those for the period 2005–2019 because of the heavier discounting effect.[15]

EGALITARIAN EQUITY

In the Egalitarian case, the global supply of permits is distributed according to projected population levels in each country/region. In this case, everyone on the

Table IV. Cost impacts of Sovereignty equity permit assignments (in billions of 1990 dollars)

Country (Area)	Year 2005				Year 2020				Year 2035			
	Annual value			Present (1990) Disc value	Annual value			Present (1990) Disc value	Annual value			Present (1990) Disc value
	Cost	Trading	Net		Cost	Trading	Net		Cost	Trading	Net	
USA	5.6	2.5	8.2	40.1	4.0	5.6	9.6	44.1	2.3	3.4	5.7	18.6
Can. & W. Europe	3.2	2.4	5.6	27.6	5.1	1.3	6.4	29.9	4.7	-0.6	4.1	12.7
Other OECD	2.4	-0.9	1.5	7.2	1.7	0.0	1.7	8.0	1.0	0.1	1.1	3.5
EEFSU	7.6	-1.4	6.2	30.6	14.4	-5.6	8.8	37.2	13.9	-7.0	6.9	19.0
China	4.0	-0.1	3.9	19.0	6.1	-0.5	5.5	23.3	4.5	1.8	6.3	14.2
Middle East	0.8	0.2	1.0	4.8	1.2	0.4	1.6	6.3	1.1	0.8	1.9	4.1
Africa	1.1	-0.2	0.8	4.1	0.6	1.9	2.5	8.1	0.3	2.9	3.2	6.8
Latin America	1.4	-0.0	1.3	6.6	1.4	0.2	1.6	7.4	2.1	-0.3	1.8	4.0
Southeast Asia	4.5	-2.4	2.1	10.3	6.4	-3.2	3.2	13.0	5.6	-1.0	4.6	9.3
Total[a]	$30.6	$0.0	$30.6	$150.3	$40.9	$0.0	$40.9	$177.2	$35.6	$0.0	$35.6	$92.2

[a] Sum of columns may not match total due to rounding.

planet implicitly receives one (ton carbon) permit per year, roughly equivalent in value to US $50 per year per capita in 2005. The results are presented in Table V. Again, the equilibrium abatement cost for each world region is presented in column 1; moreover, the cost figures in Table V are the same as the cost figures in Table IV, as well as for the results of all other criteria. This follows from the Coase Theorem, which stipulates that the assignment of tradeable permits will result in a uniquely efficient outcome, regardless of how the permits are distributed.

The distribution of permits does affect the amount of permit trading by each region, as shown in column 2. For the Egalitarian criterion, we see that all the industrialized countries are buyers, and that all the developing countries are sellers. The permit allocation to developing countries are so high that all but the Middle East have negative net cost impacts, i.e., positive gains (see column 3). The U.S. takes on the greatest cost burden, and Southeast Asia, which contains especially populous countries such as India and Indonesia, receives the greatest net gain. Total net cost are again $30.6 billion, however, and the present discounted value for the initial period is again $150.3 billion.

The outcome for the second period is similar to that of the first, except that EEFSU are projected to incur the largest net cost, $80.7 billion. The rank order of net gains and losses is the same for the third period, though the gains for China fall significantly as population growth slows.

HORIZONTAL EQUITY

The results for the Horizontal Equity criterion (for the total GDP version) are presented in Table VI. We reiterate that this is an outcome-based criterion, so that net costs are required to be an equal proportion of GDP for all countries, or 0.1% ($30.6 billion ÷ $30,916 billion), for example, in the Year 2005. Permit allocations are derived from this constraint and, in the Year 2005, call for OECD countries and the Middle East to buy permits and EEFSU, China, Africa, Latin American, and Southeast Asia to sell permits. Again, the U.S. suffers the largest absolute cost burden.

The situation changes only slightly in the Year 2020, with Latin America and Africa shifting from the permit selling to the permit buying side. Moreover, the change is even less significant for the Year 2035, when Latin America switches back to being a seller. The individual country net cost burden ranking over the entire time horizon hardly changes, since the relative ranking of GDPs is projected to change very little.

VERTICAL EQUITY

The results of the Vertical Equity criterion (on a per capita GDP basis) are presented in Table VII. These results differ somewhat from the Horizontal Equity results. The major differences are the significantly greater burden for Other OECD

Table V. Cost impacts of Egalitarian equity permit assignments (in billions of 1990 dollars)

| Country (Area) | Year 2005 | | | | Year 2020 | | | | Year 2035 | | | |
| | Annual value | | | Present (1990) Disc value | Annual value | | | Present (1990) Disc value | Annual value | | | Present (1990) Disc value |
	Cost	Trading	Net		Cost	Trading	Net		Cost	Trading	Net	
USA	5.6	62.1	67.7	332.5	4.0	70.7	74.7	354.5	2.3	56.8	59.1	161.7
Can. & W. Europe	3.2	26.5	29.8	146.3	5.1	27.9	33.0	156.2	4.7	20.0	24.7	69.8
Other OECD	2.4	10.1	12.5	61.3	1.7	12.0	13.8	65.3	1.0	8.8	9.9	28.6
EEFSU	7.6	48.2	55.9	274.4	14.4	66.2	80.7	337.6	13.9	55.6	69.5	181.1
China	4.0	−29.4	−25.4	−124.8	6.1	−24.0	−17.9	−109.1	4.5	−7.0	−2.5	−25.5
Middle East	0.8	−0.5	0.3	1.4	1.2	−1.0	0.2	1.1	1.1	0.3	1.4	1.8
Africa	1.1	−37.4	−36.3	−178.1	0.6	−56.0	−55.4	−226.3	0.3	−58.3	−58.0	−136.0
Latin America	1.4	−11.9	−10.6	−51.9	1.4	−13.6	−12.2	56.6	2.1	−10.6	−8.5	−25.1
Southeast Asia	4.5	−67.7	−63.3	−310.7	6.4	−82.2	−75.8	−345.5	5.6	−65.7	−60.1	−164.2
Total[a]	$30.6	$0.0	$30.6	$150.3	$40.9	$0.0	$40.9	$177.2	$35.6	−$0.0	$35.6	$92.2

[a] Sum of columns may not match total due to rounding.

Table VI. Cost impacts of Horizontal equity permit assignments (total GDP basis) (in billions of 1990 dollars)

Country (Area)	Year 2005				Year 2020				Year 2035			
	Annual value			Present (1990) Disc value	Annual value			Present (1990) Disc value	Annual value			Present (1990) Disc value
	Cost	Trading	Net		Cost	Trading	Net		Cost	Trading	Net	
USA	5.6	3.9	9.5	46.8	4.0	7.5	11.5	52.2	2.3	6.6	8.9	24.7
Can. & W. Europe	3.2	3.8	7.0	34.4	5.1	3.3	8.4	38.1	4.7	1.9	6.7	18.2
Other OECD	2.4	1.4	3.8	18.7	1.7	3.1	4.9	21.6	1.0	2.8	3.9	10.6
EEFSU	7.6	−3.6	4.1	20.0	14.4	−8.7	5.7	24.2	13.9	−9.1	4.8	12.7
China	4.0	−2.8	1.2	5.7	6.1	−3.9	2.2	8.3	4.5	−2.0	2.5	5.6
Middle East	0.8	0.5	1.3	6.3	1.2	0.9	2.1	8.4	1.1	1.1	2.2	5.2
Africa	1.1	−0.3	0.8	3.7	0.6	0.8	1.4	5.2	0.3	1.2	1.5	3.5
Latin America	1.4	0.0	1.3	6.6	1.4	0.6	2.0	8.1	2.1	−0.2	1.9	4.6
Southeast Asia	4.5	−2.8	1.6	8.0	6.4	−3.6	2.8	10.9	5.6	−2.5	3.1	7.1
Total[a]	$30.6	$0.0	$30.6	$150.3	$40.9	$0.0	$40.9	$177.2	$35.6	$0.0	$35.6	$92.2

[a] Sum of column entries may not match total due to rounding.

countries (e.g., Japan) and for the Middle East, and the significantly lower burden for Canada/Western Europe and EEFSU, as well as most developing countries, especially Southeast Asia. Also, the sets of permit buyers and sellers differ between the two criteria.[16]

The results of the Vertical Equity criterion (on a GDP basis) are not presented in detail, but they do resemble features of both the Horizontal Equity and Vertical Equity (per capita) criterion results. The rank order of burdens for the various regions is about the same as the former, but, as expected, the variance of the burdens is significantly greater, more closely resembling the latter. The major permit buyers and sellers are the same between the Horizontal and Vertical (GDP) cases, with a few minor sellers in the former becoming buyers in the latter. Also, the same countries are permit buyers and sellers for the two Vertical Equity cases in the Year 2005, though the results begin to differ in the Years 2020 and 2035, when, for the total GDP case, Canada and Western Europe remain permit buyers.[17]

CONSENSUS EQUITY

The results of the simulation of Consensus Equity, where equal weight is given to population and GDP, are presented in Table VIII. These results differ significantly from the Horizontal and Vertical Equity criteria, and, as would be expected, are closer to the Egalitarian Equity results presented in Table V. The major difference is that the EEFSU grouping is projected to take the greatest hit, and China is projected to suffer a positive net cost burden for the Consensus case. Moreover, by the Year 2035, nearly all OECD country groupings are projected to incur a negative cost burden (i.e., a financial gain).

The results differ significantly for the case where GDP is given a weight of 0.75 (not shown). Here, by the Year 2020, the U.S. is projected to have a negative net cost burden, and by the Year 2035, China is projected to incur higher net costs than any other country. The results for a Consensus Equity simulation where GDP is given a weight of 0.25 (also not shown) move in the opposite direction, with the U.S. having the second highest net cost burden, and China having negative net costs through the Year 2020.

6. Conclusion

This paper has provided an in-depth analysis of several alternative arrangements for the international sharing of benefits and costs of greenhouse gas mitigation. We have presented a non-linear programming model capable of simulating allocation-based, outcome-based, and some aspects of process-based equity criteria. We have specified these criteria formally and shown that several other approaches to burden-sharing, often labeled as "objective" or "acceptable," may appear to be philosophically distinct from equity criteria on the surface, but are mathematically equivalent and therefore have the same welfare outcomes. Our simulations show that the

Table VII. Cost impacts of Vertical equity permit assignments (per capita GDP base; $Y = 2$) (in billions of 1990 dollars)

| Country (Area) | Year 2005 | | | | Year 2020 | | | | Year 2035 | | | |
| | Annual value | | | Present (1990) Disc value | Annual value | | | Present (1990) Disc value | Annual value | | | Present (1990) Disc value |
	Cost	Trading	Net		Cost	Trading	Net		Cost	Trading	Net	
USA	5.6	11.7	17.3	84.8	4.0	17.3	21.3	95.7	2.3	15.4	17.7	47.0
Can. & W. Europe	3.2	0.1	3.3	16.4	5.1	-0.7	4.4	19.2	4.7	-0.7	4.0	10.2
Other OECD	2.4	5.8	8.2	40.2	1.7	10.7	12.4	50.9	1.0	10.2	11.2	28.4
EEFSU	7.6	-6.5	1.1	5.5	14.4	-12.5	1.9	7.5	13.9	-12.1	1.8	4.5
China	4.0	-4.0	0.0	0.0	6.1	-6.1	0.0	0.1	4.5	-4.4	0.0	0.1
Middle East	0.8	-0.2	0.6	2.8	1.2	-0.5	0.7	3.2	1.1	-0.4	0.7	1.7
Africa	1.1	-1.1	0.0	0.0	0.6	-0.6	0.0	0.1	0.3	-0.3	0.0	0.0
Latin America	1.4	-1.3	0.1	0.4	1.4	-1.3	0.1	0.5	2.1	-2.0	0.1	0.3
Southeast Asia	4.5	-4.5	0.0	0.0	6.4	-6.4	0.0	0.1	5.6	-5.6	0.0	0.0
Total[a]	$30.6	$0.0	$30.6	$150.3	$40.9	$0.0	$40.9	$177.2	$35.6	$0.0	$35.6	$92.2

[a] Sum of column entries may not match total due to rounding.

Table VIII. Cost impacts of Consensus equity permit assignments (50–50 weighting) (in billions of 1990 dollars)

Country (Area)	Year 2005				Year 2020				Year 2035			
	Annual value			Present (1990) Disc value	Annual value			Present (1990) Disc value	Annual value			Present (1990) Disc value
	Cost	Trading	Net		Cost	Trading	Net		Cost	Trading	Net	
USA	5.6	19.7	25.3	124.4	4.0	19.1	23.0	121.1	2.3	11.6	13.9	45.0
Can. & W. Europe	3.2	1.5	4.8	23.3	5.1	-2.8	2.3	17.8	4.7	-8.2	-3.4	-1.0
Other OECD	2.4	-5.7	-3.3	-16.3	1.7	-8.9	-7.2	-25.7	1.0	-10.0	-8.9	-19.2
EEFSU	7.6	38.2	45.9	225.2	14.4	49.6	64.1	272.0	13.9	38.9	52.8	141.1
China	4.0	-0.7	3.3	16.1	6.1	8.6	14.6	43.2	4.5	19.3	23.8	45.5
Middle East	0.8	-2.3	-1.5	-7.3	1.2	-4.2	-3.0	-11.0	1.1	-3.8	-2.7	-6.9
Africa	1.1	-17.3	-16.2	-79.7	0.6	-24.7	-24.1	99.6	0.3	-24.7	-24.4	-58.2
Latin America	1.4	-5.5	-4.1	20.2	1.4	-5.9	-4.5	-21.4	2.1	-4.5	-2.4	-8.3
Southeast Asia	4.5	-28.0	-23.5	-115.3	6.4	-30.8	-24.4	-119.3	5.6	-18.8	-13.1	-45.8
Total[a]	$30.6	$0.0	$30.6	$150.3	$40.9	$0.0	$40.9	$177.2	$35.6	$0.0	$35.6	$92.2

[a] Sum of column entries may not match total due to rounding.

net costs of mitigation for several criteria were very similar (e.g., Sovereignty, Horizontal, and Vertical Equity, and therefore also for differentiation rules such as Grandfathering, No Harm, and No Income Divergence). However, some seemingly reasonable criteria have rather extreme outcomes (e.g., Egalitarian, and Consensus Equity).

Our model can be applied to any burden-sharing or benefit-sharing rules that can be mathematically specified. There is an increasing need for such a framework as the number of differentiation proposals emanating from the group of industrialized countries increases nearing COP-3, and especially as we look beyond to a time when it will be imperative to have developing countries as part of an agreement that requires them to mitigate greenhouse gases as well.

Acknowledgements

The authors wish to thank two anonymous and most astute referees and also Snorre Kverndokk, Robert Kohn, James Shortle, Duane Chapman, Lester Lave, Kenneth Richards, James Kahn, and Deborah Nestor for comments on earlier versions of this paper. The usual disclaimer applies. Also, the views expressed in this paper are those of the authors, and do not necessarily represent the positions of the institutions with which they are affiliated.

Notes

1. *Equity* in this paper refers to distributional justice of emission permit trading, the redistribution of carbon taxes, or unilateral transfers across countries, i.e., *international equity*. This differs from *intergenerational equity*, which is another major consideration in global warming policy. It is the authors' contention that these two types of equity can be analyzed separately.
2. The First Conference of the Parties in Berlin in 1994 (COP-1) established the basis of such an agreement (known as the "Berlin Mandate"). Commitments by industrialized countries are the focus of most ongoing analyses by the Intergovernmental Panel on Climate Change (IPCC) and individual researchers (see, e.g., Stanford Energy Modeling Forum, 1997).
3. Differentiation is defined more narrowly in FCCC (1996) as follows: "That some Annex I parties or groups of parties would have commitments that are different from those of other Annex I parties or groups of parties." Essentially this is a way of requesting special treatment with respect to the GHG mitigation commitment by attempting to use a term intended to be more neutral than equity. For Annex I countries equity is a two-edged sword – the relative gains from differentiation on the up-side are likely to be small in comparison to the loss of position with the respect to the more numerous developing countries on the down-side.
4. This is also true of other recent work on the subject, which includes: d'Arge (1989), Chapman and Drennen (1990), Rose (1990, 1992), Toman and Burtraw (1991), Grubb and Sebenius (1991), Richards (1991), Solomon and Ahuja (1991), Kverndokk (1993), Eyckmans et al. (1993), Chichilnisky et al. (1993), Musgrave (1994), and Chao and Peck (1996). All of these studies have at least one of the following limitations: examination of only a single equity criterion, examination of "rules of thumb" (e.g., population, land area) rather than equity criteria, analysis at a theoretical level only, or use of hypothetical data. Exceptions are some of the papers reviewed in this section and Eyckmans et al. (1993).
5. There are alternative equity criteria we did not include in our list. For example, Kneese and Schulze (1985) define various ethical systems, some of which overlap with our criteria. They also provide an excellent discussion of a non-humanistic environmental ethic, but not to the point

where it can be operationalized. Eyckmans et al. (1993) present an axiomatic framework for equity analysis that differs from ours as well.

6. We emphasize the difference between the aforementioned formal equity criteria and the use of *reference bases*, which are merely implementation indices (see Rose, 1992). Examples of reference bases are GDP, population, energy use, emissions, and land area; some have an obvious equity criterion counterpart (e.g., population), others apply to more than one criterion (e.g., emissions), and still others have in fact no obvious equity counterpart (land area). Reference bases do have the desirable properties of focal points, a term Schelling (1960) coined to represent a key facilitating feature of negotiation processes. Toman and Burtraw (1991; p. 12) suggest that "negotiators will seek out rules of thumb...," but also note that because of strategic considerations, it is unlikely that "... simple rules of thumb alone can successfully guide the negotiation process." They go on to state: "Thus strategic and procedural aspects of negotiation can be viewed as essential to the evolution of a commonly shared standard of equity that must accompany an international agreement. Morrisette and Plantinga (1991; p. 6) have likewise stated: "Success, however, will depend on how the different stakes of nations can be dealt with in the negotiation process in an equitable manner." We thus ascribe primacy to equity principles. If global warming were an uncomplex issue that could be settled in a short time, we would endorse the more pragmatic "rule of thumb" approach. Since the issue is complex, negotiations likely to take years, and to go through several stages, it is important to have a solid foundation. It is likely that equity principles will need to be thoroughly articulated and their full implications understood before a lasting agreement can be reached.

Also, our criteria deal with static aspects of equity. In addition to the literature on intergenerational equity aspects of global warming, there are other dynamic considerations relating to the responsibility for cumulative build-up and the opportunity cost of future foregone development. We contend that these can be addressed, to a great extent, by using historical or future emissions as a reference base (see Rose and Stevens, 1993, 1998).

7. The compensation aspects of this criterion can be thought of as related to the Hicks-Kaldor test, which is only an endorsement of potential compensation. The matter of actual compensation is left to the policy-maker, and is always characterized as an equity decision.

8. We should acknowledge some additional aspects of arbitrariness of the criteria put forth. One of these is "partition dependence," which refers to the fact that applications of a given criterion are not unique but may depend on the grouping involved. (We thank one of the reviewers for calling this to our attention.) For example, for the case of Vertical Equity, the distribution of permits would be altered if we treat, say, Western Europe and Canada as one entity or split this grouping in two (or further divided Western Europe). We agree, but suggest this may not be as serious a problem in actual policy-making applications. First, one can readily conceive of applying Vertical Equity to all the individual countries entering into an agreement, rather than to regional groupings. Therefore, the individual country application may be considered a superior partition. (Our example below is only intended to be illustrative of the general principle.) Second, even if one concedes the variations associated with the Vertical Equity criterion on this basis, is this sufficient to reject it from consideration? The principle is a hallmark of even traditional Welfare Economics, is widely applied in policy-making in general, and, as Table II indicates, is often at the core of so-called objective criteria for global warming policy.

9. Applied to our context, the Coase Theorem means that efficient abatement of CO_2 is independent of the distribution of a fixed global supply of emission permits among countries, assuming the absence of significant transactions costs and income effects. We believe these assumptions are reasonable. Tietenberg (1992) has made a good case for the absence of market power in a global CO_2 permits market. The empirical analysis in this paper, as well as Chao and Peck (1997), suggests that income effects from nearly all recommended permit distributions are likely to be small (typically less than 1% of GDP), and for practical purposes can be ignored. Note this is also below the current annual level of foreign aid transfers and below the World Bank's recommended target of 0.75% of GDP for donor countries. Most of those who have examined marketable GHG permits believe the costs of finding a buyer or seller and concluding a sale are likely to be an infinitesimal fraction of the tens of billions of dollars of projected permit transactions (see, e.g., Tietenberg, 1992). Negotiating a greenhouse gas treaty will not be easy, and voluntary exchange

may still fail to eliminate all of the Pareto-relevant portion of the greenhouse externality. Inability to forge an agreement, however, is not due to monetary transactions costs but rather to factors such as differing views of the problem and cultural attitudes that are stumbling blocks to an international treaty (transactions costs is a misnomer here).

10. As will be shown below in Table III, the calculation of individual country net benefits can be accomplished by the mathematical specification of permit distribution criteria. However, in most cases, it is necessary to know *global* net benefits first. This is a straightforward calculation with the information already discussed. The global marginal cost function is the horizontal summation of individual country marginal cost functions, and the global marginal benefit function is the vertical (public good) summation of the individual country marginal benefit functions. Since the cost-effectiveness approach stipulates an abatement level exogenously, this is the value of the independent variable for both the global benefit and cost function. For the more general global efficiency case, this abatement level must be determined endogenously by the maximization of net benefits, thus necessitating a formal programming solution. In the cost-effectiveness case here, the necessary global net benefits can be computed by a side-calculation. An equation such as (3a) is needed to calculate individual country net benefits in the allocation model as well. It can simply be treated as a side-calculation, once the values of R_i and P_i are determined, or the equation can be added to the equation set (2a) through (2c), with the net benefit constant transformed into a variable.

11. Once the least-cost abatement levels for individual countries have been determined, both allocation-based and outcome-based permit distributions can be analyzed with a simple spreadsheet program. Another approach to simple distribution cases is a simultaneous equation system solution (see, e.g., Bohm and Larsen, 1994). We have chosen the details of a more elaborate programming model, which will be needed for the more complex analyses of real world problems, including additional constraints and the mitigation of more than one greenhouse gas (when mitigation is joint-product).

12. A controversy has recently arisen over whether uniform permit prices and the equalization of marginal abatement costs between nations will lead to a Pareto optimal or even cost-effective allocation of resources given the public good character of GHG abatement, which some suggest requires a Lindahl (multiple price) equilibrium (cf., Chichilnisky and Heal, 1993, 1994; and Chao and Peck, 1997). The Chichilnisky-Heal approach is to assume different marginal utilities of income across countries and to analyze the problem using Negishi weights, the typical implication of which is to automatically allocate a relatively larger share of permits to developing countries. We believe our approach does a better job of separating efficiency and equity considerations in general, and of allowing for a wide variety of equity principles in particular.

13. We acknowledge that there is considerable ambiguity and arbitrariness inherent in some of the equity criteria and their specification. For example, Horizontal Equity can be interpreted in terms of both total GDP and per capita GDP reference bases. The same is true of Vertical Equity, though most applications of the principle have been in the per capita version (consider, for example, the difference between the two versions for the Middle East). In addition, our example of the Consensus criterion is arbitrary and essentially invokes an outcome-based proxy for a process. One of the reviewers has questioned the legitimacy of the Market Justice criterion, but there is extensive belief among economists and political scientists that the market is inherently fair. This is the prevailing attitude in conservative approaches to the New Welfare Economics and by other social scientists (see, e.g., Lane, 1986). Note that we have listed this approach also because of its congruence with a global carbon tax. For this criterion, all permits are auctioned off (hence, the designation $\lambda P_i \geq 0$ in Table III, indicating that no country receives any permits, or entitlements, for free). The optimal permit purchases would be equivalent to the optimal response to a carbon tax, and hence carbon tax revenues. But this still begs the question of which equity rule might be used to redistribute the global carbon tax revenues or permit auction revenues. In these cases, yet another equity or differentiation rule would need to come into play. The Compensation principle is also indeterminate with use of the formal model alone because it begs the question of which countries should pay the compensation. Finally, we have not included the Rawls Maximin criterion in Table III because of the difficulty of its specification. One interpretation would be that the poorest of developing countries (those officially designated as LDCs) would be favored,

and therefore this criterion would be similar to the "No Purchase" rule (rather than a "No Harm" criterion because Rawls is not a "Welfarist"), but there is little guidance on how the burden would be shared among other countries.

14. In the analyses of the Berlin Mandate case, simulations were run that: a) required unilateral compliance by Annex I countries alone and b) a type of "joint implementation" in which non-Annex I countries are allotted emission permits equal to their projected baseline levels, which they can then sell to OECD countries. However, because energy markets in the model are global, the emission reductions in the OECD will have an effect on emissions in non-OECD regions, even when they are not participating. These deviations were not large, so that we have abstracted from them and used ordinary baseline projections. The situation does, however, indicate the difficulty of establishing policies independent of implications for developing countries. That is, even the Berlin Mandate case is likely to require adjustments for developing countries that involve at least an implicit equity consideration.

15. Note that mitigation costs before trading are not shown, but are available from the authors upon request. Also, the present analysis does not include benefits associated with mitigation. Though this is potentially an important consideration, we omitted it because of the tenuous nature of benefit estimates. The reader is referred to Rose and Stevens (1993) for an analysis that includes benefits; in that study, the optimal level of CO_2 abatement, i.e., one that maximizes net benefits, was 14.9% of baseline emissions in the Year 2000.

16. The Vertical Equity criterion (as well as Ability to Pay) would not be partition dependent if they were implemented on a per capita basis. Moreover, an example worked out by one of the referees for Vertical Equity indicates the results would not change much.

17. Note that the Vertical Equity results resemble an outcome-based version of the "No Harm to Developing Countries" rule. This has become a very popular policy proposal recently because it is viewed as an excellent strategy for obtaining developing country involvement in a truly global agreement in the aftermath of Kyoto.

Appendix

Table A. reference bases for marketable permit distributions

Region	Gross emissions[a]			Gross domestic product[b]			Population[c]		
	2005	2020	2035	2005	2020	2035	2005	2020	2035
United States	1,721	1,934	2,068	9,617	13,171	16,124	275	295	299
Canada & W. Europe	1,089	1,234	1,294	7,066	9,564	12,042	460	470	467
Other OECD	441	496	499	3,852	5,601	6,982	160	164	163
EEFSU	1,695	2,341	2,638	4,118	6,542	8,732	462	487	505
China	950	1,545	2,229	1,175	2,533	4,438	1,467	1,657	1,776
Middle East	214	343	526	1,303	2,443	3,981	205	297	384
Africa	256	448	738	771	1,549	2,794	1,013	1,444	1,862
Latin America	351	523	743	1,360	2,232	3,433	565	672	751
S.E. Asia	736	1,268	2,024	1,654	3,212	5,660	2,039	2,487	2,853
Total	7,453	10,132	12,759	30,916	46,847	61,186	6,646	7,973	9,060
Global Abatement (%)	15.7	16.5	14.6						
Permit Price ($)	50	50	38						

[a] In gigatons of carbon. [b] In billions of 1992 constant U.S. dollars. [c] In millions of persons.

References

Agarwal, A. and S. Narain (1991), *Global Warming in an Unequal World: A Case of Environmental Colonialism*, New Delhi: Centre for Science and Environment.

Barrett, S. (1992), 'Acceptable Allocations of Tradable Carbon Emission Entitlements in a Global Warming Treaty', in S. Barrett et al., *Combating Global Warming*, Geneva: UNCTAD.

Barrett, S., M. Grubb, K. Roland, A. Rose, R. Sandor and T. Tietenberg (1992), *Combating Global Warming: A Global System of Tradable Carbon Emission Entitlements*, Geneva, Switzerland: UNCTAD.

Bertram, G. (1992), 'Tradable Emission Permits and the Control of Greenhouse Gases', *Journal of Development Studies* **28**, 423–446.

Bohm, P. and B. Larsen (1994), 'Fairness in a Tradable-Permit Treaty for Carbon Emissions Reductions in Europe and the former Soviet Union', *Environmental and Resources Economics* **4**, 219–239.

Brooke, A., D. Kendrick, and A. Meeraus (1989), *GAMS: A User's Guide*, Redwood City: Scientific Press.

Chao, H. and S. Peck (1997), 'Pareto Optimal Environmental Control and Income Distribution with Global Climate Change', Discussion Paper, Electric Power Research Institute.

Chapman, D., and T. Drennen (1990), 'Economic Dimensions of CO_2 Treaty Proposals', *Contemporary Policy Issues* **8**, 16–28.

Chichilnisky, G. and G. Heal (1993), 'Global Environmental Risks', *Journal of Economic Perspectives* **7**, 65–86.

Chichilnisky, G. and G. Heal (1994), 'Who Should Abate Carbon Emission?' *Economics Letters* **44**, 443–449.

Cline, W. (1992), *Economics of Global Warming*, Washington, DC: Institute for International Economics.

Coase, R. (1960), 'The Problem of Social Cost', *Journal of Law and Economics* **3**, 1–44.

d'Arge, R. (1989), 'Ethical and Economic Systems for Managing the Global Commons], in D. Botkin et al., eds., *Changing the World Environment*, New York: Academic Press.

Edmonds, J. and Barns, D.W. 1992. "Factors Affecting the Long-Term Cost of Global Fossil Fuel CO_2 Emissions Reductions', *International Journal of Global Energy Issues* **4**(3), 140–166.

Edmonds, J. and J. Reilly (1985), *Global Energy: Assessing the Future*, New York: Oxford University Press.

Edmonds, J., M. Wise, and D. Barns (1995), 'Carbon Coalitions: The Cost and Effectiveness of Energy Agreements to Alter Trajectories of Atmospheric Carbon Dioxide Emissions', *Energy Policy* **23**, 309–335.

Edmonds J., J. Reilly, R. Gardner and A. Brenkert (1986), *Uncertainty in Future Global Energy Use and Fossil Fuel CO_2 Emissions 1975 to 2075*, TR036, DO3/NBB–0081, Dist. Category UC–11, National Technical Information Service, U. S. Department of Commerce, Springfield, VA.

Edmonds, J., M. Wise, R. Sands, R. Brown, and H. Kheshgi (1996), *Agriculture, Land-Use, and Commercial Biomass Energy: A Preliminary Integrated Analysis of the Potential Role of Biomass Energy for Reducing Future Greenhouse Related Emission*, PNNL–11155, Pacific Northwest National Laboratories, Washington, DC.

Eyckmans, J., S. Proost, and E. Schokkaert (1993), 'Efficiency and Distribution in Greenhouse Negotiations', *Kyklos* **46**, 363–397.

Framework Convention on Climate Change, Ad Hoc Group on he Berlin Mandate (1996), 'Strengthening the Commitments in Article 4.2(A) and (B) Quantified Emission Limitation and Reduction Objectives within Specified Time-Frames: Review of Possible Indicators to Define Criteria for Differentiation Among Annex 1 Parties', Geneva, July 8.

Framework Convention on Climate Change, Conference of the Parties (1997), 'Kyoto Protocol to the United Nations Framework Convention on Climate Change', Kyoto, December 10.

Grubb, M., and J. Sebenius (1991), 'Participation, Allocation and Adaptability in International Tradable Emission Permit Systems for Greenhouse Gas Control', Paper prepared for OECD Workshop on Tradable Greenhouse Gas Permits, Paris, France.

Hahn, R., and K. Richards (1989), 'The Internationalization of Environmental Regulation', *Harvard International Law Journal* **30**, 421–446.

INTERNATIONAL EQUITY AND DIFFERENTIATION IN GLOBAL WARMING POLICY   51

Intergovernmental Panel on Climate Change (IPCC) (1996), *Climate Change 1995: Economic and Social Dimensions*, Cambridge: Cambridge University Press.

Kneese, A., and W. Schulze (1985), 'Ethics and Environmental Economics', in A. V. Kneese and J. Sweeney, eds., *Handbook of Natural Resource and Energy Economics, Vol. 1*, New York: Elsevier Science Publishers.

Kverndokk, S. (1993), 'Global CO_2 Agreements: A Cost-Effective Approach', *Energy Journal* **14**, 91–112.

Kverndokk, S. (1995), 'Tradable CO_2 Emission Permits: Initial Distribution as a Justice Problem', *Environmental Values* **4**, 129–148.

Lane, R. (1986), 'Market Justice, Political Justice', *American Political Science Review* **80**, 383–402.

Larsen, B. and A. Shah (1994), 'Global Tradable Carbon Permits, Participation Incentives and Transfers', *Oxford Economic Papers* **46**, 841–856.

Leggett, J., W. J. Pepper, R. J. Swart, J. Edmonds, L. G. Meira Filho, I. Mintzer, M.X. Wang, and J. Wasson (1992), 'Emissions Scenarios for the IPCC: An Update', in *Climate Change 1992: The Supplementary Report to the IPCC Scientific Assessment*, Cambridge: University Press.

Manne, A., and R. Richels (1991), 'Global CO_2 Emission Reductions: The Impacts of Rising Energy Costs', *Energy Journal* **12**, 87–107.

Morrisette, P., and A. Plantinga (1991), 'The Global Warming Issue: Viewpoints of Different Countries', *Resources* **103**, 2–6.

Musgrave, P. (1994), 'Pure Global Externalities: International Efficiency and Equity'. Paper presented at the 50th Congress of the International Institute of Public Finance, Cambridge, MA.

Nordhaus, W. (1993), 'Rolling the DICE: The Optimal Transition Path for Controlling Greenhouse Gases', *Resource and Energy Economics* **15**, 27–50.

Pezzey, J. (1992), 'The Symmetry Between Controlling Pollution by Prince and by Quantity', *Canadian Journal of Economics* **25**, 983–991.

Rayner, S. and E. Malone, eds. (1997), *Human Choice and Climate Change: An International Social Science Assessment*, Columbus, OH: Battelle Press.

Richards, K. (1991), 'Tradable Permits in the Global Climate Convention', Discussion Paper, University of Pennsylvania Law School.

Richels, R., J. Edmonds, H. Gruenspecht, and T. Wigley (1996), 'The Berlin Mandate: The Design of Cost-Effective Strategies', paper prepared for the Stanford Energy Modeling Forum, February 3, 1996.

Rose, A. (1990), 'Reducing Conflict in Global Warming Policy: The Potential of Equity as a Unifying Principle', *Energy Policy* **18**, 927–935.

Rose, A. (1992), 'Equity considerations of Tradable Carbon Entitlements', in S. Barrett et al., eds., *Combating Global Warming*, Geneva: UNCTAD.

Rose, A. and B. Stevens (1993), 'The Efficiency and Equity of Marketable Permits for CO_2 Emissions', *Resource and Energy Economics* **15**, 117–146.

Rose, A., and B. Stevens (1998), *The Marketable Permits Approach to Global Warming Policy*, Chicago: University of Chicago Press (forthcoming).

Rose A., B. Stevens and G. Davis (1988), *Natural Resource Policy and Income Distribution*, Baltimore: John Hopkins University Press.

Solomon, B. and D. Ahuja (1991), 'An Equitable Approach to International Reductions of Greenhouse Gas Emissions', *Global Environment Change* **1**, 343–350.

Stanford Energy Modeling Forum (1997), 'Economic Impacts of Climate Change Policies', Stanford, CA.

Tietenberg, T. (1992), 'Implementation Issues', in S. Barrett et al., eds., *Combating Global Warming*.

Toman, M. and D. Burtraw (1991), 'Resolving Equity Issues: Greenhouse Gas Negotiations', *Resources* **103**, 10–13.

Weitzman, M. (1974), 'Prices vs. Quantities', *Review of Economic Studies* **41**, 447–491.

[31]

Should the north make unilateral technology transfers to the south?
North–South cooperation and conflicts in responses to global climate change

Zili Yang *

Center for Energy and Environmental Policy Research, E40-267 Massachusetts Institute of Technology, 1 Amherst St., Cambridge, MA 02139, USA

Received 24 June 1996; accepted 15 November 1997

Abstract

Whether developed countries should make unilateral technology transfers to developing countries in order to address global environment problems is debatable. This paper discusses the issue in a framework that recognizing nations' joint production of environmental externalities. Unlike the existing literature on unilateral transfers, this paper presents a North–South environmental–economic optimal growth model that allows transfers to mitigate externalities only. The paper derives criteria that would make such transfers feasible. By solving the transfer problem in a modified RICE model [Nordhaus, W.D., Yang, Z., 1996. A regional dynamic general equilibrium model of alternative climate change strategies, Am. Econ. Rev., 86 (4) 741–65], this paper also provides information on the timing and the amount of unilateral transfers from North to South to address potential global warming problem, one major global environmental externality. A policy implication from this study is that moderate employment of unilateral transfers would benefit North along with the world as a whole. © 1999 Elsevier Science B.V. All rights reserved.

JEL classification: F35; H23; Q29
Keywords: Foreign aid; Climate change; Stock externalities

1. Introduction

The international community has been keenly aware of the urgency of such global environmental issues as global warming, ozone-layer depletion, and species' endangerment. The June 1992 international environmental summit held in Rio de Janeiro, Brazil, reflected such awareness. Among the possible policy responses to global environmental issues, one of the foremost in importance is a call for international cooperation and joint partnerships to cope with global environmental problems. The 1987 Montreal Protocol on Substances that Deplete the Ozone Layer, signed by major countries, is one successful example of international cooperation in solving global environmental problems. The 1992 United Nations Berlin Conference and 1997 Kyoto Conference on global climate change offered for the evidence that the international community can work toward cooperatively addressing global climate change—an environmental externality on a scale much larger than any other.

Even before the Rio summit, politicians from developing countries had appealed to leaders of industrialized nations for unilateral transfers of technology and capital from developed countries ('the North') to developing countries ('the South') as a tangible form of international cooperation. Some western economists have also proposed, in discussions of policy responses to potential global warming, that a portion of carbon tax revenue should be used to fund environmental projects in developing countries (Schelling, 1991).

Following World War II, industrialized nations transferred vast sums to developing countries for political, economic, and humanitarian reasons. Nonetheless, the sufficiency of developed countries' concern for global environmental issues to motivate the continued flow of substantial funds flowing from North to South—private or public—is still in question.

In a policy regime of international cooperation to deal with global environmental issues, if industrialized nations willingly finance the amelioration of environmental deterioration elsewhere, the motivation behind the transfers could be anything but philanthropic. One major incentive for such unilateral transfers is economic: once such unilateral transfers are made, developed countries' welfare improves. [1]

In many large-scale modeling endeavors relating to global climate change issues, the international monetary transfers in joint implementation schemes

---

[1] The term 'unilateral transfer' in this paper differs slightly from its usual meaning. While a recipient is not required to repay monetary inflows, as 'unilateral transfer' generally implies, the recipient must use the money for environmental improvement. Therefore, commodities flowing as a result of such transfers are necessarily environmental preservation technologies. Such technological transfers have other terminologies in policy discussions of climate change, as subsequent sections of this paper will show.

(sometimes called 'side payments' and 'tax recycling') serve as major instruments for policy analysis. Two models developed early that have addressed transfer issues are Global 2100, developed by Manne and Richels (1992), and GREEN, developed by the economists of OECD (1992). More recently, the EPPA model, developed by MIT's Joint Program on the Science and Policy of Global Change (Yang et al., 1996) has also been employed to examine transfer issues. And several other large-scale models on climate change are now available, as well, for such studies. For a detailed survey of these models, see the work of Weyant et al. (1996). The literature on various aspects of unilateral transfers in dealing with global environmental issues is extensive. Most studies do not focus on particular large-scale models, but instead provide insights on many theoretical and empirical issues related to transfer problems. For example, Hoel (1991) discusses the problem of unilateral actions taken by one country to deal with global environmental issues; Bohm (1994) raises joint implementation as a possible international policy response to climate change; Kverndok (1995) and Rose et al. (1997) examine distribution issues such as burden-sharing schemes in international cooperation to deal with climate change; Wirl (1994) also probes several of the aforementioned issues via a game theoretic approach.

In this paper, I formulate the problem of unilateral transfers in a North–South optimal growth model with cumulative environmental externalities, [2] and analyze conditions under which such transfers might be feasible. Unlike the conventional formulation of unilateral monetary transfers which allows transfers to be used for anything, the explicit assumption here is that such transfers do not contribute directly to the GNP of southern nation: money from the North goes only toward purchasing technology to reduce externalities in the South, so that, essentially, unilateral transfers are restricted to ameliorating environmental externalities. This feature is integrated into a modified version of the RICE (Regional Integrated Model of Climate and the Economy) model, developed by Nordhaus and Yang (1996), a dynamic general equilibrium model focusing on climate externalities. The timing and volume of unilateral transfers as the North's policy response to potential global warming, one of the most important environmental dilemmas facing the international community, are derived in the modified RICE model.

The remainder of this paper is organized as follows: Section 2 introduces a North–South optimal growth model involving cumulative environmental externalities with unilateral transfer features. Section 3 incorporates the unilateral transfer mechanism described in Section 2 into the RICE model and presents economic

---

[2] Externalities with similar properties are termed 'stock externalities' by Brito (1972) and Intriligator and Brito (1976) in their discussion of arms race. Such externalities build up over time, their impact (positive or negative) depending on their stock at the time of valuation. Implications of stock externalities in the context of environmental issues have been discussed by various authors, such as Tietenberg (1992).

analysis of the simulation results from the modified RICE model. Section 4 offers concluding remarks.

2. A North–South environmental–economic optimal growth model

2.1. The model

The North–South environmental–economic optimal growth model presented here assumes a world economy consisting of two regions: North and South. Each region produces an aggregate private good, namely, GNP. As a byproduct of the production, each region contributes to the build-up of cumulative environmental externalities. [3] If the North sacrifices a portion of its consumption or capital formation to make unilateral transfers to the South, it can reduce the level of externality flows from the South. The model thus can be expressed as a joint optimal control problem for both North and South. Appendix A formally presents this model, including a key to notations.

In the model, Eqs. (A-1) and (A-8) are intertemporal utility functions of the North and the South, respectively; Eqs. (A-2) and (A-9) are these regions' GNP identities; Eqs. (A-3) and (A-10) are their respective aggregate production functions; Eqs. (A-4) and (A-11) are the respective capital formation functions; Eq. (A-5) is the accumulation process of environmental externality stocks; Eqs. (A-6) and (A-7) are flows of environmental externalities in the North and the South, respectively. Because the North and South jointly produce environmental externalities, Eqs. (A-5), (A-6) and (A-7) appear in the optimal control problems of both regions.

In the model, $Tr(t)$ is the volume of unilateral technological transfer from North to South during period t. Unlike the case with conventional unilateral transfers, $Tr(t)$ here does not directly contribute to southern GNP but instead affects only the level of externality flows in the South during period t, namely, $b^S(t)$. This formulation demonstrates that unilateral transfers' sole purpose is to reduce the stock building of environmental externalities from the South; such transfers directly alter neither the pattern of private goods production nor the consumption behavior of the South.

The functional forms in the model can be quite flexible; we assume only that all functions are twice differentiable. In addition, U and F are concave functions, and the following first-order derivatives have the following signs: $g_J < 0$, $g_Y > 0$, $f_T < 0$, $f_Y > 0$.

---

[3] Cumulative environmental externalities include global climate change and ozone-layer depletion.

In this model, the South does not control environmental externalities using its own money. This assumption reflects a consensus that a nation's valuation of global environmental externalities correlates with its level of economic development. While the South might increasingly attend to local pollution problems, this region is not as likely as the North to significantly address global environmental issues. Within such a framework, the South clearly would not play a strong role in unilateral technological transfers. The South could not generate higher externality flows than the maximal value of Eq. (A-7) allows. Suppose the South is on an optimal production path $Y^{S*}(t)$. No unilateral transfers would occur from North to South if the North considers the maximal amount of externality created by the South, $b^{S*}(t) = f(0, Y^{S*}(t))$, to be acceptable.

The whole issue of unilateral technology transfers can therefore be expressed as follows: From a northern viewpoint, is it in the best interests of the North to have $\mathrm{Tr}(t) > 0$? If so, what is the optimal timing and level of $\mathrm{Tr}(t)$? [4]

The discussion below focuses on the behavior of the North, considering $b^{S*}(t)$ to be an exogenous variable fed into the system of the North. Based on this assumption, the problem faced by the North, as described in Appendix A, can be simplified as follows:

$$\max_{I^N, \mathrm{Tr}, J} \int_0^\infty U^N\big(F^N(K^N(t)) - I^N(t) - \mathrm{Tr}(t) - J(t), -B(t)\big) e^{-\gamma_1 t} \mathrm{d}t \quad (1)$$

$$\text{s.t. } \dot{K}^N(t) = I^N(t) - \delta_1 K^N(t) \quad (2)$$

$$\dot{B}(t) = h(J(t), K^N(t)) + G(\mathrm{Tr}(t), t) - \sigma B(t) \quad (3)$$

$$I^N(t) \geq 0, \mathrm{Tr}(t) \geq 0, J(t) \geq 0$$

$$B(0) = B_0, \quad K^N(0) = K_0^N$$

The optimal control problem of the North, i.e., System (1), has three control variables: investment $I^N(t)$, unilateral transfers $\mathrm{Tr}(t)$ and domestic mitigation cost $J(t)$. System (1) also has two state variables: capital stock $K^N(t)$ and externality stock $B(t)$. In Eq. (3), the contribution to $B(t)$ by the North is a function of h: the North's own control efforts and capital stocks. On the other hand, the South's contribution to $B(t)$ is related to G, which is a function of unilateral transfers from the North and an exogenous trend of southern growth level. Assuming that the southern economy is growing, the following derivatives have the signs: $h_1 < 0$, $h_2 > 0$, $G_1 < 0$, $G_2 > 0$.

---

[4] Similar to this is a social planner's problem in which unilateral transfers from North to South are determined at a socially optimal level (a weighted sum of the welfare of North and South). Because of external effects, the two problems are not identical. If $\mathrm{Tr}(t) > 0$ in a 'North-only' problem, then it is true in the 'global' problem, providing constraints are the same. The reverse is not necessarily true, however. For simplicity, only the 'North-only' problem is considered in the present section. Section 3 compares the two cases in an empirical context.

2.2. Conditions for Tr(t) > 0

Despite its simplicity, Problem (1) requires a crucial decision by the North on unilateral transfers in the presence of environmental externalities. Because $\text{Tr}(t)$ and $J(t)$ are perfect substitutes and the flow contributions by the two regions to environmental externalities are additive, the efficiency conditions for $\text{Tr}(t) > 0$ are very easy to obtain.

From the Lagrangian of Problem (1), [5]

$$\mathscr{L}(t) = U\big(F(K(t) - I(t) - \text{Tr}(t), -J(t)) - B(t)\big)e^{-\gamma_1 t} + \mu_1(t)\big(I(t)$$
$$- \delta K(t)\big) + \mu_2(t)\big[h(J(t), K(t)) + G(\text{Tr}(t), t) - \sigma B(t)\big]$$
$$+ \lambda_1(t)I(t) + \lambda_2(t)\text{Tr}(t) + \lambda_3(t)J(t)$$

we can obtain the Euler equations of Problem (1). The following efficiency conditions for $\text{Tr}(t) > 0$ can then be obtained from the Euler equations (see Appendix C for proof).

Proposition: A necessary condition for $\text{Tr}(t) > 0$ is:

$$\lambda_3(t) = \frac{G_1(\text{Tr}^*(t), t) - h_1(J^*(t), K^*(t))}{\mu_2(t)} \geq 0 \qquad (4)$$

holds for the optimal solution of Problem (1). In particular, the necessary condition for the North to curb its contribution to environmental externalities ($J(t) > 0$) and make transfers to the South ($\text{Tr}(t) > 0$) concurrently is:

$$G_1(\text{Tr}^*(t), t) = h_1(J^*(t), K^*(t)) \qquad (5)$$

The sufficient condition for the North to make unilateral transfers only ($J(t) = 0$), in an extreme case, is:

$$G_1(T^*(t), t) > h_1(J^*(t), K^*(t)) \qquad (6)$$

The economic interpretation of conditions (4), (5) and (6) is simple. The North is willing to make unilateral transfers only when a dollar can reduce externalities at least as much in the South as in the North at the margin. In Problem (1), the decision to make transfers or not depends on the shapes of functions G and h in the optimal solutions. Obviously, if $G_{12} > 0$, conditions (4), (5) or (6) are likely to be met for a sufficiently large t. Thus, transfers are likely to be made at the end, if

---

[5] For simplicity, superscript N is omitted in the following discussion.

not at the beginning, of the planning time span. Also, conditions (4), (5) and (6) imply that the northern decision on whether to make transfers is not dependent on levels of externalities in either North or South. Such a decision is based on how effectively transfers can change the level of externalities in the South; the level itself may be high or low. This issue brings out a basic assumption in this paper: that the unilateral transfer problem is actually a technology transfer problem. If a technology can mitigate environmental externalities generated by the South more effectively, the monetary transfers representing such a technology should be made by the North.

While discussions within the framework of a theoretical, stylized model are useful, they are not very helpful in empirical policy analysis, because without specifying Problem (1), we cannot provide definite answers to many concrete concerns about unilateral transfers and relevant policy issues. Section 3 therefore introduces unilateral technology transfers in a modified version of the RICE model —an applied model having the major features of generic Problem (1)—discusses the issues of unilateral technology transfers in an empirical context.

3. The RICE model with unilateral technological transfers

3.1. Background of the model

The RICE model, developed by Nordhaus and Yang (1996), is an expansion of the DICE (the Dynamic Integrated Model of Climate and the Economy) model by Nordhaus (1994). The DICE model is an optimal economic growth model of the global economy incorporating impacts of global warming and mitigation costs of CO_2 emission reduction. The RICE model, by dividing the global economy in the DICE model into six regions, treats CO_2 emissions (a major contributor to global warming) as public 'bads,' or externalities, produced by regions. Each region reaches its own optimal CO_2 emission level by maximizing a social welfare function weighted by a set of time-variant Negishi weights. [6] In the RICE model, capital flows are allowed in a conventional sense: capital flows into regions' GNP accounts directly and each region must maintain a zero balance of payments at the end of the planning horizon.

In the modified RICE model that is introduced in this paper, the six regions in the original RICE model are merged into two regions: the North and the South, [7]

---

[6] For a technical treatment of welfare weights in the RICE model, see Nordhaus and Yang (1996).

[7] More precisely, 'the North' here represents the USA, Japan, and the European Union, while 'the South' includes the Former Soviet Union, China, and the rest of the world in the original RICE model. 'The North' here is a subset of OECD bloc.

and no capital flows between regions in a conventional sense. However, unilateral transfers from North to South are allowed in a manner similar to that described in Section 2. (A complete description of the modified RICE model is in Appendix B.)

The modified RICE model is clearly a special case of the generic North–South environmental–economic optimal growth model presented in Section 2: In the modified RICE model, each region contributes to CO_2 emissions, $E^i(t)$, while producing an aggregate product $Q^i(t)$. $E^i(t)$ here corresponds to $b^i(t)$ in Section 2. Global CO_2 emissions are the sum of CO_2 emissions from both North and South and are additive. Atmospheric CO_2 concentration, $M(t)$, is similar to $B(t)$ in Section 2. Finally, atmospheric temperature $T_1(t)$, a monotonic function of $M(t)$, affects the utility function negatively. Regions can reduce or even stop CO_2 emissions by sacrificing a portion of current consumption and exerting a control rate $\mu^i(t)$ on CO_2 emissions. The nature of $\mu^i(t)$ is similar to $J(t)$ in Section 2.

A major difference between the modified model described here and the original RICE model is that an additional control variable, unilateral transfers, $Tr(t)$, is introduced. When $Tr(t) > 0$, the disposable GNP of the North is reduced by incurring mitigation costs in Eq. (A-23). $Tr(t)$ enters the CO_2 emission function of the South Eq. (A-19) and reduces the South's emissions. Empirically, $Tr(t)$ represents the unilateral transfers from North to South, embodied in technologies for controlling CO_2 emissions in the South. The CO_2 emission function of the South Eq. (A-19) is crucial for examining transfer issues. The symmetric expressions of $Tr(t)$ and $\mu_S(t)$ in Eq. (A-19) imply that indigenous and transferred CO_2 reduction technologies are not distinguished here. [8] However, the distributional implications of $Tr(t)$ and $\mu_S(t)$ do differ. When $Tr(t) > 0$ and $\mu_S(t) = 0$, the North bears mitigation costs; when $Tr(t) = 0$ and $\mu_S(t) > 0$, the South bears mitigation costs; when both $Tr(t) > 0$ and $\mu_S(t) > 0$, North and South share the mitigation costs. From a global social planner's perspective, CO_2 emissions from the South need to be reduced through Eq. (A-19). The issues in policy-making and welfare analysis are whether the North could benefit from scenarios in which $Tr(t) > 0$. For a social planner, the relevant question is whether the North, and the world as a whole, could benefit from the North's paying the South for its CO_2 emission reductions by transferring mitigation technologies.

Note that the system Eqs. (A-12), (A-13), (A-14), (A-15), (A-16), (A-17), (A-18), (A-19), (A-20), (A-21), (A-22), (A-23), (A-24) and (A-25) is a global social planner's problem. In this regime, the optimal control rate in the South, $\mu^S(t)$, is not 0, in general. This outcome differs from that defined in Section 2, namely, a totally passive South in dealing with global environmental externalities. If the social planner thinks the South is too poor to pay, however, zero control by

---

[8] For an aggregate model like the RICE, such a relatively strong assumption is necessary.

the South may be played out as a feasible 'second-best' scenario. Also, the social planner can change the relative weights of North and South in the social welfare function, which is based on the utilitarian principle, to control the flow of optimal transfer amounts. In all of the above cases, the unilateral transfers from North to South are higher compared with the problem defined in Section 2 because the South would assume a large share of the social welfare function.

To obtain a problem equivalent to the model defined in Section 2, the following changes are needed in System (A-12) through (A-25). First, the objective function (A-12) should be a 'North only' intertemporal utility function:

$$\max_{c^N(t)} U^N\big(c^N(t)\big) = \sum_{t=0}^{\infty} \frac{P^N(t)\big[c^N(t)^{1-\alpha} - 1\big]}{(1-\alpha)(1+r)^t} \tag{7}$$

In addition, CO_2 concentration function (A-21) is modified as:

$$M(t) = m + \beta\big(E^N(t) + \tilde{E}^S(t)\big) + (1 - \delta_M)M(t-1) \tag{8}$$

where $\tilde{E}^S(t)$ represents CO_2 emissions from the South, with $\mu^S(t) = 0$. Having made these changes, the system comprising Eqs. (7) and (8), and Eq. (A-13) through Eq. (A-25) (except Eq. (A-21)) presents an optimal control problem of the North where the North can decide whether to make transfers based solely on its own interests.

3.2. Model calibration and data sources

The base year of the modified RICE model is 1990. The time span of the model is 30 periods, with each period representing a decade. For purposes of simulation, 12 periods (from 1990 to 2100) are reported in this paper for analysis. Such treatment balances considerations of computer capacity, policy relevance, and numerical accuracy of the solutions. Most parametric specifications in Eqs. (A-13), (A-14), (A-15), (A-16), (A-17), (A-18), (A-19), (A-20), (A-21), (A-22), (A-23), (A-24) and (A-25) are drawn directly from either Nordhaus (1994) or Nordhaus and Yang (1996). Those regionally specific parameters in the original RICE model are either aggregated into North and South or treated as weighted averages in the modified RICE model.

The only new parameters in the modified RICE model are β_1 and β_2 which appear in the mitigation cost function of the North Eq. (A-24). The unilateral technology transfer, $Tr(t)$, enters the South's CO_2 emission function in a symmetric way as the South's own CO_2 emission control rate. When $Tr(t) > 0$, the North incurs mitigation costs. Setting $\beta_2 = b_{2,N} = b_{2,S}$, coefficient β_1 is calibrated according to the following assumption: during the periods of policy implementation (2000–2100), the average unit costs (dollars per ton of carbon) in the North are the same for domestic control and unilateral transfers. This assumption reflects the homogeneity of the North's environmental technology, implementing in the North or in the South. Because the aggregate economic activity level in the South

Table 1
The summary of simulation scenarios

Scenarios	Control variables	Objective function
(i)	$\mu_N(t)$, Tr(t)	Social welfare function of North and South
(ii)	$\mu_N(t)$	Social welfare function of North and South
(iii)	$\mu_N(t)$, $\mu_S(t)$	Social welfare function of North and South
(iv)	$\mu_N(t)$, $\mu_S(t)$, Tr(t)	Social welfare function of North and South
(v)	$\mu_N(t)$, Tr(t)	Welfare function of North
(vi)	$\mu_N(t)$	Welfare function of North

is higher than that in the North during the periods examined, benchmark value coefficient β_1 is larger than $b_{1,N}$. [9] A sensitivity analysis has been conducted on alternative values of β_1 around the benchmark value.

3.3. Simulation results

The following six scenarios have been simulated using the modified RICE model to examine North–South transfer issues. Table 1 displays a summary of these scenarios.

(i) Maximizing the social welfare function (A-12) with no CO_2 control efforts by the South, the social planner decides on the optimal unilateral transfer path and control rate path for the North.

(ii) Maximizing the social welfare function (A-12) with no CO_2 control efforts by the South; the North makes no unilateral transfers. Under these conditions, the social planner selects the optimal control rates for the North.

(iii) Maximizing the social welfare function (A-12) with no unilateral transfers from North to South, both North and South exert optimal control efforts on CO_2 emissions.

(iv) Maximizing the social welfare function (A-12) where the social planner decides the optimal CO_2 control efforts in both North and South, as well as the North's optimal unilateral transfer path.

(v) Maximizing the welfare function of the North (7) with no control efforts by the South, the North determines the optimal unilateral transfer path and control rate path.

(vi) Maximizing the welfare function of the North (7) with no control efforts by the South; the North makes no unilateral transfers and selects optimal CO_2 control rates.

---

[9] The assumed economic growth potential of the South is very optimistic in the original RICE model, resulting in higher economic activity levels in the South during later periods. Nonetheless, the South is assumed always to remain behind the North in GNP per capita during the planning time horizon.

Amounts of Transfers

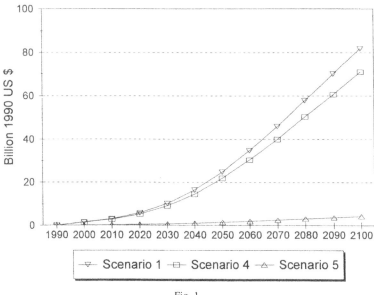

Fig. 1.

These six scenarios represent mutually exclusive policy regimes. The optimal solutions obtained from those scenarios reveal many interesting properties of optimal unilateral transfers under different situations. A summary of observations follows.

First, whenever unilateral technology transfers are allowed, as in Scenarios (i), (iv) and (v), they take place during the whole time horizon (Fig. 1). The unilateral transfer amounts are different but close in Scenarios (i) and (iv). However, the amounts in Scenarios (i) and (iv) are much higher than they are in Scenario (v). In all scenarios, the amounts of unilateral transfers increase over time, both in absolute terms and as shares of total northern GNP (Fig. 2). The share of unilateral transfers in the GNP is relatively small. It is 0.13% at peak in Scenarios (i) and (iv), and is 0.01% at peak in Scenario (v). [10]

Second, the decision to make unilateral transfers does not strongly impact domestic control rates in the North (Fig. 3). When maximizing the welfare function of the North, as in Scenarios (v) and (vi), control rates are drastically

---

[10] Overall mitigation costs in the RICE model are relatively low, compared with those used in other integrated assessment models. This low-cost assumption affects the amount of unilateral transfers. Results of the present study show a lower share of transfers than is indicated by other models that include joint implementation or tradable carbon permit schemes.

78 *Z. Yang / Resource and Energy Economics 21 (1999) 67–87*

Share of Transfers in GNP

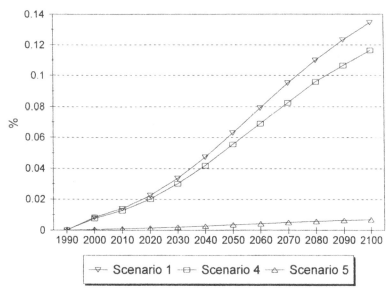

Fig. 2.

CO2 Emission Control Rates
North

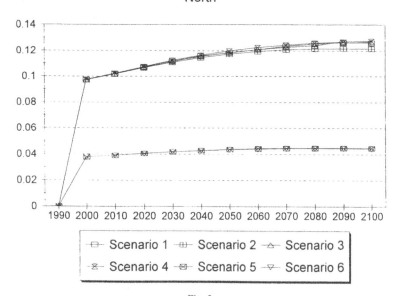

Fig. 3.

Global CO2 Emissions

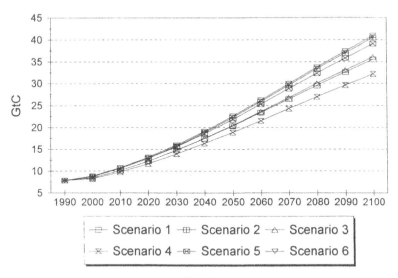

Fig. 4.

lower than they are in the scenarios of maximizing global welfare functions. Also, whether or not the South controls CO_2 emission does not significantly affect the optimal control rates of the North.

Third, unilateral technology transfers from North to South reduce global CO_2 emissions and concentrations under comparable situations. As a consequence, the atmospheric temperature increase is lower. When maximizing the social welfare function (A-12), as in Scenarios (i), (ii), (iii), and (iv), the paths of flows ($E(t)$) and damages ($T_1(t)$) of environmental externalities clearly differ, depending on whether unilateral transfers are made or not (Figs. 4 and 5). On the other hand, when maximizing the welfare function of the North, as in Scenarios (v) and (vi), the effects of unilateral transfers on those variables are noticeable, though not as obvious as in the previous case.

Finally, unilateral transfers from North to South improve both the welfare of the North and global welfare, where they are relevant. The welfare of the South, which receives transfers, improves directly. Table 2 displays the values of those welfare functions.

3.4. Policy implications

From simulations on the modified RICE model, the following conclusion can be drawn: if conditions in the model are met, the North should make unilateral

80 *Z. Yang / Resource and Energy Economics 21 (1999) 67–87*

Temerature Changes

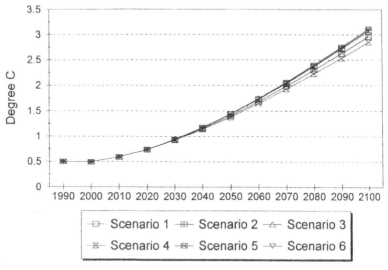

Fig. 5.

technology transfers to facilitate the South's CO_2 emission reductions. This conclusion supports policy suggestions advocating such technology transfers by many southern politicians and some northern economists. Due to the external effects of global climate change, the argument for transfers is strong from a global point of view and clearly positive from the North's point of view.

In Table 2, the values of global social welfare function yield a preference ranking (from high to low) of (iv), (iii), (i) and (ii). In other words, from a global

Table 2
The welfare function values

Scenarios	North	South	Global
(i)	− 3.35647	− 38.61344	− 13.93356
(ii)	− 3.35626	− 38.61438	− 13.93370
(iii)	− 3.35619	− 38.61412	− 13.93357
(iv)	− 3.35637	− 38.61330	− 13.93345
(v)	− 3.35619	n.a.	n.a.
(vi)	− 3.35621	n.a.	n.a.

The negative values in this table are due to the specific scaling of the objective function in the RICE model, which has a form of logarithm function of per capita consumption. Hence, the smaller the absolute value, the larger the utility value. Also, logarithmic transformation of per capita consumption, renders seemingly small differences in the table relatively significant.

welfare perspective, the ranking of policies regarding the North–South relationship in dealing with potential climate change, from the most preferable to the least, is: both the North and the South control CO_2 emissions, and the North also makes unilateral transfers; both the North and the South control CO_2 emissions, with no transfers from the North; the North controls CO_2 emissions and makes transfers while the South does nothing; only the North controls CO_2 emissions, and makes no transfers. From a global point of view, the world would be better off if the North transfers and the South controls, *ceteris paribus*.

This policy preference ranking results largely from the following features of the modified RICE model. First, the model maximizes the social welfare function, in which the South has a substantial share (the social welfare weight of the South is set at 0.3 and the North at 0.7). [11] Improving the South's welfare by reducing environmental damage promotes global welfare significantly. Second, the South is a fast-growing economy that contributes increasingly to global CO_2 emissions. From an efficiency standpoint, CO_2 emission reductions in the South might be more effective and less costly, than similar measures taken in the North. Third, the North is rich and the South is poor in per capita terms. From an equity viewpoint, the North should share the heavier burden of mitigation costs. Because of these facts, a socially optimal level of environmental externalities (i.e., global CO_2 emissions) requires both North and South to control CO_2 emissions domestically. In addition, the North should help the South control CO_2 emissions by transferring environmental technologies. If the South cannot afford to pay for technology to control CO_2 emissions, the North should bear the whole burden of mitigation costs to benefit itself along with the rest of the world.

To achieve the best of the four policy alternatives listed above, namely, Scenario (iv), full cooperation and communication between North and South is necessary. The optimal solution to a social planner's problem (though the social planner does not exist in an international institution setting) of providing environmental externalities is feasible only when parties fully internalize external effects through cooperation. If such cooperation does not occur, and parties engage instead in decentralized self-serving activities to respond to environmental externalities, the optimal policy is unattainable. From a one-sided (say, the North's) perspective, the policy ranking relating to CO_2 emission controls and unilateral transfers can be quite different, as illustrated by the arguments below.

According to Table 2, the North's preferential ranking of the scenarios discussed above is: (iii), (ii), (iv), and (i). Policy option (iii), however, is in second place from the global social planner's standpoint. The North would prefer that both parties contribute their 'fair share' of domestic CO_2 emission controls first, as in Scenario (iii). In contrast, a global social planner would prefer to open

---

[11] The welfare weights used here are estimated from weights in the original RICE model.

another channel, namely, unilateral transfers of CO_2 emission control technologies from North to South, to improve the global welfare. From the global social planner's perspective, (iii) is inferior to (iv). The North prefers (iii), a second-best scenario, over (iv), because almost all its investments in transfers improve the South's welfare.

Interestingly, if the North does not cooperate with the South, deciding instead to maximize its own utility (as in Scenarios (v) and (vi)), the North is still better off making unilateral transfers to the South, though such transfers would be very small, as indicated by the last two rows of Table 2. Therefore, if the South were unable or unwilling to pay for its own CO_2 emission controls, the North would likely still make at least small unilateral transfers in its own best interests. This result could be used by the global social planner to achieve a 'second-best' outcome, if the South is unable to pay for CO_2 emission controls. The result can also be used by the South as a credible threat to the North for certain minimum transfers, if the South is unwilling to pay for CO_2 emission controls.

Finally, the unilateral technological transfers in all scenarios discussed above represent only a tiny portion of the North's wealth. Therefore, no substantial financial obstacles should prevent such transfers. As long as these unilateral transfers represent technology for controlling CO_2 emissions, the North should benefit. This argument applies other global environmental externalities as well. Institutional and political barriers will always be issues, however, for even small unilateral transfers.

4. Conclusion

This paper has presented some aspects of unilateral technology transfers from developed countries to developing countries to address global environmental externalities such as ozone-layer depletion and global climate change. Conclusions from the simple North–South environmental–economic optimal growth model in Section 2 and results from simulations using the modified RICE model in Eq. (3) all indicate that, if certain conditions for efficiency are met, it is feasible and advisable for developed countries to make unilateral transfers of environmental technologies to developing countries.

Acknowledgements

This research is supported by the U.S. Department of Energy and the Joint Program on the Science and Policy of Global Change at Massachusetts Institute of

Z. Yang / Resource and Energy Economics 21 (1999) 67–87 83

Technology. I also wish to thank two anonymous referees for their insightful comments.

Appendix A. The North–South environmental–economic optimal growth model

(i) The Northern model:

$$\max_{I^N, \text{Tr}, J} \int_0^\infty U^N\big(C^N(t), -B(t)\big)e^{-\gamma_1 t}\mathrm{d}t \tag{A-1}$$

$$\text{s.t. } C^N(t) = Y^N(t) - I^N(t) - \text{Tr}(t) - J(t) \tag{A-2}$$

$$Y^N(t) = F^N\big(K^N(t)\big) \tag{A-3}$$

$$\dot{K}^N(t) = I^N(t) - \delta_1 K^N(t) \tag{A-4}$$

$$\dot{B}(t) = b^N(t) + b^S(t) - \sigma B(t) \tag{A-5}$$

$$b^N(t) = g\big(J(t), Y^N(t)\big) \tag{A-6}$$

$$b^S(t) = f\big(\text{Tr}(t), Y^S(t)\big) \tag{A-7}$$

$$I^N(t) \geq 0, \ \text{Tr}(t) \geq 0, \ J(t) \geq 0.$$

$$B(0) = B_0, \ K^N(0) = K_0^N.$$

(ii) The Southern model:

$$\max_{I^S} \int_0^\infty U^S\big(C^S(t), -B(t)\big)e^{-\gamma_2 t}\mathrm{d}t \tag{A-8}$$

$$\text{s.t. } C^S(t) = Y^S(t) - I^S(t) \tag{A-9}$$

$$Y^S(t) = F^S\big(K^S(t)\big) \tag{A-10}$$

$$\dot{K}^S(t) = I^S(t) - \delta_2 K^S(t) \tag{A-11}$$

Also Eqs. (A-5), (A-6) and (A-7).

$$I^S(t) \geq 0.$$

$$B(0) = B_0, \ K^N(0) = K_0^N.$$

In Models (i) and (ii) above, superscripts N and S represent the North and the South, respectively. A key to the other notations (omitting superscripts) follows:

$U(t)$	Utility function
$Y(t)$	Aggregate production function of GNP
$C(t)$	Consumption function
$I(t)$	Investment function
$B(t)$	Stock of environmental externalities
$b(t)$	Flow of environmental externalities
$Tr(t)$	Volume of transfers from the North to the South
$J(t)$	Cost of domestic externality control (by the North)
$\gamma > 0$	Pure time preference
$\delta > 0$	Capital depreciation rate
$\sigma > 0$	Dissipation rate of stock externalities

Appendix B. The modified RICE model

$$\max_{c^i(t)} V(c^i(t)) = \sum_{t=0}^{\infty} \frac{\phi^N U^N(c^N(t)) + \phi^S U^S(c^S(t))}{(1+r)^t}$$

$$= \sum_{t=0}^{\infty} \sum_{i=N,S} \frac{\phi^i P^i(t)\left[(c^i(t))^{1-\alpha} - 1\right]}{(1-\alpha)(1+r)^t} \tag{A-12}$$

$$\text{s.t. } Q^i(t) = A^i(t)\left[K^i(t)\right]^\gamma \left[P^i(t)\right]^{1-\gamma}, i = N, S \tag{A-13}$$

$$Y^i(t) = \Omega^i(t)Q^i(t), i = N, S \tag{A-14}$$

$$C^i(t) = Y^i(t) - I^i(t), i = N, S \tag{A-15}$$

$$c^i(t) = \frac{C^i(t)}{P^i(t)}, i = N, S \tag{A-16}$$

$$K^i(t) = (1 - \delta_K)K^i(t-1) + I^i(t), i = N, S \tag{A-17}$$

$$E^N(t) = (1 - \mu^N(t))\sigma^N(t)Q^N(t), 0 \le \mu^N(t) \le 1. \tag{A-18}$$

$$E^S(t) = (1 - \mu^S(t))(1 - Tr(t))\sigma^S(t)Q^S(t), 0 \le \mu^S(t) \le 1. \tag{A-19}$$

$$M(t) = m + \beta(E^N(t) + E^S(t)) + (1 - \delta_M)M(t-1) \tag{A-20}$$

Z. Yang / Resource and Energy Economics 21 (1999) 67–87 85

$$T_1(t) = T_1(t-1) + \frac{\tau_2[F(t) - \lambda T_1(t-1)] - R_2[T_1(t-1) - T_2(t-1)]}{R_1\tau_2}$$

(A-21)

$$T_2(t) = T_2(t-1) + \frac{T_1(t-1) - T_2(t-1)}{\tau_2}$$

(A-22)

$$F(t) = \tau\frac{\log(M(t)/m)}{\log 2} + f(t)$$

(A-23)

$$\Omega_N(t) = \frac{\left(1 - b_{1,N}\,\mu^N(t)^{b_{2,N}}\right)\left(1 - \beta_1 Tr(t)^{\beta_2}\right)}{1 + \theta_{1,N}T_1(t)^{\theta_{2,N}}}$$

(A-24)

$$\Omega_S(t) = \frac{1 - b_{1,S}\,\mu^S(t)^{b_{2,S}}}{1 + \theta_{1,S}T_1(t)^{\theta_{2,i}}}$$

(A-25)

A key to notations (omitting superscripts and subscripts of N and S) in the modified RICE model:

$V(t)$	Intertemporal social welfare function
$U(t)$	Utility function of the regions
$C(t)$	Consumption function of the regions
$Q(t)$	Aggregate production function of the regions
$A(t)$	Exogenous technological progress level
$P(t)$	Population (also labor input) of the regions
$K(t)$	Capital stocks of the regions
$Y(t)$	Adjusted GNP level of the regions
$c(t)$	Per capita consumption of the regions
$I(t)$	Investment level of the regions
$\mu(t)$	CO_2 emission control rate of the regions
$Tr(t)$	Unilateral transfers (by the North)
$\sigma(t)$	CO_2 emission/output ratios
$E(t)$	CO_2 emissions by the regions
$M(t)$	Atmospheric CO_2 concentrations
$T_1(t)$	Atmospheric temperature change
$T_2(t)$	Oceanic temperature change
$F(t)$	Total radiative forcing
$f(t)$	Exogenous radiative forcing
$\Omega(t)$	Mitigation cost and climate change damage function

All other lower-case Greek and Roman letters without the time dimension are coefficients. For their definitions and values, see Nordhaus and Yang (1996) and Nordhaus (1994). For simplicity, only the values of those coefficients related to

North–South transfers, mitigation cost function, and climate damage function are given here:

$$b_{1,N} = 0.07, \qquad b_{1,S} = 0.12, \qquad b_{2,N} = 2.887, \quad b_{2,S} = 2.887,$$

$$\theta_{1,N} = 0.01155, \quad \theta_{1,S} = 0.01600, \quad \theta_{2,N} = 1.5, \qquad \theta_{2,S} = 1.5,$$

$$\beta_1 = 1.015, \qquad \beta_2 = 2.887.$$

Appendix C. Proof of the proposition in Section 2

The parts of the Euler equations of model (1) are:

$$\frac{\partial \mathcal{L}}{\partial J} = -U_1 e^{-\gamma_1 t} + \mu_2(t) h_1 + \lambda_3(t) = 0 \tag{A-26}$$

$$\frac{\partial \mathcal{L}}{\partial \text{Tr}} = -U_1 e^{-\gamma_1 t} + \mu_2(t) G_1 + \lambda_2(t) = 0 \tag{A-27}$$

$$\lambda_2(t) \text{Tr}(t) = 0 \tag{A-28}$$

$$\lambda_3(t) J(t) = 0 \tag{A-29}$$

From Eq. (A-28), a necessary condition for $\text{Tr}(t) > 0$ is $\lambda_2(t) = 0$. And from Eqs. (A-26) and (A-27), we have,

$$\lambda_3(t) = \mu_2(t)[G_1 - h_1] + \lambda_2(t) \geq 0 \tag{A-30}$$

When $\lambda_2(t) = 0$, from Eq. (A-30) we have Eq. (4).
From Eqs. (A-28) and (A-29), we have Eqs. (5) and (6).

References

Bohm, P., 1994. On the feasibility of joint implementation of carbon emissions reductions, University of Birmingham Department of Economics Discussion Paper, pp. 94–105.

Brito, D.L., 1972. A dynamic model of an armaments race. Int. Econ. Rev. 13, 359–375.

Hoel, M., 1991. Global environmental problems: the effects of unilateral actions taken by one country. J. Environ. Econ. Manage. 20 (1), 55–70.

Intriligator, M.D., Brito, D.L., 1976. Strategy, arms races and arms control. In: Gillespie, J., Zinnes, D. (Eds.), Mathematical Systems in International Relations Research. Praeger, New York, 1976.

Kverndok, S., 1995. Tradable CO_2 emission permits: initial distribution as a justice problem. Environ. Values 4 (2), 129–148.

Manne, A.S., Richels, R.G., 1992. Buying Greenhouse Insurance: The Economic Costs of CO_2 Emission Limits. The MIT Press, Cambridge, MA.

Nordhaus, W.D., 1994. Managing the Global Commons. The MIT Press, Cambridge, MA.

Nordhaus, W.D., Yang, Z., 1996. A regional dynamic general equilibrium model of alternative climate change strategies. Am. Econ. Rev. 86 (4), 741–765.

OECD, 1992. The Economic Costs of Reducing CO_2 Emissions, Special Issue, OECD Economic Studies, No. 19, Winter 1992.

Rose, A., Stevens, B., Edmonds, J., Wise, M., 1994. International equity and differentiation in global warming policy. Forthcoming in Environ. Resour. Econ., 1997.

Schelling, T.C., 1991. Economic responses to global warming: prospects for cooperative approaches. In: Dornbusch, R., Poterba, J. (Eds.), Global Warming: Economic Policy Responses. The MIT Press, Cambridge, MA.

Tietenberg, T., 1992. Environmental and Natural Resource Economics, 3rd edn. Harper Collins Publishers, New York.

Weyant, J. et al., 1996. Integrated assessment of climate change: an overview and comparison of approaches and results. In: Climate Change 1995: Economic and Social Dimensions of Climate Change. Cambridge Univ. Press, New York, pp. 367–96.

Wirl, F., 1994. Global warming and carbon taxes: dynamic and strategic interactions between energy consumers and producers. J. Policy Modeling 16 (6), 577–596.

Yang, Z., Eckaus, R.S., Ellerman, A.D., Jacoby, H.D., 1996. The MIT emissions prediction and policy analysis (EPPA) model, MIT Joint Program on the Science and Policy of Global Change Report No. 6.

[32]

The Kyoto Protocol and developing countries

Mustafa Babiker, John M. Reilly*, Henry D. Jacoby

Joint Program on the Science and Policy of Global Change, Room E40-267, Massachusetts Institute of Technology, 77 Massachusetts Avenue, Cambridge, MA 02139-4307, USA

Received 12 November 1999

Abstract

Under the Kyoto Protocol, the world's wealthier countries assumed binding commitments to reduce greenhouse gas emissions. The agreement requires these countries to consider ways to minimize adverse effects on developing countries of these actions, transmitted through trade. Using a general equilibrium model of the world economy, we find that adverse effects fall mainly on energy-exporting countries, for some even greater than on countries that are assuming commitments. Removing existing fuel taxes and subsidies and using international permit trading would greatly reduce the adverse impacts and also reduce economic impacts on the countries taking on commitments. Another approach, preferential tariff reduction for developing countries, would benefit many developing countries, but would not target those most adversely affected. If instead, OECD countries directly compensated developing countries for losses, the required annual financial transfer would be on the order of $25 billion (1995 $US) in 2010. © 2000 Elsevier Science Ltd. All rights reserved.

Keywords: Climate change; Trade; Developing countries

1. The obligations of Annex B nations

Economic trade links among countries will transmit effects of greenhouse gas control measures adopted by one set of nations, in a ripple effect, to countries that may not have agreed to share the burdens of control. For example, emission restrictions under the Kyoto Protocol will increase the cost to Annex B regions of using carbon-emitting fuels, thereby raising manufacturing costs of their energy-intensive goods, some of which may be exported to developing countries. The restrictions also will lower global demand for carbon-emitting fuels, reducing their international prices. In addition, emission controls may depress economic activity in countries subject to emission restrictions, lowering these countries' demand for imports, some of which come from developing countries. In combination, these changes in trade volumes and prices can have complex consequences, harming some developing countries while benefiting others.

Beginning with the Framework Convention on Climate Change (United Nations, 1992), the Parties have agreed that implementation of any agreement should give special attention to the concerns of vulnerable economies. Article 4.8 of the Convention states:

> In the implementation of commitments the Parties shall give full consideration to what actions are necessary to meet the specific needs and concerns of developing country parties arising from adverse effects of climate change and/or the implementation of response measures .

Among a list of nine specific points of focus for this concern is the following:

> (h) Countries whose economies are highly dependent on income generated from the production, processing and export, and/or on consumption of fossil fuels and associated energy-intensive products.

Article 4.9 of the Convention calls for special attention to the least developed countries "with regard to funding and transfer of technology."

The Kyoto Protocol restates this obligation, using somewhat stronger language (United Nations, 1997). Its Article 2.3 holds that:

> The Parties in Annex I shall strive to implement policies and measures in such a way as to minimize adverse effects, including effects on international trade, and social, environmental and economic

526   *M. Babiker et al. / Energy Policy 28 (2000) 525–536*

impacts on other Parties, especially developing country Parties and in particular those identified in Article 4, paragraphs 8 and 9 of the Convention, which consist mainly of energy exporting and small island countries.[1]

Article 3.14 goes on to call for early consideration by the Parties of "what actions are necessary to minimize the adverse effects," and expands the list of mechanisms to be considered to include "the establishment of funding, insurance and transfer of technology."

Building on an earlier analysis of these issues (Babiker and Jacoby, 1999), we here explore mechanisms by which implementation of Annex B commitments in the Kyoto Protocol may affect developing economies, and how these effects might be mediated. While we focus on possible adverse effects, we note positive effects, as well. Moreover, our analysis is designed to highlight effects on those countries that seem to be the special concern of the Convention's Article 4.8(h) above, i.e., those in the Non-Annex B group that are heavily dependent on exports of energy.

We do not consider all possible instruments that might be applied to mitigate these effects. For example, the mention of "insurance" in article 3.14 of the Protocol is a reference to means of alleviating the impacts of climate change itself; it is thus outside the scope of our analysis, which includes only the economic effects of proposed emission restrictions. In addition, the possible uses of technology transfers are not well defined and not easily subjected to economic analysis, so we do not consider them here. We do, however, consider two sets of actions that Annex B countries could take to limit negative impacts on Non-Annex B countries. The first is a set of policy measures, not specific to any particular disadvantaged country, that could accompany implementation of Annex B controls:

- revision of fuel taxation policies,
- removal of coal subsidies,
- trading of emission permits.

The second set of policy measures includes actions that Annex B countries might consider to meet the needs of particular developing countries. These actions include:

- special tariff concessions,
- direct financial compensation.

We explore these two sets of possible responses to the stated Annex B obligations in the context of the specific Kyoto emissions targets and timetable, i.e., a reduction in Annex B country emissions below 1990 levels (a reduction that averages around 5% for the 2008–12 commit-

ment period (United Nations, 1997)). For the task, we apply a general equilibrium model of the world economy; briefly described in Section 2 of this paper.

In Section 3, we consider the distribution of burdens resulting from the Kyoto Protocol, and the mechanisms that could lead to such a distribution, taking the year 2010 as representative of the first commitment period. We assume in the first case that none of the possible measures listed above is adopted. For this case, our results are similar to those of previous analyses (Babiker and Jacoby, 1999; Babiker et al., 1997; Montgomery et al., 1998). We find that, in the absence of corrective measures, the welfare loss attributable to Kyoto for some Non-Annex B countries could exceed that for countries accepting emission restrictions. A key contributing factor is a shift in the terms of trade (i.e., the ratio of a country's export prices to its import prices, suitably weighted). As noted earlier, cost penalties on carbon emissions will increase the costs of energy-intensive goods (if manufactured in a country under restriction), even if the international prices of carbon-intensive fossil fuels fall. In this circumstance, for example, an oil-exporting Non-Annex B country will suffer economic losses because it (1) will have less revenue from oil exports and (2) will face higher prices for imports of energy-intensive goods from Annex B regions. Other Non-Annex B countries with a different mix of imports and exports may be better off under the same set of Annex B restrictions. The vulnerability of nations to this phenomenon is roughly related to the "weight" of fossil energy exports in their economies.

For our reference case, we establish a policy scenario that presumes no special effort is expended to mitigate developing-country effects of the Kyoto Protocol. In Section 4, we consider the extent to which these economic impacts might be mitigated using one or more of the first set of instruments mentioned above. We find that the latter "accompanying policies" could significantly reduce, though not completely offset, the adverse influence of Kyoto implementation on the most seriously affected developing countries.

Section 5 considers specific actions that may be invoked to compensate Non-Annex B countries that are adversely affected by response measures adopted by Annex B nations, beyond the mitigation options offered by emissions-reducing policies' implementation mechanisms. We first consider preferential tariff reductions granted to Non-Annex B countries, and find that beneficiaries of such a measure do not closely match those countries that suffer adverse consequences from Annex B carbon restrictions. Next, we estimate the direct level of financial transfers that would be needed to compensate adversely affected developing countries. We set up a mechanism for compensation within our model so that general equilibrium effects are considered in establishing the magnitude of transfer needed.

---

[1] The list of parties to the Convention in Annex I differs only slightly from the Annex B grouping developed in the Kyoto Protocol and used in this analysis. The composition of Annex B is shown in Table 1.

M. Babiker et al. / Energy Policy 28 (2000) 525–536 527

Section 6 draws conclusions from these sample calculations about (1) the nature and magnitude of spillovers from Annex B policies onto Non-Annex B economies, and (2) the feasibility of the various policy measures that might be considered to reduce adverse spillover effects.

Before we turn to the analysis methods and results, a cautionary note is in order. Our purposes in conducting these numerical exercises are to explore the mechanisms by which policies adopted by Annex B countries might influence Non-Annex B economies, and to develop a rough impression of how various attempts to limit these effects might work. The absolute magnitudes of these effects are, of course, subject to considerable uncertainty (Webster, 1997; Webster and Sokolov, 1998). For example, the cost of attaining any fixed emissions target is highly sensitive to growth rates in the forecast period. Experiences in Russia, the United States, Japan, and several Asian developing countries over the last decade indicate that one can expect large errors in growth forecasts over a period as short as a decade. Few foresaw the collapse of the Soviet Union or the economic problems that beset Asian economies in the 1990s. Nearly all forecasters have underestimated economic growth in the United States over the 1990s. By the same token, the precise effects of changes in tax and tariff regimes, or of real-world emissions permit-trading schemes are influenced by many details of implementation and market adjustment, and so are uncertain in themselves, as well. Still, it is worth pointing out that the *mechanisms* of burden transfer would remain the same (though the magnitude of effect might change) across the wide range of possible estimates of growth, ease of economic adjustment, and performance of any corrective measures taken.

A further caveat regarding our results is the fact that they are computed assuming no economic, environmental, or political shocks other than those attributable to the Kyoto Protocol. In reality, other shocks are inevitable, and the magnitudes of policy effects studied here are such that, although it may be possible to identify and roughly quantify them ex ante, their influence would not likely be separable from general economic variability ex post. Finally, our economic model is based on the most highly disaggregated data set of its type, yet we are still only able to identify regional groupings of countries such as the Middle East or North Africa. These regions contain diverse countries in which the magnitude of impacts from Annex B actions will certainly vary (e.g., Egypt vs. Libya in North Africa); we cannot be sure even that the direction of impact would be the same for all countries in a region. If direct financial transfers to compensate for adverse consequences of Kyoto implementation were to be considered as a practical matter, these difficult problems would have to be dealt with.

2. The analysis method

For analysis of these burden-reducing measures, we apply the MIT Emissions Prediction and Policy Analysis (EPPA) Model (Babiker *et al.*, 2000; Yang *et al.*, 1996). EPPA is a recursive dynamic, multi-regional general equilibrium model of the world economy. The current version of EPPA is built on a comprehensive energy-economy dataset that extends the existing GTAP system (Hertel, 1997). Denoted GTAP-E, this dataset accommodates a consistent representation of energy markets in physical units as well as detailed accounts of regional production and bilateral trade flows. The base year for the model is 1995, and the model is solved recursively through 2100 in five-year intervals.

The GTAP-E database identifies 22 sectors and 45 nations or regions. Its underlying detail allows aggregation of the model to suit the specific analysis task. For the studies presented here, the model was aggregated to eight sectors, plus two future "backstop" energy sources, and 25 regions. As shown in Table 1, nonenergy goods are aggregated to three sectors, whereas the energy sector is

Table 1
Dimensions of the EPPA-GTAP model

Production sectors	Countries and regions
Non-Energy	*Annex B*
1. Agriculture	USA United States
2. Energy-intensive industries	JPN Japan
3. Other industries and services	EEC Europe[a]
Energy	OOE Other OECD[b]
4. Crude oil	FSU Former Soviet Union
5. Natural gas	EET Central European Associates
6. Refined oil	*Non-Annex B (Selected regions)[c]*
7. Coal	KOR Korea
8. Electricity	IDN Indonesia
Future energy supply	CHN China
10. Carbon liquids	IND India
11. Carbon-free electric	MEX Mexico
Primary factors	VEN Venezuela
1. Labor	BRA Brazil
2. Capital	RME Rest pf Middle East[d]
3. Fixed factors for fuel and agriculture	RNF Rest of North Africa[e]
	SAF South Africa

[a]The 15 nations of the European Union as of 1995.
[b]European Free Trade Area (EFT), Australia, New Zealand, Canada, Turkey.
[c]Other Non-Annex B regions included in the model but not in the reported results are: Malaysia (MYS), Philippines (PHL), Thailand (THA), Argentina (ARG), Chile (CHL), Colombia (COL), Morocco (MAR), Rest of Sub-Saharan Africa (RSS), and Rest of the World (ROW).
[d]Includes the Arabian Peninsula, Iran, and Iraq.
[e]Tunisia, Algeria, Libya, and Egypt.

528

M. Babiker et al. / Energy Policy 28 (2000) 525–536

represented in terms of fossil fuel type and electricity. Annex B is aggregated into six regions. Non-Annex B is modeled in greater detail, allowing the study of impacts of Kyoto-style restrictions on developing countries. Within the calculations, the Non-Annex B group is modeled as 19 separate countries or multicountry aggregates, but for ease of presentation, only the ten regions listed in Table 1 are shown in our tables and figures.

The model's equilibrium framework is based on final demands for goods and services in each region, arising from a representative agent. Final demands are subject to an income balance constraint with fixed marginal propensity to save. Investment is savings-driven, and capital is accumulated subject to vintaging and depreciation. Consumption within each region is financed from factor income and taxes. Taxes apply to energy demand, factor income, and international trade, and the proceeds are used to finance an exogenously grown level of public provision. International capital flows in base year accounts are phased out gradually, and the government budget is balanced each period through lump-sum taxes.

Along the baseline, fossil energy resources through 2010 are calibrated to an exogenous price path for fuels. Afterward, prices are driven by a long-run resource depletion model. Energy goods and other commodities are traded in world markets. Crude oil is imported and exported as a homogeneous product, subject to tariffs and export taxes. All other goods, including energy products such as coal and natural gas, are characterized by product differentiation, with an explicit representation of bilateral trade flows calibrated to the 1995 reference year of the GTAP database. Energy products (i.e., refined oil, coal, natural gas, and electricity) are sold at prices that differ between industrial customers and final consumers.

The analysis presented here focuses on CO_2 only, and the Kyoto targets are assumed to apply to a 1990 baseline of fossil carbon emissions, and to be achieved by a reduction in fossil fuel burning. In fact, implications of the Kyoto Protocol will depend also on the treatment of carbon sinks and the six non-CO_2 gases included in the agreement. Depending on the region, including sinks and all gases in the baseline and in the control regime yields an average OECD control cost that is 20% to 35% lower than the cost estimated from a carbon-only analysis (Reilly *et al.*, 1999a, b). Were this analysis extended to all gases and carbon sinks, therefore, the welfare effects would likely be reduced somewhat because fewer reductions in fossil fuel emissions would then be needed to meet the emissions targets under Kyoto.

3. The reference case, with and without the Kyoto Protocol

Carbon emissions (in megatons of carbon, MtC, by year) under the reference conditions are shown in

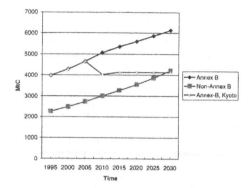

Fig. 1. Reference and Kyoto carbon emissions.

Fig. 1 for the Annex B and Non-Annex B aggregates. Also shown is the trajectory of Annex B emissions under the Kyoto emissions restraint, assuming the agreement stays in place at the 2008-12 level in succeeding decades. Under Kyoto-type constraints, the emissions of Non-Annex B countries may vary from their reference levels because of carbon leakage, but that difference is not shown here because it varies from case to case.

Under our reference conditions, with no climate policy, we assume the world oil price will fall somewhat by the year 2010 from its level in the 1995 GTAP base year. The scenario is a smoothed approximation of the realized price behavior over the period of price volatility experienced from 1995 to 1998, based on U.S. Department of Energy statistics (DOE/EIA, 1998). The oil price turns up after 2010 as the oil market comes under control of the EPPA Model's long-run resource depletion model. All the comparisons below are developed in relation to this reference case, with its underlying price model.

For a version of this reference case with the Kyoto Protocol in place, we chose a policy scenario with no trading in emissions permits and no attempt to correct distortions resulting from Annex B existing fuel taxes and tariffs. (Coal subsidies are removed by 2010 in the EPPA reference case, as discussed further in Section 5.2) This case is labeled NT-D, for No permit Trade with tax Distortions. As suggested earlier, the imposition of Kyoto emissions reductions would reduce the demand for the more carbon-intensive fuels, oil and coal, and thus lower their international prices below the levels under the reference with no climate policy. For example, in this case, the 2010 oil price is 15% below its level under no-climate-policy conditions. This oil price change is a key determinant of the burdens imposed on oil-exporting developing countries, and of the gains realized by others.

M. Babiker et al. / Energy Policy 28 (2000) 525–536

529

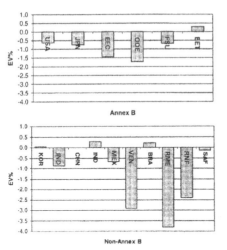

Fig. 2. Welfare effects of Kyoto Protocol: EV% (NT-D, 2010).

Table 2
Decomposition of impacts of the Kyoto Protocol (2010)

Region	Percent change with the Kyoto Protocol		
	EV	GNP	Terms of trade
Annex B			
USA	n 0.64	n 1.18	1.31
JPN	n 0.75	n 1.84	1.41
EEC	n 1.45	n 3.68	1.07
OOE	n 1.73	n 3.70	n 0.62
FSU	n 0.68	n 0.38	n 2.27
EET	0.30	0.42	0.27
Non-Annex B			
KOR	0.04	0.19	0.48
IDN	n 0.86	n 0.71	n 2.13
CHN	n 0.01	0.06	n 0.30
IND	0.29	0.55	1.12
MEX	n 0.67	n 0.58	n 1.98
VEN	n 2.92	n 2.56	n 8.82
BRA	0.22	0.23	0.72
RME	n 3.81	n 3.12	n 8.65
RNF	n 2.40	n 2.77	n 6.79
SAF	n 0.13	0.06	n 0.26

Fig. 2 shows the welfare losses from Kyoto implementation under reference-case conditions, expressed as percentage changes in the equivalent variation index for year 2010. (Equivalent variation, here denoted EV, is a measure of welfare that shows by how much regional well-being, roughly the level of consumption, changes as a result of a policy intervention.) As seen in previous analyses (Jacoby et al., 1997; Jacoby and Sue Wing, 1999; Kolstad et al., 1999), the Kyoto Protocol generates welfare losses across Annex B countries in the range 0.5–2.0%, except for Eastern European countries in transition (EET: countries that have moved or are moving from planned economies/communism to market/democratic economies/governments), a block of nations that realizes minor short-term welfare gains from its improved comparative advantage in relation to the rest of Annex B. For Non-Annex B, the results show welfare losses in excess of those in Annex B for some regions, such as the Persian Gulf (RME), and net welfare gains for others, such as India (IND). As a general rule, the results suggest that non-Annex B energy importers would likely gain from implementation of the Protocol, whereas energy exporters would lose. Among the oil-exporting regions, those depending most heavily on oil proceeds would be most adversely affected by Annex B emissions control.

Annex B emission controls are translated into welfare gains or losses in Non-Annex B regions through shifts in international trade and prices. Imposition of emission controls by Annex B regions reduces their demand for domestic and imported energy and raises the prices of their energy-intensive exports. The GTAP database

shows that the 1995 oil imports by Annex B countries amounted to more than 65% of international energy trade, so the world oil price is affected strongly by the control policy. Hence, energy exporters face adverse movements in their terms of trade, while most Non-Annex B energy importers may experience improvements. While important, these first-round energy trade and price effects do not represent the whole story. Energy price changes spur broader effects on terms of trade within a larger set of income and price effects that propagate through the international economy, influencing the distribution of gains and losses. Comparative advantages in energy-intensive and other goods are also affected (Babiker and Jacoby, 1999), in ways that differ depending on the energy efficiency and price effects in each country.

To illustrate this transmission process, Table 2 displays the impact of the Kyoto agreement on welfare, GNP, and terms of trade. Focusing first on terms-of-trade effects, we see clearly that not all Annex B countries experience favorable movements in their terms of trade, and neither do all Non-Annex B countries experience adverse movements. Indeed, the data reveal generally favorable movements in terms of trade for energy importers and adverse movements for energy exporters. Second, the results for welfare change (based on equivalent variation, EV) indicate how misleading GNP can be as a measure of the burdens of an emissions-control program. In particular, the higher GNP losses of Annex B are mitigated by favorable movements in these nations' terms of trade, whereas the relatively lower GNP losses for oil-exporting countries are aggravated by unfavorable movements in their terms of trade. Further, an interesting contrast is that both China and South Africa suffer welfare losses from Kyoto due to adverse movements in their terms of trade, even though they experience gains in GNP.

4. Implementation measures to reduce effects on developing countries

Our analysis of possible instruments for mitigating impacts on developing countries is based on a set of eight cases. These cases are described in Table 3 along with the legends used in the figures. Section 3 compared a reference case with no climate policy (REF, listed as Case 1 in the table) to a case in which the Kyoto Protocol is carried out with no emissions permit trading and with the existing domestic energy distortions in place (NT-D, shown as Case 2). Now we turn to Cases 3–6, which represent various ways in which Kyoto constraints could be implemented *within* individual Annex B countries to reduce their economic effects on Non-Annex B parties. Each case is compared with the NT-D results.

In the first of these cases (NT-ND), covered in Section 4.1, existing fuel taxes are assumed to be eliminated and the carbon emissions policy is put in place without these existing distortions. Other changes that might reduce impacts, even in the presence of fuel tax distortions, include the removal of coal subsidies (discussed in Section 4.2). Section 4.3 considers the extent to which permit trading among Annex B countries (T-AB) would reduce the impact on oil prices and limit the negative effect on developing economies that depend on oil exports. These measures are then considered in combination in Section 4.4.

4.1. Removal of fuel tax distortions

Most analyses of Kyoto-type emissions agreements assume that the Protocol is imposed in the form of a tax

on fossil fuels that reflects the fuels' differential carbon content, or a cap-and-trade system that results in a common price of carbon emissions across sources. The circumstances are more complicated than what such an assumption implies, however, because most countries already have a variety of fuel taxes, focused mainly on automotive fuel; many such taxes have been in place for decades. The original justifications for these taxes were many and varied, depending on the country. For some, the taxes were a way to limit the foreign exchange drain of fuel imports, or to limit national dependence on foreign suppliers. In other cases taxes were a source of general revenue or a "user fee"-like source of funding for highway construction and maintenance. More recently, relief of road congestion and reduction of urban air pollution have offered additional justifications. The approach in our NT-D case is to accept these taxes as the status quo and apply carbon constraints on top of them. If there are legitimate economic externalities or unrecovered public costs (such as highway construction) to which these taxes are an efficient response, then applying a carbon constraint on top of them could well be the most economically efficient approach.

If these taxes are not efficient responses to external effects of fuel use then they distort economic decisions, so removing them would improve economic efficiency and economic welfare, absent interactions with other distortions. For example, if fuel taxes exist mainly to collect revenue, then carbon permit sales could replace this source of revenue, making separate fuel taxes unnecessary. Fuel taxes may also have ill-defined objectives or serve as highly inefficient mechanisms for achieving stated objectives. A complete analysis of the justification and effectiveness of these taxes is well beyond the scope of this paper. While our model does not measure any welfare benefits (such as reduced pollution or congestion) deriving from these taxes, the GTAP database does identify the magnitude of the taxes, and thus we are able to consider a case with No Trade and No Distortions (NT-ND), in which we treat all energy taxes as pure economic distortions. This case should be considered bounding (or limiting) case to the extent that external market effects exist which justify some of these taxes. The welfare losses associated with their removal would, thus, partly offset the efficiency gains we estimate.

The graph in Fig. 3 shows that the negative economic effects on oil-exporting regions are reduced significantly in NT-ND compared with the NT-D case.[2] The reason

Table 3
Reference and policy cases

No.	Case	Legend
1	Reference	REF
2	Kyoto, no trade, existing distortions	NT-D
	Policies accompanying Kyoto implementation	—
3	Remove distorting fuels taxes	NT-ND
4	Remove coal subsides	—
5	Add emissions permit trading	T-AB
6	Combined effect of all	—
	Country-specific policies	—
7	Tariff concessions	NT-TC
8	Direct compensation	—

[2] In these welfare comparisons, we do not impose the condition that total revenue raised from these two components of the tax system remains the same; thus, our calculation is not exactly equivalent to the tax treatment in most analyses of the double-dividend issue. However, imposition of a revenue-neutral condition would not likely change the implications for Non-Annex B countries of removing these distortions.

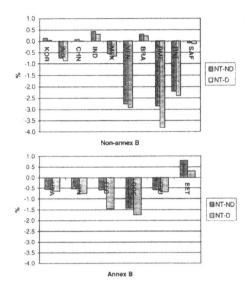

Fig. 3. Kyoto and welfare: The implication of pre-existing distortions in Annex B's energy markets (2010).

for the change is straightforward. The oil price declines by only 9% if tax distortions are removed (Case NT-ND), compared to the previously discussed 15% decline if tax distortions are maintained. With a harmonized system, therefore, deterioration in terms of trade for oil-exporting regions is reduced, lowering their welfare losses.

For Annex B, shown in the lower part of the figure, a switch to a carbon-based increase in fuel prices is favorable for all regions. The gain is greatest in Europe because fuel tax distortions are greatest there. Interestingly, a choice of carbon-based rather than distorted fuel surcharges also benefits non-oil-exporting Non-Annex B countries such as Korea (KOR), India (IND), China (CHN), and Brazil (BRA).

4.2. Removal of subsidies for coal use

Another distortion in the energy system arises from subsidies provided to coal producers in several Annex B countries. These subsidies encourage use of Annex B coal at the expense of imported coal, and encourage coal usage at the expense of oil and natural gas. Removing coal subsidies from Annex B nations should therefore reduce effects on developing-country energy exporters. Such subsidies clearly distort economic activity in Annex B regions, and their removal might therefore increase welfare in Annex B regions, as well. Among the Annex B

regions that will be under restraint in 2010, the main region where these subsidies are currently in place is Europe (EEC). Such subsidies also remain in effect in some countries of the Former Soviet Union (FSU) and Eastern Europe (EET), but these regions are not under restraint in 2010, so no change is considered there.

As noted earlier, our reference case (REF) assumes that these coal subsidies are removed from all countries by 2010. However, we can test the implications of this change by performing a calculation under the assumption that the subsidies will remain in place in OECD countries. This calculation reveals that the effects of removing all coal subsidies from the OECD are in the expected direction, but very small. The welfare effects of removal are neutral or positive everywhere, but not significant for any oil-exporting developing region. The coal sector is too small to make a difference to the OECD regions as defined in our model, and the effect on oil prices is also insignificant. Only in South Africa, where coal exports to the OECD are important, is the effect observable with rounding: the country's 2010 welfare loss is reduced from 0.15% to 0.13% when OECD coal subsidies are removed.

4.3. Emissions trading

The details of international emissions trading, covered under Article 17 of the Kyoto Protocol (United Nations, 1997), are the subject of continuing debate. Although the complexities of alternative implementation schemes may prevent attainment of the cost savings of an ideal trading regime (Hahn and Stavins, 1999), many studies have shown that the potential for cost reductions is great (e.g., Montgomery *et al.*, 1998; Jacoby *et al.*, 1997; OECD, 1992; Ellerman *et al.*, 1998). The analysis conducted here shows the same result. Gains from unrestricted emissions trading are substantial not only for those engaging in such trade, but often for others as well.

The results are displayed in Fig. 4, which shows a case with permit trade only among Annex B countries. Given our reference forecast, FSU and EET share a total of 165 MtC of "hot air" in 2010. They benefit from selling it, and the four OECD regions benefit from lower-cost carbon control when they buy it. In the United States, for example, the carbon price in 2010 drops from $205 per ton under autarchy to $92 per ton with Annex B trading (T-AB). In welfare terms, the cost is lowered most in Japan (by 58%) and in other OECD regions, as well (by 28% to 40%), compared to the case with no emissions trading.

The introduction of Annex B trading means that the 2010 oil price would fall from the reference by less than in the no-trading case (10% as compared to 15%). The reduced impact on energy prices would tend to mediate effects transmitted through the mechanisms of

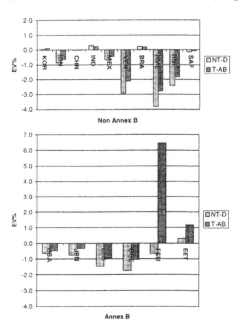

Fig. 4. Kyoto Protocol: The welfare implications of alternative emissions trading schemes, 2010.

Table 4
Reference welfare loss under Kyoto implementation, and the change in loss under various accompanying policies

	VEN (%)	RME (%)	RNF (%)
Reference EV loss	n 2.92	n 3.81	n 2.40
Change in EV loss with:			
Removal of distorting fuel taxes	e 0.16	e 0.96	e 0.37
Removal of coal subsidies	0.0	e 0.01	0.0
Addition of emissions trading	e 0.81	e 1.03	e 0.59
Combined effect of the above	e 2.47	e 3.26	e 1.80

The table also shows the effect if all measures were to be taken together. It is interesting to note that, contrary to what might be expected, the effects are not additive. Indeed, the combined effect is more than twice the sum of the separate effects for VEN, twice the sum of the separate effects for RNF, and about 50% higher than the sum of the separate effects for RME. This magnification of effect when combining the removal of existing energy distortions with emission-rights trading is explained by what happens to the international price of oil in the combined measure compared to the two separate measures. Whereas the oil price falls by 9.2% when only existing energy taxes are removed and by 10.1% when only emissions trading is considered, it falls by only 2.5% when all the measures are considered jointly (recall that dropping coal subsidies has no appreciable effect on oil prices). On the other hand, no Annex B region is adversely affected by the combined measure compared to the case NT-D. Thus, combining the two measures almost offsets the welfare costs inflicted on some developing countries by the Kyoto response measure without resulting in additional costs to Annex B regions.

Two main points can be drawn from the results in this section. First, the way emission restrictions are implemented substantially affects Non-Annex B countries. Second, the implementation options considered here, for the most part, both reduce the cost of the Kyoto emission restrictions for Annex B countries *and* limit the impacts on Non-Annex B countries. The implementation options we considered do not completely eliminate all negative consequences for all Non-Annex B countries, but they go a long way toward doing so. The other side of this coin is that the implementation options we considered also reduce the unintended beneficial consequences of Annex B actions on Non-Annex B countries, some of which are the poorest members of this group.

Basically, a more efficiently implemented policy has smaller costs and smaller unintended consequences. Furthermore, while we have not been able to consider the

international trade discussed earlier. So, for example, oil exporters (e.g., IDN, MEX, RME and RNF) would suffer lower welfare losses than they would in a world without trading. On the other hand, those regions that benefited under no-trade conditions (e.g., KOR and IND) would be somewhat less advantaged by Kyoto if trading is in effect. These effects are enhanced if a large developing country joins the trading regime, as explored in Babiker and Jacoby (1999).

4.4. The combined effect of accompanying policy measures

In this section, we combine all three of the above actions to evaluate the extent to which they reduce impacts on Non-Annex B regions. Table 4 shows the results for a subset of the developing countries that are of interest: Venezuela (VEN), the Persian Gulf (RME), and North Africa (RNF). The table shows the reference EV loss if the Kyoto Protocol is implemented, then presents the change in impact resulting from each associated policy, considered alone. Again, removal of coal subsidies is shown to be insignificant. Depending on the region, on the other hand, emissions trading and removal of distorting fuel taxes could soften the effect of Kyoto implementation.

influence of non-CO$_2$ greenhouse gases and sinks, the
work of Reilly *et al.* (1999a, b) cited earlier, indicates that
efficient use of these control options would reduce burdens even further.

5. Direct measures to reduce effects on developing countries

The ways in which emissions constraints are implemented can substantially reduce impacts on Non-Annex
B countries, but as long as policies lead to reductions in
fossil fuel use, fuel exporters will experience consequences. In this section, we consider two options that
go beyond the general policies that might accompany
the imposition of Kyoto emission restrictions. These
are preferential tariff reductions for Non-Annex B
countries, and direct compensation of countries suffering losses from Annex B implementation of the Kyoto
agreement.

5.1. Tariff concessions

Here we consider preferential removal of tariffs for Non-
Annex B countries from goods imported into Annex B
countries. When applying these preferential tariffs in our
model, we exclude energy (oil, gas, and coal) and energy-
intensive goods. Our reasoning is that reducing tariffs on
energy-intensive goods would be inconsistent with the
objectives of the Climate Convention, as this would encourage leakage of carbon emissions from Annex B to
Non-Annex B regions. Tariff reductions extended to oil,
gas, and coal would effectively shift production of these
goods from Annex B countries to Non-Annex B countries. Such a shift in production of oil, gas, and coal
would further concentrate Kyoto-related losses on the
energy-producing sectors in Annex B. Tariff levels are
included in the GTAP data set. The effect of tariff concessions can be computed by comparing the Kyoto case
under current conditions (with Annex B tariffs in place)
to a case assuming one-way reduction in tariffs by Annex
B countries on goods from all Non-Annex B countries.
We denote this case NT-TC, indicating No Emissions
Trading and Tariff Concessions. All fuel-specific taxes
(distortions) are in place.

The results of such tariff concessions are shown in
Fig. 5. Not surprisingly, the one-way preferential removal
of Annex B tariffs from Non-Annex B goods causes
welfare losses in all Annex B regions except FSU, which
seems to realize minor gains from the resulting trade
diversion. In contrast, EET is most affected by such
a concession policy, losing all the welfare gains it might
have achieved from Kyoto. This is because the concession policy diverts Annex B imports away from EET
toward Non-Annex B regions. This is not true for FSU
because, as reflected in the GTAP base-year trade statis-

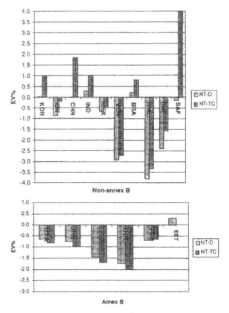

Fig. 5. Kyoto Protocol with and without tariff concessions on non-
energy intensive products.

tics, FSU has lower tariff rates and a smaller volume of
trade with OECD than does EET.

The effect of the concession on developing countries is
highly variable. A number of countries benefit substantially, South Africa being the most prominent example.
A number of regions that would suffer welfare losses from
Kyoto implementation, on the other hand, are little affected by such tariff reductions. For example, benefits to the
Persian Gulf countries (RME) and Venezuela (VEN) are
quite small.

The basic conclusion is that a policy of country-specific preferential reductions in tariffs on Non-Annex B exports to Annex B nations would benefit many developing
countries, but not target the benefits to those countries
negatively affected by Annex B implementation of
the Kyoto Protocol. Furthermore, even if, in principle,
trade concessions could target countries that experience
economic losses, predicting the dynamic effects of
trade concessions targeted to closely compensate those
adversely affected by Annex B climate policies would
raise many difficult issues.

5.2. Direct compensation

We consider, finally, the level of financial transfer that
would be required to compensate losses to Non-Annex

B regions. Even if such a direct transfer mechanism is not likely to be established, the calculations can offer some indication of the attention that should be given to other mitigation measures, both those discussed above and others we are unable to model, such as technology transfer. Naturally, the amount of compensation required to "minimize" Kyoto effects would depend on the stringency of the emissions control measures taken, how the measures are implemented, and other uncertain economic developments between now and 2010. We make the calculations on an ex ante basis, using our reference scenario as a representation of conditions in this future period. We do not attempt to resolve the institutional question of how the adverse effects would be calculated in the year in which they are to be paid.

Here we explore the potential magnitude of these financial transfers, focusing only on those regions that suffer welfare losses. We make no correction for Non-Annex B regions that may actually benefit from the imposition of Kyoto restrictions. Using the EPPA-GTAP Model, we analyze financial transfers by assuming an implicit allocation of emissions permits from selected Annex B countries to those Non-Annex B regions that are disadvantaged. Since the regions of the former Soviet Union (FSU) and Eastern Europe (EET) are not under restraint in 2010, the transfer of permits must come from the four OECD regions only (see Table 1 for their compositions). The obligation to transfer is allocated across the four OECD regions as a percentage of their individual post-reduction emissions targets.

The permit transfers are modeled such that each receiving region in Non-Annex B gets the same percentage of permits from each OECD region, with the objective of meeting the welfare criterion stated in the transfer scenario. For example, if RME requires 1% of the permits allocated to OECD to meet the prescribed welfare level in the scenario, then 1% of these permits allotted to each OECD region are transferred to RME. The recipient

nation is then assumed to sell the permits back to the corresponding source at the marginal value in the source region. By this method, we can calculate the financial transfer that would be required, in the face of Kyoto implementation, to maintain all Non-Annex B regions at their reference levels of welfare, or with only some limited decrease in welfare. The calculation of the level of permits allocated was made endogenously in the model. Thus, the estimate takes into account the general equilibrium adjustment of the world economy to these transfers. To explore the magnitude of these general equilibrium adjustments, we also consider a case in which the effects of the financial transfers on goods flows and prices are ignored.

Table 5 presents the results. Considering first the general equilibrium adjustment, and assuming no trade in emissions permits, we can see that the "minimization" of adverse impacts to Non-Annex B regions (noted in the table as ΔEVr 0) would require an overall annual financial transfer from OECD nations to Non-Annex B regions of $27.6 billion in the year 2010. Somewhat over half this amount would comprise transfers to the Persian Gulf nations (RME). Other nations needing substantial transfers would include North Africa (RNF), Venezuela (VEN), Mexico (MEX), and Indonesia (IDN). If the objective were to mitigate these effects but not necessarily eliminate them, the overall transfer required would be substantially reduced. For example, the table includes a calculation for the 2010 loss in welfare within Non-Annex B nations limited to 1%. The overall transfer is cut to $14.5 billion, and in this case, roughly 80% of the transfer is to the Persian Gulf region.

The allowance of permit trading among Annex B nations would lower the financial transfers required to hold EV at zero. Direct transfers would be reduced by about 25%, to a total of $20 billion, as shown in the table.

The EPPA-GTAP Model computes a general equilibrium adjustment to these financial transfers. That is,

Table 5
Financial transfers from OECD countries required to reduce Non-Annex B welfare losses in 2010 to zero, or to a maximum of 1.0% (1995 $US billions)

| Region | General equilibrium | | With trading | Partial equilibrium |
| | No permit trading | | | No permit trading |
	ΔEVr 0	ΔEVg 1.0%	ΔEVr 0	ΔEVr 0
IDN	1.59		1.16	1.52
CHN	0.13			0.09
MEX	1.75		1.16	1.60
VEN	1.97	1.29	1.44	1.84
RME	15.6	11.5	11.5	14.7
RNF	2.96	1.72	2.26	2.69
SAF	0.14		0.06	0.15
Total	27.6	14.5	20.0	25.7

M. Babiker et al. / Energy Policy 28 (2000) 525–536 535

compared to a solution without these transfers (NT-D), their addition increases the aggregate demand levels, creating an upward pressure on prices in the recipient countries and decreasing the level of incomes in the donor countries. Thus, global adjustments occur in economic activity, international trade, and prices in response to the compensation plan. An alternative estimate would simply calculate the financial transfers needed to return Non-Annex B countries to the reference level of welfare (in effect, calculate the EV loss in monetary terms), ignoring the fact that these transfers influence economic activities in both recipient and donor regions. As can be seen from the table, this partial equilibrium approach differs only slightly from the EPPA-GTAP general equilibrium answer. The total transfer in 2010 is approximately $25.7 billion; thus, the partial equilibrium approach to estimating this figure underestimates the needed transfers by about 7%.

6. Discussion and conclusions

It is no surprise that emissions control actions by the large developed countries, which dominate world trade flows, will have ripple effects on the global economy, affecting countries that have not volunteered to share any burdens of the emissions control regime. The magnitudes of these impacts are highly uncertain, but the analysis above does give an idea of what these impacts might be. Clearly, the greatest loss is imposed on energy exporters, and the more dependent a country is on energy exports, the greater the effect will be on its economic welfare. A country like Mexico, therefore, with a large, diversified economy, will be affected much less than will nations of the Persian Gulf (RME), for which oil revenues constitute a much larger fraction of GNP.

Our analysis leads to two broad conclusions. First, the way in which emissions targets are implemented can have a major effect on a policy's impact on Non-Annex B countries. In particular:

- Unrestricted emissions trading would reduce impacts substantially. With the accession of Non-Annex B regions to the agreement, the reduction could be even greater.
- Removing fuel price distortions in Annex B countries would also substantially reduce impacts.
- Removing coal subsidies would have a very small effect, though it would reduce negative consequences for South Africa measurably because of the importance of coal exports to the South African economy.
- We did not consider the effect on Non-Annex B of including other gases in the mitigation strategy of Annex B. Other work we have conducted leads us to believe that a "multi-gas" strategy would further reduce negative impacts on Non-Annex B countries.

Second, all of the above implementation options would also reduce the cost of restrictions for Annex B countries by increasing the cost-effectiveness of the emissions-reduction policies or by eliminating other economic distortions.

Third, as long as energy markets are affected, Non-Annex B countries that export energy are likely to experience some negative consequences. A broad policy of preferential tariff reduction on Non-Annex B exports to the OECD would benefit many developing countries but not target the benefits to those countries negatively affected by Annex B implementation of Kyoto. Therefore, the only remaining methods of mitigation may be a selective use of preferential tariffs or some form of direct compensation. If direct compensation is invoked, the required transfers could be substantial, concentrated on a few countries. We estimate the annual transfer for 2010 to be around $25 billion, the annual amount transferred would, of course, change over time.

Acknowledgements

For crucial contributions to the preparation of the EPPA-GTAP Model used here, and for helpful criticism of the paper, thanks are due to R. S. Eckaus, A. D. Ellerman, and D. M. Reiner. The EPPA component of the MIT modeling system has been developed with the support of a government–industry partnership including the U.S. Department of Energy (901214-HAR; DE-FG02-94ER61937; DE-FG0293ER61713) and the U.S. Environmental Protection Agency (CR-820662002), the Royal Norwegian Ministries of Energy and Industry and Foreign Affairs, and a group of corporate sponsors from the United States and other countries.

References

Babiker, M.H., Jacoby, H.D. 1999. Developing country effects of Kyoto-type emissions restrictions. Joint Program on the Science and Policy of Global Change Report No. 53. Massachusetts Institute of Technology (MIT), Cambridge.

Babiker, M.H., Maskus, K.E., Rutherford, T.F., 1997. Carbon tax and the global trading system. Working Paper 97-7. University of Colorado, Boulder.

Babiker, M.H., Reilly, J., Eckaus, D., Jacoby, H., Sue Wing, I., 2000. The emissions prediction and policy analysis (EPPA) model, version 3, MIT Joint Program Report, forthcoming.

DOE/EIA, 1998. International Energy Outlook.

Ellerman, A.D., Jacoby, H.D., Decaux, A., 1998. The effects on developing countries of the Kyoto Protocol and CO₂ emissions trading. Joint Program on the Science and Policy of Global Change Report No. 41. MIT, Cambridge.

Hahn, R.W., Stavins, R.N., 1999. What has Kyoto wrought? The real architecture of international tradable permit markets. Working Paper. John F. Kennedy School of Government. Harvard University, Cambridge.

536 *M. Babiker et al. / Energy Policy 28 (2000) 525–536*

Hertel, T.W., 1997. Global Trade Analysis: Modeling and Applications. Cambridge University Press, Cambridge.

Jacoby, H.D., Eckaus, R., Ellerman, D., Prinn, R., Reiner, D., Yang, Z., 1997. CO_2 emissions limits: economic adjustments and the distribution of burdens. The Energy Journal 18(3), 31–58.

Jacoby, H.D., Sue Wing, I., 1999. Adjustment time, capital malleability and policy cost. In: Weyant, J.P. (Ed.), The Energy Journal Special Issue: The Costs of the Kyoto Protocol: A Multi-Model Evaluation. International Association for Energy Economics, Cleveland.

Kolstad, C., Light, M., Rutherford, T., 1999. Coal markets and the Kyoto Protocol. Working Paper. University of Colorado, Boulder.

Montgomery, D., Bernstein, P., Rutherford, T., 1998. Carbon abatement, permit trading and international trade. Working Paper. Charles River Associates and University of Colorado, Boulder.

OECD, 1992. The Economic Costs of Reducing CO_2 Emissions. OECD, Paris.

Reilly, J.M., Mayer, M., Harnisch, J., 1999a. Multiple gas control under the Kyoto Agreement. Paper presented at the Second International Symposium on Non-CO_2 Greenhouse Gases (NCGG-2), Noordwijkerhout, The Netherlands, 8–10 September.

Reilly, J., Prinn, R., Harnisch, J., Fitzmaurice, J., Jacoby, H., Kicklighter, D., Melillo, J., Stone, P., Sokolov, A., Wang, C., 1999b. Multi-gas assessment of the Kyoto Protocol. Nature 401 (7 Oct.) 549–555. An early version is also available, with the same title, as Joint Program on the Science and Policy of Global Change Report No. 45. MIT, Cambridge.

United Nations, 1992. Framework Convention on Climate Change. United Nations, New York.

United Nations, 1997. Kyoto Protocol to the United Nations Framework Convention on Climate Change, Conference of the Parties on Its Third Session, FCCC/CP/1997/L.7/Add.1, 10 December.

Webster, M.D., 1997. Exploring the uncertainty in future carbon emissions. Joint Program on the Science and Policy of Global Change Report No. 30. MIT, Cambridge.

Webster, M.D., Sokolov, A., 1998. Quantifying the uncertainty in climate predictions. Joint Program on the Science and Policy of Global Change Report No. 37. MIT, Cambridge.

Yang, Z., Eckaus, R.S., Ellerman, A.D., Jacoby, H.D., 1996. The MIT Emission Projection and Policy Analysis (EPPA) Model. Joint Program on the Science and Policy of Global Change Report No. 5. MIT, Cambridge.

Name Index

For Product Safety Concerns and Information please contact our EU
representative GPSR@taylorandfrancis.com Taylor & Francis Verlag GmbH,
Kaufingerstraße 24, 80331 München, Germany

Printed and bound by CPI Group (UK) Ltd, Croydon, CR0 4YY
01/05/2025
01858422-0014